Five Centuries of
English Book Illustration

Plate I. William Blake. William Blake, *Jerusalem* (1820). Reproduced from the Blake Trust facsimile (1952) of the unique illuminated copy now at Yale.

Five Centuries of
English Book Illustration

EDWARD HODNETT

SCOLAR PRESS

First published in 1988 by
SCOLAR PRESS
Gower Publishing Company Limited
Gower House, Croft Road
Aldershot GU11 3HR
Copyright © The Estate of Edward Hodnett, 1988
Reprinted 1990

Edward Hodnett died in 1984, before the editorial
work on this book was complete. In addition to those
named in the author's Preface on page vii the
Publishers wish to express their thanks to Irene Pavitt
for her work in preparing the typescript for setting
and in correcting the proofs.

British Library Cataloguing in Publication Data

Hodnett, Edward
    Five centuries of English book illustration.
    1. Illustration of books——England——
    History
    I. Title
    741.64'0942   NC978

ISBN 0–85967–697–8

Printed in Great Britain by Galliard (Printers) Ltd, Great Yarmouth, Norfolk

Contents

Preface

This book has been on my mind for a long time. In 1928, I proposed something of the sort for my doctoral dissertation in English literature at Columbia University. My unorthodoxy raised no eyebrows, but I was told to limit myself to the late fifteenth century. The Bibliographical Society generously published the result. In 1967, the original idea served as an excuse to live in London for a few months. The stay lasted for nine years and, as I was drawn into the magnetic field of research, yielded four books all of which grew out of the main study. These years also included several months of labor on additions and corrections for a reissue of the long neglected dissertation. Since 1976, I have lived in Washington, D.C., and the research for and writing of the chapters on the eighteenth and nineteenth centuries and further research for and rewriting of the other chapters took place here. I give this account of the genesis of this book for whatever admonitory value it may have.

To avoid misunderstanding, let me say at once that I approach the study of book illustration as an independent discipline. That it *may* be considered a subdivision of art history, literary history, bibliography, graphics, book production, publishing, or anything else does not mean that it *must* be so considered. Indeed, to do so may lead to the neglect of central realities because of preoccupation with what are often side issues in English book illustration – iconography and harmony between illustration and type, for instance. This has resulted in a much longer book than I had any intention of writing, in spite of rigorous cutting and condensing of successive drafts.

Additions and corrections will inevitably be necessary. Apart from omissions through oversight, gaps in the holdings of the libraries used (including the delay in availability of recent publications), and deliberate exclusions that some readers may deem unwarranted, there will be yearly additions to the books and artists discussed in this study who were working in the mid- and late twentieth century – and the twenty-first century soon will be here. Corrections are equally certain. The vast quantity of factual material to be dealt with covering five centuries of English publishing makes error-free efforts by one unassisted person beyond reasonable expectation. Furthermore, the judgments of one person on so many matters are fallible and subject to review. Most significantly, additions and corrections will be forthcoming from studies of individual artists in the future.

I have not written for specialists, it hardly needs saying, but have tried to keep in mind the needs of persons without extensive knowledge of English book illustration or graphics, on the one hand, or of English literature, on the other. I have, however, been particularly mindful of the needs of the young literary scholars who are now beginning to study the functional aspects of English book illustration and who will be the authors of the many monographs about it that have yet to be written. They will correct my errors, fill in my omissions, and challenge my judgments. That is as it should be. Good luck to them.

Foremost among my debts is the one I owe to the library catalogers, those anonymous, conscientious, unsung benefactors of all scholars, without whose aid I could hardly have begun. My second debt is to the authors of the many books and articles that I consulted, often without being able to acknowledge their contributions. More personally, I am deeply indebted to members of the staffs of the British Library, the Department of Prints and Drawings of the British Museum, the Folger Shakespeare Library, and the Library of Congress. Many librarians have served me without my having been able to thank them in person, and so I thank them now. Some became valued friends and advisers, and I thank them warmly for their interest and advice. Among these, I am especially indebted to Ian R. Willison and David L. Paisey, the British Library; Nati Krivatsy, the Folger Shakespeare Library; and Don C. Marcin, Peter M. Van Wingen, and the late Peter M. Petcoff, the Library of Congress, for their many kindnesses. Lia Hunt of the Limited Editions Club, Grey Hodnett, Dee Cook, and Mike Crump also gave valuable help.

E.H.

Chevy Chase, Maryland, 1982

List of Plates

For

JESSIE

With love and gratitude

Introduction

Through all recorded history, illustrations have accompanied literary works. After the introduction of printing in Europe, only a few years passed before the publication of *Der Edelstein* (Bamberg, 1461), the first dated illustrated book. It was a collection of Aesopian fables compiled by Ulrich Boner, a Swiss monk, and illustrated with 103 woodcuts derived from manuscript illuminations. As we shall see, William Caxton, the first English printer, delayed illustrating his books for a time but soon built up an extensive collection of woodcuts, which he employed liberally. Since the late fifteenth century, illustration has been a steadfast element in English publishing and in the cultural history of the English people. The extent of its role has varied with social, technological, and economic conditions, and the role of the illustrator likewise has varied from anonymous handyman to title-page celebrity. The number of illustrated books published in England during the past five centuries is enormous. Yet remarkably little serious critical attention has been given to the functional aspects of English book illustration, even to the extent of differentiating among the different kinds. Leading illustrators have been the subjects of bibliophilic, biographical, bibliographical, and technical studies, but not until recently has the work of any – and few at that – been subjected to scholarly criticism. Several useful summary accounts of groups of artists and periods of illustration, such as Forrest Reid's *Illustrators of the Sixties* (1928), have dispensed judgments without either clear criteria or concrete analyses to support them. The artists, book designers, collectors, librarians, printers, and print experts who until recently did the bulk of the writing about English illustration were interested almost exclusively in how illustrations look. According to their orientation, they wrote about illustrations in one of two ways: either as independent works of art or as units of the book as an aesthetic whole.

Rarely in the past – and not frequently in the present – has anyone systematically differentiated among the three broad functions of illustration: to decorate, to inform, and to interpret. As a result, entirely dissimilar kinds of designs from books as unlike one another as works of fiction, architecture, horticulture, and travel have been lumped together for praise and censure. (Pictures in any kind of book are illustrations; here, the reference is the usual one – images in literary works.) Furthermore, this confusion has taken place without a clear statement of criteria of excellence except by those writers who make harmony between illustration and printed page their prime consideration and frankly say so. Judgments about illustrations based solely on the way they look are understandable and, when so stated, wholly proper. They are misleading when this single criterion is not expressed and when they convey the impression that no other considerations are relevant.

The primary reason for illustrating literature, as every ordinary reader understands and as the vast majority of illustrators and authors, printers and publishers in England during the past five centuries have understood, is to contribute to the reader's comprehension and enjoyment of works of the imagination – fiction, poetry, plays, and essays – and of other forms when they are something more than factual communications. That literary illustrations of generally recognized excellence – Hans Holbein's, say – are often highly decorative, harmonious with the printed page, and handsome as independent works of art is obvious. The majority of English illustrations possess these qualities in only modest degrees. The essential creative act of literary illustration is interpretation of the text, and that should be the center of criticism of an illustrator's work. (One may quibble about the word *interpretation. Realization* is a more precise word for what is meant here, but it has no adjectival form.) We find support in Johann Sebastian Bach's instructions to one of his organ students: "When playing hymns, do not treat the melody as if it were important but interpret the words through the melody."

Aims

The main aim of *English Book Illustration* is to present the first one-volume selective, comprehensive, and critical record of literary illustration in England during the five centuries since the introduction of printing. (The year 1976 was celebrated internationally as the Caxton Year, and it is as far in modern times as this account can conveniently go.) To accomplish this aim required two separate but related actions. The first, which is printed second, was the compilation of a catalog of the illustrators (or, for the mid-fifteenth to early seventeenth centuries, of the printers of books with anonymous illustrations) who seem worthy of being remembered in this arbitrary manner and of a selection of those books of reasonable importance illustrated by each artist (or, before 1600, issued by printers) that support the choices made. The result is "A Selective Catalog of Illustrators and Illustrated Books", Part II of this book. It lists about 250 illustrators and 2700 books (including those of a score of early printers) chosen from the multitude reviewed.

Tentative judgments about the merits of illustrators and books formed during the clearing of the field to compile the Catalog were preliminary to the studies of individual periods, illustrators, and books that compose Part I, "A Critical Account of Five Centuries of Literary Illustration", the main text. Accompanying the text are reproductions of 201 black-and-white illustrations and 6 color plates.

Together, the Critical Account and the Catalog are intended to introduce the general reader to the main developments in and contributors to this relatively neglected chapter of English cultural history, to be a reference aid for workers in related fields, and to serve as a starting point for more intensive and scholarly studies. To realize these ends, selection was limited (1) to artists resident in England and to books printed in England, (2) to works with at least a modest claim to recognition as imaginative adult literature, and (3) to works that contain pictures (except photographs) of some artistic value that can be said to interpret the text. Exceptions were made when they serve a useful purpose. Except in Chapter Two and except for important visual interpretations of individual books in or passages from the Bible, Bible illustrations are not discussed. Their range is so enormous and the borrowing of motifs is so pervasive that only a separate study would be satisfactory.

The expression "books of reasonable importance" has no defensible exactness. Various considerations came into play. What is generally accepted as serious literature took precedence over lighter forms, and substantially illustrated books took precedence over books with two or three routine designs. Books with only a frontispiece occasionally were included to give a balanced view of illustration from the mid-fifteenth to mid-seventeenth centuries, but were omitted in the accounts of later centuries. The aim has

been to include all those books that contain each artist's most successful, or at least most ambitious, examples of literary illustration. That there are unjustified omissions is regrettably certain. They came about because of the author's poor judgment, ignorance of a book's existence, or inability to inspect a copy. The Catalog lists certain books that were not examined when there is reason to believe that they belong there.

The three overriding reasons for circumscribing the scope of this work are (1) to ensure some hope of examining enough of the thousands of illustrated books published in the past five centuries to be able to form opinions about them, (2) to have room in one volume to discuss with some definiteness the selected illustrators and representative examples of their work, and (3) most important, to have sufficient uniformity of kind to afford a firm basis for critical judgments. Critical accounts of the vast domains of Bibles, children's books, light humorous works, and periodicals, not to mention the even vaster array of history, science, travel, and other books of factual information, which are often handsomely illustrated, would require the application of a variety of special criteria, take years of further research and writing, and result in separate publications. There already are excellent studies of illustrated children's books; the other fields are challenges to scholarly investigation. But flexibility, even inconsistency, may be desirable – as when a leading illustrator, such as George Cruikshank, does a series of children's book designs with serious adult qualities.

One incidental aim of this book is to encourage librarians, dealers, and collectors to identify and preserve, by microform if necessary, the best illustrated books of the past and of the present, which so soon becomes the past. James Northcote's *Fables* (1828, 1833), illustrated by William Harvey; William Allingham's *Music Master* (1855), illustrated by Arthur Hughes, John Everett Millais, and Dante Gabriel Rossetti; Elizabeth Gaskell's *Cranford* (1898), illustrated by Hugh Thomson; and other treasures of nineteenth-century illustration are disintegrating in the stacks of the general collections of libraries, and much of the finest work of the twentieth century cannot be found at all in many libraries.

Organization

Among the usual ways of organizing a work of this sort – alphabetical, chronological, stylistic, and technical – the chronological was adopted as the most convenient for reference. More exactly, the progression is by centuries; but for manageability, the eighteenth, nineteenth, and twentieth centuries are divided into periods defined by the work being done. To take the eighteenth century as an example, Louis Cheron, Gravelot, Louis du Guernier, Francis Hayman, William Kent, and other illustrators of the first half of the century have much in common, and John Miller, Samuel Wale, Anthony Walker, and other artists of the third quarter are not different or important enough to be given a chapter by themselves. But artists as important and different from their predecessors as Thomas Bewick, William Blake, Henry Fuseli, and Thomas Rowlandson, all of whom were active in the fourth quarter of the eighteenth century, clearly constitute a distinct group and therefore were assigned a separate chapter. Because only three or four illustrators who worked before the seventeenth century can be named, Chapter One and Chapter Two are organized chiefly around the printers who were most active in using illustrations, and Chapter Two also includes sections on illustrated books of some interest by other printers. The Catalog follows a parallel arrangement. Within the remaining chapters, the presentation of illustrators in alphabetical order seemed to be the only practicable approach and the one most likely to meet most needs. Although this arrangement of the book does not formally group artists related to one another by style or interests, such relationships become apparent in the discussions and from inspection of their work. The introductory note to each chapter points out briefly some of the major characteristics and developments of the period as well as certain artists and books of special interest.

Critical Account of Literary Illustration

The degree of success of a literary illustrator must be measured first of all by how effectively his or her designs convert the author's words into complementary images. This is a complex and elusive matter that the text of this book, the Critical Account, explores with no pretense of finality. On the whole, English illustrators, particularly those who have made their living by illustrating, have been men and women of modest views of their own importance. They have generally aspired to do three things: (1) represent accurately the characters, incidents, and settings of scenes from the works entrusted to them in a way that makes clear what is taking place; (2) convey through the expressiveness of their drawings the emotional effects evoked by the words of the author; and (3) make drawings that deserve respect for competent draftsmanship, arouse interest, and provide pleasure additional to that of the text. Only during the past century has decorative harmony of the illustrations with the rest of the book been a conscious concern of English illustrators.

Keen sensitivity to literature distinguishes a true illustrator from other artists. It is often missing in the work of many illustrators of unimpeachable technical credentials. The images of an artist who has been genuinely successful as an illustrator generate an intensity of awareness of the author's purposes similar to that effected by the text, at times transcending it. This is a far cry from simply representing how characters look and what they are doing, although the majority of illustrations have always done that. Let us imagine what would be required in an illustration of the moment in the last scene of *King Lear* when Lear re-enters, carrying the body of his faithful daughter, Cordelia, who has been hanged just as Lear has come to realize how he has wronged her. The drawing of this moment may be a masterpiece of draftsmanship, but if it does not communicate the anguish of the old king and the cumulative horror of the events, it is a failure. If it does convey that poignant feeling and at the same time arouse aesthetic delight comparable with that which Shakespeare's poetry bestows along with the shattering experience of tragedy, then the artist is worthy to share the page with the poet.

Largely stimulated by the prodigious efforts of William Blake scholars to clarify the fascinating interplay between his illustrations and his poems, literary scholars have begun to investigate the long-neglected functional aspect of illustration, the relationship of image and text that we have been discussing. Ideally and practically, any serious criticism of the illustration of literature must start with knowledge of the work that has been illustrated, with the kind of understanding of works within their fields that literary scholars possess generally to a superior degree than do the rest of us. Only when armed with knowledge of a text in all its particulars – which is altogether different from school-day memories or from a flip through the pages to learn what "happens" – can one answer even the first question about a series of illustrations: How wisely has the artist chosen the moments to be illustrated? Critics have rarely raised this question. Yet every illustrator – or the author or publisher – must decide which of the thousands of moments recorded in words he or she will record in images. The exigencies of publishing usually require the distribution throughout a book of a fixed number of designs, which may be as general as one design to a chapter; but the decision always comes down to a single moment for each image, exactly as though the artist held a camera. Examination of the illustrations in several editions of a familiar classic will reveal that the moments chosen vary from the illuminating to the downright pointless and trivial. Twentieth-century artists have sometimes used the occasion to make the sort of drawings they like to do with something close to indifference to the intent of the author. Some

3

illustrators – and some critics – have defended their right to draw what they please. If they prize their independence so much, one wonders, why do they not create original drawings and prints – and bind them within covers, perhaps – unfettered by a text or by having to share credit with a Shakespeare or a Cervantes?

The insistence expressed here that the primary function of the literary illustrator is to interpret the text must not be taken to imply that his or her skill as an artist is not important. On the contrary, leading illustrators have rarely been anything but first-rate draftsmen, and those rare illustrators who are deemed great, in the strict sense of the term, have been great artists. Yet, as we have said, a good illustration is something much more than a good drawing. In a general way, the primary intent of imaginative literature is to arouse emotional responses, whereas other forms aim first to inform or persuade. Take again the example of King Lear with the dead Cordelia in his arms: Would not Rembrandt have been the supreme illustrator of this heartbreaking scene? One may speculate about the relative influences on Rembrandt's greatness of his compassionate humanity and his technical mastery. But it is clear that although neither quality would have been sufficient in itself, the second would have been indispensable to the creation of the profoundly expressive designs needed to convey the almost unbearable emotional impact of the tragic climax of Shakespeare's play.

Estimating the relative merits of illustrators, illustrated books, series of illustrations, and single illustrations is a subjective, unscientific procedure. It is beset by booby traps. Probably the most common is judging an illustration as an original design when it is not. There can be failure to distinguish between autographic designs and those that have passed through the hands of reproductive woodcutters, engravers, or etchers. Then there can be failure to recognize that part of or all of a design has been borrowed. Such borrowing may be an open expression of homage, a nefarious piece of plagiarism, or something in between. For works done before 1850 and to a diminishing degree thereafter, the question of originality of designs is a difficult one to answer when it is a matter of importance. Only in special instances does there exist readily available evidence that permits certainty that a given design is entirely original or, if not, that indicates the source and degree of borrowing. At the most elementary level, illustrators cannot possibly know how people of all times and classes of society have dressed or what their artifacts have looked like. They must often borrow from pictures. Sometimes an artist, because of pressure of time or lack of imagination, adapts the designs of a predecessor, not always an illustrator of the same book or even an illustrator. T. S. R. Boase in his

article "Illustrations of Shakespeare's Plays in the Seventeenth and Eighteenth Centuries" (1948) shows that Sir Joshua Reynolds borrowed the arrangement of his painting *Death of Cardinal Beaufort* in *2 Henry VI* for the Boydell Shakespeare Gallery from Nicolas Poussin's *Death of Germanicus* and that in subsequent illustrations of the same scene, often apparently different from one another, the outstretched hand of the cardinal is usually present (and so is the upraised arm of the king), as in Poussin's work. Henry Fuseli's 1802 illustration "Satan, Sin, and Death" in *Paradise Lost* bears little resemblance to William Hogarth's painting of the same scene (ca. 1764). But Marcia Pointon in *Milton and English Art* (1970) reproduces an intervening drawing, which Fuseli made in 1776. It clearly proves that his 1802 design evolved from Hogarth's. Notwithstanding that it is impossible to know always when an artist has taken part of or all of a composition from someone else's work, judgments have to be made without qualifying constantly.

Almost from the beginning of printing, artists with established reputations have been called on to illustrate books. The disciplined masters of the fifteenth, sixteenth, and seventeenth centuries had no trouble accepting the restrictions placed on them by their interpretive role. By the eighteenth century, a certain indifference to the texts on the part of illustrators begins to show. In the nineteenth and twentieth centuries, artists called on to illustrate books had often won their fame through their prints and their work for popular periodicals. That familiarity to a wide audience was the chief reason for the assignment. Much of the time, the success of a popular artist depends to a great degree on easy recognition of a distinctive style. Humorous artists with the widest followings have had the most individual styles – George Cruikshank is a conspicuous example. In the twentieth century, this easy identifiability has extended to serious painters and graphic artists – Pablo Picasso is the leading example. When the publisher matches the book to the artist – the humorous works that Cruikshank was called on to illustrate, for instance – no problem occurs. But when artist and book are not matched, the artist faces a dilemma because his or her characteristic way of drawing is not only the reason for the assignment, but also his or her artistic identity. Should the artist preserve that identity or adjust the designs to the nature of the text? Instances of successful adjustment are rare, probably because artists have not recognized the problem or could not or would not solve it if they did. Thus, how much does a distinctive style distort the reader's impression of the author's intent?

Many other special problems arise bearing on the judgment of illustrations done over the course of 500 years. Most of them come up in the discussion of individual illustrators. Many are discussed at length in my *Image and Text: Studies in the Illustration of English Literature* (1982).

In order to focus this study, to accomplish the aims noted earlier in the Introduction, neither extensive biographical data nor analyses of books of secondary importance are included in the entries in the Critical Account. Portraits, maps, and diagrams usually are not noted. Otherwise, quality and interest are the determinants, with quantity cautiously recognized as an indicator of the importance attached by the publisher to a series of illustrations. Since information about almost anything starts with numbers, the account of an artist's work usually includes the number of illustrations in every book discussed and, when it seems useful to know (mainly for the mid-fifteenth through to the eighteenth century) measurements of designs. After 1800, the great increase in the number of illustrated books published, the dominance of the octavo size, and, later, the practice of reducing drawings in photographic reproduction make exact measurements seem rarely necessary. Full-page, half-page, headpiece, small vignette, and similar descriptions adequately indicate the approximate size of the illustrations in relation to standard pages. The discussion usually specifies the technique used. When it does not, the characteristic one of the artist or of the period is to be assumed.

The desire to be of service to others who will someday study these illustrators requires the inclusion of a good deal of this matter-of-fact information. Each discussion also tries within a limited space to give a general impression of an artist's work, describe the subject matter of his or her designs, note his or her relation to other illustrators, comment on the most important or representative of his or her books, and analyze one or more works, with special attention to the design chosen for reproduction. Each analysis attempts to make an evaluation of the artist's relative achievement as an interpretive illustrator, subjective and tentative as the evaluation may be.

In addition to the more than 200 illustrators discussed in the Critical Account, about 50 artists of secondary importance and about 25 early printers are listed in the Catalog. The books published by several of these printers receive extended attention in the text. Some of the secondary illustrators, whose work seems too limited, or undistinguished to warrant separate discussion, are commented on in the text in relation to the major artists or in the introductory remarks to a chapter, but they usually are not represented by a reproduction of an illustration. For economy, reproductions of illustrations were restricted to one per artist. For illustrators of distinction, considerable productivity, or variety of styles, one reproduction is in-

adequate. But it still can be representative of an artist's serious literary work and was chosen for that reason, not necessarily as his or her best drawing. The reader with a serious interest in certain illustrators or books will have to go to the original works. Reproductions, especially when reduced, can be misleading, and one or two or three reproductions can never provide a safe basis for judgment of an entire series of illustrations as it actually appears in a given book.

Selective Catalog of Illustrators and Illustrated Books

The Catalog follows the organization of the Critical Account by periods, with the illustrators and printers listed in alphabetical order and their books, in chronological order. Those illustrators and printers whose names are in roman type are discussed in the Critical Account. Those whose names are in italics are not.

With a few exceptions, illustrators are listed in the Catalog and discussed in the Critical Account in the period in which their work first appeared. Frequently, however, their earliest work did not seem important enough to record. If an artist illustrated only one or two books in the last years of a period and then went on to do the work for which he or she is best known in the succeeding period, the artist is placed in that second period. If, however, several of an artist's earliest books are included in the Catalog, his or her work is discussed in the earlier period, even though most of the books that the artist illustrated were published later and he or she is generally associated with the later period.

When an artist shared with one or more other artists in illustrating a book, "With anr." or "With others" appears at the end of the entry. Giving the names of all collaborators each time would be repetitious. The identity of these artists sometimes is noted in the Critical Account, and it almost always can be found in the books. Seldom do all the contributors to multiple-artist books merit notice.

As already mentioned, the identity of illustrators who worked during the fifteenth and, with a few exceptions, sixteenth centuries is unknown; therefore, almost all the Catalog entries for those centuries are of printers.

Until the latter part of the seventeenth century, the printer of books was also, in effect, the publisher. Then the bookseller and gradually the publisher came to assume the planning, financing, and distributing functions separate from the printing, and their names, not the printers', appear in the entries. In all the later periods, however, printers sometimes have controlled the illustrations. For entries before the nineteenth century, the initials of publishers'

5

first names are given once under each illustrator. Publishers became fewer, more firmly established, and better known in the nineteenth and twentieth centuries; initials are usually omitted in the later entries. Further, to conserve space, an ampersand instead of *and* is used in the name of a publishing firm of two or more partners; and the firms of Longman and Routledge, both of which have had various partners through the years but have retained the family names, are designated as only Longman and Routledge.

The place of publication of a book is London unless otherwise stated. Exceptions are university presses with the same name as the place – for example, Oxford – and the frequently listed Gregynog Press of Newtown, Montgomeryshire, Wales; Golden Cockerel Press of Waltham Saint Lawrence, Berkshire; and Limited Editions Club and Heritage Press, its former affiliate, of New York. The relationship between LEC and Heritage began in 1935. The Heritage books almost always were photo-offset reprints of LEC editions and came out a year or so later. This arrangement was subject to exceptions; therefore, in any instance of special importance, the reader should investigate further. If there is a London publisher, others – for example, in Edinburgh or New York – that shared an edition are not mentioned. Editions published abroad are not listed, except for an occasional first edition in English or in a few instances when the only edition available to the writer was a virtually simultaneous and identical American one.

Dates of publication are meant to be those of first printing, but in a work of this scope, verification of every date has been impossible. Among other variables, books often are issued for sale before or after the date on the title page, the first by design – just before Christmas usually – the second because of delay. Later printings are not listed in the Catalog and rarely are discussed in the text. In the Catalog, the order in which books are listed under a date does not indicate the known order of publication, which usually is beyond discovery. In the text, the statement that an artist illustrated a book in a certain year generally means that the illustrations appear in a book published in that year. The drawings generally would be made during the preceding months; but a year or more might be needed for the many designs in a long work, and instances of gaps of several years between drawing and publication exist. It is possible, therefore, that the illustrations published in one year could have been drawn before those in a book of an earlier date.

Bibliographical studies of the printing of many books have disclosed curious and not always explicable aberrations in print-shop procedures and in the behavior of fallible human beings dealing with common day-to-day problems of printing books. They also have disclosed confusion in the records. Differences between information given in this study and that found in other records or in copies of books other than those cited here may indicate errors, but not necessarily. For example, the sharing of editions among several booksellers, each of whom usually had only his name printed on the title page of the copies he sold, occasionally took place in the eighteenth and nineteenth centuries.

Considerable effort has gone into trying to make the Catalog comprehensive, representative, and accurate, although selective. Where accuracy is paramount, the reader will have to review the work of an illustrator afresh, with more care about editions, issues, and perfect copies than has been possible in this study.

Bibliographies

This study contains three bibliographies: a general bibliography follows the Catalog; bibliographies for all eleven chapters follow the general bibliography; and a bibliography relevant to the work of a specific illustrator is included in his or her Catalog entry. The books and articles listed in the general, chapter, and individual bibliographies are limited to those that seem particularly useful, especially recent ones. References in the general and chapter bibliographies often contain valuable material about individual illustrators and should be consulted in addition to any references in the Catalog – and, of course, when none is given. Standard biographical dictionaries, histories of art, and social histories also should be consulted as a matter of course. The reader who wishes to be fully informed about an illustrator, especially a minor one, must scan the indexes of appropriate art, bibliographical, and literary journals. The absence of any references for numerous illustrators signifies that the general and chapter references seemed adequate or that some, especially in periodicals, may have been overlooked.

Index

The comprehensive, alphabetical Index of illustrators, printers, booksellers, presses, engravers and others should help in locating specific artists and craftsmen in the Critical Account and in the Catalog.

PART I

A Critical Account of Five Centuries of Literary Illustration

CHAPTER ONE

The Fifteenth Century
1476–1500

For most of the first century of publishing in England, the story of book illustration has to be traced through printers and the woodcuts they used, not through illustrators. Strictly speaking, there were no illustrators. English graphic art was in a sad state and remained that way – except for portraits and decoration – well into the seventeenth century. During the early years of English printing, only an occasional minor artist of any kind, such as "Gilbert" and William Baker, putative painters of the fresco of the Miracles of the Virgin in Eton College Chapel (completed 1486–87), can even be named. Nor did any foreign artist, even Hans Holbein, apply his talents to lift English illustration to the level of the best on the Continent. (Much of the work there was poor, too.) Indeed, we cannot attach a name to anyone who can seriously be called an illustrator until Marcus Gheeraerts the Elder arrived in London from Bruges in 1568. Yet during the years before Gheeraerts's arrival, English printers issued many books abundantly illustrated with woodcuts.

Conditions of Early Illustration

The books published by early English printers can be divided into two groups: religious and nonreligious. The latter can be subdivided into three categories: information (law, medicine, science, history, travel, husbandry), education (Latin grammars, dictionaries), and literature (poetry, satire, prose and verse romance). Sometimes, as in saints' lives and Sir John Mandeville's *Travels*, popular religious and informational books had a strong literary, not to say fictional, element. Episodes from the lives of Jesus, Mary, and saints and from the Bible and Apocrypha had a long tradition of illustration in manuscripts and paintings. Legal, doctrinal, philosophical, and other scholarly works, especially in Latin, were rarely illustrated beyond an identifying cut or two, such as of a saint or a coat of arms. Grammars and wordbooks do not lend themselves to illustration; yet they generally had a cut of a scholar or a master and pupils as a frontispiece or on the title page. Indeed, the most ubiquitous early English woodcuts are those of scholars and schoolmasters, the best being of French origin. Richard Pynson used about two dozen times a handsome copy of the French printer Jean Du Pré's cut of a scholar sitting on a canopied seat and turning the pages of a book that rests on a Λ-shaped lectern with a round base. This thoughtful scolar was copied by other English printers. The schoolmasters are droll: usually the master sits on a thronelike chair with a birch at the ready above a huddle of students. Such blocks cheer up a multitude of editions of Latin grammars. Wynkyn de Worde used a miserable one about three dozen times, the record for any English woodcut. In spite of the ominous birch, the presence of such illustrations suggests a more humane pedagogical outlook than might be expected. Hundreds of early books, and later ones for that matter, with just a cut or two at the beginning are illustrated in only a bibliographical sense. Fortunately, the commercial drive of the early printers led them to extend their markets by printing, after translation if necessary, and illustrating abundantly, books of knowledge and literature that previously had been the privilege of only the learned to read and the delight of only the rich to own.

Seven printers issued illustrated books in England before 1500. (The eighth English printer, John Lettou, seems not to have used illustrations.) In order of the appearance of their first book with illustrations (according to generally accepted dates that are subject to revision), they were William Caxton (1481), William de Machlinia (1484?), Theodoric Rood and Thomas Hunte (1486), the St. Albans Printer (1486), Richard Pynson (1492?), Wynkyn de Worde (1493), and Julyan Notary (1498). Since all but two of Notary's numerous illustrated books are said to have been issued in the sixteenth century, he will be considered in the next chapter. Machlinia printed a *Horae ad usum Sarum* (1484?), and Rood and Hunte in Oxford printed John Mirk's *Liber festialis* (1486), but both used worn blocks and thereafter printed no other illustrated books. *The Bokys of Haukyng and Huntyng and Blasyng of Armys* (1486), issued by the St. Albans Printer, contains, for the first time in England and only a little later than in Germany, colored woodcuts produced by the impression of a color block instead of by hand illumination. Since the designs are simple coats of arms and nothing came of the innovation, the book is of only historical interest. That leaves the three major printers of illustrated books in England during the fifteenth century: Caxton, de Worde, and Pynson.

Because de Worde and Pynson continued to print well into the sixteenth century, the first period of English book illustration actually extends from 1481 to around 1535. In the last two decades of the fifteenth century and the first three of the sixteenth, more than two dozen printers in Great Britain issued illustrated books. Yet Caxton, de Worde, and Pynson printed 650 of the almost 900 known illustrated books published in England before 1535, and their editions contained about 2000 of the approximately 2700 woodcuts recorded. (For bibliographical purposes, the presence of one woodcut classifies a late-fifteenth- or early-sixteenth-century book as illustrated; but, with a few exceptions, books discussed in the Critical Account and listed in the Catalog contain more than one.) Among the other printers, Julyan Notary, Robert Copland, and Peter Treveris were the leaders in using a substantial number of illustrations, but neither they nor any other printer of this first period was able to bring together on English soil a first-rate original draftsman and a skilled woodcutter. They occasionally commanded the services of competent cutters, some of whom possibly worked for them abroad, but these artisans directed their efforts almost entirely to copying Continental designs. This was natural, since the illustrations already were in the established texts being translated into English. In a sense, the illustrations were being translated, too. But for the same reason, the best woodcut illustrations in English books of the first period are impressions of imported blocks, although some of the copies are good facsimiles of foreign originals. Most of the best importations and copies of both religious and secular illustrations are those from France.

Woodcuts in Early Printed Books

A few words about woodcuts may not be superfluous. Throughout this book, the word *woodcut* is used in the strict sense, never as a synonym for *wood engraving*. The essential point is that the wood is *cut*. The cutting is done with a knife drawn toward the cutter across a block of relatively soft wood, such as pear, apple, holly, and service, which has been cut along the grain, or "on the plank". The wood on both sides of every line or shape that is meant to print black has to be cut or chiseled away. Wood engrav-

ings differ from woodcuts in the method, tools, and wood used, and in the effects achieved. Wood engraving did not come into use until three centuries after the death of Caxton; metal engraving, not until a century. The engraved metal relief block is a variant form of the woodcut that was used for early Continental book illustrations and religious prints and occasionally was imported from France to England in the early sixteenth century. Fine detail, fluent tapering lines, white-line shading, neat white dotted areas, and bent borders instead of breaks in used blocks are evidence of metal relief engraving.

Woodcuts were the natural substitutes for hand-drawn manuscript illustrations when, around 1450, Johannes Gutenberg began printing by movable type, which yielded editions of hundreds of copies of one text. Woodcuts already were being used for other purposes: single-sheet religious images, playing cards, block books, textile patterns, and even manuscript illustrations. Woodcuts are just right for the printed book because they can be printed at the same time as type and by the same surface pressure on the common screw-and-lever press, on which all books were printed until the early nineteenth century. Wood blocks, therefore, have to be the same height as type. Today, the standard height is .918 inch (23.317 mm). It was virtually the same in Cologne and Augsburg in Caxton's day, although it varied in other places. At their best, woodcuts produce on the page strong, simple patterns congruous with the heavy typefaces used by early northern European printers. Cutting wood blocks is tedious work. They tend to split under pressure or during temperature changes, and when wanted, they may be locked up in the forms of another book, have been mislaid, or have been lent to another printer. Thus many early English books contain a hodgepodge of woodcuts of different styles and sizes drawn from whatever supply of blocks the printers had on the shelves, often for years, as the dates of the books, the breaks in borders, and the round drill marks of worms attest. Condition of the impression of blocks and dates of any previous uses often help date fragments and undated books.

Cutting an illustration on a block of wood with knife and chisel is not an easy feat; but the adjective *crude*, as used by literary scholars, is an imprecise description of early English woodcuts. We know nothing about the activities of the men who illustrated the books of the first English printers beyond what we infer from the impressions themselves. Someone had to draw the designs that were not traced (as the majority were); someone had to transfer the designs to the wood blocks if they were not drawn directly on the wood; and someone had to cut the blocks. Since there were no master artists and therefore no specialized

Formschneider, or cutters, as on the Continent, tracing or drawing and cutting were probably more often than not done by one hand – the poor blocks by anyone in the print shop who wanted to have a go, the better ones by someone with comparable skills, such as an illuminator, a scribe, a metalsmith, or a wood-carver. Using the term *hand* is one way to avoid repeating *designer* and *cutter* and speculating on whether one or more persons were involved.

In 1968, the publication in facsimile of an illuminated manuscript of Caxton's translation of Ovid's *Metamorphoses* afforded a unique opportunity to examine late-fifteenth-century drawings done in England as illustrations for a text clearly intended to be printed. This elegant manuscript, however, was apparently in preparation for presentation, not for printing, but doubtless to a prospective patron of a projected edition. Only four of the fifteen planned illustrations were completed and colored. The manuscript is dated "Westminster, 22 April 1480", but no copy printed by Caxton, de Worde, Pynson, or other first-generation printer is extant. It is difficult to understand why, with the best part of his career ahead, Caxton would have taken the trouble to translate this popular work and then not print it. He almost certainly did not print an illustrated edition, for no stray blocks from an easily identifiable *Metamorphoses* series turn up in later books, as they almost certainly would had Caxton printed such an edition.

In any case, we miss what would be an enlightening comparison of late-fifteenth-century English drawings and woodcuts of the same design. Nevertheless, these drawings seem to be representative examples of late-fifteenth century draftsmanship, if we may judge by another – the Lambeth manuscript illumination of Lord Rivers, attended by a monk (probably the scribe Haywarde), presenting a book to Edward IV. The line drawings beneath the color of the *Metamorphoses* and Lambeth manuscript designs seem to be not much more sophisticated than the woodcuts of the period. Thus we may be led to speculate that less of the essence of the original drawings escaped the inexperienced cutters than we might have assumed. But in early English woodcutting, as distinct from nineteenth-century facsimile wood engraving, the character of the drawn line would seem to have had relatively little influence on the quality of the cut line. Given the general excellence of traditional compositions, particularly of religious designs, expert cutters could have endowed even weak drawings and tracings with dignity and charm. The mediocre quality of much early English woodcut illustration, therefore, seems on the whole to be more the consequence of the cutting than of the drawing.

Major Printers

William Caxton

Besides having been the first printer in England, William Caxton (1422?–91) was the first English publisher, almost in the modern sense of the term. In order to determine the market for printed books in England, he supplemented his own discriminating taste with canny inquiries into the literary preferences of others. In consequence, his list of about eighty titles is notable for its popular appeal. In addition to religious and educational works, it is strong in belles-lettres, including most of the works of Geoffrey Chaucer, Sir Thomas Malory's *Morte d'Arthur* (1485), *Fables of Esope* (1484), and several romances. It would therefore seem likely that Caxton would have found woodcut illustrations an asset. He must have been familiar with them: as already mentioned, the first dated illustrated book was printed in Germany in 1461; the first appeared in France in 1478; and illustrated books were first published in Italy and the Netherlands between those two dates. Yet from 1474, when he probably printed his first book in Bruges, Caxton did without illustrations entirely for several years, during which he published more than two dozen books. Between 1481 and 1486, however, by copying and buying, he accumulated at least 381 woodcuts. Then for five more years, the rest of his printing career, he reused blocks from this store. Still, he issued only twenty illustrated publications, not all of which were books. Among the literary works that Caxton printed and might have had illustrated, but did not, are Chaucer's *Troilus and Criseyde*, John Gower's *Confessio amantis*, Virgil's *Aeneid*, *Reynart the Foxe*, *The right plesaunt and goodly historie of the foure sonnes of Aymon*, *Recuyell of the Historyes of Troye*, and *Paris and Vienne*.

The illustrations that Caxton had freshly prepared were technically poor, even when they were copies. Those he imported were much better, but they were shopworn. Yet Caxton had had exceptional opportunities to become familiar with the arts. Bruges, his home for more than thirty years, not only was the home of a long line of great artists, but also was a famous center of illumination; and Margaret of York, duchess of Burgundy, who encouraged Caxton in his translating and printing, owned many rich manuscripts. Notwithstanding, Caxton seems to have regarded illustrations as a vehicle intended only to extend the sales of his printed books to a wider circle of readers than the manuscript producers ever thought of reaching. There is no evidence that he took any pleasure in pictures in books or that he was displeased with any of those in the books from his press. In none of his otherwise revealing prologues and epilogues did he discuss them. It was Caxton's bad luck that no artists and trained woodcutters were working in late-fifteenth-century England, but we cannot help wishing that he had shown the vision as the founder of English book illustration that he showed as the founder of English book publishing. It is idle, however, to judge his woodcut illustrations solely in terms of technical proficiency.

Caxton came close to getting the credit for having introduced metal engraving with a burin to English book illustration. In the Huntington Library copy of the first book printed in English, *Recuyell of the Historyes of Troye* (Bruges, 1474?), is an engraving of a contemporary interior scene that shows Caxton (presumably a reasonably close likeness) presenting the book to Margaret of York. Since the plate was inserted and does not appear in other copies of the book, there is little doubt that it was made for only this presentation. The work is Flemish and did not inspire Caxton to use engraving as a medium of illustration after he moved to Westminster in 1476.

The Myrroure of the Worlde (1481) by Vincentius (Vincent de Beauvais) is the first illustrated book printed in England. For it, Caxton had a series of eleven woodcuts made. (Two of them also appear in a book formerly, but no longer, thought to have been printed in 1480.) The designs, a mixture of diagrams and simple figures, such as a couple playing music, are wretched. For his second illustrated book, Jacobus de Cessolis's allegorical *Game and Playe of the Chesse* (1483), Caxton turned to another hand, who was from then on his chief but not sole reliance. He was in no sense an artist, only a copyist, and he probably never had cut a wood block before, but he was a considerable improvement on his predecessor. Since he also prepared many of the blocks for Caxton's editions of Jacobus de Voragine's *Legenda aurea* and of *Fables of Esope* and all those for *The Canterbury Tales*, he was the first person in England who might loosely be called a book illustrator. These three books were published at around the same time, perhaps all in 1484.

The illustrations in Caxton's translation of *Fables of Esope* (26 March 1484) have exceptional interest because Aesopian fable books have engaged the attention of several leading English illustrators. *Fables of Esope* is the first major volume of belles-lettres printed in England to have been substantially illustrated – a wholesale 186 woodcuts, the first 27 of which picture incidents from Planudes's "Life of Aesop". The 186 designs are copies of copies made in Lyons (1480) of the famous series of Johann Zainer of Ulm (ca. 1476). Caxton's heavily outlined representations of the human and animal characters in his succinct versions of the fables are childish affairs. But many of Caxton's readers probably had childlike tastes in art and literature, and his simplified woodcuts must have enhanced

their delight in the shrewd fables of talking animals and birds. From the first design, that of the cock finding the precious but inedible gem on the dunghill (fig. 1), to the last, that of the fox trying to beguile the cock and hens out of a tree, the woodcuts show the northern European impulse to communicate with the reader, to retell the story in naturalistic pictures – a deviation, not necessarily for the better, from the medieval, oriental, and Italian urge to celebrate through decoration, to add beauty to the page.

Caxton decided that illustrations would help the sale of his second edition of Chaucer's *Canterbury Tales* (1484?). The twenty-three blocks, all by the chief hand, were probably based on manuscript drawings and seem to be English, for they are much like the designs in the Ellesmere and Cambridge manuscripts. Apart from whatever loss there is in the cutting, the illustrations are dismally inadequate. Twenty-two represent the pilgrims mounted for the journey to Canterbury. They are barely identifiable by their dress and the symbols they carry. The last cut – it should have been the first – shows the company eating at a round table at the Tabard Inn before setting out from Southwark. Rude as it is, this cut is the first genuine illustration of a scene from English literature to appear in a book printed in England.

Sometime after 20 November 1483, Caxton published his largest and most important religious book, the comprehensive *Legenda aurea* of Voragine (or Varagine). The illustrations, copied from a Continental edition, are ambitious: a full folio frontispiece of a Saints in Glory and seventeen page-wide and fifty-four column-wide representations of the life of Jesus, Old Testament scenes, and saints with their symbols. Several of the saints do double and triple duty when their symbols are not too specific. The page-wide biblical scenes are the most interesting. They are not prepossessing, but they serve to instruct the simple reader and to make a large volume approachable.

Caxton's second important religious book was St. Bonaventura's *Speculum vitae Christi* (1486), illustrated with blocks imported from the Low Countries. The twenty-seven traditional designs of the life and Passion of Jesus fit neatly into the space of the blocks, and the even distribution of line work makes them seem to belong on the type-page. Superior to these conventional designs, although not cut with the grace of many French religious series, are five Flemish designs that Caxton acquired: the Crucifixion, Lazarus and Dives, the Tree of Jesse, David and Goliath, and the Three Rioters. The Crucifixion, with twenty-five appearances by 1502, was the most popular early English religious illustration. Caxton also brought to England from the Low Countries three dozen much-used small religious woodcuts, probably for first use in a *Horae ad Usum Sarum*

1. Anon. *Fables of Esope* (1484). William Caxton.

2. Anon. Sir Thomas Malory, *Morte d'Arthur* (1498). Wynkyn de Worde.

(1490), of which no copy is known. These crowded little blocks were reprinted for years in the religious books of Wynkyn de Worde and other printers.

Wynkyn de Worde

William Caxton's chief printer and successor, Wynkyn de Worde (d. 1534) – Jan van Wynkyn from Worth in Alsace – lacked Caxton's literary inclinations, but he had a great deal of indiscriminate enthusiasm for illustrated books and rarely failed to tuck in a cut or a handful of cuts when the opportunity offered. In the forty years of his career as a master printer, he issued almost 450 illustrated titles, of which not all were really books and many were reprints. Somewhat fewer than one-third of the extant titles are secular; of these, about two dozen are substantially illustrated works of literature. Fragments of others indicate that the number printed probably was close to fifty. De Worde had a stock of at least 1000 blocks, a great many of which saw multiple service. About one-half of these woodcuts were of religious subjects. He published the same number of illustrated titles in the second half of his career as in the first half; yet he added few blocks to his collection after 1520.

De Worde's first illustrated books were those in which he could use his master's blocks, which became his on the death of Caxton in 1491, and he continued to use them as long as he could. He used them in Geoffrey Chaucer's *Caunterbury Tales* (1498) and in many popular religious works, including Jacobus de Voragine's *Legenda aurea* (1493), St. Bonaventura's *Speculum vitae Christi* (1494), *Horae beatissime virginis Marie*, John Mirk's *Festyuall* (1508), and *Nicodemus Gospel*. He reprinted these books often throughout his career, and he stuffed them all with woodcuts. His cuts are apt, but since they vary in size, style, and condition, they give his religious books an untidy appearance. Even when he had a set of new cuts, de Worde could not refrain from incorporating some of his old ones and so spoiling the possibility of a unified effect. But he had at his disposal at least one hand who was a good copyist and a clean cutter. This chief hand provided the printer with the best of his blocks; the cuts that de Worde imported from the Continent were usually old and miscellaneous. Because this hand could copy so faithfully, some of de Worde's woodcuts suggest standards that do not actually prevail.

Three books testify to de Worde's early commitment to illustrations, although all the woodcuts in them were copied from Continental originals. The thirty-nine single-column cuts of saints in the *Vitas patrum* (1495) of St. Jerome are poor, but de Worde achieved a certain opulence by repeating each an average of four times. He never again used the unskilled cutter of these blocks. His chief hand copied nineteen illustrations from a Flemish and a French edition for *De proprietatibus rerum* (1495) of Bartholomaeus Anglicus. This encyclopedic view of the large and small affairs of the world as seen 250 years earlier was greatly helped by simple outline cuts of the universe, Creation, doctors practicing their arts, the elements, animals, birds, plants, miners, and a four-compartment representation of savor, color, liquor, and odor (a suspicious woman inspecting eggs at a market). In 1499, the same hand cut about seventy blocks for that ancestor of science fiction, Sir John Mandeville's *Wayes of the Holy Londe*, popularly known as Mandeville's *Travels*. He probably followed copies done in Lyons of the original series, which had been commissioned by the Augsburg printer Anton Sorg. Shakespeare mused over these woodcuts of strange creatures and customs in faraway places, probably as they appeared in Thomas East's edition of 1568 or 1583(?), and he transmuted them into the golden poetry of Othello's explanation of how Desdemona came to fall in love with him. The language of early writings about science and technology was often vague; woodcuts, therefore, were a vital ally of the early printing press in the spread of knowledge and error.

On rare occasions, the first English printers were forced to have original interpretive designs cut (and drawn, if there was no manuscript model to follow). Among these, by far the most interesting is de Worde's series for his 1498 edition of Sir Thomas Malory's *Morte d'Arthur*. It is the only major work of English literature printed during this early period that contains a substantial number of woodcuts made in England that create for the modern reader a true world of the imagination. Twenty-one generously-sized designs project bravery, marvels, dishonor, and slaughter with uninhibited zest. The unknown artist did his best to lead the reader into each book with an anticipatory glimpse of the crowded events to follow, although he failed to reverse his drawings on the blocks and so got the sequences backward. He visualized scenes such as those of the mother of the newborn Tristram handing a monkeylike baby to a gentlewoman, on the left, and stretched out in labor, on the right, and of Gawayne and Ector asleep in an abandoned chapel and then happily greeting each other on the road to it. Yet it is instructive to compare the cut for Book IV (fig. 2) – "How Merlyn was assoted and dooted on one of the ladyes of the lake; and how he was shette in a roche under a stone and there dyed" – with Aubrey Beardsley's drawing of the same moment four centuries later.

To the modern eye, both drawing and cutting in this *Morte d'Arthur* series are wild and wonderful, and it is easy to believe that the illustrations delighted de Worde's customers. That the extravagant effect was unintentional is beside the point. Whoever drew the designs – the circular eyes and other details suggest an artist from the Low Countries – had a novice's troubles with anatomy and proportion. Figures sometimes vary from the diminutive in the foreground to tower high farther away; horses seem to be rented from a carrousel; knights and horses sometimes have long jointless legs; and Arthurian ladies come extraordinarily short in the waist. These forms are boldly outlined and given definition by restrained open parallel-line shading, and they are supplemented by tall castle gates, sugar-loaf hills, feathery white-line foliage, and airplane-like birds. Lacking clear horizon lines, and with form uncertainly related to form, knights and ladies, horses and castles tend to float with an abandon that turns the legends into a visual fantasy curiously in harmony with Malory's burled prose. This 1498 edition has missed oblivion by only one copy, now in the Rylands Library in Manchester. When thirty-one years later de Worde decided to reissue Malory's work, he had lost several blocks and was forced to piece out his set with cuts from early romances; but ten of the originals, snowy with wormholes, survived to serve William Copland in 1557. In the *Morte d'Arthur* series, we meet the first truly interpretive illustrator to work in England.

Had de Worde been blessed with artistic taste and with the artists and artisans to express it, he could have been lord of the English illustrated book. His determination to carry out Caxton's decision to put the printing press at the disposal of all Englishmen who could read led him to publish many more romances and other secular books of entertainment with illustrations than anyone else in England before the eighteenth century. His opportunities were Aladdinian. Beginning in 1498 with *Morte d'Arthur* and *Caunterbury Tales*, his list includes book after book that better woodcuts might have made memorable: Mandeville's *Travels* (1499), Raoul Le Fèvre's *Y^e Hystoryes of Troye* (1502), *Robert the Deuyll* (1502?), *The Four Sons of Aymon* (1504), *King Ponthus* (1505?), Pierre Gringore's *Castell of Laboure* (1506), *The Dystruccyon of Jherusalem by Vaspazian and Tytus* (1508), three poems by Stephen Hawes – *Pastyme of Pleasure*, *Example of Vertu*, and *Comfort of Lovers* (1509) – Sebastian Brant's *Shyppe of Fooles* (1509), *Kynge Rycharde Cuer du Lyon* (1509), Antoine de La Salle's *Fyftene Joyes of Maryage* (1509), *The Knyght of the Swanne* (1512), *The Chronycles of Englonde* (1515), Chaucer's *Troylus and Cresyde* (1517) and *Parlement of Foules, Olyuer of Castylle* (1518), two translations of Boccaccio by William Walter – *Tytus and Gesyppus* (ca. 1525) and *Guystarde and Sygysmonde* (1532) – *Chevalier Paris, Valentine and Orson, Seven*

Wise Masters of Rome, Generides, John of Hildesheim's *Three Kings of Cologne, Flowers of Ovid, Hyckescorner, Sir Degore,* Alexander Barclay's *Cytezen and Uplondyshman, Gesta Romanorum, Cocke Lorell's Bote, Squire of Low Degree, Frederick of Jennen, Reynard the Fox, Ipomydon, Sir Bevis of Hampton, Capystranus,* and a dozen other diverting shorter pieces. Among these works, *Guystarde and Sygysmonde* (1532) is notable because its four blocks are apparently the last romance illustrations freshly cut for de Worde. (It would seem likely that *Tytus and Gesyppus* was issued at or near the same time, rather than at the date [ca. 1525] assigned. It contains two fresh blocks.) The *Guystarde and Sygysmonde* illustrations, although certainly copied, summarize the gruesome love story in four woodcuts, which, uniquely, are printed together on the page following the colophon.

Because de Worde's chief hand made clean, strongly outlined copies of neat French illustrations, the early editions of these popular works, with woodcuts made for them, are sometimes creditable illustrated books. As is true of all early illustrated books for nonscholars, they were immensely popular. Copies of all of them are rare: some editions are known from one copy; some, from fragments; and some, only from woodcuts belonging to unmistakable series, such as *Reynard the Fox*, that appear in other books and in later editions by later printers, even well into the seventeenth century.

Wynkyn de Worde missed the chance for glory that his fifty or so illustrated popular literary works offered, but in regretting the absence of originality and technical excellence in his illustrations, we must not deny him a place of importance in the history of English book illustration.

Richard Pynson

Although Richard Pynson (d. 1530) was the first printer in England to produce well-designed books, his output of fewer than 200 illustrated books was not one-half that of Wynkyn de Worde. He began printing in London in the early 1490s and was printer to Henry VIII from 1509 until his death. Yearbooks, legal works, indulgences, and schoolbooks kept his press busy, so that he was able to enter the popular market judiciously. Born and well trained in France, Pynson borrowed, bought, or copied illustrations that had appeared first in the books of French printers such as Jean Du Pré, Philippe Pigouchet, and Antoine Vérard, as well as some from the Low Countries. His able chief hand, who apparently was French, was the best resident woodcutter of the period, but he was a facsimile copyist. Like Caxton and de Worde, Pynson slacked off in acquiring new blocks in his later years.

3. Anon. Pierre Gringore, *The Castell of Laboure* (1505?). Richard Pynson.

Pynson's first illustrated book – possibly his first English book – was Geoffrey Chaucer's *Tales of Canterburie* (1492?), which has woodcuts that are little improvement on Caxton's. The copyist must have read the Prologue (or had it translated) because in the cut of the dining scene at the Tabard Inn, he added differentiating details to some of the pilgrims – the Knight quaintly wearing a suit of armor, for instance. Among religious books and indulgences, Pynson, as official printer, issued a few handsome missals and Books of Hours for Sarum use. From France, he imported four large blocks: a relief metal engraving of the Resurrection, a Saints in Glory, and two Crucifixions. They are technically the best illustrations to appear in any early English religious books. The seventeen illustrations that adorn John Lydgate's *Falle of Princis Princessis & Other Nobles* (27 January 1494), a translation of Boccaccio's *De casibus virorum*, are the first fine interpretive illustrations of belles-lettres in an English book. They are, however, imports that were originally used in Du Pré's edition, *Les Cas et Ruynes des nobles hommes et femmes* (Paris, 1483–84).

In the Huntington Library is an edition of *Fables of Aesop* printed by Pynson's type and illustrated with Caxton's blocks. It is dated "1497" with some certainty. In 1500(?), Pynson brought out another edition, with a complete series of smaller woodcuts based on the Caxton set. These facts point up the gaps in our knowledge of early

printing in London. Although de Worde took over Caxton's stock of woodcuts, as far as is known, he did not print the *Fables*. Did Pynson borrow the 186 blocks for his first edition? It seems unlikely that de Worde would have been that generous to even a friendly competitor. Did Pynson buy the blocks? It seems unlikely that if he had, he would have gone to the expense so soon afterward of having all 186 blocks recut. Pynson probably did not buy them; one of the Caxton blocks was used later in a de Worde book. On 4 September 1507, de Worde supplied the cuts for a joint edition of Jacobus de Voragine's *Legenda aurea*, which he and Pynson issued with separate colophons. In a similar venture, *The Boke Named the Royall*, also assigned to 1507, they pooled their collections of appropriate religious cuts. In 1497, with so large a venture as *Fables of Aesop*, it would have been as reasonable for the rivals to divide the cost – Pynson to do the printing and de Worde to supply the blocks. Since only one imperfect copy of that edition exists, it would not be statistically strange for all those with de Worde's colophon to have disappeared. A few years later, for whatever reason, Pynson elected to reissue the *Fables* on his own and had a series of smaller, neater blocks made for his sole use. The popularity of Aesop in England from the earliest days of printing cannot be doubted.

Dutch, Flemish, and French printers early issued books

for export to England, some in English. In 1503, Antoine Vérard of Paris entered the English market with a translation of Pierre Gringore's placid allegory *The Castell of Laboure*, and Pynson pirated this edition a year or two later (1505?). The translator was Alexander Barclay, who usually was associated with Pynson, as the poet Stephen Hawes was with de Worde. These were two of the earliest author–publisher teams in the history of English letters, although, of course, Caxton in his own person was the earliest. The twenty-eight *Castell of Laboure* illustrations were copied with almost photographic precision from the edition printed by Philippe Pigouchet and Simon Vostre in 1499. The detailed designs of domestic scenes have a nice linear quality, excellent composition, and enough well-distributed shading to evoke an illusion of volume and depth rarely present in the woodcuts of the period in England (fig. 3). As a commentary on the state of the art of illustration in this period, it must be added that *The Castell of Laboure* (1506) was also one of de Worde's most successfully illustrated books – with woodcuts faithfully copied from Pynson's.

In 1503, Vérard also invaded the London market with a *Shepherd's Calendar* written in an extraordinary approximation of English, which Pynson roundly denounced in *The Kalender of Shepherdes* (1506). Yet he procured Vérard's blocks to illustrate his translation. They make up an assorted lot of stargazing shepherds, symbolic figures of the planets, tortures of the damned from the *Ars moriendi*, occupations of the months and the days of the months, saints to go with the saints' days, and signs of the zodiac. Along with this assortment came the first all-purpose cuts to appear in English books: little borderless men, women, trees, and castles. They had been used by German and French printers for some time, and their economy appealed to the English printers, who used them generously. A human figure often appears with the name of a character above his or her head, but the function of these all-purpose cuts seems to have been more to decorate the page than to pretend to illustrate the text.

Barclay was the translator for another of Pynson's ambitious illustrated-book ventures, the 1509 edition of Sebastian Brant's verse satire *Shyp of Folys*. It contains 109 large diverting woodcuts of the doings of Brant's collection of knaves and fools. Perhaps de Worde learned of the enterprise after it was in progress and rushed through a prose translation with inferior illustrations, for halfway along, Pynson's copies of the French designs were made hastily, as much detail as possible being omitted. Had the work progressed as it had begun, *Shyp of Folys* would have been one of the most satisfactory of early English illustrated books. The designs were copied from those in the 1497 edition of Geoffroy de Marnef and Maystener, which are, in turn, copies of the original designs in Johann Bergmann van Olpe's first edition (Basel, 1494) as they appeared in his Latin edition (1499). The originals possibly were drawn by the young Albrecht Dürer under Brant's direction. De Worde's less-well-executed series was copied from copies made in Lyons. This sort of devious genealogy makes one cautious about accepting apparent sources of English woodcuts without considerable research among editions rarely found in one library.

Pynson printed fifteen illustrated romances and similar popular works, one-quarter of de Worde's production of this sort. Similarities among a number of cuts in literary works printed by de Worde, Pynson, and Julyan Notary and their occasional mixture in one book raise baffling questions about ownership and printing practices. Shrewdly chosen, Pynson's popular works include Lydgate's *Falle of Princis Princessis & Other Nobles* (1494), *Fables of Aesop* (1497, 1500?), *Beuys of Southamtowne* (1503?), Guido delle Colonne's *Hystorye Sege and Dystruccyon of Troye* (1513), *The Dystruccyon of Jherusalem by Vaspazyan and Tytus* (1513), and Chaucer's *Troilus and Criseyde*, *Boke of Fame* (1526), and *Parlement of Foules*. Their illustrations are cleanly cut, apt, and homogeneous. The ability of Pynson's chief hand to cut facsimile blocks gives Richard Pynson's illustrated books the honor of representing the highest standards in the first period of publishing in England.

CHAPTER TWO

The Sixteenth Century
1501–1600

For convenience, illustration in the sixteenth century can somewhat arbitrarily be divided into three roughly equal periods: 1501 to 1535, 1536 to 1562, and 1563 to 1600. The most important books of the first period are those printed by Wynkyn de Worde and Richard Pynson. The other printers of the first third of the sixteenth century either used Continental blocks or copies of them or derived their designs from the blocks of de Worde or Pynson. During the second period, religious controversy gave prominence to books on religion; printers of occasional literary works had to resort to using badly worn blocks handed down from earlier printers. In this period, the Great Bible (1539) was the first of the Tudor Bibles to bring splendid illustrations to all the English people, but the Tudor Bibles were almost entirely the productions of Continental printers, artists, and woodcutters. Independent creativeness is rare among the other illustrated books of these middle years. Two notable events were the introduction of metal engraving and the presence of Hans Holbein the Younger in London; yet neither had any direct effect on English illustration. The third period began with the publication by John Day of the first English edition of John Foxe's *Actes and Monuments of the Church* (*The Book of Martyrs*) (1563). It is one of the significant books in the history of English illustration, the first great work by an English author that was issued by an English printer-publisher and contains a distinguished series of original illustrations. Although its subject matter continues the religious concerns of the middle period, it marks a break with the past in illustration and was followed in the remaining years of the sixteenth century by several individual works of considerable interest but little continuity.

Among these works are several books illustrated with woodcuts, some of which, like those in *Actes and Monuments*, are remarkable and had to be especially designed for the works they illustrate. Furthermore, in this period appeared the first book printed in England that is illustrated with etchings and the first that contains engraved literary illustrations. The etchings are original; the engravings,

copies. It is important to remember two facts about the use of these media at this time: (1) both were adopted as rapid means of reproducing drawings, not, as later, for their intrinsic aesthetic effects; and (2) artists customarily combined both media on a plate, so that it is often difficult to determine which is dominant. Statements here and elsewhere that one or the other method was used mean that one appears dominant to the observer, who may be wrong. A third fact of importance about these media is that they cannot be printed simultaneously with type, a limiting expense in illustrating books. (Books listed in the General Bibliography contain authoritative explanations with illustrations of these and other media. The reader who is not familiar with graphics should consult them now in order to avoid confusion hereafter.)

A look through the Catalog reveals how book illustration reflected the social and literary conditions of the sixteenth century. Only two or three literary works by living authors were published before 1563. The early printers continued William Caxton's policy of using the printing press mainly to make more widely available the religious, informational, and recreational reading of the past. The reigns of Henry VIII and Mary I saw the publication of new serious books on religion and history; not until England settled down under Elizabeth I did illustration take on a more literary aspect, although the cuts in Edmund Spenser's *Shepheardes Calendar* (1579) and *Faerie Queene* (1590) fail to signal the flowering of Elizabethan literature. In terms of illustration, England moved into the Renaissance with John Harington's translation of Ludovico Ariosto's *Orlando Furioso* (1591), which contains the first important series of copper engravings.

Early Printers: 1501–1535

Whether because of the times or the accident of personalities, none of the score of printers who published illustrated books in the early sixteenth century ever matched the initiative of the three fifteenth-century leaders in this respect. Most of their books contain blocks that were borrowed, copied, or descended from those of Caxton, de Worde, Pynson, and Continental sources. A few points of interest, however, might be noted briefly.

Julyan Notary seems to have issued twenty-eight illustrated books before he stopped printing in 1520. It is difficult to be certain about the number because, on occasion, he may have printed for de Worde, rather than for himself. His designs are uniformly presentable but unoriginal. He imported some metal relief cuts of religious subjects, and his woodcut copies of such metal cuts are primitive English white-line antecedents of the eighteenth-century work of Elisha Kirkall and Thomas Bewick and of modern wood engraving in this style. Five heavily illustrated books appeared from his press: soon after 1500 were published *Hore beate Marie virginis*, Jacobus de Voragine's *Legenda aurea*, and *Cronycle of Englonde*; about 1515, *Huon of Burdeux*; and in 1518(?), *The Kalender of Shepardes*. Several of the cuts in *Legenda aurea* (16 February 1503 [1504]), such as the Ascension (fig. 4), are copies in wood of French metal relief cuts in the *manière criblée* – white flicks on black. There is only one extant copy of the only English edition of *Huon of Burdeux* known to have been printed in this early period. It followed soon after the printing of the first edition by Michel le Noir (Paris, 1513), from which Lord Berners made his translation. It contains thirty-four woodcuts, nineteen not otherwise listed. Some seem to be copies of le Noir's blocks; some come from a *Four Sons of Aymon* series; and ten appear earlier and later in de Worde books. Notary's edition of *Huon of Burdeux* points up the need for gathering more information about the relationships among early English printers and for sorting out the Continental sources of the illustrations in English romances printed in the sixteenth century – not a formidable task.

Peter Treveris, who printed 25 illustrated books and used more than 100 woodcuts, was the first English publisher clearly to aim at scientific readers. His first book, a translation of Hieronymus von Braunschweig's *Handywarke of Surgeri* (1525), which originally had been published in Strasbourg, is made more useful by its roughly copied and extremely vivid illustrations, such as those of screw-operated trepanning mechanisms. The next year, he brought out the first of his two editions of *The Grete Herball*. It contains over 100 neat copies of Continental cuts of plants and illustrations of husbandry, such as a woman making wine or cider. In 1527, Treveris printed the first of three editions of Braunschweig's *Boke of Distyllacyon*, with strong illustrations of equipment and processes. It was the headspring of all subsequent English chemistry books. Treveris deserves some credit for having

had the verse in Alexander Barclay's *Certayne Egloges* (1530?) illustrated with three suitable and relatively sophisticated designs. The one of Cordix and Coridon, whatever its source, might be taken as a model image for all subsequent pastorals (fig. 5). Treveris probably never had an illustration "invented", but he had more sense of the function of illustration than did any other minor printer of the period. The count of Treveris's illustrated books includes a Huntington Library fragment of a collection of Christmas carols tentatively assigned to him (1525?). It has a roughly copied Day of Judgment (91 × 69 mm), which is not listed in *English Woodcuts, 1480–1535* (1973).

A typographically satisfactory book with fresh, if limited, illustrations is *The Pastyme of People* (1529), written and printed by John Rastell. The eighteen large, boldly treated kings of England from William the Conqueror to Richard III are happily matched with the tall folio pages. That the designs were made by a superior draftsman who understood the strength and limitations of the woodcut is apparent in the way the widely spaced, cleanly cut shading follows the contours of the body and drapery (fig. 8). These designs had to have been made to order but, one would guess, by a foreign hand, as usual.

Thomas Berthelet, Richard Fakes, William Faques, Charles Kyrfoth, Notary, Rastell, John Scolar, John Skot, Treveris, and Robert Wyer all had cuts of scholars or schoolmasters. Some were copies of de Worde's or Pynson's cuts, and some had other sources. Among these, one used in Oxford by Scolar and another used by his successor Kyrfoth seem to represent university scenes. The shadowy Scolar used his cut three times in June 1518 (fig. 6). Then the Welsh printer Thomas Berthelet acquired the block. In spite of rough cutting, the small design of a pupil reciting to his tutor in a study has considerable charm because of its intimacy. Since another version of the same design appears in a French book of 1537, Scolar's cut undoubtedly had a Continental origin. The design used by Kyrfoth in *Compotus manualis ad vsū Oxoniēsiū* (1519) is a decorative three-panel scene of a master and seven pupils in a fascinating study (fig. 7). This illustration had a dissolute but long-lived career after leaving Oxford, until, with the top compartment and half of the bottom lopped off, it heads a broadsheet ballad entitled "London's Ordinarie" (ca. 1660). Treverìs had one of the best cuts of a master teaching, which depicts master and five attentive pupils in a schoolroom with arches, but it had belonged to Godfrey Back of Antwerp in 1510.

The debasement of standards of illustration in England after the deaths of de Worde, Pynson, and Notary shows up with leaden lackluster in the books of Robert Wyer, who printed before and after 1535. Except for one Book of

4. Anon. Jacobus de Voragine, *Legenda aurea* (1503 [1504]). Julyan Notary.

5. Anon. Alexander Barclay, *Certayne Egloges* (1530?). Peter Treveris.

21

6. Anon. Whittinton, *De heteroclitis nominibus* (1518). John Scolar.

7. Anon. *Compotus manualis ad vsū Oxoniēsiū* (1519). Charles Kyrfoth.

Hours (1533?) with thirteen illustrations that might have been Notary's, Wyer usually limited himself to one or two perfunctory woodcuts. Before 1535, he did not issue a single illustrated romance. Around 1540, he had about sixty-five fresh woodcuts made for Guido delle Colonne's popular *Hystoryes of Troye*, which his predecessors had filled with pictures of knights and ladies and love and violence. But, typical of the times, Wyer was content to illustrate his edition with abominable copies of familiar designs drawn from several romances.

With less than the usual arbitrariness, it can be said that the first period of English book illustration ended around 1535. Of Caxton's blocks, only a few stragglers survived that long. After around 1520, de Worde and Pynson relied largely on the blocks piled on their shop shelves. They continued to issue illustrated books without cease, but they ordered new blocks cut only when they had to. Pynson died in 1530; de Worde, in 1534. An "acte conccrnyng prynters and bynders" passed by Parliament in 1534 banned the importation into England of books printed abroad; after 1538 all books had to be licensed before publication; and the rise of Protestantism diminished the sale of the most popular Catholic illustrated books.

The Middle Years: 1536–1562

Tudor Bibles

The scope of this book permits only a passing glance at five of the most famous Tudor Bibles. Their often wonderful illustrations are not native in design or cutting; they all originally appeared in Continental editions. Because translating the Bible into English was banned at the time, the first three Bibles with English texts were printed abroad. Nevertheless, their illustrations must have helped to give definition to the biblical imagery that bloomed with so much vigor in Tudor minds.

The first complete printed Bible in English, translated by William Tyndale and Myles Coverdale, was printed by Eucharius Cervicorn and Johannes Soter, probably in Marburg, Germany, on 4 October 1535. The illustrative title border (272 × 166 mm), designed by Hans Holbein the Younger before he settled in England, is one of the finest examples of this hybrid form. It is made up of four blocks that were cleverly planned to appear to be one. The seventy or so illustrations by Hans Sebald Beham had been made for a Catholic Bible printed in Mainz in 1534. Most are one-column blocks (49 × 71 mm), minor masterpieces, often with numerous figures, architectural details, and distant background scenes (fig. 9). Even with a good deal of repetition, they are somewhat lost in the folio. Beham cannot be

claimed as an English illustrator; but the presence of this substantial body of his work in a book of such historic importance in England suggests that he was the major individual force in early English book illustration, even though it is difficult to claim a school of followers for him. The same blocks were used in the Southwarke Bible (1537), said to have been printed by Jacob van Meteren in Antwerp for James Nycolson.

The Matthew Bible (1537), edited by John Rogers and believed to have been printed by Matthew Crom in Antwerp for Richard Grafton and Edward Whitchurch, contains four kinds of cuts: (1) the title border and an Adam and Eve in Paradise; (2) facsimiles of a number of Beham's Old Testament series and his portrayals of the Evangelists writing; (3) one highly finished cut each for Psalms and for Proverbs, and one of Esau; and (4) twenty-two used cuts of a full Revelation series.

Thomas Cranmer's Great Bible (April 1539) had a curious history. François Regnault first printed it in Paris for Grafton and Whitchurch, but most of the sheets were lost in a fire. Using French printers and presses brought to London and salvaged waste sheets as a guide, Grafton and Whitchurch published this finally authorized edition. The great title frame (343 × 234 mm) is handsome, but as the often repeated legend *Vivat Rex* makes unmistakable, it was meant to glorify Henry VIII rather than God. The sixty or so illustrations consist of about forty-five woodcuts (56 × 77 mm) – of which thirty-two were also used to make up two title borders – and seventeen of Regnault's worn metal relief cuts – fifteen of his life of Christ series, one of St. Matthew, and one of St. Paul. The woodcuts look like first copies of better models, but they must belong to earlier times, before Beham.

The Bishops' Bible (1568), printed by Richard Jugge, contains a title-page portrait of Elizabeth I that was engraved on copper, perhaps by Franciscus Hogenberg during his visit to England, and two other engravings – of Leicester and of Burghley – seemingly by the same hand. The strange odyssey of the approximately 140 woodcut illustrations (77 × 117 mm) has been traced by Colin Clair in his article "The Bishops' Bible, 1568" (1962). Surrounded by ornate strapwork woodcut frames and centered on the great two-column pages, they make a fine show, in terms of book design a better one than the small Beham blocks in the English *editio princeps*. They are, however, facsimiles of the brilliant series by Virgil Solis in the Lutheran Bible (Frankfurt, 1560). According to Clair, the copies were cut for a Dutch Bible (Cologne, 1566) by various hands, including Arnold Nicolai, Christopher Plantin's fine woodcutter. The copyists preserved Solis's monogram – in tribute, not as a deception, one would like to think. After second use in the Bishops' Bible, the blocks returned to the Continent and were used to illustrate a Latin Bible (Antwerp, 1570) and a Danish Bible (Copenhagen, 1589). Nevertheless, these copies of Solis's designs, although perhaps over-refined in comparison with the earlier illustrations by Holbein and Beham, brought variations on traditional compositions in their vigorous action and luxuriant Late Renaissance detail that English readers must have found appealing.

Jugge also brought out a quarto edition of the Bishops' Bible in 1569 with an illustrative woodcut title page (170 × 125 mm). In the upper half, Elizabeth I, holding a scepter and an orb, is being crowned by female figures of Justice and Mercy, while below at the sides, Fortitude and Prudence perch on the strapwork. Directly beneath the throne in an oval cartouche is the title "The holi-bible", unusual for having been cut in the wood. Beneath the cartouche and out of scale with the rest of the design, a congregation listens to a preacher, and cut in the block is the inscription "God save the Queene". Arthur Hind's suggestion that the "IB" of John Day's edition of William Cuningham's *Cosmographical Glasse* (1559) might have been responsible for this block seems doubtful. The long-bodied, small-headed allegorical women seem to belong to the Antwerp tradition, as does the strapwork festooned with vegetables and fruit.

From 1535 to the end of the sixteenth century, many editions of the Bible appeared with illustrations of mixed ancestry. Because of the official status of the Bible, more people may have been acquainted with these images than with any other illustrations. Yet in spite of the general excellence of the illustrations in Tudor Bibles, their influence is not demonstrable beyond the fact that the best Elizabethan woodcuts resemble them in their firm outlines and parallel-line shading.

Thomas Geminus

The first metal intaglio engravings, as distinct from metal relief cuts, used in an English book are four poorly executed copies of German woodcut diagrams of eighteen birth positions in *The Byrth of Mankynde* (1540), a treatise on midwifery translated by Richard Jonas from a Latin edition of Eucharius Rösslin's *Rosengarten*. They are not the work of a trained artist or engraver.

Thomas Geminus (d. 1562), said to have been a Belgian also called Gemyny and Lambrit, is the first known designer-engraver on metal to have practiced in England. He was not an interpretive illustrator in the sense of this study, and Arthur Hind and other authorities have discussed his work in meticulous detail. His only important

work is *Compendiosa totius Anatomie delineatio aere exarata*, dedicated to Henry VIII and printed by John Herford in October 1545. It contains forty pages of large plates on "brass" (that is, copper), most of which are 330 × 190 mm. They depict skeletons and anatomical figures. There also are pages of smaller body parts. With minor variations, Geminus traced the extraordinary woodcuts in Andreas Vesalius's two historic folios, *De humani corporis fabrica libri septem* and *De humani corporis fabrica librorum epitome*, both of which were first published by Johannes Oporinus in Basel in 1543.

Although Vesalius sneered at Geminus's plagiarism, the engravings are almost perfect copies of the masterly woodcuts. The title page of royal arms and allegorical figures, substituted for the title-page scene of Vesalius demonstrating and lecturing to a crowd in a domed operating theater, reveals that Geminus was a draftsman of modest talents. His fame rests on his being the first known burin engraver on metal in England and on his having had the good luck to copy the most famous of all medical woodcuts. His plates had no direct influence on illustration. Metal engraving did not become common in England until the end of the sixteenth century and was not used widely for interpretive illustration until the 1700s.

Hans Holbein the Younger

One of the greatest of book illustrators, Hans Holbein the Younger (1497–1543) visited England for eighteen months and then lived there from 1532 until his death, but he illustrated no English books. Impressions of small stray blocks (ca. 42 × 59 mm) – "The Pharisee and the Publican" and "Christ Exorcising a Demonias" (suspiciously signed "HANS HOLBEN") in Thomas Cranmer's *Catechismus* (1548), "The Hireling Shepherd" in Urbanus Regius's *Lytle Treatyse* (1548), and a unique proof of "Christ Before Pilate" in the British Museum (also signed incorrectly) – may have been drawn during the 1530s for a series no longer extant or, more likely, not completed. Their origin and originality are uncertain. In 1581, Henry Bynneman used a neat reduced and reversed copy of one of Holbein's cuts for Esdras on the title page of a Latin edition of the dialogues of Jean Tixier de Ravisy. Almost entirely linear, modest in size and treatment, these woodcuts are models of lucid situational statement and animated movement, and have a dignity and tension reflective of the scenes they depict, but their use in England was too fortuitous to accord them the serious attention they deserve.

Holbein certainly must have drawn before 1543 the splendid design (206 × 135 mm) of Henry VIII and his council that first appeared in Edward Halle's *Union of the*

8. John Rastell. John Rastell, *The Pastyme of People* (1529).

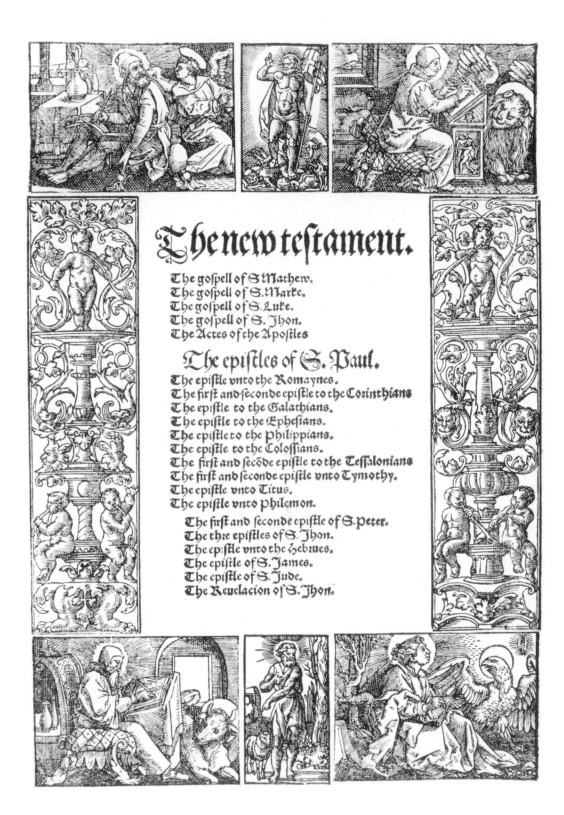

9. Hans Sebald Beham. Bible (1535). Eucharius Cervicorn and Johannes Soter.

Two Noble and Illustre Famelies of Lancastre and Yorke, commonly called Halle's *Chronicle*, published by Richard Grafton, the Bible printer, in 1548. The scene is beautifully spacious and symmetrical. The king, head turned and gesturing, animates the semicircle of advisers, twelve on either side of him, in the second quarter of the design. Above him rises the back of a canopied throne and tapestried walls and above them, a fan-vaulted ceiling. In an oblong cartouche at the bottom is printed "God save the Kyng". Oddly, Grafton put the cut at the end of the book as a sort of reverse frontispiece, possibly on receiving the news of the death of Henry VIII in 1547. Arthur Hind thought that the initials "I.F." are those of Jacob Faber, a Basel woodcutter who worked in France. The fastidious work surely was not executed in England. Hind listed the design as a woodcut, but it may be a metal relief engraving. Twenty-eight years later, the block was used in the third edition of John Foxe's *Actes and Monuments* (1576); the impression shows none of the usual signs of wear of a wood block. Under the circumstances, one wonders that so far in advance of publication Holbein would have drawn this one elaborate design for a book. Hind suggested that it "might have been designed for some larger purpose, perhaps for wall decoration in Whitehall Palace". It is not an illustration, but it is indisputably an English scene in an English book.

Holbein's ornamental borders, initial capitals with background scenes, trim little portrait of the poet Thomas Wyatt ("Holbenus nitida pingendi maximus arte/Effigiem expressit graphice") in John Leland's *Naniae in mortem Thomae Viati* (1542), and device of three children plundering an apple tree (borrowed by the printer Reginald Wolfe) – the most charming ever to adorn an English book – are all melodious notes in the inharmonious chorus of Tudor printing. But they cannot be seized on to inflate Hans Holbein's importance in English book illustration.

Books of Some Interest: 1548–1562

In his brief English appearance, 1547 to 1548, Anthony Scoloker gives us a revealing glimpse of sixteenth-century illustration. He printed several small illustrated books. The most interesting are his own translations of two books of Christian instruction, one from the Dutch of Cornelis van der Heyden and the other from the French of Pierre Viret. Of the first, he printed two varying editions: (1) a perfect copy of *The Ordynarye for All Faythfull Chrystians* (n.d.) consists of "The ordenary for all degrees" (n.d.) and "A right goodly rule (An ordenary to praye)" (1548) and contains thirty-three cuts (ca. 53 × 66 mm); (2) an imperfect copy is in four parts: an introduction called "A bryefe

summe of the whole byble," "A christian instruction for all persons," "The ordenary for all degrees," and "A Right Goodly rule (An ordenary to praye)" and contains at least forty-nine cuts, including those in (1). The state of two or three of the blocks suggests that (1) was printed before (2). The translation of Viret's *Notable Collection of Diuers and Sondry Places of the Sacred Scripture* (after 7 June 1548) is similar to "An ordenary to praye" and contains seven blocks from the series used in van der Heyden's book; therefore, Scoloker probably printed Viret's book after he had printed van der Heyden's. Two blocks from the series appear in a little translation of Martin Luther's sermon on John 20 that Scoloker printed or pretended to have printed in Ipswich, according to the title page, also in 1548.

Scoloker got all these woodcuts from Ghent, where they had been used in a series of sixty-four appropriate illustrations for one of the books he translated, van der Heyden's *Corte Instruccye* (1545). The talented Joost Lambrecht printed the book, cut the blocks, and perhaps drew the designs for them. Although Scoloker's illustrations are, therefore, secondhand foreign woodcuts, the designs of Old and New Testament scenes, social degrees and occupations (including a detailed view of a print shop, the earliest in a book printed in English), and occasions for prayer make up one of the best uniform series in an English book printed during the Tudor period (fig. 10).

In *A History of Printing in Britain* (1965), Colin Clair says that Scoloker's books were probably printed in the Low Countries, not in Ipswich. If so, Lambrecht of Ghent must have worked closely with him. In 1566, nevertheless, eight of the Scoloker blocks were used in David Lyndsay's *Dialogue betweene Experience and a Courtier*, printed by Thomas Purfoote and William Pickering in London; and in 1581, the print-shop block turned up in Stephen Bateman's *Doome Warning All Men to the Iudgemente*, printed by Ralph Newbery for Henry Bynneman. Many of the Continental woodcuts used in sixteenth-century English books must have been handed around in much the same way as Lambrecht's. For example, the eighteen neat and appropriate small woodcuts in Richard Jugge's edition of Bishop John Bale's *Image of Bothe Churches* (1548?) look as though the blocks had become worn and seem to be copies of a better executed traditional Revelation series. Bale wrote the book in exile, and the cuts clearly came from abroad.

John Heywood's long Catholic "parable", *The Spider and the Flie* (1556), printed by Thomas Powell, is one of the few books of the mid-sixteenth century to boast an extensive series of presentable illustrations specifically made for it. The frontispiece (178 × 112 mm) is a full-length portrait of Heywood, identified by his initials, as though seen through a heavy oval frame. Then follow – in a spirited, if not inspired, effort to enliven the long-worded philosophical debate in seven-line stanzas – almost fifty illustrations and many repeats. Most of these are neat scenes (93 × 103 mm) of the poet sitting first at one end of a table and then at the other and observing a spider and a fly in a web on a lattice window with slightly varying arrangements of flies, spiders, and a butterfly around the main actors (fig. 11). These curious scenes are relieved by several double spreads (122 × 175 mm). In the end, a maid (Mary I) kills the spider, sweeps the window (the realm) clean, and establishes order so that the spiders and flies can carry on in their accustomed state. The excessive repetition of blocks dulls the effect of these illustrations – a startling exhibition of enterprise in early illustration.

One of the most unusual Tudor woodcut books is *Genealogie of the Kings of England* (1560–62), a folio of half-length portraits of the monarchs of England from Noah to Elizabeth I issued by Gyles Godet. Beneath the royal arms of each is a two-stanza verse account of his or her reign. Some of the blocks depict only one monarch, and some have as many as four figures. The likenesses of Henry VIII and Mary I are sufficiently close to the Hans Holbein and Antonio Moro paintings to make clear that a fair draftsman made the drawings. The cutting is coarse but strong and effective, especially as a base for coloring, as in the British Library copy. In *A Century of the English Book Trade* (1905), E. Gordon Duff writes that Godet "seems to have been a wood engraver [*sic*] and his publications consist almost entirely of woodcuts". If so, he was the first print-maker, printer, and publisher, but not interpretive illustrator, on record in England.

The mid-sixteenth-century printer Richard Tottel exemplified the undiscriminating attitude of Tudor printers toward illustrations. He missed the fresh opportunities offered by John Lydgate's *Falle of Princis* (1554) and Stephen Hawes's *Pastyme of Pleasure* (1555) and introduced badly worn old romance cuts and some copies with indifference to effect. In Gerard Legh's handbook of heraldry, *Accedens of Armory* (1562), however, along with many simple shields and devices, there are an illustrative title page (158 × 101 mm), for which the text provides four pages of description (one of the earliest examples in an English text of images preceding words), and three other newly cut explanatory designs.

Later Printers: 1563–1600

Until 1563, not one important illustrator, let alone a school, had emerged in England despite the great early popularity of the woodcut-illustrated book. After the flood of wood-cuts copied, bought, borrowed, or inherited by William Caxton and his successors, the stream of illustrations slowed to a trickle. In the third quarter of the sixteenth century, with the great creative surge of Elizabethan literature still to come, English taste had not yet assimilated the mannered characteristics that had established the burin-engraved metal plate as the successor of the woodcut on the Continent. Yet in this slack period were published some of the most significant English illustrated books, and with one exception, they are illustrated with woodcuts. The men who were responsible for most of these books, according to our limited information, were the printers John Day and Henry Bynneman and the artist Marcus Gheeraerts the Elder. Among the large number of Calvinists who fled from the Low Countries and France at this time were Gheeraerts and other artists, such as those in the atelier of John de Critz, as well as artisans described in the rolls of aliens as "engravers". The artists continued the prevailing concentration on portraits and seem to have paid little attention to illustrating books. Yet there is no doubt that both the anonymous designs and the cutting of the wood blocks were the work of these refugees. Surprising in view of the troubled conditions on the Continent was the flourishing traffic in Continental books during the late six-teenth century. For instance, in *Christopher Plantin* (1960), Colin Clair says that the London bookseller Nicholas England stopped in Antwerp on his way home from the Frankfurt Book Fair in 1567 and bought 222 books from Plantin – 44 titles, including emblem books.

John Day

Like William Caxton, John Day (1522–84) was a publisher in a broad sense as well as a printer, and he used illustrations more effectively than did any other printer in the sixteenth century after the death of Wynkyn de Worde. His illustrated books include William Cuningham's *Cosmographical Glasse* (1559), John Foxe's *Actes and Monuments* (1563, 1570), Jan van der Noot's *Theatre* (1568), Stephen Bateman's *Christall Glasse of Christian Reformation* (1569), Robert Grosseteste's *Testaments of the Twelve Patriarches* (1575), and John Derricke's *Image of Irelande* (1581). All except *Het Theatre* were illustrated with woodcuts.

Cuningham's *Cosmographical Glasse* (1559) does not contain interpretive illustrations, but it has a handsome wood-cut title-page border of allegorical figures; initial capitals embellished with figures; and astronomical and geographi-cal diagrams, charts, and tables. The title-page border, two of the initials, and a terrestrial globe are signed "IB". These initials appear twice in Halle's *Chronicle* (1548), printed by Richard Grafton. It has been suggested that

10. Joost Lambrecht (?). Cornelis van der Heyden, *Corte Instruccye* (1545). Anthony Skoloker.

11. Anon. John Heywood, *The Spider and the Flie* (1556). Thomas Powell.

29

12. Anon. John Foxe, *Actes and Monuments of the Church* (1563). John Day.

they are the initials of John Bettes, who signed a portrait painted in 1545, but the identification is too tenuous and the cuts are too incidental to entitle Bettes to be called the first known English book illustrator.

The book forever associated with Day is Foxe's *Actes and Monuments of the Church,* better known as *The Book of Martyrs.* Day, a Protestant who was imprisoned during the reign of Mary I, must have taken a deep personal interest in this history of English Protestantism, with its vivid accounts of the Protestant martyrs. The grim realism of the many woodcut illustrations contributed enormously to the long life of the work. The first of Day's editions (1563) was largely a translation of the book that Foxe had published in Latin on the Continent with no woodcuts. While working closely with Day on the first and second English editions, Foxe almost certainly had an important advisory role in regard to the illustrations. The identities of the artists are not known; there seem to have been two, refugees from the Low Countries or France in all probability.

In the 1714-page, two-column folio edition (1563), the cuts include a large title page, initial capitals decorated with portraits of Elizabeth I and Edward VI, and fifty-three genuine illustrations. Forty-seven are page wide (ca. 125 × 176 mm), and six are 25.4 mm wider than one column (65 × 97 mm). In the 2314-page, two-volume second edition (1570), there are 104 cuts: the 47 large blocks from the first edition, 18 new ones (ca. 127 × 181 mm), and 39 smaller blocks, almost all one-column wide, together with numerous repeats. There are no new illustrations in Day's later editions.

The large illustrations of the recent martyrdoms are among the earliest examples of graphic journalism in England. They are wonderfully detailed in their realization of Foxe's passionate prose: martyrs being scourged, burned, hanged, and stretched on the rack. The horror is heightened by the stoicism of the martyrs and the businesslike manner of the torturers. Typical is the martyrdom of Sir John Oldcastle (fig. 12). Other illustrations in both editions deal with less violent events but are almost as interesting. The additions by a new designer in the 1570 edition include a series that attacks the papacy. The compositions throughout both editions depict numerous figures and are clearly the work of experienced draftsmen. The cutting was equally professional. The fascination that these woodcuts held, and still hold, for generations of readers is a tribute to Day's vision of the importance of illustrations.

Van der Noot's *Theatre* is discussed later in this chapter under Marcus Gheeraerts.

Bateman's *Christall Glasse of Christian Reformation* (*wherein the godly maye beholde the coloured abuses used in this our present tyme*) (1569) contains thirty-seven woodcuts (97 × 112 mm), each of which is enclosed in a thick-and-thin double border. It seems to be the first book by an English author with some, although not all, of the essential characteristics of an emblem book. This essence is an interaction and mutual dependence of didactic text and allegorical picture. While image and word in *A Christall Glasse* have a reciprocal relationship, the illustration seems to have come into existence first. Since the designs are central to the book and since Bateman says nothing about their source, perhaps they were conceived by him. This is the first series of illustrations in England to have been signed extensively, although we have seen some signed single blocks. Twenty-two of the *Christall Glasse* illustrations are signed "G"; four are signed "G-L", with the separating mark looking like a flattened *M* or a bat; and eleven are unsigned. "G" and "G-L" may be the signatures of one cutter, and he may have cut all the blocks. It would not be surprising if he had worked in Antwerp or even had continued to work there, although he is not good enough to have been Christopher Plantin's cutter Gerard Jansen van Kampen, who used a "G" on some of his blocks.

Who drew the designs for the *Christall Glasse* woodcuts? Unless the blocks were imported from the Low Countries, Marcus Gheeraerts the Elder is the most likely choice, partly because he was the only illustrator available, as far as we know. He had arrived in London as an exile in 1568 and had found work at once on Day's edition of van der Noot's *Theatre.* It is natural that he would have illustrated another book for Day immediately afterward. Unless, again, the book had a Continental source, the content of the designs almost had to have been dictated by Bateman. But uncommon animals, round towers on bumpy hills, bearded men with bent noses and slashed doublets, and harbors and ships suggest Gheeraerts's hand beneath that of the cutter. They do not prove it.

A Christall Glasse is a sort of tour through the vices and virtues with a Rome-hating Puritan as a guide. The usual format is of double spreads: a sermon with biblical references is on one page, and on the facing page is an epigraph from a classical author above a woodcut, beneath which is "the signification of the picture" in five or six lines. One of the Gluttony cuts shows a fine naturalistic brawl at a stag dinner party. The illustrations that depict the virtues are unexpectedly fine. The one of Faith, a knight in armor standing on a recumbent devil, has as its setting a harbor scene with a small boat sailing before the wind, towers on a hilly shore across the bay, and, shining from among ropy clouds, a sun with concentric circles of radiance. These details occur often in Gheeraerts's etchings. The cut for Hope shows some of the crew of a disabled storm-tossed ship ("the dispersed churche of god") finding safety with

31

Christ on a rocky isle. The ship is much like those in Gheeraerts's known illustrations.

Day's edition of *A Book of Christian Prayers* (1569), sometimes called *Queen Elizabeth's Prayer Book*, contains the well-known woodcut of the queen kneeling at prayer before elaborate parted curtains. The likeness of the queen's profile is unusual. The many border units of biblical and dance of death subjects are both metal cuts and woodcuts that had definitely seen service on the Continent. *The Testaments of the Twelve Patriarchs, the Sonnes of Jacob* (1575), translated by Anthony Gilby from the Latin of Robert Grosseteste, bishop of Lincoln, has thirteen fresh emblematic woodcuts (75 × 59 mm), one signed "RB". The first shows Jacob dispensing advice on his deathbed, and the rest portray his sons and their symbols. Finally, Derricke's *Image of Irelande* (1581) is a contemporary celebration in doggerel verse of the subduing of the uncouth Irish "woodkerns" by Sir Henry Sidney for Elizabeth I in 1575. Six of the twelve large woodcuts (181 × 318 mm) are probably the finest ever specifically made for an English book. The drawing and cutting of massed cavalry and foot soldiers are extraordinary both for the vividness of the observation, as if drawn on the spot, and for their consummate execution (fig. 13). They resemble the engravings and woodcuts in Jean Tortorel and Jacques Perrissin's *Quarante tableaux ou histoires diuerses qui sont memorables touchant les guerres, massacres, & troubles aduenus en France en ses dernières années* (1570). The other six woodcuts have documentary value but are technically inferior.

Marcus Gheeraerts the Elder

On 26 August 1567, the Flemish painter and etcher Marcus Gheeraerts (ca. 1520–90?) published in Bruges at his own expense *De warachtighe Fabulen der Dieren*, an Aesopian fable book by the lawyer Edewaerd de Dene. His 107 etched illustrations are a landmark. Etching, a relatively new medium, had rarely been used for illustrating books. Gheeraerts adapted many of the traditional Aesopian fable motifs that had descended to him from earlier editions, but the detailed naturalism of his treatment of birds and animals and Flemish settings was a significant departure from the simple linear effects of the preceding woodcuts. The series, to which he added eighteen designs in a French edition (Antwerp, 1577), was reprinted and imitated throughout Europe well into the eighteenth century.

In March 1568, Gheeraerts fled from Bruges with his young son to join the Dutch, Flemish, and French Protestant refugees in London. (The son, also named Marcus, became one of the leading Elizabethan portrait painters. He never etched or illustrated books.) The Protestant printer John Day at once hired Gheeraerts to illustrate *Het Theatre* (September 1568), a book of prose and verse by Jan van der Noot, another Calvinist exile. Although the plates are unsigned, careful comparison with the *Fabulen der Dieren* etchings leaves no doubt that Gheeraerts etched the twenty emblematic yet naturalistic designs (88 × 71 mm) for the poems in this book. The Dutch edition was followed in October by one in French and in 1569 by an English translation – *A Theatre for Voluptuous Worldlings* – printed by Henry Bynneman, with woodcut copies of the illustrations. (Some of the poems in the English edition were translations from the French by Edmund Spenser, then probably sixteen, who must have studied the etchings with fascination.) Gheeraerts is thus the first known book illustrator to have practiced in England. The twenty plates are the first etchings known to have been made in England, the first emblematic designs in a book printed in England, and, indeed, the first complete series of illustrations of belles-lettres by an identifiable artist to have been printed in England. The nature of these contributions can be seen in a before-and-after design of a triumphal arch as an emblem of the transitory character of earthly things (fig. 14). Gheeraerts was a genre artist, and his realism turns nymphs and other supernatural figures into lumpy plebeians. He used etching, however, to get refinements of detail, such as animals and birds in motion, and to indicate tonal effects and the illusion of distance, which is impossible to do in a woodcut. In the sixteenth illustration, typical of his humanizing touch, three tiny peasants trudge along an empty road and a riverman guides a boat with a long sweep, exactly as in *Fabulen der Dieren*.

Circumstantial and stylistic reasons also make it seem likely, as already noted, that Gheeraerts designed the 37 woodcuts in Stephen Bateman's *Christall Glasse* (1569), printed by Day, and, as we shall see, about 100 of the 138 woodcuts in Raphael Holinshed's *Chronicles of England, Scotlande, and Irelande* (1577), printed by Bynneman. Without further evidence, Gheeraerts's participation in these books remains speculative. But even at that, Marcus Gheeraerts the Elder has a modest place in English book illustration because of his *Theatre* etchings and, as we shall note in the next chapter, the direct relation between his Aesop illustrations and those of Francis Cleyn, Wenceslaus Hollar, and Francis Barlow in the seventeenth century.

Henry Bynneman

The only Elizabethan printer who published illustrated books that in any way rival those of John Day was Henry Bynneman (fl. 1556–83). He and Day enjoyed the patronage of Archbishop Matthew Parker and were presumably on a

13. Anon. John Derricke, *An Image of Irelande* (1581). John Day.

14. Marcus Gheeraerts the Elder. Jan van der Noot, *Het Theatre* (1568). John Day.

friendly footing. They may have been working together in 1569 when Bynneman printed *A Theatre for Voluptuous Worldlings*, the English edition of Jan van der Noot's *Theatre*, which Day had issued the year before in Dutch and French editions. The twenty woodcuts are copies of the illustrations etched by Marcus Gheeraerts. Most are facsimiles of the main outlines only, and, as is natural in direct tracing, they print in reverse; but five are not reversed. The fourth and sixth are slightly altered. Bynneman may have taken over the printing of the English edition because Day's three presses were engaged with the second edition of John Foxe's *Actes and Monuments* (1570). But why Bynneman did not use Gheeraerts's etchings is a puzzle. The wood blocks reappear in *Theatrum das ist Schawplatz* (1572), printed in Cologne, probably taken there by van der Noot in 1571.

In 1575, Bynneman printed for Christopher Barker two related books containing six remarkable woodcuts of special interest because they anticipate Francis Barlow's sporting prints. Two of the six are in George Turbervile's *Booke of Faulconrie or Hauking*, and four are in the shorter anonymous twin compilation, *The Noble Arte of Venerie or Hunting*, attributed to Turbervile. In four of the six illustrations, Elizabeth I is represented in outdoor scenes. In addition, the first volume contains ten vignettes – an eagle, a vulture, and eight hawks – all derived from Conrad

Gesner's woodcuts. The second volume contains many vignettes of animals and hunting scenes by an inexpert hand. The first of the two true illustrations in *The Booke of Faulconrie* decorates the title page and is reprinted once. Above a stream stands a noble in ballooning trunk hose with a hooded falcon perched on his gloved hand. He is attended by two handsomely appareled gentlemen and four dogs. In the second, Elizabeth I on horseback watches hawks attacking cranes. Similarly, the title page of *The Noble Arte of Venerie* is decorated with a kennel-yard scene of two well-padded sportsmen starting off on foot with hounds as one blows a hunting horn. In three scenes of remarkable intimacy for Tudor book illustration, Elizabeth I enjoys a picnic in the woods during a hunt (fig. 15), stands amid trees in the forest while a huntsman on bended knee proffers fruit, and is handed a knife in order to take assay of the meat of a slain stag by cutting it "from the brisket to the belly". These six illustrations give the impression of having been drawn from direct observation, if not on the spot. The style is not that of either Gheeraerts or the *Image of Irelande* artist. The principal cutter might have been the man who two years later did the fine work for Bynneman's edition of Holinshed's *Chronicles*. In 1611, Thomas Purfoote had the figure of James I substituted for that of the queen in the three surviving Elizabeth I blocks. This seems to have been the earliest substantial example in an English

34

15. Anon. George Turbervile, *The Noble Arte of Venerie or Hunting* (1575). Henry Bynneman.

16. Anon. Raphael Holinshed, *Chronicles of England, Scotlande, and Irelande* (1577). Henry Bynneman.

book of the correction of a wood block by plugging.

Bynneman's chief hand seems to have made one of the first original English metal relief cuts (48 × 56 mm) for *The Mirror of Mans Lyfe, Englisshed by H. K.* (1576). An ill-clad holy man intercepts a noble in the dress of *The Booke of Faulconrie* astride a rearing plumed horse. He calls the noble's attention to a skeleton on the ground and presumably utters the grim words cut around the border of the block: "O wormes meate: O froath: O vanitie: Why art thou so insolent."

Bynneman printed in two folios the first edition of the famous *Chronicles of England, Scotlande, and Irelande* (1577), assembled for publication and partly written by Raphael Holinshed. The revised edition (1587) – Shakespeare's source for *Macbeth*, *King Lear*, *Cymbeline*, and the British historical plays – was not illustrated. It seems probable, although not provable, that Gheeraerts made the majority of the designs for this notable English illustrated book. It contains 138 fresh woodcut illustrations, not counting two or three dozen small torso vignettes of kings. Many of the 138 blocks are repeated so many times that they make a total of more than 1000 impressions. As always, the first volume got the better treatment, 123 original illustrations, with only 15 in the second volume. The second volume has over 200 more reprints than the first, 556 to 330. The repetition is not offensively monotonous. The brief descriptions of Britain, Scotland, and Ireland preceding the histories are not illustrated.

The 138 *Chronicles* illustrations fall into several two-column and one-column groups of varying sizes, scales, and styles. In spite of wholesale repetition, they can be divided roughly into a uniform majority of great interest as illustrations and a miscellaneous remainder of less interest. Except for the series made for Foxe's *Actes and Monuments* and for Derricke's *Image of Irelande*, no woodcuts designed for an English book have been so complex in composition, acute in representing emotional situations, well drawn, and well cut. The compositions are cleverly varied in perspective and in grouping of major and minor elements. Incidental detail of dress, furnishings, weapons, ships, animals, and architecture has an appeal that was new to English illustration. Through gesture and a certain amount of innovative facial expression, the characters are remarkably expressive. With these advances, the naturalistic story-retelling nature of English book illustration can be said to have become established.

The violence that surges through the pages of the *Chronicles* gives the illustrations their vitality; their diverse subjects give them an independent interest, often documentary. In the first illustration, Brutus shoots an arrow at a stag and kills the king, his father. In the National Gallery of Scotland is a drawing of a stag hunt signed by Gheeraerts and dated "1575" that closely resembles this design in treatment. An account of the Scots and Picts using fire and sword to make "sharpe warre agaynst the Britains wasting their Countrey" gives rise to a spectacular view of three walled cities filling the sky with flames and smoke while tiny figures with bundles flee into a watery Netherlandish countryside. One of several elaborate illustrations of sieges shows cannon firing from between rolls of wattles and soldiers, armed with muzzle-loading muskets, sportingly attacking the high walls of a town. A sea battle with ships spewing cannon fire broadside at one another must have seemed to the Elizabethans as immediate as a television newscast. The sheer literalness of contemporary dress, settings, and mechanisms, together with imaginative stage management, gives sundry murders, rapes, executions, and martyrdoms an almost photographic conviction of reality.

The quiet scenes have their own appeal. The stonemasons and carpenters in two illustrations of buildings under construction use the kind of scaffolding that is still in use in England. Soldiers with their camp followers straggle past a thatched farmhouse – one little boy riding behind his father on a bedroll, a woman striding beside her husband with a baby slung on her back and a child clutching her hand. A synod is convened with eleven elders seated on a U-shaped bench and a secretary and a scribe at a table in the open end. Mealtime in an army camp, two idyllic hunting scenes, kings receiving delegations, and "Makbeth and Banquho" meeting the three attractive "weird sisters or feiries" – all are handled with freshness and dignity. The scene of a bareheaded suitor presenting himself before a princess as she dines on an outdoor porch takes much of its sense of life from the accessory flagons of wine, livery of the servants, musicians playing, couples strolling in the street, and ape eating an apple in the shade (fig. 16). No early English woodcut has more charm.

Two questions about the illustrations have to be answered briefly: (1) Were they designed for the *Chronicles*? (2) Which were perhaps designed by Gheeraerts? The answer to the first question seems to be that 66 of the 138 illustrations have demonstrable relevance to the text; 50 have relevance but lack particularizing detail to prove it; 17 are general-utility blocks, chiefly battle scenes but including two Gheeraerts-style hunting scenes; and 5 include erroneous details, such as a battle on ice when no ice is mentioned and a king receiving nobles instead of clergy, indicative of borrowing or error in understanding. Careful study suggests that Gheeraerts drew the designs for ninety-four of the illustrations and probably for another sixteen. The remaining twenty-eight are uncertain. A pull-out panoramic view of the 1573 siege of Edinburgh (272 × 379 mm), at the end of the second volume, seems not by Gheeraerts. The initials "CT" in a square presumably are those of the cutter, but he may have been the designer, too. CT seems to have cut a few of the miscellaneous blocks. He also signed a border or two in Day's edition of *A Book of Christian Prayers* (1569) and an ornate broken-arch title border in Augustine Marlorat's *Catholike Exposition upon the Revelation of Sainct John* (1574), printed by Bynneman.

The belief that Gheeraerts's drawings lie beneath many of these woodcut impressions is based on his availability, the presence of subject elements common in his illustrations and prints, certain of his stylistic effects as they would probably look when interpreted in wood, and the general resemblance to his compositions and "color". If the assignment of most of the designs for Holinshed's *Chronicles* to Gheeraerts is correct, it is a major addition to his works; in any case, *Chronicles of England, Scotlande, and Irelande* is one of the most remarkable of English illustrated books.

The illustrations in *Actes and Monuments, An Image of Irelande*, and *Chronicles* came at the end of the first century of English book illustration. William Caxton, Wynkyn de Worde, Richard Pynson, Julyan Notary, Peter Treveris, and the other early printers who had crowded books with hundreds of illustrations were long dead, and the popularity of the woodcut was long spent. Yet all the illustrations in the books by Foxe, Derricke, and Holinshed are woodcuts, the best presumably made in England during the sixteenth century, and together with Gheeraerts's *Theatre* etchings, they are the forerunners of the naturalistic, particularized, expressive English illustration of the following centuries.

Stephen Bateman's *Doome Warning All Men to the Iudgemente* (1581), a history of marvels of all sorts, was printed by Ralph Newbery "under assignment" from Bynneman. Most of the seventy-eight illustrations seem freshly cut; those borrowed from other series are apt enough. A series of animals in thick-and-thin borders has an almost modern simplicity and strength. Several human monstrosities are less decorative. Various other cuts have other affiliations. A surrealistic profile "portrait" of a pope was created from a montage of subjects, such as a fish for the nose and a pitcher for the mouth and chin. On the facing page is a one-column block of a martyr being suspended from a Γ-shaped support over a fire, which was originally printed by Day in Foxe's *Actes and Monuments*. And Joost Lambrecht's remarkable cut of a print shop with four printers at work, previously seen in Anthony Scoloker's edition of Cornelis van der Heyden's *Ordynarye for All Faythfull Chrystians* (1548), illustrates a sketchy account of printing in which William Caxton sets up his press in Westminster around 1471. A female seven-headed beast (the Church of Rome) seems more likely to have been cut for Bateman's *New Arival of the Three Gracis, into Anglia about 1580* (1581), printed by Thomas East.

Other Late-Sixteenth-Century Printers

On the verso of the title page of *An Enchiridion of Chirurgerie* (1563), one of the four books in *Certaine Workes of Chirurgerie*, compiled by Thomas Gale and printed by Rouland Hall, is a block (102 × 72 mm) of a surgeon making an incision in the chest of a man seated on a tussock beneath a tree. A cocked-hatted attendant bends watchfully over the patient. The fine rhythms of the design are enhanced by discreet curved-line shading. The block reappears in Wylliam Clowes's *Prooved Practice for All Young Chirurgians* (1588). On the title page of *Certaine Workes* is an illustration of a naked figure stuck with swords and other sharp weapons, and distributed through the work are a portrait of Gale at fifty-six that is dated "1563" and illustrations of surgical instruments and of a muscular infant with a winged arm. All these cuts are by the same hand, which differs from those employed by John Day and Henry Bynneman by a lighter touch and the use of some irregular crosshatching. The dated portrait suggests that the work was done in England. The winged figure is a copy of number XV of Bernard Salomon's designs for Andrea Alciati's *Emblematum libri duo* (Lyons, 1547).

The printers Thomas Purfoote and William Pickering illustrated David Lyndsay's *Dialogue betweene Experience and a Courtier* (1566) (called in the running head *The Boke of the Monarche*) with twenty-two cuts. Eight of them are from Joost Lambrecht's Bible series, which Anthony Scoloker had used in 1548, and twelve are from almost perfect copies of Hans Sebald Beham's Old Testament designs, some twice removed. A cut of a battle scene is common to Lyndsay's book and Thomas Becon's *New Pollecye of Warre* (1542), printed by John Mayler – another instance of the relationships among sixteenth-century printers still to be clarified by bibliographical comparisons of their books.

The most illustrated author in the second half of the sixteenth century was Stephen Bateman (Batman) (d. 1584). This scholar-cleric, who collected Archbishop Matthew Parker's library, now at Corpus Christi College, Cambridge, wrote in a popular way on a wide range of social, religious, and pseudoscientific subjects and was a transitional figure in both euphuism and emblemism. Since each of the four illustrated books noted here was brought out by a different printer, presumably much of the enthusiasm for illustration was Bateman's. His illustrated books appeared at two times a decade apart: in 1569, *A Christall Glasse of Christian*

17. Anon. Stephen Bateman, *The Trauayled Pylgrime* (1569). Henry Denham.

18. Anon. *The Morall Philosophie of Doni* (1570). Henry Denham.

39

19. Anon. *Three Lordes and Three Ladies of London* (1590). Richard Jhones.

June.

20. Anon. Edmund Spenser, *The Shepheardes Calendar* (1579). Hugh Singleton.

Reformation, printed by John Day, and *The Trauayled Pylgrime*, printed by Henry Denham; in 1581, *The New Arival of the Three Gracis*, printed by Thomas East, and *The Doome Warning All Men to the Iudgemente*, printed by Ralph Newbery. The four books contain about 140 woodcuts; astonishingly, almost all seem to have been designed specifically for Bateman's texts, and they are among the most interesting and best-cut designs of the period.

A Christall Glasse has been discussed under John Day. When Henry Denham was active as a printer, from 1560 to 1589, he showed a certain initiative about illustrating his books. In 1569, he printed Bateman's allegorical *Trauayled Pylgrime*, with twenty woodcuts (ca. 94×110 mm). The series is fresh and apt, but the cutting is inferior. Several blocks are signed with a swash "A". It is possible that these are copies of Christopher Plantin designs cut by Arnold Nicolai, who used this signature. The woodcuts follow the languid doggerel-verse account of the author's journey through time. He appears in each cut, and underneath each is an explanatory legend. The first, for instance, shows a knight on foot with spear and shield, a man with a book on one side and a young boy with a birch on the other. The legend reads: "Here the Author beginnes his voyage, being ready armed, bidding Infancie farewell, and now growing by Reason to further possibilitie and strength." Many cuts merely show the author as a mounted knight, vizor down, meeting figures that symbolize such abstractions as memory. Three are varied designs of considerable interest. In one, three men sit at a round table in a rose arbor – the author banqueting with Understanding and Diligence. In a larger design, the author on his horse Will arrives in front of the "palace of disordered livers", whose inhabitants embrace one another and blow horns from windows (fig. 17). The third, also larger, presents Elizabeth I "passing by" in a canopied wagon, an angel flying ahead and blowing a twisted horn, as the author beholds the contention of Dolor and Debility. As noted above, Thomas East printed Bateman's *New Arival of the Three Gracis, into Anglia about 1580*, presumably just before Bateman's *Doome Warning* but also in 1581. (See Bynneman.) A cut of a ship arriving in a harbor and three women descending a rocky path toward an author reclining on the shore must have been made for this work, although it is too large for the title page. An appropriate Day of Judgment seems to be a companion cut, as does a female seven-headed beast (the Church of Rome) that is apparently giving birth to a pope while two devils use bellows to keep the fires of hell blazing around both the pope's head and a covetous soul held by the tail of the beast.

Among sixteenth-century illustrated books, perhaps the most entertaining is *The Morall Philosophie of Doni* (1570),

also printed by Denham. It is a collection of fables and tales deriving from Bidpai, "englished out of the Italian" by Sir Thomas North. The forty-nine woodcuts (ca. 70×80 mm), no doubt descended from Italian originals, are genuine illustrations that were prepared for Denham's edition. Some represent fairly elaborate scenes for a block of this size. In one, a robber dressed in women's clothes plunges headlong to the ground while trying to escape from the top of a house on a ladder of moonbeams (fig. 18). In another, a wife opens the door to admit her husband while her lover tiptoes away from a bed in the background.

It has never been customary in England to illustrate plays beyond the title page, and then rarely with anything but decorative designs. This seems curious, since plays are built by scenes and thus are especially suitable for representation in pictorial terms, and illustrations can visualize for the reader characters, costumes, action, and settings with little competition from the text. Among plays printed in England, one of the earliest with interpretive illustrations is Theodore Beza's *Tragedie of Abraham's Sacrifice* (1577), translated by A. G. and printed by Thomas Vautroullier. The three illustrations, perhaps copied from a French edition, are of interest only because of the date and their aptness. In 1590, Richard Jhones placed on the title page of *Three Lordes and Three Ladies of London* an unusual woodcut of two men (perhaps an actor and a playwright) apparently explaining the morality play to a group of women seated in another room on a platform (fig. 19). But for the most part, the title-page woodcuts in those Elizabethan plays that appeared in book form were done in the degraded manner that was common to ephemeral broadsides and ballads. They suggest that woodcutters of the modest competence of those who had cut the blocks for the two plays just mentioned were dying out.

Among sixteenth-century English books, herbals make a pleasant impression that is not attributable to native talent. The folio *Niewe Herball* (1578), translated by Henry Lyte from a French edition of Rembert Dodoens's Latin original and printed by Gerard Dewes, has the vivacious title-page border and hundreds of plants designed by Pieter van der Borcht and cut by Arnold Nicolai and Gerard Jansen van Kampen for Plantin. Better known is John Gerard's *Herball: or General Historie of Plants* (1597), printed by Edmund Bollifant for John Norton, followed in 1633 by an enlarged edition. The chaste outlines with restrained shading to indicate form only and the absence of backgrounds or borders suggest that the woodcuts in these two editions, said to number 1800 and 2850, were imported from Frankfurt and Antwerp. They are the very model of harmony between illustration and type-page, but they are not, of course, English or interpretive.

A small oasis of interest in the barrens of Elizabethan illustration is Edmund Spenser's *Shepheardes Calendar*, printed by Hugh Singleton in 1579. The twelve oblong woodcuts (ca. 59 × 102 mm) are modest enough, but they are original, if limited, illustrations of the pastoral allegory (fig. 20). The artist pictured the visible incident for each month as he deduced it from reading the text and not unnaturally ignored the serious discourse about love, poetry, faith, and so on that Spenser sums up in an "Embleme" at the end of each eclogue. He extracted little from his charming possibilities except the elementary facts, usually two shepherds talking in the foreground with only meager atmospheric detail. For Spenser's January, for instance – the sad season of the year, with frozen trees and "winter-beaten flock", when Colin Clout, the unfortunate lover, "breaketh his pipe and casteth himself on the ground" – a leafless tree and a broken bagpipe are the chief interpretive symbols. For March, the artist amusingly gave a literal representation of a shepherd who scorned love for so long that he finally became entangled in its net. April is notable for showing Elizabeth I alfresco surrounded by her ladies, some playing musical instruments, while to one side, a shepherd boy joins in on his pipe. On the side of the May design, a couple in a carriage drawn by winged horses, is an Aesopian scene of a fox flattering a kid.

Among Denham's later books, Thomas Bentley's pious three-part *Monument of Matrones* (1582) might be mentioned for its evidence of the occasional availability of a skilled craftsman. The three title-page borders, although of modest size, have rightly been praised as among the best examples of Elizabethan work. They were especially made for Denham, for his initials appear on the sides of the first; they diplomatically make way for "ER" on the other two. Therefore, since the same hand seems to have cut the one illustration that appears in the long work, he apparently was in London. The design (148 × 104 mm) is an oval Last Judgment within a frame of four allegorical figures, fruit, and strapwork. In the upper half of the oval is Christ in heaven; in the lower half, the dead arise beside the effigy of a queen on a tomb. On the side of the tomb in a space that earlier must have held another name is printed "Q. Katherine". The fineness of the detail in the four blocks and the excellence of the lettering indicate that they probably are metal relief cuts. The lettering closely resembles that in a small title-page cut in Bynneman's edition of *The Mirror of Mans Lyfe* (1576), which seems more certainly engraved in relief on metal. Both the borders and the illustration were probably made for Denham much earlier.

Spenser's *Faerie Queene* (1590) is a symbol of the waning state of the illustrated book in the last years of the sixteenth century. In the two volumes of the first edition of the long narrative poem – so susceptible to illustration, yet so rarely illustrated well – William Ponsonby introduced just one woodcut. This fresh-looking vignette (127 × 79 mm) of an appropriate St. George slaying the dragon is tucked away in the first volume facing the opening of the second book, the legend of Sir Guyon, or Temperance. The design is cramped, but the effect is pleasing. Presumably, it was merely copied for use in this edition. It is typical of the times that the printer was content to make a gesture so pointless that it might better not have been made at all.

Arthur Hind attributed to the Dutch cartographer Jocodus Hondius, a visitor in England from 1583 to 1593, the engraved title page, two maps, and five allegorical plates (ca. 143 × 94 mm) in Hugh Broughton's *Concent of Scripture* (1588). John Harington, in his translation of *Orlando Furioso*, mistakenly says that these are the first copperplates engraved in England, but the allegorical plates seem to be the earliest burin-engraved interpretive illustrations in an English book. They represent biblical texts and are bound together at the end of the book. The execution has little grace. Within formal borders are symbolic figures not unlike those etched by Gheeraerts in the 1568 *Theatre*: a warrior with a scepter before a background resembling those of Joachim Patinir, a falling apple tree, four mythological beasts, a ram fighting a buck, and the whore of Babylon mounted on her multiheaded beast (fig. 21). The industrious English engraver William Rogers followed these designs roughly to make a similar but inferior series of larger plates for a 1590 edition of *Concent of Scripture*.

Among the most impressive of illustrated Elizabethan books is the John Harington translation of Ludovico Ariosto's *Orlando Furioso* (1591). The 400-page folio of the allegorical romance of Ruggiero and Bradamante in stanzas of ottava rima has forty-six numbered engraved plates (198 × 137 mm), one as frontispiece to each book. With numerous deviations, they are burin-engraved copies of Girolamo Porro's engravings in Francesco Franceschi's edition (Venice, 1584), which, in turn, were ultimately derived from the superb woodcuts in Vincenzo Valgrisi's edition (Venice, 1556). Had the latter been the model for the line-by-line reproduction of 1591, beauty would have come to English illustration and might have taken root. As it is, the copies from Porro are welcome visual summaries. They are filled with dozens of labeled figures enacting the chief events of each canto, diminishing in size from bottom foreground to top background. Men in armor, ladies, battles, horses, tents, castles, rivers, and ships fill the tall plates with rich narrative detail.

Orlando Furioso was the chief ornament of engraved illustration in England for a long time, but after a century

21. Jocodus Hondius (?). Hugh Broughton, *A Concent of Scripture* (1588).

of English book production, we can hardly bestow our admiration on facsimiles. About the best we can say is that Thomas Cockson, who signed the title page and probably took the lead in making the plates, and the anonymous engravers were little inferior to Porro in handling a burin. Harington may have been responsible for changes in the plates, since some are substantive architectural elements. It has also been suggested that he called for the explicitness of the foreground scene of the nude Lydia in hell in plate XXXIV (fig. 22) in order to tease his godmother, Elizabeth I, who had banished him from court and set him the task of translating *Orlando Furioso* because he had circulated among her ladies-in-waiting his translation of an indecorous episode from this work.

Harington was the first writer to say anything of consequence about English book illustration. In his paragraph on "the pictures", he writes, "They are all cut in brasse [copper], and most of them by the best workmen in that kinde [engraving]." He continues disingenuously, "Yet I will not praise them too much, because I gave direction for their making" – without mentioning the plagiarism. He adds that he has not seen any of "this kind" (that is,

engraving) in any book except Broughton's *Concent of Scripture*, in which there are "some 3. or 4. prettie figures (in octavo) cut in brasse verie workemanly". Then he lists other books illustrated with woodcuts, which he rates inferior to metal engravings according to the old proverb "The more cost, the more worship." The use of illustrations, he says sententiously, is that once people have read the book, they can read it again in the pictures; and he notes that not everyone observes perspective, "which is the chief art in a picture". These pronouncements light up the progress of art appreciation in Great Britain by 1591.

Of passing interest is *The Strife of Love in a Dreame*, printed for Simon Waterson by J. Charlewood in 1592. This partial translation of Francesco Colonna's cloying *Hypnerotomachia Poliphili* is illustrated with copies of the anonymous woodcuts from the celebrated edition printed by Aldus Manutius (Venice, 1499). Even in the hands of an Elizabethan cutter, the twenty-two outline designs, including ten full-page (ca. 145 × 105 mm) and five half-page, are effective – although artless. One wonders what fine books England might have had if the inspiration of the Venetian school had been felt more acutely and 100 years earlier.

43

22. Anon (Thomas Cockson?). Ludovico Ariosto, *Orlando Furioso* (1591).

44

CHAPTER THREE

The Seventeenth Century
1601–1700

Illustration ran an erratic course during the seventeenth century. External events had a great deal to do with this state of affairs. The Civil War and the Puritan Commonwealth caused an upheaval in society that directly affected book publishing as well as the reading habits of the public. Portrait painting had continued since the time of Henry VIII to be the staple of the leading painters. The novel did not exist; plays were hardly ever illustrated; and poetry, only occasionally. Most of the books with plates of some distinction are books of travel, topography, architecture, portraiture, and natural history – often, essentially, bound collections of prints. Emblem books are a special genre. During the century, in spite of adverse circumstances, three significant changes occurred: (1) the publication of a respectable number of well-illustrated editions of works of English literature and translations of classics, including the first illustrated editions in England of *The Pilgrim's Progress* (1680), *Don Quixote* (1687), and *Paradise Lost* (1688); (2) the virtual disappearance of the woodcut from serious illustration in favor of intaglio engraving on copper and, surprisingly, etching; and (3) the emergence of two illustrators of international stature – long-resident Czech-born Wenceslaus Hollar and English-born Francis Barlow.

The presence in London of such experienced engravers as William Hole, Renold Elstrack, Francis Delaram, William Faithorne, and Crispin van de Passe and his sons Simon and Willem would seem sufficient in itself to have generated good literary illustration, but it did not. Nevertheless, engraving was central to the development of illustration in England for the next two centuries. Metal engraving had become a common medium for book illustrating on the Continent a century before it did in England. Its great attraction to the artists of the time was the ease with which it reproduces fine detail, far beyond the capability of a woodcut. Another attraction was that every stroke or touch of the engraving tool on the copperplate registers as a black line or dot when printed. In normal intaglio engraving, the plate is inked, the surface is wiped clean, and dampened paper is forced by a rolling press into the ink-filled channels made by the engraving tool. This procedure is the reverse of getting an impression from printing type and woodcuts, whose surfaces are inked. Therefore, an engraved illustration and the type-page have to be printed on different presses. This involves extra cost, as do the copperplates themselves. As a result, seventeenth-century English books containing engraved plates were, on the whole, luxuries, often had only a frontispiece and an ornate title page, and, if more elaborate, often had to be underwritten in advance by patrons and subscribers. High costs, war, and Puritan disapproval of frivolity helped limit the number of illustrated books printed during the seventeenth century compared with other centuries. As early as 1568, as we have seen, etching had been used to illustrate one book. It has not, however, been a method popular with illustrators; that it was the method used by the two leading illustrators in England in the seventeenth century seems largely coincidental. In etching, the design is produced on a plate – usually copper – by acid "eating" into the metal, and the printing is similar to that of engraving and has the same disadvantage of expensiveness.

It is important to remember that although illustrations are called either engravings or etchings, in practice the two methods were routinely combined – virtually always in the eighteenth and early nineteenth centuries. Outlines of designs on engraved plates might be etched first; parts of etchings, such as architectural forms, engraved; and each method might be used to reinforce passages done by the other. Drypoint also might be used on etched plates. To the early artist, the object was to reproduce a drawing as expeditiously as possible. Another point to bear in mind is that the engraver frequently signed his own name to plates and left off the designer's. The usual abbreviation after the name of the designer was "del." or "delin." (*delineavit*) or "inv." or "inven." (*invenit*); "sc." or "sculp." (*sculpsit*) came after the engraver's; and "et." was used after the etcher's. If the designer was also the engraver, he used both – for example, "del. et sc." The term *fecit* is ambiguous: in addition to referring to the designer, engraver, or etcher, it can refer to a special process, such as aquatint; and on occasion, it seems to indicate that the artist based his design on a previous one. It behooves those of us who are not print experts to be discreet in our technical statements about intaglio plates unless we have firsthand evidence to support us. In this study, use of the term *engraving* or *etching* means that the plates are so signed, that the title page so states, that the dominant impression is that of one or the other, or that the hand habitually used one technique.

Anonymous illustrators were responsible for much of the somewhat miscellaneous body of seventeenth-century illustrations. Therefore, to give some sense of order, the discussion is divided into three parts: Anonymous and Minor Illustrators; Emblem Books; and Major Illustrators.

Anonymous and Minor Illustrators

In Thomas Coryate's account of his travels on the Continent, which has the misleading title *Coryat's Crudities* (1611), William Hole has one delightful semi-interpretive engraving among the half dozen he did for the book. Coryate explains: "The name of Cortezan of Venice is famoused over all Christendome. And I have here inserted a picture of one of their noble Cortezans, according to her Venetian habites, with my owne neare unto her, made in that forme as we saluted each other." In the full-page plate (170 × 119 mm), Hole followed Coryate's instructions to the letter: at the left, "Il Signior Tomaso Odcombiano" (Coryate came from Odcombe, Somerset), hat in hand, is warmly greeted by "Margarita Emiliana bella Cortesana di Venetia," richly gowned and bare breasted, Venetian fashion, as Coryate reports (fig. 23).

Among Jacobean engravers, Francis Delaram did some book work besides portraits and title pages, but he cannot be considered a book illustrator. Arthur Hind says that the forty-eight unsigned plates in George Sandys's *Relation of a Iourney [to] the Turkish Empire* (1615) "might well be by Delaram after drawings provided by George Sandys". That would make Sandys the illustrator. The plates are factual representations of buildings and scenes in Turkey, Egypt, the Holy Land, and several parts of the Mediterranean.

The number of natural-history books published in the seventeenth century is evidence of the widespread increase in scientific investigation, which found expression in the research of Sir Isaac Newton and the establishment of the Royal Society. Most of the early illustrations, however, were not based on firsthand observation, but evolved from Continental sources of the sixteenth century: those in Edward Topsell's *Historie of Four-footed Beastes* (1607) and *Historie of Serpents* (1608) were copied from the works of Conrad Gesner, for example. The early-seventeenth-century books about animals, birds, fish, insects, flowers, and plants are wholly functional. The designs are often quaint, but the occasional handsome series is almost always composed of originals brought from the Continent. Two examples of such imports are John Parkinson's folio *Paradisi In Sole Paradisus terrestris : or, a Garden of All Sorts of Pleasant Flowers* (1629) with 110 exceptional, huge woodcuts (397 × 191 mm), including the astonishingly detailed title page signed "A. Switzer", and Payne's *Flora : Flowers Fruict Beastes Birds and Flies* (1658) with 11 rectangular engraved plates (140 × 200 mm). A. Switzer probably was the grandson of the wood engraver Christopher Switzer, who had emigrated to England from Germany around 1574 and had a son named Christopher, also a wood engraver.

Although woodcuts had long ceased to be the medium for series of literary illustrations, through the seventeenth century, they commonly enlivened – in a primitive form – printed lyrics of popular ballads and other broadsides. They also survived as title-page designs for plays. *The Spanish Tragedie* (1615) by Thomas Kyd has an unusual title page with speeches in ribbons and four figures: Horatio, just murdered and hanged; Hieronimo, his father; Bel-imperia, Horatio's secret beloved; and one of the murderers (fig. 24). Christopher Marlowe's *Tragicall History of Doctor Faustus* (1624) is another one of the few enlightening examples. Faustus, gowned as a scholar, stands in his study within a necromancer's circle and calls up Mephistopheles, a grotesque black creature with a human head. These woodcuts are technically naïve, but they are penetrating illustrations, for they get at the heart of the plays. They also underscore the paucity of available talent.

The first edition of Izaak Walton and Charles Cotton's *Compleat Angler* was published in 1653 with an attractive, small title-page frame engraved by Pierre Lombart and several nice illustrations of different kinds of fish. Many editions since the first have been adorned with similar functional designs, and some with fine illustrations that crystallize the warm human experiences of Piscator and his friends.

Argalus and Parthenia (1656), a long, dull narrative poem in couplets by Francis Quarles, has, in addition to the title page, twenty-nine engraved plates (ca. 153 × 102 mm) that attempt to offer images parallel to the text. The original designs, by Edmund Marmion, are in the Ashmolean Museum, Oxford. All but two of the engravings are poor; they are attributed to Thomas Cross, an engraver of shorthand symbols. Numbers 3 and 7 were done in mixed engraving and etching by a more experienced hand, perhaps

23. William Hole. Thomas Coryate, *Coryat's Crudities* (1611).

24. Anon. Thomas Kyd, *The Spanish Tragedie* (1615).

25. Edmund Marmion. Francis Quarles, *Argalus and Parthenia* (1656).

MEMORIE.

26. Anon. Thomas Jenner, *Work for None but Angels & Men, or A Book Shewing What the Soule Is* (1658).

48

a pupil of Wenceslaus Hollar. In number 3, three women watch a young horseman carrying a lance (fig. 25). Despite their poor execution, the twenty-nine designs match the action as it unfolds, and thereby constitute a rare sustained effort to illustrate a narrative.

By mid-seventeenth-century standards, the eight engraved illustrations (ca. 155 × 120 mm) in Thomas Jenner's *Work for None but Angels & Men, or A Book Shewing What the Soule Is* (1658) are unusual. They are emblematic without having a specific relation to the text. Two show men, one an author ("Memorie") writing at a table and wearing a hat and a cloak (fig. 26) and the other a painter ("Fancie") with a heart device on his easel. Six show women, including one wearing a flower-trimmed hat and carrying well-drawn flowers and another playing a carefully detailed organ. The women seem to have been inspired by Hollar's *Ornatus muliebris Anglicanis*. These engravings may have been designed for another purpose, but they were intended to be bound in this edition, for they have the correct signatures and text printed on the verso. Four plates have four lines of English verse engraved below the figures; the other four may have lost their verses by cropping, as in the British Library copy.

How artists relied on the past for parts of designs – and how far back they sometimes reached – can be seen in a random instance, *A New Book of Flowers & Fishes* (1671). Below the elaborate, flower-decked scroll cartouche enclosing the title is a realistic harbor fishing scene derived from the background in Marcus Gheeraerts's "Eagle and Snail" Aesopian fable illustration of 1567.

We noted in Chapter Two that the three woodcuts in a translation of Theodore Beza's *Tragedie of Abraham's Sacrifice* (1577) are among the earliest illustrations of a play published in England. A century later, Elkanah Settle's *Empress of Morocco: A Tragedy with Sculptures. As It Is Acted at the Duke's Theatre* (1673) contains the first genuine detailed representations of a play. The frontispiece, engraved by William Sherwin, is a front elevation of the Duke's Theatre. The other five engravings seem to have been designed and engraved by William Dolle, an engraver of portraits; three are signed by him. They have as their diverse subjects a picture-frame stage with musicians in a gallery, a harbor, Moors dancing to the beat of African drums, a masque in hell (fig. 27), and a torture chamber.

The History of Prince Erastus and the Seven Wise Masters of Rome (1674) by Francis Kirkman is more interesting for its preface than for its illustrations. It contains eighteen full-page engravings (ca. 130 × 75 mm), each divided into two or three scenes, and several smaller engravings. The figures are small; the detail is slight; and the engraving is unskilled. The drawings might have been better than the

engravings. This is one of the books that mark the descent from the magnificent etchings of Hollar and Barlow to the undistinguished engravings that fill modest eighteenth-century books of fiction. Nevertheless, in the preface, Kirkman confides to the reader:

My cost hath been extraordinary in the Pictures, for I have bestowed more on this book than on any book of this bigness [small octavo] in English; so that the Reader may read every particular of all the Histories in Picture; and indeed Picture is not only convenient, but necessary in all Histories of this nature, there is so great affinity between them, that Picture is said to be Dumb or silent History, & History to be speaking picture there being a Poetical Art to be used in both, Pictoribus atque Poetis. This book being chargable to me, I hope the Reader will consider me in the price. If the former [*The Famous History of Don Bellianis of Greece* (1673)] were so well accepted, I doubt not but this will be as well received; for as it exceeds that in price, so do I assure thee it exceeds that in worth.

Somewhat in Hollar's manner are the five plates (ca. 60 × 81 mm) in John Quarles's *Triumphant Chastity: or, Joseph's Self-Conflict* (1684), "Illustrated with several Copper-Plates and Emblems suitable to the Subject." The poem, by Francis Quarles's son, is an extended debate. The plates are worthy of mention because they are etched, fully interpretive, and naturalistic; but they are signed by Adrian van de Venne, who died in The Hague in 1662.

Not until the fifth edition of the first part of John Bunyan's *Pilgrim's Progress* (1680) is there a series of illustrations beyond the engraved portrait of the uncomfortably sleeping author. Nathaniel Ponder's advertisement for the fifth edition says: "The Publisher, observing that many persons desired to have it illustrated with pictures . . . besides those that are ordinarily printed to this Fifth Impression, hath provided Thirteen Copper Cutts." "Those that are ordinarily printed to this Fifth Impression" apparently refers to the portrait and an aberrant woodcut of the martyrdom of the Faithful. The thirteen plates are simple, unskilled attempts to represent key moments, the stations on the Pilgrim's way, but since they are the first of many *Pilgrim's Progress* series, they are listed here for comparison: (1) Christian meeting Evangelist, (2) Christian meeting Worldly Wiseman, (3) Christian at the Wicket Gate, (4) Christian in the Arbor, (5) Christian losing his Burden, (6) Christian passing the Lions, (7) Christian in complete Armor, (8) Christian in the Valley of the Shadow of Death, (9) Faithful before Judge Hategood, (10) Martyrdom of Faithful, (11) Giant Despair before his Castle, (12) Pilgrims with Shepherds of the Delectable Mountains, and (13) Pilgrims riding the Clouds.

In the eleventh edition, woodcut copies replace the original thirteen engravings, and the subsequent history is replete with changes in kinds of illustrations.

The Pilgrim's Progress probably exists in more illustrated editions than does any other work of English literature. Many leading illustrators have done series for it, as have dozens of unremembered hands. In his introduction to William Blake's illustrations in *Engravings* (1950), Geoffrey Keynes says: "In no instance, however, were the refined productions of a Stothard or a pre-Raphaelite artist suited to the plain style of Bunyan's writing. The rough and homely woodcuts of a chapbook are more in tune with the tinker-preacher's spontaneous art than the polished products of the sophisticated book-illustrator." This sounds true, but the response of readers to illustrations may not be so straightforward; it varies with their relation to the work illustrated and with the spirit of the age. Still, Christian sticking his sword in Apollyon's belly and making blood spurt, a plain Vanity Fair seen close up, and the rest of the plates and woodcuts in early editions do help readers of today to imagine how the great "Similitude" may have looked through Bunyan's eyes.

The first English illustrated edition of another classic among illustrated books, the folio *Don Quixote* (1687), translated by John Philips and "Adorned with Several Copper Plates", contains a frontispiece and sixteen amusing illustrations, two on a plate (ca. 265 × 165 mm), without signatures of artist or engraver. With two exceptions, they are the prototypes of the designs in many editions to the present day: the barber dubbing Quixote a knight, Quixote tilting at the windmills (fig. 28), Sancho Panza being tossed in a blanket, Quixote taking a hand in the puppet show, and so on. The two designs on the final plate are less common: the Enchanted Head, and Quixote conquered by the Knight of the White Moon. The intelligent selection of incidents and the good composition beneath the artless drawings and engravings indicate borrowing from a Continental series. This 1687 series was itself reproduced in reduced size in Samuel Buckley's edition (1700–03).

Emblem Books

Not a single edition of an accepted emblem book printed in England before 1700 can claim a set of native illustrations notable for artistic excellence or conceptual originality. Yet some discussion of English emblem books is desirable because the genre has received so much scholarly attention and is one literary form in which the image is indispensable. The fad began with the *Emblematum liber* of Andrea Alciati, an Italian lawyer, printed in Augsburg in 1531. The book was instantly a best seller, and subsequent edi-

tions and similar collections flooded Europe well into the nineteenth century. A pure example of this esoteric form is distinguished from other kinds of illustrated allegory by the interdependence of a moral text (always short and often in verse) and the device, or picture. Neither is fully understandable without the other. For this synergistic exercise to be ideal, one would think, the text and the image would have to be conceived and roughed out, if not executed, at the same time. One way to make sure that the device was not self-evident was to use symbols having no actual equivalents in nature – a hand holding a burning heart, say. Mythological elements, such as the phoenix reborn from fire, were also favorite devices. But many of the emblem images were ordinary objects endowed with hidden symbolic meanings.

Throughout Elizabethan times, the still flourishing medieval love of allegory and the fashion for extravagant "conceits" led to the incorporation in verse and prose of images derived from emblem-book devices and impresas that the writers had seen, as in the line "His helmet now shall make a hive for bees" in George Peele's poem "Farewell to Arms". The English emblem books have been listed and analyzed thoroughly by Rosemary Freeman, *English Emblem Books* (1948); Henry Green, *Andrea Alciati* (1872); and Mario Praz, *Studies in Seventeenth Century Imagery* (1938). We shall comment on a few of special interest.

The first true emblem book written in English after the Alciati model was Geffrey Whitney's *Choice of Emblemes* (1586). Whitney was then a student at the new University of Leiden, and the book was printed by Francis van Ravelingen in the shop that his father-in-law, Christopher Plantin, had established at the university. The 248 illustrations are a miscellaneous assortment, mostly impressions of worn blocks from the several editions of Alciati, Ioannis Sambucus, Junius, and Claude Paradin that Plantin had been printing in Antwerp for twenty years. Although *A Choice of Emblemes* was published abroad and used old woodcuts, it offered to the English public a large share of the traditional devices that had so caught the fancy of Europeans. Whitney's faltering English versions of the emblem texts, with the illustrations cut by Arnold Nicolai and Gerard Jansen van Kampen, must have stimulated that brilliant literary generation that emerged during the last years of Elizabeth I's reign, although most Elizabethans were well acquainted with similar forms of symbolism, and many, with foreign emblem books. But in seventeenth-century England, the moralizing element in emblem books came to supersede the intellectual play that had so appealed to men like Sir Philip Sidney, and religious emblem books preempted the field.

An exception is *Minerva Britanna* by Henry Peacham.

27. William Dolle (?). Elkanah Settle, *The Empress of Morocco: A Tragedy with Sculptures* (1673).

28. Anon. Miguel de Cervantes, *Don Quixote* (1687).

29. Henry Peacham. Henry Peacham, *Minerva Britanna: or a Garden of Heroical Devises* (1612).

30. Crispin van de Passe. George Wither, *A Collection of Emblemes* (1635).

As a graduate of Trinity College, Cambridge, and a writer on the graphic arts and heraldry, Peacham was a rarity among English illustrators, but he is more memorable for being the first known English artist who can be called an illustrator than for his illustrations. He was the author of *The Art of Drawing with a Pen* (1606), *Graphice* (1612), and *The Compleat Gentleman* (1622). A sketch by him of the supplication scene from *Titus Andronicus* (III.i) can be said to be the first known illustration of a Shakespearean play, although it did not appear in a book, and an extant title page dated "1639" indicates that he produced an edition of Aesop's *Fables*, apparently no longer in existence. That leaves him with one extant work of interpretive illustration. *Minerva Britanna: or a Garden of Heroical Devises, furnished, and adorned with Emblemes and Impresa's of sundry natures, Newly devised, moralized, and published, by Henry Peacham, Mr. of Artes* (1612) indicates that Peacham was publisher, author of the 204 versified emblems, and designer – and, not unlikely, cutter – of the title-page device and 204 woodcut illustrations (51 × 73 mm), each with a neat frame. He seems to have revived the woodcut as part of the proof of his contention that the English were as clever as the foreign followers of Alciati. Both verse and woodcuts are marked more by plain substance than by art. Typical and fascinating is a woodcut of a football game (fig. 29). The first stanza of the accompanying verse reads:

> The country Swaines, at footeball heere are scene,
> Which each gapes after, for to get a blow,
> The while some one, away runnes with it cleane,
> It meetes another, at the goale below
>   Who never stirrd, one catcheth heere a fall,
>   And there one's maimd, who never saw the ball.

Worldly wealth is like a football, at which – "like Brutes" – each strives to get a kick, says Peacham. Some of his material came from traditional fables – two travelers and a bear and the cat and cock seem to be derived from designs by Marcus Gheeraerts –, which suggests that he may have used the blocks later in his edition of Aesop.

George Wither's *Collection of Emblemes* appeared in two volumes (1635, 1634). The 200 circular engravings (diameter 100 mm) are the finest in any English emblem book, but they were printed from the plates designed and engraved in Utrecht by Crispin van de Passe and his family for Gabriel Rollenhagen's *Nucleus emblematum selectissimorum* (Arnheim, 1611) and can hardly be claimed as part of English illustration. In "To the Reader", Wither says that the book, with his verse moralizing the already existing designs, would have appeared many years before but that the plates "could not be procured out of Holland upon any reasonable conditions" earlier. Yet he derogates the

engravings as "being onely dumbe Figures, little delightfull, except to Children and childish-gazers". Then he wrote exactly thirty lines of prosy verse explaining item by item the meanings he found in each device.

The tall pages, with the engravings and text neatly balanced, make up a distinguished-looking book. Each engraving, encircled by a Latin motto, shows in the foreground carefully drawn but often unnatural figures or objects against a background scene, usually of countryside with a city and often a harbor in the distance. The meaning of the foreground device usually is impenetrable, or at best uncertain, without the verse interpretation. A sword standing point up in defiance of gravity with a rope looped around the blade and a gallows in midground leads Wither to warn readers who may be inclined toward crime what is in store for them, and yet he adds that Death will get any guilty judges who sentence poor thieves to death (fig. 30). Wither's daughter published his *Divine Poems* (1688) after his death with copies of a friend's twelve lost plates, which Wither had "illustrated" with poems. The plates show punishments inflicted on transgressors of the Ten Commandments – for instance, three virtuous fellows stoning a transgressor who is tied to a tree.

The poet and benefactor Edward Benlowes persuaded Francis Quarles to write his *Emblemes* (1635) to go with the illustrations in two Jesuit emblem books that had been published in Antwerp. William Marshall and William Simpson copied with minor adjustments all but two of the seventy-eight illustrations in the five books into which *Emblemes* is divided. In a law suit, Quarles said that the plates had cost him more than £120. The vignettes (ca. 60–80 × 60 mm) in Books I and II were copied from those in *Typus mundi* (1627), and the illustrations (83 × 52 mm) in the other three books, from those in Herman Hugo's *Pia desideria: or Divine Addresses* (1624). Both of these series used as the main actors a nimbused cherub – pagan Cupid transformed into Infant Jesus – and another small child – Anima, or the Soul. In a brief and unpretentious note to the reader, Quarles writes: "An Embleme is but a silent Parable. Let not the tender Eye checke [hesitate] to see the allusion to our blessed Saviour figured in these Types. In holy Scripture He is sometimes called a Sower, sometimes a Fisher, sometimes a Physitian: and why not presented so as well to the eye as to the eare?" Quarles followed his *Emblemes* with *Hieroglyphikes of the Life of Man* (1638). The title-page design and fifteen illustrations were based on an effective series of candle-motif devices that was engraved by Marshall after Continental designs.

Pope's *Dunciad* sneer that "the pictures for the page atone" notwithstanding, the popularity of Quarles's emblem books among his contemporaries and his survival as a literary figure derive mainly from his having been a competent practitioner of manneristic seventeenth-century verse. His evangelical fervor and ingenious metaphors have had wide appeal among pious readers. Quarles was much more independent of the illustrations than was Wither; he often was well along in his two-page poems before he worked in overt references to the engravings. Nevertheless, one of the reasons that his *Emblemes* and *Hieroglyphikes* have been reprinted in many editions is the challenging oddity of the engravings, by which, like Quarles's Soul, the reader's understanding "From Sense she climbs to Faith". Wither and Quarles gave century-old emblem books a new religious existence in England, but Quarles incorporated the emblematic image into his thinking to create fresh subjective poems. In so doing, even though the illustrations preceded his own compositions, he contributed to establishing in England the idea that illustrations might in themselves be transcriptions of visions of emotional intensity, an idea soon to be brilliantly realized in Francis Barlow's etchings for Benlowes's *Theophila* (1652).

Major Illustrators

Francis Barlow

The first major English-born book illustrator was Francis Barlow (1626?–1704). He was also the first English etcher, modern animal and bird artist, recorder of sporting scenes, political cartoonist, and, possibly, modern landscape artist. The lifelikeness of his animal and bird drawings, prints, and paintings attracted the admiration of the founders of the Royal Society and allied him with the scientific spirit of the seventeenth century. Barlow was, moreover, an interpretive illustrator of great freshness and vigor; the art historian Otto Benesch wrote that he was "one of the greatest illustrators of all time". His drawing is perhaps too subordinated to purpose, with much of his etching too heavily outlined, sometimes with the aid of an engraving burin, and the work he did not etch was too often poorly etched or engraved to justify this high estimate on artistic grounds.

Barlow's first book work of consequence seems to have been an unsigned, charming etched portrait in the open Van Dyck style of the twelve- or thirteen-year-old Elizabeth Stuart, wearing mourning for her recently executed father, Charles I. It is the frontispiece in a translation by C. W. (Christopher Wase) of Sophocles's *Electra* (1649). The book was printed secretly in England and not "At the Hague, for Sam. Brown". This seems to be the earliest known etching by an English-born artist. The attribution to Barlow is firmly supported by comparison with his signed work, beginning with the autographic etched frontispiece and two illustrations, which include wild and domestic creatures, in Sir William Denny's *Pelecanicidium: or the Christian Adviser against Self-Murder* (1653).

Among other frontispieces designed by Barlow, the one for James Howell's *Parley of Beasts, or Morphandra* (1660), which includes a group of nine animals, also serves as a basis for identifying later plates that Barlow did not etch. It is signed "F. Barlowe Inu: R Gaywood fecit". Richard Gaywood, a longtime friend of Barlow, often signed only his own name or failed to sign any name on the plates he etched and engraved after drawings by Barlow. In accordance with a contemporary custom on the Continent, Barlow designed several collections of prints of animals and birds as manuals for apprentice artists, engravers, goldsmiths, and other artisans. The first seems to be one published in 1654 with plates etched by Wenceslaus Hollar. Hollar and Gaywood etched and engraved the plates for what probably was Barlow's own verse text in *Seuerall Wayes of Hunting, Hawking, & Fishing according to the English Manner* (1671), a valuable early book for foreign sportsmen.

Barlow's reputation as an interpretive illustrator must rest mainly on the plates he etched for two works, Edward Benlowes's *Theophila* (1652) and *Aesop's Fables* (1666), and on the designs he drew for the "Life of Aesop" in the second edition of *Aesop's Fables* (1687), most of which were etched by another hand. His illustrations for John Ogilby's *Androcleus: or the Roman Slave* (1668) are an important series, but their virtues are diminished by the inept etching and engraving by Gaywood and others. Two large signed plates in Sir Robert Stapylton's translation of Juvenal's *Mores Hominum, The Manners of Men Described in Sixteen Satyrs* (1660) cannot be ignored. One is a satire of the proconsul Marcus Aurelius Marius in a drinking bout with a thief, a hangman, and other low fellows, and the other shows Juvenal and a friend feasting on plain food and poetry, with four delightful small boys in attendance. Barlow's drawings of these figures show great variety and naturalness. The other contributors were Johan Danckerts, Robert Streater, and, possibly, Wenceslaus Hollar, and Hollar etched all the plates. Much later, in Richard Blome's *Gentlemans Recreation* (1686), only two of the numerous plates bear Barlow's name; but thirteen others seem to be his, and he may have designed some of the dozen others. Extant drawings indicate that in this encyclopedic folio of country sports and occupations, some of Barlow's most characteristic work lost its excellence through poor engraving.

The pious, eccentric, and generous Edward Benlowes's *Theophila: or Love's-Sacrifice. A Divine Poem* (1652) first consisted of eight cantos, but by increments reached thirteen. Extant copies differ because Benlowes, who paid for the printing, made up individual presentation copies from the sheets in varying sequences and with some variation in illustrations. It seems probable that for the earliest version he hired Barlow to do only a portrait of the poet and a facing frontispiece of Theophila (Divine Love or the Soul) triumphing over the serpent Evil. The two plates are unsigned and are engraved as well as etched. Benlowes then seems to have decided on a smaller format and had Barlow etch an illustration for each of the eight cantos. He later extended the poem and had Barlow etch two more illustrations. As time went on, he also inserted in presentation copies an incongruous assortment of previously used plates by Hollar, Francis Cleyn, Jan Baptist Gaspars, and others; two old woodcuts; and his cropped portrait and Theophila triumphant. Benlowes's verse is composed of fervent disconnected religious affirmations that must have been virtually impossible to illustrate without the poet's help. Yet Barlow's allegorical, sometimes emblematic, designs are sensitive realizations of significant moments in Theophila's progress heavenward.

Barlow's ten main plates include designs as varied as the poet musing while an eagle flies upward with his book and an angel crowns a young woman, Theophila; Theophila praying, surrounded by seven snarling beasts, symbols of the deadly sins; David playing a harp, Theophila holding Moses's tablets, and Christ bleeding; the poet, sitting in an alcove bed, beholding a vision of Theophila, while an owl, a cat, and a dog add a characteristic Barlow touch; two angels supporting Theophila in her ascent toward heaven while condemned souls fall into hell; and, the two late additions, the virtuous man resisting temptations and the poet as a courtly youth in a pastoral setting.

The inking and printing of some of the plates in the British Library copy and in other copies are atrocious. Two of the drawings are extant, easily identified as Barlow's, although, like the plates, they are unsigned. Benlowes was enamored of emblem books (he encouraged and subsidized Francis Quarles). Thus with Barlow's plates or proofs before him, he wrote four-couplet commentaries on them. These verses were engraved on separate plates that were printed beneath the first six illustrations but not, probably because of the crowding, the last four. What makes Barlow's ten etched *Theophila* illustrations unique in English book illustration is their blending of unaffected naturalism with mystical intensity. With the aid of Benlowes's explications and, doubtless, advice, Barlow turned the poet's intentions into images of convincing clarity and fervor, a remarkable feat for a youth of twenty-five or so.

Barlow's best known contribution to book illustration is the series in his edition of *Aesop's Fables* (1666), with its French, English, and Latin text, including eighty unillustrated pages of the "Life of Aesop". The English version of each fable, by Thomas Philipott, was engraved at the bottom of each plate in six couplets. The plates in this first edition include a beguiling etched frontispiece depicting Aesop surrounded by animals and birds, an engraved title page (dated "1665") with five etched animals around a cartouche surmounted by an eagle, and 110 etched illustrations (ca. 130 × 160 mm). About half the motifs for the illustrations were derived from those of Marcus Gheeraerts; twenty-five seem to be original; and the rest appear to have been based on designs by Cleyn and other predecessors. But while inspired directly by Gheeraerts's naturalistic etchings of the fable creatures and their surroundings, Barlow handled his material with so much freedom and imagination that only 14 of the 110 designs are closely similar to their apparent sources. The great difference between Barlow's designs and those of his predecessors, even Gheeraerts, is the extraordinary accuracy with which he recorded the appearance and movements of his animals and birds and the immense dignity that he bestowed on them. His human beings tend to have character rather than charm, but in one crucial respect, Barlow is supreme among Aesopian fable illustrators – both animals and humans are always interacting, always expressive, always physically and emotionally involved in the action. The design for the fable of the vixen that set fire to an eagle's nest in revenge for the eagle's having seized her pup shows how Barlow combined precision of observation and drawing with dramatic involvement (fig. 31).

In 1668, Barlow came to the aid of his neighbor John Ogilby, who had lost his stock in the Great Fire of 1666, by helping with the reprint of the second edition of *Aesop Paraphras'd*, which Ogilby published with three other works in one volume. (See Hollar.) Since Barlow did not etch any of the plates in Ogilby's *Aesopic's: or a Second Collection of Fables Paraphras'd in Verse* – also in the 1668 volume – it is not clear how many of the seventeen plates neither by Hollar nor by Josiah English he designed, possibly all seventeen. Some of the animals in plates etched by Gaywood are recognizably by Barlow, but on the whole, some fine drawings seem to have been sadly degraded. Barlow also drew thirteen of the eighteen illustrations in Ogilby's verse *Androcleus: or the Roman Slave*, another work in the volume, and may have drawn three of the others. Ogilby's satirical reworking of the tale of Androcles and the lion did not offer Barlow the opportunities that the fables had; yet the drawings must have been up to his usual standard of draftsmanship and far better than Gaywood's etching makes them seem.

After the Great Fire, it took Barlow until 1687 to bring out the second edition of his *Aesop's Fables*, although he had begun work on it before 1678. He had Philipott's English couplets burnished off the bottom of the plates to make room for new versions by the well-known Restoration woman playwright Aphra Behn. He also added thirty-one illustrations to the "Life of Aesop", which had not been illustrated in the edition of 1666. Five of the designs he etched, and twenty-six were capably etched by Thomas Dudley, a pupil of Hollar. The motifs seem to be derived from a series close to the woodcuts in Jerome de Marnef's *Aesopi Phrygis Fabulae* (Paris, 1585) and from Pieter van der Borcht's etchings in *Les Fables et la Vie d'Esope* (Antwerp, 1593). Barlow's usual freedom of invention and the elaboration of detail in dress and accessories make this one of the most impressive of all "Life of Aesop" series. In the British Museum are 114 of Barlow's *Aesop's Fables* and "Life of Aesop" wash drawings. They were worked up with remarkable certainty. The plates etched by Barlow and Dudley, although reversed, are faithful renderings of the drawings. The small inconsistencies between some drawings and the plates that were made from them strengthen the purpose, not just the appearance, of the illustrations.

Other issues, but not editions, of the Aesop made up of Barlow's sheets of 1687 appeared – in 1703, for example – and in 1704, Étienne Roger brought out *Les fables d'Esope* in Amsterdam. He had acquired the frontispiece of Aesop with the animals and birds, 26 of the 31 "Life of Aesop" plates, and 107 of the 110 fable plates. On the title page, he paid tribute to Barlow and emphasized the value of the animals and birds as models for painters, sculptors, engravers, and other artists. Barlow's plates were copied in France and Germany for more than a century and by generations of English artists, including Elisha Kirkall in Samuel Croxall's long-lived *Fables of Aesop and Others* (1722) and the leading engravers of the day in the edition published by John Stockdale in 1793.

Francis Barlow's eminence rests not only on his having been the first major English-born etcher and book illustrator and a great animal and bird draftsman, but also on the way his dynamic, expressive images realize the spirit as well as the events of the texts they serve.

Francis Cleyn

A German who had studied in Italy and had been employed to do paintings for the palaces of Christian IV of Denmark, Francis Cleyn (1582–1657/58) was brought to England in 1625 by James I to be chief designer at the Mortlake tapestry factory. To supplement his income during the reign of Charles I, Cleyn also designed prints and illustra-

tions. His illustrations for a folio edition of George Sandys's *Ovid's "Metamorphosis"* [*sic*] *English'd, Mythologiz'd, and Represented in Figures* (1632) are the first important series of the seventeenth century in England. The fifteen plates for the fifteen books, all of which apparently were engraved by Salomon Savery of Amsterdam, follow the archaic method of presenting several incidents in receding planes (fig. 32), and Cleyn used *fecit* instead of *invenit* or *delineavit* on the one plate on which his and Savery's names appear. These facts suggest that he probably based his designs on a Continental series. He did, indeed, borrow the motifs for most of his wholly different compositions for eighty illustrations in John Ogilby's *Fables of Aesop, Paraphras'd in Verse and Adorn'd with Sculpture* (1651) from Marcus Gheeraerts's *De warachtighe Fabulen der Dieren* (1567). Comparison with other signed etchings by Cleyn confirms that he etched these plates, wholly without grace. He disguised his plagiarism by making otherwise pointless changes but also included details required by Ogilby's contemporary satire in his paraphrases of the traditional fables.

Seventy-four of the 101 full-page plates in Ogilby's folio translation of Virgil's *Works* (1654) carry Cleyn's name. He may have made the drawings for all but one. Wenceslaus Hollar etched at least forty-two; the rest were engraved by others. Ogilby, who was his own publisher, used the series again in his Latin edition (1658), and Jacob Tonson used it in John Dryden's translation (1697). The elaborate plates are useful and impressive visualizations of the multitudinous martial and pastoral scenes in the *Aeneid*, *Georgics*, and *Bucolics*, and make this edition of Virgil's *Works* one of the grand illustrated volumes of the seventeenth century. Again, it is likely that Cleyn derived his designs from an earlier Continental edition. He seems to have been forced by ill health to turn over the illustrating of Ogilby's translation *Homer His "Iliads"* (1660) to Abraham van Diepenbeeck of Antwerp after having drawn an unknown number of the forty-nine designs. Van Diepenbeeck probably designed all twenty-four plates in Ogilby's *Homer His "Odysses"* (1665). He seems not to have worked in England.

After Gheeraerts, Francis Cleyn is the first known illustrator of significance to have practiced in England, and he is the link between Gheeraerts's etched Aesopian fable illustrations and those of Hollar and Francis Barlow.

William Faithorne

In *A Descriptive Catalogue of the Engraved Work of William Faithorne* (1888), Louis Fagan of the British Museum identified Faithorne (1616?–91) as the illustrator of four books in addition to having been the leading Elizabethan engraver of portraits and other frontispieces. The impression given

31. Francis Barlow. *Aesop's Fables* (1666).

32. Francis Cleyn. *Ovid's "Metamorphosis" English'd, Mythologiz'd, and Represented in Figures* (1632).

58

is that Faithorne was the designer as well as the engraver of the plates in these four books, but Fagan did not commit himself. Examination of the plates reveals that Faithorne did not claim to be the original designer of even one.

In the first of the four books, Jeremy Taylor's *Great Exemplar of Sanctity and Holy Life* (1653), Faithorne signed the title-page plate of Mary and Child and the Evangelists with the abbreviation "fe.", which undoubtedly meant that he had made up the design from common sources. All eleven illustrations are signed with Faithorne's name and "sc.", indicating that he was the engraver but not the "inventor". The fine "Marriage Feast in Cana of Galilee" and "The Resurrection", however, were etched by Wenceslaus Hollar, who was living in Faithorne's house at the time. The plates are larger than the type-page, a sign of probable borrowing. *Antiquitates Christianae: or, The History of the Life and Death of the Holy Jesus and Apostles* (1675) by Taylor and William Cave contains over ninety plates, some etched. Faithorne signed only the frontispiece Annunciation, and only as the engraver. Hollar etched fourteen plates. Fagan implicitly assigned to Faithorne the sixty plates in Samuel Wesley's *Life and Death of Our Blessed Lord and Saviour Jesus Christ: an Heroic Poem* (1693), but only one main plate is signed and that by the engraver Nicholas Yeates.

It seems certain that Faithorne and his engravers copied all these traditional Catholic designs for these three Protestant works from readily available sources. The "fe." rather than "inv." or "del." after Faithorne's name on the two undistinguished illustrations of Hero and Leander in a volume of the poems of Moschus, Bion, and Theocritus (1655) in Latin and Greek strongly suggests adaptation from a Continental edition.

The importance of William Faithorne in English engraving and the large number of plates in these books make it desirable to clear up the facts about his role before passing judgment on him as a literary illustrator. So far, there seems to be no evidence that he was one.

Jan Baptist Gaspars

Known mainly as an assistant to Sir Peter Lely and Sir Godfrey Kneller, Jan Baptist Gaspars (Jaspers) (1620–91), from Antwerp, may have been a brilliant interpretive book illustrator. He cannot be praised as unreservedly as he may deserve because he seems to have illustrated only one book, *Lysis: or, the Extravagant Shepherd* (1653), a translation of Charles Sorel's *Le Berger extravagant* (Paris, 1628) by John Davies of Kidwelly. Furthermore, the etched plates have been removed from the copies examined by this writer. Four have been preserved as inserts after publication in a copy of Edward Benlowes's *Theophila* (1652); possibly there were more. Gaspars came to London toward the end of the reign of Charles I and stayed long enough to do two portraits of Charles II. He also designed tapestries. His Rubenesque drawing of figures is strengthened by an admirable open etching style in the manner of Sir Anthony Van Dyck.

The Extravagant Shepherd is described as an "anti-romance" by its author, and Gaspars's illustrations wittily sustain the parody. In the frontispiece (ca. 272 × 185 mm), Lysis, the hero, and Charite, the heroine – both dressed in the height of fashion – stand below a naked female figure (symbolizing fleshly love), while Venus and Cupid disapprove from their pedestal. Facing the first book is an etching (230 × 140 mm) of Anselm, a fashionable young man from Paris, conversing with his friend the shepherd Lysis, who is seated on the ground beside his sheep (fig. 33). An amusing surrealist bust of Charite (235 × 166 mm), with lilies and roses on her cheeks and other literal representations of the excesses of romantic imagery, precedes the second book. (A prototype, engraved by Crispin van de Passe, is in the French edition [Paris, 1628].) To illustrate the "Banquet of the Gods" in the third book, Gaspars etched a large folding plate (260 × 383 mm), signed "Ianbattest Iaspers Inv: et Fec". It mixes gods and goddesses in contemporary dress, servants bearing bowls of nectar, drunken satyrs and Pan, and many other figures seething about the personification of fate. The success of these *Extravagant Shepherd* plates lies in their excellence as etchings that express amusing ideas. There is nothing quite like them in the whole of English book illustration. It is regrettable that Jan Baptiste Gaspars did not illustrate at least one book by an English author so that the degree of his originality might be more clearly assessed.

Wenceslaus Hollar

Nearly all the 2700 etchings attributed to Wenceslaus Hollar (1607–77) are prints, even those issued in books. Many of the prints and illustrations cataloged as his are plates that he etched after paintings, prints, and drawings by others. In his own right, Hollar was primarily a great topographical and architectural draftsman. He worked in England for more than thirty years, with a break of eight years on the Continent in exile with the Royalists. Besides a number of documentary plates of historical value, frontispieces, title pages, and decorative initials, he designed and etched eighty-five interpretive illustrations. Except for a brief period before the Civil War when he was in the employ of the earl of Arundel, Hollar was forced by his need for money to work without rest at any assignment offered him. His plates depict with almost photographic precision a wide range of subjects: women's costumes, animals, butterflies, insects, plants, Windsor Castle, St. Paul's Cathedral, tombs in Westminster Abbey and Canterbury Cathedral, reconstructions of biblical temples, churches in Nottinghamshire, fortifications in Tangier, London before and after the Great Fire, and such contemporary events as the trial and execution of the earl of Strafford and the coronation of Charles II. The modest body of literary illustrations designed and etched by Hollar must be viewed against this background of unceasing labor under pressure.

Before undertaking any extensive interpretive illustration of his own, Hollar must have given the subject a good deal of thought as he etched at least 42 of the 101 large plates for the second edition of John Ogilby's translation of Virgil's *Works* (1654) after designs mainly by Francis Cleyn, and later the frontispiece and all sixteen plates in Sir Robert Stapylton's translation of Juvenal's *Mores Hominum* (1660) after drawings by Johan Danckerts, Robert Streater, Francis Barlow, and, possibly, himself.

Hollar's serious efforts as an illustrator of imaginative literature are associated with works by Ogilby. A man of several careers, Ogilby had decided to become his own publisher after the success of the first edition of his translation of Virgil's *Works* (1649) and his *Fables of Aesop, Paraphras'd in Verse* (1651), illustrated by Cleyn. Following the second edition of Virgil (1654), Ogilby published the second edition of *Aesop Paraphras'd* (1665) with fifty-seven plates (for fifty-eight fables) designed and etched by Hollar and, unfortunately, twenty-four by Dirk (Roderigo) Stoop (ca. 1610–86). Although a native of Utrecht, Stoop had come to England from Portugal in the entourage of Catherine of Braganza at the time of her marriage to Charles II in 1662 and was the official painter to the queen. In spite of his experience as an artist, he merely copied Cleyn's designs to fit the larger size of the new pages, not unlikely because Ogilby had instructed the two artists to do so. In addition, however, his etchings are singularly unappealing. Hollar, however, did not follow Cleyn blindly or exclusively, and his plates would have made up a series of great unity and grace had it not been for the jarring presence of Stoop's plates.

There are eighty-two fables in the 1665 edition of *Aesop Paraphras'd*, the last one being a timely satire of the Dutch that Ogilby added to the eighty-one tales reprinted from the 1651 edition. There are eighty-one plates (ca. 220–50 × 165–95 mm) because Hollar followed Cleyn in illustrating two related fables in one design. Hollar based forty-four of his designs on Cleyn's versions (which, as previously noted, were derived from Marcus Gheeraerts's *Fabulen der*

Dieren [1567] series, with minor changes), nine on Gheeraerts's original plates, and four on both. For Ogilby's new fable, he drew a new design. Hollar had become acquainted with Gheeraerts's work during his years on the Continent, and some of his copies of the Aesop plates are in the British Museum. Conceptually, Hollar contributed nothing new, again, probably because he and Stoop were not expected to. He did not have Gheeraerts's or Barlow's special competence in drawing animals and birds, nor did he have their commitment to linear illustration. Instead, he was mainly concerned with the whole tonal effect of illustrations. However, since the plates for Ogilby's folio are large, and Hollar, always pressed for time, neglected detail in many of the settings, a number of the plates contain too much dark crosshatched shading and monotonous foliage. But he often improved on Cleyn's designs by omitting literal details of Ogilby's references to current social conditions and by redrawing the characters and their settings with fastidious delicacy.

The Great Fire of 1666 destroyed Ogilby's stock. He bounced back in 1668, not merely with a reprint of *Aesop Paraphras'd* (1665), but with the addition of three fresh works in the same volume: *Aesopic's: or a Second Collection of Fables Paraphras'd in Verse*, fifty more Aesopian fables applied to contemporary affairs; *Androcleus: or the Roman Slave*, an uncertain retelling of the tale of Androcles and the lion; and *The Ephesian Matron, or Widow's Tears*, another ancient tale retold. Some sort of difficulty, perhaps conflict with other assignments, seems to have interfered with Hollar's work on the new pieces. Ogilby's neighbor Barlow was called in to assist by drawing about half the plates, including most of those in *Androcleus*.

In *Aesopic's*, one plate sometimes does duty for more than one related fable, and three of Hollar's *Aesop Paraphras'd* plates of 1665 were used again. Thus there are only thirty-six new plates for the fifty fables. Of these, Hollar designed and etched eighteen; Josiah English, a pupil of Cleyn but an imitator of Hollar, etched one (which he probably drew); and Barlow seems to have designed the remaining seventeen. Richard Gaywood etched some of Barlow's designs, and an unknown hand engraved the rest. Again, the sources are varied, but since they do not include any by Cleyn and since ten of the designs have to be original because the fables are not traditional, the effects are livelier, if not harmonious. Some, such as Hollar's "The Swan and the Stork" and "The Crab and Her Mother", are among the delights of English illustration.

The only wholly original series of interpretive illustrations by Hollar consists of ten large etched plates (ca. 245 × 195 mm) in *The Ephesian Matron*. Ogilby's verses retell Petronius's unpleasant *Satyricon* tale of the newly widowed

33. Jan Baptist Gaspars. Charles Sorel, *Lysis: or, the Extravagant Shepherd* (1653).

34. Wenceslaus Hollar. John Ogilby, *The Ephesian Matron, or Widow's Tears* (1668).

matron of Ephesus who substitutes on the gallows the corpse of her husband for that of a malefactor in order to save her lover, a Roman soldier facing execution because the malefactor's body, which he was guarding, was stolen while he entered the husband's tomb to get out of the cold and stayed to dally with the widow. The first two plates gave full scope to Hollar's incomparable skill in drawing broad scenic and architectural effects: the Matron and her husband strolling on a terrace above a formal sunken garden, with the walled city of Ephesus in the background (fig. 34); and the funeral procession coming out of the gate of Ephesus after the husband dies suddenly of the plague. Then follows a sequence showing the helmeted Roman soldier entering the tomb (which is furnished with candles and a fireplace), having supper with the widow while her maid watches in the shadows, and being repulsed at knifepoint by the Matron when he attempts to force his attentions on her. Hollar next pictured an interlude between Venus and Cupid, in which Ogilby has Venus approve of the Matron's sudden (unillustrated) capitulation. After the soldier discovers the theft of the malefactor's body, the Matron is shown cutting off those parts of the husband's corpse that, according to law, had been cut off the malefactor before he was hanged. Then, the Matron, soldier, and maid are depicted substituting the husband's corpse on the gallows in what is a grim travesty of the Deposition. In the final plate, Hollar was forced to follow Ogilby's absurd text by showing Venus restoring the husband to life and connubial bliss. The two Venus plates are distractions, through no fault of Hollar's. The other eight etchings make up a most unusual series of illustrations, in which the images have more distinction, sincerity, and emotional power than does the text they serve.

The only other comparable illustrations by Hollar are the seven etchings (132×81 mm) of the Passion in *The Office of the Holy Week According to the Missal and Roman Breviary* (1670). Sir W. K. Blount translated the work from the French, and it was printed by the "Widow Chrestien" in Paris. Although Hollar signed all the plates, he added the ambiguous *fecit* after his name. Four of them are said to be after designs by Jacobo Palma and Stella – that is, possibly after paintings in London or engravings in Blount's possession – and all are traditional Passion scenes. Yet, unoriginal as these designs are, Wenceslaus Hollar's sensitive etching makes this one of the finest native religious series in an English book.

Sir John Baptist Medina

After the enterprising young Jacob Tonson bought a half-interest in the copyright of *Paradise Lost* – in association with Richard Bentley – he published the first illustrated edition of *Paradise Lost* by subscription in 1688, twenty-one years after the first edition and fourteen years after John Milton's death. It was the earliest serious effort to illustrate an important work of English poetry. The plates in this edition also appear in Tonson's editions of 1692 and 1695. (In 1709, Tonson published the first illustrated collection of Shakespeare's plays.) Tonson's edition of *Paradise Lost: A Poem in Twelve Books*, printed by Miles Flesher, is the fourth edition and the first folio. As announced on the title page, it is "Adorn'd with Sculptures": a portrait of Milton and an engraved frontispiece (ca. 284 × 181 mm) for each of the twelve books. Eight of the thirteen designs were drawn by John Baptist Medina (de Medina) (1659–1710) and engraved by Michael Burghers (d. 1720), who then and for about fifty years worked for the Oxford University Press. (He designed as well as engraved a number of frontispieces. Two of the best are one of schoolboys picking up apples shaken from a tree in an edition of William Lily's *Grammar* [1687] and one of four scholars in a Bodleian Library alcove for Thomas Benson's *Vocabularum Anglo-Saxicum* [1701].) The Victoria and Albert Museum possesses Medina's drawings – for Books III and V to XI. They prove that Burghers's plates are exact transcriptions. The plate for Book IV was designed by Bernard Lens, Sr. (1631–1708) and engraved by Peter Paul Bouche of Antwerp; it is signed "B Lens Senior invent: P P Bouche sculpsit".

Until recently, it had been assumed that Medina designed the remaining three *Paradise Lost* illustrations, although they were signed only by Burghers. He signed all the plates except the one by Lens: "Burgesse", six times; "Burg.", four; and "Burghers", once. In 1972 in the *Metropolitan Museum Journal*, Suzanne Boorsch presented convincing evidence that Henry Aldrich (d. 1710), of Christ Church College, Oxford, initiated the designs for Books I, II, and XII. Aldrich, an authority on architecture, music, logic, and other subjects, was closely associated with the Oxford University Press and had a collection of about 2000 prints (still at Christ Church College), which he had gathered on the Continent. Boorsch argues persuasively that he selected elements from his prints of biblical subjects, mostly after Italian paintings, for Burghers to adapt as designs for the three books. She suggests that either Aldrich was too busy to continue beyond the three designs or Tonson insisted on original designs. Another possibility is that Aldrich and Burghers may have found that the rest of the poem demanded designs of more originality than they were capable of creating. Boorsch suggests that Tonson then hired Lens, an enamel painter from the Netherlands, but was dissatisfied with his first design and dismissed him. Lens's drawing for Book IV is in the archaic tradition of continuous representation of several scenes on one plate, and the effects, perhaps because of the engraving by Bouche, are not polished. But Tonson later tolerated many illustrations much worse than this – the Shakespeare series of 1709, for example. Why Lens did plate IV, not plate III, is an unanswered question. (On stylistic grounds, the signed frontispiece of a ship, whale, and cask [but not the unsigned illustrations] in Jonathan Swift's *Tale of a Tub* [1710] seems to be the work of his son Bernard II [1659–1725], an etcher and mezzotint engraver.)

John Baptist Medina, the son of a Spanish army captain, was born in Brussels and studied painting there, as his Rubenesque figures suggest. He must have begun work on the Milton soon after his arrival in London in 1686 at the age of twenty-seven. He almost certainly had not illustrated a published book before, and he never illustrated another. The Ovid for which he is said to have drawn designs was not published, and the assertion that he illustrated *Paradise Regain'd* for Tonson in 1713, twenty-five years after *Paradise Lost*, after having established himself as a portraitist in Edinburgh and three years after his death, seems improbable on the face of it and untenable because the feeble designs bear no resemblance to those of 1688. (See Pigné.) Tonson, a Milton enthusiast who did as much as anyone to build the poet's reputation, probably advised Medina closely about the eight 1688 illustrations, for it seems unlikely that young Medina's command of the English language or appreciation of English poetry would have extended to a perceptive reading of *Paradise Lost*. The summary "argument" that precedes each book and familiarity with biblical art would have helped, of course.

The designs for Books I, II, and XII, those thought by Boorsch to have been fabricated from Aldrich's prints, are the most memorable of the twelve. They are also inaccurate. The plates for Books II and XII copy similar scenes from known prints that do not follow the text. And the design for Book I seems to have been derived from an as yet undiscovered source because it, too, does not correspond to Milton's lines. Since Burghers signed these three plates, they were engraved in Oxford, but since Aldrich's name does not appear at all, it seems safe to assume that his role was limited to finding what he thought were acceptable parallel scenes among his prints or other readily available biblical prints and book illustrations and suggesting how Burghers might adapt them.

In the plate for Book I, familiar because it is the one usually reproduced (although it is wholly unlike the rest, except that for Book II), the large figures and Caravaggesque effects give the scene an adventitious melodramatic quality.

Satan alone stands amid flames on the "burning marle", prodding the fallen angels with a thin pole to no clear purpose. In the poem, however, he has a moonlike shield and stands on the beach with Beelzebub while rousing his followers with a speech. More logically, the illustration for Book II pictures the confrontation between Satan and Sin and Death at the gates of Hell. Hideous Sin is accurately rendered, but Death – described by Milton as black, shapeless, and crowned – becomes a skinny living figure with a skull as a head, akin to Death in fifteenth-century woodcuts. In the air are three demonic forms like flying shrimp, which have no counterparts in the poem. Satan stands on a shattered half-gate that he apparently has battered down – a serious error, since the point of the scene is that Sin opens the gate with a key when Satan recognizes her as his daughter and mother of his son, Death. Boorsch traces the background and the flying monsters to Andrea Mantegna's *Descent into Limbo*; the three main figures seem to have been copied from a print or a book illustration. The design for Book XII is a facsimile of an engraving of the Expulsion scene in Raphael's Vatican fresco. Raphael's despairing, guilt-ridden Adam and Eve do not fit the ambiguous, almost hopeful last lines of *Paradise Lost*.

The main element in the Book IV plate by Lens shows Uriel descending from heaven to warn Gabriel, on guard at the Gate of Paradise, to watch out for Satan. Uriel, swathed in yards of gown, seems to be coming in for a crash landing. Gabriel, seated on a stone, appears to be beckoning to Ithuriel and Zephon, who stand behind him beneath a display of armor. Next in the multiple receding scenes, Ithuriel and Zephon foil Satan, in the form of a toad, by pricking him with a spear as Adam and Eve sleep in a bower. This Lens design differs from those by Medina in its greater amount of detail and its attempt to suggest the bountifulness of Paradise. For the fourth illustrated edition – published by Tonson in 1705 with inferior, reduced plates – Heinrich (Hans) Eland copied all the original plates except the one for Book IV. For that, "J. Gweree" (J. Goeree) drew the bower scene as a single-incident design that resembles those by Medina.

In the plates for Books III and V to XI, Medina made an effort to represent significant scenes, sometimes with other scenes indicated sketchily, but not so comprehensively as did Lens. He placed the main figures large in the foreground but did almost nothing to make their surroundings seem authentic or even habitable. In some plates, there are also Italianate cloudborne celestial scenes, notably in Book VI, where Medina pictured surprisingly well (perhaps by borrowing) the two armies of angels on separate islands of cloud, with the rebel host being toppled without visible force. Beyond credit for presenting for the first time

35. John Baptist Medina. John Milton, *Paradise Lost: A Poem in Twelve Books* (1688).

65

in elementary graphic notation what takes place in two-thirds of *Paradise Lost*, however, Medina's illustrations merit little praise. They are uninspired renderings of an inspired text. At no time does he convey anything of the vastness of the action, the opulence of the scene, or the grandeur of the theme of Milton's epic. He is not even good at filling his large plates with enlightening tableaux or revelations of character; his Satan is a stock satyr, more comic than Miltonic.

Medina suffered from two disabling limitations: his inability to comprehend the high seriousness and beauty of his subjects, and the inadequacy of his drawing to suggest either. Like many another artist who was not an illustrator by experience or feeling, Medina relied on technique. Unfortunately, he had only two outmoded Manneristic tricks: anatomical extravagance, and exaggerated bodily gesture.

What he made of *Paradise Lost* can be amply demonstrated by reference to any one of the eight plates; the frontispiece to Book VII, Raphael's account of Creation in his long recapitulation of previous events – the least demanding scene in the entire poem – will do (fig. 35). The gesticulating Raphael seems to be delivering an oration, not quietly talking; the muscular Adam suggests a model in a life class; and poor ignored naked Eve looks miserable, as though having a chill. Medina's series may shed light on the flow of Continental art into England following the Restoration, but it casts little light on Milton. In his 1717 portrait by Sir Godfrey Kneller, Tonson holds conspicuously the 1688 edition of *Paradise Lost*, which he said was his most profitable book. Perhaps the plates by Medina and Burghers contributed to this happy outcome by bringing Milton's lofty verse down to earth.

CHAPTER FOUR

The Eighteenth Century (I)
1701–1775

Changes brought about by the restoration of Charles II in 1660 did not fully affect English book illustration until the eighteenth century. The relaxation of social attitudes had given the lighter forms of literature and the theater a considerable vogue. In early-eighteenth-century England, as in France, illustrated editions of belles-lettres, including plays, appeared in profusion in illustrated duo-decimo editions, handy for people with the time and taste for reading fashionable authors. The admiration for French art that Cavalier refugees had brought back to England led to the importation of skilled French artists and engravers. They introduced to English book illustration neoclassic elegance, romantic rustic folk and scenes, mild eroticism, fastidious attention to costume, dainty ornamentation, small vignette head- and tailpieces, illustrations within neat borders, and a general impression of lightness and languor. The engravers raised the standards of the craft in England and helped give the practitioners more prestige. Because of the strong French presence, specific relationships between English and French illustrated books of the eighteenth century – the several editions of *Don Quixote* and Charles-Antoine Coypel's immensely popular series, for instance – offer numerous neglected opportunities for research.

While French artist-engravers were the leading influence in English book illustration in the first half of the century, native artists were responsible for the majority of the illustrations in the books published between 1700 and 1775 that were chosen for inclusion in the Catalog. As an interpretive illustrator, Francis Hayman is the leading figure of the period. Within circumscribed limits, Richard Bentley and William Kent are also of considerable interest. William Hogarth has a place in English book illustration for reasons other than his limited contributions to books. The realism of and moral indignation in his satirical prints depicting the weaknesses and depravity of English society were an invigorating counterpoise to French effeteness and a permanent inspiration for "Englishness" in the graphic arts, including illustration. And almost single-handedly,

Hogarth was instrumental in effecting the enactment, around 1735, of the first copyright laws to protect engravers. Since all book illustrations of the period were engraved, these copyright acts were a bulwark against the widespread piracy of designs. They led in 1862 to the extension of copyright to artists and photographers.

The literary development with the greatest effect on illustration was the rise of the novel. Two of the works of prose fiction most widely read in England and most often illustrated – Cervantes's *Don Quixote* and John Bunyan's *Pilgrim's Progress* – had been published in the seventeenth century. They were followed in the early years of the eighteenth century by Daniel Defoe's *Robinson Crusoe* and Jonathan Swift's *Gulliver's Travels*. But the modern novel with characters, including women, facing contemporary social problems began somewhat later, with Samuel Richardson's *Pamela, Clarissa Harlowe*, and *Sir Charles Grandison*. Henry Fielding's urge to satirize Richardson led him into the field, followed by Tobias Smollett, Laurence Sterne, and Oliver Goldsmith. They all wrote novels that gave illustration an enormous impetus. Ever since, the novel has been the literary form that has appealed to the widest public and, until our time, that has been most closely identified with serious illustration.

Publishing practices throughout the eighteenth century tended to obscure the individuality of many illustrators. A great many books contain only a frontispiece, sometimes augmented by one or two other plates. Having more than one artist – anywhere from two to ten – engage in illustrating one book became common. Many of them often designed only one or two plates. Some of these group illustrators were painters of repute who occasionally made drawings or permitted their paintings of literary subjects to be copied to lend prestige to a publisher's venture; such designs can hardly be considered to be illustrations. The prevalence of costumed figures posturing in pastoral and drawing-room settings and the leveling effect of engraving give the illustrations of the eighteenth century an interchangeable, look-alike character that reduces the claim of a very large

67

number of volumes to be significant examples of illustrated books. Under the circumstances attending publishing, therefore, numerous artists have no substantial work that can be viewed in isolation in order to give them a clear identity or sustain a critical analysis. Consequently, more illustrators were at work than are listed in the Catalog, and some are listed there but are not discussed in the text. All known illustrators of the century, however, are represented in Hanns A. Hammelmann and T. S. R. Boase's *Book Illustrators in Eighteenth-Century England* (1975). The importance of copper engraving as the vehicle of visual communication in these years before wood engraving and photography can be inferred from the following title alone: *A Series of One Hundred and Ninety-Six Engravings, (in the Line Manner,) by the First Artists of the Country, Illustrative of* [Hume's] *"The History of England"* . . . *Upon the Execution of Which Have Been Expended Forty-Four Thousand Pounds* (1812). The artists included Edward Burney, William Hamilton, Philippe Jacques de Loutherbourg, Robert Smirke, Thomas Stothard, and Richard Westall; the engravers, Francesco Bartolozzi, Edward and William Finden, James Fittler, and John Landseer.

Richard Bentley

Son of the famous master of Trinity College, Cambridge, Richard Bentley (1708–82) was one of Horace Walpole's correspondents and helped design Strawberry Hill. He was also a friend of Thomas Gray, who wrote a poem in his honor. As an amateur artist, Bentley's only signal achievement was *Designs by Mr. R. Bentley, for Six Poems by Mr. T. Gray* (1753). The unusual precedence given to Bentley in the title was requested by Gray because he feared ridicule for having published six "little matters thus pompously [magnificently] adorned". Walpole had the thin folio handsomely printed and added a useful "Explanation of the Prints".

Bentley drew the designs for nineteen engravings. There is a whimsical title-page vignette of a monkey painting and Apollo playing a lute. Each poem has a full-page frontispiece (ca. 250 × 200 mm), a rectangular headpiece, and a vignette tailpiece. In the frontispieces, Bentley combined within decorative rococo frames both scenes from the poems and scenes made up of motifs from the poems and from his imagination. Even the absence of straight borders was an act of liberation for English design. All but one or two of the head- and tailpieces also make interpretive comments. For example, the frontispiece to Gray's supreme example of light verse, "Ode on the Death of a Favourite Cat, Drowned in a Tub of Gold Fishes", has an inner illustration of Selima, Walpole's cat, perched on a "lofty

vase's side", but the two mock-heroic caryatids – a river god stopping his ears to Selima's cries and Destiny snipping the nine threads of her lives – and other units in the enclosure are Bentley's extensions of Gray's wit. The headpiece of Selima swimming in the tub has two cats on the side dressed as mourners and a standish (writing set) above as a sign that the poet will write her elegy. The tailpiece playfully goes beyond the demise of the friendless favorite and shows Selima in the bow of Charon's boat arching her back at the welcoming committee of three-headed Cerberus.

The frontispiece to "Elegy Written in a Country Church Yard" presents – in the words of Walpole's "Explanation of the Prints" – "A Gothic gateway in ruins with the emblems of nobility on one side; on the other, the implements and employments of the Poor. Thro' the arch appears a church-yard and village-church built out of the remains of an Abbey. A countryman showing an epitaph to a passenger." Bentley most happily matched wit with Gray in the frontispiece to "A Long Story" (fig. 36). In mock-heroic couplets, Gray recounts how he had taken sanctuary in a private place in the rear of his mother's house in order to escape two visiting ladies from the manor house. Bentley has the Muses convey the hunted poet under their hoops to a "small closet in the garden", pursued by two winged female warriors.

Few English poets have been so well served by an illustrator as Gray in these nineteen engravings. Had he been sufficiently employed, Richard Bentley unquestionably would have become one of the brightest stars among English illustrators.

François Boitard

Jacob Tonson, who had published the first illustrated edition of *Paradise Lost* in 1688, published *The Works of Mr. William Shakespeare. In Six Volumes Adorn'd with Cuts*, also the first illustrated edition, in 1709 and 1710. It is often referred to as the Rowe edition because the editor was Nicholas Rowe, the playwright. Until 1969, the identity of the designer of the frontispieces, each of which illustrates a scene from each of Shakespeare's thirty-seven plays and six apocryphal plays, was unknown. Michael Vander Gucht was the usual candidate because his name is on the portrait of Shakespeare used as a frontispiece to each of the volumes. After comparing these unsigned plates with those in Tonson's edition of *The Works of Mr. Francis Beaumont and Mr. John Fletcher* (1711), seven of which name "F. Boitard" as the artist (an exercise that anyone could have done during the previous two and a half centuries), Hanns A. Hammelmann stated cautiously that he considered François Boitard (ca. 1670 – ca. 1717) to have

36. Richard Bentley. *Designs by Mr. R. Bentley, for Six Poems by Mr. T. Gray* (1753).

37. François Boitard. William Shakespeare, *Hamlet*, in *The Works of Mr. William Shakespeare* (1709).

been the designer of "most, very possibly all", of the *Shakespeare* illustrations. After Hammelmann's death, the editor of the "Boitard" entry in *Book Illustrators in Eighteenth-Century England* toned down Hammelmann's judgment to "many of the plates can be attributed to François Boitard". Careful examination of the two sets of plates and other books and reflection on the circumstances of publication of the two works make it seem certain that Boitard drew all the designs in both collections and that Elisha Kirkall engraved them, as well as the Vander Gucht portrait of Shakespeare.

The *Shakespeare* and *Beaumont and Fletcher* sets of illustrations are much alike and can be discussed together. The forty-three plates in the *Shakespeare* and the fifty-two in the *Beaumont and Fletcher* are markedly French in style. Their aim seems to be to re-create scenes observed in the theater or to imagine them as they would look on the stage. Since Boitard could have had only a superficial knowledge of Elizabethan plays, Rowe – who, in this edition, was the first editor to divide Shakespeare's plays into acts and scenes and to provide stage directions – selected the scenes to be illustrated and, possibly aided by his friend Thomas Betterton, a Shakespearean actor-manager, suggested how they would look when played. In the early eighteenth century, Elizabethan plays were considered to be uncouth and were often rewritten to meet contemporary notions of good taste and good theater before being put on the stage. They were then played in eighteenth-century costumes, including knee breeches and periwigs and tight-waisted bodices and flowing skirts, together with standardized apparel for classical times and armor for military figures. The result can be seen in the plate for *Hamlet* (IV.iv), in which the ghost of his father appears to Hamlet in Gertrude's apartment after he has killed Polonius (fig. 37). The overturned chair so conspicuous in the foreground is a bit of contemporary stage business. Much of the unattractiveness of the plates in these two series must be attributed to Kirkall, who until then had had little experience in engraving human figures in such profusion.

Boitard seems to have illustrated only one other book besides the *Shakespeare* and *Beaumont and Fletcher*, although he may have been the designer of unsigned plates in other contemporary publications. For *The History of Joseph* (1712), a poem by the Reverend W. Rose that was printed by Tonson, Boitard provided a frontispiece for each of the six "books". The fact that all the plates bear the signatures of Boitard and Kirkall strengthens the probability that the two were responsible for all the *Shakespeare* and *Beaumont and Fletcher* illustrations. Then, too, Boitard designed and Kirkall engraved a crowded allegorical frontispiece of Britannia receiving homage from Neptune for

William Howell's history of the kings of England, *Medulla Historiae Anglicanae* (1712). The book is mainly of interest in relation to Kirkall.

Boitard's son, Louis Philippe (d. ca. 1760), designed and engraved plates for a number of miscellaneous books, but he was a draftsman and interpretive illustrator of limited talents. Perhaps in the history of science fiction he will be remembered for having anticipated flying machines in his drawings for the first edition of Robert Paltock's *Peter Wilkins, a Cornish Man* and two other books in 1751.

Louis Cheron

A Calvinist refugee from France in 1695, the painter and teacher Louis Cheron (1655–1735) – he dropped the accent from his name on arrival – turned to book illustrating at a late age. His draftsmanship is excellent but somewhat formal and decorative, reminiscent of his style of painting. To a number of books, he contributed only a frontispiece.

Ovid's "Metamorphoses" in Fifteen Books. Translated by the Most Eminent Hands (1717) is one of Jacob Tonson's celebrated publications and one of the most impressive eighteenth-century English books. It is a grand folio in the seventeenth-century fashion with a cast of translators headed by John Dryden. Hammelmann says that the fifteen magnificent plates (ca. 345 × 210 mm) are by Cheron and Louis du Guernier. Since no artist's name is on them, the absence of a reason for the attribution is regrettable. Both artists may have been employed by Tonson at this time. But since du Guernier signed his name on three plates as one of the four engravers – the others were Elisha Kirkall, Michael Vander Gucht, and Robert Smith – it is difficult to imagine that he would not have signed even one with "inv. et sculp." if he was also the designer, as he invariably did in other books. The most reasonable explanation for such total reticence about naming the designers is that the designs were not original but were copies of a Continental series. The archaic multiple-scene compositions support this explanation. It is extremely unlikely that any artist available to Tonson, especially Cheron in light of his *Paradise Lost* series, would have adopted this outmoded artistic style for one book. We can believe that Hammelmann had good reason for saying that Cheron and du Guernier drew the designs without our believing that they invented them. Since it is impossible to guess which designs Cheron drew, there is no point in saying more about his role in this grand volume.

The four illustrations signed by Cheron for *Rapin of Gardens: A Latin Poem* (1718) are pleasantly varied, from an allegorical design of Flora on a cloud to a realistic one of a muscular workman digging a hole in which his mate will plant a tree. This second plate has a sugar-loaf mountain in the background, almost the signature of Kirkall, who engraved the four plates.

Cheron's chief contribution to English illustrated books is in Tonson's two-volume edition of *The Poetical Works of John Milton* (1720). Cheron had collaborated with Sir James Thornhill, a painter of historical subjects, on an edition of the Bible (Oxford, 1717), and their designs were to some extent models for those in the *Poetical Works*. After the title-page portrait "Milton Inspired" by Cheron, each of the twelve books of *Paradise Lost* has a rectangular headpiece (89 × 170 mm), an illustrative initial, and a tailpiece (ca. 102 × 140 mm). The tailpieces tend to be simplified and crowded to fit within heavy oval frames, but most are active scenes, such as "Satan Disputes with the Angelic Guard".

Thornhill drew "Satan Summons His Legions" as the headpiece for Book I, and Cheron drew the rest of the designs. All things considered, Cheron's eleven headpieces are one of the most satisfactory series of *Paradise Lost* illustrations. While the wide rectangular measure imposed constraints, Cheron met them in most plates by filling the foreground with figures that are linked firmly to one another through action and gesture. He drew normal, attractive figures and molded them and their immediate surroundings by a complex interplay of light and shadow that ties the figures together, yet gives each solidity. Cheron (or more probably Tonson) chose moments of critical importance and did not turn Satan into the hero of the epic. The following twelve subjects, revising those of Tonson's first edition of 1688, come close to being the norm from which later artists deviate but do not often depart significantly: Book I, "Satan Summons His Legions"; Book II, "Satan at the Gates of Hell"; Book III, "The Son in Heaven"; Book IV, "Adam and Eve in the Garden"; Book V, "Raphael Discourses"; Book VI, "The Battle of the Angels"; Book VII, "The Creation"; Book VIII, "Adam Asks Raphael about Celestial Motions"; Book IX, "Adam Tempted"; Book X, "Sin and Death in Paradise"; Book XI, "Michael Foretells the Future"; and Book XII, "The Expulsion".

Cheron could not transmit the music of Milton's verse or the grandeur of his thought, but he realized dramatic moments in terms as expressive as the text and space allowed. "Adam and Eve in the Garden" is a charming, relaxed arrangement: Adam, seated cross-legged, turns to Eve, who is kneeling and stretching toward him affectionately. With utter naturalness, the design fills the imposed space and conveys a sense of the happiness then prevailing in the Garden of Eden. "Raphael Discourses" makes Paradise palpable and Raphael's visit as natural as a friend's

dropping in for tea. In contrast, "The Battle of the Angels", a scene avoided by other illustrators, gives the illusion of full-scale combat with only four foreground figures and five others. Cheron's professionalism is apparent in the contrast between the dominant forward thrust of the figures of the good angels – tall, winged, urbane – and the backward movement of the beaten-down figures of Satan and his rebel host – horned, nude, evil looking (fig. 38). Finally, Cheron created a convincing variant of Raphael's Vatican fresco of the Expulsion to fit the imperatives of his space. He presents the moment in which Michael, with his fiery sword, stands on the bottom one of the steps down the cliff from the eastern gate of Paradise before disappearing. Adam's and Eve's feet are for the first time on the "plain" – the threatening world outside Paradise – and Eve turns in anguish toward Adam, whose hand supports his bowed head. Cheron not only brings home the emotional impact of the Expulsion, but also suggests the drawing together of Adam and Eve as they face their unknown future.

Paradise Regained, for which he drew five illustrations, did not offer Cheron the same opportunities for dramatic designs. For *Samson Agonistes*, he drew "Samson and Manoa", a powerful evocation of the blind, chained Samson seated in prison in Gaza as his father pleads with him. For "Lycidas", he drew one design. Cheron's five illustrations for *The Countess of Pembroke's Arcadia* (1724) by Sir Philip Sidney are suitable, but like the first, which depicts the shepherds Strepton and Claius pulling Musidorus from the sea, they are not in key with the young Sidney's fanciful pastoral mood.

Cheron's most extensive series of interpretive illustrations is the thirty-seven of the forty-five in Tonson's eight-volume edition of Plutarch's *Lives* (1727). Each presents as comprehensively as possible in a full-page design an incident in the tempestuous lives and deaths of Plutarch's subjects. The best of the thirty-six plates in Samuel Croxall's anthology *A Select Collection of Novels and Histories* (1729) are the four by Louis Cheron.

Gravelot [Hubert François Bourguignon]

In the dozen or so years that Gravelot (Hubert François Bourguignon) (1699–1773) worked in England – as both illustrator and engraver – after his arrival in 1732 or 1733, he was a major force in bringing the fashionable-society style of Jean Antoine Watteau and François Boucher, with whom he had studied, to the England that William Hogarth was rudely revealing to the English. This paradox tends to make the pliant grace of his figures – he used large dolls as models – the fastidious attention to contemporary dress

38. Louis Cheron. John Milton, *Paradise Lost* in *The Poetical Works of John Milton* (1720).

39. Gravelot. Samuel Richardson, *Pamela: or, Virtue Rewarded* (1742).

and furniture, and the delicate handling of light and shade seem a little incongruous in some of the English works he illustrated. His right to a place in English book illustration, however, is ensured by his having been one of the earliest illustrators of some leading literary works: John Dryden's *Dramatick Works* (1735), John Gay's *Fables* (1738), William Shakespeare's *Works* (1740), Samuel Richardson's *Pamela* (1742), Sir Thomas Hanmer's edition of Shakespeare (1744), and Henry Fielding's *Tom Jones* (1750). Some of these assignments he shared with Francis Hayman. Gravelot returned to France in 1745. It has been said that he illustrated only one English work thereafter; yet numerous books with his designs came out in England after 1745. He was also one of the finest engravers and teachers of engraving of his time. During Gravelot's residence in England, most of the books for which he designed and engraved illustrations either were not belles-lettres or had only a frontispiece or one or two vignettes by him.

In his first important English work, Gravelot drew twenty-seven frontispieces (132 × 76 mm) for Jacob Tonson's six-volume duodecimo edition of John Dryden's *Dramatick Works* (1735). The plates for the comedies tend to be graceful French-style conversation pieces that reveal little about the plays. In his illustrations for the tragedies, Gravelot overdid scenes in which someone has just been or is about to be stabbed. Gerard Vander Gucht's engraving obscures much of the charm of Gravelot's drawings, but not their other fine qualities.

The fifteen illustrations (158 × 100 mm) that Gravelot drew and Gerard Scotin engraved for *Fables. By the Late Mr. Gay* (1738), the posthumous second series, are larger and finer than those by William Kent and John Wooton in the first series (1727). Gravelot's superiority is technical. Aided by Scotin's excellent engraving, he made his figures a part of a fully realized scene, while Kent and Wooton's stand apart. In dress, posture, manner, and expression, Gravelot endowed Gay's human characters with a sophistication that Gay would have liked them to have.

Gravelot was not so well tuned to Shakespeare's *Works* (1740). He drew one design for each of the thirty-six plays (*Pericles* was omitted) and engraved eight of the plates. Vander Gucht engraved the rest, not so well. Gravelot's limitations are exemplified by an excellent design for the banquet scene in *Macbeth* (III.iv) that loses its force because Banquo's barefoot ghost stands on tiptoe, like a ballet dancer. Yet Gravelot projects the tension in most scenes, as in the plate for *3 Henry VI* (V.v), in which Queen Margaret cries to the dying Prince of Wales, "O Ned, sweet Ned! speak to thy mother, boy," while the noble assassins stand tensely by with bloody swords. His depiction of Othello smothering Desdemona (V.ii) is another surprising example of savage realism.

With his friend Hayman, Gravelot shares the credit for having illustrated the first "modern" English novel, Richardson's *Pamela: or, Virtue Rewarded* (1742). Gravelot contributed fifteen designs for illustrations (126 × 76 mm) and Hayman, twelve; Gravelot engraved and etched all twenty-seven plates. Both drew designs for the first three volumes, and Gravelot drew all seven for the fourth. His plates are especially good in realizing the scenes that show the domestic rewards of virtue that make *Pamela* a main source of English sentimental fiction and of serious analysis of human relations. Gravelot's depiction of Pamela forcing Mr. H. to return Polly's note exemplifies the elegance and sensitivity that he brought to English illustration (fig. 39).

Gravelot was a man of generous spirit. For Hanmer's sumptuous quarto edition *The Works of Shakespear* (1744), he not only played second fiddle to Hayman by engraving all the plates, which he did superbly, but also drew the five illustrations (ca. 210 × 147 mm) for Volume IV, perhaps to safeguard Hayman's fee by helping to complete the contract. (See Hayman.) The plays illustrated by Gravelot are *1, 2,* and *3 Henry VI, Richard III,* and *Henry VIII*. Hanmer's choice of scenes offered little in the way of colorful action, but Gravelot evoked the drama in moments such as that in *3 Henry VI* (II.v) during the battle near Towton when the king, standing apart, observes a son with the body of his father, whom he has killed, and a father with the body of his son, whom he has killed.

After Gravelot returned to Paris, he illustrated a French four-volume duodecimo edition of Fielding's *Tom Jones* (1750) with sixteen plates (125 × 75 mm). (The first edition had been published in 1749.) The almost dainty hero is far from Fielding's image of Tom. The polite boudoir and drawing-room scenes seem more suitable to the works by Boccaccio, Jean Racine, and Jean-Jacques Rousseau that Gravelot also illustrated. Five of Gravelot's original drawings for *Tom Jones* are in the Rosenwald Collection in the Library of Congress.

Louis du Guernier

Since Louis du Guernier (1687–ca. 1735?) arrived in London from Paris in 1708, and books with his plates appeared regularly between 1714 and 1735, he probably died around 1735 and not in 1716, as has been assumed. As an artist-engraver, du Guernier was much less accomplished than were his countrymen Louis Cheron and Gravelot. The six plates in Alexander Pope's *Rape of the Lock* (1714), the first complete edition, have none of the elegance and wit that one expects from a French artist and that *The Rape of the Lock* demands. They are painfully literal and plain, even though Pope may have given them his approval. In Canto II, for example, Belinda and her companions are "Launch'd on the Bosom of the Silver Thames" in a clumsy dory propelled by sail and oars, possibly drawn from observation, certainly not from imagination. Du Guernier designed and engraved (and etched) the seven plates in the first edition of John Gay's burlesque pastoral, *The Shepherd's Week* (1714). Their content and execution are an improvement on those for *The Rape of the Lock*. The frontispiece of villagers dancing around a maypole has a special appeal because of the inclusion of an artist – clearly du Guernier – sitting on the ground and sketching. Jacob Tonson's publication in 1714 of another illustrated edition of William Shakespeare's *Works* failed to give du Guernier a really satisfactory chance to prove his worth. For the same forty-three plays as in the 1709 edition (thirty-seven by Shakespeare and six by other authors), du Guernier signed eight plates "inv." and eight "inv. et sculp.", Elisha Kirkall signed two "scu.", and twenty-five were not signed. Most of the designs are reduced versions of the plates of 1709, often reversed, and most have minor changes, as of costumes. They do not suggest that du Guernier had any more than an elementary grasp of the dramatic action or the ability to present even that in other than elementary terms. In the scene on the heath in *King Lear* (III.iv), he lined up the characters with Lear in the middle, as he may have seen them on the stage but in a way that reveals nothing of the ironic interplay among Edgar, Lear, Gloucester, Kent, and the Fool.

Several of the scenes in the eleven plates in Tonson's six-volume *Works of Ben. Johnson* (1716) are crowded with figures in natural relationships, as though drawn on the spot. Some suggest stage productions, but others, such as the street scenes in *Volpone* (fig. 40) and *Bartholomew Fair*, seem to have been based on sketches of London streets. In their unadorned way, a number of these plates have a sense of immediacy usually absent from eighteenth-century illustrations of English plays.

Hanns A. Hammelmann names du Guernier and Cheron as the illustrators of Tonson's edition of *Ovid's "Metamorphoses" in Fifteen Books. Translated by the Most Eminent Hands* (1717); but as indicated in the discussion of Cheron, it seems doubtful that either artist designed any of the plates, although they may have copied the designs from a Continental edition of the seventeenth century. The relationship of the six plates in *Ovid's "Art of Love"* (1712) to those in this 1717 edition requires further study. The ten plates that du Guernier added to those by Cheron for Tonson's eight-volume edition of Plutarch's *Lives* (1727) are among his best efforts, especially that depicting the founding of Rome.

Francis Hayman

Friend of William Hogarth, David Garrick, Sir Joshua Reynolds, and other prominent figures of his time and one of the founders of the Royal Academy of Arts (1768), Francis Hayman (1708?–76) was a "literary" painter and the leader among the few early- and mid-eighteenth-century English-born book illustrators. He drew the designs for early editions of several important literary works. The first was Samuel Richardson's *Pamela: or, Virtue Rewarded* (1742), for which he drew twelve illustrations (126 × 76 mm) and Gravelot, fifteen. Gravelot engraved and etched all the plates. Hayman derived surprisingly animated scenes from Pamela's decorous letters about her problems and even made apparent her varying relationships with the other characters in this study of eighteenth-century society from a feminine point of view. Since *Pamela* was the first modern English novel, and this edition was published the year after the complete *Pamela* first appeared, it is the first illustrated English novel.

In a contract dated 28 November 1740, Sir Thomas Hanmer, acting as editor and publisher, engaged Hayman to illustrate an edition of Shakespeare's plays. Hayman was to be paid three guineas by the one-time Speaker of the House of Commons for a frontispiece to each of the thirty-six plays (*Pericles* was not included). If all the plates were not finished by 25 March 1741, Hayman would not be paid. This harsh proviso was not enforced. Gravelot, who engraved all the plates, designed the five in Volume IV, clearly because Hayman had fallen behind schedule. The contract also stated that Hanmer would choose the subjects for the designs and that they were to be finished in "Indian ink in such manner as shall be fit for the Ingraver to work after them and approved by the said Sʳ Thomas Hanmer". Extant instructions for twenty-seven of the illustrations and comments on four preliminary drawings reveal that the imperious Hanmer had perceptive ideas about how scenes should be illustrated, particularly in regard to gestures, expressions, and historical accuracy of costumes. The Hanmer contract and all the drawings by Hayman and Gravelot are bound into the copy of the edition in the Folger Shakespeare Library. The wash drawings were worked up with fastidious care, and Gravelot re-created them as engravings with superb fidelity.

The published work appeared in 1743 and 1744 under the imposing title *The Works of Shakespear. In Six Volumes. Carefully Revised and Corrected by the Former Editions and Adorned with Sculptures designed and executed by the best hands. Oxford: Printed at the Theatre, 1744.* Volumes II, III, and IV are dated 1743. It is difficult to say how much of the final result, good and bad, was Hanmer's responsi-

40. Louis du Guernier. Ben Jonson, *Volpone*, in *The Works of Ben. Johnson* (1716).

41. Francis Hayman. William Shakespeare, *Hamlet*, in *The Works of Shakespear* (1744).

bility. He was a pioneer with few precedents to influence his choice of the scenes to be illustrated and the effects to be stressed. Limited to one plate to a play, his choices ranged from those that became traditional, through the unusual but acceptable, to the nonessential and eccentric. One of his unusual choices was the scene in *Julius Caesar* (IV.iii) between Brutus and Cassius in Brutus's tent before the Battle of Philippi. Hanmer's blunt but shrewd comment on Hayman's preliminary sketch was that Brutus looked older than Cassius. Shakespeare had called him "the lean and wrinkled Cassius", he reminded the artist. Furthermore, he added, "You have put too much fury into his looks and action. He looks more like a Russian than a great man earnest in discourse. . . . Mend his looks and his hair, to give him a little more dignity mix'd with his hasty temper." As for Brutus, Hanmer pointed out that he should not be shown leaning on books because it "gives him too great an affectation of wisdom", and since Brutus and Cassius have just entered the tent from a march, books would not be lying around. Hanmer also made an acute comment: "I reckon one of the hardest tasks you have is the drawing for *Julius Caesar*, where two eminent men being in conference, not only characters of each are to be set forth but even their manner of discourse which requires great nicety." Yet in the final plate, Brutus seems too young, and his casual posture does not accord with the harsh charges that he has been making against Cassius. Hayman's thirty-one illustrations (ca. 210 × 147 mm) do not project Shakespeare's characters as the unique flesh-and-blood people we now tend to imagine them to be. He perceived them as players – for he was illustrating plays – and naturalism had not reached the London stage. His design for the play scene in *Hamlet* (III.vii) is signally successful in separating the action on the stage so that the focus is on Hamlet's tense observation of Claudius's terrified reactions to the dumb show (fig. 41). Hayman's plates may not be sensitive responses to the ultimate humor, poetry, and tragedy of Shakespeare's plays, but they are clear and elegant illustrations, admirable representatives of the best English work of their period.

In *Fables for the Female Sex* (1744), satirical verse by Edward Moore and Henry Brooke, Hayman's frontispiece and sixteen illustrations are workmanlike rather than original. His fashionably dressed ladies owe much to French models; his animals, to Francis Barlow; and his satire, to Hogarth. The designs for "The Colt and the Farmer" and a few others show signs of a fresh English realism. Hayman drew appropriate frontispieces (68 × 92 mm) for the eight duodecimo volumes of *The Spectator* (1747). The first shows the Spectator's Club in session at Mr. Buckley's in Little Britain, the members sitting at a round table and drinking spirits. The other seven plates are as urbane as the essays they illustrate. The four frontispieces (133 × 90 mm) for *The Tatler* (1759) are equally apt, but less atmospheric.

Hayman's illustrations apparently were well received, for Jacob Tonson and Draper had him design twelve new plates (213 × 170 mm) for their two-volume quarto *Paradise Lost* (1749) with notes by Thomas Newton. The original plates and copies had a long life in later editions. Yet Satan in knee breeches is more amusing than sinister; Adam and Eve are a comely young nudist couple in an English pastoral setting; and the archangels Raphael and Michael are young and ordinary. Even the Fall seems a domestic, not an epic, tragedy. It probably was the clarity of the "story line" and the way Hayman's neat drawings turn the loss of Paradise into Adam and Eve's personal reverse that gave the series its popular appeal.

In 1752, Tonson and Draper brought out a companion edition in three volumes of *Paradise Regain'd, Samson Agonistes,* and *Poems on Several Occasions,* also edited by Newton. Hayman drew five designs (215 × 167 mm), one each for *Paradise Regain'd, Samson Agonistes,* "L'Allegro", "Il Penseroso", and *A Mask [Comus]*. The *Samson Agonistes* and *Comus* designs are the liveliest, but also the most quaintly anachronistic. The most successful is the one for "L'Allegro" – Euphrosyne leading the sober Milton, presumably to join the young people who are dancing and courting in the background.

Hayman may have felt most at ease as an interpretive illustrator in doing the nine designs (128 × 80 mm) he contributed to the nine-volume edition of *The Works of Alexander Pope* (1751), with others by Nicholas Blakey, Samuel Wale, and Anthony Walker. He drew three designs for Volume IV, five for Volume V, and one for Volume VI. The editor, William Warburton, may have had something to do with selecting the passages to be illustrated, but Hayman had to have read "Epistle to Dr. Arbuthnot", *Imitations of Horace,* and *The Dunciad* with care to have dealt with the satire as exactly as he did. In Book IV of *The Dunciad,* for instance, in which the Empress of Dullness, the sleeping Cibber at her feet, commands her offspring to be dull in the several ways that Pope itemizes, Hayman scrupulously included even the lepidopterist.

One of Hayman's most natural and appealing designs illustrates "The Hop-Garden" in Christopher Smart's *Poems on Several Occasions* (1752). It is a rollicking scene of hop pickers tossing a youth into a hop bin, into which they have deposited a young girl. The only other illustration is by Thomas Worlidge (1700–66). Two mowers, quaintly wearing hats and coats, eat their noontime "dinner" under a tree. The plate is more interesting because it is etched and realistic than because it is aesthetic. The small frontispieces that Hayman drew for the five plays in William Congreve's *Works* (1753) fail to create much interest by means of characterization or pantomime.

Hayman's twenty-eight engraved plates (255 × 175 mm) in the two-volume quarto Tobias Smollett translation of *Don Quixote* (1755) are a surprisingly original series. Even when Hayman chose a traditional scene, such as Quixote's somnambulistic attack on the wine-skins, the effect is fresh. But the unhackneyed feeling about Hayman's designs comes from the way in which, without downplaying Quixote and Sancho Panza, they bring to life individuals in the large supporting cast who have been totally ignored or only lightly indicated by other illustrators, as in the charming engraving by Charles Grignion of Cardenio and the Curate discovering Dorothea, disguised as a youth, bathing her feet in a forest pool. There is more than a hint of Hayman's knowledge of the theater in his grouping of characters, such as those surrounding Quiteria, who is kneeling beside Basilius. Quarto-size plates, of course, permit a fullness of treatment that is not possible in duodecimo editions and is difficult in octavos. But Hayman failed to create definitive personalities for the immortal pair – in several plates, Sancho Panza appears to be a dwarf – and like most other artists, he was unable to communicate Cervantes's interplay of fantasy and reality, satire and faith.

William Hogarth

In his satirical prints, William Hogarth (1697–1764) "illustrated" the London of the first half of the eighteenth century with passionate realism, vivid anecdote and action, and strenuous expressiveness. Potentially, he was one of the great English book illustrators; but he did not fulfill that potential. Perhaps he preferred to maintain the independence of a painter, designer, etcher, engraver, seller of prints, and teacher.

Although all five frontispieces in *Cassandra* (1725) by Gaultier de Coste La Calprenède are signed "Hogarth Inv^t et Sculp", one cannot help wondering whether they may not have had French prototypes. Because Hogarth etched them, they have a freedom that is absent from his familiar engravings, which were often executed by engravers in his employ; but the handling of posture and gesture also makes these plates, if wholly original, the work of a true illustrator. The same sense of action likewise makes it not extravagant to compare Hogarth's small documentary plates for John Beaver's *Roman Military Punishments* (1725) with Jacques Callot's *Misères de la Guerre*. Two baroque designs (134 × 75 mm) for the Council in Hell in *Paradise Lost* (1725) are convincing attempts to realize this vast gathering, but they are wholly uncharacteristic and derivative trial efforts, not members of a published series.

Hogarth's only claim to importance as a book illustrator is his series for Samuel Butler's *Hudibras* (1726). (It seems to have been made before his much larger series of individual *Hudibras* prints, dated "1725".) The sixteen illustrations are perfectly keyed to the burlesque spirit of Butler's satire of the Puritans. Yet in spite of the "Invenit et sculpsit" on the plates, all but two of Hogarth's designs derive directly from the unsigned engraved series in an edition of *Hudibras* first published by George Sawbridge in 1709. (The Library of Congress copy is so dated, not "1710".) One of Hogarth's original designs is "Burning the Rumps at Temple Bar", an almost documentary recreation of a London mob protesting against the Rump Parliament by hanging and burning stolen rumps of beef. The other is a long fold-out of Hudibras as a "skimmington". That the composition is a parody of a painting by Annibale Carracci only slightly diminishes Hogarth's wonderful image of Hudibras being subjected to the English rural custom of an erring wife or husband being ridden through the town tied to the spouse (fig. 42). These two plates demonstrate better than do most of Hogarth's prints that he might have become not merely a good illustrator, but a great one.

Hogarth apparently was commissioned to supply illustrations for an edition of *Don Quixote* because six plates were owned by Jacob Tonson, passed on to Robert Dodsley, and inserted in later editions, such as that of 1755 (which also has illustrations by Francis Hayman). It has been assumed that Hogarth's designs were intended for what became the 1738 edition in Spanish, edited by Lord Carteret, but were rejected by him or Tonson in favor of those by John Vanderbank. If true, this rebuff would help explain why Hogarth did so little illustrating of literature thereafter. The six plates, signed "Inv^t et Sculp", are vigorous and at the same time endow Quixote with considerable sensitivity. The handling of Quixote's attack on the itinerant barber in order to claim his brass basin as a helmet of gold is especially spirited. But Hogarth's poor anatomy, harsh lines, and uncoordinated crosshatching gave him no chance against better drawing by Vanderbank and engraving by French professionals. Hogarth is said also to have prepared illustrations for the second edition of *Pamela* at the request of Samuel Richardson. They were not used and are now lost.

Hogarth designed the two plates used as frontispieces for the first and second volumes (1760) of the nine-volume first edition of Laurence Sterne's *Tristram Shandy*. Corporal Trim reading a sermon on conscience to the sleeping Dr. Slop, Uncle Toby, and Walter Shandy catches the elusive humor of Sterne perfectly. The baptism of Tris-

42. William Hogarth. Samuel Butler, *Hudibras* (1726).

tram, although not so amusing, also makes one regret that William Hogarth did not illustrate the whole of this classic, with suggestions from the admiring author.

William Kent

Derided by Horace Walpole and William Hogarth, yet versatile and influential, William Kent (1685–1748), in association with the earl of Burlington, left his mark on England with his Palladian architecture and landscape gardening. His book illustration was incidental to his work as a portrait painter and decorator of interiors and is of interest mainly for its factual content. The influence of Kent's study in Rome is apparent in the neoclassic pastoral-allegorical nature of two of his three designs for John Gay's *Poems on Several Occasions* (1720), which are nicely tuned to Gay's satire, and of his four popular designs for James Thomson's *Seasons* (1730). The latter might be said to document as well as illustrate the Augustan verse meditations on an ideal relation between man and the environment through the year. Kent also did headpieces and tailpieces for each book of Alexander Pope's translation of Homer's *Odyssey* (1725).

With John Wooton, Kent shared the fifty-two designs (78 × 97 mm) for Gay's verse *Fables* (first series, 1727). Kent did the headpiece for the introduction and twenty-one illustrations; Wooton did twenty-nine illustrations; and one design, probably by Kent, is signed only by the engraver. Wooton drew most of the designs for animal fables, and Kent drew the rest. Gay's handling of the fable is free, discursive, and critical of court life. Kent and Wooton, therefore, did not use traditional Aesopian motifs. Kent read Gay's scenes with intelligence and supplied detail that the poet may or may not have imagined – for instance, a huge fireplace and a wicker crib in a nursery where a mother and nurse observe a baby. When possible, Kent also introduced columns, arches, and Roman public buildings. Kent and Wooton's poorly engraved plates and Gravelot's fine ones in the second series (1738) supplied many motifs for later editions, including those of Thomas Bewick (1779), John Stockdale (1793) (several artists), and William Harvey (1854). To Pope's philosophical poem *An Essay on Man* (1734), Kent contributed six head- and tailpieces.

Kent's thirty-two designs (158 × 231 mm) for Edmund Spenser's *Faerie Queene* (1751) are the first serious effort to illustrate the whole of this long poem with some appreciation of its medieval and picturesque aspects. The title-page inscription, "Adorn'd with thirty-two Copper-Plates, from the Original Drawings of the late W. Kent, Esq., Architect and principal Painter to his Majesty," shows how much

Jacob Tonson and Barnaby Lintot counted on Kent's illustrations to sell their three-volume quarto edition. Most of Kent's designs represent literally the encounters of the chief characters in their wanderings through generalized landscape. Occasionally, however, Kent's imagination was stirred, as in his substitution of a Chinese parasol and other decorative details for the "boughs and arbours ... like a little forest" on the "gondelay" in which the distracting Phedria ferries Guyon across the Idle Lake (fig. 43). Had not circumstances led Kent to drop from twenty illustrations in Volume I to seven in Volume II and then to five in Volume III, this edition of *The Faerie Queene* would have been one of the considerable efforts, if not achievements, of eighteenth-century English book illustration.

Elisha Kirkall

Elisha Kirkall (ca. 1682–1742), one of Jacob Tonson's busiest engravers (see Boitard), was the first and one of the finest English makers of chiaroscuro reproductions of paintings. He was almost certainly also the first English artist – perhaps the first European – to illustrate a book with wood engravings, and he was certainly the first English artist – but not European – to illustrate a book with engravings in relief on metal (Thielman Kerver's Book of Hours [Paris, 1498] is an example, perhaps on pewter). In both instances, the engraving technique is called white-line. Engraving in relief on metal, he illustrated one of the most popular editions of Aesopian fables ever printed in England. He was not, however, an interpretive illustrator of any originality.

The problem that Kirkall, as a professional engraver, set himself to solve was how to reduce the cost of illustrating books. What was needed was a medium that combined the inexpensiveness of woodcuts (which had not been used in important books for more than a century) with the ability to reproduce detail comparable with that achieved by metal intaglio engraving. In two editions of William Howell's popular *Medulla Historiae Anglicanae* (1712, 1719), a history of the British monarchs, Kirkall tried out his solutions. For the edition of 1712, he designed sixty spirited illustrations (ca. 78 × 97 mm) (not all original) of coronations, battles, assassinations, and other royal events. All but one he engraved with a burin on wood. In a note, the publishers say: "The Cutts added in this Edition are intended more for use than shew. ... And if it be objected That the Graving is in Wood, and not in Copper, which would be more beautiful; we Answer, that such would be much more expensive too." The work is coarse, but the lines do not rip. This suggests that Kirkall engraved across the grain of a block of a hard wood, but not boxwood; the technique was

43. William Kent. Edmund Spenser, *The Faerie Queene* (1751).

44. Elisha Kirkall. Samuel Croxall, *Fables of Aesop and Others* (1722).

good but not good enough for fine detail, as in a small face. The exceptional illustration in the 1712 edition of *Medulla Historiae Anglicanae* is that of William the Conqueror. Kirkall engraved it in relief, as he did the wood engravings, but on a relatively soft metal, probably type metal (an alloy consisting chiefly of lead and antimony) or pewter.

The four bookseller-publishers clearly were not enthusiastic about the wood engravings. In 1719 (with the same François Boitard and Kirkall intaglio-engraved frontispiece that was in the 1712 edition), Kirkall began the experiment of redoing the earlier designs by engraving them in relief on metal. He did only the first three, in reverse. They are improvements on the wood versions. But the publishers were still not satisfied, for they had him engrave the remaining illustrations in the orthodox intaglio manner, although they settled for only half as many as in 1712.

The 196 illustrations (54 × 69 mm) engraved in relief on metal for the first edition of Samuel Croxall's long-enduring *Fables of Aesop and Others* (1722) served to vindicate Kirkall's innovation. They introduced an important technical advance in book illustration. Without doubt, Kirkall's neat oval designs within rectangular frames contributed much to the wide appeal of the modest work. The illustration for the fable "The Boar and the Ass" (fig. 44) shows what Kirkall accomplished in reproducing relatively fine detail on an inexpensive block that could be printed simul-

taneously with the type. It also shows how, by doing what it is natural to do in engraving in relief, Kirkall got his tonal effects – by cutting white lines on black, and using black lines largely for outlines. A generation later, Thomas Bewick founded his wood-engraving technique on Kirkall's designs for *Fables of Aesop*. Unfortunately for English book illustration, the practical and aesthetic advantages of white-line wood engraving were not given due recognition until the twentieth century.

Like his predecessors from the beginning of printing, Kirkall felt no need to invent original designs for the traditional fables. For Croxall's retelling of the often told fables, he drew on Francis Barlow for almost half his designs, Marcus Gheeraerts for one, and French sources for the rest. But he assimilated their motifs into his own unified series so that in their modest way, Elisha Kirkall's 196 blocks form one of the most attractive of all English editions of Aesop's fables.

John Miller [Johann Sebastian Müller]

A German engraver who came to England in 1744 from Nuremberg, Johann Sebastian Müller (ca. 1715–ca. 1789) changed his signature from "J. S. Müller" to "J. S. Miller" and then in 1760 to "John Miller". His distinction lies in his botanical and topographical prints, especially those in

45. John Miller. James Thomson, *Works* (1762).

Philip Miller's two-volume folio *Figures of the Most Beautiful, Useful and Uncommon Plants Described in the Gardners Dictionary* (1760) and the three-volume folio *Illustratio Systematis Sexualis Linnaei* (1773–77). The plates in Jonathan Swift's *Works* (1755), James Thomson's *Works* (1762), and Edward Young's *Passions Personify'd in Familiar Fables* (1773) are his only interpretive ones of any significance. The five plates in the second volume of Thomson's *Works* reveal Miller to have been a conscientious reader of the text and an able draftsman and engraver whose theatrical effects, as in the double-death finale of "Tancred and Sigismunda", perhaps reflect the staging of the hyperbolic tragedies of the day (fig. 45).

Nicolas Pigné

It has been suggested, without evidence, that Sir John Baptist Medina designed the illustrations in Jacob Tonson's duodecimo edition of *Paradise Regain'd, Samson Agonistes, and Poems on Several Occasions* (1713). It contains eleven plates, all of which are the same size (118 × 63 mm), including portraits of Milton and Shakespeare used as illustrations. There is no resemblance of any kind between Medina's big plates of 1688 and these little ones of twenty-five years later – during which he had been painting portraits in Edinburgh – and three years after his death. The

first six plates are standard scenes from the life of Christ, certainly adapted from some easily available source. Only the plate for "L'Allegro" is signed – "N. Pigné:f:". It and the "Il Penseroso" designs are companion figures of no merit. The question is whether the Pigné *fecit* can be taken to mean that he designed as well as engraved the "L'Allegro" plate and, if so, whether he designed the rest, except the last, a crude experiment by a novice for "The University Carrier".

Nicolas Pigné (1690?–1718?) was a pupil of Bernard Picart of Paris and Amsterdam. His large posthumous frontispiece portrait of John Urry in Tonson's folio Chaucer (1721) is a superb exhibition of engraving. He signed that "sculp.", which suggests that the "L'Allegro" *fecit* included the drawing. Attractive but not faultless headpieces showing the pilgrims leaving the Tabard Inn and oval designs depicting individual mounted pilgrims are unsigned. The evidence is inconclusive: Pigné may have designed and engraved all the Milton and Chaucer plates, but there is no firm evidence that he did.

John Pine

By publishing Latin editions of Horace's *Opera* (1733–37) and Virgil's *Bucolica et Georgica* (1755, 1774) with engraved texts in imitation of letterpress, John Pine (1690–1756) (with assistance from his son Robert [1730–88]) earned a note in the annals of English books. The very perfection of the imitation makes the effort pointless, except that the head- and tailpieces could be engraved on the same plates as the text. Most of the illustrations are functional and decorative. The only reason to mention Pine among illustrators rests on one frontispiece, said to be his contribution to the first edition of Daniel Defoe's ageless *Robinson Crusoe* (1719). The castaway appears much as he has appeared ever since, in an exceedingly warm sheepskin outfit. He also is heavily armed with two muskets over his shoulders and a long sword dangling from his waist, details modified in time. The battles, beheadings, babes in the woods, and other diverting scenes – forty-five in all – that Pine designed as well as engraved for *A Collection of Old Ballads* (1723) are poor both functionally and decoratively.

Isaac Taylor the Elder

Although his name is on plates in a large number of books, Isaac Taylor the Elder (1730–1807) was an engraver whose original frontispieces and miscellaneous illustrations are neither substantial nor better than routine. The frontispiece for the Newcastle edition of John Cunningham's *Poems, Chiefly Pastoral* (1766) – a reposeful millstream with cows standing in the water, a bridge, a thatched cottage, and, for good measure, a background ruin – standardizes pre-Romantic enthusiasm for idyllic English country life. It hardly warrants Thomas Bewick's extravagant praise or the adjective *enchanting*, which has been applied to it by other critics. Typical of Taylor's limitations are those apparent in the four plates in *A Collection of Poems by Several Hands. Intended as a Supplement to Mr. Dodsley's Collection* (1775). For "Abelard and Eloisa", he drew a monk sitting beside the sea below a monastery; for "Oriental Eclogues", he put a turban on the head of a shepherd and minarets in the background; for "Mary Queen of Scots", he borrowed John Vanderbank's design of 1729; and for "The Valetudinarian", he thought of nothing better than the small figure of a man sitting beneath a great tree.

John Vanderbank

London-born John Vanderbank (1694–1739) studied with Sir Godfrey Kneller and became a successful but debt-ridden portrait painter. In addition to frontispieces for a number of books, he contributed illustrations to the six-volume *Select Collection of Novels and Histories* (1729), translations edited by Samuel Croxall, and to *Don Quixote* (1738, 1742). Among his ten of the thirty-six designs for the first work, only a few, such as those of Essex unsuccessfully

petitioning Elizabeth I and of Mary Queen of Scots seeking solace from a crucifix before her execution, seem more than passable. Besides Vanderbank, the illustrators were Joseph Highmore, ten designs; Louis Cheron, four; Gerard Vander Gucht, four; Joseph Goupy, two; Moses Vanderbank (John's younger brother), two; and Louis du Guernier, Peter Tillemans, and Peter Monamy, one apiece. One plate is unsigned.

In a pioneering venture, Jacob Tonson published a three-volume quarto *Don Quixote* in Spanish in 1738, although a plate dated "1723" indicates how long a project can be in the making. In addition to a portrait of Cervantes by G. Kent and a second one by Vanderbank, this edition contains an allegorical frontispiece and forty-one plates by Vanderbank. In 1742, Tonson published a two-volume English translation by Charles Jarvis. He dropped the portrait by Kent and added twenty-five plates by Vanderbank in the second half of the work. In total, a portrait, an allegorical frontispiece, and sixty-six other plates – all full-page (ca. 250×175 mm) – in this ambitious venture entitle Vanderbank to some recognition. Vander Gucht engraved all but four of the plates. In his "Advertisement concerning the Prints", Dr. John Oldfield offers the first extended (and still enlightening) analysis in English of illustration. Its detailed application to *Don Quixote* suggests that Oldfield had a good deal to do with the choice of moments to be illustrated and their treatment in accordance with his theories. This accounts for the absence of the attack on the windmills and other familiar scenes and the inclusion of a number of episodes not portrayed in other series. By following Oldfield's directions, Vanderbank recorded a considerable diversity of events; but in not having Don Quixote seem the butt of the satire, he often made him only a passive on-looker, a spare man with an aquiline nose, a thin uptwirled mustache, and no definite personality. Sancho Panza, however, is clearly defined as an amusing peasant, yet no buffoon. In sixty-six illustrations marked by English realism, Vanderbank has a number of successes, of which pretty Altisidora singing to Don Quixote and Sancho Panza is one of the most attractive (fig. 46).

Michael and Gerard Vander Gucht

There seems to be no evidence that Michael Vander Gucht (1660–1725) invented any of the plates that he signed "sculp." He did not, as has been asserted, reengrave the 101 plates in John Dryden's translation for Jacob Tonson of Virgil's *Works* (1697). The plates are those designed by Francis Cleyn for John Ogilby's 1654 edition and bear his name and those of his engravers. The only change ordered by Tonson was the hasty "Romanizing" of the

46. John Vanderbank. Miguel de Cervantes, *Don Quixote* (1738, 1742).

nose of Aeneas on eight plates, in an effort, it is said, to flatter William III after Dryden had refused to dedicate the work to the king.

Gerard Vander Gucht (1697–1776), son of Michael, was one of the busiest reproductive engravers during the first half of the eighteenth century. Although he sometimes signed his name in the orthodox way, he seems to have preferred "Vander", usually abbreviated "V^{dr}". He designed some undistinguished plates, but can hardly be called an illustrator.

Samuel Wale

Not a dozen of the 100 books containing designs by Samuel Wale (1721?–86) can be listed as imaginative works substantially illustrated by him. The others are books of information in various fields, as well as many for which he designed only a frontispiece or two or three plates. He apparently was a good draftsman, for he was one of the founders of the Royal Academy of Arts and occupied the Chair of Perspective. But perhaps because of indifferent work by his engravers and the profusion of the drawings he turned out, his illustrations have a prosaic look. Wale should, however, be remembered as the first in a long line of interpretive illustrators of Izaak Walton's *Complete Angler*, published with Charles Cotton's *Discourse on Rivers, Ponds, Fish, and Fishing* (1760). Wale's frontispiece and eight plates (142 × 78 mm) seem stiff as engraved by the unfortunate forger William Ryland, but they give body to some of the most captivating passages of this much loved and illustrated classic. These include Piscator, the angler, overtaking Venator, the hunter, and Auceps, the falconer, at the top of Tottenham Hill; Piscator and Venator asking the inn hostess to cook the chub they have caught; the milkmaid and her mother singing "Come Live with Me and Be My Love" to them; Piscator teaching Venator how to fish for trout as they lounge beside a stream; and Venator's repayment with a "bottle of sack, Milk, Oranges and Sugar . . . a drink like Nectar" as they rest in a flowery arbor (fig. 47).

Anthony Walker

A professional engraver who could draw his own designs when called on, Anthony Walker (1726–65) had few substantial assignments as an illustrator. Fineness of detail and early wear, perhaps caused by extensive etching before engraving, tend to make his plates a little blurry. Nevertheless, Walker would surely have made more of a name for himself had he lived longer because he had the ability to draw designs that catch the attention.

To the nine volumes of *The Works of Alexander Pope* (1751), Walker contributed only two illustrations, both of which he engraved. The first illustrates the crucial moment in *The Rape of the Lock* – when the Lord on tiptoe behind Belinda does his dastardly deed as she sips her steaming coffee. Although the scissors are not visible and the faces printed gray in some impressions, the elegance of the two gentlemen and two ladies (an excellent imitation of the French style by the young Walker), the authenticity of the table full of coffee paraphernalia, and the naturalness of the serving woman watching in the background raise Walker's design above the artificiality that pervades so much eighteenth-century illustration (fig. 48).

William Somervile's *Chace* (1757), Tobias Smollett's *Sir Launcelot Greaves* (1760), John Ogilvie's *Poems on Several Subjects* (1762), John Philips's *Poems Attempted in the Style of Milton* (1762), and Ogilvie's *Providence: an Allegorical Poem* (1764) contain most of the rest of Walker's slender output of interpretive illustrations exclusive of single frontispieces. Hanns A. Hammelmann says that *Sir Launcelot Greaves* (in its initial publication) was the first illustrated serialized novel. Four headpieces are exactly right in substance and mood for a group of odes in Ogilvie's *Poems on Several Subjects* (1762). For example, Father Time using his foot and a scythe handle to topple the last stones of a once-proud building is an ingenious projection of the theme of "Ode to Time". For Philips's bucolic "Cyder", Walker redrew with changes Michael Vander Gucht's design, in the 1708 edition, of the grafting of a branch to an apple tree, which, in turn, was derived from one by Francis Cleyn in John Ogilby's edition of Virgil's *Works* (1654).

47. Samuel Wale. Izaak Walton, *The Complete Angler* (1760).

48. Anthony Walker. Alexander Pope, *The Rape of the Lock* (1751).

CHAPTER FIVE

The Eighteenth Century (II) 1776–1800

The decision to follow a natural chronological order by centuries results in a certain awkwardness in this chapter because the five most important illustrators – Thomas Bewick, William Blake, Henry Fuseli, Thomas Rowlandson, and Thomas Stothard – did much of their most significant work after 1800. Nevertheless, their beginnings were in the last quarter of the eighteenth century, the first period that belongs almost entirely to English artists. Fuseli was a Swiss, but his career as an artist and art teacher took place entirely in England. Furthermore, the French were no longer dictating taste. Except for Fuseli's *Sturm und Drang* excesses, lingering French pastoralism and drawing-room politesse in the illustrations by secondary figures and by Stothard, and some overt imitation of Italian artists, the leading illustrators were their own masters. In all English book illustration, there are no artists more individualistic or more successful in their different ways than Bewick, Blake, Fuseli, and Rowlandson. This chapter will attempt to determine how successful they and their contemporaries were as literary illustrators.

The multiple-artist productions of the early and mid-eighteenth century, mentioned in the introductory remarks to Chapter Four, continued to be common in this period. A development that reflected an increase in the number of middle-class readers and a response by enterprising publishers was the multivolume collection: *The Poets of Great Britain Complete from Chaucer to Churchill* and *The British Theatre*, published by John Bell; *British Classics* and *The Novelist's Magazine*, published by Thomas Harrison; and pocket editions of British novels, poems, and classics, published by John Cooke and his son Charles. The few designs in each volume usually are small and are surrounded by heavy standard borders; they were engraved on copper by skilled members of a team, so that it is virtually impossible to tell the work of one illustrator from that of another. In the interest of harmony, the engravings sacrificed whatever personal qualities the original drawings may have possessed. There seems to be so little to say about them that just a few are discussed, briefly, and others are only mentioned in passing or are ignored entirely. For instance, the circular plates by John Hamilton Mortimer (1740–79), a painter of historical subjects, in seven volumes of *The Poets of Great Britain* are too small and insignificant to justify his inclusion in the Catalog. We are left with a handful of more independent but not especially original artists to add to the five well-known ones. Yet we must not forget that William Hazlitt in "On Reading Old Books" wrote: "*Tom Jones*, I remember . . . came down in numbers once a fortnight, in Cooke's pocket-edition, embellished with cuts. . . . Ah, never again shall I feel the enthusiastic delight with which I gazed at the figures and anticipated the story and adventures. . . ."

Other publishers brought out ambitious editions of the work of one author. To give a concrete idea of what they were like, *The Plays of William Shakespeare* (1788–91), published by Bellamy and Robarts in eight volumes, might be cited as an example. The seventy-two oval illustrations for the thirty-six plays – there are also two allegorical tributes to Shakespeare in the front of each volume – are neat and attractive but undistinguished. Nine artists contributed, and one plate is unsigned. The chief artists were Henry J. Richter, nineteen designs; Edward Dayes, fifteen; Richard Corbould, fourteen; and Edward Francesco Burney, eleven. Others represented were Charles Ansell, Conrad Metz, Daniel Dodd, Charles Ryley, and William Walker. Part of the pleasant impression that the series makes is due to the elaborate deep frame, reengraved for each plate, and to the polished work of the engravers. This series is one of a large number made during the eighteenth century in which illustration has a strong decorative function akin to that of dress, furnishings, and manners.

John Bewick

Quantitatively, John Bewick (1760–95) was more of an interpretive illustrator than was his famous older brother, Thomas. He seems to have drawn upward of 250 designs and engraved most of the blocks for at least 7 books, includ-

49. John Bewick. William Somervile, *The Chase* (1796).

ing 4 for children. They are simple and literal, but adequate. The draftsmanship seems to be no better than the engraving, which runs from poor to fair. Bewick occasionally introduced his monogram, as in the first of thirty-two blocks for Joseph Ritson's *Robin Hood: A Collection of All the Ancient Poems, Songs and Ballads* (1795), which are larger, more open, and more figure oriented than are the usual designs by Thomas. Bewick may have drawn and engraved them all. He had a share in designing the thirteen blocks for Oliver Goldsmith and Thomas Parnell's *Poems* (1795). His only memorable illustrations, however, are his last – those in William Somervile's *Chase* (1796). There are thirteen vignettes: one on the title page; a formal frontispiece to each of the four "books"; and the eight illustrations – a leafy hunting headpiece and tailpiece to each book. In a note "To the Patrons of Fine Printing", William Bulmer, the printer-publisher of the volume, announced the untimely death of John Bewick. He stated that Bewick had "finished on the wood the whole of the designs except one" and that Thomas had engraved them. Thomas drew the last, small tailpiece. His superb engraving and some redrawing – no apprentice hands could have touched these blocks – must have added grace and authority to the series. Nevertheless, Bewick's hunting scenes in nine of the vignettes are truer to Somervile's subjects than is the bombastic verse. In the tailpiece to Book II, he met the most

extreme demands of the text by designing a well-composed tiger kill. But the four elegant decorative frontispieces are so fine in their balance between eighteenth-century formalism and nineteenth-century naturalism that the one for Book II seems a fitting memorial to young John Bewick (fig. 49). They are very like some frontispieces designed by John Thurston and engraved by Charlton Nesbit in Somervile's *Hobbinol, Field Sports, and the Bowling Green* (1813), which was printed by Bulmer for Rudolph Ackermann.

Thomas Bewick

Essayists and bibliographers have celebrated the charm and technical skill of the wood engravings of Thomas Bewick (1753–1828). Their enthusiasm has obscured two facts: few of his designs are original imaginative illustrations, and no one knows for sure which of those attributed to him he personally drew and engraved. On the title pages, he and his publishers claimed work done in his shop as his, no matter how much had been done by apprentices. Some of the books listed in booksellers' and libraries' catalogs as having been illustrated by Bewick represent errors of ignorance or cupidity.

Bewick was apprenticed as an engraver on metal and made his living for sixty years by performing the routine jobs of a professional metal engraver in Newcastle-upon-

Tyne, except for nine months in London (1776–77). A self-taught draftsman, he got his start as an illustrator and a wood engraver in *Select Fables, in Three Parts* (1776) by imitating the white-line burin engraving in relief on metal of Elisha Kirkall, which he admired, in Samuel Croxall's *Fables of Aesop and Others* (1722). For the designs in *Fables by the Late Mr. Gay* (1779), he followed those in William Kent and John Wooton's 1727 series; and for the designs in the enlarged *Select Fables, in Three Parts* (1784), he and John Bewick used the Croxall edition and other sources. Bewick's technical contribution was the substitution of blocks of boxwood cut across the grain for soft metal. Commercial engravers before him had used boxwood, but only for limited purposes. His other contribution was the refinement of Kirkall's approach to tonal effects – engraving from black to white, relying on white lines, and not crosshatching black lines.

Bewick spent a lifetime exploring a narrow range of effects. As a practicing engraver, not primarily an artist, he used his drawings merely as guides and worked up the detailed effects on the blocks with his tools. His burin was part of him. He could think and draw with it. The result is the subtle gradation of values from black through the grays to white. The vivacity of his best work results from his repertory of different white strokes that give realistic textures to earth, grass, bark, foliage, fur, feathers, and so on. He surpassed all his assistants and imitators in his ability to manage masses and transitions so that the elements of the composition are in perfect harmony with one another, a remarkable achievement for a man facing a bit of wood with only his vision to control his hands – and at night, after a long day of engraving on metal, it is said. No matter how small his design, Bewick always made the major elements dominant. The work of his apprentices and followers can often be identified or at least suspected by the absence of cohesion of the elements and the limited range of values. But such identification remains an area of speculation, except where trustworthy documentation exists.

Bewick cannot be regarded as an important illustrator of literary works because he seems not to have invented a series of imaginative interpretive designs for a single example of belles-lettres of any consequence. For example, one would think that his second Aesop effort, *The Fables of Aesop and Some Others. With designs on wood by Thomas Bewick* (1818), would have evoked his most original mature work, since he had loved the fables of Aesop since boyhood. Yet virtually all the motifs for the 188 headpieces (and the text, word for word with casual variations) were, again, taken from Croxall's edition. It is said that William Harvey and other pupils assisted with the drawings and engraved the blocks because Bewick had gout in his hands. Neverthe-

less, this edition of Aesop is Bewick's most appealing series of literary illustrations. How derivative the designs in other books attributed to him with varying degrees of authority may be and how many were drawn and engraved by pupils are questions still to be satisfactorily answered.

Bewick's only really imaginative original designs are the vignette tailpieces that he placed in the empty space on short pages, principally those in his and Ralph Beilby's *General History of Quadrupeds* (1790) and *History of British Birds. Vol. I, Land Birds* (1797), and his *Vol. II, Water Birds* (1804). The animals and birds themselves are sometimes handsome, but they aim at accurate representation above everything, and some of the animals are copies from books on natural history. The tailpieces are illustrations without text, unrelated in any specific way to the account that precedes them. They are in themselves rural essays, close to the preoccupations of countrypeople – farming, domestic and wild animals, hunting and fishing, unemployment, natural functions, and death. They often are humorous, with a Yorkshireman's sardonic edge; and they often tell an anecdote, as in "Keep on This Side", a vignette in *Land Birds*, in which a naughty boy leads a blind man into a stream instead of to the stepping stones on which his dog waits anxiously (fig. 50). These realistic vignettes may have helped promote a pre-Wordsworthian view of rural England, but their earthiness had no significant influence on book illustration, as can be seen in the superficially similar vignettes of Birket Foster.

Bewick was a creative force as a wood engraver, not as a book illustrator, the main influence in the revival of autographic white-line wood engraving in the 1920s. His books proved what Kirkall had set out to prove: that relief engraving could supersede intaglio engraving and bring inexpensive, amply illustrated books within the reach of a newly literate public. Bewick's pupils figured prominently in this development. Besides his brother John, the chief wood engravers trained by him were Luke Clennell, Charlton Nesbit, and John Thompson. Charles Thompson went to Paris and trained a whole school of French wood engravers. Two engravers who were briefly apprenticed to Bewick and later became influential were John Jackson and Ebenezer Landells. Jackson initiated the important *Treatise on Wood-Engraving* (1839) by William Chatto and himself, and Landells was involved in the founding of *Punch* (1841). Four of Bewick's pupils turned from engraving to illustrating. The sickly youth Robert Johnson (1770–96) drew a number of designs credited to Bewick. William Harvey, Bewick's favorite pupil, became an illustrator. He and John Thurston, who had not been a pupil of Bewick, were key figures in the transition from metal-engraved and steel-etched to wood-engraved illustrations; they were quite as important as Bewick in bringing this about, since they worked in London and were prolific illustrators of literature of all sorts. Thurston and Harvey collaborated with some of Bewick's alumni and other wood engravers in establishing a mode of drawing and engraving that could have benefited all nineteenth-century book illustration had it prevailed.

William Blake

The illustrated work of William Blake (1757–1827) is unique in almost every way. From childhood, poetry and art were equal interests, and both were vehicles for expressing Blake's strongly held, unorthodox, and often obscure ideas. With an exception or two, he illustrated only poetry. As a professional intaglio metal engraver for most of his life, he engraved many plates for books after the designs of other artists. Not one of his own works was issued by a commercial publisher during his lifetime. Blake was forced to try, ineffectually, to be his own publisher by devising various ways to reproduce his poems and illustrations. This body of work differs so much from most of his illustrations for books by others that we will consider the latter first. In this way, too, we can get a better idea of what sort of interpretive illustrator Blake was.

Books by Others

Listed in the Catalog are thirty-six titles, eighteen by Blake and eighteen by other authors. If Blake had never illustrated a book of his own, he still would be one of the leading illustrators of England. His illustrations for Edward Young's *Night Thoughts* (1797); Thomas Gray's *Poems* (1797–98); John Milton's *Paradise Lost* (1807–08), *Paradise Regain'd* (1825?), and minor poems; Robert Blair's *Grave* (1808); Ambrose Philips's "Imitation of Virgil's First Eclogue" (1821); and the Book of Job (1825 [1826]) compose a body of work unsurpassed in range, sensitivity to the text, technical variety, and artistic distinction.

As early as 1791, Blake had engraved six dry little designs perfectly suited to Mary Wollstonecraft's didactic *Original Stories from Real Life*, but his first important set of illustrations for the work of another poet was for *The Complaint, and the Consolation: or, Night Thoughts* (1797) by Young. He spent two years in preparation, painting 537 watercolors. From this massive collection, now in the British Museum, he etched and engraved forty-three plates (357 × 320 mm) to illustrate the first four of the nine nights. This half-work was published with thirty lines of printed text in a box imposed off-center on each of the full-page illustrations, so that the visible design is L-shaped. These *Night Thoughts* illustrations are revelations of Blake's inventive

power and ability to engrave lines of almost revolutionary freedom. The volume did not sell; the rest of the project was abandoned; and Blake did not engrave the remaining watercolors.

As a gift for his wife, the sculptor John Flaxman commissioned Blake to illustrate Gray's *Poems*. Between 1796 and 1798, he painted 116 watercolors and mounted printed pages of text (cut from a book) on them in the manner of *Night Thoughts*. They were not intended for publication and seem to have been done with great spontaneity, an expression of the joyousness that Blake wrote about so earnestly. They were reproduced in 1972, with only sixteen in color.

Blake was a great reader of Milton and, one would think, should have made the illustration of Milton's poems one of the main achievements of his career. Perhaps that inhibited him. At different times between 1801 and 1825, he made sets of watercolors for *Paradise Lost* (1807–08), *Paradise Regain'd* (1825?), *L'Allegro and Il Penseroso* (ca. 1817), *On the Morning of Christ's Nativity* (1809), and *Comus. A Mask* (1801). They were not published until the twentieth century. Strangely, the nine carefully finished designs (ca. 255 × 205 mm) for *Paradise Lost* seem influenced unduly by the work of earlier artists. The twelve illustrations for *Paradise Regain'd* show a fresher reaction to the text but not the originality of interpretation to be expected. The six illustrations each for "L'Allegro", "Il Penseroso", and *Comus* are more relaxed and Blakean. Blake painted two sets of six watercolors for *On the Morning of Christ's Nativity*. They include "The Descent of Typhon and the Gods into Hell", an example of the extraordinary images that Blake was able to extract from other poets' lines. Either Blake did not illustrate "Lycidas" and *Samson Agonistes* or his drawings have been lost. He could have done an excellent series for both.

Despite having his portrait as a frontispiece to Blair's poem *The Grave* (1808), Blake was unhappy about the fee of £20 for the twelve designs and about having them etched and engraved by Louis Schiavonetti, after he had been told that he was to do the engraving. *The Grave* would seem to have provided a greater stimulus to Blake's imagination than *Night Thoughts*, but the designs are more formal. "The Soul Exploring the Recesses of the Grave", however, is one of Blake's most memorable illustrations of another poet's lines.

In a completely isolated action, Blake engraved on wood a frontispiece and twenty small rectangular illustrations (ca. 35 × 75 mm) for Philips's "Imitation of Virgil's First Eclogue" in *The Pastorals of Virgil Illustrated by 230 Engravings* (1821). This is the third edition of a schoolbook published by Dr. Robert Thornton of Guy's Hos-

50. Thomas Bewick. Thomas Bewick and Ralph Beilby, *History of British Birds. Vol. I, Land Birds* (1797).

pital, a physician and botanist who also published the celebrated *Temple of Flora* (1807) with gorgeous aquatints and mezzotints of flowers. Blake had to turn his hand to wood engraving for the first time because all the illustrations retained in this edition from the first two had been engraved on wood. Yet his series has done more than any other single work to establish wood engraving in England as an art form capable of liberating the imagination and creating works of beauty. Thornton thought them crude and ordered a new set by professional wood engravers. Before he was persuaded to change his mind, three of Blake's blocks had been replaced. The twenty original blocks for the illustrations were to have been printed on five pages, four on a page. The printer put the three variant blocks on a page by themselves. Thus one of Blake's blocks was left over at the end, and it was discarded. (The drawing is extant.) Then, to correct what may or may not have been Blake's error, his sixteen blocks were trimmed to fit the page. The larger frontispiece, of the shepherds Thenot and Colinet, remained untouched.

The five-page poem ostensibly is a dialogue between the philosophic Thenot and his young friend Colinet, who bewails the troubles of his occupation. But Colinet represents Philips, and his complaints are aimed at Alexander Pope because of Pope's attack on him for daring to compete in the writing of pastorals. Blake stuck to the pastoral ele-

ments, and from the moment that Thenot spies the troubled Colinet leaning against a tree, through the efforts of Colinet to improve his shepherd's lot, to the peaceful evening when Colinet and his sheep return to enjoy Thenot's hospitality, the little blocks are suffused with a romantic glow. This modest little sequence enchanted Blake's young admirers – Samuel Palmer, John Linnell, and Edward Calvert – and the finest modern wood engravers also have offered their homage. Yet Blake never engraved another wood block, although a finished drawing is on a block in the British Museum. He certainly recognized the beauty he had wrought, but he probably did not care for working in wood. To an engraver on metal whose burin incised the sharp sweeping lines of the *Night Thoughts* plates, the short coarse lines required by a little piece of wood must have been exasperating. Blake may have used one of his metal engraver's burins. Each push produced a ragged white line instead of a sharp black one. He had worked for too many years as a metal engraver to find this technique congenial. In addition, the surface of the blocks was not polished as smooth as it should have been.

Among the illustrations of works he did not write, Blake's greatest series came late in his career – the twenty-one intaglio engraved plates (ca. 90 × 118 mm and ca. 135 × 105 mm) for the Book of Job. They were commissioned in 1821 by Linnell to give Blake an income and were based on

95

a set of watercolours painted in 1820 on a commission from another friend. To avoid the expense of printing the text, Blake engraved appropriate passages on the margins of the plates. For three years, Blake labored over the plates. They are dated "8 March 1825", but the first sets appeared in 1826 as *Illustrations of the Book of Job*. Old, ill, poor, and neglected, Blake could not help identifying with Job. In images of marvelous graphic and emotional power, he traced the tribulations that Job had to withstand before the Lord finally granted him peace. Typical of the tremendous effects that Blake attained in this series is the plate for "The Just Upright Man Is Laughed to Scorn". With his wife crouched in fear on one side of him, Job kneels patiently, while three erstwhile friends stare at him madly and point accusingly with both hands.

Two unfinished series for famous books by others that Blake was working on at the end of his life have been published: John Bunyan's *Pilgrim's Progress* (1941) and Dante's *Divine Comedy* (1922). Among the 28 *Pilgrim's Progress* watercolors, done in 1824, and the 102 *Divine Comedy* drawings, of which Blake had engraved 7 before his death, there are some splendid individual designs, but they do not constitute successful series of illustrations.

Books by Blake

Blake is the great exception in still another way: he is the one English illustrator whose work has been cataloged, reproduced, and analyzed plate by plate in relation to its text by literary scholars. For most of us, appreciation of Blake's images for his obscure long poems requires help from literary specialists. We shall limit our discussion to summary remarks.

Forced to become his own publisher, Blake circumvented the cost of printing his poems by devising a "secret method" to reproduce texts and illustrations and by coloring some of the impressions, mostly by hand. According to Robert N. Essick in *William Blake, Printmaker* (1980), Blake used a fine brush and an acid resistant to draw his design and write his text directly on the plate. He lettered the text in reverse, an ability common among professional engravers. A brief bath in acid ate away the bare parts of the plate and left the illustration, decoration, and poem in low relief. But Blake was experimental and varied his technique as he went along, especially in coloring, and he often revised completed work, so that the methods used to get impressions of any one plate may differ extremely. A relief plate is printed by surface pressure, as is a woodcut, wood engraving, or modern photo-process block. The prints are called relief etchings and with color added, illuminated relief etchings. Whatever the aesthetic value of an individual design, when finished in color by Blake's hand, it became a new work of art of greater substance and, usually, of beauty.

That Blake's work went unrecognized by all but a few friends is understandable. He would print a small edition of a poem, color a few copies, and wait for buyers. Illuminated copies often differ materially from one another because the coloring was done at long intervals and on some impressions by Blake's wife, Catherine. Blake's books, therefore, can be said to be individual works of art more closely related to illuminated manuscripts than to illustrated printed books. They are, however, available today in splendid photographic reproductions and can be considered as though published in the usual way.

The number of Blake's actual illustrations of his own poems, as distinct from decorative designs, is difficult to pin down. The distinction is often debatable. The books in the following list, compiled from numerous and sometimes differing scholarly studies and facsimile editions, contain plates that were etched in relief, with two exceptions. Color is unique to individual copies. Blake's chief series of illustrations of his own works are in *Tiriel* (ca. 1785–88) (incomplete), nine drawings apparently antedating the relief etchings; *The Songs of Innocence* (1789) combined with *The Songs of Experience* (1794), numerous marginal and interlinear designs; *The Book of Thel* (1789), five designs; *The Marriage of Heaven and Hell* (ca. 1790–93) (mostly prose), thirteen small designs; *Visions of the Daughters of Albion* (1793), five main designs; *America: A Prophecy* (1793), frontispiece and sixteen illustrated pages, of which about eight are main designs; *Europe: A Prophecy* (1794), three full-page plates with no text and eleven pages with substantial designs; *The Book of Urizen* (1794), title page, and ten full-page and seventeen other designs; *The Song of Los* (1795), three full-page designs; *The Book of Ahania* (1795) (intaglio etched, only one copy extant), frontispiece, title page, and tailpiece; and *Jerusalem* (1818–26), eleven full-page, thirty-six one-third to three-quarter page, and fourteen smaller illustrations.

Blake's illustrations of his own books vary in comprehensiveness – not only from incidental decorations to full-page designs, but also in number and complexity. In order to emancipate his art from a sense of the particular, Blake drew most of his figures either nude or garbed in shapeless gowns. Thus they take on a timeless, placeless aspect that is in keeping with the universals with which he deals in his poetry. They are also suitable to do the decorative bending and floating to which Blake assigned them; such figures in everyday dress would look ludicrous. Blake's human and heavenly figures reflect his admiration for the paintings of Michelangelo, Raphael, and Guilio Romano, but he found inspiration in a number of other sources. Sharp variations in size, shape, location, and spacing of designs give most of Blake's books the appearance of spontaneity. *The Book of Urizen* (1794) is an exception. The ten full-page and several almost full-page boldly colored plates dominate the twenty-eight-page poem and create a unified and concentrated effect.

In relation to his own work, Blake exercised a freedom of interpretation made possible by his certain knowledge of the total meaning – of which his words are only a partial expression - and by his ability to embody visual aspects of that meaning in graphic images. The result is often an illustration that amplifies the text through a parallel graphic statement rather than merely represents what the text "says". No other English writer or artist of equivalent stature has had this duality of talent. And since Blake usually drew text and image on the same page or on adjacent pages, the reader of Blake's poems reproduced in their original state receives these dual appeals to mind and eye almost simultaneously. As Blake gradually evolved a philosophy in his sequence of more than a dozen long poems from *Tiriel* (ca. 1785–88) to *Jerusalem* (1818–26), he created mythic characters and relationships and embodied them in successive series of illustrations of increasing importance in conveying his thoughts. *Jerusalem* was the culmination of his life's effort as a poet-seer.

Although Blake began the plates for *Jerusalem: The Emanation of the Great Albion* in 1804, the date on the title page, the date of printing of the six complete copies has been determined by the watermarks in the paper and by Blake's testimony as having been no earlier than between 1818 and 1826. The complicated 100-page poem, according to one exegesis, traces the reunion of Albion (materialistic Britain) with Jerusalem, which is Albion's spiritual "emanation" (feminine counterpart), through the efforts of Los (Imagination) and thus Man's recovery of his lost soul. Text, decorations, and the approximately three dozen main illustrations and many smaller ones were first etched in relief. On eight of the larger plates, Blake achieved tonal effects by what looks like the method used by twentieth-century white-line wood engravers – apparently by adding relief engraving with a burin. Two plates thus treated – one of Albion drawn in a chariot by two bulls with human heads, wings, lion manes, and horns (suggested by the bulls of Persepolis) and the other of the vanquished evil Queen Vala, her prime minister Hyle, and the soldier Skofield in chains (he once accused Blake of sedition) shown in deep despair (pl. I) – epitomize interpretive book illustration at the outer reaches of expressiveness. Before his death, Blake completed only one illuminated copy, which is now at Yale University. The text is in orange ink, and the watercolors make the dynamic black-and-white figures wonderfully rich and strange.

Blake's illustrations are unique creative achievements. They are too unusual, however, and until recently not accessible enough, especially in their illuminated states, to have had much influence on the mainstream of English illustration. The handful of his wood engravings inspired twentieth-century illustrators not only to adopt the white-line technique, but also to go beyond Thomas Bewick's modest realism; and what Blake called his "bounding line" was perpetuated by the Pre-Raphaelites, Walter Crane, Aubrey Beardsley, and later artists of the 1890s and early 1900s. Nevertheless, even slight acquaintance with his work has been sufficient to imbue sensitive artists with an urge to transcend the inhibitions of the literal and to strive to charge their images with the same power and beauty as the poetic word, as did William Blake.

Edward Francesco Burney

The shy cousin of Fanny Burney and nephew of the musicologist Charles Burney, Edward Burney (1760–1848) was a watercolorist who supported himself for most of his life by drawing book illustrations and miscellaneous designs. Sharing in the family amateur theatricals doubtless helped him visualize the scenes he drew, but his work usually has more grace than force. Burney's fourteen illustrations in Samuel Richardson's *Pamela* (1786) record the epistolary account of the penalties and rewards of virtue with what emotion the small engravings can convey. Mr. Colbrand putting on "one of his deadly fierce looks" and threatening to *ching* with a huge carved sword any villain who dares touch Pamela, who has just escaped through an open window, must have delighted the readers of this new genre.

Burney contributed designs to two editions of Shakespeare. He drew seven circular plates for *The Dramatick Writings of Will. Shakespeare* (1788), including one of the moving scene in *King John* (IV.i) in which young Arthur pleads with Hubert not to carry out the king's orders to blind him (fig. 51). The text offers no guide to the disposition of the two figures, and one cannot assume that Burney had seen *King John* played. The unhappy Hubert slumped on what looks like an execution block, head on chest and looking away from Arthur, who sits on the edge of a chair behind him and touches him trustingly as he speaks in his ear, is excellent theater and illustration. Associated with Burney in this edition, which was published by John Bell, were the painters William Hamilton and Philippe Jacques de Loutherbourg. The eleven designs by Burney of the seventy-two illustrations (not counting the "allegories") in *The Plays of William Shakespeare* (1788–91), published by

51. Edward Francesco Burney. William Shakespeare, *King John* in *The Dramatick Writings of Will. Shakespeare* (1788).

Bellamy and Robarts, are neoclassic in their blending of the pastoral and the histrionic. The most refreshing is the stagy one in *Romeo and Juliet* (II.ii) of Juliet leaning out over her balcony while Romeo, not far below, declaims his passion, as in an opera.

The seventy illustrations for John Stockdale's two-volume edition of John Gay's *Fables* (1793) are said to have been designed by Burney and Charles Catton the Younger. William Blake engraved twelve of the plates, and several other engravers signed the rest. Since no artist's name appears on any plate, it is not possible to say how well Burney's designs relate to those by William Kent and John Wooton (1727) and by Gravelot (1738) in earlier editions of Gay's *Fables*. The designs for "The Two Owls and the Sparrow" and "The Vulture, the Sparrow, and Other Birds" derive ultimately from paintings by Francis Barlow.

The four designs in *Paradise Regained and the Minor Poems* (1796) – "Baptism of Christ", "Samson", "L'Allegro", and "Il Penseroso" – show Burney using the vignette with excellent decorative results, as he did again in the 1800 edition of *Paradise Lost*. The twelve larger illustrations in *Paradise Lost* are mainly distinguished by an unusual sense of depth and an abundance of fruits and flowers. Some of the designs are derivative; some of the compositions are crowded and tangled; and some of the effects are quaint – the ostrich-headed serpent standing on its tail and

tempting a comely Eve, who is bowered by hollyhocks, and a coy-looking Eve who spoils a vigorous Expulsion scene, for example. Burney designed plates for a number of other books, but they tend to be scattered, one or two to a volume.

Richard Corbould

In spite of his academic competence and great productivity as an illustrator, Richard Corbould (1757–1831) came close to achieving anonymity. He can be remembered best only as one of the names most frequently found on the pleasant but unmemorable small plates in dozens of the standard volumes published by Thomas Harrison, John Bell, and John and Charles Cooke. Corbould disposed of his assignments in a uniform manner, whether he was illustrating Mrs. Sheridan's *Memoirs of Miss Sidney Bidulph*, John Shebbeare's *Lydia: or, Filial Piety*, John Dryden's *Poems*, Tobias Smollett's *Humphrey Clinker*, or Miguel de Cervantes's *Don Quixote*. In most of these popular books, his stint was only one to four designs. Even when Corbould had a more challenging opportunity, as he had as one of the leading contributors to Bellamy and Robarts's edition of *The Plays of William Shakespeare* (1788–91), he failed to rise above his routine level. Among his fourteen plates, that of the fight between Macbeth and Macduff in the last scene of *Macbeth* (V.viii) shows Corbould at his most animated.

52. Richard Corbould. James Thomson, *The Seasons* (1802).

"Autumn", in James Thomson's *Seasons* (1802) (fig. 52), can stand as representative of a great number of decorative-interpretive designs by him and other artists of similar talent in the many volumes of popular editions of fiction, poetry, and drama that were published in the eighteenth and early nineteenth centuries.

Corbould's sons George and Henry are said to have spent thirty years making drawings for engravings of the Elgin Marbles. Henry drew some uninspired illustrations, including a stiff frontispiece depicting bodies being unloaded into a pit by moonlight for Daniel Defoe's *History of the Great Plague* (1819), which may have influenced George Cruikshank's design. (The work of Henry's son Edward Henry is discussed in Chapter Six.)

John Flaxman

The neoclassic sculptor John Flaxman (1755–1826) was not in the usual sense a book illustrator. He drew designs, engraved by others, for five foreign classics, but the engravings were published with only captions and legends. These sets of prints were extraordinarily popular all over Europe, but more as revelations of what the classic spirit was supposed to be than as illustrations of familiar literature. Flaxman drew the designs for four of the books in Rome in 1792 and 1793, and three of the series were engraved

there in 1793. The books are *The Odyssey* (1805) and *The Iliad* (1795) of Homer, 34 plates each; *Compositions from the Tragedies of Aeschylus* (1795), 30; *The "Divine Poem" of Dante Alighieri* (1807), 110; and *Compositions from the "Works Days and Theogony" of Hesiod* (1817), 36. The last series was drawn in England and engraved by William Blake (1817). The Aeschylus was also engraved in England (1795).

It is difficult now to be enthusiastic about these engraved outline drawings of figures, which are said to have been inspired by Greek vase designs but are devoid of the timeless mystery of those stylized forms. As a sculptor, Flaxman felt compelled to get his anatomy right. To a modern, his figures, mostly in profile and without background, suggest statues, not poetry or drama. But to Flaxman's contemporaries, they meant far more; Byron did not publish the first two cantos of *Childe Harold* until 1812, and the Elgin Marbles did not reach the British Museum until 1816. The designs for *The Odyssey* and *The Iliad* have often appeared with the entire texts. One of the illustrations of Titan from the Hesiod series is reproduced (fig. 53) because it was admirably engraved in a soft dotted-line technique by Blake and suggests how Flaxman influenced Blake. Flaxman's outline style also inspired the German artists known as Nazarenes, who in the first half of the nineteenth century devised a technique with which they hoped to emulate the work of sixteenth-century woodcutters.

53. John Flaxman. *Compositions from the "Works Days and Theogony" of Hesiod* (1817).

Henry Fuseli

Leaving behind his native Switzerland and his Zwinglian ministry, Johann Heinrich Füssli (1741–1825) arrived in London in 1764. With the encouragement of Sir Joshua Reynolds, he spent eight years (1770–78) in Rome studying art. On his return to England, he changed his name to Henry Fuseli and began his belated career as an artist. Although he taught art and in 1799 became professor of painting at the Royal Academy, Fuseli never was a master of drawing or color. He made up for his technical weaknesses by borrowing liberally from artists whom he admired, especially Michelangelo and the Mannerists, and by creating sensational designs in which human figures exhibit exaggerated postures and states of abnormal sensibility. His earliest success was a painting called *The Nightmare*. Fuseli's paintings and illustrations came as a shock after the decorum of his Anglo-French predecessors. His emotional extravagance, reflecting the early influence on him by the *Sturm und Drang* movement, only anticipated the Byronism soon to sweep Europe. His work received mixed reactions during his lifetime but has enjoyed an enthusiastic revival in our day, largely because of its violence and psychological idiosyncrasies. This belated popularity has shed little light on Fuseli's ability as an interpretive illustrator.

Four illustrations, done for Tobias Smollet's *Peregrine Pickle* as early as 1769, helped Fuseli in his decision to become an artist, and his designs for Erasmus Darwin's odd poems *The Botanic Garden* (1791) and *The Loves of the Plants* (1789) – published as one volume in 1791, with two plates engraved by William Blake – and *The Temple of Nature* (1803) foretold the unconventional images to come. Fuseli contributed designs to a number of books, most of which have illustrations by other artists as well. In Thomas Gray's *Poems* (1800) and James Thomson's *Seasons* (1802), William Hamilton shared the assignment. Fuseli made more of an impression in a translation of C. M. Wieland's *Oberon: a Poem* (1805), for which thirteen steel engravings were made after his romantic paintings, and in Homer's *Iliad and Odyssey* (1810), to which he was the leading contributor, with seventeen of the forty-eight illustrations. Typically, in the pitiful scene of old Priam begging Achilles for the body of Hector, Fuseli dissipated the pathos by giving Priam the arms of a blacksmith.

Fuseli's reputation as an illustrator rests on his series for John Milton's *Paradise Lost* (1802) and William Shakespeare's *Plays* (1805). From the beginning, many of Fuseli's paintings were of scenes from the works of Milton and Shakespeare. Indeed, he was engaged to illustrate an edition of Milton, modeled after the Boydell Shakespeare, but it was abandoned when the editor, William Cowper, suffered a mental breakdown. Financial troubles delayed until 1799 the opening of the Milton Gallery to display Fuseli's paintings based on Milton's works. The gallery failed. In 1802, Fuseli's long preoccupation with *Paradise Lost* finally resulted somewhat ingloriously in an illustrated edition with a meager six engravings after paintings by Fuseli and six after drawings by Hamilton.

Fuseli's designs are in Book I, "Satan Summons His Host"; Book II, "Satan at the Gates of Hell"; Book III, "Uriel Watching Satan"; Book IV, "Satan Starting from Ithuriel's Spear"; Book VI, "Battle of the Angels"; and Book XII, "Adam and Eve Leave Paradise". It is not fair to judge plates after Fuseli's paintings as though they were planned illustrations. Would he have devoted five of his six designs to Satan, or, if he had, would his small drawings have been designed in the same way as his paintings? With these reservations, we can dismiss Fuseli's plates as absurd images of Milton's great poem. For example, in the design for Book I, Satan stands naked on a rock with both arms stretching upward and forefingers pointing. In that for Book II, Sin pitches herself perilously in a great swirl between her athletic young father, Satan, and their dim offspring, Death. The design for the battle in Book VI consists almost entirely of a ludicrous winged Messiah, with a peculiar helmet on his head and strips of cloth about his waist, charging straight ahead through the air without apparent purpose. Surprisingly, the Expulsion is a languishing affair, with Adam tenderly supporting Eve, who here has hand to face. In the background, a naked Michael is apparently running away. These amazing designs indicate that *Paradise Lost* deeply stirred and aroused strange images in Fuseli.

The Plays of Shakespeare (1805), published in ten volumes by forty-one booksellers, was a tribute to Fuseli's rise in public esteem. He was the sole illustrator and on the title page was given precedence over the editor, Alexander Chalmers. His thirty-seven illustrations (ca. 165 × 90 mm) were expertly engraved by fourteen engravers, of whom Blake was one. Fuseli was an enthusiastic theatergoer, but his imagination had too long been fired by Shakespeare's lines for him to take eighteenth-century stage productions as models, although some may have given him ideas for designs. The vehemence of his images was his response to Elizabethan passion. In his rectangular designs, Fuseli concentrated on individualizing a single manneristic figure with one or two supporting figures. This gave him little space for settings. He also introduced arbitrarily rhythmic compositions, which help give some of his designs a dynamic quality not seen before in England.

Fuseli was limited to one plate for each of the thirty-seven

54. Henry Fuseli. William Shakespeare, *Hamlet* in *The Plays of Shakespeare* (1805).

plays, but he selected his own scenes and treated them as he thought best. There is a sense of fresh vitality in many of his interpretations. In the first play, *The Tempest* (I.ii), Prospero is not a venerable wise man in a cloak but a figure of authority standing on a rocky coast. In the trial scene in *The Merchant of Venice* (IV.i), Shylock grimly sharpens a knife. In *Richard III* (V.iii), the king, troubled by a dream in which appear the ghosts of his victims, draws his sword as he springs out of bed. In *Hamlet* (I.i), instead of a wraith-like presence, the ghost in armor thrusts out his arm to point as he takes a vigorous stride (fig. 54). Most expressive is King Lear, not a confused old man but an Old Testament prophet, who half kneels as he holds the dead Cordelia in his arms (V.iii).

But Fuseli corrupted his illustrations as a result of three faults. The first was his borrowing. Two serious examples are the designs for *The Taming of the Shrew* (Induction i) and *Titus Andronicus* (II.iii). In the first, the drunken Sly asleep on the floor with his legs spread is a redrawing of Baldung Grün's *Bewitched Groom*; in the second, Martius trying to climb out of the pit is an Italian artist's composition. The second fault was Fuseli's eccentric selection of certain moments, each the basis for the only illustration of an entire play, in order to draw figures in accordance with his own preoccupations. These eccentricities are either outrageous or ludicrous; for example, the drunken Sly in *The Taming of the Shrew*, the striding ghost in *Hamlet*, Romeo in silken tights seen from the rear in the apothecary's shop in *Romeo and Juliet* (V.i), and a comic treatment of Falstaff's death in *Henry V* (II.iii). His third fault was his inability to convey in any of the thirty-seven illustrations anything of Shakespeare's humor or tenderness. Falstaff looks heavy and dull; and women characters, even the innocent Miranda and Desdemona, are modeled on Parisian courtesans.

Henry Fuseli brought to English art an energy and a freedom from stereotypes that, fusing with similar qualities in the work of Blake, had a beneficial effect on book illustration. He was, however, too self-absorbed and obsessive in his enthusiasms to be anything but an imperfect interpretive illustrator.

William Hamilton

The popularity enjoyed by William Hamilton (1751–1801) as a painter led to the inclusion of plates after his paintings and drawings in a number of books. Without the warmth of color, these plates often substitute sentimentality for charm. His most popular illustrations were those in James Thomson's *Seasons*, three editions of which contain his designs. The best known (1797) is his only important solo effort, a folio for which he painted twenty designs, including five reproduced as full-page engravings, some by Francesco Bartolozzi. Of greater interest are the six plates in Du Roveray's two-volume edition of *Paradise Lost* (1802). Hamilton (not Richard Westall) drew designs for the quieter scenes of Books V and VII to XI, and Henry Fuseli designed the rest, the dynamic ones. Hamilton's ability to be faithful to the text and yet to present a scene in its idyllic aspects is evident in his lush treatment of the Awakening of Eve (fig. 55).

Philippe Jacques de Loutherbourg

Born in Strasbourg, Philippe Jacques de Loutherbourg (Lauterburger) (1740–1812) studied art in Paris and in 1771 moved to London, where he was for ten years influential as stage designer for David Garrick. He contributed twenty-one designs to *The Dramatick Writings of Will. Shakespeare* (1788) and seven spirited battle scenes to David Hume's *History of England* (1812). His biblical paintings were the source of engravings for the Bible (1791–1800) and the Apocrypha (1816). He might have been a significant illustrator had his other interests not been so absorbing. Loutherbourg dabbled in faith healing and invented the Eidophusikon, a miniature theater.

Thomas Rowlandson

After studying at the Royal Academy schools and for two years in Paris, Thomas Rowlandson (1756–1827) gave up the effort to be a portrait painter for the less confining life of a designer of prints and book illustrations. He drank, gambled, and wenched like the heroes of Fielding and Smollet; he loved to travel, as do the characters of Sterne; and he was as good-natured and carefree as the leading men and women of Goldsmith. Although influenced by William Hogarth and given to rude caricature, Rowlandson indulged in the satire of laughter, not moral indignation, and offset it by his fondness for youth, lovely ladies, snug interiors, and picturesque places.

The eight aquatints – Rowlandson was the only prominent artist to use aquatints extensively for literary interpretation – in Henry Wigstead's *Excursion to Brighthelmstone* (1790) gave early evidence of Rowlandson's talent as a landscape artist. Then followed an exceptional engagement with the Edinburgh printer-publisher Sibbald: Henry Fielding's *History of Tom Jones, a Foundling* (1791) and *Adventures of Joseph Andrews* (1792), and Tobias Smollett's *Novels* (1791) – a six-volume collected edition – *Humphrey Clinker* (1793), *Adventures of Peregrine Pickle* (1805), and *Roderick Random* (1805). Except for *Humphrey*

55. William Hamilton. John Milton, *Paradise Lost* (1802).

Clinker, Rowlandson etched the plates for these books. He then tinted with watercolors a set of impressions for each as a model to be followed by the publisher's hand-colorists. The episodic narratives of Fielding and Smollett move along without much complexity of plot or subtlety of characterization, and Rowlandson easily identified with the heroes and their misadventures, as in the one of Roderick Random joining a party of French soldiers. All the heroes resemble Rowlandson as he appears in his self-portraits and anticipate the cinema hero – handsome, virile, and unintellectual. All the ladies, nice and not so nice, are freshfaced and buxom. The caricaturing of the supporting cast of villains, eccentrics, and vulgar folk is excessive, but the contrast with the leading men and women supplies an energy that is absent from the French-influenced illustrations of the eighteenth century. Rowlandson seized on the ample opportunities for vigorous and comic action, such as Peregrine Pickle bounding down the staircase of the burning inn with the scantily clad Emilia in his arms while Pipes follows with Sophy in his.

In 1808, Rowlandson became associated with Rudolph Ackermann, a German who between 1808 and 1834 published at his "Repository of the Arts" – 101, The Strand – two illustrated periodicals and numerous books with colored plates. Rowlandson drew the figures to go with buildings and interiors drawn by the architect Augustus Pugin on the 104 plates (ca. 194 × 259 mm) that first appeared in installments in Ackermann's *Poetical Magazine* (1808–11) and then were issued in three volumes as *The Microcosm of London* (1808–10). The union of talents brilliantly fixed the features of early-nineteenth-century London. Rowlandson etched the outlines on the plates and then tinted on proofs the areas to be aquatinted. After Ackermann's aquatinters had finished their tasks on the plates, Rowlandson completed a master print with watercolors as a model to be followed by Ackermann's handcolorists.

Almost all of Rowlandson's remaining illustrations were done for Ackermann. The best known works to come out of this relationship are the Doctor Syntax books, with verse texts by William Combe. The first appeared in serial form in Ackermann's *Poetical Magazine* as *The Schoolmaster's Tour* (1809–11) and then in book form as *The Tour of Doctor Syntax, in Search of the Picturesque* (1812). Two more volumes followed: *The Second Tour of Doctor Syntax, in Search of Consolation* (1820), and *The Third Tour of Doctor Syntax, in Search of a Wife* (1820–21). Each volume has the subtitle *A Poem*. There are eighty plates (112 × 193 mm) in all. The volumes are a burlesque of guidebooks by the Reverend William Gilpin, a schoolmaster, but they also serve as a vehicle for drawings based on sketches that Rowlandson had made on tours with friends. The illustra-

56. Thomas Stothard. Daniel Defoe, *Robinson Crusoe* (1790).

tions in the first volume record the misadventures suffered by Syntax as he rides off on Grizzle, his mare, to make his fortune by illustrating his account of his travels. Typical of Rowlandson's plates is one of Syntax happily reading from his manuscript to a bored and sleeping audience. The main weakness of the series is unaccountable; Doctor Syntax is neither comic nor memorable.

As each of the *Doctor Syntax* drawings was finished, it was taken to Combe, an old Etonian, in debtors' prison. He pinned up the drawing and invented two or three pages of narrative and commentary in humorous couplets to go with it. It is said that artist and author did not meet. In the same manner, Combe supplied what the title page calls "metrical illustrations" for Rowlandson's seventy-two designs (123 × 206 mm) for the two-volume *English Dance of Death* (1815–16). They emulate Hans Holbein's famous small woodcuts with complete originality and display some of Rowlandson's finest draftsmanship and dramatic compositions. In them, Death sardonically surprises widely assorted members of English society – antiquarian and insurance broker, statesman and bishop, virago and coquette, glutton and sot, hunter and prize fighter.

The twenty-four colored aquatints (110 × 190 mm) for Oliver Goldsmith's *Vicar of Wakefield* (1817) make up Rowlandson's most agreeable, least exaggerated literary series. They represent Rowlandson's disciplined willing-ness to direct his energies to bringing out the best in Goldsmith and to not let his proclivity toward satire and grotesquery interfere. In addition to those scenes that picture the affection and cohesiveness of the Primrose family, Rowlandson seized on those that introduce something special: villagers dancing by moonlight, Olivia and Sophy having their fortunes told by a gypsy, Dr. Primrose riding through a village street on top of the strolling players' cart with their musical instruments, the play being staged in a provincial theater, and the charlatan connoisseur in an art gallery. Toward the end of his search for his erring daughter, Olivia, the Vicar puts up for the night at a wayside inn and asks the landlord's company over a pint of wine. The landlord's wife complains bitterly about having to do all the work, but the Vicar placates her with wine and is rewarded by the discovery that Olivia is at the inn (pl. II). Instead of depicting the obvious reunion, Rowlandson portrayed the diverting moment when the landlady is at the top of her tirade but is about to accept the wine, and at the same time, he celebrated the inn as the Englishman's sanctuary. As with Doctor Syntax, Rowlandson, strangely, failed to create a convincing Vicar; on the frontispiece, he is young and potbellied. Still, Thomas Rowlandson's aquatints for *The Vicar of Wakefield* are one of the great delights of English book illustration.

Thomas Stothard

In the fifty years of his career, Thomas Stothard (1755–1834) illustrated more than fifty books and moved from copper engraving to wood- and steel engraving, always by other hands. Among the three dozen novels in Thomas Harrison's series, *The Novelist's Magazine* (1780–86), for which he designed small engravings are *Tom Jones, Robinson Crusoe, Tristram Shandy, Don Quixote,* and *Gulliver's Travels*. He did four to sixteen designs for these classics, but he was allowed twenty-eight plates in Samuel Richardson's *Sir Charles Grandison* (1783?) and thirty-four in *Clarissa Harlowe* (1784?). Stothard showed an awareness of his responsibility to transmit an author's intent in such diverse series as the fourteen illustrations for Geoffrey Chaucer's poems (1782–83) in John Bell's pocket-edition *The Poets of Great Britain,* six for Robert Paltock's *Peter Wilkins, a Cornish Man* (1783), ten for *The Arabian Nights' Entertainments* (1785), and fourteen for another edition of *Robinson Crusoe* (1790), published by John Stockdale. The last come close to being models of straightforward illustration, with nothing slighted or exaggerated. The plate of Crusoe and Friday building a boat is an example of this integrity (fig. 56).

Stothard functioned best in the middle range of emotions. The six illustrations in Oliver Goldsmith's *Vicar of Wakefield* (1792) are sentimental, although excusably so. Lacking a sense of grandeur, his thirteen illustrations for *Paradise Lost* (1792–93), made pretty by Francesco Bartolozzi's mezzotinting, are not Miltonic. Nor do the sixteen engrav-

ings after his paintings of scenes from Shakespeare's plays (1807) reveal feeling for the tragic and comic, although Stothard experienced tragedy in his own life. During the first third of the nineteenth century, Stothard added Homer, Sir Walter Scott, Robert Burns, Byron, and Boccaccio to his catalog of major authors without demonstrating any advance in his powers.

In 1810, the banker-poet Samuel Rogers published a new edition of *The Pleasures of Memory,* for which Stothard drew thirty-four simple vignette head- and tailpieces, mostly of *putti*. Engraved on wood by Luke Clennell in strong outlines with curved-line shading, they are decorative and charming. They helped fix the idea of a sentimental Stothard. In 1830, Rogers published his *Italy: A Poem,* illustrated with nineteen small vignettes of scenes with people by Stothard and twenty-three of places by J. M. W. Turner. The two artists divided the illustrations in the same way in Rogers's *Poems* (1834), Stothard doing thirty-three and Turner, thirty-one. All these small vignettes were engraved on steel, the most famous series of steel engravings in English works of literature. More effective as interpretive illustrations are the four charming engravings on copper for Izaak Walton and Charles Cotton's *Complete Angler, or Contemplative Man's Recreation* (1836), published after Stothard's death.

Thomas Stothard deserves respect for the large number of works of literature that he illustrated, for the decorum that he brought to pre-Victorian books, and for the clarity of his insights, especially in works of moderate emotional intensity.

Plate II. Thomas Rowlandson. Oliver Goldsmith, *The Vicar of Wakefield* (1817).

CHAPTER SIX

The Nineteenth Century (I)
1801–1854

During the first half of the nineteenth century, privilege, license, and the royal prerogative were reduced, Parliament gained in power, people moved into the cities and towns to work in the new industries, public education took root, and a literate middle class increased in size and demanded appropriate reading matter. After Victoria became queen in 1837 and prosperity and public decorum came to prevail, literature began to reflect the changes, and illustration did likewise. Most directly, inventions in all phases of book production – presses, type, typesetting, paper, and binding – increased output many times over, reduced costs and prices, and created more publishers and better channels of distribution. In the early years of the nineteenth century, the copper engraving of book illustrations began to be superseded by aquatinting, etching on steel, and steel engraving, all of which were prevalent until wood engraving became universal.

The first half of the nineteenth century was the great period of English book illustration. During those five decades, more of the most original and most productive literary illustrators were at work than at any other time. With increasing frequency, publishers gave illustrators equal prominence with authors on title pages, specified in advertisements and on title pages the number of illustrations, and listed the titles and page numbers of individual illustrations, with the name of the illustrator of each one in multiple-artist gift books. Since this elevation of the illustrator occurred in first editions of novels as well as in easily available classics, the common reader had come to prize illustrations and to discriminate among illustrators. William Blake, Henry Fuseli, and Thomas Rowlandson, all of whom had begun their careers in the last quarter of the eighteenth century, were still creating, in the early years of the nineteenth, designs of an imaginative force and exuberance not seen in England before or since. Thomas Stothard also contributed his pleasant illustrations to many books that were published in the early decades of the century.

Then came Hablot Browne, George Cruikshank, Birket Foster, John Gilbert, William Harvey, John Leech, John Tenniel, John Thurston, Richard Westall, and numerous lesser illustrators. Although these nine major figures varied in their talents, all were immensely productive and popular, and all were dedicated professional illustrators who averaged about thirty working years each. Their success was to a considerable extent due to a fortunate coincidence of their personal outlook with the tastes of the new middle-class reading public and with the kind of contemporary literature being published to entertain this expanding market. They offered hearty fare: broad but not offensive humor, exciting melodrama, escapist romance, and reassuring sentimentality. With amazing energy, they created hundreds of imaginary characters and scenes for long lists of books of poetry, fiction, and humor.

Novels were frequently first published in "parts" – issued every month or at other intervals – which increased sales by dividing the total price into small sums. (The parts were often later issued bound in three volumes.) It was not unusual for the illustrator to deliver finished designs for one installment before the author had written the next. Yet those who illustrated novels met their deadlines week in and week out with illustrations that have created indelible images for generations of readers. The combined pressures of time and heavy work loads for low pay inevitably forced rapid execution – without models, as a matter of course. One result was a good deal of imperfect draftsmanship, but another was a vitality and lack of self-consciousness that permeate the work of this period as they do that of no other in the history of English book illustration.

The variety of books required to meet the changing tastes of the expanding reading public led to specialization among illustrators. It seemed useful to include in the Catalog some of the noninterpretive work as representative samples. The Romantic poets had taught their readers to gaze on the wilder aspects of nature with awe and exaltation and on the tamer aspects of country life with approbation. J. M. W. Turner and John Martin were the leading celebrants of the first kind of aspect, and Birket Foster was that of the second. Travel became less exclusive, and Clarkson Stanfield and Edward Lear gave both travelers and stay-at-homes much pleasure with their handsome plein-air drawings reproduced in books as plates accompanied by text. The scientific curiosity of the seventeenth century, manifested in Francis Barlow's special attention to birds and animals, had passed on to Thomas Bewick and was inherited by Harvey, Samuel Howitt, Lear, and other nineteenth-century illustrators. The drawing of flowers, which went back to the woodcuts in sixteenth-century herbals, derived more exactness from the researches of Carl von Linné (Linnaeus) and more charm from the application of color. The most famous flower book of the period was Dr. Robert Thornton's *Temple of Flora* (1807), with richly colored aquatint and mezzotint plates by Victor Reinagle and others. (Thornton was the villain in 1821 in the handling of Blake's only wood engravings.)

Also descended from the seventeenth century but reflective of the rising aspirations of the nineteenth-century English middle class were serious and jocular illustrations featuring horses in sporting books, in fiction about landed and Rotten Row gentry, and in derisory accounts of tradesmen on horseback. Among the leading illustrators in this genre, Henry Alken is still popular. The upsurge of graphic humor was a major development of the first half of the nineteenth century. Rowlandson was followed by George Cruikshank, Robert Cruikshank, Richard Doyle, Leech, and William Makepeace Thackeray, all of whom contributed vastly to the spirit of genial good cheer throughout the English-speaking world with their book illustrations. Doyle and Leech were even better known for their contributions to *Punch*, which was founded in 1841.

Among the "numerous lesser illustrators" dismissed anonymously were several of considerable ability. Edward Henry Corbould, John Franklin, Joseph Kenny Meadows, Henry Courteney Selous, and Robert Smirke were productive and popular, but their work was uninspired. George Cattermole, Frederick Pickersgill, Daniel Maclise, Noel Paton, and William Mulready, although limited in their output, were more original.

Contributing to the great diversity that permeates book illustration of the first half of the nineteenth century is the variety of technical forms used after a century of almost nothing but copper engraving. During this period and the next, some English artists were influenced by the "shaded-outline" method of some German artists, including Peter von Cornelius (1783-1867) and other so-called Nazarenes, who had been inspired by John Flaxman's illustrations. The nearer the shaded-outline designs approached the look of sixteenth-century woodcuts, as in Alfred Rethel's illustrations for *Niebelungenlied* (1840) and *Totentanz* (1849),

the more attractive, if archaic, they seemed. A few English illustrators tried the cold pure outline style, but Franklin, Maclise, John Everett Millais, Paton, Pickersgill, Frederick Sandys, and Tenniel sometimes achieved excellent results by molding the outline of figures and objects with short restrained lines of shading and leaving the background white. It was a sensible compromise between the severe simplicity of early-Italian woodcuts and the labored imitation on wood of the tonal effects of metal engraving. It went well with the type-page. Yet the sanity and potentialities of the shaded-outline designs were ignored and then forgotten until the end of the century.

The growth of the market for illustrated books after 1820 – not only for popular literature, but also for books of scenic views, architecture, portraits, and copies of paintings – led to engraving on steel plates rather than on copperplates, which are good for only a short run before showing wear. The hardness of steel both guaranteed durability and permitted a fineness of line, brilliance, and graduated range of tone beyond the capability of a copperplate. But steel was extraordinarily difficult to engrave. According to Basil Hunnisett in his definitive *Steel-Engraved Book Illustration in England* (1980), the design on steel plates was always etched first, and the engraving was very slow – months and even years for large plates. Processes for engraving on softened steel and on hardened copper eventually were introduced. Mezzotint engraving on steel was also popular, mainly for portraits, landscapes, and reproductions of paintings.

The great period of steel engravings and mezzotints was the twenty years between 1825 and 1845. Neither medium was well adapted to literary illustration, and steel engravings in books for the general reader tend to be small, with indistinct detail. A typical example of how steel plates were used is *The Life and Works of Lord Byron* (1832-33), with designs by Stanfield, Turner, Cattermole, and several other artists. Turner and Stanfield were leaders in the use of the medium for book illustration. Stothard and Westall were the most prominent illustrators to have many of their interpretive designs engraved on steel. Martin was the only English artist ever to produce memorable interpretive illustrations by means of mezzotint.

Another variant form was etching on steel. Especially in the hands of Cruikshank and Browne, it was a peculiarly appropriate technique for illustrating both moderately priced eighteenth-century classics and the lively popular literature of such new authors as Charles Dickens, Charles Lever, and Harrison Ainsworth. Etching on steel was widely used for book illustration in England only in the first half of the nineteenth century; indeed, during the years in which Cruikshank and Browne produced their

57. Henry Alken. *The Real Life of London* (1821–22).

popular work, it was the leading technical mode of English literary illustration.

Wood engraving, previously not much used except for small cheap printings, had developed in a special way, which has been little noted and should be investigated further. In the eighteenth century, Elisha Kirkall and Thomas Bewick had demonstrated that engraving in relief on blocks that were the same height as the type was the practical way to circumvent the high cost of copper-engraved book illustrations. Kirkall experimented with soft metal blocks, but Bewick adopted fine-grain boxwood cut across the grain, which far outlasted metal engravings and etchings. Kirkall reinvented white-line technique as an alternative to black-outline woodcutting and black-line intaglio metal engraving, and Bewick proved its usefulness. As designer-engravers, Kirkall and Bewick, and their follower Blake, realized that there was no point in making careful black-line drawings for themselves to copy in fac-simile. They created forms, details, and degrees of light and dark with their gravers, working from black to white. But when Thurston, trained as both a metal engraver and a wood engraver, began to design literary illustrations of figures in action to be engraved on wood by hands who were not artists, he seems to have realized that compromise was desirable and developed what might be called the "modi-fied-Bewick" or "post-Bewick" technique. Figure 77 is an

excellent example.

The main characteristics of the modified-Bewick technique are strong black outlines with somewhat stylized shading, notably along arms and legs; white-line treatment of foliage and other areas; absence of black crosshatching; and free use of white space. The technique is sensible in terms of human labor, aesthetically stimulating, harmoni-ous with the type-page, and emphatic in producing literary illustrations. The method was taught to a group of wood engravers who worked first with Thurston and then with Harvey, Cruikshank, Thomas Landseer, and others. The leaders among the dozen or so practitioners, some of whom had been trained by Bewick, were George Wilmot Bonner (1796–1836), Robert Branston (1778–1827), Luke Clennell (1781–1840), John Jackson (1801–48), Ebenezer Landells (1808–60), Charlton Nesbit (1775–1838), Samuel M. Slader (d. ca. 1861), and John Thompson (1785–1866).

Lithography also had a vogue in England during the early nineteenth century. The process had been developed by Aloys Senefelder in Munich in 1798 and introduced to England a few years later. In 1819, Rudolph Ackermann published *A Complete Course of Lithography*, his translation of Senefelder's treatise of 1818. In spite of the wonderful work of Eugène Delacroix, Honoré Daumier, and Paul Gavarni in France, the great potential of lithography for serious literary illustration was ignored in England. It was used mostly for topographical illustrations and for portraits and later, in the form of chromolithography, for color plates in topographical, botanical, and children's books. George Baxter and Edmund Evans used multiple wood blocks for color printing, with particularly charming results in children's books, but, again, with virtually no effect on the illustration of adult literature.

Henry Thomas Alken

Most of the many illustrations by Henry Alken (1784–1851) in more than a dozen books are smaller versions of the familiar prints of pink-coated fox hunters associated with his name. They have an honorable place in the specialized history of English sporting books, but need not be discussed here. Yet early in his career, Alken proved that he could have become a major literary illustrator, very like Hablot Browne, who followed him. His opportunity came with *The Real Life of London: the Adventures of Bob Tallyho, Esq. and His Cousin the Hon. Tom Dashall by an Amateur* (1821–22). This was not a brazen cashing in on the success of Pierce Egan's *Life in London* (1821), illustrated by Robert and George Cruikshank, but an awkward response to that book in an effort to lure readers with a similar humorous narrative in what is, in fact, a fat two-volume compendium of serious information, including dollops of statistics, about the "real London".

The fifteen color plates, most of which are signed "Drawn & Etched by H. Alken, Esqr.", demonstrate that although Alken did not share the Cruikshanks' sense of life's absurdities, he was just as observant, could develop with acuity and imagination the scenes as written, and was at home in their London – as they were not in his fields. His ability to follow an author's cues and at the same time build complete scenes of which the author mentions only parts is evident in such amusing yet serious documentary designs as "Exhibition, Somerset House: Tom & Bob among the Connoisseurs" and "Billingsgate: Tom & Bob taking a Survey after a Night's Spree" (fig. 57). In the first illustration, he carefully drew the several "characters" as they are described in the text and added others drawn from observation. In the second, he included the fishwife being upset, the two others fighting over a fisherman, and the woman stall owner about to send for a half pint of "blue-ruin" gin, at Tom's expense; but he subordinated them – as Cruikshank never would have done – to his record of the famous Thames Street fish market.

Hablot Knight Browne [Phiz]

As Phiz, Hablot Knight Browne (1815–82) shared in the fame of Charles Dickens, but there are other reasons for placing him among the major English book illustrators. He illustrated more than seventy-five books, few of which were reprinted classics; most were the first editions of novels by living authors. No other English artist has ever approached this record. Even more extraordinary, Browne usually illustrated parts of stories for publication as they were being written. Thus he frequently was deprived of what illustrators ordinarily take for granted – the chance to read and analyze a book and make preliminary studies before beginning a series. Browne often worked against urgent deadlines, with only a few days to do an assignment of two illustrations. He became established during the years when etching on steel was the most popular technique for book illustration – between the copper engraving of the eighteenth century and the wood engraving of the mid-nineteenth century – but his technical procedure was unusual. He transferred his drawing from paper to a steel plate prepared for etching by his associate Robert Young, redrew it through the ground with an etching needle, and then returned the plate to Young to be bitten with acid. Because of the tendency of the plates to wear, Browne sometimes did more than one plate for designs for a work with a long run. Furthermore, Browne habitually worked on the books of more than one author at the same time. Taken together, these conditions imposed handicaps that were endured by no other English illustrator.

Although Dickens and Browne are the most celebrated author–artist team in the history of English book illustration, it is well to realize that in addition to his designs for ten major and three minor works by Dickens, Browne illustrated seventeen books by Charles Lever, six by Harrison Ainsworth, and more than forty by a score of other authors (not all in the Catalog). His usual assignment for Dickens and Lever was thirty or forty plates; for other authors, it was fewer. For clarity, it is better to examine his work by author, rather than chronologically.

Dickens began his career with *Sketches by Boz* (1836, 1837), illustrated by George Cruikshank. He then wrote sketches about a cockney sportsman, which were issued in parts under the title *The Posthumous Papers of the Pickwick Club* (1837). Browne became illustrator after Robert Seymour, the originator of the project, committed suicide after having done eight plates, and Robert Buss was dropped after having done two. He took the pseudonym Phiz to go with Dickens's Boz. The usual arrangement was for him to do two plates to be inserted together at the beginning of each part, which the reader bought in a paper

58. Hablot Knight Browne (Phiz). Charles Dickens, *The Personal History of David Copperfield* (1850).

wrapper. When *Pickwick Papers* appeared in book form, Dickens wrote in the introduction that most of the illustrations had been executed from "the author's mere verbal description of what he intended to write". Throughout his association with Browne, Dickens, even while living on the Continent, selected the scenes to be illustrated – indeed, invariably wrote them with illustrations in mind – gave directions as to how they should be treated, and criticized preliminary drawings. In spite of the concreteness and increasing realism of his descriptions, Dickens considered illustrations to be a necessity.

Browne etched thirty-four plates for the book edition of *Pickwick Papers*. Its lasting literary success and the identification of the illustrations with the text have obscured the fact that young Browne, who had had little training or experience and who drew from memory, did not yet draw well and overdid comic exaggeration in his imitations of Cruikshank's style. Popular delight in the endless predicaments of Mr. Pickwick and his friends and in the sayings of Sam and Tony Weller lent luster to the illustrations. The same is true of Browne's next series – thirty-nine illustrations for *The Life and Adventures of Nicholas Nickleby* (1839) – except that his drawing and his characterization perceptibly improved when Dickens developed the humorous episodes around the Kenwigs family, the Mantalinis, Vincent Crummles and his provincial theatrical company,

Miss La Creevy, and Charles and Ned Cheeryble.

Through the rest of Browne's association with Dickens, his effectiveness, or readers' perception of it, varied with his material. *The Old Curiosity Shop* and *Barnaby Rudge* are unusual because they are stories within *Master Humphrey's Clock* (1841). Because of weekly publication, the drawings were engraved on wood, and George Cattermole shared in the designs for *Barnaby Rudge*. The hypocritical Seth Pecksniff in *The Life and Adventures of Martin Chuzzlewit* (1844) was Browne's first genuinely successful character. In the last five novels on which they worked together, both Dickens and Browne matured, which did not necessarily make either one more popular. *Dealings with the Firm of Dombey and Son* (1848) marked technical advance for both, but Paul Dombey was neither attractive nor eccentric enough to arouse popular enthusiasm. Browne, however, etched single figures and group scenes more decisively and expressively than he had previously, with little of the excess crosshatching he had used before, and he made the most of the comic scenes without burlesque. In *Dombey and Son* appeared the first of what have been called the "dark plates", "ruled plates," or "mixed mezzotints" because, apparently at first to save time, Young produced dark tonal effects quickly by engraving areas of a plate with a multiple-line machine. The "dark plates" are often handsome, but they are not compatible with linear etchings.

The most popular success of the team of Dickens and Browne was *The Personal History of David Copperfield* (1850). The reasons are clear. The semiautobiographical background of the novel makes the story believable, and the constant presence of the sympathetic David gives cohesiveness to its episodic progress. The abundance of vivid but not caricatured characters – Uriah Heep, the Murdstones, the Peggottys, Steerforth, Traddles, Aunt Betsy Trotwood, Mr. Dick, and, Dickens's brilliant creation, Wilkins Micawber – all of whom are actively involved in the events, gave Browne splendid opportunities, which he was now able to handle with easy competence. Among the forty plates are many complex ones – "Mr. Micawber delivers some valedictory remarks" (fig. 58), for example – in which Browne visualized situations so immediately that the scenes are made clear with no apparent effort.

Bleak House (1853) and *Little Dorrit* (1857) offered no opportunities equal to those of *David Copperfield*. In the first, moreover, the presence of ten "dark plates" out of thirty and in the second, eight out of forty takes away from the importance of Dickens's characters and events because the "dark plates" are used primarily for settings, perhaps at Dickens's request. The short *Tale of Two Cities* (1859), however, gave Browne good characters and dramatic scenes, and his sixteen steel etchings are well done. The almost humorous mob scene during the Reign of Terror and the failure to choose as the last illustration Sydney Carton either comforting the little seamstress or taking Charles Darnay's place on the guillotine (Dickens's decision, presumably) make clear the extent to which the success of illustrations depends on more than artistic ability.

For a quarter of a century after *Pickwick Papers* had brought Browne to public notice, he was also the illustrator of the books of the Irish novelist Charles Lever, all of which were first issued in parts. At first, Browne not only showed the same technical weaknesses as in Dickens's early novels, but also was handicapped by a lack of familiarity with Irish life. Lever dealt in the comic, the convivial, and the sensational, and he habitually used real persons, places, and incidents for fictional purposes. Browne's rude comic treatment of the Irish characters in the first seven of Lever's novels, beginning with *The Confessions of Harry Lorrequer* (1839), sometimes annoyed the Irish, including Lever. After 1845, the author lived on the Continent, another handicap for his illustrator. But Browne's draftsmanship and outlook matured, as we have noted. *The Knight of Gwynne* (1847), *Roland Cashel* (1850), *The Daltons: or Three Roads in Life* (1852), *The Dodd Family Abroad* (1854), *The Martins of Cro' Martin* (1856), *Davenport Dunn: A Man of Our Day* (1859), and *One of Them* (1861) contain

many plates of quiet distinction. They often depict scenes with a number of figures, such as a masquerade ball, a murder trial, a market day, a whist party, and a man reading to a group of people outdoors at night. "Going Home" in *Davenport Dunn* is one of the best of Browne's "dark plates". Among Browne's series, that in *Roland Cashel* is unique: the forty plates are lighter mixed mezzotints. They are extremely attractive, but these tonal plates cannot equal the subtlety of expressiveness, especially in faces, of Browne's usual etchings. The decline that overtook Browne in the 1860s affected his work on his last two of Lever's books, *Barrington* (1863) and *Luttrell of Arran* (1865).

Both Browne and Harrison Ainsworth were in their prime when Browne succeeded Cruikshank as Ainsworth's illustrator. Yet only two of Ainsworth's six sensational historical tales brought out the best in Browne. One was *Crichton* (1849), the adventures of a young Scot, the "admirable" James Crichton, during the times of Henry of Navarre. The other was *Mervyn Clitheroe* (1858), a fictional account of Ainsworth's early life in Manchester, which was far more congenial material for Browne than were historical thrillers. Half of the twenty-four plates are dark mixed mezzotints, but they are unusually fine. Browne dealt with great skill with a wide variety of scenes, including boys in a sweet shop, "Twelfth Night Merrymaking in Farmer Shakeshaft's Barn", "The Duel on Crab-tree Green", "The Stranger at the Grave", and "I Find Pounell in Conference with the Gypsies".

Through the years of demanding activity with Dickens, Lever, and Ainsworth, Browne managed to illustrate books by a score of other writers. They include Robert Smith Surtees, Douglas Jerrold, Frances Trollope, George Payne Rainsford James, William Carleton, Joseph S. Le Fanu, Augustus and Henry Mayhew, and Harriet Beecher Stowe – all of whom were leading writers in their day. Among these many volumes, the plates for Augustus Mayhew's *Paved with Gold: or the Romance and Reality of the London Streets, An Unfashionable Novel* (1858), mainly mixed mezzotints, are a documentary treasure portraying the London streets.

Browne continued to etch long after wood engraving had become the standard method of reproducing illustrations. After *A Tale of Two Cities* (1859), Dickens cast him off, and Anthony Trollope discontinued his services before he completed *Can You Forgive Her?* (1864–65). Neither author ever received from other artists and wood engravers interpretations as sensitive as Browne's. In 1867, Browne suffered a stroke and remained partly paralyzed; his last years were difficult. His drawings for the wood engravings in *Pickwick Papers* (1874) and for an edition of Lever's novels (1876–78) are lifeless in comparison with his etchings.

59. George Cattermole. Charles Dickens, *Barnaby Rudge* (1841).

Working under trying conditions much of the time, unspectacular because he always put the author's interests before his own, Hablot Browne is nevertheless one of the foremost English literary illustrators.

George Cattermole

An architectural draftsman who made designs for many books, George Cattermole (1800–68) has slight connection with the mainstream of English book illustration. The thirty-nine wood-engraved vignettes in his friend Charles Dickens's serial *Master Humphrey's Clock* (1841), which turned into *The Old Curiosity Shop* and *Barnaby Rudge*, are his one memorable contribution. They would have gone unremarked among the 157 illustrations by Hablot Browne had they not shown a certain fantastic excess, very like Dickens's way with words. Typical examples are the interior of the Old Curiosity Shop (with Little Nell, her father, and Quilp present to prove that Cattermole could draw figures when he wanted to), the now famous Maypole Inn headpiece of Chapter I of *Barnaby Rudge*, and the two Maypole interiors – one in days of peace (fig. 59), and the other in days of trouble. Almost all of Cattermole's numerous other designs were reproduced by steel engravings in historical works. He was felicitous in capturing the romantic past in scenes such as "West Row, Edinburgh" and

"Melrose Abbey" in *Scott and Scotland* (1845?), edited by H. I. Stevens and A. Stevens.

Edward Henry Corbould

Grandson of Richard Corbould and son of Henry, a respected painter in oils and watercolors, and tutor to the royal family, Edward Henry Corbould (sometimes listed as Edward) (1815–1905) achieved no single success in forty-five years of illustrating. From the beginning of his career, his designs appeared with those of other artists, as did the six, engraved on steel, in Tom Moore's *Lalla Rookh* (1838). The one of a villainous Indian moved by the innocence of a child, for "The Peri's Second Pilgrimage", received the tribute of being adapted by John Tenniel for his once-celebrated 1861 edition. The seven carefully detailed wood engravings in a solo engagement with *The Faerie Queene* (1853) reduce Edmund Spenser's allegory to an adventure story set in a past devoid of wonder. Corbould seems to have found melodrama congenial, which is evident in the twenty-one large horizontal vignettes for *The Rye House Plot; or, Ruth, the Conspirator's Daughter* (1883), a sixpenny historical thriller by George William MacArthur Reynolds. Barbara Villiers, duchess of Cleveland and mistress of Charles II, demanding favors from the king in return for £25,000, which he needs to fill his empty

60. Edward Henry Corbould. George William MacArthur Reynolds, *The Rye House Plot; or, Ruth, the Conspirator's Daughter* (1883).

exchequer, is representative of Corbould's best work (fig. 60).

George Cruikshank

One of the most productive and individualistic of English illustrators, George Cruikshank (1792–1878) not only drew, but also etched hundreds of illustrations, most, it is said, on copperplates faced with steel. Excluding children's books, collections of humorous designs, and numerous didactic and other ephemeral works, the Catalog contains almost seventy titles. Cruikshank had no formal art training. He and his older brother, Robert (Isaac Robert), learned to draw and etch as young boys in the workshop of their father, Isaac, a popular caricaturist. In his early years, roughly 1811 to 1821, Cruikshank succeeded his father and James Gillray as England's chief artist in comic ephemerae of all sorts. His etchings gradually began to appear as book illustrations, although many of them came out first in periodicals or par s.

Cruikshank's fame as a book illustrator is generally associated with the novels of Charles Dickens, but before Dickens began writing for the *Monthly Magazine* in 1833, Cruikshank already was a successful illustrator. The thirty humorous aquatints in *Life of Napoleon: A Hudibrastic Poem* (1815), with verse "illustrations" by William Combe,

the earliest Cruikshank book in the Catalog, at times approach serious reporting. Also of historical interest are the twelve hand-colored etchings of life on a British man-of-war in Matthew Barker's *Greenwich Hospital* (1826). But Pierce Egan's *Life in London* (1821) and David Carey's *Life in Paris* (1822), emulations of Thomas Rowlandson's *Microcosm of London* (1808–10), were the first books to bring Cruikshank widespread public attention. The drawings are stiff (most of those in *Life in London* were by his brother Robert), and the coloring of the aquatints by unskilled hands is sometimes muddy.

Cruikshank moved away from Rowlandsonian social satire into interpretive illustration in his etched plates for two translations. His twelve designs in Volume 1 of *German Popular Stories* (1823), the first English translation of the Brothers Grimm collection *Kinder- und Hausmärchen* (1812), fixed the way we think of fairyland. The title-page vignette of three generations of a family seated in front of a huge fireplace, laughing as they listen to the stories being read, is one of the best-known English illustrations. The designs for "The Elves and the Shoemaker", "The Golden Goose", and "The Jew in the Bush" are marvelous illustrations. Cruikshank made no more concession to young readers than did the Grimms (in the objectionable third story, for instance). Yet Cruikshank's dozen etchings have enchanted and have stirred the imaginations of children and adults for 150 years. In 1826, he etched ten plates for Volume 2 of *German Popular Stories*. His eight illustrations for Adelbert von Chamisso's *Peter Schlemihl* (1823), the man who cast no shadow, are a revelation of his flair for the bizarre.

Memoirs of the Life and Writings of Lord Byron (1825) – extended quotation, running summary, and commentary compiled by George Clinton – is illustrated with forty-three unsigned and uncredited wood engravings attributed to Cruikshank by A. M. Cohn in *A Catalogue Raisonné of the Printed Works Illustrated by George Cruikshank* (1924). Some are dated between June 1824 and July 1825. Although these illustrations were probably not drawn by Cruikshank, for he routinely signed even his slightest sketches, they seem to have been made after his drawings. Without pretense to artistic distinction, they respond forcefully to Byron's verse. There are blocks as romantic as "Childe Harold at Zitza, near the Chimariot Mountains"; as charged with melodrama as "The Prisoner of Chillon", in which the prisoner is breaking his chains; and as amusing as "Beppo's Return", in which Laura is distracting Beppo from her infidelity with questions about and criticism of his beard. The series of six vignettes in William Cowper's comic poem *The Diverting History of John Gilpin* (1828) were also engraved on wood. They perfectly record the linen draper's wild ride on his wedding anniversary against a background of astonished rustics, dogs, and fowl in village streets. This little masterpiece sold for one shilling. The companion piece, *The Epping Hunt* (1830), Tom Hood's comic poem about a cockney tradesman who aspires above his class, is more obvious. John Huggins is one of the direct precursors of Mr. Pickwick. In *Life and Writings of Byron*, *John Gilpin*, *Epping Hunt*, and other books with wood engravings, Cruikshank had the good fortune of having John Thompson, Robert Branston, George Wilmot Bonner, and other fine engravers interpret his designs in the post-Bewick manner.

The twenty-four watercolor sketches, now in the Princeton University Library, from which Cruikshank etched the illustrations for *Punch and Judy* (1828) were reproduced in a 1937 edition of the book. The drawings were made in the Drury Lane lodgings of the puppeteer Piccini at a private performance for the publisher Septimus Prowett, Cruikshank, and John Payne Collier, who recorded the dialogue. The color sketches and the black-and-white illustrations affirm Cruikshank's close identification with the theater and comic pantomime and might be said to be forerunners of the animations of Walt Disney.

In 1831, besides doing surprisingly literal illustrations for Daniel Defoe's *Robinson Crusoe*, Cruikshank etched designs for four novels in the Novelists Library series,

edited by Thomas Roscoe: Tobias Smollett's *Humphrey Clinker*, *Roderick Random*, and *Peregrine Pickle*; and Henry Fielding's *Tom Jones*. They were followed in 1832 by others in the same series: Fielding's *Joseph Andrews* and *Amelia*; Oliver Goldsmith's *Vicar of Wakefield* and Smollett's *Sir Launcelot Greaves* in one volume; and Laurence Sterne's *Tristram Shandy*. It was a notable effort by the publisher James Cochrane to supply a wide public with inexpensive illustrated editions of novels that had become classics. Although the subjects are congenial, the plates are not attractive. Cruikshank used short scratchy outlines and overdid crosshatched shading on his small etched plates. The farcical scenes are far better than are those of critical importance to the main characters. Typically, he seized the opportunity to show Humphrey Clinker spilling the custard, stepping on the dog, and dropping the china as he serves dinner to the Brambles; Molly Seagrim in *Tom Jones* attacking her tormentors with a leg bone in the churchyard; and Parson Adams in *Joseph Andrews* sprawling in Parson Trulliber's pigsty. His six designs for *Tristram Shandy* are both too robust and too matter-of-fact to reflect Sterne's slithering humor.

In 1833, Cruikshank illustrated Miguel de Cervantes's *Don Quixote*, Alain René Le Sage's *Gil Blas*, John Wight's *Sunday in London*, and Defoe's *Journal of the Plague in London, 1665*. In his long career, he could hardly have found any texts more to his liking than Le Sage's picaresque satire and Cervantes's masterpiece. Some of the plates are marred by facetiousness. Don Quixote and Sancho Panza returning home, for instance, would have just the right degree of pathos and dignity but for Sancho's appearance as a comic fat boy. The fourteen small vignette street scenes in the episodic *Sunday in London* were well served by the wood engravers Bonner, Branston, John Jackson, and Williams. The four designs that Cruikshank drew for Defoe's *Journal of the Plague in London, 1665* were engraved on metal by another hand. Still, "The Great Pit in Aldgate" – showing men with torches about to unload a death cart into a huge pit – and "Solomon Eagle" – showing the Quaker stripped to his waist, eyes staring, a pot of fire on his head, and running through a narrow Whitechapel street with hands lifted, crying, "Spare us, Good Lord, Spare thy People!" – are unforgettable designs thoroughly in harmony with Defoe's grim prose. Cruikshank owed something to Henry Corbould's illustrations for an 1819 edition, and, in turn, Cruikshank's interpretations were the inspiration for the illustrations in an 1863 edition, for which Frederick Shields has been highly praised.

As a true-born Londoner, an artist who could toss off city types and scenes from memory, an etcher who had an inimitable style, and the possessor of an enthusiastic middle-class following, Cruikshank brought a great deal to the illustration of the works of Charles Dickens. Furthermore, both had been immersed in the social criticism of William Hogarth and of Gillray at an early age and saw life in much the same extreme terms, leavened by tolerant laughter. The alliance between Cruikshank and Dickens was limited, but fruitful. (One fruit has been lengthy discussion, which we will not prolong, of the extent of Dickens's indebtedness to Cruikshank for suggestions.) Their relation began in the *Monthly Magazine* of December 1833 and yielded two series of *Sketches by Boz*. The production resembled Rowlandson's *Doctor Syntax* and *Microcosm of London* and the Cruikshank brothers' edition of Egan's *Life in London*. Dickens was then a novice of twenty-four and Cruikshank, an established artist of forty-four.

The sixteen etched vignettes in the First Series of *Sketches by Boz* (1836) illustrate only about half the prose sketches. Young Dickens's aim of presenting "little pictures of life and manners as they really are" sometimes led him into tasteless satire and sometimes, as in "A Visit to Newgate" and "Gin Shops", into pompous preaching. Cruikshank's etchings, with their incisive authenticity, good humor, and lack of sentimentality, had much to do with the favorable public response to the *Sketches* and to Boz himself. In the Second Series of *Sketches by Boz* (1837), Cruikshank's designs for the breakfast-stand in "Streets by Morning", the secondhand clothes stall of Monmouth Street, a pickpocket being trundled off to the police station in a wheelbarrow, and two women quarreling in the street at Seven Dials give us unforgettable impressions of London life at the beginning of Victoria's reign.

Oliver Twist (1838), which appeared in three volumes, is one of the few illustrated books that is well enough known to be considered famous. Of the fifty-one chapters, twenty-five are illustrated with etched vignettes. The success of Cruikshank's most famous illustrations has to be judged in the light of the melodramatic nature of Dickens's novel. Both men loved amateur dramatics and sought to achieve effects, whether literary or graphic, that were inherently theatrical. Dickens made Oliver singularly obtuse and must have concurred in Cruikshank's picturing him in the early chapters as a ninny, a boy with a young man's head. Dickens and his times were responsible for the characterization of Fagin with anti-Semitic prejudice, but Cruikshank was responsible for the brutal caricature. Dickens gave ignoble roles to Bill Sikes, the Artful Dodger, and Noah Claypole, but Cruikshank dehumanized them. The most satisfactory illustrations in *Oliver Twist* are the humorous ones: "Mr. Bumble and Mrs. Corney taking tea" (fig. 61), "Mr. Claypole as he appeared when his master was out", and "Mr. Bumble degraded in the eyes of the Pauper". In scenes

that include Oliver, the well-known one of the Dodger picking the pocket of the old gentleman at the bookstall and the one of Nancy and Sikes catching Oliver outside the bookshop have the appeal of their realistic London street settings.

Oliver sees little action in the illustrations in the second half of the book. They are given over to the unfolding of the absurdities of Monks's plot against Oliver and of Nancy's counterplot. The climax forced Cruikshank into unrestrained sensationalism. The murderer Sikes trying to escape is depicted mad with terror on the rooftop (he falls off and neatly hangs himself in his own noose, while his dog jumps after him and dashes its brains out). Fagin, also mad with terror, bites his nails in the jail cell. The cell scene has been repeatedly praised as a great illustration and a great etching. It is undeniably memorable. But it is difficult to believe that any readers but those of tender years or conventual innocence can look on it or on the illustration of Sikes on the roof with any serious concern. As for the quality of Cruikshank's etching in this plate, Fagin's face, with its irisless eyes, might be that of a comic-strip character.

It is a pity that Dickens did not realize that Cruikshank would have been particularly well suited to illustrate *Pickwick Papers* (1837). Collaboration was made very difficult because each had to be the star. Cruikshank did etch twelve vignettes for the *Memoirs* (1838) of the clown Joseph Grimaldi, which Dickens edited. The stage scenes are done with affection.

Cruikshank's association with Harrison Ainsworth began with *Rookwood* (1836). The other Ainsworth books that he illustrated followed the last of his Dickens books. Ainsworth wrote without grace, economy, or humor. He tied his stories closely to well-known historical settings – as indicated by the titles *The Tower of London* (1840), *Guy Fawkes* (1841), *Windsor Castle* (1843), and *St. James's* (1844) – which led Cruikshank into the error of making self-conscious drawings of buildings. Ainsworth's wooden narratives permitted Cruikshank little scope for comic liberties. In numerous scenes, such as those in *The Miser's Daughter* (1842) (with a Westminster Abbey purlieu) in which the miser Scarve discovers the loss of the mortgage money and Abel Beechcroft finds the body of Scarve in the grave dug in the cellar, Cruikshank failed to rise above the level of a boy's thriller.

The best series of illustrations that Cruikshank made for Ainsworth's books is the one for *Jack Sheppard* (1839). The twenty-seven etched plates are larger than Cruikshank's usual vignettes and are enclosed in borders. They record the highwayman's imprisonment, escapes, and captures on his path to Tyburn. As etchings, these illustrations

61. George Cruikshank. Charles Dickens, *Oliver Twist* (1838).

are poor; they were drawn with indecisive lines and were shaded with disorderly crosshatching. This spoils the effects in what are excellent interpretations of Ainsworth's lurid melodrama.

A few other books that Cruikshank illustrated are worth noting. His assignment to supply "scenes of mirth, of merriment, of humour" in a forty-eight-volume edition of Sir Walter Scott's *Waverley Novels* (1836–39) was the publisher's misjudgment. In association with Scott's texts and the designs after J. M. W. Turner and other academic landscape and historical painters, his comic etchings seem out of place. The two etched scenes aboard men-of-war – "Saturday Night at Sea" and "Tars Carousing" – make Charles Dibdin's *Songs: Naval and National* (1841) a book for which one would gladly leave shelf space. Cruikshank's trite text in his *Bachelor's Own Book: Being the Progress of Mr. Lambkin, Gent.* (1844) is offset by twenty-four amusing, if unspontaneous, etchings. They are more attractive when properly colored. Lambkin's journey from foolish bachelorhood to connubial bliss is no *Rake's Progress*, but the plates are a treasury of early-Victorian interiors. Lambkin sitting glumly on a bench in a barn while waiting for a farmer's wife to finish milking a cow is an example of what Cruikshank's etching looks like when he took pains. Cruikshank was well attuned to Charles Lever's *Arthur O'Leary* (1844). His five etchings for the humorous, high-spirited, and

anecdotal account of O'Leary's (Lever's) European wanderings are just right. For instance, the *Maire de Grivet* imperturbably waiting for the *notaire* to draw up a *procès verbal* before releasing the plump O'Leary, who has been bound to a tree (against his will, he insists), is funny to the same degree as the text. Lever may have employed Cruikshank rather than Hablot Browne just this one time because Browne was fully occupied with Dickens's *Martin Chuzzlewit* (1844) and with Lever's *Tom Burke of "Ours"* (1844).

Late in his career, Cruikshank proved his extraordinary reportorial powers in the twenty-one plates that he etched for William Hamilton Maxwell's one-sided *History of the Irish Rebellion in 1798* (1845). They reconstruct in unflinching detail the atrocities recorded in Maxwell's pages. Cruikshank reveled in scenes crowded with dozens of figures, such as "The Camp on Vinegar Hill". In the background, the commanding officer conducts business outside his tent while a priest says Mass; in the foreground, camp followers prepare a meal while a group execution takes place nearby. "The rebels storming 'The Turret' at Lord Tyrrell's" is one of Cruikshank's fine etchings.

In 1903 appeared a sumptuous edition of John Bunyan's *Pilgrim's Progress*, "Illustrated with 25 Drawings on Wood by George Cruikshank from the Collection of Edwin Truman". These are not Cruikshank's drawings, but wood engravings of them. Many are signed "GC^K", as are those

62. Robert Cruikshank. Charles Molloy Westmacott, *The English Spy* (1825–26).

in Richard Harris Barham's *Ingoldsby Legends* (1840, 1842) and other wood blocks, and one is signed by the engraver "Dalziel". Cruikshank drew the designs around 1860, according to Truman, who did not say why they had not been used then. They suffer from Cruikshank's search for the sensational rather than for the sense of the text and from the dulling effect of mechanical shading. "Vanity Fair" is the design in which Cruikshank is most himself.

How quickly Cruikshank passed beyond the limits of his capacity to feel and interpret can be seen in such books as *The Beauties of Washington Irving* (1835), in which he caught the humor but missed the humanity; Francis Smedley's *Frank Fairleigh* (1850), in which the unamusing scenes of school days, society, and domesticity fall flat; Harriet Beecher Stowe's *Uncle Tom's Cabin* (1852), which includes a series of tasteless caricatures that, as William Feaver says in *George Cruikshank* (1974), "brings out the worst in him", including his caricatures of blacks; and Robert Brough's *Life of Sir John Falstaff* (1858), in which his efforts to secure historical authenticity led to a loss of verve and character. When Cruikshank deserted comedy and melodrama, he often became commonplace.

Cruikshank was at his best as an interpretive illustrator in those few books and chapters of books that permitted him to exercise his talent for comic exaggeration without distorting the author's intent. With Hogarth and Rowland-

son, he helped create a spirited English style that was to have a strong influence on Victorian book illustration, especially of the humorous sort. That Cruikshank etched most of his hundreds of illustrations instead of having them engraved demonstrated the soundness of etching as a medium for illustration, even though wood engraving proved to be less expensive and more durable. His etching varied greatly; it was often hasty and ordinary, but the ease and sureness of his line as he created his extraordinary characters and exuberant street scenes put George Cruikshank, at least occasionally, in the company of Jacques Callot, Adriaen van Ostade, and Francisco de Goya.

Isaac Robert Cruikshank

Although he was not the equal of his younger brother, George, as draftsman, etcher, caricaturist, or master of laughter and indignation, Robert Cruikshank (1789–1856) – he soon dropped the Isaac – was a shrewd enough observer and a good enough draftsman to have left a valuable record of the recreations of high and low society during the unsavory reign of George IV. This record is embodied principally in early work: the thirty-six plates in Pierce Egan's immediately popular *Life in London* (1821), which he shared with George, although he is said to have designed most of the plates; sixty-six of the sixty-nine plates in Charles

63. Richard Doyle. William Makepeace Thackeray, *The Newcomes* (1854–55).

Molloy Westmacott's *English Spy* (1825–26), with its revelations of life at Eton, Oxford, Bath, Brighton, and London; and thirty-five of the thirty-six plates in Egan's sequel, *Finish to the Adventures of Tom, Jerry, and Logic* (1829). The full-page plates in these and a few other books are hand-colored aquatints, with the application of the color sometimes little better than that of a daub, which perhaps it sometimes was. Properly applied, the watercolor gives body to crowded scenes of eating, drinking, gaming, wenching, slumming, and other often brutish entertainments of the day. One of Cruikshank's less crowded and better drawn compositions from *The English Spy*, "Capping a Proctor", preserves an example of high spirits at Oxford (fig. 62).

Color covers the shortcomings of Cruikshank's drawings. His uncolored etching was amateurish when he went beyond outlining, as in *Divine Emblems* (1837), some of the plates in *The Playfair Papers* (1841), and Matthew Barker's *Jem Bunt* (1841) and *The Old Sailor's Jolly Boat* (1844). *The Playfair Papers: or, Brother Jonathan, the Smartest Nation in All Creation* shows Cruikshank's ability to develop images from texts. For this anti-Yankee account by the mythical Hugo Playfair, he created a sense of believability, as in an aquatint of a turbulent communal meal.

Like his brother, Cruikshank was lucky to have many of his drawings given a new, unmistakable personality by being translated by practitioners of modified-Bewick wood engraving. These clean-cut vignettes appear in a number of volumes, particularly twenty-five by Sears in *Don Quixote* (1824); thirty-seven by George Wilmot Bonner in Egan's *Life in London* (1821); twenty (unsigned) in Westmacott's *Points of Misery* (1823); eighty-five by Samuel Slader, Bonner, and others in Jonathan Birch's *Fifty-One Original Fables* (1833); and thirty-nine by Slader in the three-volume *Cruikshank at Home* (1840?).

Even at its best, the etched work of Robert Cruikshank has largely only a documentary appeal. But the color plates and wood engravings after his drawings make up a body of well-conceived illustrations that is too substantial and interesting to be neglected.

Richard Doyle

By trade a professional humorist, *Punch* artist Richard (Dicky) Doyle (1824–83) is remembered for his long-familiar cover of *Punch*, his drawings in three of Charles Dickens's Christmas books, and his sixteen large wood engravings, printed in color by Edmund Evans and published with William Allingham's poem *In Fairyland* (1870). Although without formal art training, Doyle was a versatile draftsman whose humorous work was strengthened by an admixture of realism. Indeed, the forty amusing illustrations of London locales and institutions – such as Hyde Park, Madame Tussaud's, and cricket at Lord's – in Percival Leigh's *Manners and Customs of Ye Englyshe, Drawn from Ye Qvick by Rychard Doyle* (1849) now have genuine documentary value. And the frontispiece to John Ruskin's quaint morality, *The King of the Golden River* (1851) – bugle-nosed South West Wind, Esq., demanding entrance at a door – is an extraordinary evocation of young Ruskin's fantastic creation. (The nose was altered in later editions.) Doyle's most characteristic sustained work probably is in his *Foreign Tour of Messrs. Brown, Jones, and Robinson* (1854), based on a visit to the Continent with friends. But his only important illustrations for a serious literary work are the forty-four etched full-page plates and forty-three wood-engraved vignettes in William Makepeace Thackeray's *Newcomes* (1854–55). Although his individual characterizations are not exceptional, Doyle was remarkably good at crowded group scenes, such as the wonderfully fecund street brawl of "Newcome vs. Newcome" at a political rally (fig. 63). Some of Doyle's best drawings are among the eighteen vignette headpieces in *A Selection from the Works of Frederick Locker* (1865). They include a Piccadilly street scene, a gentleman tying a lady's shoe in a field, and three couples playing croquet in the garden of the Villa Aldobrandini. The last exemplifies Richard Doyle's special blend of humor and accurate social reporting: although the setting is Rome, the scene is a precious bit of Victoriana.

Myles Birket Foster

Encouraged by the wood engraver Ebenezer Landells, to whom he was apprenticed, Birket Foster (1825–99) became an artist. He opened his career as an illustrator with a congenial book, Thomas Miller's *Country Year Book* (1847). Of the 140 illustrations, he did about half, all of which are landscapes and rustic scenes with unobtrusive human figures – his stock in trade for the rest of his career. Between 1850 and 1860, Foster drew an astonishing number of illustrations for books and periodicals, and he painted assiduously, chiefly in watercolor. Foster was a landscape artist, not an interpretive illustrator. For many of the books to which he contributed illustrations, another artist drew the narrative designs. When he did include figures, they tend to be documentary, as in "Whitsuntide", an outdoor dance, and "Hop-Picking" in *The Country Year Book*.

Foster first attracted attention as an illustrator with his thirty-one designs for Henry Wadsworth Longfellow's *Evangeline* (1850), and other Longfellow assignments

64. Birket Foster. William Wordsworth, *Poems of William Wordsworth* (1859).

followed. He went to Scotland to do the scenic effects for four of Sir Walter Scott's verse tales, while John Gilbert drew the action pictures. Foster drew twenty-eight designs for *The Lady of the Lake* (1853), forty-five for *The Lay of the Last Minstrel* (1854), forty-six for *Marmion* (1855), and thirty-eight for *The Lord of the Isles* (1857). These designs are attractive vignettes engraved on wood by Foster's friend Edmund Evans. A composite Foster drawing might seem to be a distant castle on a mountain seen by moonlight through an arch of trees over a rocky stream. But the variety is much greater than is at first apparent. Foster was a competent architectural draftsman and drew a number of buildings and ruins in the Scott series. The combined talents of Foster and Gilbert made the illustrations almost ideal for Victorian readers, while the thirty-three designs in James Beattie's *Minstrel* (1858) are one of the best of Foster's solo series on wood.

Because he specialized in landscapes, Foster found a place for most of his work in books of poetry in company with other artists. Among these volumes are Robert Willmott's anthology *The Poets of the Nineteenth Century* (1857), twenty-six designs; Charles Mackay's collection *The Home Affections, Pourtrayed by the Poets* (1858), twenty; James Thomson's *Seasons* (1859), twenty-one; *Poems of William Wordsworth* (1859), seventy-one; and *The Poems of James Montgomery* (1860), forty. In these five books, Foster main-

tained his high quality and changeless style. Because his spirit was so akin to that of Wordsworth, it seems fitting to reproduce a typical Foster illustration from that series – the one for "The Fountain", which shows the young poet and old Matthew seated beside a brook (fig. 64).

Foster entered a new phase in 1856, with the publication of *Sabbath Bells Chimed by the Poets*. Evans added four oil-based colors to wood engravings of fifteen Sabbath-oriented designs. *Sabbath Bells* is one of the most charming English books of the mid-nineteenth century. Other books with color added to Foster's designs are *The Poems of Oliver Goldsmith* (1859), *Odes and Sonnets* (1859), and *A Book of Favourite Modern Ballads* (1860), which Evans printed in bright colors. Evans and Foster finally arrived at outlines and color blocks in Miller's *Common Wayside Flowers* (1863). The largest and most fully worked up wood engravings after Foster's designs are the thirty in *Birket Foster's Pictures of English Landscape. With Pictures in Words by Tom Taylor* (1863). This collection of prints attests to the popularity of Foster's work among persons who could not afford his watercolors. As J. M. W. Turner's steel engravings popularized the wilder aspects of nature, Foster's wood engravings helped make appealing the tamer aspects as well as country life. But when around 1860 the sale of his watercolors permitted, Foster cut down on the tedious task of making drawings on small pieces of wood.

SIR PATRICK SPENS

THE king sits in Dunfermline town,
    Drinking the blude-red wine:
'O where will I get a skeely skipper
    To sail this new ship of mine?'

O up and spake an eldern knight,
    Sat at the kings right knee:
'Sir Patrick Spens is the best sailor
    That ever sailed the sea.'

Our king has written a braid letter,
    And sealed it with his hand,
And sent it to Sir Patrick Spens,
    Was walking on the strand.

65. John Franklin. *The Book of British Ballads* (1842).

Birket Foster's illustrations are open to the charge of similarity and sentimentality, but they were close to the heart of the nineteenth-century reading public and so have a special place in any account of Victorian illustration.

John Franklin

A sound draftsman with an immediately recognizable Germanic shaded-outline style, Irish-born John Franklin (ca. 1800–68) had little chance to assert himself in the books that he shared with other illustrators. He was a good illustrator, consistently searching out centers of interest and inventing expressive, if not especially original, designs for them. His designs have the virtues of being decorative, easy to engrave on wood in facsimile, and agreeably related to the type-page. He etched some of his designs.

Franklin's most ambitious assignments were fifty-six of the illustrations for the First Series of *The Book of British Ballads* (1842), edited by Samuel Carter Hall, and forty for the Second Series (1844). In both volumes, the several artists had to adapt their drawings to fit awkward spaces and shapes on pages with stanzas of the ballads. Franklin's headpiece illustration for "Sir Patrick Spens" shows how well he solved even so difficult a problem as a three-quarter page (fig. 65). The sleeping toper and the curved staircase fill the lower quarter admirably, while the "eldern knight" answering the king's first-stanza question sets the stage. An almost pre-Pre-Raphaelite touch is the emphasis given such accessories as the lantern and the wine carafe and goblet carried by the boys on the stairs. Franklin encapsulated the rest of the ballad in three more illustrations: the richly gowned Sir Patrick receiving from a page the king's dread orders to sail in spite of threatening weather; a terrified sailor clinging to the shattered mast of the sunken ship while two others hang on to him desperately and another clasps his hands in prayer as he is about to drown; and, a century before Eric Gill, a group of their ladies entwined in an L-shaped floral scroll and grieving for their dead with an agonized intensity demanded by the great ballad and unknown to Gill.

Jean Ignace Isadore Gérard. See Grandville.

Sir John Gilbert

Largely self-taught, John Gilbert (1817–97) in 1871 was knighted by Queen Victoria and was elected president of the Royal Water-Colour Society, even though his main professional activity was making drawings on wood to be engraved, mostly by the Dalziel brothers, for periodical and book illustrations. A bachelor, he lived all his eighty years in the London suburb of Blackheath. Spurred by love of money, he was noted for his dependability, speed, and extraordinary productivity. As a consequence, it would seem, too many of his designs consist of two or three figures that fade into a vague crosshatched background. (The background parts of his wood blocks usually were lowered so that the foreground figures stand out.) Gilbert seldom individualized characters beyond elaborating the costumes of persons of rank, and he only fitfully took much interest in settings. In the majority of the books that he illustrated, he seems not to have entered imaginatively into the emotional life of the characters. In a few important exceptions, however, his interpretations are as natural and appealing as those of any nineteenth-century illustrator.

Among Gilbert's early books, Richard Harris Barham's *Ingoldsby Legends* (1840, 1842), Miguel de Cervantes's *Don Quixote* (1841), William Cowper's *Poems* (1841), and Samuel Carter Hall's collection *The Book of British Ballads* (1842) give evidence of Gilbert's prodigal talents. In *Don Quixote*, the rather quiet moments he chose show the knight and Sancho Panza looking more as we imagine Cervantes thought they looked than they usually do. The depictions of Sancho sitting on a stool at the feet of the duchess and protesting that he is unfit to govern an island and of him as governor holding an audience could hardly be better. The twenty-two designs for three poems in the First Series of *The Book of British Ballads* (1842) reveal Gilbert's flair for medieval costumes. Costumes are also the main element in the exotic atmosphere of *The Arabian Nights' Entertainments* (1844). About a dozen of Gilbert's forty-six illustrations for Charles Mackay's *Salamandrine* (1853) offset the banality of the poem. George and Edward Dalziel proudly reproduced one – a large vignette of the preparation of a marriage feast, with the groom's mother presiding over a mountain of food and drink – in *The Brothers Dalziel: A Record of Fifty Years' Work, 1840–1890* (1901). Through the 1850s, Gilbert contributed 150 illustrations to 4 of Sir Walter Scott's verse tales. Birket Foster shared the bulk of the task with him, and J. M. W. Turner had a steel-engraved frontispiece and a title-page vignette in each volume. In *The Lady of the Lake* (1853), Gilbert's twenty-nine illustrations and the Highlands scenes by Foster were engraved on wood to resemble steel engraving. Gilbert was in his element in this and in the succeeding volumes: *The Lay of the Last Minstrel* (1854), fifty-five designs; *Marmion* (1855), thirty-four; and *The Lord of the Isles* (1857), thirty-two. Gilbert's facility in drawing groups of warlike and costumed figures in motion is conspicuous throughout the four books. His drawings, such as the one in *The Lay of the Last Minstrel* of Margaret manning a cannon on the ramparts with her soldiers, are more eloquent than are Scott's

66. John Gilbert. William Shakespeare, *King Lear* in *The Plays of William Shakespeare* (1858).

Humpty-Dumpty couplets: "The noble Dame, amid the broil,/Shared the grey Seneschal's high toil." Harrison Ainsworth also gave Gilbert scope for his special talents in *The Lancashire Witches* (1854) and *The Flitch of Bacon* (1854).

In 1857 appeared *The Poets of the Nineteenth Century*, with thirteen of Gilbert's illustrations scattered among those of other leading Victorian illustrators, including Foster, William Harvey, Frederick Pickersgill, Arthur Hughes, John Everett Millais, and John Tenniel. Three or four of his designs, such as one for Heman's "Coronation of Inez de Castro", stand out. The approximately 100 illustrations by Gilbert in *The Poetical Works of Henry Wadsworth Longfellow* (1856) include a number printed earlier in volumes of individual poems. The collected edition contains a hodgepodge of shapes, but it is appealing because of the unexpected studies of old trees, a vase of flowers, beguiling children, the decorating of an altar, a village smithy, a family musicale, a Spanish herdsman blowing a horn, and the monks of Croyland making merry at Christmas. In these illustrations, Gilbert seems to have entered into the life of what he was illustrating. (He also borrowed George Cattermole's Maypole Inn from *Barnaby Rudge* [1841].)

The chief accomplishment of Gilbert's career are the 831 illustrations in Howard Staunton's edition of *The Plays of William Shakespeare* (1858), in three handsome volumes. This is one of the memorable English illustrated works. It came out first in parts between 1856 and 1858 at the bargain price of one shilling a play. Gilbert labored for four years to produce his incredible number of designs for the thirty-seven plays – an average of twenty-two designs for each play, including a full-page frontispiece for each. The sonnets and four other poems were added at the end of the third volume. Most of the illustrations of the plays are vignettes of various sizes that were placed above the two-column text and tailpieces that were placed at the end of scenes. Gilbert faltered in some of his interpretations and often in his drawing, especially of faces, hands, and horses. But the intelligence of his reading of the plays, the naturalness of the behavior of his characters, the sustained diversity, and the opulence of his designs make this one of the most successful illustrated editions of Shakespeare, the greatest challenge to any illustrator.

In his wood engravings, Gilbert was able to illustrate a great many scenes that had never before been illustrated. They embrace not only much more of the action of each play, but also many more of the subordinate characters and changing moods, an impossibility for an artist limited to two or three or often only one design for each play. In *The Merchant of Venice*, for instance, Gilbert followed

Shylock outdoors after he has agreed to the harsh terms at the end of the trial scene (IV.i). He imagined Shylock as leaning on a stick in bitter defeat, no longer an object of revilement but one of compassion. In *Romeo and Juliet*, after killing Tybalt in a duel, Romeo hides in Friar Lawrence's cell (III.iii). Again, without textual authority but credibly nevertheless, Gilbert chose an imaginary moment when Romeo kneels before a crucifix and holds his head in anguish as the friar tells him of his banishment from Verona and Juliet. Gilbert was always at his best in drawing noble and military figures in all their trappings. In this edition of Shakespeare, he presented them in many impressive groups with more than usual care for detail, but also with sensitive revelation of their feelings, as in the early scene (I.i) in which King Lear rejects Cordelia while Goneril and Regan watch scornfully (fig. 66).

Gilbert's later books offer no surprises. *Poems of William Wordsworth* (1859) belongs mainly to Foster. Gilbert's share of the 100 illustrations was only 17. A few, such as one of the poet leaning over a rustic gate and listening to the disputatious child in "We Are Seven" and one of Sir Eustace and Hubert, his false brother, on horseback before the gate in "The Horn of Egremont Castle", enliven the volume. Gilbert drew forty-one designs for *The Poems of James Montgomery* (1860). They include twelve vignettes for "The World before the Flood" that help elevate Montgomery's effort to be Miltonic. The eight designs in Alexander Pope's *Poetical Works* (1866) misfire, with the exception of the concept for the crucial moment in *The Rape of the Lock*. Belinda sits demure, lovely, and natural as she listens to the compliments of a coffee-sipping admirer, while the Baron, scissors at the ready, leans on the back of her chair, and the naughty Clarissa watches in the rear. In *The Book of Brave Old Ballads* (1879?), perhaps meant for the young, the sixteen full-page designs are vigorous but unusual only as colored wood engravings after designs by Gilbert.

Grandville [Jean Ignace Isadore Gérard]

Although the works of the French master of anthropomorphic fantasy, Jean Ignace Isadore Gérard (1803–47), who signed himself Grandville, were first published in Paris, they became well known in England. Grandville has a place in English book illustration mainly by reason of having had some influence on Lewis Carroll and John Tenniel. Among the English editions of books that he illustrated, however, Daniel Defoe's *Robinson Crusoe* (1840) is marked by the convincing naturalism of its approximately 300 designs.

67. William Harvey. Edward T. Bennett, *The Tower Menagerie* (1829).

William Harvey

William Harvey (1796–1866), Thomas Bewick's most successful apprentice, went on in 1817 to study art and anatomy in London and then succeeded John Thurston as the leading designer for wood-engraved book illustrations in the 1830s and 1840s. His assistance on Bewick's *Fables of Aesop and Some Others* (1818) had a lasting effect on him. In time, Harvey became an animal artist of distinction. He "adapted or freely translated on the blocks for the engravers" the pasted-up cut-out suggestions of the eighty-year-old painter James Northcote for Northcote's *One Hundred Fables, Original and Selected* (1828) and *Fables, Original and Selected* (1833). In addition, Harvey supplied an illustrative initial and a tailpiece for each of the 201 fables. The strong contrasts and the combination of black-line and white-line wood engraving by John Jackson, Charlton Nesbit, the team of Robert Branston and Wright, and several other practitioners of the modified-Bewick technique produce bright modern effects. Harvey's tailpieces are literary scenes that ingeniously illustrate the "applications" of the fables.

Concerning the fifty-eight vignette headpieces and fifty-eight tailpieces for *The Tower Menagerie* (1829), the author-editor Edward T. Bennett wrote that Harvey "confined himself to the chastity of truth" in "seizing faithful charac-

teristic portraits of animals in restless and almost incessant motion". These "portraits", often of pairs of animals, were smartly engraved on wood by Branston and Wright. There followed the companion work, *The Gardens and Menagerie of the Zoological Society Delineated* (1830–31), also under Bennett's supervision. For Volume I, *Quadrupeds* (1830), Harvey and the same two engravers produced a frontispiece, sixty-four headpieces, and thirty-nine tailpieces. For Volume II, *Birds* (1831), they did a frontispiece, seventy-three headpieces, and fifty-one tailpieces. With *The Tower Menagerie* series, this comes to an impressive total of 197 main life studies and 148 tailpieces, 345 blocks in all. These studies of animals and birds drawn from life – especially those of the lioness and cubs (fig. 67), jaguar on a cliff edge, Malaysian rusadeer, and Indian antelope in *The Tower Menagerie* and of the Barbary mouse, Indian ox, zebu, and wild turkey in the Zoological Society volumes – seem more animated and captivating by far than do those of Bewick, who had had few live models in Northumberland.

Harvey probably designed nineteen or twenty of the twenty-two illustrations in John Bunyan's *Pilgrim's Progress* (1830). Several have his signature, and two are after paintings by John Martin: "The Valley of the Shadow of Death" and "Celestial City". The faithful recording of the narrative and the fine wood engraving make this one of the most agreeable editions of this classic. The 100 designs by

68. Thomas Landseer. Robert Burns, *Tam O' Shanter and Souter Johnny* (1830).

Harvey for an 1850 edition, engraved by the Dalziels, are more inclusive, but they do not have the directness and relevance of this series. Daniel Defoe's *Robinson Crusoe* (1831), "Illustrated with forty-six characteristic wood-engravings, finely executed from drawings by William Harvey", is another English classic in an edition long popular with Victorian readers, although it contains no innovations.

The steel-engraved frontispieces and title-page vignettes in the fifteen-volume edition *Life and Works of William Cowper* (1836) include scenes and figures associated with Cowper's life as well as illustrations of the text, such as John Gilpin's ride and Odysseus and his men among the beasts on the Isle of Circe. They reveal not only Harvey's versatility, but also the suitability of steel for translating his drawings. The growing skill of the practitioners of reproductive wood engraving, however, led to ill-advised imitation of steel engraving. The result was a seeming decline in Harvey's powers during the remaining twenty years of his career. He seems to have suffered no loss of invention or skill in drawing, but his designs were often too small and too crowded for the new fashion. Therefore, the more than 500 illustrations for Knight's often reprinted three-volume edition of *The Thousand and One Nights* (1839–41) – forty engravers are said to have been kept busy on the blocks – 37 for Thomas Campbell's *Poetical Works*

(1840), 120 [50?] for *The Poetical Works of John Milton* (1843), 100 for Bunyan's *Pilgrim's Progress* (1850), 14 for Robert Willmott's anthology *The Poets of the Nineteenth Century* (1857), and almost 100 for Defoe's *Robinson Crusoe* (1858) are, with some exceptions, more impressive for numbers than for originality.

Harvey's most pleasing late work appears in three books. His 450 vignettes for the Reverend John G. Wood's *Illustrated Natural History* (1853), although small, are a good substitute for photographs. His 67 main illustrations of the 126 in John Gay's *Fables* (1854) lack the satirical edge of their text and the artifice of the eighteenth-century couplets, but the confrontations between human and animal characters are lively. And the 117 delightful drawings of birds, bugs, flowers, and rustic scenes in Alphonse Karr's *Tours Round My Garden* (1859) ensure that although he did not make the most of his possibilities as an interpretive illustrator, William Harvey earned a secure place in the ranks of illustrators of fable and nature books.

Thomas Landseer

Among the most amusing examples of English literary illustrations are the two short series by Thomas Landseer (1795–1880), brother of the Victorian painter Sir Edwin Landseer. They are in companion poems by Robert Burns,

An Address to the Deil and *Tam O'Shanter and Souter Johnny*, issued by different publishers in 1830. For the first, Landseer designed a full-page view of hell, a head-piece, and seven vignette illustrations of the crimes against mankind for which the poet blames the Devil. They range from terrifying benighted travelers to taunting Job in his direst misery. For *Tam O'Shanter*, Landseer drew four full-page vignettes and a small title-page portrait of Tam. Because this poem is a single climactic episode – and the dialect is not impenetrable – the four illustrations form an almost perfect sequence of images. Only the realism of the "sulky sullen dame" nursing her wrath at home clashes with the humerous tone of the poem. This lapse is offset by the rollicking scene of Tam and Souter Johnny drinking and singing the stormy night away in the local alehouse. On the way home, the frightened mare Meg communicates to the drunken Tam her terror of the threatening super-natural forces (fig. 68). But Tam soon spies on a revel of witches, warlocks, and the Devil and is bewitched by one of them, Nan, dancing wildly in her cutty sark (short chemise). The drawing of this merrymaking includes a wasplike crea-ture dancing with Nan and a wolf playing the bagpipes, closely related to the creations of Grandville and Walt Disney. Tam's admiring cry of "Weel done, Cutty-sark [naughty girl]!" angers the revelers, breaks up the party, and sends Tam and Meg in flight. The final design shows Meg bearing the terrified Tam to safety by springing across a stream (Scottish witches cannot cross running water), leaving only a fistful of her tail in the grasp of the furious Nan. These eleven main illustrations – superbly engraved by George Wilmot Bonner, Gorway, Ebenezer Landells, Charlton Nesbit, Samuel Slader, John Thompson, and Williams – warrant Landseer a mention in the annals of English books. They also exemplify good interpretive illus-tration and demonstrate the superiority of post-Bewick white-line wood engraving for illustrating over the facsimile work of the Dalziels, Swain, and other mid-Victorians.

Edward Lear

In spite of appalling personal problems, Edward Lear (1812–88) achieved fame as an artist in three fields: natural history, landscape, and humor. Apart from his more than 400 immensely expressive and humorous lithographed sketches that accompany the limericks in his four *Nonsense* books, originally begun to entertain the children of the earl of Derby at Knowsley Hall, Lear never attempted literary illustration. (The vignettes and plates in Tennyson's *Poems* [1889] are landscapes.) It might be noted that Lear used lithography for his astonishing *Illustrations of the Family of Psittacidae, or Parrots* (1832) and for most of his fine travel books. But to a vast public, Lear is known for only the limerick illustrations, which he tossed off with blithe disregard for academic proprieties. Like the limer-icks, they are uneven in quality. Among the better ones is the drawing in *A Book of Nonsense* (1846) (fig. 69) for

There was an Old Man with an owl, who continued to
bother and howl;
He sate on a rail, and imbibed bitter ale,
Which refreshed that Old Man and his owl.

John Leech

After attending Charterhouse School and studying medi-cine for two years at St. Bartholomew's Hospital, John Leech (1817–64) learned etching from George Cruikshank. From the time he joined *Punch* in 1842, a year after its founding, until his death, he was one of its mainstays, and much of his book work appeared first in *Punch*. He offset the vulgarity of some of his ridicule of people whom middle-class Victorians considered vulgar by the care that he took to bring out the beauty of young women and thoroughbred horses. With a few exceptions, the books in which Leech's designs appear are humorous at a level of obviousness that makes good draftsmanship a sufficient substitute for imagination or subtlety.

Having applied unsuccessfully for the deceased Robert Seymour's job as illustrator of *Pickwick Papers* (1837), Leech was lucky to be chosen by Charles Dickens to illustrate *A Christmas Carol* (1843), probably because Hablot Browne was busy drawing the illustrations for *Martin Chuzzlewit* (1844). He also was lucky that Dickens had color added by hand to four small etched vignettes. Four even smaller designs were wood-engraved tailpieces. Leech's drawings record some instantly famous scenes, and like Browne before him, he borrowed from that fame. We still look on the frontispiece of the Fezziwigg Ball and the final wood engraving of Scrooge and Bob Cratchit enjoying a cup of punch together with a suffusion of good will that obscures their technical deficiencies. Leech was only one of the illustrators of Dickens's four subsequent Christmas stories, but he was the leading one. He drew five of the thirteen designs in *The Chimes* (1845), seven of the fourteen in *The Cricket on the Hearth* (1846), three of the fourteen in *The Battle of Life* (1847), and five of the sixteen in *The Haunted Man* (1848) – twenty of fifty-seven or, counting *A Christmas Carol*, twenty-eight of sixty-five. The other illustrators were Daniel Maclise, Richard Doyle, Clarkson Stanfield, Edward Landseer, John Tenniel, and Frank Stone. In 1852, the first collected edition of the five stories appeared as *Christmas Books* with all the original

69. Edward Lear. Edward Lear, *A Book of Nonsense* (1846).

illustrations. Despite the notion that Dickens invented yᵉ jolly olde English Christmas, there is more depression than gaiety in the illustrations of his Christmas stories.

Leech had first chance at his *Punch* colleague Douglas Jerrold's popular *Mrs. Caudle's Curtain Lectures* (1846), but he was limited to a steel-etched frontispiece. It may have been the prototype of hundreds of later comic drawings. Mr. Caudle, in stocking feet, is about to sneak up a staircase, while on the floor above, Mrs. Caudle waits grimly by candlelight to lecture him. In 1866, Charles Keene illustrated the entire book. The twenty colored etchings in Gilbert à Beckett's two-volume *Comic History of England* (1847–48) are meager. (A merry party at Charles II's court has had a face-lift from Peter Paul Rubens and Sir Anthony Van Dyck.) The 240 wood-engraved vignettes are stronger and simpler, usually only two or three figures acting out a *Punch* line, such as "Canute Performing on His Favourite Instrument" in a pre-New Orleans jazz session. In 1852, *The Comic History of Rome* was published with ten colored etchings and ninety-eight wood engravings by Leech.

Robert Smith Surtees, his cockney grocer sportsman Mr. Jorrocks, and Leech are permanently linked, although Browne preceded Leech as illustrator of *Jorrocks's Jaunts and Jollities* in 1838. Leech first illustrated Surtees's *Mr. Sponge's Sporting Tour* (1853) with thirteen color plates

and eighty-four wood engravings before Surtees returned to Jorrocks in *Handley Cross: or Mr. Jorrocks's Hunt* (1854). The beefy, opinionated Jorrocks has none of the appeal of Mr. Pickwick, but the red and pink hunt coats in the seventeen hand-colored plates and the graceful horses, eager hounds, and hedged fields in the eighty black-and-white wood engravings have ensured his survival. Mr. Jorrocks "hoisting himself on [his horse] like a great crate of earthenware" shows how Leech combined humor with serious drawing (fig. 70). Leech illustrated three more books by Surtees, including *Mr. Facey Romford's Sporting Hounds* (1865), which Browne finished after Leech died.

John Leech individualized secondary figures much as Browne did to create interesting situations, but he did not command Browne's variety of posture and gesture or his economical and lively expressions.

Daniel Maclise

Illustrating was an occasional activity for Cork-born Daniel Maclise (1806–70), one of the most vigorous and popular Victorian painters of literary and historical themes. His best work in books followed his early adoption of the German firm-outline and limited parallel-line-shading style. The results seem best, however, in metal engravings after his linear designs, an exceptional medium for full-page

70. John Leech. Robert Smith Surtees, *Handley Cross: or Mr. Jorrocks's Hunt* (1854).

interpretive illustration after the eighteenth century. In Tom Moore's *Irish Melodies* (1845), the text and leafy borders were also engraved by the "omnigraphic process", along with 158 plates signed by Maclise, of which about one-third are genuine illustrations. He seems to have engraved and etched perhaps five. These Germanic engravings may seem cold. Yet, as the plate for one of Moore's drinking songs makes clear, Maclise went well beyond the poet in rendering the scene concrete and contemporary (fig. 71). The title page and six large illustrations within ornate poppy borders for a translation of Gottfried Bürger's macabre Gothic verse tale *Leonora* (1847) are strong but derivative engravings on wood in misguided imitation of steel plates. Maclise's two illustrations for "Morte d'Arthur" in Edward Moxon's edition of Tennyson's *Poems* (1857) stand up well to the competition from the Pre-Raphaelites. His drawing of Arthur beholding Excalibur, which is held by a hand rising out of the lake, is one of the best conceived and executed designs in the book. What is missing is a sense of the supernatural. The lady under the water seems too mortal to perform any wonders. Maclise's last important series was twenty-six designs for Tennyson's *Princess* (1860).

John Martin

Paradise Lost (1827) with designs by John Martin (1789–1854) is one of the most famous illustrated books published in England. It is also the only book for which Martin is remembered. An edition of the Bible published in 1837 contains wood engravings after sepia drawings by Martin and Richard Westall, and in 1838, Charles Tilt bought and published in book form – as *Illustrations of the Bible* – twenty mezzotints of Old Testament scenes from a series of Bible prints that Martin had begun (1831–35) but abandoned for lack of sales – or, rather, salesmanship. Virtually all his designs, mostly frontispieces, in other books have biblical subjects, including eleven mezzotints in a long poem by Thomas Hawkins, *The Wars of Jehovah, in Heaven, Earth, and Hell* (1844). The *Paradise Lost* illustrations are, of course, also biblical. The work is an epic poem; but John Milton first planned it as a biblical drama, and it still has a strong dramatic development.

Martin's huge paintings of Bible scenes, particularly *Joshua Commanding the Sun to Stand Still* (1816), *The Fall of Babylon* (1819), and *Belshazzar's Feast* (1820), had made him popular and had turned him to printmaking to reach a wider public. He mastered the demanding art of mezzotint, in which the artist works from black to white. The surface of a metal plate is roughened with a cradle, or rocker.

130

71. Daniel Maclise. Tom Moore, *Irish Melodies* (1845).

72. John Martin. John Milton, *Paradise Lost* (1827).

This creates a burr that will hold ink and print as gray to velvety black, depending on the degree of burr. Lights from gray to white are created by scraping the burr and wiping parts of the plate clean. Engraving and etching are used for linear detail. Martin apparently worked from oil sketches and first etched his design. He also used soft steel instead of copper. The medium was ideal for Martin's purposes in *Paradise Lost* because many of his designs consist of huge walled edifices, vast sweeping landscapes, and tiny human and celestial beings. The effect is one of grandeur, a stage for supernatural forces.

Septimus Prowett, a venturesome publisher, paid Martin the exceptional sum of £2000 to do twenty-four mezzotints (ca. 200 × 275 mm) to illustrate *Paradise Lost* and, before this set was completed, ordered a smaller set of the same designs (ca. 150 × 200 mm) for £1500. The large plates were sold beginning in March 1825 in twelve monthly parts with forty-eight pages of text. The book was published in 1827 in several forms. The mezzotints in the two-volume quarto edition are much superior to those in the smaller octavo. Apparently – or so it seems in the examples inspected – Martin did not completely finish parts of a few plates and seriously marred others by etching small additions, such as a tree or two, that stand out as distracting black lines. These examples may be unusually worn.

Because of the fame of Martin's designs for *Paradise Lost*, it is useful to inquire how he went about illustrating this classic. He chose his subjects deliberately. While his contract for twenty-four plates allowed him two for each of the twelve books of the poem, he distributed them irregularly: four in Books I and IV; three in Books V and X; two in Books II, III, IX, and XI; one in Books VII and XII; and none in Books VI and VIII.

Seven of the illustrations in the first three books have Satan as the central figure. Two of these designs are representative. After being cast out of Heaven into Hell with his rebel horde, Satan addresses his followers in a fantastic Great Consult in Pandemonium. He is seated atop a huge globe; in the light of "naphtha and asphaltus" lamps, thousands of his followers encircle him at a great distance. They decide not to resume the fight against God but to send Satan to seek out and corrupt the new race that, it is rumored, God has created. At the portal of Hell, Satan encounters his daughter, Sin – a "snaky sorceress" – and the offspring of their incestuous union, Death, guarding the gate. In general, where Martin presented panoramic views, as of Pandemonium, the design is wholly or almost wholly original. Where figures were depicted close up, as in the Gate of Hell scene, the design is likely to have been based on an earlier illustration – Henry Fuseli's in this instance.

There follow two grand designs of angels in Heaven.

But the high drama of Book III is the scene between God and his Son, in which Milton enunciates in lofty verse the theme that Christ will die for humanity. Martin avoided this crucial scene. But when in Book IV the action shifts to Paradise, Martin is superb in his realizations of Adam and Eve's delectable surroundings, although his Paradise resembles a Buckinghamshire park more than a tropical garden. Nor is it well stocked with game or adorned with flowers and fruits, as Milton prescribed, probably because Martin found it difficult to draw small objects in mezzotint. But Eve looking at her reflection in a lake, Adam and Eve in morning adoration (fig. 72), and Adam and Eve in two scenes with the archangel Raphael are surrounded by a Paradise of Miltonic splendor.

Martin made the unusual decision not to illustrate Book VI, as we have noted. Why? One possible reason is that Books VI and VII recapitulate the events that took place before the poem opens, in order that Milton might begin "in the midst of things". Martin may have thought that to introduce pictures of those events so belatedly would confuse the sequence. But the real reason may have been his unwillingness to come to grips with the most dynamic scenes in the entire epic: the great rebellion in Heaven, including the climax when the Messiah drives a chariot between legions of good angels and forces the rebels toward the edge of Heaven. Martin also did not illustrate Book VIII, in which Milton's purpose was expository. Martin may have considered illustrations of expository verse to be mere visual digressions and may have passed over the usual illustration of the birth of Eve as conspicuously out of sequence.

To span the gap left by not illustrating Books VI and VIII, Martin introduced in Book VII one magnificent, if dark, design of God creating light. (He had painted it earlier as a Bible picture.) God casts the sun ahead of him with one hand and drops the moon and stars behind him with the other. Milton's verse version of Genesis 1: 3–5 and 16–18 is one of his grandest passages, but it is not concrete. Martin's image is a justifiable illustration endowed with contributory virtues.

In Book IX, Martin presented in a traditional way the Temptation of Eve and Eve's tempting of Adam. What his mezzotints do that had not been done so emphatically before is make the coming loss of Paradise manifest by setting the figures off against the peace and luxuriance of the landscape. The loss is signalized in Book X by a remarkable design of the guilty Adam and Eve caught in shafts of light as they try to hide from God's voice in a dark wood. A long passage in the same book about a bridge over Chaos from Hell built by Sin and Death to enable them to make their way to the world of Man brings about another meet-

73. William Mulready. Oliver Goldsmith, *The Vicar of Wakefield* (1843).

ing between Satan and his offspring. It also gave Martin justification for imagining them as tiny figures in a spectacular scene suggested by the bridges and tunnels of the England of the Industrial Revolution.

For contrast in Book XI, Martin engraved a vast radiant Celestial City to which a host of angels is supposed to be hurrying to hear God's judgment on humanity, although no hurry is apparent. It is an impressive use of space. The design was moved to be the frontispiece to the edition. In the next plate, the archangel Michael appears as a small figure in a radiance seen at a distance by Adam and Eve as he brings God's decision about their punishment. It is a handsome and pertinent design, but its impact is lessened because plates 12 and 14 in Books IV and V have the same composition. The final illustration is the traditional one – the Expulsion. The text says that Michael led Adam and Eve by the hand to the eastern gate of Paradise and down the cliff to the plain, and then disappeared. Martin elected to show Michael not at all and Adam and Eve while they are on their way down. But he followed Milton in showing them hand in hand, brought closer together as they face their uncertain future.

Comparison of Martin's images with Milton's text suggests that he successfully projected the elevated nature of the epic events by the scale and magnificence of his designs and that he made Paradise palpable by the beauty and opulence of the mezzotints. But his preference for such scenes and perhaps his lack of experience in normal figure compositions led him to omit some of the critical dramatic scenes and not to make the most of others. John Martin achieved an aesthetic unity in his series, which might have been great had he been more of a literary illustrator concerned primarily with interpreting *Paradise Lost* rather than staging it.

James Northcote. See Harvey.

William Mulready

Born in Ireland but a Londoner from 1792, William Mulready (1786–1863) became popular for genre and landscape paintings distinguished mainly by their painstaking detail. Illustrations for children's books have been attributed to him, but the thirty-two vignette headpieces in *The Vicar of Wakefield* (1843) are his only important solo series of illustrations. The vignette for Chapter V depicts the Vicar and his family, still untroubled after the loss of their wealth, being approached for the first time by the villain Thornhill, their landlord, "with a careless superior air" (fig. 73). The design is representative of Mulready's compact handling of several figures within a small composition and command of bodily gesture. Its responsiveness to

134

74. Frederick Pickersgill. *The Home Affections, Pourtrayed by the Poets* (1858).

Oliver Goldsmith's blend of realism and sentimentality makes Mulready's series one of the most satisfactory chronicles of the occasional joys and many misfortunes of the Primrose family. The illustration of "The Goose", one of four by Mulready in Edward Moxon's edition of Tennyson's *Poems* (1857), realizes perfectly the turmoil of the uncharacteristic, humorous poem by the poet laureate.

Samuel Palmer

His discipleship to William Blake and his unusual life, no less than the charm of his paintings, prints, and drawings, have made Samuel Palmer (1805–81) the object of much attention in recent years, but it is idle to think of him as a book illustrator. In spite of his great enthusiasm for Blake's wood blocks, he turned over his heavily loaded landscape drawings for Charles Dickens's *Pictures from Italy* (1846) and for three collections of poems to professional engravers, with conventional results. A small headpiece and tailpiece for William Shakespeare's *Songs* (1853), "Illustrated by the Etching Club", are little more than technical exercises. Palmer's reputation as an illustrator rests on his designs for the posthumous *English Version of the Eclogues of Virgil* (1883), which he translated, and John Milton's *Minor Poems* (1888). It seems, however, more accurate to say that he drew two sets of similar landscapes suggested by the

eclogues and the minor poems than that he illustrated them. In the poems of neither Virgil nor Milton is human activity so negligible and darkness so pervasive as in these illustrations. Furthermore, these are not the complete series of etchings that Palmer planned for many years, and he had nothing to do with their publication. His son supervised the publication of both books. Of the fourteen *Eclogues* plates, Palmer etched only one, his son completed four, and nine are "orthophotographic" reproductions of drawings. The twelve designs for Milton's *Minor Poems* are drawings reproduced by photo process, and they have a lithographic density.

Phiz. See Browne.

Frederick Richard Pickersgill

Had Frederick R. Pickersgill (1820–1900) been asked to illustrate more books by himself, he would have been one of the most prominent Victorian illustrators. As a member of the Royal Academy, he was often among the artists asked to contribute to the illustrated gift books of the period. He was a careful draftsman whose drawings vary considerably in quality. The seven "hard-line" designs in the Second Series of *The Book of British Ballads* (1844) and the six similar ones in Philip Massinger's *Virgin Martyr* (1844)

75. Robert Smirke. *The Arabian Nights* (1802).

are unattractively drawn and reflect nothing of the spirit of the folk ballad or of Elizabethan drama.

In his later interpretations of religious and Victorian themes, Pickersgill improved immensely. His 6 illustrations for 6 poems in *The Home Affections, Pourtrayed by the Poets* (1858), a typical Victorian anthology edited by Charles Mackay, stand out in their bold clarity among the 100 designs by such leading artists of the period as John Gilbert, William Harvey, and John Everett Millais. In Leigh Hunt's retelling of "Hero and Leander", instead of showing the doomed Leander striving against the billows or Hero plunging from the tower, Pickersgill united the lovers in death at the foot of the tower (fig. 74). His choice of the moment to illustrate and his realization of it rank Frederick Pickersgill among the few successful artists among the many who have undertaken to illustrate that popular myth.

Robert Smirke

An illustrative painter – and member of the Royal Academy – rather than a book illustrator, Robert Smirke (1752–1845) tried to be both by choosing subjects from literature and making small monochromatic paintings that could be easily engraved. A contemporary of Henry Fuseli, Thomas Stothard, and William Blake, he contributed with them to the Boydell Shakespeare Gallery. As early as 1783, thirty-two of the forty steel engravings in *The Picturesque Beauties of Shakespeare* were from his designs, and only seven were from those of Stothard and one was from that of Charles Ryley. The best of his work is in five books that recount events taking place in countries bordering the Mediterranean Sea and the Red Sea. He designed twenty-four illustrations for *The Arabian Nights* (1802); twenty-four for Alain René Le Sage's *Gil Blas of Santillane* (1809); six of forty-eight for *The Iliad and Odyssey* (1810), in which Fuseli had the leading role; seventy-four for *Don Quixote* (1818); and four for Samuel Johnson's *History of Rasselas, Prince of Abyssinia* (1819).

Smirke was an artist of solid worth and little distinction. The twenty-four illustrations in the five-volume *Arabian Nights* (1802), engraved by seven engravers, are among the best of the early English efforts to do justice to this popular import. In his design of Sindbad's encounter with the Old Man of the Sea (fig. 75), Smirke managed the problem of factual credibility by the accuracy of his drawing and suggested both the exotic setting and Sindbad's mixture of perplexity and fear.

Don Quixote (1818) is Smirke's most extensive and typical effort. It contains forty-four full-page steel-engraved illustrations and thirty vignettes. The tonal effects of the engravings by Abraham Raimbach, Charles Grignion, and other proficient hands betray the painted origins of the

76. William Makepeace Thackeray. William Makepeace Thackeray, *Vanity Fair* (1848).

77. John Thurston. James Puckle, *The Club: in a Dialogue between Father and Son* (1817).

plates. At times, Smirke seems too obviously to have posed his figures, but his chief weakness is the absence in his illustrations of a humor equivalent to that of Cervantes. But Smirke did make his characters Spanish, which English illustrators usually have not done. Don Quixote is dark, aquiline, and proud – an aristocrat; Sancho Panza is dark and squat – a peasant but no clown. They could do with a touch of exaggeration, but they are more convincing than are the too frequent comic figures.

William Clarkson Stanfield

Clarkson Stanfield (1793–1867) was a respected seascape and landscape artist best known for his designs in several scenic and travel books, especially the forty splendid steel engravings after his drawings in *Stanfield's Coastal Survey* (1836). Many of the steel engravings in editions of works by Sir Walter Scott issued during the first half of the nineteenth century were from his designs. Among his interpretive illustrations, the best are the twenty steel engravings in Frederick Marryat's *Pirate, and the Three Cutters* (1836). Designs such as the title-page "Mast-head Midshipman" and the stormy "Bay of Biscay" and "Wreck of the *Avenger*" are prize examples of illustrations that depict scenes better than their texts. Stanfield was not so well served when in Charles Dickens's Christmas books – *The Chimes* (1845),

The Cricket on the Hearth (1846), *The Battle of Life* (1847), and *The Haunted Man* (1848) – and in Tennyson's *Poems* (1857), his tonal drawings were turned into wood engravings.

William Makepeace Thackeray

Like most novelists, William Makepeace Thackeray (1811–63) had an illustrator's eye; he also had a minor talent for drawing. With little art training, for the first dozen or so years of his career, he drew comic pictures for the ephemeral burlesques and satires that he contributed to *Fraser's Magazine* and other periodicals. When he elected to illustrate his first major work, *Vanity Fair* (1848), his literary powers had grown far beyond his artistic ability. Most of his thirty-eight steel etchings and eighty-three wood engravings are inadequate visualizations of the scenes that flow like a mighty river through his massive novel. He was at ease only with humorous incidents, as in the steel-etched "Jos performs a Polonaise" (fig. 76) and in the droll vignettes that go with the initial capitals notched in chapter openings. He illustrated *The History of Pendennis* (1849, 1850) and *The Virginians* (1858, 1859) and contributed to other works with the same meager results before wisely letting others illustrate his novels.

Some of Thackeray's best efforts are in his Christmas

78. J. M. W. Turner. John Milton, *The Poetical Works of John Milton* (1835).

books. For instance, a woman with a parasol and a Pekingese dog being stared at by neighbors, illustrating "The Lady Whom Nobody Knows" in *Our Street* (1848), is Victorian social satire at its most refined. The seventeen etched and tinted designs in *Doctor Birch and His Young Friends* (1849) make it the surprise of Thackeray's books. The humor is broad and gentle, as in "A Young Raphael" – a schoolboy caricaturist being observed from behind by his schoolmaster victim – but the tinting transforms the spare line drawings into one of the most delightful Victorian series. A complete chronological catalog of Thackeray's illustrations is needed.

John Thurston

Like his predecessor Thomas Stothard and his successors George Cruikshank, William Harvey, Hablot Browne, and John Gilbert, John Thurston (1774–1822) was a professional who got the job of illustrating books done by drawing designs on demand, with a clear understanding of the needs and limitations of his craft, without affectation, and yet with no loss of integrity. Trained as a metal engraver by James Heath, Thurston followed the trend of the times by turning to wood engraving before devoting himself entirely to illustrating. By a happy conjunction of events, he came along in time to work closely with Charles Whittingham

of the Chiswick Press and with George Wilmot Bonner, Robert Branston, Charlton Nesbit, Samuel Slader, John Thompson, and other early wood engravers, and it seems that he was in large measure responsible for creating what we have called the modified- or post-Bewick technique. Thurston dominated wood-engraved book illustration during the first twenty years of the nineteenth century.

Several of the books listed in the Catalog were assigned to him with varying degrees of certainty because his name does not appear in them. It is said that he drew every line of his designs on the blocks and that engravers reproduced them exactly. In different books and working with several engravers, Thurston achieved markedly similar effects, which were repeated by the same engravers in books illustrated by the Cruikshanks, Harvey, and Thomas Landseer, so that Catalog attributions of his unidentified works are subject to review.

In addition to the number of books he illustrated, Thurston is notable for the number of designs he drew, seemingly with ease. He was not daunted by the demands of David Hume's ten-volume *History of England* (1818) or of two or three editions of Shakespeare. His most impressive feat was designing 1000 little vignettes for Thomas John Dibdin's twelve-volume collection of plays, *The London Theatre* (1815), to which Stothard contributed 250 designs. Thompson was the engraver. All of Thurston's

79. Richard Westall. John Milton, *The Poetical Works* (1794, 1795, 1797).

small illustrations are distinguished by the clarity and vigor of figures in action, even in battle scenes, rather than by any subtlety of interpretation or richness of detail. Limited space usually made such desiderata unrealistic. Some are stiff, a little like broadside cuts, but many are charming. The delightful small headpieces for the twenty books of Torquato Tasso's *Godfrey of Bulloigne: or, Jerusalem Delivered* (1817), also engraved by Thompson, make the well-printed two volumes an edition to covet.

Thurston will be remembered primarily for his collaboration with the early wood engravers on three books. The first is Bishop Thomas Percy's *Hermit of Warkworth: A Northumbrian Ballad* (1806). On the title page, the names of the engravers, Charlton Nesbit and Luke Clennell, are displayed in larger type than is that of Thurston. The nine vignettes offer harmonious accompaniment to the romantic notes of the ballad. The drawing of figures and the strength of line are markedly superior to those in Thomas Bewick's work as a literary illustrator. (The same cuts, with three others, in an 1834 edition are said on the title page to be by "Mr. Craig" and "Engraved by Mr. Bewick".)

The second of the three books is William Somervile's *Hobbinol, Field Sports, and the Bowling Green* (1813), handsomely printed by William Bulmer for Rudolph Ackermann. Among the fifteen designs (nine signed by Nesbit), the technical distinction lies with four formal decorative vignettes, including a wonderful scarecrow frontispiece for Canto I and an elegant scroll and willow-tree frontispiece for Canto III, both engraved by Nesbit; the four are curiously like the fine ones said by Bulmer to have been designed by John Bewick for Somervile's *Chase* (1796) and engraved by Thomas Bewick. They embody about everything in the way of drawing on the block and engraving that wood engravers came to believe basic more than a century later.

Finally, Thurston's title-page design and twenty-four small rectangular headpieces for the two dozen "characters" in *The Club: in a Dialogue between Father and Son* (1817) by James Puckle, generally retitled *Puckle's Club*, are a prime example of felicitous illustration. They were admirably engraved by Thompson (who did thirteen), Branston, Nesbit, and others, including Harvey, "a pupil of Mr. Bewick". The text takes the form of graphically satirical accounts of a drunken party by a smug young man followed by a didactic commentary by his father. Each section presents a character: "Antiquarian", "Buffoon", "Critic", and so on to "Xantippe", "Youth", and "Zany". "Detractor" slandering a passing couple is representative of this series and of the fine wood engraving by the post-Bewick group (fig. 77). The 1817 series appears in Charles Tilt's 1834

edition with improved printing of the blocks at Whittingham's Chiswick Press and with the subtitle *A Gray Cap for a Green Head*. Although Thurston's scenes are more decorous than they would have been had William Hogarth or Thomas Rowlandson done them, his incisive drawings and the wood engravings of the early-nineteenth-century masters have given this cross section of English tavern society a modest fame.

Joseph Mallord William Turner

The several hundred drawings that J. M. W. Turner (1775–1851) made for books fall into two groups: those for books of the scenery and sights of Britain, Italy, and France; and those for four or five books of poetry and for the works of Sir Walter Scott. In the main, they are fastidious small landscapes, seascapes, and townscapes, often with appropriate but tiny incidental figures. Under Turner's supervision, a number of engravers – including Edward Goodall, Charles Heath, Edward Finden, William Miller, and Robert Wallis – turned his watercolors into steel engravings of unsurpassed brilliance. In literary works, they are most effective when combined with interpretive illustrations, beginning with the twenty-three vignettes in Samuel Rogers's *Italy: A Poem* (1830) and thirty-one in Rogers's *Poems* (1834) accompanied by Thomas Stothard's illustrations. The twenty-four designs in Scott's *Poetical Works* (1833–34) and forty-one in Scott's *Miscellaneous Prose Works* (1834–6) had the advantage of being derived from a productive sketching trip to Scotland and were, as they were planned to be, an important sales asset in the enterprise. Turner and Clarkson Stanfield contributed most of the frontispieces and added title-page designs to the seventeen-volume *Life and Works of Lord Byron* (1832–33). Turner's depiction of Waterloo after the battle is one of the few action pieces. Since Turner had never been to Greece, many of his drawings were based on sketches by others.

In 1835, John Macrone published a six-volume edition of *The Poetical Works of John Milton*, "With Imaginative Illustrations by J. M. W. Turner, Esq. R.A.". Turner's seven steel-engraved vignettes are on an appropriately grand scale. The design of "St. Michael's Mount, Shipwreck of Lycidas" (fig. 78), for instance, shows what Turner could have done had he devoted himself to making "Imaginative Illustrations". If these seven vignettes were two or three times larger, they would be among the most impressive illustrations of Milton's works, even though the poor drawing of the figures would be more conspicuous.

Except for his part in the short-lived ascendancy of steel engraving and in the plethora of landscapes in Victorian books, Turner had little influence on book illustration. He had an important supporting role, however, in initiating and maintaining the Romantic way in which the English were learning to view the world around them.

Richard Westall

A painter of attractive watercolors and a member of the Royal Academy by the time he was thirty, Richard Westall (1765–1836) was a professional illustrator for more than thirty years. In that long span, he illustrated most of the standard works of English literature popular at the time. Westall's drawings, especially those done with brush and sepia, are often bold and fluent, but almost all the designs he prepared for books had to fit the constricted space of small steel engravings. This compression sometimes results in staring-eyed melodramatics. Westall illustrated primarily books of narrative verse, and thus he was able to present figures in moments of action and stress, just as he did for such prose works as Oliver Goldsmith's *Vicar of Wakefield* (1818) and John Bunyan's *Pilgrim's Progress* (1820). His designs for the domestic themes of Thomas Campbell, Goldsmith, James Thomson, Thomas Gray, and Robert Burns are as felicitous as those for the more flamboyant ones of Sir Walter Scott, James Beattie, Tom Moore, and William Falconer.

Westall's two series of designs for works by John Milton reveal the reason for his popularity as well as his limitations. In the twenty-eight plates for the three-volume *Poetical Works* (1794, 1795, 1797), Westall and his engravers dealt more convincingly with terrestrial than with celestial events. Among the twelve *Paradise Lost* plates, for instance, muscular, staring Satan in "The Birth of Sin" derives from his portrayal by Henry Fuseli, and Sin is a pretty young woman apparently emerging from Satan's shoulder in a burst of light. For "Eve Going Forth among Her Flowers", Westall conceived a Godiva-like Eve standing idly beside a luxuriant growth of hollyhocks and other cottage flowers (fig. 79). In the minor poems and in Volume II of his long popular series of twelve vignettes for *Paradise Lost* (1817), he frankly created idyllic visions to accompany Milton's verse. In the Romantic mood of the times, he and his engravers also made a contribution to Orientalism with their illustrations for Samuel Johnson's *History of Rasselas, Prince of Abyssinia* (1817), Moore's *Lalla Rookh* (1817), and *The Tales of the Genii* (1820).

In general, Richard Westall maintained a high level of workmanship rather than of imagination in representing scenes from many authors with simplicity, dignity, grace, and feeling for the texts and the times, and in so doing helped crystallize the Romantic vision in the early-nineteenth-century reader.

142

CHAPTER SEVEN

The Nineteenth Century (II)
1855–1885

The second period of illustration in the nineteenth century is bracketed by the publication of two books. The illustration by three Pre-Raphaelites of William Allingham's *Music Master* (1855) has come to mark the beginning of what are called the "'sixties". The terminal date of 1885, rather than of 1870, was chosen because pen-and-ink illustration of books can be said to have been fairly launched with Hugh Thomson's drawings for Joseph Addison's *Days with Sir Roger de Coverley* (1886). Indeed, few of the book illustrators of the 1860s were working in the 1880s, but their successors introduced no major developments before 1886.

As a convenience for remembering them, the numerous illustrators of the mid-nineteenth century can be sorted into groups. The six leaders of what might be called the standard illustrators are George Du Maurier, Arthur Boyd Houghton, John Everett Millais, Noel Paton, George Pinwell, and John Dawson Watson. In the same rank but separate are three Pre-Raphaelites: Arthur Hughes, Dante Gabriel Rossetti, and Frederick Sandys. Other top-rank illustrators of diverse talents are the humorists Charles Keene and John Tenniel, the foreigner Gustave Doré, and the naturalist Joseph Wolf. That leaves two other groups: a small one of artists of ability but less distinction or productivity, such as Frederick Barnard, William Holman Hunt, William Small, Marcus Stone, Frederick Walker, and a few others who are discussed in the text; and one that includes a number whose work is listed in the Catalog but not discussed in the text.

The nostalgic enthusiasm of Gleeson White's *English Illustration: "The Sixties," 1855–70* (1897) and its successor Forrest Reid's *Illustrators of the Sixties* (1928) has fostered the idea that the mid-nineteenth century was the golden age of English book illustration. In profusion and popularity of illustrated books, it was. The expansion of the British Empire had helped make England the leading industrial and commercial nation in the world, with a consequent increase in prosperity, middle-class literacy and affluence, publishers, and illustrated magazines and books. The pressure to turn out illustrations for inexpensive and moderately priced editions in greater abundance and with more speed and economy than ever before made wood engraving the universal means of reproducing illustrations. With the mass of work to be done against tight schedules, groups of wood engravers had to be assembled to deal with the flow of wood blocks in an organized way. The Dalziel and Swain firms dominated the trade. The need for hands gave work to many men and boys, and to some women and girls, who, in addition to doing odd jobs around the shop, mastered the difficult craft of engraving by working on the easier passages on blocks and on less important orders.

Victorian wood engraving was strictly facsimile reproduction of designs, which for some years all but a few professional illustrators drew on the blocks. By the 1870s, the drawings were being photographed onto the blocks. The process is thought to have been introduced in the first series of *Lyra Germanica* (1861) by the engraver Thomas Bolton. It was infinitely more convenient than drawing on the block or tracing a drawing on the block, permitted drawings to be two or three times larger than the blocks, and preserved the drawings. Engravers laboriously reproduced every black line and squiggle as the artist had happened to make them. An exception was the practice for the artist to work up much of a drawing by brush and wash or even color and leave to the engraver the task of getting equivalent tonal values by means of lines. The skill of the experienced Victorian engravers was astonishing. Unfortunately, it was sadly misdirected. In the 1840s, engravers had lost their standing and had accepted the role of facsimile engraver, which allowed no leeway for original effects. This role included the onerous, deadening, and time-wasting drudgery of reproducing vast amounts of pen-and-ink crosshatching used by the artist to suggest the tonal effects of a painting. In contrast with intaglio etching or engraving on metal, black-line crosshatching on wood can be simulated only by removing all the square or lozenge-shaped interstices to give the illusion of continuous crossed lines.

The number of hours devoted by clever engravers to this profitless exercise over the years was appalling. Furthermore, with all their skill, the Victorian facsimile engravers were unable to obtain the freedom and spontaneity of the original, rapidly drawn pen lines. Thus a certain stiffness in the best reproductive engraving of the period descends to total deadness in the mediocre examples.

Other depressing aspects of this protracted demonstration of human stupidity are, first, that George Wilmot Bonner, Robert Branston, Charleton Nesbit, and other wood engravers in the early nineteenth century had shown, as we have seen, how well adapted to book illustration the modified-Bewick method was, and, second, that in all these years, no one protested and no one except the practitioners of the German shaded-outline method attempted to revive or devise a better technique than facsimile engraving. Another occasional deviation was a borrowing from the wood engravers who copied paintings for the art journals. In the days before the advent of halftones and color photographs, these engravers achieved painterly effects by the use of neat patches of close parallel white-line shading and produced the darkest tones by the use of *criblé*. Engravers who used this technique often ruined drawings by unrestrained tint-tool shading. The technique was not widely used for illustrating books. Perhaps the best examples are in the 1882 edition of *Works of Henry Fielding*, illustrated by William Small.

The Victorian novel gave the illustrators a great opportunity. The public not only had money to buy novels, but also had time to read them. They acquired a taste for long narratives with lifelike characters and situations. But more engagement with "real" characters and problems necessitated more analysis and calm conversation and less action. The effect on illustration was an endless repetition of ladies and gentlemen in conventional attire (the billowing dresses must have been a compositional blessing) talking together while sitting or standing, dining, or clustered about in drawing rooms or at garden parties. These static scenes reflect the importance attached to middle-class respectability and upper-class leisure, but too often seem lethargic and as fit for one novel as another. As a result, although mid-Victorian artists made many splendid drawings, they rarely produced a book full of vital interpretive illustrations.

The distance between the artist and the engraver – and, indeed, the text – lengthened with the increase in the publication of gift books and Christmas annuals, which had begun to be the vogue in the earlier decades of the nineteenth century. This stimulated the already widespread practice of dividing the illustrations among several artists. To attract buyers, publishers – or sometimes printers or engravers acting as subcontractors – often included in books the designs of well-known painters who had little experience as illustrators. Although mid-Victorian painting was heavily "literary" and anecdotal, with scenes taken from literary classics, history, and family life, designs by painters more often than not seem to be composed "pictures" rather than illustrations. The illustrations for gift books occasionally were drawn first, and verse or other text was written to "illustrate" the pictures.

Even experienced illustrators who were limited to one or two or a scattered few designs in a book full of illustrations by others could not feel the same sense of obligation to the text or to the engraver that they would have felt had they been the sole illustrator. Many leading illustrators took their painting careers seriously and in these gift books felt constrained to compete with established painters by also producing pictures using carefully posed models. The sentimentality of many of the multiple-artist gift books, extending from the celebration of childhood to the acceptance of the familiar presence of death, added to the impression that they were collections of prints rather than illustrated books. Still, these volumes were an important Victorian phenomenon and contain enough fine illustrations to justify including in the Catalog those that have good examples of an artist's work.

One characteristic of mid-nineteenth-century publishing was the practice of reprinting in book form fiction, poetry, and humorous pieces that had first appeared in such popular periodicals as *Good Words*, *Cornhill Magazine*, and *Punch*. Many illustrators earned double reputations, in periodicals and in books. Since not all of any artist's magazine illustrations were republished, the judgments made here by reference only to the books in the Catalog do not always agree with those of critics like White and Reid, both of whom included magazines in their surveys and judged illustrators primarily as draftsmen.

Distinct from volumes in which publication in parts or in magazine serial form preceded book publication are volumes of magazine illustrations published either without text or with text different from that for which they were designed. *The Cornhill Gallery* (1864) was the prototype of those without text (but with the sources correctly indicated), and George Walter Thornbury's *Historical & Legendary Ballads & Songs* (1876) is the most conspicuous example of those with substitute texts. *Dalziel's Bible Gallery* (1881) is one collection of illustrations without text that can be justified as not just a bound collection of prints because the text is so well known – or was at the time.

Another characteristic of the mid-nineteenth century that is reflected in illustrated books was a serious interest in nature. William Coleman, Harrison Weir, Joseph Wolf, Thomas W. Wood, and Johann Zwecker, all of whom were

80. Frederick Barnard. Charles Dickens, *David Copperfield* (1872).

81. Charles Henry Bennett. *The Fables of Aesop and Others: Translated into Human Nature* (1858 [1857]).

82. Randolph Caldecott. Washington Irving, *Bracebridge Hall: Selections from the "Sketch Book"* (1877 [1876]).

146

not truly interpretive illustrators, contributed richly to this interest with their carefully studied drawings of birds and animals in works of literature shared with other artists as well as in more specialized natural-history books of their own. John G. Wood's *Common Objects of the Country* (1858), illustrated by Coleman, is said to have sold 100,000 copies in one week.

For the record, (Mary) Ellen Edwards (who signed her work "M.E.E.") should be mentioned here as an example of a rarity – a Victorian woman illustrator who did not limit herself to children's books. Unfortunately, the characters in *The Claverings* (1867), her one major effort, seem to be unaware of what Anthony Trollope expected of them.

Frederick Barnard

In 1863, after having studied in Paris, Frederick Barnard (1846–96) became in his drawings for the *Illustrated London News* a prominent proponent of the social realism that was replacing the livelier illustrating of the first half of the century and the genteel work of the " 'sixties". (Vincent van Gogh was an admirer of Barnard.) With a certain ambiguity, someone once called him "the Charles Dickens of black-and-white artists". It is true that his reputation rests mainly on the twenty-one volume *Works of Charles Dickens. Household Edition* (1871–79). In it are his illustrations for ten of Dickens's works and for John Forster's *Life of Charles Dickens* – 472 of the 866 wood engravings. Furthermore, they illustrate most of the important works with generous numbers of designs: *David Copperfield* (1872), sixty-one; *Martin Chuzzlewit* (1872), fifty-nine; *Bleak House* (1873), sixty-one; *Master Humphrey's Clock and Other Stories* (1874), nine; *Barnaby Rudge* (1874), forty-six; *A Tale of Two Cities* (1874), twenty-five; *Nicholas Nickleby* (1875), fifty-nine; *Sketches by Boz* (1876), thirty-four; *Dombey and Son* (1877), sixty-two; *Christmas Books* (1878), twenty-eight; and Forster's *Life of Charles Dickens* (1879), twenty-eight.

Barnard worked out every composition with care for balance and variety. He never lapsed into formulas, never slighted any of the 472 designs. He reconstructed the scenes with concern for the emotional interaction of Dickens's strongly marked characters within appropriate but not overdone settings. Wisely, he did not attempt to invent a new Dickensian mythology but accepted the chief characters as they had been shaped by Dickens and Phiz, although with fresh conceptions of most of the scenes. (He did not, of course, have the advantage of the author's advice; Dickens had died in 1870.) But the times had changed, and Barnard tempered the raffish appearance and behavior of some of Phiz's characters and generally gave the novels a more normal surface. In doing so, however, he was in spirit denying Dickens, whose word enchants because it is imaginary and its people vary from normalcy. How Barnard preserved and invented can be seen in a full-page design from *David Copperfield* (1872), in which Micawber impresses the names of the streets on David (fig. 80). Paradoxically, Barnard's attempts to depict eccentrics like Wackford Squeers and Uriah Heep embarrass because they lack the saving grace of humorous exaggeration. Barnard usually handled groups well, as in *Dombey and Son* (1877), but these scenes tend to lose their Dickensian edge.

Barnard's other major effort consisted of 66 illustrations among the 100 in an edition of John Bunyan's *Pilgrim's Progress* (1880). With the exception of that depicting the Giant Despair, they are too domestic and sentimental to achieve an effect of either piety or drama. The rest of his work seems too miscellaneous to justify comment. The underlying drawing in many of Barnard's illustrations is concealed by a superfluity of lines. The Dalziel engravers made them worse. They exerted no restraint to relieve the obscurity and sometimes used a ruling machine in a mechanical fashion on random blocks in a poor imitation of Phiz's "dark plates". Thus every one of Barnard's series of illustrations has some excellent designs, and every one is spoiled by unattractive ones.

In the end, Frederick Barnard becomes a sort of exemplar of this period of reproductive wood engraving. We cannot be sure to what extent he was responsible for these mixed impressions and to what extent he was a victim of the engraving practices of the times.

Charles Henry Bennett

The one book illustrated by Charles H. Bennett (1829–67) to be remembered is *The Fables of Aesop and Others: Translated into Human Nature* (1858 [1857]). The frontispiece and twenty-two slightly shaded outline drawings are hand-colored wood engravings. Although they fall short of Grandville's fantasies, Bennett's satirical drawings of animals playing human roles in human attire are among the best examples of this anthropomorphic treatment by a mid-Victorian artist. Bennett shrewdly rejected adaptation of traditional fable motifs and projected his characters into contemporary applications of the morals. In "The Fox and the Crow", for example, the fox, a flattering swindler, is shown on bended knee proposing to the crow, a wealthy widow. To the complete originality of these designs, Bennett added equal freshness of characterization and expression, as in "The Frog and the Ox" (fig. 81). The Dalziels considered Bennett's illustrations for John Bunyan's *Pilgrim's Progress* (1859) to be the best of all series for this book, but his almost three dozen drawings for *London People: Sketched from Life* (1863) are much more fascinating to a twentieth-century eye. The individualized types as Bennett saw them in the law courts, on trains, at the theater, up a back court, and in Belgravia are valuable bits of Victoriana, their accuracy not impaired by friendly satire.

Randolph Caldecott

In his brief career, Randolph Caldecott (1846–86) illustrated only four adult works of literature of any importance. His illustration of them preceded his success in children's books. Besides the influence of his simplified outline designs in the sixteen children's *Picture Books* produced in color by Edmund Evans, Caldecott was influential in reviving the vigor and good-natured realism of John Leech's mode of drawing, and he had some influence on the development of the open style and benign outlook of Edwin Austin Abbey and Hugh Thomson. It is unfortunate that Caldecott came along just before photo process was firmly established and that he chose, as others did at the time, to have his designs engraved on wood (although they were photographed on the block first). Modern reproductions of his original broken-outline drawings show a stenographic quality that was not preserved by his facsimile engraver, James Cooper, skillful as he was.

Caldecott's first successful effort at book illustration was Washington Irving's *Old Christmas: Selections from the "Sketch Book"* (1876 [1875]). It was followed late in 1876 by Irving's *Bracebridge Hall: Selections from the "Sketch Book"*. The first contains 112 drawings of various sizes, and the second, 120. Caldecott's style settled down in *Bracebridge Hall* to approximately what we recognize as that of Thomson and the pen-and-ink school, as can be seen in one of the eight full-page illustrations, "The Wedding", which depicts a gathering of villagers in the churchyard to cheer the happy couple (fig. 82). Temperamentally, Caldecott was perfectly attuned to Irving's genial essays, and he re-created characters and scenes with the equivalent of Irving's unlabored charm. Yet the two series no longer make the impression that they made before it became possible to compare them with the livelier and lighter direct reproductions of the pen-and-ink drawings of Abbey, Thomson, Charles Brock, and Henry Brock.

The last adult book on our list illustrated by Caldecott is *Some of Aesop's Fables with Modern Instances* (1883). For each of the twenty short, straightforward translations by his brother Alfred (with no moral or modern instance in the text), he supplied one headpiece fable vignette and one tailpiece vignette of the "modern instance". Again, Cooper engraved the designs on wood. The volume manages to be both elaborate and insignificant. In a smaller format with two or three times as many fables and the facetious tailpieces omitted, the book would be an acceptable but commonplace collection.

Joseph Crawhall

Joseph Crawhall (1821–96), a rope maker who lived in Newcastle-upon-Tyne, put together a half-dozen or more volumes in the forty years before 1889, of which *Chapbook Chaplets* (1883) is a good example. In all but the first, he adapted and cut old ballad and chapbook woodcut designs and invented some of his own. Except for a rare one blessed with charm by hand-coloring, they are crude and without merit as literary illustrations. They came along, however, when reproductive wood engraving was giving way to pen and ink, and they suggested an alternative not only to those two media, but also to most of the woodcuts of the fifteenth and sixteenth centuries. In spite of their humble ballad and chapbook derivation, they ultimately go back to the broad, free brush drawings of medieval manuscripts and unsophisticated woodcut copies, such as those in Ulrich Boner's *Der Edelstein* (Bamberg, 1461). The idea bore fruit in the work of William Nicholson, Gordon Craig, Claud Lovat Fraser, and their followers and thus earned Crawhall a note in the history of English graphics.

The Dalziels

Until photo process put an end to reproductive wood engraving, the most familiar name in Victorian book illustration was Dalziel. It was on hundreds of blocks (often when the designer's signature was not), usually of remarkable faithfulness to the drawings and sometimes of superb, if misdirected, technical excellence. In addition to being the foremost firm of wood engravers in England, the Dalziels were a force in stimulating book illustration. They often hired the illustrators, and initiated and produced a Fine Art Books series for publishers to distribute. In these gift books, the Dalziel name also appears among those of well-known illustrators.

The Dalziels were numerous. Only four need be mentioned here. The older brothers were born in Northumberland and spent their boyhood in Thomas Bewick's Newcastle-upon-Tyne. George (1815–1902) and Edward (1817–1905) studied with Charles Gray in London, and in 1839 founded their own firm. Thomas (1823–1906), who had been apprenticed as a copper engraver, soon joined them. Edward Gurden (1849–88) became associated with his father, Edward, and his uncles in the 1870s. George concentrated on business, but Edward and Thomas are

THE CALIPH LOOKING THROUGH THE LATTICE.

this for a reason, which makes me blush for shame whenever I think of it—because she called me her son, as in truth I am, and would not acknowledge me to be the Commander of the Faithful, as I maintained, and actually believed myself to be. You, too, are the cause of that offence I gave my neighbours, when running to our house at the cries of my poor mother, they found me so exasperated against her that I beat her violently,

83. Thomas Dalziel. *Dalziel's Illustrated Arabian Nights' Entertainments* (1865).

84. Gustave Doré. Samuel Taylor Coleridge, *The Rime of the Ancient Mariner* (1876).

represented among the illustrators of magazines and of numerous books, some of which are not listed in the Catalog because they contain few designs by the Dalziels or they were for children. Edward Gurden illustrated several books before his early death, just as photo process was becoming established.

Thomas was the best draftsman and the most professional illustrator. His chief efforts were his 100 designs in John Bunyan's *Pilgrim's Progress* (1863), 90 in *Dalziel's Illustrated Arabian Nights' Entertainments* (1865), 20 in Jean Ingelow's *Poems* (1867), and 25 in Robert Buchanan's *North Coast and Other Poems* (1868). An example of how good he could sometimes be is the *Arabian Nights' Entertainments* design of the caliph Haroun Alraschid secretly enjoying the elaborate trick he has played on Abou Hassan in the tale "The Sleeper Awakened" (fig. 83). His illustrations, in the main, use white space surprisingly well.

In *The Illustrators of the Sixties*, Forrest Reid dismissed Edward Gurden as "decadent" because he was "completely out of touch with the whole spirit of the sixties". That is hardly an indictable offense. In truth, however, he did not draw well, had an unattractive mannerism of outlining his figures heavily, and either used or permitted far too much dark multiple-tint-tool background shading.

Dalziel's Bible Gallery (1881), a collection of some of the finest biblical designs, without text, by Victorian artists, was a gallant farewell to the era of facsimile wood-engraved book illustration, to which the Dalziels had contributed so much. (Their use of the singular-possessive form of their name was not generally followed by publishers.) *The Brothers Dalziel: A Record of Fifty Years' Work, 1840–1890* (1901), written by George and Edward in their old age, is a polite, not always illuminating, but valuable reminiscent account of the activities of the firm that was at the center of mid-Victorian illustration.

Paul Gustave Doré

Among book illustrators most widely known to the English-speaking peoples, Gustave Doré (1832–83) is certainly one. His illustrations for the Bible, for works by Dante and François Rabelais, and for *Don Quixote* (1863), *Paradise Lost* (1866), and *The Rime of the Ancient Mariner* (1876) have been on family and public-library bookshelves throughout the English-speaking world since they first appeared in English editions. But since Doré lived in France and was only a visitor to England, although in time a regular one, his appearance in this study is by indulgence. Doré's pen-and-wash illustrations for books published in England were, with one exception, either drawn or photographed on wood blocks and were engraved by a highly skilled but

wrong-notioned group of Paris engravers. Their prize folio full-page blocks, featuring dark border-to-border shading that was made with a mechanical tint tool and is seldom relieved by white, grow tedious. Their exercise of their own tricks misrepresented Doré. His strength was the spontaneity and gusto of his incredibly swift drawings, usually done from a photographic memory and an exuberant imagination – all triumphantly manifest in his vignettes.

Although first published in France, Doré's folio *Don Quixote* (1863), with 118 illustrations, perhaps did most to capture the English public. It is one of the great illustrated books, probably the greatest of all editions of *Don Quixote*. But Milton and Tennyson were so far removed from the world that Doré knew or could imagine that his fifty designs for *Paradise Lost* (1866) and nine apiece for *Elaine* (1867), *Guinevere* (1867), *Vivien* (1867), and *Enid* (1868) interrupt the poems rather than intensify their effects. The steel-engraved designs for Tennyson's *Idylls of the King* (1868) are even less compatible with the poems. With his friend Blanchard Jerrold to take him around and write a supporting text, Doré drew from memory and the slightest of notes 182 theatrically realistic illustrations for Jerrold's *London. A Pilgrimage* (1872). These wood engravings, especially those that record the dreadful living conditions of the poor, are now a part of social history. Doré had little success with Edgar Allan Poe's *Raven* (1883). The twenty-six huge wood engravings are both too grandiose and too literal.

The one great series of Doré's interpretive illustrations of an English work of literature is in his folio of Samuel Taylor Coleridge's *Rime of the Ancient Mariner* (1876). It consists of forty-two wood engravings: four assorted introductory designs, and thirty-eight enormous full-page ones. Although the illustrations overwhelm the short ballad stanzas, they induce the simple words of the poem to expand infinitely in the imagination, like fireworks. Like Noel Paton, whose *Ancient Mariner* (1863) series he apparently studied, Doré failed to communicate a sense of the supernatural, but he did make the amazing events of the Mariner's voyage as believable as the Preface to Wordsworth and Coleridge's *Lyrical Ballads* (1798) stipulated supernatural events should be. The alienation and anguish of the Mariner are symbolized by his retreat to the masthead, where he stands on his tilted perch as if crucified (fig. 84). Doré had no visual equivalent to Coleridge's ballad stanza to keep the shore scenes from seeming mundane, but few English book illustrations hold their own with a great work of imaginative literature as well as his ship and harbor-boat scenes do with Coleridge's *Ancient Mariner*.

Gustave Doré failed in two solemn undertakings: he was never taken seriously as a painter, and he never completed the series of illustrations of Shakespeare's plays on which

85. George Du Maurier. George Du Maurier, *Trilby* (1895).

he labored for years. That might have been the masterpiece overtopping all his others, as he boasted it would be.

George Louis Palmella Busson Du Maurier

Anglo-French George Du Maurier (1834–96) is now more widely known as an author than as an illustrator, although he did not write the first of his three autobiographical novels until he was fifty-seven. Like his associates John Tenniel and Arthur Boyd Houghton, he lost the sight in one eye, which limited his working day drastically. In 1860, nevertheless, he began drawing for *Punch* and was a weekly fixture for the rest of his life. He also contributed regularly to the *Cornhill Magazine, Once a Week, Good Words,* and other magazines. Leaving street life, horsy people, and middle-class families to John Leech, Charles Keene, John Everett Millais, and other artists whom he admired, he became a gifted recorder of Victorian drawing-room society. His pencil drawings are firm and cleanly shaded; yet too often, they became wood engravings filled with scratchy unidirectional lines on faces and dresses and with masses of unfunctional crosshatching.

Critics have thought that Du Maurier's best illustrated books are his early ones. During the first four years of his career, Du Maurier illustrated eight books by Elizabeth Gaskell, and twenty years later, he illustrated two more.

Here and there among the insufficient four designs for each volume is a good drawing, often overshaded. In *The Grey Woman and Other Tales* (1865), the illustration of a woman holding up a small child to show to a man who is in bed is very good. Yet Du Maurier clearly chose the scene in order to draw his wife and one of his children – his wife and children were his habitual models – not to illustrate a significant passage in the story; indeed, the man is the narrator, not even an active member of the cast. The thirty-two illustrations in Douglas Jerrold's *Story of a Feather* (1867) are animated and realistic. The twenty in William Makepeace Thackeray's *History of Henry Esmond* (1868) have the continuity, the seventeenth-century costumes, and the sense of the dramatic equal to that of Thackeray to give them strength, as in the illustration showing the death of Lord Castlewood at the hands of Lord Mohun in a duel. Taken as a whole, however, even the *Henry Esmond* series cannot be singled out for distinction. The same verdict seems to be unavoidable on the rest of the books that Du Maurier illustrated early in his career.

Du Maurier's last illustrations were done for his own three novels, and they are pen-and-ink drawings reproduced by photo process. Unfortunately, the eighty-five vignettes in the first one, *Peter Ibbetson* (1892), were cruelly reduced. The dozen or so designs in the first part are scattered mementos of Du Maurier's early childhood in Paris.

86. Luke Fildes. Charles Dickens, *The Mystery of Edwin Drood* (1870).

Even with later flashbacks, the shift to adulthood in London breaks the continuity. The main difficulty with the book as a whole, however, is that the moony love theme is not even faintly convincing and does not lend itself to concrete visual development.

Trilby (1895) is Du Maurier's most effective illustrated book. (It also made him affluent.) The 120 pen-and-ink vignettes of various sizes cover all aspects of the story, which, although melodramatic, is believable within the conventions of popular fiction – and probably for many readers, as pseudoscience. The extraordinary number of illustrations and the tight progression of the narrative enabled Du Maurier, as artist, to give coherence and credibility to the main and incidental events: in Paris, English art student Little Billee's doomed love for the model Trilby; and in London, the death of the musician Svengali, followed by the failure of Trilby as La Svengali, the singing sensation of Europe, to sing without Svengali's mesmeric influence, Trilby's madness and death, and Billee's hurried demise. Nonsensical as this story is, it translated into closely related drawings of easily identifiable characters in moments of drama and of relaxation. Whatever may have been the effect of *Trilby* as a play, an opera, and a film, Du Maurier's illustrations did not contribute to the myth that the coast of Bohemia is on the Left Bank of the Seine, although the novel was influenced by Henri Murger's *Scènes de la vie Bohème*. The early full-cast scene in the spacious studio shared by Billee, the Laird, and Taffy (fig. 85) looks like a tea in Cheyne Row, and Trilby is no Mimi or even Eliza Doolittle. But these designs are more original than is any conventional celebration of bohemianism, for they are warranted to be closer to the laminate of fact and fable in Du Maurier's mind – the way things were at that far-off time and the way he wished they had been – than to the conventional view.

Du Maurier's third novel, *The Martian* (1898), a curious exercise in self-admiration, contains forty-eight pen-and-ink illustrations, almost all of which are full-page. A few, such as the one of a Dominican priest playing the 'Moonlight Sonata" (a descent from *Trilby* to nil degrees of dramatic tension), have strength as drawings. But as in *Peter Ibbetson*, fantasy submerges memories of Paris school days, and Du Maurier gave himself little chance to put together a convincing series of designs or to create any illusion of a carefree life to which a reader might temporarily escape.

George Du Maurier's many years as one of the foremost social satirists of Europe must outweigh his uneven accomplishments as a book illustrator. Yet, at the age of fifty-seven, to write so popular a classic as *Trilby* and to illustrate it with 120 vigorous, original drawings is one of the exceptional achievements of English book illustration.

Sir Samuel Luke Fildes

After a brief stint, from 1866 to 1879, as an illustrator, Luke Fildes (1844–1927) devoted the rest of his long career to being a successful painter "in the anecdotal and melodramatic vein" and a fashionable portraitist. Most of his black-and-white illustrations – among the first to be photographed onto the block – were for magazines; his book work was incidental. (He apparently was not the illustrator of Anthony Trollope's *Way We Live Now* [1875], although he is so identified by Forrest Reid; the inferior designs are signed "L G F".) Among the contributions to John Foxe's *Book of Martyrs* (1866) by the leading illustrators of the period, however, his drawings of Ridley writing in prison and of Marsh reading the Bible on his way to his execution seem the most convincing. But he is remembered as an illustrator only because of his association with the unfinished *Mystery of Edwin Drood* (1870). Before Charles Dickens died suddenly, Fildes had completed twelve of the twenty-four illustrations contracted by Dickens. Fildes's realism, for which Dickens had chosen him at George Du Maurier's recommendation, is apparent in his illustration of the scene in which John Jasper, guardian of young Edwin Drood (and heavily clued as his probable murderer), falls unconscious on learning from dry-as-dust Mr. Grewgious, guardian of Miss Rosa Bud, that just before Drood's disappearance, she and Edwin had agreed not to marry (fig. 86). Perhaps Fildes's realism lent a mite of credibility to this strained and sometimes disagreeable tale, but the extremism of George Cruikshank's illustrations for *Oliver Twist* (1838) would have been more fitting.

Sir William Schwenck Gilbert

In the Preface to *The "Bab" Ballads* (1869), William S. Gilbert (1836–1911) wrote that he ventured to publish the illustrations with the ballads "because, while they are certainly quite as bad as the Ballads, they are not much worse". Not all critics have been so tolerant. Gilbert was not a trained draftsman, but like Edward Lear and G. K. Chesterton, he was proof that correct drawing is not indispensable to good humorous illustrating. In his simple, lightly shaded outline drawings for *The "Bab" Ballads*, with not a jot of effort spent on nonessentials, he transmitted not only the appearance and behavior of his imaginary characters, but also, as in the portrait of Lorenzo de Lardy and his inamorata (fig. 87), the irresistible drollery of his verse. He ad-libbed the same whimsical running visual commentary on *More "Bab" Ballads* (1873) and on *Songs of a Savoyard* (1890), but, alas, not on his Savoy operas. He also illustrated, conventionally, books written by his father, the novelist William Gilbert.

87. William Schwenck Gilbert. William Schwenck Gilbert, *The "Bab" Ballads* (1869).

Ernest Henry Griset

Although born in Boulogne, Ernest Griset (1844–1907) lived in London from his childhood on. He studied painting briefly in Belgium, but supported a large family as a comic illustrator for *Fun*, *Punch*, publications for children, and books of little account. In spite of being close to being the equal of his master Grandville in both draftsmanship and the depiction of fantasy, he did not create the masterworks of which he was capable. His substitutions of beasts, birds, and bugs for human beings derive much of their fascination as well as their authority from the superb life studies – some of the best in watercolor – that he regularly made at the London Zoo. Some good animal and insect drawings are among the thirty-six illustrations for each of three far-fetched and sometimes offensive narratives by James Greenwood. His two most popular books probably were *Griset's Grotesques; or Jokes Drawn on Wood, with Rhymes by Tom Hood* (1867), with 100 wood engravings accompanied by the wooden verses of Hood, and *Our London* (1884), reprints of *Fun* drawings. They demonstrate that Victorian illustrations need not have been cloaked in a pall of crosshatching. Griset's limited work as an interpretive illustrator was marred. Clearly, as Lionel Lambourne speculates in his study *Ernest Griset: Fantasies of a Victorian Illustrator* (1979), the publishers sought to capitalize

on Gustave Doré's success in England through imitating his effects by hiring Pannemaker et Fils of Paris to engrave the blocks for Daniel Defoe's *Robinson Crusoe* and for *Aesop's Fables*, both of which were published in 1869. Many of the almost 100 illustrations for *Robinson Crusoe* now seem to be in poor taste rather than amusing, but a few, such as the one of Crusoe's habitation within a stockade, show what Griset might have done had he devoted himself to serious illustration.

Aesop's Fables should have been Griset's masterpiece, but the thirty-two full-page designs were degraded by Pannemaker's allover tint-tool shading. Most of the sixty linear headpieces and tailpieces (some are partly tonal) are wonderfully fresh, but Victorian readers were probably more enthralled by the full-page Doréan designs. When they are not too Stygian, we can find them tolerable; and when we strip them in imagination to Griset's basic line drawings, we can admire them wholeheartedly. Even when he adopted a traditional Aesopian motif, as he did occasionally, Griset added his own inventions, as in "The Wolf and the Lamb", one of the less spoiled full-page designs (fig. 88). The ragged garb and club of the voracious wolf, the basket and posture of the lamb, and the flume that indicates that the stream flows toward the lamb – a problem not solved by most earlier illustrators – seem to be Griset's additions. Only the occasional lack of correspondence between image and text raises any question that Ernest

88. Ernest Henry Griset. *Aesop's Fables* (1869).

89. Henry Holiday. Lewis Carroll, *The Hunting of the Snark: an Agony in Eight Fits* (1876).

Griset's ninety-two illustrations form one of the most original English Aesop series.

Henry Holiday

Lewis Carroll's *Hunting of the Snark: an Agony in Eight Fits* (1876) is the one book illustrated by Henry Holiday (1839–1927) to achieve notice. He had a much easier task than had John Tenniel and Harry Furniss. He had only an eighty-three-page poem to deal with, and so his nine full-page wood engravings have a unity denied other series of illustrations for books written by Carroll. Furthermore, *The Hunting of the Snark* is witty, and, with its echoes of "Jabberwocky", much of it amuses children. For instance, children can connect Holiday's rousing illustration (fig. 89) with the stanza in which the Baker's uncle prophetically tells the Baker that if he discovers that the Snark is a Boojum, he will vanish. (He does.) Taken as a whole, however, the literal draftsmanship and the portraits of actual people tend to make Holiday's drawings seem more painstaking than humorous.

Arthur Boyd Houghton

Like John Tenniel and George Du Maurier, Arthur Boyd Houghton (1836–75) was blind in one eye. The other

troubled him throughout his career. He trained himself to draw from memory and, in time, to draw on the block with no preliminary sketches. The Dalziels added him to their team of illustrators when they enlarged their domain as engravers by producing and printing illustrated books to be sold by George Routledge, William Strahan, and other young publishers – a Victorian anticipation of the "creative" modern "package" plan. (The Dalziels refer to "A. Boyd Houghton", but he signed his drawings "A. Houghton" and "AH".) Houghton painted diligently but never escaped from the pressure of black-and-white drawing for books and periodicals. Perhaps because of his eye troubles and perhaps because of frustration with his lot, in spite of his devotion to his family, he drank himself to death before he was forty. Yet in one way, the times were right for Houghton. There was much work for an artist who combined speed and extreme conscientiousness, as he did. The burgeoning periodical press had to have just such talent at hand, and Houghton drew hundreds of blocks for numerous now-forgotten publications. The times also yielded a broader-based reading public for the Dalziels' gift books. Houghton's contributions to these volumes lose their individuality in mixed company. Thus in spite of the quantity and general excellence of his drawings, few books containing Houghton's illustrations can be singled out for special comment.

Mainly in company with Thomas Dalziel, but also with contributions by George Pinwell, John Everett Millais, Tenniel, John Watson, Thomas Morten, and Edward Dalziel, Houghton was the chief illustrator of *Dalziel's Illustrated Arabian Nights' Entertainments* (1865), edited by H. W. Dulcken. It came out first in parts and then in two volumes. The high standard of the illustrations, together with their number and generous size, made this one of the most popular Victorian books. Houghton's share of the 211 illustrations was 92, a task that occupied him for many months in addition to his other assignments. The portrayal of the unhappy Princess of Bengal (fig. 90) from "The Enchanted Horse" is an example of Houghton's best work. He applied two principles to his designs that not only improved the appearance of the resulting wood engravings, but also made the work of the engraver easier and faster. First, he used white extensively, but with limited contrasting dark passages. Second, he used curved single-line shading when the forms made it feasible. In this illustration, it gives the Princess's dress a graceful sweep. Houghton or the Dalziels crosshatched small areas for extra darkness only. (The lute with a broken string and the fountain are not in the text, but are legitimate additions.) For these drawings, according to the Dalziels, Houghton borrowed costumes and objects collected by his family and friends in India. Houghton's main appeal in this design and throughout the series is the sense of conviction he conveys. We believe in the deep depression of the Princess, who, having feigned madness to avoid marrying the Sultan of Cashmere, now yearns for Prince Firouz Shah just before he rescues her with the aid of the enchanted horse. Yet in the end, ironically, what *Arabian Nights' Entertainments* calls for is more remoteness, more mystery, not the immediacy and everyday acceptability that Houghton achieved in this, his most admired series.

Although not interpretations of a text, the most attractive series of wood engravings after drawings by Houghton is one of his earliest: the thirty-five designs commissioned from him alone by the Dalziels on the theme of child life. Accompanied by one page of awful verse written to order for each design by Jean Ingelow and six other "lady authors", the series appeared first as *Home Thoughts and Home Scenes* (1865) and later as *Happy Day Stories* (1875), with new text by Dulcken. This Dalziel enterprise contains large blocks printed on thin card. No doubt drawn from observation of Houghton's own family, the designs are now of considerable sociological interest for reasons not intended to be of interest: the large number of very young children in what must have been a typical middle-class Victorian family; the resident grandparents; the children's capacity for self-entertainment; and, in the one deviation

from the pleasant, the children's familiarity with death. Seldom can there have been published so thorough, loving, and unsentimental a record of the play and home life of young children. The remarkable variety of posture and planes in which the children are shown explains why Houghton has been held in such respect as a draftsman.

The laudable effort to be both original and authentic led Houghton into difficulties in his 107 designs for *Don Quixote* (1866). Because of their abundance, the illustrations are inevitably fresh in many respects. Even in standard scenes, such as Don Quixote's encounter with the three peasant girls who Sancho Panza leads him to think are Lady Dulcinea del Toboso and two of her damsels, Houghton's concepts were his own. In that illustration, he dressed Don Quixote in ballooning trousers and armor that look as they should look, a fair imitation of the real thing. During Sancho Panza's governorship, he presented the fat little man with his head buried in the enormous ruff of a quilted coat with a long train, a delicious invention. But the realism that focuses attention on such details tends to subdue both laughter and compassion. Then, too, the faces are so obscured by crosshatching that the two leading characters lack consistent identity.

Houghton's other illustrations often appeared first in periodicals. They are not memorable. The most extensive, all of which accompany designs by others, are the nine designs in *Ballad Stories of the Affections* (1866), seventeen in *A Round of Days* (1866), seven in John Foxe's *Book of Martyrs* (1866), sixteen in Ingelow's *Poems* (1867), twelve in *Golden Thoughts from Golden Fountains* (1867), thirteen in Robert Buchanan's *North Coast and Other Poems* (1868), twenty-four in William Ralston's *Krilof and His Fables* (1869), and six in Valentine's *Nobility of Life* (1869).

Arthur Hughes

During his long career, Arthur Hughes (1832–1915) was a painter who supplied his family's wants principally by designing wood-engraved illustrations for children's fairy tales and fantasies. It is said that between 1860 and 1865, he drew 231 designs for *Good Words* alone. He seems originally to have been chosen as the sole illustrator of the Irish poet William Allingham's *Music Master: A Love Story and Two Series of Day and Night Songs* (1855). He drew six of the eight illustrations; the two added at the end were by his friends John Everett Millais and Dante Gabriel Rossetti. It was a notable first for all three and for English book illustration. Hughes's frontispiece of a youth helping a young woman over a stile has the same spare manner as Millais's "Edward Gray". All the designs by Hughes have a quiet intensity new among Victorian illus-

90. Arthur Boyd Houghton. *Dalziel's Illustrated Arabian Nights' Entertainments* (1865).

91. Arthur Hughes. Christina Rossetti, *Sing-Song: a Nursery Rhyme Book* (1872).

92. William Holman Hunt. Alfred, Lord Tennyson, *Poems* (1857).

93. Charles Samuel Keene. Douglas Jerrold, *Mrs. Caudle's Curtain Lectures* (1866).

trations. For Tennyson's *Enoch Arden* (1866), he drew twenty-six designs. They indicate that he might have become one of the most successful illustrators of adult books had his bent been that way.

Among the juvenile books illustrated by Hughes, three are well known. As first illustrator of Thomas Hughes's *Tom Brown's Schooldays* (1869), he has long been identified with that classic. For young boys, his thirty-four illustrations have the virtue of obviousness; for Old Boys, the vice of nostalgia. Otherwise, the only design that escapes from the constrictive didacticism of the author is that showing a school servant locked in a cagelike cubicle and doling out money for the holiday coach ride home to impatient boys at four o'clock in the morning. Of the several children's books by George MacDonald that Hughes illustrated, *At the Back of the North Wind* (1871) is most praised. It is one of the longest books for young children ever published, a strange mixture of the fantasies of Diamond, a boy named after a horse, and the North Wind in the form of a woman, and the exploits of Diamond, when he is older, among London cabmen. Hughes's seventy-five illustrations do much to lend credibility to MacDonald's curious entertainment for the young.

The 118 drawings for Christina Rossetti's *Sing-Song: a Nursery Rhyme Book* (1872) give Hughes his place in English book illustration apart from his work for children.

Rossetti's stanzas only pretend to be for children. Hughes's vignette headpieces have the same disarming simplicity of form, usually with little shading or background, and the same range of humor, love, compassion, and grief as the lyrics. He sometimes failed to imagine a fresh design, but the variety of his images indicates how sensitively he followed the swallowlike flight of the verse. There are charming drawings of domestic animals and birds, including a lovely one of a swan. A drawing of a child happily clasping her countryman father as he carries a bundle of faggots suggests that Ernest Shepard's designs for *When We Were Very Young* (1924) owed something to the *Sing-Song* series (fig. 91). The frontispiece of a child amid the gnarled shapes of a forest in Gordon Hake's verse *Parables and Tales* (1872) is representative of the occasionally fine designs scattered among the other books illustrated by Arthur Hughes.

William Holman Hunt

One of the founding brothers of Pre-Raphaelitism and the epitome of the Victorian painter, William Holman Hunt (1827–1910) made drawings for only fifteen illustrations scattered among a number of books. In almost every instance, he was invited to contribute to a volume with other artists. He never drew an entire series of designs for one work and thus cannot be seriously regarded as a book

Oh, think ye na my heart was sair,
When my love dropt down and spake nae mair!
There did she swoon wi' meikle care,
    On fair Kirkconnell lee
                        HELEN OF KIRKCONNELL

94. John Lawson. *Ballads: Scottish and English* (1867).

illustrator. The seven designs in Edward Moxon's edition of Tennyson's *Poems* (1857) are his only extended effort. Together with the designs by John Everett Millais and Dante Gabriel Rossetti, they hold promise of a new spirit in English illustration. Only Hunt's headpiece for "The Lady of Shalott", however, has any of the sense of strangeness that permeates young Rossetti's designs. Her hair somehow floating horizontally, the Lady stands within a curious circular horizontal loom, forgetful of her weaving as she watches sideways in a round mirror Lancelot approaching Camelot. Better drawn are Hunt's headpieces for Tennyson's "Recollections of the Arabian Nights", "The Ballad of Oriana", and "Godiva". The second shows the warrior-narrator pledging his troth to Oriana on the ramparts of a castle before going into battle below the walls (fig. 92). The scene is indicated but not described in the verse. Hunt suggested the urgency of the moment by showing the lover stringing his bow and his horse neighing impatiently, and he foreshadowed the tragic outcome by showing Oriana looking away into space.

The few other book illustrations that Hunt drew are more conscientious than either inspiring or suffused with Pre Raphaelite mystique. His one contribution to Margaret Scott Gatty's first series of *Parables from Nature* (1861) derives its interest from the subject matter of the parable "Active and Passive". A sailor with a spyglass under his arm studies an inscription on a sundial, while below him, a sexton digs a grave. "The Lent Jewels", the frontispiece to Robert Willmott's anthology *English Sacred Poetry of the Sixteenth, Seventeenth, and Eighteenth Centuries* (1861), is a fine drawing of a couple walking in the courtyard of a palace. More evocative is the figure of a young woman kneeling on a bed as she prays beside a dormer window, in Isaac Watts's *Divine and Moral Songs for Children* (1863). The frontispiece to the medieval poem *The Pearl* (1891), a young woman, rather than the infant protagonist of the poem, with a large crown held on her hip and a large pearl on her breast, fails to convey any of the mystic fervor and lyricism of the verse.

Charles Samuel Keene

Apprenticed for five years to the wood engraver Charles Whymper, Charles Keene (1823–91) never went to art school. He differed from his fellow Londoners George Cruikshank, Hablot Browne, and John Gilbert in basing his drawings on life studies, however. His work, which has been widely admired, appeared chiefly in periodicals, most of it as illustrations of unamusing jokes in *Punch*, where he succeeded John Leech as chief humorous cartoonist in 1864. Although he was an excellent etcher, his work was reproduced by wood engravers.

Keene's book illustration was incidental. His first substantial mature effort was fifteen designs for Charles Reade's *Good Fight*. This historical romance first appeared in *Once a Week* in 1859 and seems not to have been reprinted as a book with all the cuts until 1910. (It was published, much enlarged, as *The Cloister and the Hearth* in 1861 without illustrations.) In *A Good Fight*, Keene stylized his drawings somewhat for the sake of the medieval matter about Erasmus's alleged parents. Only one of the designs has a sense of permanence, that of Gerard leaning across a table to clasp Margaret's hands, a partial anticipation of Frederick Sandys's "Old Chartist" (1862), also in *Once a Week*.

The Cambridge grisette (1862) by Vaughan Morgan deserves mention only because Keene's eight full-page and eight initial chapter vignettes – which go with legends such as "Your Name and College, Sir?" "Chocolate and Madeira", "The Langham Rooms", and "The Boudoir Bar" – are now of almost anthropological interest. Something of the reason for the adulation of Keene by the intemperate Joseph Pennell and others is apparent in *Legends of Number Nip* (1864), translated from the German by Mark Lemon, first editor of *Punch*. Keene's six vignettes are sturdy folktale designs, so cleanly drawn that they served as models for the pen-and-ink draftsmen of the next generation. Among the dissimilar efforts illustrating ten of Tom Taylor's translations of the viscount de La Villemarqué's *Ballads and Songs of Brittany* (1865), Keene's one full-page illustration, "The March of Arthur", stands out. First, the warriors are carrying rifles, instead of spears and bows and arrows, up a rocky mountain path; the erroneous weaponry suggests that the careful Keene did not have the text before him. Second, the files of men form an unusual design handled so firmly that it is in strong contrast with most of the others, particularly the fussy ones by John Everett Millais. "The March of Arthur" is one of the most modern of Victorian illustrations.

Keene's drawings for Douglas Jerrold's *Mrs. Caudle's Curtain Lectures* (1866) have been regarded as masterpieces of book illustration. The frontispiece is a colored lithograph of the sober Mr. Caudle on his doorstep at night without a key, while Mrs. Caudle's silhouette on the window shade indicates her state of readiness. There follow thirty-seven small illustrations, which accompany initials, and nineteen larger vignettes. The crisp unsigned wood engravings must be the remains of some of Keene's most lifelike drawings. But, like many in *Punch*, they are too true to life to be funny. For one thing, the couple look like their children's grandparents throughout. As a graphic humorist, Keene needed the grace of a bit of caricature even more than did Leech.

The scene illustrating the thirty-second lecture looks grimly serious. Although Jerrold's tone is jocular, Mrs. Caudle accuses Mr. Caudle of flirting with Kitty the maid and threatens to dismiss her for stealing when her quarter is up on Tuesday (fig. 93). (On Tuesday, she does just that.)

On balance, it seems too bad that Charles Keene did not illustrate serious literature, for his realistic studies seem better adapted for it than for the trivia to which he devoted his career.

John Lawson

The assignments given the Scottish artist John Lawson (fl. 1865–89) in books by now-forgotten minor authors and by some who wisely remained anonymous would excuse his omission from this study. But the title-page vignette and seven full-page designs for *Ballads: Scottish and English* (1867) deserve recognition because they are one of the really satisfactory nineteenth-century series. Much of the credit for the good impression they make is due to the sensitive engraving by Robert Paterson. The illustration for "Fair Helen of Kirkconnell", Helen dying in the arms of her lover after she has shielded him from being shot by a jealous rival, exemplifies Lawson's meticulous drawing of main figures and detail, to both of which he gave emphasis through an uncrowded setting and spare crosshatching (fig. 94). (He might have omitted the rival's face and had better luck with the broken-hearted lover's expression.) There is nothing remarkable about Lawson's best work; it was good by the professional standards of the time because it was what both the ballads and the readers required.

Fredercik, Baron Leighton

Among the many mid-nineteenth-century painters who occasionally submitted their drawings to the mercies of the wood engravers of illustrations for magazines and books, Frederick Leighton (1830–96) was one of the most distinguished. What sets him apart is that he demonstrated the capabilities of a true illustrator. Since he was a busy painter and sculptor, and the president of the Royal Academy after 1878, not an illustrator, his contributions to a few minor works and his celebrated designs for *Dalziel's Bible Gallery* (1881) can be passed over. Leighton's one major effort as an illustrator in a close working relationship with an author is his series for George Eliot's *Romola*, which was serialized in the *Cornhill Magazine* in 1865 and was published in two volumes in 1880. About twelve of the twenty-four illustrations are among the best of the period. Inferior engraving by some of Swain's hands probably accounts for the less satisfactory look of the rest. Leighton's firmly outlined, careful drawings and restraint in crosshatching made facsimile engraving of his designs reasonable. His concentration on main characters interacting against lighter backgrounds gives precedence to situation rather than scene.

"The Blind Scholar and His Daughter", the first design in the *Romola* series, exhibits how sincerely Leighton entered into his task as illustrator (fig. 95). According to Leonée Ormond and Richard Ormond in *Lord Leighton* (1975), Eliot was delighted that the artist "knew Florence by heart", but she engaged in spirited correspondence with him about his drawings. After Leighton had overruled her objections to the look of the daughter in this design, she agreed tartly that "the exigencies of your art forbid perfect correspondence between the text and the illustration". She later concluded that "illustrations can only form a sort of overture to the text".

James Mahoney

Like Frederick Walker and George Pinwell, James Mahoney (fl. 1865–79) began his career as an apprentice to the wood engraver and mountain climber Edward Whymper. Before drink ruined him, Mahoney did enough good work, most of it in magazines, to offset the ordinariness of the rest. His 150 or more designs for *Oliver Twist*, *Our Mutual Friend*, and *Little Dorrit* in the twenty-one volume *Works of Charles Dickens. Household Edition* (1871–79) make up the main body of his book work. In spite of the Dalziels' capable engraving (the edition was one of the projects they managed), many designs are overloaded with crosshatching; but they are generally natural and expressive of Dickens's intentions.

Sir John Everett Millais

In 1848, at the age of nineteen, John Everett Millais (1829–96) was one of the founders of the Pre-Raphaelite Brotherhood, but he soon edged away to paint portraits, landscapes, and historical, literary, and anecdotal subjects in his own fashion. In time, he gathered public honors that included a baronetcy, the presidency of the Royal Academy, and burial at St. Paul's Cathedral. His first significant book illustration was his single wood-engraved design in William Allingham's *Music Master: A Love Story and Two Series of Day and Night Songs* (1855). His Pre-Raphaelite friends Arthur Hughes and Dante Gabriel Rossetti drew the other illustrations in the little collection of poems. Millais's illustration shows a charming group, composed of a mother telling a story to five children and an older woman in front of a

95. Frederick Leighton. George Eliot, *Romola* (1880).

fireplace. It evokes the trancelike mood of the poem and anticipates the much-loved "Grandmother's Apology", which Millais did for *Once a Week* in 1859.

Young Millais was the leading contributor to the memorable Edward Moxon edition of Tennyson's *Poems* (1857), with eighteen illustrations. The traditional artists represented in the volume are Thomas Creswick, William Mulready, John Callcott Horsley, and Clarkson Stanfield; but the volume is a landmark in English illustration because of the thirty designs by the Pre-Raphaelites Millais, William Holman Hunt, and Rossetti. Millais's work reveals a basic confusion that he had difficulty in resolving. He used two conflicting styles, tonal and linear. His design for "St. Agnes's Eve" – a nun holding a candle as she stands on a dark tower stair – is an example of the first, and the one for "Edward Gray" – the heartbroken citified Gray holding hands with a sympathetic lady as they stand in a pasture – exemplifies the second. In the "St. Agnes's Eve" design and in numerous others, Millais covered most of the block with crosshatching. The "Edward Gray" drawing is perhaps too severely in the German hard-outline style. When he struck a balance and molded the forms of his cleanly linear figures with a minimum of shading and blended them into their surroundings, as he did beautifully in the dressing of the bride at the end of "The Talking Oak", he arrived at a model for wood-engraved illustration. Even he ignored its virtues. In several other multiple-artist collections, the one or two designs by Millais stand out because of their intense feeling without melodramatics, although good compositions often suffer from surplus crosshatching.

The reputation of Millais as an interpretive book illustrator rests largely on his designs for four of Anthony Trollope's novels: *Framley Parsonage* (1861), six designs; *Orley Farm* (1862), forty; *The Small House at Allington* (1864), eighteen; and *Phineas Finn, the Irish Member* (1869), twenty. Heretical as it may be to say so, these illustrations contribute so little to the books that they could be omitted. Millais drew figures in dark clothing, which he represented by closely scratched crosshatching with few highlights. But the chief deficiency is of interpretation, beginning with the choice of moments to be illustrated. "Bread sauce is so ticklish" and "Please, ma'am, can we have the pease to shell?" are the inspirations for two designs in which a servant stands with folded hands before a seated figure. Of the forty illustrations in *Orley Farm*, eight are of one figure and fifteen, of two. Typical of the single-figure designs with their legends are a woman seated ("There was sorrow in her heart, and deep thought in her mind"), a man seated ("Von Bauhr's dream"), a man standing by a table ("Why should I not?"), and a woman standing and looking toward the corner of a room ("And how are they all at Noningsby?") as she addresses a visitor who is outside the frame of the illustration. Among these immobile single figures and the numerous two figures who rarely do anything but look at each other are several graceful drawings, such as "The Crawley Family" in *Framley Parsonage*, "Guilty" (an exceptional, emotional scene) in *Orley Farm*, and " 'Mama,' she said at last, 'it's over now, I'm sure' " in *The Small House at Allington*.

Although Millais's series for Trollope's novels depict with authority the more sedate and affluent aspects of Victorian domestic existence, it is difficult to find grounds for the admiration they have aroused, beginning with that of the novelist himself. The charitable thing to say is that Millais may have subordinated his own interests in order to do what he thought Trollope's narratives required, and guessed wrong. (The illustrations for *Framley Parsonage* and *The Small House at Allington* were reproduced superbly by the Dalziels in *The Cornhill Gallery* [1864] from the original wood blocks instead of from the electrotype casts used in the *Cornhill Magazine*, in which Trollope's novels first were serialized.)

Millais worked hard for six years on *The Parables of Our Lord and Saviour Jesus Christ* (1864 [1863]), so hard that he wearied and completed only twenty of the thirty illustrations he had contracted to draw for the Dalziels, who occasionally combined publishing with engraving. Twelve of the designs first appeared in the magazine *Good Words*. The series was immensely popular, and the Dalziels made money from Millais's drawings and even from his blocks in addition to the profit on the 10,000 copies printed. Millais's approach was fresh. He ignored traditional biblical motifs and fitted the characters into rural Scotland, where he was staying at the time. Conceptually, the designs are moving, clearly because the words of Jesus moved Millais. The compositions – particularly "The Good Samaritan", "The Prodigal Son", and "The Unjust Judge" (perhaps Millais's leading Pre-Raphaelite illustration) – are unusual, almost monumental. "The Sower", "The Pearl of Great Price", and "The Pharisee and the Publican" are mainly in the linear style, with restrained molding of figures. But, again, he was inconsistent. He repeated his effort to paint with crosshatching in a number of designs, including his unfortunate night scenes: "The Tares" and the frequently praised "Lost Piece of Silver". As a whole, the series is too uneven to be the masterwork that it has been said to be. It excels in the intensity and sincerity of the feeling that it communicates.

When fifteen years later, Millais came to illustrate William Makepeace Thackeray's *Memoirs of Barry Lyndon* (1879) with four vignettes, he had arrived at a style that looked back to eighteenth-century engraving and that

96. John Everett Millais. William Makepeace Thackeray, *The Memoirs of Barry Lyndon* (1879).

anticipated the best of the pen-and-ink work of the next three decades. Barry sitting sideways and reading one of Lady Lyndon's letters in the "whisky shop" while the servant he has bribed sits in the shadows with his back to Barry and drinks is as suave as anything by Edwin Austin Abbey or Hugh Thomson (fig. 96).

John Everett Millais might have been one of the most important English book illustrators. Numerous critics say he is. His sensitive response to literature, his ability to compose groups of figures in easy and revealing relationships, and his early mastery of the molded-outline style made him potentially the ideal artist of Victorian wood-engraved illustration. To reach that eminence, however, he would have had to illustrate more books by himself, to illustrate novels that are more physically animated than are the four by Trollope, and to hold steady to the molded-linear style. He certainly would have fared better had his drawings been reproduced by photo process without the intervention of engravers. The widely varying effects produced by different engravers can be seen in *Millais's Illustrations* (1866).

Thomas Morten

Troubled by epilepsy and money problems, Thomas Morten (1836–66) wavered between progression and retro-

gression as a painter and an illustrator. At thirty, he ended his short career by hanging himself. His skill as a draftsman would have earned him a respectable place in an account of Victorian book illustration had he not plagiarized some of his designs and thus made the rest suspect. In *The Illustrators of the Sixties*, Forrest Reid mentioned Morten's indebtedness to Gustave Doré in Jonathan Swift's *Gulliver's Travels* (1865) and scolded him for other "cribbing", including an exact copy of a drawing by John Dawson Watson from *Good Words* for John Foxe's *Book of Martyrs* (1866). Yet Reid and others have praised the eighty main illustrations in *Gulliver's Travels* for their originality, and Gordon N. Ray, in *The Illustrator and the Book in England from 1790 to 1914* (1976), rated the edition the best in English before that of Rex Whistler (1930). In 1973, however, Allan R. Life pointed out that in addition to the borrowings from Doré and others, the entire series was heavily indebted to illustrations by John Gordon Thomson, then an amateur (later a *Fun* cartoonist), which appear in an edition of *Gulliver's Travels* published as one of S. O. Beeton's Penny Books: "Thomson's designs often function as studies for Morten's far more elaborate and accomplished works." To observe the proprieties, let us call this the Morten–Thomson edition, with contributions from Doré. It is one of the books of the period to be preserved and studied, not rejected.

The full-page illustrations – there are many smaller decorations – do not turn Swift's masterpiece into a completely successful series of images, but many designs are more spontaneous and convincing than those in any other English edition. In the frontispiece, Gulliver's legs serve as a triumphal arch through which the Lilliputian army can march. Two scenes in the introductory "Life of Jonathan Swift" give intimate glimpses of the author: in the garden at Moor Park with Stella; and "bereaved and miserable", with his bald head lowered on a table. The first twenty Lilliput illustrations are the most appealing, probably because Gulliver is large – man seems important. The drollery of the satire is apparent, and amusing detail is abundant, as in the cuts of Gulliver kneeling while 300 tailors make him a suit of clothes (fig. 97), of a crowd of savants examining his watch through a telescope, of Gulliver using a Lilliputian hogshead to toast the King and Queen, and of Gulliver about to leave Lilliput, shown first in a rowboat and then in a sailboat.

In the twenty-two illustrations in the Brobdingnag section, where the relative sizes are reversed, designs of the quality of that showing the Queen taking Gulliver in her hand to the King as he reads and the terrifying one of Gulliver being attacked by monstrous bees and other insects make manifest Swift's theme of man's insignificance. In the third section, set on the flying island of Laputa, Lagado, and island of the sorcerers, Thomson and Morten faced difficulties in translating the verbal extravagances into concrete terms, but among the twenty designs are some successes – ghosts serving meals, for instance. In the country of the Houyhnhnms, as Swift's satire darkens, the artists lost their grip. The horses look unnatural rather than superior. Finally, the beastly human Yahoos – or Mrs. Grundy – defeated them, and they let them go unpictured. The Morten and Thomson illustrations are an imperfect but often fascinating set of adult interpretations of a classic that seldom is illustrated without enfeebling concessions to young readers. It is also a memorial to the flawed but talented Thomas Morten.

Sir Joseph Noel Paton

From textile designing in Paisley, the Scot Noel Paton (1821–1901) became a painter of literary, historical, and allegorical subjects who had a flair for illustrating, which he indulged sparingly. He developed a clear, well-balanced Germanic linear style in which shading plays a limited modeling and accenting role. In his twenty-three drawings for William Edmonstoune Aytoun's *Lays of the Scottish Cavaliers and Other Poems* (1863), he revealed an unusual faculty for handling pages full of costumed figures in scenes

of war. A number of his illustrations have more emotional force than do the poems. For the first poem, "Edinburgh after Flodden", for example, there are moving designs of Randolph Murray, the broken captain of the Scottish forces, returning alone from Flodden in defeat and giving the Provost of Edinburgh the torn Scottish ensign that his young son had carried into battle.

Paton's twenty large wood engravings for Samuel Taylor Coleridge's *Ancient Mariner* (1863) form one of the superb series of English illustrations. The drawings are impeccable, and the engraving is facsimile technique at its best. The series deals with all aspects of the Mariner's discourse – from his stopping one of three Wedding Guests (in Renaissance costume), through the shipboard crises, to the return of the stricken ship to its home harbor and the Mariner's resumption of the life of Christian grace. This complete visual embodiment is enriched by all sorts of concrete detail. The compatibility of Paton's effects with Coleridge's magic lines can be seen in the design of the Mariner, alone with his dead shipmates, so moved by the beauty of the water snakes on the "rotting sea" that he blesses them unawares and is able to pray, whereupon the Albatross drops from his neck into the sea (fig. 98). (Paton placed the Mariner on the bowsprit just forward of the anchor.) The series is not perfect. In three designs, the souls in flight are far from ghostly, and at no time do the sailors look as emaciated as their ordeal demands.

Most of the twenty large designs in the posthumous deluxe *National Shakespeare* (1904) are overworked, overposed, and understated, but there are exceptions: the lively illustrations for *Henry IV*, the figure of Macbeth, Othello telling Desdemona and her father the story of his life, and Lear holding the dead Cordelia are indeed Shakespearean.

George John Pinwell

An uneducated boy who liked to draw, George J. Pinwell (1842–75) studied briefly at two art schools and in the studio of the wood engravers Charles and Edward Whymper and then went on to become a respected illustrator. Like most of his artist friends, he expended much of his energies on work for *Good Words*, *Once a Week*, and other magazines of the day. He had a long illness in 1870 and died at the age of thirty-three in 1875, the same year as Arthur Boyd Houghton and Frederick Walker. The first important assignment of Pinwell's career was 10 illustrations of the 211 in *Dalziel's Illustrated Arabian Nights' Entertainments* (1865). Like Houghton, Pinwell shared most of his assignments in this standard Dalziel manner. While seven of Pinwell's *Arabian Nights' Entertainments* designs are for the popular Sindbad episodes, they reassert facts rather

97. Thomas Morten. Jonathan Swift, *Gulliver's Travels* (1865).

98. Noel Paton. Samuel Taylor Coleridge, *The Ancient Mariner* (1863).

than stir wonder. Sindbad arranging his escape from the Valley of Diamonds by means of a roc and Sindbad about to kill the drunken Old Man of the Sea with a rock are his liveliest contributions.

Pinwell's finest hour came a little too early in his career. The Dalziels entrusted to him alone one of their most ambitious projects, *Dalziel's Illustrated Goldsmith* (1865), which is uniform in design with *Arabian Nights' Entertainments*. It contains designs of varying sizes, some of which are vignettes and the rest, within borders. Pinwell still had limitations as a draftsman. His faces are rarely clear cut or attractive because of messy shading around the main features, and the dark shadows behind foreground figures sometimes became arid tracts of crosshatching. Nevertheless, Pinwell's illustrations make this edition of Oliver Goldsmith's works one of the goodly volumes among Victorian illustrated books. The accumulation of scene after scene of homely, natural, and expressive groupings builds up a trust in the illustrations as an extension of the text. In the illustration of a scene from *The Vicar of Wakefield* (fig. 99), the reader can believe that Mrs. Primrose is actually greeting her erring daughter with the absurd words that Goldsmith put in her mouth and that Olivia is overcome with shame. The forty-three illustrations for *The Vicar of Wakefield* record without artifice the affections and afflictions of the unfortunate but resilient Primrose family. Whether it is a sociable evening with Farmer Flamborough and the blind piper, the itinerant limner painting a portrait of one of the daughters, Dr. Primrose preaching to his fellow prisoners, or Burchell's final test of Sophia, all seem uncontrived.

In 1866, the Dalziels and George Routledge brought out an edition of Alain René Le Sage's *Adventures of Gil Blas*, with eight unsigned illustrations identified as Pinwell's by Forrest Reid. If they are his, he may have had his monogram removed because he recognized that he had completely failed to capture the spirit of the picaresque tale. His two main interpretive efforts after this are in Jean Ingelow's *Poems* (1867), for which he drew twenty of the ninety-seven illustrations, and in Robert Buchanan's *North Coast and Other Poems* (1868), for which he drew six of fifty-three. The seven he did for Ingelow's "High Tide on the Coast of Lincolnshire" are refreshing. Those he did for *North Coast* are not. Among the remaining books listed in the Catalog, Pinwell was only rarely represented by a fine design, such as the Charles Keene-like street scene for "Only a Lost Child" among his eight in the large coffee-table volume *Touches of Nature* (1867) and the interior of a barn, "The First Swallow", among his eighteen in *Wayside Poesies* (1867).

Dante Gabriel Rossetti

Poet and translator as well as painter, Dante Gabriel Rossetti (1828–82) joined William Holman Hunt and John Everett Millais in the short-lived but influential Pre-Raphaelite Brotherhood (1848–51). Illustrating was for him a brief and unsatisfactory episode. His total book output was only ten illustrations in four books. Yet today he seems a figure of greater interest and consequence than many more productive artists.

William Allingham, an Irish poet and friend of Rossetti, Millais, and Arthur Hughes, seems to have arranged that first Hughes and then the three of them illustrate his collection of poems, *The Music Master : A Love Story and Two Series of Day and Night Songs* (1855). Always dilatory, Rossetti drew only one design, the well-known "Maids of Elfen-Mere". He had never drawn on a wood block and tried to cover his inexperience by complaining about the Dalziels' engraving, which was superb. (He even failed to allow for the reversal of the design in printing.) Yet the drawing has about it a sense of mystery rarely seen before except in the designs by William Blake and Henry Fuseli. Rossetti did not introduce anything not in the poem; "The Maids of Elfen-Mere" deals with the supernatural. To put into one design the idea of how disturbed the sensitive Pastor's Son is by the recurrent visitations of the Three Damsels and their disappearance at eleven o'clock, Rossetti drew the Damsels – white-robed, strongly lighted, and otherworldly – filling the block vertically as they sing. Then, in a brilliant inspiration, he seated the Pastor's Son on the floor, a dark substantial figure of this world seen from the back against the light, his troubled face averted in profile. (The design should be viewed in a mirror.) This one wood block has been mainly responsible for dating the beginning of mid-Victorian book illustration with *The Music Master*.

Five of Rossetti's book illustrations are in Edward Moxon's edition of Tennyson's *Poems* (1857), shared with Millais, Hunt, and five other illustrators. In a comment on the Moxon edition of Tennyson, Laurence Housman wrote in *Arthur Boyd Houghton* (1896) that the main difference between the Pre-Raphaelites and the other artists was that the others did nothing to show that they had any sense that they were illustrating literature. Hunt did the opening illustration for "The Lady of Shalott", but let Rossetti do the concluding one: Lancelot gazing down on the dead Lady in the boat in which she has floated to Camelot (fig. 100). It is a strong design weakened by the addition of candles, which are not in the text, and of small figures in the background. But Lancelot bending forward is the great knight of Arthur's court, and he could indeed be saying, "God in his mercy lend her grace". The second design, for "Marian in the South", must be meant to illustrate the lines

Low on her knees herself she cast,
Before Our Lady murmur'd she . . .
And on the liquid mirror glow'd
The clear perfection of her face.

But Marian is at the feet of Christ on the Cross, and the mirror, behind her, reflects the back of her head. The coarse engraving by Linton pleased Rossetti.

The third design, the first of two illustrations for Tennyson's "Palace of Art", is Rossetti's famous St. Cecilia. It illustrates just one stanza:

Or in a clear-walled city on the sea,
    Near gilded organ-pipes, her hair
Wound with white roses, slept St. Cecily;
    An angel look'd at her.

The design, which Tennyson said he did not understand, has brought forth some far-fetched explanations. St. Cecilia kneels in front of what seems to be a miniature organ above a portcullis arch: her hands rest on the keys as though playing; her head is thrown far back; and her eyes are closed. It is clear that Rossetti preferred to think of her not as being asleep, but as enraptured. She is being kissed (one critic says "munched") by a cloaked male figure. It is not clear where his hands are or how the object on his back, which looks inflated, can function as wings. That the soldier in the lower corner, who is placed with his back to the intense scene above and is eating an apple, symbolizes the indifference of the ordinary world is obvious, excessively so. We are left with a cluttered, willfully implausible design full of passion and wonder.

The second "Palace of Art" design illustrates the stanza that comes next but one after the St. Cecilia stanza. It represents King Arthur, wounded, "dozing in the vale of Avalon,/And watch'd by weeping queens". In a crowded oval arrangement, ten queens sit on the grass, their spiky coronets close together and their identical faces expressing curiosity rather than grief. They are not weeping. It takes a while to discover the bearded face of Arthur as he lies within the enclosure of queens. Neither "Palace of Art" design illustrates the poem, only special references within it; but, again, both designs are faithful to Tennyson in their conveying a sense of events that transcend the ordinary.

The fifth illustration, for "Sir Galahad", is also factually confused. It illustrates Galahad's stop at a "secret shrine" where he hears voices and where tapers are burning, not a critical instant in the poem. Linton's engraving does not

do all that it might do for Rossetti's drawing, and Rossetti's illustration does not do much for Tennyson's poem.

After the Tennyson effort, Rossetti had had about enough of the rigors of book illustration. Thus he never illustrated any of his own poems, which he unquestionably would have done with distinction. He relented to the extent of drawing four designs for two of his sister Christina's slight volumes of verse. The first, *Goblin Market and Other Poems* (1862), reveals Rossetti's ability to adjust to his material. The frontispiece shows the wicked anthropomorphic goblin men – post-Grandville and pre-Tenniel clothed birds and small animals, including a wombat – wheedling a curl from Laura as payment for their baskets of fruit (worldly pleasures), which she craves, while in the background, sensible sister Lizzie flees. It is a delightful drawing, and if the crowding goblin men are clearly up to no good, they do not seem so sinister as they are in Christina's allegorical fantasy. On the added title page, the sisters, "Golden head by golden head", sleep wrapped in each other's arms. Victorian readers may have found the image disconcerting, but Lizzie and Laura belong to the fleshy rather than the fleshly school. (One hand is much larger than the other three.)

Rossetti also contributed a frontispiece and a title-page design to Christina's *Prince's Progress and Other Poems* (1866). The prince, who has been mysteriously delayed on the journey to his wedding, arrives as the body of his betrothed is carried by. For this scene, Rossetti invented an illustration of a vault with the prince weeping, maidens praying, and the bride-to-be lying in the upper tier of a tomb. The design stresses the maudlin and fails to suggest he strange evil forces that have brought about this conclusion. The square title-page design of the young bride-to-be sitting by an overly dark casement window, her hands extended before her as she waits for the prince, fits the mood of the key line: "The long hours go and come and go."

Dante Gabriel Rossetti's ten illustrations did nothing to cultivate the nonacademic naturalism that he and the other Pre-Raphaelites and John Ruskin talked about so earnestly. But, as Edward Burne-Jones testified, these designs did a great deal to encourage the artist as illustrator to take his role seriously and to fulfill it creatively.

Frederick Sandys

Because he never drew an extensive series of illustrations for a book and because almost all his twenty-five designs in books first appeared in magazines, Frederick Sandys (1829?–1904) was only marginally a book illustrator. He was an open imitator of Albrecht Dürer and his nineteenth-century follower Alfred Rethel and developed an "un-

99. George Pinwell. *Dalziel's Illustrated Goldsmith* (1865).

173

100. Dante Gabriel Rossetti. Alfred, Lord Tennyson, *Poems* (1857).

101. Frederick Sandys. *Touches of Nature* (1867).

174

equivocal line" admirably suited for reproduction by wood engraving. Several of his magnificent designs have had a life of their own apart from their texts, particularly "The Old Chartist", "Rosamond, Queen of the Lombards", "The Waiting Time", "Danaë in the Brazen Chamber", "Amor Mundi", "Manoli", and "The Death of King Warwolf". "Amor Mundi" illustrated Dante Gabriel Rossetti's poem of that title in the *Shilling Magazine* in 1865. Typical of Sandys's contributions to several volumes are the two illustrations in Robert Willmott's anthology *English Sacred Poetry of the Sixteenth, Seventeenth, and Eighteenth Centuries* (1861): the fine "Life's Journey", a man bending over the body of his son, who had been lost in a wood; and the familiar "Little Mourner", a girl on her knees in the snow in a graveyard. His nine blocks in George Walter Thornbury's *Historical & Legendary Ballads & Songs* (1876) were originally designed for different texts in *Once a Week*.

Three of Sandys's illustrations were reproduced in *Touches of Nature* (1867), an anthology from William Strahan's magazines, with the poems for which they had been designed. They afford a chance to look beyond Sandys's superb draftsmanship to estimate his potential as an interpretive illustrator. The first one illustrates Christina Rossetti's "Hoping Against Hope", a plaint for the return of a lover. A young woman sits on a headland and gazes out to sea, her tension revealed only by a hand gripping a tuft of beach grass and her teeth clenched on a strand of hair. She is perhaps too much like Electra waiting for the return of Orestes to be the woman in Rossetti's brittle verse, but she is one of the nobler Victorian creations. For "Sleep", a mother's soliloquy over her sleeping daughter, Sandys skillfully solved the problem of how to make clear that the girl is not dead. The illustration says everything that Dora Greenwell's verse tried to say, without the embarrassing explicitness. The third poem, "Until Her Death", by Dinah Mulock Craik, even more embarrassingly speculates about the future death of a beloved person. Sandys accepted the theme but gave it his own, larger interpretation (fig. 101). A woman in a Renaissance gown leaning forward in contemplation, chin in hand, may seem to pay homage too directly to Dürer's *Melancholy*.

Frederick Sandys may have remained rooted in the past for too long. But he was a superb draftsman who would have been an excellent interpretive illustrator had he illustrated major works by authors who had the same order of imagination as his own.

Frederick James Shields

After early hardships, Frederick Shields (1833–1911) won the friendship of leading literary and artistic figures, including Dante Gabriel Rossetti and Ford Madox Brown, with whom he is generally associated as an artist. Inspired by Pre-Raphaelite designs in Edward Moxon's edition of Tennyson's *Poems* (1857), he began a series of illustrations for *The Pilgrim's Progress* in 1859. John Ruskin praised a photograph of the "Vanity Fair" drawing on a wood block, and Charles Kingsley helped Shields with the costumes and other details. He completed seventeen illustrations in 1861, but they were not published until 1864 as *Illustrations for Bunyan's "Pilgrim's Progress"*, with, to his bitter chagrin, only brief quotations instead of the full text. They were generously admired by Ruskin and others.

Meanwhile, Shields had published the work on which his reputation as a book illustrator rests, a series of six designs for Daniel Defoe's *History of the Plague of London* (1863). The book is rare, but the drawings are in the British Museum. Designs such as "The Plague Pit", with corpses sliding out of a tip cart into a pit by torchlight (fig. 102), and "The End of a Refugee", with a dead body being dragged by a long hooked pole to a hurried grave, have a stark objectivity that is in harmony with Defoe's bare prose. The design that has caught the imagination of later generations is that of the Quaker Solomon Eagle running nearly naked through the streets of London and crying that the plague, which he had predicted, has come to punish the impenitent. The designs of Solomon Eagle and of the plague pit, as well as others among the final four designs in *History of the Plague of London* – the best – owe a good deal to the four metal engravings made after George Cruikshank's drawings for an edition of 1833, but they are not copies. Shields thought that the engravers had botched his drawings. Perhaps because of his double disappointment, he gave up illustrating – except for one drawing of Christ and the disciples in *Touches of Nature* (1867) – for painting, mainly in watercolor.

William Small

To almost all the books listed under his name in the Catalog, the painter and lithographer William Small (1843–1931) contributed only one or two pleasant designs. No surprises are among the four in Jean Ingelow's *Poems* (1867) and the four in *Touches of Nature* (1867). One of a child watching a carpenter shaping a beam outdoors, in *Touches of Nature*, exemplifies his idyllic picture making. But Small demonstrated two verities that are often ignored: first, illustrators, like politicians, sometimes rise above their ordinary performance when faced with a large challenge; second, engravers hold the artistic fate of illustrators in their hands, literally.

In the ten-volume *Works of Henry Fielding* (1882), Small had his one big opportunity; he was the only illustrator of the first five volumes, which embrace Fielding's novels: *Tom Jones* (two volumes), *Amelia*, *Joseph Andrews*, and *Jonathan Wild*. For each volume, he was allowed eight full-page illustrations, a generous forty in all. His engraver was the little known Robert Paterson, described in U. Thieme and F. Becker's *Allgemeines Lexikon der bildenden Künstler* (1907–50) only as a "copper-engraver in Edinburgh and London 1870–79". Paterson employed the parallel-white-line tonal wood-engraving technique. How amply Small's drawings realize Fielding's un-Victorian episodes and how rich a presence Paterson gave them by his suave burin work are apparent in "Mr. Allworthy Assisted in Carrying Off the Captain to a Warm Bed" (fig. 103) in *Tom Jones*. Captain Blifil has endured his unpleasant marriage by making elaborate plans for spending the fortune that his wife will inherit at Mr. Allworthy's death. Now, while taking his evening walk, the captain has died of apoplexy and has kept dinner waiting, greatly upsetting Mrs. Blifil. The formality of Small's drawing seems better suited to Sir Walter Scott than to Henry Fielding, whose rough irony is better matched by the etched line of Thomas Rowlandson, George Cruikshank, and Hablot Browne. But there can be no doubt that Small read Fielding with sound understanding of what are significant scenes and that the forty designs in the realistic mode of the times were appropriate for their Victorian public. They still give impressive style and substance to Fielding's characters.

According to Forrest Reid in *The Illustrators of the Sixties*, Small in his later years drew in wash on the blocks and left the interpretation to the engravers, as undoubtedly he did in the Fielding volumes. The result, Reid asserts solemnly, was "the beginning of the decadence, for it was on these later drawings that the new school was founded, bringing our period of illustration to an end".

Marcus Stone

Whether or not Charles Dickens intended young Marcus Stone (1840–1921) to supplant Phiz, Stone has been remembered as a book illustrator principally for seeming to have done just that. He also has been said to represent a new generation of realistic illustrators. Stone was in no way the equal of Phiz, but he deserves a brief mention for another reason. Examination of his designs for works of various authors as engraved by the Dalziels, Swain, and Green indicates that while his drawings vary in quality, they usually give an impression of freshness and excellence. For instance, in the illustration "The Boofer Lady" for *Our Mutual Friend* (1865), the lady is not only beautiful,

but also interesting. James Mahoney, however, in the fifty-eight illustrations for a later edition of *Our Mutual Friend* (1871–79), chose scenes of much more vitality than did Stone for his forty.

Stone freed himself and his engravers from the tyranny of excessive crosshatching. Although he drew careful preliminary sketches of figures and settings, he simplified his designs to essentials. Then he used strong crosshatching and white areas for emphasis and lighter line work for subordinate elements. Comparison of the works by Stone proves that his control of effects was deliberate. The dinner scene between Dorothy and her Aunt Jemima in the excellent series of sixty-four designs for Anthony Trollope's *He Knew He Was Right* (1869) is a good example of his work (fig. 104).

Marcus Stone showed that the detailed comprehensiveness of so much wood-engraved illustration of the nineteenth century was as much a reflection of the mid-Victorian state of mind as were parlor furnishings.

Sir John Tenniel

Before he illustrated *Alice in Wonderland* – that is, *Alice's Adventures in Wonderland* and *Through the Looking-Glass, and What Alice Found There* – John Tenniel (1820–1914) was known internationally for his weekly political cartoons in *Punch*. He had joined *Punch* in 1850, was the head cartoonist from 1862 to 1901, and was knighted in recognition in 1893. He also had contributed illustrations to a number of books; indeed, his career as a book illustrator was almost finished. Yet the two books by Lewis Carroll made Tenniel one of the best known and universally admired English illustrators.

Tenniel, who had lost an eye in an accident, had little training in art, was an early practitioner of the German shaded-outline style, and drew from memory. He began illustrating as early as 1844, but is so firmly identified with the mid-Victorians that he is included with them in this study. Tenniel's first solo effort was *Aesop's Fables* (1848). He and Joseph Wolf had to redraw some of the animals in 1851; but his cartoons eventually became identified with animals, such as the Russian bear. He usually made his drawings on paper, traced them in reverse on wood, and redrew them for the engraver. His series of twenty-two etchings on steel for Shirley Brooks's novel *The Gordian Knot* (1860), however, are among his best illustrations. For a long time, his sixty-nine wood engravings in Tom Moore's *Lalla Rookh* (1861) were extravagantly praised. The decline in the taste for oriental romances makes it necessary to read *Lalla Rookh* to appreciate their excellence.

In a dozen or so books, Tenniel suffered from having a

102. Frederick James Shields. Daniel Defoe, *History of the Plague of London* (1863).

103. William Small. Henry Fielding, *Tom Jones* (1882).

small number of his designs lost among those of other artists. Among his most substantial contributions to these joint efforts were ten in Robert Pollok's *Course of Time* (1857), thirty of sixty in Richard Harris Barham's *Ingoldsby Legends* (1864), and eight in *Dalziel's Illustrated Arabian Nights' Entertainments* (1865). Paradoxically, Tenniel's illustrations in books other than Carroll's that now seem most convincing are not romantic, fantastic, or humorous but are serious, as in *The Gordian Knot* and *The Mirage of Life* (1867), a collection by William H. Miller of examples of the unsubstantiality of fame, for which he drew twenty-nine designs.

The genesis of *Alice's Adventures in Wonderland* (1866) is well documented. The Reverend Charles Lutwidge Dodgson (1832–98) was a mathematics don at Christ Church College, Oxford, who adopted the nom de plume Lewis Carroll (Lewis from Lutwidge, Carroll from Charles) to keep his lighter writings separate from his scholarly work. He was unusually fond of little girls. On 4 July 1862, he made up a story as he and a clergyman friend rowed the three daughters – Lorina, thirteen; Alice, ten; and Edith, eight – of Dean Liddell of Christ Church College up the Isis to Godstow for a picnic. When they returned, Alice, his favorite, begged him to put the story in writing for her. Carroll began writing immediately, made an uncommon arrangement with Macmillan in February 1863 for publication at his own expense, secured Tenniel as illustrator in April 1864, and received the first galleys from his printer, the Oxford University Press, in May 1864. As batches of proof were delivered, Carroll went up to London to confer with Tenniel and the Dalziel brothers, the engravers. By the end of June 1865, 2000 copies of *Alice's Adventures in Wonderland* were ready.

The illustrating of *Alice's Adventures in Wonderland* was a cooperative effort. Carroll was a fussy man who had definite ideas about the illustrations, but he was also one of the best early photographers in England, had a strong interest in art, and could draw a bit. He had hand-lettered and illustrated with thirty-seven pen drawings a manuscript that he called "Alice's Adventures Under Ground", which he had promised Alice Liddell in July 1862 but did not deliver to her until November 1864. Tenniel must have seen these drawings or versions of them because a few of his designs are quite similar. It seems that Carroll was persistent but polite in making suggestions but that Tenniel never accepted any against his judgment. Both men were influenced by the surrealistic work of the French artist Grandville, whose humorous drawings of animals, birds, flowers, and inanimate objects in human roles were popular in England. They could not help also being familiar with somewhat similar personifications in the work of George

Cruikshank and Richard Doyle.

Including the frontispiece, which is an illustration for Chapter XI, Tenniel drew forty-two designs for *Alice's Adventures in Wonderland* at the rate of £3 5s. each. Fourteen of the larger ones have borders; the vignettes, which are of different sizes, are distributed throughout the book in an unattractive manner. Tenniel was not satisfied with the printing of the wood engravings, and Carroll obligingly and at considerable expense had the edition reprinted by the London firm of Richard Clay. It was issued before Christmas 1865 but, as was customary, with the publication date of 1866. The Oxford edition was sold to the New York publisher Appleton with a new title page, also dated "1866". In the books printed in London, the quality of the printing of the type is better than in the Oxford edition, but the illustrations seem to have printed too light, at least in the copies examined for this study.

Analysis of Tenniel's forty-two illustrations for *Alice's Adventures in Wonderland* in relation to Carroll's text yields both concurrence in the expert and popular judgment that the two are bound in an indissoluble union and agreement with the minority opinion that the union is not perfect. The strongest negative reaction arises from the passive, even incidental, treatment of Alice (whose feet are too small and head sometimes is too large). The main reason for Tenniel's success is the compatibility of his drawings with Carroll's narrative style. What Gleeson White called Tenniel's "decisive, unsympathetic line" when engraved in wood created images of detailed literalness that vouch for the truthfulness of Carroll's unexaggerated manner of telling his dream tale. This is apparent in the pivotal scene of Alice's encounter with the King and Queen of Hearts, in which the demure Alice is surprisingly rude to the ferocious Queen (fig. 105). There is an identity of spirit between image and text that required no special adjustment on Tenniel's part; his illustrations for *Alice's Adventures in Wonderland* have the same factuality as do his political cartoons for *Punch*.

A few specific examples of the pluses and minuses of the series can be briefly noted. The most popular designs probably are those for the poem "Father William". The four illustrations occupy the top half of successive pages and present Father William and his young questioner in animated action: Father William standing on his head, doing a backward somersault, and balancing an eel on his nose; and the young man bending forward in astonishment as he uncovers the empty platter. Negatively, however, these four outweigh the illustrations in any other part of the book, and "Father William" was inserted as a divertimento, not as part of Alice's adventure. The rest of the book is well balanced, with the trial of the Knave of Hearts for

104. Marcus Stone. Anthony Trollope, *He Knew He Was Right* (1869).

105. John Tenniel. Lewis Carroll, *Alice's Adventures in Wonderland* (1866).

106. George Housman Thomas. Anthony Trollope, *The Last Chronicle of Barset* (1867).

stealing the tarts, the most elaborate full-page design, given the prominence of the frontispiece and with Alice taking the lead in two full-page vignettes at the end: upsetting the jury box, and being attacked by the pack of cards before awakening.

The immense success of *Alice's Adventures in Wonderland* led to popular demand for a second volume. *Through the Looking-Glass, and What Alice Found There* (December 1871, dated "1872") followed. Circumstances had changed. Carroll no longer was writing down for young readers the improvisations of a summer day. He was a celebrity writing "another Alice book", consciously or not for an adult audience. A logician as well as a mathematician, Carroll not only considered the metaphysical implications of such events as Alice's passing through a looking glass, but also involved her in a game of chess and subjected her to a great deal of adult play on words. Thus *Through the Looking-Glass* resembles *Alice's Adventures in Wonderland* only in being a fantasy built around a ten-year-old girl named Alice. (Alice Liddell was now approaching twenty.) The illustrations, consequently, are more sophisticated.

Tenniel agreed reluctantly to again be Carroll's illustrator. He drew fifty designs, all vignettes except the frontispiece, that are more uniform in size than are those in *Alice's Adventures in Wonderland*. As a series, they also are more varied, more complex, and more interesting on an adult level. They present difficulties for children to understand. The chief improvement is that Alice has an active role throughout. Her vigorous presence makes inconspicuous her absence from two famous poems, "Jabberwocky" and "The Walrus and the Carpenter", with their well-known illustrations. Alice's involvement with the chess pieces gives her a share in the main episode, but her encounters with Tweedledum and Tweedledee, Humpty Dumpty, and the White Knight stimulate more entertaining illustrations. Carroll again has Alice throw a tantrum for a climax, a second interesting psychological development; and Tenniel brilliantly recorded in precise terms Carroll's description of the spirited scene of Alice pulling the cloth and dishes off the table at the dinner in her honor at her becoming a queen. Carroll wisely discarded a superfluous episode between Alice and a wasp wearing a wig when Tenniel protested that a wasp in a wig was "altogether beyond the appliances of art".

John Tenniel's success in illustrating Lewis Carroll's *Alice's Adventures in Wonderland* and *Through the Looking-Glass, and What Alice Found There* can be attributed to several elements: the intense and permanent appeal of the dream narratives to many children and adults; the perfect way in which a sizable number of the drawings turn Carroll's special blend of everyday event and outrageous fantasy into memorable scenes; the contribution of Tenniel's stiff, literal style to this sense of credibility; and the international popularity of Tenniel as a *Punch* artist. Yet the illustrations are uneven: some are much less necessary, imaginative, or completely realized than others; and Alice too often is unexpressive and uninvolved. The episodic nature of both books accounts for the fact that Tenniel's best remembered designs are for interpolated poems, but numerous other drawings are, in all respects, fine illustrations. Except for the peculiar realm of emblem books, never in England have text and image been so indivisibly fused as in the two books that go by the title *Alice in Wonderland*.

George Housman Thomas

After his apprenticeship as a wood engraver, George Thomas (1824–68) is said to have been successful as a wood engraver in Paris, as the publisher of an illustrated newspaper in New York, and as the engraver of bank notes before he returned to London as a magazine and book illustrator shortly before his death. It is difficult to determine how he managed at the same time to be continually productive illustrating books for English publishers in the 1850s and 1860s. His most sustained efforts are the eleven designs in *A Book of Favourite Modern Ballads* (1860), twenty in Wilkie Collins's *Armadale* (1866), and thirty-two in Anthony Trollope's *Last Chronicle of Barset* (1867). He achieved professional caliber without a special identity. And yet he sometimes showed a superior grasp of the function of illustration. For instance, in his illustration of the scene in which Lochinvar rides off with Ellen in *A Book of Favourite Modern Ballads*, he avoided triteness by playing down the lovers and by giving full rein to the consternation caused by the abduction. Thomas's ability to individualize characters and employ pantomime and emotional play can be seen in his illustration of the quiet scene in *The Last Chronicle of Barset* in which Mr. Toogood arrives at Mr. Crawley's schoolroom to tell him that he is no longer under suspicion of theft (fig. 106).

Frederick Walker

A poor London boy, apprenticed first to an architect and then to the wood engraver Edward Whymper, Frederick Walker (1840–75) gradually edged into book illustration by way of *Once a Week* and the *Cornhill Magazine*, which brought him to the attention of William Makepeace Thackeray. He was one of the conscientious but undistinguished social realists of the mid-nineteenth century who hold our attention precisely because their drawings so literally preserve the Victorian scene and spirit. His designs in the several gift books whose illustration he shared with better known artists tend to be attractive pictures rather than illustrations, but some are convincing expressions of honest sentiment: a woman knitting while she reads the Bible and a child praying in Robert Willmott's collection *English Sacred Poetry of the Sixteenth, Seventeenth, and Eighteenth Centuries* (1861), and "Only a Lost Child" in *Touches of Nature* (1867), for example. In his short career, Walker had little chance to assert himself as an interpretive illustrator of serious literature. Among the designs in the second of two novels by Anne Thackeray Ritchie – *The Story of Elizabeth* (1867 and *The Village on the Cliff* (1867) – that of Monsieur Fontaine blowing a cornet while his wife plays the piano is up to the standard of any work by his more admired contemporaries. Walker's only substantial series, however, is the one for Thackeray's *Adventures of Philip* (1868). Among the sixteen illustrations, scenes such as "Laura's Fireside", "Morning Greetings", and "A Letter from New York" suggest that Thackeray was an arrant sentimentalist. Only "Judith and Holofernes", the nurse Caroline standing over the drunken Reverend Mr. Hunt, whom she has banged on the head with a cupboard door and then knocked out with chloroform, shows the robust side of Thackeray. "The Poor Helping the Poor" in *The Adventures of Philip* is a fair example of Walker's best illustrating (fig. 107). Denis Duval and Tom Parrot examining a pistol is the best of the four designs that Walker drew for Thackeray's unfinished *Denis Duval* (1882) before the novelist's death.

John Dawson Watson

Without unusual distinction, John D. Watson (1832–92) was still one of the leading mid-nineteenth-century illustrators. Primarily a painter of genre subjects in watercolor, he conceived of his function as an illustrator in modest terms: to be factually faithful in his restatements of an author's words. Because he held to that purpose, his illustrations have the sincerity that the times demanded; his work is a reminder that novelty may not always be vitally necessary. Yet the Dalziels chose Watson to do all 110 designs for *The Pilgrim's Progress* (1861) because the publisher wanted a fresh look. The figures sometimes seem posed, and unrelieved crosshatching grows tedious. Nevertheless, Watson's realism consorts well with John Bunyan's bare narrative, as in the drawings "Vanity Fair" and "Little Faith Robbed".

The illustrations must have pleased, for Watson's twenty-eight of eighty wood engravings made him the leading contributor to Robert Willmott's anthology *English Sacred Poetry of the Sixteenth, Seventeenth, and Eighteenth Centuries* (1861). His collaborators included John Gilbert, eight designs; the Pre-Raphaelites William Holman Hunt, one, and Frederick Sandys, two; Charles Keene, two; Henry Marks, seven; Frederick Pickersgill, one; Frederick Walker, three; Harrison Weir, four; Joseph Wolf, seven; and several other lesser known artists, seventeen. On the whole, Watson caught the spirit of the early poets very well, although the ten realistic designs for Thomas Gray's "Elegy Written in a Country Churchyard" evoke neither a unified theme nor a graphic impression. But his illustrations of a family reading the Bible, a congregation praying, a child embracing its mother, a child saying grace, and a father sitting on the side of the bed of his dying daughter are among the best in the volume. He also made three drawings for the similar *English Sacred Poetry of the Olden Time* (1864). The one for Henry Vaughan's "Morning", an exhortation to morning prayer, is a design of unaffected simplicity: a woman kneeling on an upholstered prie-dieu.

Another major assignment was Daniel Defoe's *Robinson Crusoe* (1864), for which Watson made 100 drawings. As in *The Pilgrim's Progress*, the unadorned images give authenticity to Crusoe's understated account. For example, on his return to the ship after the wreck, Crusoe states,

My difficulty was still greater to know how to get on board. . . . I swam around her twice, and the second time I espied a small piece of rope hanging down the fore-chains so low that with great difficulty I got hold of it, and by the help of that rope got into the forecastle of the ship.

Watson showed Crusoe in the middle of his climb, hauling himself up by the shrouds with one foot still in the fore chains and the bit of rope dangling (fig. 108). The literalness of the close-up has a good deal of the magic of Defoe's concrete prose. Watson never again had so challenging an assignment, but he was a frequent contributor with other popular illustrators to the periodicals and anthologies of the 1860s.

Harrison William Weir

After seven years of apprenticeship to George Baxter, a color printer, during which he also learned to engrave on wood, Harrison Weir (1824–1906) became a painter of birds and animals. Apart from specialized works in his field, such as Miller's *Sports and Pastimes of Merry England* (1859), for which he drew twenty-one designs, his book illustrations usually ranged from one to six and were incidental to the interpretive illustrations or landscapes by other artists. Weir's major solo effort is his series for the Reverend George F. Townsend's *Three Hundred Aesop's Fables: Literally Translated from the Greek* (1867). The title page

107. Frederick Walker. William Makepeace Thackeray, *The Adventures of Philip* (1868).

108. John Dawson Watson. Daniel Defoe, *Robinson Crusoe* (1864).

109. Harrison William Weir. George F. Townsend, *Three Hundred Aesop's Fables: Literally Translated from the Greek* (1867).

110. Joseph Wolf. John G. Wood, *The Illustrated Natural History* ([1859], 1862, 1863).

184

111. William Stephen Coleman. John G. Wood, *The Illustrated Natural History* ([1859], 1862, 1863).

112. Thomas W. Wood. John G. Wood, *The Illustrated Natural History* ([1859], 1862, 1863).

of this Routledge edition lists 114 illustrations. These vignettes are marked by clearly drawn characters, little foreground, virtually no background, and, usually, a minimum of crosshatching. Weir's animals sometimes are exceedingly appealing, as in the headpiece for "The Town Mouse and the Country Mouse" (fig. 109). The naturalist John G. Wood said about Weir's birds and animals – he contributed to two of Wood's books – that they were "always picturesque but never correct". In *Three Hundred Aesop's Fables*, that failing would have been tolerable if Weir had shown more imagination in depicting his creatures acting out the fables. This edition, reprinted in 1874 with fifty fables and illustrations, is not to be confused with *The Fables of Aesop. Translated by Samuel Croxall. With New Applications, Morals, etc. by Rev. George Fyler Townsend* (1866), with 110 fables and anonymous illustrations, similar to Weir's, also cut down to fifty in an 1869 edition.

Joseph Wolf

A German country boy who had an avid interest in wild creatures, Joseph Wolf (1820–99) had been well trained as an artist before he migrated to London. In England, he enjoyed a solid reputation as a painter of birds and animals and eventually was appointed Special Artist to the Zoological Society. His drawings of birds and animals in numerous books supplemented the illustrations of other artists, but he was not an interpretive illustrator and is included in this study because of his achievement in the illustration of nature books. His best work appears in *The Illustrated Natural History* ([1859], 1862, 1863) by the Reverend John G. Wood, then chaplain of St. Bartholomew's Hospital. This extremely readable work first came out in 1853 with 450 vignettes by William Harvey, then appeared in larger monthly parts over almost four years, and finally was published in three volumes: I, *Mammalia*;

II, *Birds*; and III, *Reptiles, Fishes, Molluscs*. Not counting diagrams, 1400 wood engravings of various sizes, almost all vignettes, adorn the 2300 pages. Wolf's associate artists were Harrison Weir, Johann Zwecker, William Coleman, Thomas W. Wood, and at least four others. The Dalziels, who were responsible for the art work, say that they and George Routledge conferred with John Wood every Monday. They praise Wolf above all the other artists. His "Koodoo", an African antelope, explains their enthusiasm (fig. 110).

More than the usual credit must go to the engravers for their incomparable burin work in this vast collection. They used the tint tool too freely for the skies, but almost no crosshatching. The results frequently are beautiful and startlingly modern. One suspects that whoever first set the style of Agnes Miller Parker and other twentieth-century wood engravers of nature subjects must have learned important lessons from Wood's *Illustrated Natural History*. Much of the charm of the autographic engravings of the 1930s can be found in the artful arrangement of the animals in "Crab-Eating Opossum" (fig. 111) by Coleman (1829–1904) and in the textures and contrasts of the lovely study of two moths (fig. 112) by Thomas Wood (fl. 1855–72).

In the numerous literary works to which Wolf usually contributed only two or three cuts, his animals fail to make much of an impression among the more dramatic illustrations with human figures. The nearest he came to interpretive illustration was in William Strahan's edition of *Aesop's Fables* (1867), in which he divided the 100 cuts with Zwecker and Thomas Dalziel. The results are not quite either fable or natural history. Some of Wolf's most attractive drawings appear as chromolithographs in several books about birds and animals, including Philip Sclater and Oldfield Thomas's authoritative *Book of Antelopes* (1894–1900), in four volumes.

CHAPTER EIGHT

The Nineteenth Century (III)
1886–1900

During the third period of nineteenth-century illustration, a wholly distinct group of artists succeeded those of the midcentury, and significant new developments took place. The most far-reaching was the introduction of photo-engraving, by which pen-and-ink line drawings can be reproduced exactly from the originals without an intermediary metal or wood engraving. In the misnamed photoengraving – or photo process, as it is more accurately called – a line drawing is photographed on a sensitized zinc plate, and the *white* areas are lowered by etching, not engraving. (New electronic methods are now in use.) Mounted on a wood block on the same level as the type, the relief design can be printed at the same time as the type, as are woodcuts and wood engravings. Perfected by Charles Gillot in France in 1872, the process began to be used in England in the early 1880s, especially by periodicals such as the *Illustrated London News*. But 1886 has been chosen as the opening date of the third period because the publication in that year of Joseph Addison's *Days with Sir Roger de Coverley* with pen drawings by Hugh Thomson can be said with reasonable justification to mark the beginning of a new era in English book illustration. Pen and ink is now second only to photography as the most economical and widely used form of graphics for reproduction.

The process block was an enormous advance in the saving of time, labor, and money. Photographing drawings onto blocks had released the artist from having to draw to the exact, cramped dimensions of wood blocks or, worse, from having to draw on the blocks. Photoengraving eliminated the block and the time-consuming engraving. A drawing can be enlarged or reduced at will, as long as its proportions are the same as those of the space to be occupied. In principle, photoengraving was an aesthetic advance, too, since it puts no constraint on the artist except to draw clean lines in black ink, which then are reproduced exactly without the intervention of another hand. Ironically, now that it would have made no difference mechanically if they had loaded their drawings with crosshatching, most of the late-nineteenth-century illustrators saw the virtue of cutting

down on it. They also relied on light vignettes to a large degree in place of heavy designs within borders. Some publishers and older artists were skeptical of or even antagonistic toward photoengraving, and a few – notably the brother and sister writer-engraver team of Laurence and Clemence Housman – clung to wood engraving long after the line cut had come into general use. Sadly, of course, the reproductive wood engraver soon became an extinct species. Before the century closed, photoengraving by the halftone process made possible the reproduction of brush drawings, but these monotone illustrations in books had to be printed on glossy coated paper and are not appealing.

The mastery of the technique of drawing with a pen for photographic reproduction by Edwin Austin Abbey, Thomson, Charles Brock, Henry Brock, Edmund Sullivan, and their more talented followers gave a new look to books in these final years of the nineteenth century. Abbey led the way, but Thomson's series of illustrations for the novels of Elizabeth Gaskell, Mary Russell Mitford, and Jane Austen and for similar gentle English classics of the past set the fashion. Close imitation of his style created a body of illustrated books of unprecedented charm. Some pen-and-ink artists aimed at something other than charm. Sullivan demonstrated how much vigor could be put into designs for the works of an author like Thomas Carlyle. Walter Crane, R. Anning Bell, and others devoted their talents to decorating rather than interpreting texts, and their mannerisms had an important part in the Art Nouveau movement of the 1890s. Then there was the young original, Aubrey Beardsley, with a head full of notions about using his pen and affronting late-Victorian sensibilities.

As it happened, the swift demise of reproductive wood engraving was followed by enthusiasm for the woodcuts of the fifteenth and sixteenth centuries, especially the Italian. It cannot be said that one led to the other. Rather, distaste for the conditions of life resulting from the industrialization of England and for machine-made products evoked an interest in socialism and handicrafts, among which printing and, theoretically, original woodcuts had a place. The leader in this movement was William Morris, whose Kelmscott Press books, illustrated by Edward Burne-Jones, are landmarks of English book publishing. Charles Ricketts had more influence as a teacher, printer, book designer, and illustrator. He adopted autographic wood engraving patterned more closely after unshaded Italian woodcuts. Other autographic wood engravers of the time were Sturge Moore, Lucien Pissarro, and William Nicholson.

Among other developments that mark this short period as one of the most stimulating in the history of English book illustration was the introduction of photographic color-plate illustrations during the last years of the nineteenth century. The first plates were two- and three-color flat tints imposed on pen drawings, which often had previously been published. Like brush drawings, they had to be printed on glossy coated paper and were separately bound in, tipped in, or pasted onto inserted sheets of thin card. They tend to be dark and muddy, but some are not and are oddly appealing. The use of etching for book illustration by William Strang was an isolated, but distinguished, phenomenon.

Photography was responsible for a good deal of mediocre illustrating during the 1890s and early 1900s. It contributed to the proliferation of magazines, which increased the demand for illustrations and decreased the time between commission and publication. Much of the poor book work of these years appeared first in magazines or was by illustrators who were accustomed to work for magazines. Thus a number of productive and competent illustrators of the period either were omitted from this study or appear only in the Catalog. (Noninterpretive specialists, such as the architectural draftsmen Herbert Austin Railton [1857–1910] and Edward Hort New [1871–1931], also are omitted.) The mediocrity of the work was often as much a matter of attitude as of execution. The ephemeral nature of many publications discouraged illustrators from imagining that they were producing serious art. The brief popularity of halftone wash drawings that simulated photographs – and sometimes were literally imposed on photographs – gave meretricious realism a temporary popularity.

Edwin Austin Abbey

Because he lived in England most of the time from 1878 until his death, became a leading member of the Royal Academy, and has a tablet to his memory in the crypt of St. Paul's Cathedral, the American Edwin Austin Abbey (1852–1911) takes his place in English book illustration with only slight reservations. As a staff artist for Harper & Brothers, he went to England in 1878 to make approximately sixty drawings for *Selections from the Poetry of*

Robert Herrick. They appeared first in *Harper's New Monthly Magazine* in New York as wood engravings, and in 1883, they were published in book form in London. Half of Abbey's drawings were in wash and look dead because the American engravers were addicted to multiple-tint tools. But Abbey's line drawings have a lifelikeness, sensitivity of line, and grace that usher in a new style. Adolf Friedrich von Menzel, Jean Louis Meissonier, and Daniel Vierge seem to have been his main influences. A look back at his vigorous but encumbered wood-engraved illustrations for an American edition of Charles Dickens's *Christmas Stories* (1876) shows what a liberating force photo process was.

The drawings for Abbey's second important work, Oliver Goldsmith's *She Stoops to Conquer* (1888), had run intermittently in *Harper's New Monthly Magazine* from December 1884 through August 1886, and Henry James had hailed them as masterly even before the first folio edition appeared in New York in 1887 and in London in 1888. The new photo-process method reproduced the delicate scratchy lines and graduated shading with a close, but far from perfect, faithfulness. (Abbey, unfortunately, still chose to do some scenes in watercolor, which required halftone reproduction.) He regularly used models. By turning and bending them, he showed them in many planes, which produced much more lifelike variety than had the repetitious postures of the drawn-from-memory figures in the illustrations of many of his Victorian predecessors. Abbey took immense pains in research to ensure accuracy of period costume, furniture, and accessories. Yet instead of seeming to be posed in a clutter of objects, Goldsmith's characters seem to be living actors and actresses seen on a stage during a performance or, perhaps more exactly, a dress rehearsal, since Abbey achieved concentration of focus by leaving blank much of the space in his dozen full-page pen-and-ink designs and his fifty assorted small ones and by giving body to only important props, without laboring over the drawing. Abbey loved literature and understood exactly the personalities, interrelationships, bearing, and behavior of Tony Lumpkin, the Marlows, and the Hardcastles. The illusion was so different from the effect of mid-Victorian illustration that Abbey was immediately popular.

In *Old Songs* (1889), Abbey turned seventeen lyrics – including "Barbara Allen", "Sally in Our Alley", and "Phillada Flouts Me" – into songs in black and white. For "Kitty of Coleraine", Abbey did a suite of four full-page vignettes, each a summary of one stanza, each light and airy with Irish sun and sentiment. *The Quiet Life* (1890) is a companion volume to *Old Songs*. Abbey contributed thirty-seven illustrations. In the ten for Alexander Pope's "Ode to Solitude", scenes of the happy man (clearly a

113. Edwin Austen Abbey. Oliver Goldsmith, *The Deserted Village* (1902).

114. Aubrey Beardsley. Oscar Wilde, *Salome* (1894).

bachelor) fishing, reading under a shady tree in summer and in a snug study in winter, and playing at bowls expand the familiar lines, as in a reverie.

The four-volume edition of William Shakespeare's *Comedies* (1899), with Abbey's 131 full-page illustrations for the 14 plays, was published only in New York. Most of the production errors of *She Stoops to Conquer* were corrected. Photogravure almost does justice to the etching-like delicacy of Abbey's pen-and-ink work. Few artists have illustrated Shakespeare so comprehensively or have equaled the liveliness, dignity, and individuality of Abbey's Shakespearean characters. He bought books, went to Italy, had mock-up sets and costumes made, and labored for years over these drawings and those for the histories and the tragedies. Only the comedies were published, probably because the other designs grew increasingly to resemble the murals for which Abbey was becoming famous.

In spite of tasteless production, mixed techniques, and excessively refined pen lines that printed gray, Abbey's illustrations for Goldsmith's *Deserted Village* (1902) are superb. A random example is his drawing for the lines about the village preacher who was "passing rich on forty pounds a year" and whose "house was known to all the vagrant train" (fig. 113). Goldsmith merely introduced the characters. Abbey assembled them in a scene, choosing that moment when the soldier takes center stage to act out his memories of "how fields are won". The bare, flagstoned room; the arrogant, slouching wastrel; the preacher, alarmed and perplexed at the violence being relived by the peglegged veteran in his old foot soldier's greatcoat; the bright-eyed listening wife; and the beggar, heedless of everything but his food – in the light from the fire, the five characters, so "real", so apparently casual, yet so artfully arranged, represent the essence of creative graphic realization.

Aubrey Vincent Beardsley

Much of the best work of Aubrey Beardsley (1872–98) can be found in the magazines of which he was the bright star, *Yellow Book* (1894–95) and *Savoy* (1896). His stature as a book illustrator, however, has to be measured by the complete series in three books: Sir Thomas Malory's *Morte Darthur* (1893–94), Oscar Wilde's *Salome* (1894), and Alexander Pope's *Rape of the Lock* (1896). To give a better idea of the range of his activity, the Catalog lists all the books that he illustrated, including several titles for which he drew only frontispieces.

While a clerk in an insurance office, Beardsley was encouraged to study art at night by Edward Burne-Jones. In 1892, he received by chance the assignment to illustrate

and decorate Malory's *Morte Darthur* in imitation of the Kelmscott Press books, which had just begun to appear. Before he finished, Beardsley may have seen drawings for the 1896 edition of Chaucer's *Works* at Burne-Jones's house. *Morte Darthur* was issued first in twelve monthly parts beginning in June 1893 and then in three volumes, the first in 1893 and the other two in 1894. For the almost 1000 pages, Beardsley made 20 full-page pen drawings and more than 300 incidental headings, initials, and initial page of each of the 21 books. The result was a clutter of inharmonious shapes and a waste of limited energy. Boredom page of each of the 21 books. The result was a clutter of inharmonious shapes and waste of limited energy. Boredom led to a change of style from respectful imitation of Burne-Jones to imitations of Andrea Mantegna, Carlo Crivelli, and Japanese woodcuts, which are woefully out of key with Malory's prose. All the illustrations exhibit weaknesses of drawing, and few add anything as realizations of the text, which Beardsley said, perhaps in exaggeration, he had not read. Two exceptions are "Merlin and Nimmue", which conveys a sense of sorcery at work, and the last illustration, which depicts Queen Guenever's withdrawal to Almesbury after King Arthur's death to become a nun. Although unsuccessful, Beardsley's illustrations for *Morte Darthur* were a remarkable feat for an inexperienced twenty-year-old youth.

In the first number of the *Studio* (April 1893), Beardsley had seven drawings, and Joseph Pennell wrote the first critical appreciation of his work. One drawing was of Salome holding the head of John the Baptist. Beardsley added an inscription in French from the first edition of Wilde's play *Salome*, which had been published in Paris earlier that year. This drawing led to Beardsley's illustrating the first English edition: *Salome, A Tragedy in One Act Translated from the French of Oscar Wilde: Pictured by Aubrey Beardsley* (1894). Beardsley made thirteen pen drawings: ten illustrations, two full-page decorative borders with figures, and a final tailpiece. The illustrations were inspired by Japanese woodcuts and, to a lesser degree, by Greek vase decorations. From the Japanese, Beardsley adopted sweeping curved lines, unshaded figures, arbitrary black areas, occasional small objects, and ample white space. His faces, however, still have a Pre-Raphaelite cast.

To a considerable degree, Beardsley used Wilde's play as an excuse to do decorative drawings and seems at times to have been making fun of both play and author, especially by using Wilde's face in a mocking manner and by giving prominence to the homosexual subplot introduced by Wilde. This resulted in his having to make some changes and to substitute illustrations that he candidly described as irrelevant. Beardsley found himself unable to take seriously Wilde's erotic and morbid rewriting of the episode of Salome and John the Baptist in Matthew 14:6–11 and in Flaubert's version, *Herodias*. As a consequence, only four of the ten main illustrations are fully concerned with the action of the play. The insertion of Wilde's likeness into the first, fourth, fifth, and sixth illustrations was immature and irresponsible. The third and eighth are irrelevant substitutions.

Of the four designs left, the second, "The Peacock Skirt" (fig. 114), definitely illustrates the moment of the imprisoned Iokanaan's (John the Baptist's) release, which Salome has negotiated with Herod, although the scene comes sixteen pages after the illustration. Salome says, "I must look at him closer," and Iokanaan says, in Wilde's flabby prose, "Who is this woman who is looking at me? I will not have her look at me." Salome bends forward, her head nearly touching that of the perturbed prophet. Unable to stomach Wilde's unctuousness, Beardsley indulged in fantasy and in an exhibition of pen virtuosity, as can be seen by Salome's wonderful peacock skirt and the utterly improbable young Iokanaan. Yet Beardsley conveyed the electric charge of the confrontation.

The seventh illustration, "The Stomach Dance", is, like "The Peacock Skirt", an extravagant image that Beardsley's imagination distilled from the text, but it also presents one of the high points of the play with a vividness that could not have been captured by naturalistic interpretation. Salome, quite rightly not dancing or encumbered with seven veils, is the epitome of Herod's lust, and a diseased gargoyle madly playing a stringed instrument is the symbol of the pervasive evil of the play.

The ninth and tenth illustrations deal with the climax of the play – Salome receiving her reward, the head of Iokanaan, for having danced. Beardsley played no tricks with either design. In the ninth, Salome grasps the bloody head of Iokanaan by the hair as the black arm of the executioner raises it on a shield from the cistern prison. The image is true to the gruesome text. Beardsley added grace by encasing the tall figure of Salome in a black gown with a rose-figured lining. The tenth is an only slightly changed redrawing of the *Studio* design – Salome kneeling as she is about to kiss the mouth of Iokanaan's severed head. The two final designs, curiously, illustrate successive lines of the play and are alternative ways of treating the same episode. That the hair of Salome and of Iokanaan were rendered one way in one drawing and a different way in the other leads to the speculation that Beardsley included the redrawing of the *Studio* design as an afterthought because it is sensational and because he was ill and did not have the energy to do a new illustration.

The third important work is Pope's mock-heroic long poem *The Rape of the Lock* (1896), "embroidered with nine drawings by Aubrey Beardsley". It is one of the successful English illustrated books. Beardsley took no liberties with his author, whose mastery of artifice, wit, and social satire so closely matched his own aspirations in another medium. And he discarded completely his Japanese effects and borrowed something of the spirit of Jean Antoine Watteau and other eighteenth-century French artists, perhaps because he was in Paris at the time. The elaborate, richly ornamented pen drawings are in perfect harmony with Pope's polished couplets, introduce no eroticism, and take no advantage of Pope's use of sylphs and gnomes. Moreover, Beardsley's series faithfully follows Pope's incremental progression of scenes to the three big ones: "The Rape of the Lock", "The Cave of Spleen", and "The Battle of the Beaux and Belles". In the first of these three climactic designs, the Baron tiptoes toward Belinda with his borrowed scissors at the ready. She is only partly visible at the left; but her ringleted hair is conspicuous, and her black dress establishes her importance. Beardsley's swift maturation is evident in the way he turned the interlocking lines of the costumes and their decoration into a masterful display of pen technique. *The Rape of the Lock* series suffers from some minor weaknesses – Belinda's doll face in some designs, for instance – but as graphic interpretation of Pope's masterpiece, it is Beardsley's most complete success in book illustration.

Increasing periods of illness brought fear of approaching death and urgent need of money. Racked by fits of hemorrhaging, Beardsley made eight drawings for a limited edition of Aristophanes's *Lysistrata* (1896), which Leonard Smithers "privately circulated" – that is, sold illegally as pornography. They are in Beardsley's most economical style – pure outlines with dotted passages but no settings, as in some of the best *Savoy* designs. They are technically excellent. They also are grossly, coldly, and dully indecent. On his deathbed, he wrote (clearly to Smithers): "I implore you to destroy *all* copies of *Lysistrata* & bad drawings. . . . By all that is holy *all* obscene drawings. In my death agony." The *Lysistrata* designs (and other "bad drawings") were part of a doomed youth's desperate effort to bolster his irregular income. They are not the witty, imaginative illustrations that he certainly would have made for a public edition of the classic. Critical responsibility, as well as compassion, excludes them from the main body of his interpretive work.

During his long and unsuccessful search for a beneficial climate on the Continent before his death in Menton on 16 March 1898, Beardsley drove himself feverishly to mount three substantial efforts. His own unfinished fantasy *Under the Hill: and Other Essays in Prose and Verse* (1904

115. Robert Anning Bell. John Milton, *Lycidas and Other Odes* (1903).

[1903]) contains four brilliant pen drawings, loosely related to the text and dense with lines to render texture and tone. The few line-and-wash drawings that he made for Théophile Gautier's *Mademoiselle de Maupin* and Ben Jonson's *Volpone: or The Fox*, both published posthumously in 1898, are proof that, had he lived, Beardsley would have continued to create fresh ways of translating literature into vivid, expressive illustrations.

Beardsley's standing as a book illustrator has to be reckoned in relation to the work of other artists in the 1890s, his lack of art instruction, his need for recognition and money, the brevity of his career, and the increasing ravages of tuberculosis. Only Edwin Austin Abbey and Hugh Thomson had used the direct reproduction of pen-and-ink drawings to much purpose in English books by 1892, the year Beardsley happened to get his first book commission, Malory's *Morte Darthur*. His imitations of what he had seen of Burne-Jones's pen-and-ink imitations of early Italian woodcuts, or wood-engraved facsimiles of Burne-Jones's drawings, were doomed to failure but not disgrace by his inexperience, bad judgment, ill health, and loss of interest. For Wilde's play *Salome*, Beardsley turned abruptly to an imitation of Japanese wood-block prints, which he recently had discovered, although they had been an influence on the aesthetic movement since the 1850s. The resulting pen drawings are unsuited to the biblical sub-

ject, cannot bear comparison with the work of Japanese masters, and are compromised by Beardsley's derision of Wilde. Yet in some of the drawings, he attained a freshness of attitude toward the illustrative process, an emotional intensity, and an originality of design that held promise that he might grow into great distinction, if not greatness, in his maturity. Instead of pushing on to develop his own economical pure-line style from what he had learned in the *Salome* series, however, Beardsley shifted once more in Pope's *Rape of the Lock* to an entirely different style, based on his sudden enthusiasm for eighteenth-century French art. The pen-and-ink designs, with their allover line work in approximation of engravings, constitute one of the most successful English series because of their scrupulous regard for Pope's witty, good-humored satire. His worries about money and about his approaching death prevented Beardsley from completing any other significant series. In only six years, he had grasped the fame for which he reached; today, if his magazine work is included, the general public can identify his drawings more readily than those by any other English artist. He was one of the few English illustrators with influence abroad – for example, on Leon Bakst in Russia, "Alastair" in Germany, and Will Bradley in the United States. But in England, he had only second- and third-rate imitators. Aubrey Beardsley endures as an inspiration to all literary illustrators to combine individual-

*Tasting some of her
home-made wines.*

116. Charles Edmund Brock. Washington Irving, *The Keeping of Christmas at Bracebridge Hall* (1906).

ity of style with fresh insights into the nature of the works illustrated.

Robert Anning Bell

At the turn of the century, R. Anning Bell (1863–1933) carried on the decorative ideas of Walter Crane and had a share in the development of Art Nouveau. The twenty or so books that he illustrated, chiefly with pen and ink, contain many limp ladies in long gowns, flowers on long sinuous stems, and similar clichés of the time, but Bell did not have the exuberance of spirit that makes Art Nouveau tolerable. He did extract the lesson of functional white space from early Italian woodcut books, and he contributed materially to the lightening of the weight of pen-and-ink drawings on the page by omitting solid blacks and extensively shaded forms.

Unfortunately, Bell reacted superficially to the literature that he illustrated. He even managed to omit Hamlet from his two illustrations of the play in Charles Lamb and Mary Lamb's *Tales from Shakespeare* (1899). His slant-eyed, goat-eared Robin Goodfellow in *A Midsummer Night's Dream* (1895), however, was probably the model for Arthur Rackham's famous Puck. In *Poems by John Keats* (1897), the more obviously the twenty full-page and almost twenty assorted-size designs imitate their early Italian prototypes, the better they are. Yet arches, columns, tesselated floors, *Primavera* gowns, and blank walls fail to add up to a reading of Keats. In one of Bell's few memorable designs, a winged Cupid climbing over a window sill by moonlight to illustrate the climactic lines of "Ode to Psyche", Cupid seems to have been derived from Charles Ricketts's illustrations for *Hero and Leander* (1894). In "The Eve of St. Agnes", Bell squandered a page on Madeline, Agnes's maid, carrying a candle up a flight of stairs. In the same poem, Porphyro waking Madeline comes close to the spirit of Keats. The illustrations in the inexpensive little Carillon edition of John Milton's *Lycidas and Other Odes* (1903) are less mannered and more aware of their interpretive function than usual (fig. 115).

Through the years, R. Anning Bell's repetitive pen-and-ink drawings helped popularize unshaded linear design, but they rarely are more than routine decoration.

Sir Frank (François Guillaume) Brangwyn

Associated with William Morris and Arthur Heygate Mackmurdo in the early days of the Arts and Crafts Movement and busy in all aspects of design, Sir Frank Brangwyn (1867–1956) was one of the active forces in Art Nouveau in England. He was not really an interpretive book illustrator,

although his pictures are in more than a dozen books. Some of his painted illustrations, such as the twenty-four in *Don Quixote* (1895), were reduced and were reproduced in monochrome, so that whatever virtue they had in color was lost. In his selection of passages from a text, Brangwyn sometimes showed flagrant indifference to literary values. From the wealth of possibilities in *The Thousand and One Nights* (1896), one of his choices among his thirty-six illustrations was "She ordered a slave girl to rub her feet". Brangwyn's main occupation was painting murals, and his illustrations were excuses for reproducing mural-like paintings of great opulence and vagueness. Robert Southey's *Life of Nelson* (1911) has seven fine color plates of ships and sea battles. Half of the twelve color plates with exotic settings, much reduced, in Alexander Kinglake's book of travels in the Near East, *Eöthen* (1913), were reproduced by courtesy of the owners of the paintings. The sixteen bold watercolor-tinted brush-and-ink drawings of mills in Brangwyn and Hayter Preston's *Windmills* (1923) help make it a book that one would like to own. The thirty-three etchings for *The Book of Job* (1948) look little better than preliminary sketches.

Charles Edmund Brock

The reputations of the prolific Brock brothers of Cambridge have been diminished, perhaps beyond their deserts, because they were imitators of Hugh Thomson both in style and in books illustrated. At first, they had uncertain command of their pens, but Charles (C. E.) Brock (1870–1938) made a bold beginning with 130 drawings for Tom Hood's *Humorous Poems* (1893) and 100 for Jonathan Swift's *Gulliver's Travels* (1894). The twelve full-page designs and numerous smaller ones for William Cowper's *Diverting History of John Gilpin* (1898) suggest that Brock had a talent for interpreting texts more robust than those assigned him. By chance, Brock substituted for Thomson in illustrating Jane Austen's *Pride and Prejudice* (1897) in Macmillan's black-and-white "Hugh Thomson" series of Austen's novels. That led to his doing thirty color plates for *Sense and Sensibility*, *Emma*, and *Persuasion* in 1898 for an edition published by Dent, while his brother did thirty for Austen's three other novels. The early tint-block process demanded firm outlines with restrained shading. The matte olive, ocher, salmon, and other earth tints are flat and formal, so that the plates seem pitched to Austen's calm voice.

In 1900, Brock drew thirty-five full-page designs and almost as many headpieces each for Charles Lamb's *Essays of Elia* and *Last Essays of Elia*. But among the perfect pen-and-ink subjects of bookish men, Christ's Hospital school, the Temple, the theater, and old china, he did not find any truly evocative themes. In "The Superannuated Man", he chose what seems to be the least desirable moment to record – the partners turning Elia loose – and nothing at all about his freedom, the stuff of the essay. Brock's single-handed illustrating of *The Prose Works of William Make-peace Thackeray* (1901–03), published in thirty 400-page volumes, was a daunting exercise. Under pressure, Brock whipped out about 300 minimal designs, most of which depict costumed characters talking to one another. Some are pen drawings and others, pencil or charcoal.

By the turn of the century, the greater refinement of color printing was able to do fair justice to the transparency and shimmer of the Brock brothers' watercolors. Color gives body and warmth and vitality, for which there is no equivalent in their pen drawings, although plates still printed too dark. Their concepts remained uninspired, but the effects are much richer. Brock was at his technical best in color plates for the English Idylls series, with twenty-five each for Elizabeth Gaskell's *Cranford* (1904) and Mary Russell Mitford's *Our Village* (1904), and twenty-four each for George Eliot's *Silas Marner* (1905) and Austen's *Northanger Abbey* (1907), *Pride and Prejudice* (1907), *Mansfield Park* (1908), *Sense and Sensibility* (1908), *Emma* (1909), and *Persuasion* (1909). The twenty-four color plates in each of Austen's novels naturally make a better show than do the earlier tint plates, but they now seem a little sweet for the tart Jane. During the first decade of the twentieth century, Brock's color plates added cheer to several of Charles Dickens's and other Christmas stories. Washington Irving's *The Keeping of Christmas at Bracebridge Hall* (1906) is a typical example (fig. 116). Then at the end of his career, he was put to the test of illustrating *Pickwick Papers* (1930) and *Nicholas Nickleby* (1931) afresh. Each of these uniform volumes allowed proper hospitality to sixteen carefully prepared large color plates. Brock rejected the humors of George Cruikshank and Phiz, but he made no effort to reconstitute the characters in a new guise. He lavished his care on dress, period furniture, and incidental detail. (Over the years, the Brocks had full-scale costumes made up and used models, it is said, to supplement their collection of prints, Regency fashion plates, and antiques.) The figures, portrayed in realistic settings, are engagingly lifelike, but since Mr. Pickwick and the Wellers, Squeers and Noggs, and the rest of the actors in *Pickwick Papers* and *Nicholas Nickleby* are not of this world but of Dickens's imagination, with these thirty-two conscientious watercolors, Charles Brock's career ended on a high level of professionalism somewhat below distinction.

Henry Matthew Brock

Because his style is somewhat firmer and tidier than that of his brother, Henry (H. M.) Brock (1875–1960) may be considered a somewhat better illustrator; but to the ordinary eye, their work seems interchangeable. His drawings are uniformly pleasant but tend to make the apparent obvious. His 16 pen-and-ink vignettes for Elizabeth Gaskell's *Cranford* (1898) are meager beside Hugh Thomson's 100. They are also too faithful to fact. Yet the drawing of two women stopping at a "little wayside public-house" to enquire the way to the home of an old woman renowned for her skill in knitting woolen stockings fixes a sunny if incidental moment in the tale of "Samuel Brown". In the same year, Brock made thirty color plates for the five volumes of *Pride and Prejudice*, *Northanger Abbey*, and *Mansfield Park* to go with those of his brother in the other Jane Austen novels. They were reproduced in the same flat tints and enjoy the same adventitious sense of perfect adaptation because of the limitations of the early color process used. In the following years, Brock's conceptualization remained restricted, as in John Bunyan's *Pilgrim's Progress* (1900), which he turned into an amiable costumed adventure story.

In the fifty or so illustrations for each of several collections of essays beginning with Oliver Wendell Holmes's *Autocrat of the Breakfast-Table* (1902), Brock's virtues of correctness and clarity of drawing are manifest, but the illustrations' success is limited; in the full-page design of the Deacon in his wonderful "one-hoss shay", all the construction and gear are beyond cavil, but the delight is missing. In the collections of the essays of Leigh Hunt (1903) and Douglas Jerrold (1903) and in Joseph Addison and Richard Steele's *"Sir Roger de Coverley" and Other Essays from the "Spectator"* (1905), this sense of qualified success remains constant. Why the Brocks just miss Thomson's level of artistry in pen and ink is apparent in drawings such that of a trio playing music, in which the music stand is drawn with such excessive care that it encroaches on the event. Still, *Sir Roger de Coverley* seems to be Brock's most satisfactory volume. Addison and Steele granted him the town and country subjects he could handle best, such as footmen in greatcoats carrying a girl in a sedan chair, Mr. Will Wimble in a stable yard with his dogs (fig. 117), Sir Roger gaily riding to hounds, and down-to-earth London scenes. But, as with his brother, Brock found the improved color process just what his drawings needed to make up for their sedateness. In Washington Irving's *Old English Christmas* (1909) and Oliver Goldsmith's *Vicar of Wakefield* (1912), the illustrations are ordinary, but the colors and highlights playing over the faces, garments, animals, and furniture communicate a warm domestic feeling that Henry

Mr Will. Wimble

117. Henry Matthew Brock. Joseph Addison and Richard Steele, *"Sir Roger de Coverley" and Other Essays from the "Spectator"* (1905).

118. Edward Burne-Jones. Geoffrey Chaucer, *The Canterbury Tales* (Prioress's Tale) in *The Works of Geoffrey Chaucer* (1896).

Brock never achieved in his black-and-white drawings.

Sir Edward Coley Burne-Jones

As friends at Oxford University in the 1850s and after, William Morris and Edward Burne-Jones (1833–98) shared enthusiasms for art, poetry, and the past. They were associated after 1862 in a firm dominated by Morris that was engaged in creating ecclesiastic and domestic furnishings and decoration. Turning to printing, Morris in 1891 brought out the first of fifty-three volumes at his Kelmscott Press. The last, in 1896, the year of his death, was the crown of his career as a designer, printer, and publisher – William Caxton's translation of the complete works of Geoffrey Chaucer. Burne-Jones earlier had done a little illustrating without distinction and had gone on to become a painter and decorative designer eminent enough to be knighted in 1894.

As chief illustrator of the Kelmscott Press, Burne-Jones drew decorative designs for eleven books, most by Morris, with little effort at interpretation. Except for four designs in Morris's *Well at the World's End* (1896), the one or two designs in each volume can hardly be called illustrations. Before the edition of Chaucer, the most ambitious project by Morris and Burne-Jones went back to their early years together when Burne-Jones had drawn 100 designs for Morris's *Earthly Paradise*. The project was abandoned after forty-four blocks for the episode of Cupid and Psyche had been engraved (thirty-eight by the inexperienced Morris, it is said); the blocks eventually were published as *Cupid and Psyche* (1974–75). Only a few of the designs have an active relation with the text. Twenty-three drawings for Robert Bridges's *Eros and Psyche* were engraved for an edition in 1935 without adding luster to the artist's record.

The Works of Geoffrey Chaucer (1896) is a thick folio containing eighty-seven wood engravings (ca. 129 × 170 mm) after drawings by Burne-Jones. It is the embodiment of Morris's efforts to create the "book beautiful" and is the only English book known and admired by the general public for its appearance. It is indeed a handsome, unified work of art; it is not, however, a book for reading. In addition to the book's size and weight, the thick floriated borders and initials drawn by Morris are overwhelming, the type is difficult to read, and the pseudomedievalism is retrogressive. It is necessary to understand that Burne-Jones's illustrations were conceived as part of Morris's plan for the book. It is also well to know how they were prepared. According to Duncan Robinson of the Fitzwilliam Museum, Cambridge, which owns all but three of the original drawings (the blocks are in the British Museum), the procedure was extraordinary. Burne-Jones made painstakingly finished soft-pencil drawings on paper. They were photographed as platinotypes, pale positives on dull paper. Under the artist's close supervision, Robert Catterson-Smith and Charles Fairfax-Murray went over the platinotypes first with a hard pencil and then with ink. After being approved by the artist, each design was photographed in reverse on a wood block and engraved in facsimile by William Harcourt Hooper. This method deadened the already much-worked-over drawings. They could have been photographed directly on the blocks in the first place or, just as well, reproduced by photo process. Much of the somewhat static effect of the illustrations came from Burne-Jones's effort to re-create something of the grave dignity of fifteenth-century Italian woodcuts, particularly those in Francesco Colonna's *Hypnerotomachia Poliphili* (1499), printed by Aldus Manutius of Venice. Many of his figures, which have heads that are too small for their height, stand passive and detached.

Although Morris and Burne-Jones worked together in the friendliest fashion, the artist clearly had the final say about what he illustrated. At first glance, the distribution of the eighty-seven illustrations is puzzling. In *The Canterbury Tales*, only seven tales are illustrated; the Prologue and fifteen tales are not. Of the twenty-eight illustrations, six are in each of three tales: the Knight's Tale, the Clerk's Tale, and the Franklin's Tale. Of the remaining ten illustrations, two are of Chaucer – one at the beginning and one at the end – and eight are in four tales, three in the Wife of Bath's Tale. Omitted are not only the prose tales, but also the enjoyable Nun's Priest's Tale of Chanticleer and Pertelote and the more robust humorous tales. Burne-Jones, therefore, did not illustrate Chaucer's *Canterbury Tales*, only about one-third of it. But he assigned fifty-nine designs to the rest of Chaucer's works, including seventeen to *The Romaunt of the Rose*, an incomplete translation from the French; twelve to *The Legend of Good Women*; and only eleven to *Troilus and Criseyde*, Chaucer's greatest single narrative.

The explanation of this curious distribution of illustrations is simple: Burne-Jones relished the allegorical, romantic, and supernatural aspects of Chaucer's writing but, as he admitted, was squeamish about its humor. The selectivity resulted in a partial, unbalanced, and unrepresentative treatment of Chaucer, but it also produced a series of illustrations that are extraordinarily harmonious in spirit as well as appearance.

With these fundamental matters clarified, Burne-Jones as an interpretive artist can still be judged by examining those poems he did illustrate. It becomes immediately apparent that he is one of the masters of English illustration, not only as an artist, but more particularly as a reader

119. Charles Conder. Honoré de Balzac, *La fille aux yeux d'or* (1896).

of texts. He knew both Chaucer's works and his times and was able to select moments of significance and turn them into concrete scenes that are merely suggested by Chaucer's conversational lines. In doing so, he often engaged in imaginative reconstruction. The two illustrations in the Prioress's Tale of the miracle of Hugh of Lincoln are examples. The first shows at the right, seven-year-old Hugh saying a prayer before an image of the Virgin; at the left, two Jews whispering at a shop stall; and in the back, pupils filing into a school. This one scene conveys visually not merely the essential facts, but also the emotion of the basic situation: the piety of little Hugh and the hatred he arouses by singing "O Alma redemptoris" daily as he passes through the Jewish quarter on his way to and from school. The second design (fig. 118) by-passes what would be the distracting factual details of the slitting of Hugh's throat, his being cast into a pit, and his burial service. Burne-Jones imagined him rising from a walled structure (presumably above the pit) as Mary leans from a cloud to place a grain of wheat on his tongue (its removal by the abbot releases his soul to heaven). This scene is based on what, in one stanza, Hugh tells the abbot he thinks happened. It concentrates the miracle into one simple, moving design.

Edward Burne-Jones was not able to manage Chaucer's conversational material so tellingly at all times, but he never failed to try. He put the poet's meaning into designs that have clarity, grace, and dignity unsurpassed by any comparable series of English illustrations.

Charles Conder

A hard-working alcoholic and a friend of Oscar Wilde, Aubrey Beardsley, Ernest Dowson, Charles Ricketts, Will Rothenstein, Max Beerbohm, Henri Toulouse-Lautrec, and other *fin-de-siècle* painters and writers, Charles Conder (1868–1909) had a minor talent in the tradition of Watteau and Fragonard. He illustrated only two published books, although he made a series of lithographs of scenes from works by Honoré de Balzac. Both books were translated from the French by Dowson. For the first, Balzac's *Fille aux yeux d'or* (1896), published by Leonard Smithers, Conder made a frontispiece and five illustrations. The title page is explicit: "With Six Illustrations Engraved on Wood by Charles Conder." By this time, it would have been usual to reproduce the drawings by photo process. But the airy effects that Conder achieved by crossing almost all his thin black lines with white lines are highly unusual. Nevertheless, only two blocks are not deadened by overall shading. One shows the meeting in the Tuileries of Henri, an exquisitely satirized dandy, and Paquita, the girl with the golden eyes, accompanied by her Spanish duenna (fig. 119); the other pictures Paquita and her duenna entering a coach

Calidore sees young Tristram slay
A proud discourteous Knight:
He makes him Squire, & of him leames
His state & present plight.

120. Walter Crane. Edmund Spenser, *The Faerie Queene* (1897).

121. Harry Furniss. Lewis Carroll, *Sylvie and Bruno* (1889).

with a footman holding the door open. These are precise realizations of Balzac's steamy romance; yet they also are Conder's odd and witty gloss on the text. They are, in addition, among the earliest modern wood-engraved English illustrations in which tonal effects were achieved almost entirely by free use of white lines (although not by true white-line technique) and by ample use of white for dramatic effect.

The four colored drawings – they seem to have been done with crayon and watercolor – that Conder made for Dowson's translation of a French version of *The Story of Beauty and the Beast* (1908 [1907]) have no equal importance The third, "Beauty in the Garden", is typical. The lady (perhaps the baroness de Meyer), wearing an enormous flowered hat, sits on a bench in a garden borrowed from Fragonard while airborne amoretti aim their arrows at her. The drawing in these four plates is execrable, but the derivative French effects have a playful artifice true to the times.

Charles Conder's example, slight as it is, might have brightened English book illustration at the turn of the century had the underlying impulse of his designs been appreciated.

Walter Crane

Walter Crane (1845–1915) now is remembered for his illustration of children's books. In his day, as head of the Royal College of Art, editor of an art journal, and author of the book *Of the Decorative Illustration of Books Old and New* (1896), he was influential in promoting linear design as harmoniously related to the printed page. He had some impact on Charles Ricketts and his associates, but, ironically, he attacked Art Nouveau, for which he was partly responsible. With a few exceptions, Crane's illustrations have no distinction as decorative designs. He was not a first-rate draftsman; his broken, ragged, thin-and-fat pen-and-ink lines are amateurish; and his hand-lettered pen inscriptions are wretched. Most of Crane's black-and-white illustrations are banal, but some of his color plates for children's books are charming.

Crane began as an apprentice to the wood engraver W. J. Linton, and as early as 1868, he turned to illustrating. Yet a quarter of a century later, the illustrations without text in *Eight Illustrations to Shakespeare's "Tempest"* (1893), *Eight Illustrations to Shakespeare's "Two Gentlemen of Verona"* (1894), and *Eight Illustrations to "The Merry Wives of Windsor"* (1895) are too ordinary for their resplendent format. The twenty-three very dark illustrations, engraved by another hand on wood, for William Morris's *Story of the*

122. Arthur Joseph Gaskin. Edmund Spenser, *The Shepheardes Calender* (1896).

Glittering Plain (1894) interpret the archaic narrative at the simple level of a boy's book. Only the frequently reproduced title-page design – a youth and three tired horsemen seeking the Glittering Plain – adds anything to the text. Edmund Spenser's *Faerie Queene* and *Mutabilitie* were issued in books of three cantos each between 1894 and 1897 to make up three large well-printed volumes. Many of the eighty-eight full-page illustrations look little different from those that Crane prepared for a boys' *King Arthur*. One of the better ones is of Calidore making Tristram a squire (Book VI, Canto II) (fig. 120). *The Faerie Queene* was Crane's chief work. It is no small achievement to have drawn 88 large illustrations (and 135 illustrative headpieces and tailpieces) for Spenser's long poem, but it is an unimportant achievement if the designs seem embarrassingly mundane in conjunction with their magnificent subjects.

The twelve full-page illustrations for Spenser's *Shepheard's Calender* (1898) are apt when they follow traditional pastoral themes. When they turn to allegorical females, they are insipid. The best design is one of Cupid as an adolescent angel drawing his bow to shoot a kneeling archer, but Cupid was borrowed from Edward Burne-Jones's God of Love in the Kelmscott Chaucer.

Sir Harry Furniss

The popular *Punch* caricaturist Harry Furniss (1854–1925) had little success in his two main opportunities as a literary illustrator. In 1889, he worked with Lewis Carroll on *Sylvie and Bruno*. The forty-six wood engravings are without continuity, unity, or special character. Indeed, it is difficult to imagine how series of images for the odd *Sylvie and Bruno* and its trailer, *Sylvie and Bruno Concluded* (1893), for which Furniss also drew forty-six designs, could be given organic treatment, but that was Furniss's task. In a preface to *Sylvie and Bruno*, Carroll said that he wrote for children in their "hours of merriment" and at the same time to suggest thoughts "not wholly out of harmony with the graver cadences of Life". He also referred to "all these (to my mind) *wonderful* pictures". The vignettes of Sylvie, a young girl, and Bruno, a little boy, are both realistic and sentimental. The badgers are imitations of the walrus in *Through the Looking-Glass* (1872). And there are drawings of adults that are right out of the *Illustrated London News*. For the poem "Peter and Paul", Furniss followed John Tenniel's "Father William" formula of four related illustrations. But this mordant satire is not for children; it is a clinical case history of Peter's "borrowing" £50 from the greedy, cheating moneylender Paul and having to repay it without having received it. The second of the four designs shows starving Peter begging for help and Paul, grown fat over the years, complimenting him on his slimness (fig. 121). Furniss realized Carroll's lines perfectly. What children in their "hours of merriment" would make of them is another matter.

One of the most dazzling assignments in all English book illustration later came to Furniss. He was commissioned to make 500 designs for a complete edition of Charles Dickens's works, with his name dominating the title – *The Harry Furniss Dickens*. He had contributed four unexceptional etchings to Dickens's book of essays *The Uncommercial Traveller* (1898). The ambitious fourteen-volume undertaking was published in New York in 1910. The publisher ruined it by reducing the pen drawings and the captions (quotations from the works) to half the size of the originals and by putting two drawings on a page, usually sideways. Apart from this disaster, Furniss remained a Victorian *Punch* artist whose 500 drawings, many of which are sketches of single characters, belong to the quasi-realistic mode of the *Works of Charles Dickens. Household Edition* (1871–79). He simply had no fresh reading of Dickens that justified giving his name to a twentieth-century edition.

Arthur Joseph Gaskin

Although Arthur Gaskin (1862–1928) of Birmingham was a wood engraver, he did little book illustrating. The five designs in a six-page, hand-printed version of the Christmas carol *Good King Wenceslas* (1895) are said to be woodcuts, but they look like pen drawings. So do Gaskin's only memorable illustrations, an elegant series of facsimile wood engravings after his designs in the Kelmscott edition of Edmund Spenser's *Shepheardes Calender* (1896), for which Gaskin received no credit in the book. The design for December demonstrates how well he combined pastoral formality and fresh seasonal effects (fig. 122). In spite of a certain fatiguing purity of line, Gaskin could have been an important illustrator had he been given important books to illustrate.

Laurence Housman

Teller of tales, poet, playwright, and espouser of causes, Laurence Housman (1865–1959) was also for about ten years a book illustrator of uneven, but sometimes highly original, talent. He also designed most of the books he illustrated; his bindings are among the most admired of the period. His sister Clemence, trained as a facsimile wood engraver just as the photographic process block was coming into use, scrupulously engraved the dense crosshatching and vermiculate foliage of Housman's designs in several books. It is difficult at first to distinguish her engravings from process blocks, except for the few that she signed with a tiny "CH sc." Housman's usual technique was much too tight and tonal for facsimile engraving. Apart from three or four designs to be mentioned, Clemence's arduous efforts were wasted. Housman's early books, with one exception, betray a beginner's uncertainties in drawing and pen technique. He drew eight realistic designs for George Meredith's verse satire of the Shakers, *Jump-to-Glory Jane* (1892), which also has Art Nouveau decorations; twelve for a translation of Jonas Lie's *Weird Tales from Northern Seas* (1893); and six for Clemence's *Were-Wolf* (1896).

The exception, and Housman's best-known illustrated dook, is Christina Rossetti's *Goblin Market* (1893). No boubt inspired by Dante Gabriel Rossetti's two designs in the first edition (1862), the twelve narrow illustrations show sudden improvement in draftsmanship, pen technique, and imaginative power. *Goblin Market* is a verse parable of two loving sisters, Lizzie and Laura, in which Lizzie rescues Laura after she has succumbed to the blandishments of the goblin men to buy their wares, a full line of symbolic fruits and berries. (Lizzie could be Christina, and Laura could be Elizabeth Eleanor Siddal, Rossetti's wife.) Housman gave most of his attention to the goblin men. Christina Rossetti found them ugly. They are ugly and evil. The anthropomorphic prototypes in her brother's frontispiece to the first edition are sly but ingratiating. Yet Christina had made them evil creatures with rodent and psittacine faces, even if her quirky verse gives them a fabulous dimension. Housman invented a grotesque visual fantasy by enveloping them in voluminous garments like nightgowns that billow and swirl and by scrunching them together with their low-crowned, broad-brimmed hats sailing about in whirlpools of drapery lines. The facing designs of the goblin men exerting their persuasive powers on Laura reveal Housman at his best as an interpretive illustrator (fig. 123).

Although the poems have much in common, the eight full-page pen drawings for Jane Barlow's *End of Elfintown* (1894) fail to equal those for *Goblin Market* as an interpretive series. First, even with pointed ears, the slim young men in *The End of Elfintown* suggest operetta extras, not elves. (The mass of crinkly hair crowning everyone, an exaggeration of a Pre-Raphaelite mannerism, reappears monotonously in later books.) Second, Barlow's poem, while not so bizarre as Christina Rossetti's, is a clever and diverting fable. It begs for witty illustration. Housman's young men and their youthful king are too ordinary, solemn, and bland.

Between 1894 and 1898, Housman illustrated four of his own works. The first two are books of tales: *A Farm in*

123. Laurence Housman. Christina Rossetti, *Goblin Market* (1893).

124. Thomas Sturge Moore. Charles Perrault, *Histoire de Peau d'Ane* (1902).

125. William Nicholson. *An Almanac of Twelve Sports: With Words by Rudyard Kipling* (1898).

Fairyland (1894), with a title-page design and twelve illustrations; and *The House of Joy* (1895), with Clemence's wood engravings of a title-page design and eight illustrations. In the second, the title-page design of Mercury as an angel in a Merry Widow hat proves that Clemence was capable of engraving a fine block when Housman made a fine drawing uncluttered by crosshatching. *Green Arras* (1896), a book of verse, and *All-Fellows: Seven Legends of Lower Redemption* (1896) contain seven designs with something of the intensity of the *Goblin Market* series. Nothing quite like Housman's strange, grim designs for "The Truce of God" and "The Merciful Drought" in *All-Fellows* had appeared before in an English book.

Housman dedicated *The Field of Clover* (1898), a volume of ten tales, "To My Dear Wood-Engraver". Clemence had received almost no recognition before, but in this book, her name is on the title page. The frontispiece of Mercury reclining as he watches sheep and the title-page design of a weary drover, both of which are virtually unshaded and are enclosed within deep scroll wood-engraved borders, are justly celebrated among English wood engravings. They show the beauty that the brother and sister team could have brought to English books had Housman shown an equal restraint in his many other designs. Unfortunately, he did not; the ten frontispieces to the tales in *The Field of Clover* have their share of strangeness, but Clemence's black-line facsimile engraving could not cope with the excess of fine line work. The frontispieces to the four books in Thomas à Kempis's *Of the Imitation of Christ* (1898), engraved by Clemence, are also unshaded. The long lines and arched interiors show the influence of Charles Ricketts and the Italian tradition, but they have the religious fervor of the text. Although the themes are familiar, the treatment is sometimes Art Nouveau.

The twelve pen drawings for Percy Bysshe Shelley's *Sensitive Plant* (1898) transcribe tonal variations of great subtlety. The one for the lines

And narcissi, the fairest of them all,
Who gaze on their eyes in the stream's recess,
Till they die of their own dear loveliness

represents a philosophy of illustration stated in the prefatory "Note upon the Illustrations", which includes the bold dogma, "If, therefore, illustration is to be an attempt to say over again what the poet has already said perfectly, it is certain to prove itself superfluous, and to be nothing better than a tautology." In the text, the narcissi are flowers. In his illustration, Housman recalled the myth of Narcissus and imposed his image of the unfortunate youth, seated on a bank of narcissi, on his vision of a seemingly endless formal garden enclosed by high meandering hedges and presided over by a Victorian lady in a garden-party gown and hat.

Failing eyesight ended Laurence Housman's career as an illustrator. Throughout it, his drawing swung from amateurish to masterly, but his best work – particularly in *Goblin Market*, *All-Fellows*, *The Field of Clover*, and *The Sensitive Plant* – opened new imaginative perspectives to English book illustration.

Thomas Sturge Moore

Although Sturge Moore (1870–1944) made fewer than twenty interpretive book illustrations, his work has been much admired. His inexperience as an engraver shows in the lack of clarity of detail in most of his prints, but he grasped the implications of the white-line approach. He got tonal and textural differences by long swirling lines that follow contours of rock, cloud, and hair and by jabs and twists for grass, bark, and leaves. His burin clumsily chewed the block and left irregular patterns of gray throughout the design, an unintentional effect that has become part of his appeal. Otherwise, the enthusiasm for Moore's illustrations must be for their pseudopastoral element.

Moore was not an original interpreter of other men's words; indeed, he was wise as well as modest to let Charles Ricketts illustrate his *Danaë* (1903). His first book illustrations are the five for his translation of Maurice de Guérin's *Centaur* and *The Bacchante* (1899). For the first, he engraved three turbid mountain scenes with centaurs. In the suffocating *Bacchante* (she lost her *e* after the title page), Moore showed her saluting the dawn and later sleeping by moonlight. Moore selected *Poems from Wordsworth* (1902) and engraved six small oblong blocks for it. The first, showing the poet sitting on the grass and beholding a rainbow, is one of his clearest designs, with ample white and the vertical shading differentiating the background from the foreground. The others tend to be too matter-of-fact.

In his friend Lucien Pissarro's edition of Charles Perrault's *Histoire de Peau d'Ane* (1902), Moore finally began to master the art of wood engraving and to unite visual imagination with manual execution. The first of the three wood engravings is an almost successful design of a woman standing between two cheval glasses; the second, a woman standing wrapped in an ass's skin; and the third, a naked woman sitting in a woodland pool, the ass's skin hanging behind her, and a gaggle of inquisitive geese standing among the trees (fig. 124). This last block is the best of Moore's book illustrations, and it is second to only a large print, *Pan and Psyche*, among his wood engravings.

Had Sturge Moore gone on from here, he certainly would

have become an important interpretive illustrator. As it is, he contributed not only to the practice of autographic wood engraving, but also to the belief that book illustrations can be imaginative and perhaps beautiful.

Sir William Nicholson

Never a book illustrator in the usual sense, Sir William Nicholson (1872–1949) contributed pictures to several books. They are noteworthy for being woodcuts, usually colored by hand for limited editions and by lithography for trade editions, and were influenced by the revival of the popular woodcut by James Catnach and Joseph Crawhall and by the posters of Henri Toulouse-Lautrec. Nicholson and his collaborator, James Pryde – "the Bickerstaff Brothers" – had more impact on the modern poster with their clean bold simplifications than Nicholson had on adult book illustration. (Pryde did not collaborate on the books.) The best-known book illustrated by Nicholson is the delightful *London Types: Quatorzains by W. E. Henley* (1898), which has thirteen 10-inch-high colored blocks. William Ernest Henley wrote verses to go with the prints. In the same year appeared *An Almanac of Twelve Sports: With Words by Rudyard Kipling*. The supporting role played by Kipling at the height of his fame testifies to Nicholson's popular regard. "Racing", the design for March, indicates the dynamic results that Nicholson could get from his stripped-down medium (fig. 125).

Paradoxically, however, through his introducing Gordon Craig to wood engraving, Nicholson can be credited with a part in the revival of autographic wood engraving, both as a medium for book illustration and as a work of art in its own right. After 1900, Nicholson went on to become a leading painter and to receive a knighthood. In 1923, he drew eight pleasant color plates of characters for John Gay's *Polly*, although they do not have the verve of Claud Lovat Fraser's set for *The Beggar's Opera* (1921). Seven heavy black-and-white drawings of characters in Siegfried Sassoon's *Memoirs of a Fox-Hunting Man* (1929) add little to the reader's enjoyment of the book.

Sidney Edward Paget

Only by chronology could the three Paget brothers – Henry Marriott (1857?–1936), Sidney Edward (1860–1908), and Walter Stanley (1863–1935) – be mistaken for *fin-de-siècle* artists. Their work is superficially realistic, even photographic. Some of their tonal designs – the wood engravings after Henry's drawings for Sir Walter Scott's *Kenilworth*, for example, as well as the wash drawings – look as though they might in part have been drawn over photographs, a

journalistic practice of the time. Their work was ephemeral. Yet Sidney Paget scored one of the great and enduring successes of illustration: first in the *Strand* (July 1891–June 1892) and then in *The Adventures of Sherlock Holmes* (1892) and the series of books that followed, he created a universally recognized image of a literary hero – Sherlock Holmes (fig. 126). His brother Walter was the model. Arthur Conan Doyle protested that Holmes was not so handsome. But no one else has ever imagined that he could look otherwise. Sidney Paget's Sherlock Holmes has been the model for every illustrator of the stories and for every stage, film, and television actor playing the part, evidence of the power that illustration sometimes wields.

Lucien Pissarro

The son of the French Impressionist painter Camille Pissarro, Lucien Pissarro (1863–1944) founded the Eragny Press at Hammersmith and printed, illustrated, and bound books there from 1896 to 1914. The large number of French titles, the limited number of illustrations in his slight publications, and the facsimile nature and mainly decorative purpose of his woodcuts keep Pissarro from being significant as an English literary illustrator. Yet the twelve blocks, some in color, in *The Queen of the Fishes* (1894), an adaptation by Margaret Rust of a French fairy tale; the five black-and-white designs in *The Book of Ruth and the Book of Esther* (1896); and the frontispiece, in color, for Samuel Taylor Coleridge's *Christabel* (1904) have been an inspiration to all who would produce books as handiworks of art.

Charles de Sousy Ricketts

That Charles Ricketts (1866–1931) designed the volumes he illustrated and many others as integrated books and published some of them at the Vale Press (Hacon & Ricketts, 1896–1904) makes him the main bridge between the Kelmscott Press and modern fine illustrated-book publishing. As in the Kelmscott Chaucer, the effects of Ricketts's illustrations are those of early Italian woodcuts, black-line facsimiles of strongly outlined drawings with parallel-line shading. As designer-engraver, he used a graver instead of a knife but with more freedom than William Harcourt Hooper had been permitted at Kelmscott. Charles Haslewood Shannon (1865–1937), a lithographer and painter and a close friend of Ricketts, collaborated on a few books. By his personal enthusiasms as well as his practice, Ricketts was a significant force in bringing a more international outlook, greater clarity of design, and beauty to English book illustration and production. He was also an important

126. Sidney Paget. Arthur Conan Doyle, *The Adventures of Sherlock Holmes* (1892).

link in the chain that extended from William Blake, through Dante Gabriel Rossetti and Walter Crane, to Art Nouveau.

The first joint effort by Ricketts and Shannon, Oscar Wilde's *House of Pomegranates* (1891), was a technical failure. Shannon's tonal drawings for the four fairy tales did not reproduce clearly and are totally at odds with Ricketts's eleven small, tight, and dark pen drawings. The five pen drawings by Ricketts for the baron de Tabley's *Poems Dramatic and Lyrical* (1893), reproduced by photogravure, as had been those in *A House of Pomegranates*, follow the Pre-Raphaelite habit of filling all available space with detail, and the line work is dark and tangled. Yet conceptually, this early work has a promising vigor, as in Ricketts's design for Wilde's tale "The Fisherman and His Soul".

The colophon of *Daphnis and Chloe* (1893) by Longus states that the thirty-six illustrations (and a colophon design) were "drawn on wood by Charles Ricketts from designs by Charles Shannon and Charles Ricketts and engraved by both". Shannon is said to have designed fifteen, which were "revised" by Ricketts before he drew them on the blocks. In 1914, Ricketts called this "early, almost boyish work". His judgment seems far off the mark for designs as arresting as those of Daphnis in the sea being towed to safety guided by the piping of Chloe on a cliff and of the lovers embracing in the shelter of a snow-covered

grape arbor. Ricketts and Shannon had learned from Venetian woodcuts the virtues of long flowing lines, little or no shading, rhythmic compositions, and plenty of white space.

Shannon also shared with Ricketts in the seven wood engravings for the Christopher Marlowe and George Chapman version of *Hero and Leander* (1894) by Musaeus. In their interpretation, they avoided the hazards of eroticism and obviousness. They gave the gods the active role they have in the poem, as in "Neptune quells the waves to stay harsh destiny" while Leander takes his last swim. The clean rhythmic compositions, with their indifference to matters of fact, are ideal accompaniments to the mannered Elizabethan verse.

The nine full-page and one half-page drawings printed in brown in Wilde's *Sphinx* (1894), with "Decorations by Charles Ricketts", are much more than decorative. The series achieves an unusual harmony by a fusion of three units – the part woman, part winged-lion Sphinx; tall, imaginary trees; and tall, fanciful rock formations – drawn with thin, slightly wavering outlines and no shading. These elegant, spacious designs embody the mystery, beauty, and terror that are demanded by the poem but are out of reach of Wilde's maudlin verse. Drawings with the emotive power of those of the poet watching the Sphinx as she drinks from a stream and of the Sphinx entering the 100-

The Prodigal Son.

127. Charles Ricketts. *The Parables from the Gospels* (1903).

cubit gate to where "dog-faced Anubis" sits, for example, transcend previous modes of English illustration.

The six round wood-engraved illustrations for *The Excellent Marriage of Cupid and Psyches* (1897), taken from William Adlington's 1566 translation of Apuleius's *Golden Ass*, are technically among Ricketts's best, but their circular composition tends to emphasize their decorative function. The five squarish wood engravings – "Tabulas invenit et sua manu sculpsit C. Ricketts" – for the same work in Latin, *De Cupidinis et Psyches amoribus fabula anilis* (1901), established what Ricketts imagined illustrations might be. The first two designs, in which solid blacks and whites and curves and angles clash, are emblematic treatments of the earthly world in which the silly girl Psyche finds herself. The third is a remarkable illustration of the young god Cupid, having been seen asleep by Psyche, rising on outspread wings while in desperation, Psyche, her arms wrapped around his leg, is pulled half out of bed. The swirl of the bodies and the counterswirl of the bedclothes form one of Ricketts's most eloquent interpretations. After an illustration of Pan calling to the despairing Psyche from across a stream, there is a tender design of Cupid awakening Psyche.

The almost square wood engravings (not woodcuts) in *The Parables from the Gospels, With Ten Original Woodcuts Designed and Engraved on Wood by Charles Ricketts* (1903) match John Everett Millais's series of twenty (1864 [1863]) in imaginative power and sincerity. Two designs serve as examples. For the Parable of the Rich Man, Ricketts rejected the easy possibilities of barns, fruit, and goods and laying up treasure and chose a difficult one: "But God said unto him, 'Thou fool, this night thy soul shall be required of thee'." The rich (young) man stretches across a table, upsetting his wine and book, to clutch the sleeping form of his soul as it floats off in the embrace of the Angel of Death. (This was the third use of this clinging motif by Ricketts.) For the first of two illustrations for the Parable of the Prodigal Son, Ricketts again rejected the obvious design – the younger son wasting his substance in riotous living – and showed the prodigal as a swineherd not merely tending the swine, but also kneeling among them beside a trough, his bent head in his arms (fig. 127). It stands as solid evidence that while Ricketts sought to create designs of beauty and decorative charm, he had an overriding sense of the interpretive function of literary illustration.

Also in 1903, Thomas Sturge Moore's *Danaë* was published in book form with three wood engravings by Ricketts. They record moments during Danaë's immurement in a tower of brass; she has been imprisoned there by her father, King Acrisius of Argos, to prevent the fulfillment of a prophecy that her child will kill him. The designs convey poignantly the claustrophobic effect of Danaë's imprisonment and the melancholy of Moore's langorous verse. The first engraving, familiar from reproductions, shows the lonely girl kissing her reflection – "In polisht walls a sister found is kissed." In the second, her lover Zeus visits her as a shower of gold – "She kneels in awe beholding lavish light." Danaë kneeling and holding her head suggests pain rather than awe. In the third design, Danaë stands on portable steps to look out a small round barred window – "Danaë at her twilit lattice ponders." In this series of three illustrations, the third one of Danaë alone in her small room seems repetitious, particularly since a few pages later comes the most graphic event in the poem and in Danaë's part of the myth: Danaë and her baby (Perseus) being set adrift at sea in a chest.

In addition to illustrating the ten books listed in the Catalog, Ricketts designed frontispieces for other books, including *Spiritual Poems* (1896) by John Gray, *Nimphidia and the Muses Elizium* (1896) by Michael Drayton, *Early Poems* (1896) by John Milton, *Sacred Poems* (1897) by Henry Vaughan, *Poetical Sketches* (1899) by William Blake, and *The Rubáiyát of Omar Khayyám* (1901) translated by Edward FitzGerald.

After Ricketts closed the Vale Press in 1904, he never again gave book illustration or wood engraving his concentrated attention. There are scene and costume designs in George Bernard Shaw's *Saint Joan* (1924) and in *Macbeth* (1933), two illustrations for Humbert Wolfe's *Troy* (1928), five poor pen drawings of nudes for a purported translation of Jean Paul Raymond's (Ricketts's) imaginary conversations *Beyond the Threshold* (1929), and six silhouettes in Ricketts's posthumous collection of short stories, *Unrecorded Histories* (1933).

Charles Haslewood Shannon. See Ricketts.

Claude Allin Shepperson

The ten full-page illustrations for William Shakespeare's *Merchant of Venice* (1899) by Claude A. Shepperson (1867–1921) are an early instance of the pen-and-ink style of Edwin Austin Abbey and Hugh Thomson applied to a schoolbook. His six designs each for George Borrow's *Lavengro* (1899), Benjamin Disraeli's *Coningsby* (1900), and Sir Walter Scott's *Heart of Mid-Lothian* (1900) are good but not numerous enough to make much contribution to the long novels. Shepperson held his own with Edmund Sullivan and Herbert Austin Railton in his designs for Leigh Hunt's *Old Court Suburb* (1902), but his nine pencil drawings, including a delightful circular composition of women drinking tea, lost a good deal as a result of reduction. "A Devon Courtship" (fig. 128) and two or three others of the eight lithographs in Eden Phillpotts's *Up-Along and Down-Along* (1905) suggest what an evocative illustrator Shepperson could have been had he been able to use this medium at all times. Unfortunately, his work in some other books seems perfunctory.

William Strang

At sixteen, William Strang (1859–1921) of Dumbarton, Scotland, began six years of study at the Slade School of Art under Alphonse Legros. He became a distinguished etcher of portraits and of architectural and anecdotal prints and a member of the small group of artists who have dedicated their etching needle to the service of book illustration. At times, he openly assumed the style of various masters, but in the main, he seems to have found the somber realism of Legros most consonant with his own outlook. The sincerity, emotional intensity, and superb storytelling quality of his designs made Strang a true interpretive illustrator. But this claim can be sustained only by waiving one of the criteria for inclusion in this study: that book illustrations appear in conjunction with the text of a book. Much of Strang's best work appeared first without text. An exception was made for him because for years, he persevered in etching a large number of what are, in fact, some of the most powerful illustrations of familiar works of literature ever published in England, and they were published in book form. He clearly thought of these uniform bound series as entities and of their continuous relation to the text and to one another as their reason for being. Some series were issued later with the complete text. The great difference between Strang and the Pre-Raphaelites and other painter-illustrators of the mid-nineteenth century is the absence in everything he did of sentimentality, pseudo-classicism, labored posing of models, and elaboration of decorative detail. (It has to be granted that the pen-and-ink drawings that Strang, in conjunction with J. B. Clark and Aubrey Beardsley, made for *Lucian's "True History"* [1894] and, with Clark, for an edition of Rudolf Erich Raspe's *Adventures of Baron Munchausen* [1895] are so heavy handed and obvious that it is difficult to believe he did them.)

As early as 1884, Strang's etchings in *Seven Illustrations to the "Ballad of Aiken Drum"*, by William Nicholson, and in *Nine Illustrations to Burns' Poems* were remarkable graphic translations of the Scottish experience. Thus Strang shares with Edwin Austin Abbey and Hugh Thomson in the opening of a new period in English book illustration. But the challenge of interpreting a major work of literature by means of illustrations drawn to be published without text came to him first in 1885 with *Fourteen Illus-*

trations for Bunyan's "Pilgrim's Progress". In the long history of this often illustrated classic, no artist has spoken more authentically than has Strang with Bunyan's seventeenth-century voice. On the title page, opposite the frontispiece portrait of Bunyan, is an engaging scene of the author's wife reading the Bible to him while a child tries to catch his attention. The twelve etched illustrations begin with Christian praying at a table with his burden on his back. In "Christian in the Slough of Despond", Strang deviated imaginatively from the text so that the dark Evangelist might stand above Christian and the unhelping Pliant kneel and pick flowers on the opposite bank of the ditch. Among the other ten subjects, Christian reaching for his dropped sword while the fiend Apollyon climbs on him is the most dramatic, but even more convincingly sinister is Christian walking fearfully through the Valley of Death, hand to sword, while flames billow from the Pit and while one of the Wicked Ones, in the form of a naked man locked in step with him, whispers blasphemies in his ear (fig. 129). Christian, relieved of his burden, praying at the foot of a cross and the marriage of Mercy and Matthew are designs of great simplicity and lasting beauty.

Except for frontispieces that he etched for two or three books, Strang's first illustrations to appear with text were those he made for his own dour but gifted ballads in Lowland Scots dialect, *The Earth Fiend* (1892) and *Death and the Ploughman's Wife* (1894). Both series were published first as sets of prints. The eleven etchings in *The Earth Fiend* record the change of luck that comes to a young farmer after he enlists the aid of a witch: he subdues a fiend, who works for him so diligently that the farmer becomes lazy and ends mysteriously with a broken neck. This series is distinguished by a memorable plate of five small children, one with a flag, discovering the fiend lying on the ground. In *Death and the Ploughman's Wife*, among the eleven illustrations and a title-page design, the most poignant is that of the mother kneeling in prayer while her child stretches forth his hands from between the knees of Death. This is stronger stuff than usually finds its way into illustrations. The supernaturalism of Strang's own two books continued in *The Christ upon the Hill* (1895) by Cosmo Monkhouse. The eight illustrations are incremental in effect. A charcoal burner and his wife worry about what will happen to their witless son, Michael, when they die. Michael believes that the Christ on the Cross on a hill is alive. In a winter's storm, he brings home on his back a wounded, living Christ, who recovers and promises ambiguously to take care of Michael. In the final scene, not explicit in the text, Michael lies crushed beneath the Cross.

Strang's *Twelve Illustrations to Milton's "Paradise Lost"* (1895 [1896]) appeared as matted prints in the same format

128. Claude Allin Shepperson. Eden Phillpott, *Up-Along and Down-Along* (1905).

129. William Strang. *Fourteen Illustrations for Bunyan's "Pilgrim's Progress"* (1885).

as his books of ballads but with only the Argument of each of Milton's books serving as text. The frontispiece portrait of Milton and the lyrical title-page etching of the poet playing a cello while his two daughters sing precede the ten illustrations. (In a 1905 edition of the complete text, the photogravured etchings lost a good deal of their quality as a result of reduction.) The *Paradise Lost* etchings do not embrace all the crucial scenes, and in being faithful to the text, they are not altogether characteristic of Strang. But the brooding figure of young Satan, his tall dark wings contrasting with a great swirl of flames that rises diagonally from the burning lake; the soft white Eve being tempted by a great python against a background of dark angular rocks; and the nontheatrical Expulsion are illustrations worthy to transmit Milton's mighty lines. In 1896, Strang etched and published his large thirteen-plate *Ancient Mariner* series without text. Except for a Holbeinish frontispiece of the bridal group and two or three designs that seem to have been conceived as prints, the *Ancient Mariner* plates are among the finest achievements of English illustration. The Mariner and the Wedding Guest, the sailors binding the Mariner with the dead Albatross around his neck, the accursed Mariner with his dead and dying mates on the deck of the ship, and the Pilot rowing his frightened boy, the Mariner, and the Hermit ashore are revelations of how the strangeness, terror, and beauty of Coleridge's masterpiece tapped the deepest resources of Strang's Scottish imagination.

The theatrical nature and Indian settings of Rudyard Kipling's tales may at first make Strang's *Thirty Illustrations to Rudyard Kipling's Short Stories* (1901) seem to be not his best work. Or it may be that his extensive use of aquatint gives this series a labored effect. Yet judged by their success in seizing on the high points of action in so many often gruesome yarns told in *Soldiers Three*, *The Jungle Books*, *Plain Tales from the Hills*, and the rest, Strang's series must be the most remarkable collection of illustrations of short stories by a British artist. Rich as English literature is in short stories and susceptible as short stories are to representation in graphic terms, they have received little attention from first-rate illustrators. Strang captured the exoticism, violence, and melodrama that made Kipling's stories so popular in the early years of the twentieth century. In 1901, Strang also published *The Doings of Death*, twelve handsome chiaroscuro woodcuts (cut by Bernard Sleigh) without text. The full-page etched illustrations that Strang contributed to a two-volume edition of Izaak Walton's *Compleat Angler* (1902) lose some of their effect among D. Y. Cameron's twenty full-page scenic etchings and numerous vignettes. Yet Strang re-created much of the unsentimental charm of Walton's prose in his re-

embodiment of Rembrandt in the second volume, especially the etchings of the hostess standing in the door of an inn and handing glasses of ale to a group of anglers, two anglers enjoying a pipe and ale with a light supper, and poachers spearing fish at night by the light of a flambeau.

No British artist has been more faithful to Cervantes's concept of Don Quixote as a man of essential dignity than Strang in his *Thirty Etchings Illustrating Subjects from "Don Quixote"* (1902), published uniformly with the Kipling folio. Here, without text, Strang had the advantages of both continuous narrative and familiar events. What Strang did brilliantly and what other illustrators usually have failed to do is keep Don Quixote consistently himself, eccentric but never foolish. Strang went to Spain to etch the series, and he paid homage to Francisco de Goya by an occasional echo of the Spanish artist's style, especially in the aquatints. The portrait of Don Quixote sallying forth with Sancho Panza, the meeting with Dulcinea del Toboso, the puppet show, the flight on the wooden horse, the depiction of Sancho as governor, and the death of Don Quixote are perceptions of the truth at the heart of this satire of the romances of chivalry that turned into a masterpiece of the ambiguous relationship between delusion and reality.

Although they are supported by the full text of the New Testament (1913), Strang's sixteen biblical etchings – with their variety of shapes and styles, from light spare figures to dark tonal full scenes – betray their original creation as separate prints. This is too bad, for their naturalism and forcefulness impose a remarkable degree of newness and feeling on the familiar events. In the oblong "Descent from the Cross", for instance, one of the finest modern etchings, the two grieving Marys are surrounded by a crowd of the curious, including children, watching the practical business of the lowering of Christ's body.

An etcher's inevitable primary commitment to printmaking prevented William Strang from establishing an unequivocal position as a book illustrator. But in the all-important matter of converting the emotional significance of works of literature into unstereotyped and moving graphic images, he was unsurpassed by any British artist.

Edmund Joseph Sullivan

In the customary way after the photographic process block had come into use, Edmund J. Sullivan (1869–1933) began his career as a pen-and-ink illustrator for newspapers and magazines. He went on to become a successful illustrator and a teacher of book illustration at the Goldsmiths' College School of Art, but something of the journalistic sense of fact persists throughout his work. He was influenced by Albrecht Dürer, Adolf Friedrich von Menzel, and Daniel

Vierge, and his illustrations for four books published in 1896 are in the manner of Edwin Austin Abbey and Hugh Thomson. Then in 1898, for Thomas Carlyle's *Sartor Resartus*, he evolved a more vigorous personal style, to which he adhered thereafter.

The four books issued in 1896 are George Borrow's *Lavengro*, Thomas Hughes's *Tom Brown's School-Days*, Richard Brinsley Sheridan's *School for Scandal* and *The Rivals* in one volume, and Izaak Walton's *Compleat Angler*. By then, Sullivan already was popular enough to compete with Thomson by having his name stamped in gold on covers. Borrow's leisurely *Lavengro* is hospitable to illustrations, but Sullivan's forty-four reduced pen drawings of gypsy life often have the look of having been drawn from photographs. For *Tom Brown's School-Days*, Sullivan drew seventy-nine full-page and half-page vignettes, many of the vignettes being of Rugby buildings. The illustrations of Tom's activities at Rugby are documentary records of Victorian public-school life. Sullivan's fifty reduced full-page pen drawings for *The School for Scandal* and *The Rivals*, published together as a volume in the Cranford series, make up two of the most complete and delightful sets of English play illustrations. The main charge against Sullivan at this stage in his career is that his work is too much like that of Thomson. But Sullivan's strength shows in the variety of posture and the expressiveness of his actors. In *The Compleat Angler*, the thirty-two full-page riverside illustrations, plus many portraits and drawings of fish, succeed in conveying Walton's faith in fishing as a gentleman's ritualistic craft and an excuse for days of idleness. Thomson never made a technically finer or more charming pen drawing than the one Sullivan invented for "The Small Bunches of Grapes Are Very Good", a mere diary entry in a fat two-volume deluxe edition of Gilbert White's *Natural History & Antiquities of Selborne & A Garden Kalendar* (1900). The main feature of the edition, however, is the forty-nine drawings of birds and small animals by J. G. Keulemans.

Sullivan's vigorous realism in the thirty-two full-page to half-page illustrations and eighteen headpieces and tailpieces for Carlyle's *Sartor Resartus* (1898) was almost as revolutionary as Charles Ricketts's and Aubrey Beardsley's antirealism. He tended now toward a more inventive style, filling his space with people and things and shading with longer, heavier, and more decisive lines. Unfortunately, he also deadened his designs – often by shading right up to the borders, and sometimes by placing heavily shaded forms against other heavily shaded forms. But he treated an extraordinary range of subjects, such as Carlyle as Herr Diogenes seated in a tub, several nudes to go with the discourse on clothes (they look naked), a lovely woman holding a lily in

the chapter on romance, grinning Death, and, in the vellum edition, Golgotha with the two thieves on crosses facing each other in front of the crucified Christ. In *Sartor Resartus*, Sullivan revealed an unusual capacity to project a set of images parallel to the text at the same level of imaginativeness, as in his transliteration of "Then is Monmouth Street a Mirza Hill, where in motley vision the whole pageant of Existence passes awfully before us" (fig. 130).

In the twentieth century, Sullivan did not succeed in Thomson's strategy of harvesting color-plate windfalls, although he might have. Perhaps because in his book work he was never the draftsman he was cracked up to be and perhaps because of the unselective abundance of his shading, his achievement is more often conceptual than executive, a paradox in view of his obsessive interest in technique. Tennyson's *Dream of Fair Women and Other Poems* (1900) and the baron de la Motte-Fouqué's *Sintram and His Companions* (1908) are the best of his twentieth-century books. In the first, he achieved much variety of effect, ranging from the grim designs for the "Vision of Sin" to the jolly ones for the un-Tennysonian "Goose". Sullivan's uncompromising drawing of the disenchanted speaker in the "Vision of Sin" embracing the skeleton of a woman is typical of an intense sincerity in his drawing that is missing from the lines he illustrated. The twenty original drawings in la Motte-Fouqué's *Sintram and His Companions* lend a convincing sense of reality to the heavy German Symbolism.

In his illustrations for some of the most illustrated works of literature, Sullivan failed to meet the high standards he wrote about so freely. John Bunyan's *Pilgrim's Progress* (1901) evoked no designs of genuine originality. Some, such as "Christian fighting Apollyon" and "Giant Despair", might have been done for boys and girls. Because Carlyle's *French Revolution* (1910) deals with the tragic facts of history, Sullivan had to find images of an order of seriousness or imaginative distortion different from those he had invented for *Sartor Resartus*. His efforts are obstructed by scores of hurried pen-and-ink copies of portraits scattered throughout the two-volume edition. His thirty-three full-page designs are more in the spirit of political cartoons than of illustrations. What should have been Sullivan's chief work, the three-volume *Works* (1911) of William Shakespeare, is a failure. His thirty illustrations, almost all pencil or charcoal drawings, look stiff and trite, as though they were based on film stills. Sixteen banal color plates and forty-eight hasty-looking pen drawings fail to do anything new for a mammoth edition of Oliver Goldsmith's *Vicar of Wakefield* (1914). Unexpectedly, Sullivan drew two series of quite satisfactory, if 1890ish,

130. Edmund Joseph Sullivan. Thomas Carlyle, *Sartor Resartus* (1898).

pen-and-ink vignettes for companion volumes of stories by Robert Louis Stevenson: *Dr. Jekyll & Mr. Hyde* and *Prince Otto* (1928), and *Weir of Hermiston* and *The Misadventures of John Nicholson* (1928). The rest of the numerous books that he illustrated seem to have been routine assignments, sometimes handled with charm, sometimes apparently corrupted by haste or ill health, but rarely charged with the simplicity of *The Compleat Angler* or the independent imagination of *Sartor Resartus*. Nevertheless, by reason of his great productivity, intelligence, and frequently powerful designs, Edmund Sullivan is a major figure in English book illustration.

Hugh Thomson

Born in Coleraine, County Derry, Northern Ireland, Hugh Thomson (1860–1920) in 1883 became an illustrator for the *English Illustrated Magazine*. Although he continued to draw for periodicals throughout his career, he was the popular illustrator of about seventy books, of which forty are in the Catalog. Thomson found success among the English classics of the eighteenth and nineteenth centuries, the gentler novels and plays that mirrored his own gentle nature. His smiling awareness of the unheroic aspect of everyday life; his relish for the counterbalancing bravery of period costumes, coaches and horses, and elegant furniture; and his brisk style give his work irresistible charm. In hundreds of pen-and-ink drawings and color plates, Thomson pictured the society of a past that was remote enough to seem serene and near enough to be remembered, a high society and a middle-class society of much formality and decorum, fringed by servants and countryfolk of quaint naturalness. With a certain gaiety of spirit and affectionate regard for the characters he drew, Thomson deserved his friend Austin Dobson's felicitous encomium of him as "the Charles Lamb of illustration".

Along with Edwin Austin Abbey, Thomson got rid of the Victorian excess of crosshatching and developed an open pen technique that in time reproduced nicely on the type-page, especially as vignettes unfettered by borders. After the heavy wood engravings of the preceding decades, Thomson's airy designs were almost like an end to mourning. When Thomson began working on the *English Illustrated Magazine*, it was still using wood engravings. But by the time of the publication of his first important book, Joseph Addison's *Days with Sir Roger de Coverley* (1886), the photographic process block for reproducing line drawings had arrived. As already noted, the date serves to open a new period – really a new era – in book illustration. *Days with Sir Roger de Coverley* is the earliest book listed in the Catalog that was illustrated by pen and ink. The fifty-one illustrations, which had appeared in the magazine, were signed "W & S Ld", evidence of the newness of photoengraving. The drawings are tight, overworked, and close to amateurish, but the research and feeling that went into them make them a pleasant addition to Addison's generalized essays. Almost all the fifty-nine pen-and-ink vignettes in William Outram Tristram's *Coaching Days and Coaching Ways* (1888) also came from the *English Illustrated Magazine* and also suffer from poor anatomy and weak pen technique. Yet they manage to recapture eighteenth-century and early-nineteenth-century types and scenes along the main coach routes. Herbert Austin Railton supplied many pen drawings of inns and old buildings. In *The Vicar of Wakefield* (1890), Thomson added to this illusion of an everyday past a sympathetic treatment of Oliver Goldsmith's familiar characters. Although he was not yet master of his own style, Thomson was the ideal illustrator of the tale. He rejoiced in the happiness that the Primrose family managed to squeeze out of their harassed existence; he smiled ruefully at their lucklessness; and he treated them with dignity in their adversities. The immediate success of the book was doubtless due in part to the abundance of the illustrations, 117 plus headpieces and tailpieces for the 32 chapters and introductory matter.

With Elizabeth Gaskell's *Cranford* (1891), the book usually associated with Thomson and the whole pen-and-ink tradition, Thomson emerged as a master of both unlabored technique and convincing interpretation. Mrs. Gaskell offered him a chance to draw varied incidents in a series of sketches that are loosely related to one another by the "humors" of a cast of characters in a village set apart in time and place so that the class roles are fixed and eccentrics "belong". Thomson exposed the feminarchy of Cranford to public view with 100 pen-and-ink drawings marked by much tact, as though these were dear friends at whose foibles he might smile with affection but never laugh. His pictures are so infused with Mrs. Gaskell's merciless perceptions, humor, compassion, and pervasive urbanity that the verbal and visual experiences merge. The publishing venture was a success, and so, unmistakably, was Thomson. Cranford became the general title of a series of gift books, although *Cranford* was not the first book published in the series.

A new "Hugh Thomson" book had become an event in the art world as well as in publishing, and Thomson's drawings were shown and sold at the Leicester Galleries. His Christmas gift book that followed *Cranford* was Mary Russell Mitford's *Our Village* (1893), with seventy-seven vignettes plus headpieces and tailpieces. In it, Thomson's pen-and-ink drawings continued to improve, as did the process for reproducing them. He relied on crisp outlines with restrained accenting, and now and then a bit of cross-hatching for darker tones. *Our Village* is both nostalgic and documentary.

In 1894, Thomson began his extended courtship of Jane Austen. It started with *Pride and Prejudice* in fulfillment of a two-year-old pledge to the publisher George Allen to illustrate a book for him. The contract for *Pride and Prejudice* – £500 plus a royalty of 7*d.* a copy after 10,000 – is evidence of how valuable an asset Thomson had become. The novel appeared in October with 160 pen drawings. To balance matters, Thomson agreed with Macmillan, his chief publisher, to do fifty illustrations for each of Austen's five other novels on the same terms as Allen had given him. The drawings took two years to execute, and the novels came out as "Hugh Thomson" books: *Sense and Sensibility* (1896), *Emma* (1896), *Mansfield Park* (1897), and, in one volume, *Northanger Abbey* and *Persuasion* (1897). To complete the series, Macmillan hired Charles Brock to illustrate *Pride and Prejudice* (1897). Until 1894, the works that Thomson had illustrated were episodic, full of outdoor scenes, and seasoned with strongly marked characters. The six novels of Austen, which he once had rejected as unsuitable for illustration, were a trying assignment. They are conversational comedies of manners in which the main characters are middle-class persons who do little besides talk to and about one another. A proposal of marriage is an exciting event. Nevertheless, Thomson's genteel, sparkling young ladies in their high-bodiced gowns gossiping with one another or acting out the rites of provincial courtship with slim young men with well-turned calves and profiles in the midst of authentic antiques probably come closer to the image that Austen had had in mind than to that which readers would have.

Some of Thomson's finest drawings are, surprisingly, those of buildings and places that he made in pencil for Macmillan's *Highways and Byways* series, to which he began contributing in 1896. Although brutally reduced, among his best are those for *Highways and Byways in Donegal and Antrim* (1899). They are not interpretive, however, and can only be mentioned with applause.

About this time, Thomson had a feeling that he was running out of material, but as he approached and passed the turn of the century, he found several texts that gave him characters, settings, and action needed for variety of illustrations. They include Charles Reade's *Peg Woffington* (1899), seventy illustrations; James Lane Allen's *Kentucky Cardinal* (1901), forty-eight; Maria Edgeworth's *Tales* (1903), forty; Fanny Burney's *Evelina* (1903), seventy-five; William Makepeace Thackeray's *Henry Esmond* (1905), fifty; and Thomas Hughes's *Tom Brown's School-Days* (1918), about fifty. Of these, *Evelina*, Burney's delightful

light comedy of manners, was the most congenial to Thomson's nature and style and stimulated the most satisfactory illustrations. "They pranced about the room, making bows" is characteristic of Thomson's mature pen-and-ink style (fig. 131).

Thomson's career was providentially sustained by the development of the color plate, at first by means of a tint added to some of the pen drawings that already had been published. The reissue of *Cranford* in 1898 with 40 of the original 100 drawings colored in irregular areas with pale tints was at once popular. There is no doubt that color enhanced the innate appeal of Thomson's drawings. Other books with some of the illustrations tinted are George Eliot's *Scenes of Clerical Life* (1906) and *Silas Marner* (1907) and a reissue of Mitford's *Our Village* (1907). Thomson's second career in color really began, however, in 1909 with the publication of the first of six plays in a sumptuous uniform format in full color reproduced by improved methods. Thomson's 172 color plates for the plays constitute one of the most substantial and successful efforts to illustrate English plays. They are Shakespeare's *As You Like It* (1909) and *The Merry Wives of Windsor* (1910), Richard Brinsley Sheridan's *School for Scandal* (1911), Goldsmith's *She Stoops to Conquer* (1912), and James M. Barrie's *Quality Street* (1913) and *The Admirable Crichton* (1914).

The forty color plates pasted on linen in *As You Like It* (1909) are unusual in a leafy pastoral way. When we linger over designs like Jacques's unwilling schoolboy creeping to school and a forester blowing his horn after having killed a deer, we realize how admirably Thomson caught Shakespeare's romantic comedy in his watercolors. Yet as soon as we open *The Merry Wives of Windsor* (1910), we see how Thomson relished its earthy comedy, its Elizabethan interiors and Windsor streets, and, most of all, its great cast of Thomson relished its earthy comedy, its Elizabethan interiors and Windsor streets, and, most of all, its great cast of characters grouped around Falstaff. The forty watercolors make this edition of *The Merry Wives of Windsor* one of the choice English illustrated books. In the two eighteenth-century comedies (with the number of plates cut back to twenty-five in each), we see again how the text limits or extends an artist's range. The characters in *The School for Scandal* (1911) are upper class, and the action takes place indoors. The play got some of Thomson's finest designs of costumes and furniture, but the most beguiling one is the frontispiece of street urchins gawking at Lady Teazle as she emerges from a sedan chair. The scenes in the companion volume, *She Stoops to Conquer* (1912), also take place indoors, but Thomson balanced his impeccable sitting-room scenes and the courting of Miss Nevill with such plates as those of Tony and his alehouse cronies singing and of Hardcastle and his servants enjoying a laugh. A play by Barrie may not seem to be a promising vehicle for twenty-two color plates, but *Quality Street* (1913) is essentially a stage treatment of *Cranford* and *Our Village*, quiet comedy and romance in a female-centered village. Thomson made the most of women sewing and gossiping, of streets with bow windows and hitching posts, and of the boon of soldiers in uniforms of the Napoleonic Wars, but Barrie's whimsy too often betrays Thomson into sweetness. The twenty color plates in Barrie's *Admirable Crichton* (1914) suffer from the basic disadvantage of modern clothes and characters, yet some of the designs – the women resting in a parlor, for instance – are superbly organized and rendered watercolors. In Acts II and III, the Edmund Dulac-like tropical-island scenes do not go well with the comic mood.

Besides these three pairs of plays, Thomson's color-plate books include two stories by Charles Dickens and a novel by Nathaniel Hawthorne. In range of feeling, Thomson was particularly attuned to Dickens. At least in his seven color plates for *The Chimes* (1913), by ignoring all the tasteless episodes in this dreadful tear-jerker, Thomson succeeded in evoking that blend of virtue, rosy good health, and geniality with which Dickens endowed the lower classes. Because the First World War closed the gift-book market, the seven illustrations that Thomson made in 1915 for *The Cricket on the Hearth* were not published until 1933. Preposterous as the story is, Thomson's depictions of the Peerybingle's domesticity and of Caleb Plummer and his blind daughter in their toy shop are engaging. The quiet golden brown and green and pink and violet hues, reproduced by collotype on the same laid paper as the text, make *The Cricket on the Hearth* one of Thomson's most harmonious and finished color-plate books.

For Hawthorne's somber tale of sin, suffering, and salvation in Puritan New England, *The Scarlet Letter* (1920), Thomson did thirty-one watercolor illustrations and some incidental pen-and-ink designs in 1915; but because of the war, the book was not published until 1920, the year of his death. Besides the local color of village scenes, Puritan dress and interiors, and visiting sailors, in this farewell offering, Thomson succeeded in something he had never before attempted. He provided a serious interpretation of a psychological drama, Hester Prynne saving her soul by accepting her fate and the pious Dimmesdale finally gaining his on the scaffold. *The Scarlet Letter* proved what deep resources Thomson possessed.

Popular enthusiasm for his early work, publishers' choice of assignments, natural inclination, and ill health led Thomson to work repetitively within a narrow band of effects during his years as a black-and-white artist. Color extended his boundaries, but only Hawthorne demanded more from him than charm – too late. Few artists have illustrated so many books so satisfactorily or have succeeded in giving delight to so many readers. Hugh Thomson was a modest man and would be content with that.

Frederick Henry Linton Townsend

A representative member of the group of productive, competent illustrators of the second rank is Frederick Henry Townsend (1868–1920). He was a *Punch* artist influenced by Edwin Austin Abbey. The Catalog lists eighteen books for the twenty years from 1890 to 1910; they indicate something of Townsend's productivity and the wide range of literature entrusted to him. The 160 line drawings for six works (in four volumes) by Thomas Love Peacock were his main effort as a book illustrator. (H. R. Millar illustrated a fifth volume, containing *Headlong Hall* and *Nightmare Abbey* [1896].) For each volume, Townsend drew forty designs, almost all full-page vignettes. "Elphin was impressed into royal favour" in *The Misfortunes of Elphin* (1897) shows how well Townsend could draw (fig. 132). The figures of Elphin, hands bound behind him, his warlike captor Maelgon, and the grooms riding through the countryside are admirably realized. But the naturalistic drawing fails even to hint at the significance of the full sentence: "So Elphin was impressed into royal favour, and was feasted munificently in the castle of Diganwy." In this spoof of Welsh literature, Maelgon is dragging Elphin off because he has declined an invitation – out of modesty, Maelgon maintains – to enjoy royal hospitality as a peace offering for Maelgon's having plundered Elphin's dwelling in his absence. Townsend failed in this illustration and in most of the 159 other designs to convey the spirit of the delightful absurdities of Peacock's satirical romances. His insensitivity was not limited to works by Peacock. Peacock's crotchety narratives lend themselves to action scenes that do not make the same demands as, say, the psychological intensities of Charlotte Brontë's *Shirley* and *Jane Eyre*, both of which Townsend illustrated in 1897. Although he was a *Punch* artist, Townsend also missed the far from subtle humor in his 240 illustrations (many halftones) for four books by Sara J. Duncan, such as *An American Girl in London* (1891).

Paul Vincent Woodroffe

In addition to illustrating books, Paul Woodroffe (1875–1954) designed books, bookplates, coats of arms, and stained-glass windows, including those in the Lady Chapel

Plate III. Edmund Dulac. Edward Fitzgerald, *The Rubáiyát of Omar Khayyám* (1909).

Plate IV. W. Russell Flint. Geoffrey Chaucer, *The Canterbury Tales* (1913).

131. Hugh Thomson. Fanny Burney, *Evelina* (1903).

132. Frederick Henry Linton Townsend. Thomas Love Peacock, *The Misfortunes of Elphin* (1897).

133. Paul Vincent Woodroffe, *The Little Flowers of St. Francis of Assisi* (1899).

of St. Patrick's Cathedral in New York. Fresh from the Slade School of Art, Woodroffe contributed twelve derivative pen drawings to *Songs from the Plays of Shakespeare* (1898), together with some charming small headpieces and floral borders. In the fashion of the moment, these designs were reproduced by photogravure and reduced, as were the eight illustrations for *The Little Flowers of St. Francis of Assisi* (1899). An angel holding a viol and appearing to St. Francis as he prays among plum trees in flower exemplifies Woodroffe's reverent translations of the words of the devout *Little Flowers of St. Francis* (fig. 133). Clemence Housman engraved the four illustrations for *The "Confessions" of St. Augustine* (1900). Augustine kissing the feet of the crucified Christ and Augustine hearing a voice as he prays beside a fig tree have religious conviction, a rare quality in book illustration. The eight pen drawings for *The Little Flowers of St. Benet* (1901), a companion volume to *The Little Flowers of St. Francis*, suffer from the demands made by the more extreme events.

For Laurence Housman's translation of *Aucassin and Nicolette* (1902), Clemence engraved Woodroffe's four illustrations on wood. It is difficult to understand why Woodroffe and Clemence, having experienced the liberation of simplicity in *The "Confessions" of St. Augustine*, returned to the slavery of dense crosshatching in this book. The designs are striking, but they owe a good deal to Dante Gabriel Rossetti's "St. Cecilia" (1857), John Everett Millais's "St. Agnes's Eve" (1857), and Housman's *Sensitive Plant* (1898) and *Goblin Market* (1893). The ten pen drawings for Tennyson's *Princess and Other Poems* (1904) resemble the engraved ones in *The "Confessions" of St. Augustine*, but they are not so graceful. Tennyson did not rouse Woodroffe to the intense responses that the saints did. Among the Art Nouveau border elements, the one of young oak leaves and acorns prefigures Eric Gill's designs by twenty years. The addition of color to the repertory of turn-of-the-century illustrators generally had a rejuvenating effect, but the opaque coloring in Woodroffe's seventeen watercolors for *The Tempest* (1908) weighs them down. On the title page, however, is a lovely black-and-white triangular design of a nude Ariel seated on an oak spray, another forerunner of Gill's drawings and quite as good.

CHAPTER NINE

The Twentieth Century (I)
1901–1918

Two world wars divided twentieth-century illustration into three periods. The First World War cut the publication of illustrated books to a trickle, subtracted four years from the careers of established illustrators, and delayed the beginnings of those of younger ones. The period was one of sporadic distinction amid a good deal of technical competence but artistic and imaginative mediocrity. Photo-engraving had greatly increased the use of illustrations in the popular press and in commercial printing and, consequently, had added to the number of journeymen illustrators. No vigorous innovative successor to Aubrey Beardsley put in an appearance. Sidney Sime might have become that person, but circumstances cast him in too specialized a role to claim the honor. Typical of artists included in the Catalog but not discussed in the Critical Account are Alfred Garth Jones and Reginald Savage, heavy-handed decorators left over from the heyday of Walter Crane, and Herbert Cole, whose drawings are too matter-of-fact to meet the demands of works as different from each other as the accounts of the travels of Gulliver and of Froissart. Byam Shaw and Maurice Greiffenhagen might be mentioned from among the many who, perhaps unfairly, are neither cataloged nor discussed. Rudyard Kipling's reactions to Greiffenhagen's drawings for a story by Kipling's friend Rider Haggard were violent: "What foul illustrations to *Ayesha*. Pity one can't sprinkle lime over illustrators – same as slugs." In *English Book-Illustration of To-day* (1907), R. E. D. Sketchley reviews the work of numerous artists who are not included in this study.

Publishers had so exploited the vogue of popular classics illustrated with black-and-white drawings similar to those of Hugh Thomson that around the beginning of the twentieth century, Thomson and other leading illustrators found themselves in mid-career worried about a waning market. As noted in the opening remarks to Chapter Eight, the simple colors that had been added to black-and-white illustrations by photography at the end of the nineteenth century had yielded results of limited appeal. In the early twentieth century, improvements in color processes brought a new round of publication of the same classics, now illustrated with fresh and faithful color plates by the familiar household names of Thomson, Charles Brock, and Henry Brock, and by newcomers, notably Arthur Rackham, Edmund Dulac, and William Russell Flint. Artists had access to a world of illustration largely denied them since the Middle Ages, the heyday of the illuminated manuscript. Color plates now were not merely tinted line drawings, but full-range autographic watercolors, although usually firmly outlined. Rackham and Dulac, both of whom managed to delight old and young, continued to work long after 1918 and became internationally known.

A serious drawback of color plates continued to be that they had to be printed on coated paper; bound, tipped, or pasted in; and often protected by a sheet of tissue. Thus they were separated from the text and broke into the reading. This probably was not intolerable for the readers of these gift books, who usually either were extending their familiarity with the text or, if young, were being induced to read it. In any case, the books were bought or given primarily for the illustrations, as evidenced by the frequent display of artists' names on the cover as well as on the title page. Nevertheless, with all the pressure on the artists to produce pretty color plates, Rackham, Dulac, and Flint were conscientious and often original in their interpretations and their drawings.

There were few other new developments in this brief period. One significant one was the entrance into the profession of several women illustrators. Of these, Jessie King was the most noteworthy because of her part in the Art Nouveau movement. Lady Eleanor Fortescue Brickdale, Evelyn Paul, Sybil Tawse, and M. V. Wheelhouse produced some charming color plates, but many more that were overworked and, because of technical problems no doubt, limited in their color appeal. Worthy of mention, too, is Gordon Craig's contribution to the revival of wood engraving in book illustration. In spirit, he was the successor to Charles Ricketts, Sturge Moore, and Lucien Pissarro, although William Nicholson was his mentor.

Lady Eleanor Fortescue Brickdale

One of the most productive women illustrators of the early twentieth century, Lady Eleanor Fortescue Brickdale (1872–1945) – usually without a hyphen – represented change in gift-book publishing from Victorian multiple-artist offerings to single-artist books. Brickdale resembled William Russell Flint in the meticulous care she gave to posture, costumes, settings, and accessories in her well-filled compositions. The effect often is that of static paintings. Color aided Brickdale's popularity, although her plates usually are not bright. In the following selection of the books that she illustrated, all except the first note the number of color plates: Tennyson's *Poems* (1905), twenty-one line drawings; Robert Browning's *Pippa Passes & Men & Women* (1908), ten, and *Dramatis Personae* (1909), ten; Tennyson's *Idylls of the King* (1911), twenty; *The Book of Old English Songs & Ballads* (1912), twenty-four; *The Golden Book of Famous Women* (1920), sixteen; and Francis Turner Palgrave's anthology *The Golden Treasury* (1924), twelve.

Edward Gordon Craig

Son of Ellen Terry, Gordon Craig (1872–1966) began acting in Henry Irving's company in 1889. William Nicholson interested him in wood engraving, and he taught himself the craft as an aid to thinking out stage productions. His long career in the theater consisted of acting, designing, producing, teaching, publishing, and writing; yet he engraved several hundred wood blocks along the way. In *Woodcuts and Some Words* (1924), he writes that he roughed in his designs on the polished boxwood blocks and then worked up his effects with a graver and a gouge. His early designs, small and restricted as most of them are, began to manifest a sense of mystery and drama that reached its height in the well-known print of the storm scene (III.ii) in *King Lear* (1920).

As early as 1904, Count Harry Kessler, a socialite and diplomat and the art-patron owner of the Cranach Press in Weimar, hired Craig to make four wood engravings to illustrate *Der weisse Fächer* (*The White Fan*) (1907), an "interlude" by Hugo von Hofmannsthal. They are an unimpressive mixed lot of black stage designs. Around 1925, at Kessler's suggestion, Craig engraved blocks to illustrate Daniel Defoe's *Robinson Crusoe*. They were not made public until about twenty-five were shown in a 1967 exhibition at the Victoria and Albert Museum. The blocks are superb examples of autographic wood engraving, which was revived in England in the 1920s. (They were printed in 1980 and offered for sale at the absurd price of £450.

It is said that there are eighty designs in the series.)

Craig holds a unique place in the history of English book illustration on the basis of only one book – the Cranach Press edition of *Hamlet*. He had worked intermittently on the blocks from 1912 until 1928, when Kessler published the German translation by Gerhard Hauptmann; in 1930, he published the English edition. Rarely have type and illustrations been so complexly and brilliantly united on facing pages throughout an entire work. Craig engraved about seventy-five blocks, and Eric Gill engraved one. They are mainly vignettes of figures in silhouette with sparse interior white lines to indicate the forms of bodies and clothing. Some of the blocks were lowered to print in an almost-black gray, and some impose black figures on gray. Craig's son Edward Anthony Craig supervised the delicate printing of the blocks. Only two blocks have touches of color added; the stern black pages could easily have borne more.

From the outset, Craig created startling, powerful images unlike any others in an English book – for instance, Hamlet's father as a tall black figure with no feet and a cadaver's face (I.i), Hamlet feigning madness and reading as he enters halfway down a twisting staircase, the dumb-show players in fantastic headpieces and masks (III.ii), Hamlet seen from the back (an echo of Henry Fuseli) opposing a surge of waves that extends across a page, Ophelia as a small white figure before a turquoise background observed by a crowd of black figures, and (another memory of Fuseli) Hamlet stretching across the left page and Laertes defending himself on the right (V.ii). These are some of the illustrations that so merge with the process of reading as to resemble a musical accompaniment (fig. 134).

Gordon Craig's illustrations for the Cranach edition of *Hamlet* make it one of the most imaginative volumes of this century because Craig – a man of the theater who was familiar with every line of the play – by his mastery of wood engraving, was able to project the tragic overtones of this monumental melodrama through suggestion, not labored realism.

Edmund Dulac

Born in Toulouse and university educated, Edmund Dulac (1882–1953) arrived in England just in time to cash in on the enthusiasm for color plates in gift books. He brought with him French elegance, the influence of Japanese prints and Persian miniatures, and experience in designing for the theater. Most of the books he illustrated are for children. His sixty color plates for an edition of the novels of the Brontë sisters (1905), reproduced by an early form of the three-color process, hover among realism, formality, and

134. Gordon Craig. William Shakespeare, *Hamlet* (1930).

strangeness, as do the narratives. The heroines are plain but interesting. The imperfect dark colors tend to be dull, but now and then French vivacity enters, as in the plate of a woman in a spotted pink dress descending from a yellow carriage with orange wheels in Anne Brontë's *Tenant of Wildfell Hall*. Some of Dulac's fifty watercolors in Laurence Housman's retelling of *Stories from the Arabian Nights* (1907), selected "mainly with a view to illustration", are technically as fine as any he ever made, but the series as a whole loses dignity because of the mixture of adult and juvenile values.

Like his rival Arthur Rackham, Dulac was both a fastidious draftsman and a fecund visualizer. Among the forty color plates for Shakespeare's *Tempest* (1908), many are too dark, but some are brilliant drawings of scenes merely mentioned, not acted out – for example, Prospero at his alchemical experiments and Prospero and the child Miranda adrift in a ship's boat. They hardly could be bettered. Many of the remainder seem pretty, the fruit of whimsy rather than of imagination, and defensible only if they were meant to enchant the eyes of children or of adults unlikely to respond to Shakespeare's poetry. The same discrepancy exists between the six decorative plates in *Comus* (1923) and John Milton's grave allegory of virtue.

The favorite gift book of Edwardian times probably was Edward FitzGerald's rendering of *The Rubáiyát of Omar Khayyám*. Dulac's illustrations for an edition published in 1909 are fresh and dignified. For the familiar fortieth quatrain, for instance, Dulac offered a quiet study of the bemused poet observing a potter in a bazaar working his wet clay (pl. III). One characteristic that separates Dulac from many other illustrators is the intelligence in the faces of his characters. In *Tanglewood Tales* (1938), Nathaniel Hawthorne's lively colloquial retelling of Greek myths, the mock classicism of Dulac's twelve plates seems more compatible with Hawthorne's amused tone than would a realistic, romantic, or comic style. But Walter Pater's affected retelling of the Cupid and Psyche episode from *The Golden Ass* of Apuleius – published as *The Marriage of Cupid and Psyche* (1951) – yielded six colorful, pretty, and lifeless oval plates.

It is a pity that an illustrator with the artistic integrity of Edmund Dulac did not have more opportunity to develop as a serious interpreter of literature.

Sir William Russell Flint

The charge against Russell Flint (1880–1969) is that his watercolor illustrations are pretty, academic, and popular. Flint was a meticulous draftsman who mastered the human figure by continually making life studies. For twenty years,

he was president of the Royal Society of Painters in Water-Colours. He considered it his duty not only to master the technical problems of anatomy, drawing, composition, and color, but also to ensure the accuracy of all details of clothing, jewelry, artifacts, architecture, furniture, and landscape in the scenes he illustrated. This authenticity adds a special value to his illustrations of literature of the past. Flint's designs are usually shallow in depth. He had a habit of pulling his flat background, or a section of it, close to his foreground figures, so that the effect approaches the formality of a mural and partly counteracts what might be an illusion of reality. Although Flint's success as a painter earned him a knighthood, for fifty years, he was a serious professional illustrator and never failed to defend the integrity of the illustrator's art.

The illustrations for Richard Whytford's sixteenth-century version of Thomas à Kempis's *Of the Imitation of Christ* (1908) were Flint's first venture into illustrations in color. The twelve four-color plates, done in the manner of illuminations, help make a cherished classic more precious without irreverence. His illustrations for *The Song of Songs Which Is Solomon's* (1909) reveal his limitations. The ten watercolors are models of academic technique, but perhaps are more suitable for Rider Haggard's *King Solomon's Mine*, which Flint had illustrated poorly in pen and ink in 1905. His twelve color plates are too lush to be in key with the sober *Thoughts* (1909) of Marcus Aurelius. Flint might be expected to have given his best efforts to Matthew Arnold's *Scholar Gipsy* and *Thyrsis* (1910) and to Robert Burns's *Songs and Lyrics* (1911); but for both volumes, he supplied unexciting landscapes. Nor did he have the proper temperament to cope with William S. Gilbert's Savoyard wit in his thirty-two illustrations for each of the librettos of *Savoy Operas* (1909) and *Iolanthe and Other Operas* (1910). His watercolors may almost as well be colored photographs.

After this unpromising start, the forty-eight color plates in Sir Thomas Malory's *Morte Darthur* (1910–11) were a major achievement for Flint and for English illustration. He said that the series had been his main preoccupation for two years but that he gladly would have spent another two on it. Flint responded naturally to Malory's tapestried prose, and his paintings have the dignity, splendor, and sheer factual authority to justify their presence. The four themes of violence, lust, magic, and piety that swirl around Arthur, Guenever, Launcelot, and the Knights of the Round Table established the continuity of the illustrations throughout the twenty-one "books", and Flint's research and imagination supplied the variety. He chose relatively few of the endless scenes of fighting, but enough to be faithful to the nature of the quarrelsome knights. He did not present a single stereotyped joust, but constantly invented something fresh from the text. Perhaps he gave women a more prominent role than Malory had assigned them. But most of the time, he depicted significant incidents in which women play a part, such as those of the Damosel of the Lake ending Merlin's evil career by imprisoning him in a rock, La Beale Isoud and Tristram discovering their love after drinking a potion in a ship at sea, and Guenever being rescued from burning by Launcelot. Several designs of much charm and dignity record quieter events. The richly ornamented design of Sir Percivale praying in a monastery while a priest offers the Sacrament to old King Evelake is an example.

For *The Heroes* (1912), Charles Kingsley's retelling of Greek legends, Flint did twelve watercolors. The exploits of Perseus, the Argonauts, and Theseus discourage prettiness or repetitiousness. The launching of Jason's *Argos*, the three Sirens sitting on a sandy beach while the Argonauts' galley passes, and Medeia offering Theseus a cup of poisoned wine are among the fine English illustrations.

Flint said that he found Geoffrey Chaucer's *Canterbury Tales* (1913) more troublesome than *Morte Darthur* because of the jump from period to period and from subject to subject – and from mood to mood, he might have added. For the same reasons, however, the thirty-six color plates in the three-volume edition are more varied, more uneven, and more surprising than are the plates in *Morte Darthur*. For example, the second illustration for the Knight's Tale, as befits that sedate account, is a deeply serious U-shaped design in blue. Tall Duke Theseus, leaning against a young chestnut tree in flower, gazes down at Queen Ipolita, who lies at his feet, while Emelye kneels at the right, as he ponders their plea for the lives of Palamon and Arcite. Then more lightly in the Miller's Tale, Flint pictured the carpenter, a bald and thick-necked man, sawing a plank in preparation for the deluge, while his pretty wife, Alison, meticulously gowned by Chaucer, casts her eyes at the merry clerk Nicholas, who is seen outdoors through a small barred window (pl. IV). Flint, without a leer, pictured the believable characters as Chaucer had presented them before the comedy turned to fabliau.

Flint's seventeen watercolors for *The Idyls of Theocritus, Bion & Moschus* (1922) are successful evocations of the characters and events of these richly sensuous, pagan narratives. Two years later appeared Flint's last masterwork, Samuel Henry Butcher and Andrew Lang's stylized and sonorous prose edition of Homer's *Odyssey* (1924) with twenty color plates. The presence throughout of a familiar hero, freshly visualized as a black-haired and black-bearded Greek, and a sequence of familiar events depicted in unfamiliar concreteness against Mediterranean settings make this one of the finest English books seriously illustrated

with color plates. For accuracy of detail, Flint went to Syracuse to study Greek vases.

During the remaining forty-five years of his career, Flint devoted himself mainly to painting and writing. The illustrations that he did for books during these years cannot be regarded as interpretive or compared favorably with his work from *Morte Darthur* to *The Odyssey*. Perhaps because of the academic correctness of his drawing and the popularity of his color plates in gift books, Russell Flint's intelligence as an interpreter of literature has not been sufficiently appreciated.

Vernon Hill

Two series of designs by Vernon Hill (1887–1953) – etcher, engraver, lithographer, and sculptor – make him a rarity among twentieth-century followers of 1890s Art Nouveau – an able interpretive book illustrator. Embedded in his work are many obvious influences, from Michelangelo to Arthur Heygate Mackmurdo. One not so obvious source was Jean Delville, a minor Belgian artist who was for a time in the 1890s a professor at the School of Art in Glasgow.

Hill's two major books are companion limited-edition folios. For Stephen Phillips's *New Inferno* (1911), he drew sixteen full-page designs with lithographic effects on black backgrounds. The unusual look of these illustrations is appropriate to Phillips's feeble effort to make Dante a denizen of Edwardian London. Hill's drawings have enough imaginative force to save them from banality. For example, to illustrate a lover's unhappy thoughts about his meeting after death with the woman he has ruined, Hill showed the two lovers, naked but enveloped in their open shrouds, floating within a circle of stars against the black sky. *L'Amour des Ames*, a painting by Delville, depicts two similar soaring figures, but in a different arrangement. Hill's composition is one of flowing grace, but his anatomical exactness in this and in other designs diminishes the mystic feeling that he tried to convey by means of long sinuous lines and such iconographic devices as mandalas, flames, snakes, and emblematic hands.

Ballads Weird and Wonderful (1912) gave Hill more varied subjects. The twenty-five large gray drawings are softly lithographic in the manner of Charles Haslewood Shannon. The marvelous old English folk ballads encouraged Hill to combine realism with a sense of strangeness. About one-third of these designs seem remarkable; one-third, only slightly less so; and one-third, vitiated by fairy-tale effects. The powerful ones illustrate ballads as familiar as "The Wife of Usher's Well" and "Edward, Edward" and as unfamiliar as "The Demon Lover" and "The Great Sealchie of Sule Skerrie". In "The Demon Lover", the demon, an athletic nude, stands as tall as the masts of a ship that is about to plunge to the bottom of the sea, with the waves rising from beneath the bow to fill the rest of the design in long, stylized, froth-topped curves. Again, the pattern resembles that of Delville's *L'Amour des Ames*. In "The Great Sealchie of Sule Skerrie", a stranger who says that he is a man on land and a seal in the sea appears to a nurse and offers gold for his child (fig. 135). He is an odd squat figure, wearing what might be fishermen's garb. He seems to be not an evil man. Only his excessively broad face and his wide-set, light eyes – staring out from under a hat that resembles a boletus mushroom – introduce the supernatural into the calm that surrounds the nurse and child. With the possible exception of Phillips's *Christ in Hades* (1911), other book work by Hill was casual and disappointingly ordinary.

Jessie Marion King

A member of the Glasgow group that contributed so much to the British brand of Art Nouveau, Jessie M. King (1875–1949) was a designer of murals, textiles, and jewelry as well as an illustrator of books for children and adults. Her illustrations are primarily decorative and are marked by long thin sweeping lines, candlelike perpendiculars, and small black motifs. She said that she had founded her spidery linear style on that of Botticelli, not of Beardsley, but there is a good deal of Beardsley in it, as well as something of Leon Bakst. The most common feature of King's illustrations is her version of Botticelli's *Primavera*, a barefoot attenuated young woman, her expressionless Pre-Raphaelite face thrust forward, her hair unbound, and her gown billowing down in a conspicuous excess of cloth. King repeatedly chose passages, often of little significance, for which she found this obsessive image adequate. The few male characters she introduced, even knights in armor, are limp and girlish.

King made no adjustment in her drawings to accommodate either subject matter or age of reader. Her five flower girls are utterly miscast in a translation of the Scottish humanist George Buchanan's gloomy Latin poetic drama *Jephtha* (1902). Some of the twenty-four illustrations for an Art Nouveau edition of Perlesvaus's *High History of the Holy Graal* (1903) are fastidiously drawn – "Perceval winneth the Golden Cup", for example – and a few touch the deeper levels of the legends. The illustrations, however, are not really concerned with the main business of the long narrative – fighting.

The twenty-four drawings for William Morris's *Defence of Guenevere and Other Poems* (1904) (fig. 136) are decorative designs of the stereotyped young woman and fragile-looking knights standing among indefinite props and artificial flowers, uninvolved in what happens in the poems. The eight photogravured illustrations in John Milton's *Comus: A Masque* (1906), although limited as interpretations, are the most successful of King's series for adult readers because she felt at home in Milton's enchanted wood. The frontispiece depicts a poet-shepherd, whose pipe, crook, inkhorn, hat, and even hair deviate delightfully from the real. But King adorned Oscar Wilde's *House of Pomegranates* (1915) with sixteen pretty watercolors that apparently were meant for little girls. She even omitted the fisherman from the long sophisticated tale "The Fisherman and His Soul".

Henry Ospovat

Before he died at the age of thirty-one, Russian-born Henry Ospovat (1877–1909) illustrated six books. His ten drawings for Shakespeare's *Sonnets* (1899) look like designs by an early Pre-Raphaelite for a mural. Among the fifteen full-page illustrations for Matthew Arnold's *Poems* (1900), the curvilinear drawing of the forsaken merman rising to the surface of the sea with his children is fashionable but prosaic. The eleven illustrations for Shakespeare's *Songs* (1901) reveal more detail and mood. Yet two of the most carefully thought-out designs show unbelievable insensitivity to Shakespeare's verse: a grim hooded priest and mourning parents beside a coffin for "Fear no more the heat o' the sun", and four drunken sailors reeling down a London street for "Blow, blow, thou winter wind". By the time Ospovat made his fifteen illustrations for Robert Browning's *Men and Women* (1903), his coarse-line style, reminiscent of that of Edmund Sullivan, had given way to imitation etching. In general, the single figures shrouded in gloom suggest no more than the possible appearance of chief characters. Beethoven was, incredibly, chosen to represent a passing reference to a man of music grown gray with nothing else to say. Lucrezia wearing a brocade gown and sitting with her face averted while Andrea del Sarto grasps her wrist and begs that they may sit quietly and quarrel no more is one of the few of Ospovat's illustrations that conveys the feeling of an author's words.

Evelyn Paul

Among the color-plate artists who were active before 1914, Evelyn Paul (1872–1945) had a pleasant gift-book style strengthened by care in introducing authentic collateral detail. By reducing the size of her figures, she gave scenes greater depth, width, and complexity than was customary. Several of the books she illustrated and illuminated, how-

135. Vernon Hill. *Ballads Weird and Wonderful* (1912).

136. Jessie Marion King. William Morris, *The Defence of Guenevere and Other Poems* (1904).

ever, are peripheral to English belles-lettres – for instance, *Stories from Dante* (1910). The fifteen color plates picture Dante in the streets of Florence and during the imaginary events of his journey and some of the exploits of the characters whom he encounters. The twenty-four color plates in Elizabeth Gaskell's *Cranford* (1910) lose their novelty because they came after the series by Hugh Thomson (1891, 1898), Charles Brock (1904), and Henry Brock (1898). Paul did enlarge the view, include more figures and more detail – particularly in the interiors – and give female dress a special veracity. The sixteen color plates for Charles Reade's *Cloister and the Hearth* (1922) do not offer anything fresh in treatment, although the "Death of Gerard", which shows the interior of a church, conveys a convincing medievalism.

Arthur Rackham

The English book illustrator most popular with the general reader undoubtedly is Arthur Rackham (1867–1939). He was a master draftsman and watercolorist who came along at the right time to make the most, artistically and financially, of the color-plate gift-book bonanza. His fanciful imagination gave his illustrations instant recognition, and his dedication to illustration kept him in the public eye for thirty years. The twenty-nine books selected for the Catalog are perhaps one-third of those that he illustrated. He had published for twelve years before color rescued him from obscurity. Oddly, Rackham never satisfactorily illustrated a book in black and white only. He frequently supplemented his color plates by a number of pen-drawn vignettes, but they seem to be intrusions. And yet underlying all his color plates are meticulous line drawings. The illustrations in a few of the books listed in the Catalog were worked up from redrawn black-and-white series.

Washington Irving's *Rip Van Winkle* (1905) first brought Rackham to public attention. The fifty-one color plates are really sepia-tinted line drawings with spots of color added; but even though a product of this early state of the art, his work has great charm. Scenes such as those of Rip and his dog Wolf flying from Dame Van Winkle, schoolmaster Van Bummel reading a newspaper to the burghers in front of the village inn, and the returned Rip among his old cronies mark the arrival of a major talent.

The book that made Rackham's reputation was *Peter Pan in Kensington Gardens* (1906), based on James M. Barrie's *Little White Bird* (1902), not on his play *Peter Pan* (1904). The format is the same as that of *Rip Van Winkle*, with the fifty illustrations following the text like a gallery exhibition. The ill-starred betrothal between Peter Pan, a naked infant, and Maimie Mannering, a four year old, is incredible. (When it ends in separation, Maimie's parting

gift to Peter is a goat.) In the year that he worked on the watercolors, Rackham steered clear of picturing Peter and Maimie together. His center of interest was Kensington Gardens (a park that is contiguous with Hyde Park in London). Twisted trees henceforth became "Rackham trees". Less obviously, the watercolors in *Peter Pan in Kensington Gardens* include images of plant life – even weeds – birds, and small animals of a precision and beauty not seen before in color in popular English books. Rackham also celebrated the Serpentine, the Broad Walk, and the Round Pond (not adequately); and he made the fairies, rather than the embarrassing humans, the chief actors. It was a great time for fairies, and Rackham gave them their most delightful embodiment: the fairy women, all ethereality; the fairy men, all long-nosed, bat-eared drollery.

It was not impertinent of Rackham to illustrate *Alice's Adventures in Wonderland* (1907). Instead of trying to outdo John Tenniel, in the thirteen color plates (mostly in neutral hues), he offered variations on themes from the Victorian classic. Only the illustrations of the pool of tears, the end of the Caucus-Race, and Alice receiving advice from the caterpillar are characteristic Rackham. Dodo, Duck, and Eaglet are superbly personable creatures. Copyright prevented him from illustrating *Through the Looking-Glass*.

For most readers, *A Midsummer Night's Dream* (1908) is probably Rackham's finest book. Through forty color plates, he was constantly at the top of his powers in establishing a conviction that the image and the word are manifestations of one spirit. Apparently, Rackham's belief that Shakespeare's – and his – first duty was to provide entertainment released him from any guilt in giving the central love story no more than its due while, with caressing imagination, picturing the blundering of Bottom the weaver and his fellow actors into the court of Oberon and Titania (III.i). Who can feel anything but a sense of rightness when Shakespeare tosses out a line like Bottom's "Mounsieur Cobweb, good mounsieur, get you your weapons in your hand, and kill me a red-hipped humblebee on the top of a thistle," and Rackham catches it and turns it into an enchanting study of thistles and a bee charging the spear of the intrepid Cobweb (pl. V)? In 1923, Rackham painted a less appealing set of thirteen watercolors to go with a calligraphic manuscript of *A Midsummer Night's Dream*. This edition was published in 1977 with no explanation of the circumstances. He also was induced to do six more watercolors, reproduced by stencil, for a 1939 edition.

Rackham's accomplishment remained high but uneven during the following years. Some of his most conscientious color plates appear in translations from the German: fifteen for the baron de la Motte-Fouqué's *Undine* (1909), thirty-four for Richard Wagner's *Rhinegold and the Valkyrie*

(1910), and thirty for Wagner's *Siegfried and the Twilight of the Gods* (1911). But for one awkward objection, the two-volume edition of Wagner's *Ring of the Nibelung* has some right to be considered Rackham's masterwork. The sixty-four full-page watercolors follow the prolonged intricacies of Wagner's libretto with tireless invention, brilliant draftsmanship, and unflagging charm. The question is their suitability to the text. The lissome feminine figures, juvenile-lead Siegfried, evil-faced and big-footed dwarfs, and horrible fanged and clawed dragon Fafner, together with the gnarled trees and delicate coloring, belong to the world of fairy tales and Shakespearean fancy, not to the world of Wagnerian gloom and doom.

Among the thirteen color plates in *Aesop's Fables* (1912) are a few lovely ones, such as "Venus and the Cat", but uncharacteristic levity and an insufficiency of birds and animals spoil the set. Almost all the fifty-one black-and-white drawings are inadequate sketches that suffer from the same drawbacks. In Charles Dickens's *Christmas Carol* (1915), however, Rackham met his obligations. As a series, his thirteen color plates are not too much like any he had done before, especially those of the heartless, frightened, and repentant Scrooge, phantoms, thieves, the amiable Fezziwigs, well-washed children, and parties. Oddly, the Cratchits are not given their usual prominence. The range of subjects in *Some British Ballads* (1918) makes Rackham's sixteen color plates one of his most diversified series, but their prettiness suggests a kind of insensitivity to the grimmer subjects. *Comus* (1921) seems to be one book in which Rackham failed for lack of sensitivity. His twenty-two illustrations are as thoughtfully drawn and attractive as ever, but they are too romantic, fairy-tale-like, and grotesque to be right for the young John Milton's grave allegorical masque. A similar failing of the imagination, possibly on the part of the publisher, turned *The Tempest* (1926) into a fairy tale in which Prospero never appears and in which Shakespeare's richer poetry is not heard. Still more obviously, Rackham failed to come to terms with Irving's *Legend of Sleepy Hollow* (1928). He seized on several inconsequential moments to illustrate, depicted Ichabod Crane as an oaf, ignored the wonderful Van Tassel party, and missed the main incident of the story – Ichabod's encounter with the Headless Horseman.

The dozen colored illustrations for *The Vicar of Wakefield* (1929) are happily fresh and free of mannerisms. (The full-page pen drawings in the early part of the book look like rejected preliminary sketches.) The older sisters cutting up the trains of their gowns to make Sunday waistcoats for their little brothers, Mr. Burchell uttering "Fudge!" as Lady Blarney and Miss Skeggs discourse on high society, and little Bill singing "Elegy on the Death of a Mad Dog"

while Sophy accompanies him on a guitar are among the most charming illustrations that Oliver Goldsmith's imperfect classic has brought forth. The twelve color plates that Rackham drew for *The Compleat Angler* (1931) – such as an angler kneeling secretly behind a pollarded willow, a coffeehouse on King's Street, Westminster, and seventeenth-century fishermen playing shuffleboard (shove ha'penny) in an alehouse – also strike fresh notes in the illustration of Izaak Walton's evergreen favorite.

Among the remaining books in the Catalog, Christina Rossetti's *Goblin Market* (1933) and Henrik Ibsen's *Peer Gynt* (1936) suited Rackham well, far better than did Edgar Allan Poe's *Tales of Mystery* (1935). But *The Wind in the Willows* (1940) was Rackham's farewell triumph, although it was published posthumously. Kenneth Grahame had invited him to be its first illustrator, and for years, he regretted having declined. Now, during his final illness, he had a second chance. His task was considerable. He not only had to do justice to a much-loved work of literature, but also had to do so after Ernest Shepard had captivated young and old with his illustrations. But Shepard's are small pen-and-ink drawings with little background. Rackham's full-page watercolors give Mole, Rat, Badger, and Mr. Toad true-to-life treatment and present their Thames-side world with endearing intimacy. The stricken hand had lost some of its authority, but it was still able to command Rackham's magic, his wonderful ability to make believe without condescension.

Popularity is no reason to deny Arthur Rackham his special place as one of England's major illustrators.

William Heath Robinson

Before the First World War dried up the deluxe color-plate gift-book market, W. Heath Robinson (1872–1944) followed his brothers Charles and Thomas Heath Robinson as a book illustrator. Four of his adult books deserve mention.

The Works of Mr. Francis Rabelais (1904), with ninety-nine full-page line drawings, was Robinson's first major effort as a serious illustrator. This long masterpiece of French humor, both tedious and brutal in translation, remains a foreign work. But Robinson was so nice a man that his gallery of endless odd characters seems to be illustrating a Victorian edition for boys and girls. A surprising Robinson emerges in the forty color plates for *Twelfth Night* (1908). Although the pasted-in reproductions are so dark that the figures are indistinct, the few that are light – especially Sir Andrew Aguecheek talking to Maria, Viola beside a sunny wall, and Sebastian and Antonio on a street with flagstones and steps – prove that this series is not an impertinence. Yet the illustrations for *Twelfth Night* are a failure because

234

137. William Heath Robinson. Rudyard Kipling, *A Song of the English* (1909).

138. Sidney H. Sime. Edward J. M. D. Plunkett, Lord Dunsany, *The Sword of Welleran* (1908).

too many of them are merely pretty pictures, and some betray poor judgment – featuring the clown in six of seven illustrations in Act V, for instance. Some of the colored drawings for Rudyard Kipling's *Song of the English* (1909), twelve plates in the small edition and thirty in the large, are more successful. The one of Sir Francis Drake's *Golden Hind* alongside a captured ship (fig. 137) must have pleased Kipling enormously. Robinson's promise as a serious illustrator ended with *A Midsummer Night's Dream* (1914). Most of the twelve color plates are as dark as those in *Twelfth Night*. And they do not have the individuality, aptness, or charm of those in Arthur Rackham's series of 1908. The thirty-two full-page line drawings seem more appropriate for a fairy tale than for Shakespeare.

W. Heath Robinson might have become an important illustrator of adult literature, but circumstances led him to concentrate on illustrating children's books, including his own, and on drawing zany inventions that have amused millions.

Noel Rooke

In the history of English book illustration, Noel Rooke (1881–1953) is important as one of those who carried the doctrine of the artist-engraver-illustrator from Charles Ricketts to the young artists – Clare Leighton, Agnes Miller Parker, Robert Gibbings, and numerous others – who were his students at the Central School of Art and Design. His own career as an illustrator was limited and undistinguished. In 1909, he did twelve full-page watercolor plates and eleven pencil drawings for Robert Louis Stevenson's *Travels with a Donkey in the Cevennes*. The watercolor scenes are muted, and the pencil drawings are stiff. His woodcut for *The Old Vicarage, Grantchester* (1916) illustrates a pamphlet edition of Rupert Brooke's poem. It is in the strong, simple linocut-like style that was popular until fine white-line technique emerged in the 1930s. For Gibbings at the Golden Cockerel Press in 1925, he engraved four full-page blocks and several smaller ones for *The Birth of Christ* according to Luke. The designs are strong, clean, and dull. In 1946 appeared Iolo A. Williams's *Flowers of Marsh and Stream*, with sixteen attractive watercolor prints by Rooke. Noel Rooke was primarily a printmaker, not an interpretive illustrator.

Sidney H. Sime

One of the ablest pen-and-ink draftsmen of the early years of the twentieth century, Sidney H. Sime (1867–1941) was handicapped by limiting his book illustrating to the five works of Lord Dunsany (Edward J. M. D. Plunkett) listed in the Catalog. Sime was a master of the fantastic, some-

Plate V. Arthur Rackham. William Shakespeare, *A Midsummer Night's Dream* (1908).

139. Sybil Tawse. Elizabeth Gaskell, *Cranford* (1914).

times lightened by wit. But some of his drawings are vitiated by uninspired effects, and even more by excessive, confusing detail. This latter defect doubtless is a result, in part, of the harsh reduction as halftones of what may have been quite clear watercolors. Dunsany's odd tales have narrow appeal and sometimes are poorly constructed. Sime created for them fanciful scenes that resemble elaborate stage sets, often of great ingenuity and technical virtuosity. "The Highwaymen" in *The Sword of Welleran* (1908) is one of Dunsany's least fantastic tales, and Sime's illustration is one of his most simple and most cogent (fig. 138). The cadaver of a hanged highwayman, Tom o' the Roads, swinging in the high wind, is about to be cut down by three solicitous but fearful cutthroat friends, who then substitute Tom's corpse for that of a newly deceased archbishop in a sacred sepulcher and thus ensure his troubled soul passage to paradise. Sime matched perfectly the tone of Dunsany's tongue-in-cheek horror tale.

Sybil Tawse

Among color-plate illustrators, Sybil Tawse earned a place of respect around the time of the First World War. Her most substantial and individual effort was twenty-four watercolors for Charles Lamb's *Essays of Elia* (1910). Tawse paid homage to her masters Hugh Thomson, Charles

Brock, and Henry Brock by imitating not only the style, but also the spirit of their color work. The plates are numerous enough to give some importance to their presence, even though the color process of 1910 still yielded dull effects. Tawse did her research carefully. The costumes, furniture, furnishings, architecture, and accessories of all sorts are true to their period, and the characters are drawn carefully as types and as individuals. But what lifts her work is that her characters and costumes and settings are harmoniously related to and subordinated to the significance of the moments chosen. An example is the illustration to accompany the last line of "Mrs. Battle's Opinions on Whist" – "Bridget and I should be ever playing". Bridget, of course, is Lamb's sister Mary. They sometimes play cards when he has a toothache or a sprained ankle, but they play for love, not, as Mrs. Battle does, for the glory of winning. The picture breathes the spirit of domestic tranquillity and affection that Lamb was celebrating.

Some of the eight illustrations for Elizabeth Gaskell's *Cranford* (1914) (fig. 139) seem too close to those by earlier artists, but they are spirited watercolors and excellent interpretations – the spinster sisters and their maid, armed with hearthside implements, making their nightly rounds of the kitchens and cellars by candlelight, for instance. In the twelve watercolors for *Tales from the Poets* (1915), a prose retelling of nine narrative poems by Geoffrey

Chaucer, Edmund Spenser, Sir Walter Scott, Henry Wadsworth Longfellow, Tennyson, and William Morris, Tawse succeeded in painting romantic scenes from the past without making the characters seem stiff from posing or the setting seem more important than the event. For "Geraint and Enid" by Tennyson, the drawing of Enid, the earl's daughter, with her mother in what seems to be a good guess as to what a bedroom in a Norman castle might have been like, is superior in every way to those designs usually found in an inexpensive wartime popular book. The moment chosen is not a revealing one, however.

The Count of Monte Cristo (1920) shows how sound and unstereotyped an illustrator Tawse was. For Alexandre Dumas's melodrama, she prepared eight sparkling watercolors (color reproduction had improved by this time) of the extensive cast of French characters with the same unobtrusive authenticity that she had brought to her other books. The forty-four pen drawings (the unexceptional frontispiece is in color) that she made for L. Allen Harker's *Miss Esperance and Mr. Wycherly* (1926) are interesting only as evidence of Sybil Tawse's greater skill as a watercolorist than as a line artist.

CHAPTER TEN

The Twentieth Century (II)
1919–1945

The second period of book illustration in the twentieth century can be said to extend from the end of the First World War to the end of the Second World War. In spite of these grim brackets, it was a time of creative energy in English illustration. It will be remembered above all as the great period of autographic wood engraving, although many artists were using pen and ink, with extremely effective results, and a few illustrators were creating a small number of distinguished etched, copper-engraved, and lithographic designs. Color was occasionally added to illustrations, with agreeable, but not remarkable, results.

Much of the credit for the excellence of illustration during these twenty-five years must go to the various persons at the Golden Cockerel Press – especially Robert Gibbings – and the Gregynog Press – especially Gwendoline Davies and Margaret Davies – for their dedication to raising book production from its low state. The number of their books in the Catalog testifies to their success. But their books suffered because of this idealism. They were designed as enduring artistic entities: typography, paper, bindings, and illustrations. Like the books of the Kelmscott Press, they tend to be large and expensive limited editions, too esoteric to be the possessions of anyone except collectors and libraries. Fortunately, trade publishers soon began to design for the general public more modest editions with excellent typography and wider scope for illustrators. Between the two was the Limited Editions Club of New York, which from 1929 to the present has commissioned numerous English artists to collaborate with leading designers and printers to produce illustrated classics for its members. Taken as a whole, the trade publishers brought out a commendable balance between classics and books by contemporary authors.

As previously noted, after the process block had come into use, pen and ink became the most common medium for illustrating, and it has remained so. It is the least troublesome and most economical of all methods. After the First World War, it enjoyed a return to favor as the medium of artists who, although adopting superficially different styles, were kin in spirit to the early- and mid-nineteenth-century illustrators. They were not, however, imitators. At the time, some seemed newfangled, but none now seems an innovative interpreter. They aimed in a forthright manner to present characters at a decisive or perhaps characteristic moment in a scene described or indicated in the text or, regrettably, limited themselves to depicting either characters or scenes only. Nevertheless, they were highly professional in their knowledge of the arts of the book and in their respect for readers' tastes.

The practitioners of etching, metal engraving, and lithography were not numerous and have to be discussed one by one. The revival of copper engraving by Stephen Gooden, however, might be cited as a reminder that in the arts, the individual is a force unto himself.

Autographic wood engraving is the special claim to fame of this period. The score or so of illustrators who both designed and engraved on wood the substantial body of illustrations that were done during these years deserve to be called the English School. They usually engraved in a manner roughly analogous to what we have called the modified-Bewick style of the early nineteenth century. Thomas Bewick had never been entirely forgotten, and the wood engravings of Sturge Moore, Lucien Pissarro, and Gordon Craig were transitional between the reproductive work of the mid-nineteenth century and the brilliant original blocks of the twentieth. Much of the stimulus came from Noel Rooke, Clifford Webb, Leon Underwood, and other teachers of wood engraving. At first – and always, in fact – the art-school teachers and students were interested in creating independent prints, and illustrations in books published in the 1920s often are heavy, solid black-and-white compositions, sometimes cut in linoleum blocks. These rarely are satisfactory as interpretive designs involving human beings. The clean linear engraving of Eric Gill, related to early Italian woodcuts and to the work of Charles Ricketts, not that of Bewick, acted as one corrective to the heavy print style.

One tradition in illustration was to draw a line around

the space to be occupied by an illustration and to draw lines up to this border or frame or to an imaginary one. The tradition has not always been followed. Bewick, Birket Foster, J. M. W. Turner, Arthur Hughes, Hugh Thomson, and others habitually used vignettes, designs without borders. Many of the artists of the 1920s and 1930s also broke out of the prison of the frame and adopted vignettes, which allow a more companionable relation of image and text. Another tradition was to apply shading in a more or less naturalistic fashion to figures and backgrounds. The wood engravers adopted a new approach to shading, or, more properly, to the treatment of that surface of the block not cut into outlines of forms. Whether or not they used this surface for shading to suggest light and shadow, shape, or material, its primary function was to give variety of pattern and texture to the block, as though the whole design were abstract. With this concept guiding them, engravers felt free to cut out areas of white in sharp arbitrary shapes. This was an exciting innovation. It eliminated areas of meaningless gray that tend to make all but the best nineteenth-century wood engravings lack contrast, and it threw light-gray and black forms into sharp relief. Engravers also used tools of different sizes and shapes to produce a variety of textures by means of parallel lines and white-line crosshatching. While their art remained representational, artist-engravers of the 1920s and 1930s – especially David Jones, Agnes Miller Parker, Gertrude Hermes, Blair Hughes-Stanton, John Farleigh, and John Buckland-Wright – created designs of great technical skill, imagination, and, sometimes, beauty. Gwenda Morgan, Reynolds Stone, and others adhered to the modified-Bewick style with charming results.

During this period, books of essays about natural history and country life were popular, and a good deal of the use of wood engravings as book illustrations was for them. Therefore, our usual idea of an interpretive design has to be stretched somewhat to accommodate these many engravings of animals, birds, flowers, and country scenes. They are, however, not merely decorations or explanatory representations. Nor are they merely incidental excuses for the artists to display their technical wizardry. They are the main subjects of the authors' discourses, and they convey the admiration, affection, or other feelings expressed in the texts. Thus they are in this special sense realizations of the text.

One of the bravest ventures in illustrated-book publishing in the twentieth century was Frederick Muller's series of anthologies of verse, New Excursions into English Poetry, each volume generously illustrated with original full-page color lithographs and wrap-around designs on linen covers. The first five were issued in 1944 and 1945:

English, Scottish and Welsh Landscape, 1700–c. 1860, illustrated by John Piper; *The Poet's Eye*, John Craxton; *Sea Poems*, Mona Moore; *Poems of Death*, Michael Ayrton; and *Soldiers' Verse*, William Scott. Then followed *Travellers' Verse* (1946), Edward Bawden; and *Poems of Sleep and Dream* (1947), Robert Colquhon. The poetry in these volumes is traditional, but these artists shared a vision of the world as a bizarre, almost Surrealistic place of harsh angles and points, jagged rocks, and twisted trees. This is a neo-Romantic outlook, and although Graham Sutherland, Piper, John Minton, and their followers eventually developed a common bag of tricks, technique in these illustrations is secondary to vision, a response to the overwhelming tension and terror, grandeur and theatricality of war on a scale never before experienced in human history. The books in this series illustrated by Piper, Ayrton, and Bawden are discussed with the rest of their work. The other four artists seem not to have been active as book illustrators. Among the five illustrators whose books are listed in the Catalog without discussion in the Critical Account, only René Ben Sussan (b. 1895) requires a word of explanation. Although he illustrated a substantial number of English books, he was born in Turkey and lived and worked in Paris, and most of the books listed were published in New York.

In spite of the large number of first-rate artists who were active and the abundance of handsomely illustrated books that were published during these twenty-five years, one significant change is disquieting. Apart from the special exception of natural-history and country-life designs, illustrations in general had become more decorative than interpretive. Various explanations may be offered. In the same way that nineteenth-century artists who had been accustomed to painting landscapes and anecdotal scenes from literature and history had repeated them as "pictures" in books, mid-twentieth-century artists who were printmakers, as many were, not accustomed to drawing human figures or accustomed to drawing them only as decorative objects, repeated their prints in books. They or their publishers chose titles that provided familiar subject matter. Some artists offered another reason: interpretive illustration is bad; the image should contribute only what the text cannot give. In practice, many illustrations of the period seem to be limited to what the artists could do easily. They do not display either depth of understanding or sensitivity to the mood and meaning of the text. At their best, these illustrations are attractive decorations; often, they are irrelevances, sometimes impertinences.

Edward Jeffrey Irving Ardizzone

"The illustrator of more than 100 books" is the extraordi-

140. Edward Ardizzone. Miguel de Cervantes, *Exploits of Don Quixote* (1959).

nary record of Edward Ardizzone (1900–82). Haiphong-born but English grown – the growing entertainingly reported with an illustration on every page in *The Young Ardizzone* (1970) – Ardizzone was a successful children's book author as well as illustrator. He was an interpretive line artist in the tradition of Phiz, John Leech, Charles Keene, and similar Victorian masters. His designs are lively and impressionistic, an antidote to both stiff academic drawing and pretentious innovation. His stenographic sketches catch the authentic posture, gesture, and expression of fictional characters in a few quick lines. Too often, however, they seem to embody a perverse refusal to draw a clean or graceful line or to make shading contribute anything to form, only to random tonal effects. Too often, the crosshatching seems careless and excessive, a direct contradiction of the economy that is Ardizzone's most admirable quality. It is, therefore, not so paradoxical that in his most satisfactory series of illustrations, he used other media besides pen and ink.

Dickens and Ardizzone should complement each other perfectly because of their similar outlook: informal, observant, indulgent, mocking – according to how their characters behave themselves. The fifty-nine pen-and-ink vignettes notched into the chapter headings of *Great Expectations* (1939), scratchy as they are, make a pleasant diversion in 457 pages, and the eight lithographs, lurid in red and gold and blue, are bound to appeal to any undemanding reader or owner. The twelve pen-and-ink illustrations in *Bleak House* (1955) seem so Victorian that the publisher might as well have reprinted a set of wood engravings from the nineteenth century. But the twelve full-page tinted lithographs for *Poems* (1946) of François Villon make up one of the most effective of Ardizzone's series. Illustrations such as those of Villon writing by candlelight on a wintry Paris night ("The Legacy"), the prisoner Villon before the bishop of Orléans ("The Testament"), and a riotous tavern scene ("Ballad of Good Doctrine") have a quality of understanding derived from close reading of the poems and commentary rather than from memories of Algernon Swinburne, Robert Louis Stevenson, and *The Vagabond King*. But color did not enable Ardizzone to meet the challenge of William Makepeace Thackeray's *Newcomes* (1954) and *Henry Esmond* (1956). Nineteen pen-and-ink drawings enlivened by stenciled pastel tints supplement the forty black-and-white drawings in the two-volume *Newcomes*, and all thirty-two illustrations in *Henry Esmond* are stenciled. *Henry Esmond* thus attains an agreeable unity, but that is no great accomplishment, and several illustrations represent Ardizzone at his best.

In "A Note on the Illustrations" accompanying his twenty-nine designs for *The Comedies* (1958) in the Heritage Shakespeare, for which John Farleigh and Agnes Miller Parker illustrated *The Histories* and *The Tragedies*, respectively, Ardizzone wrote:

The illustrator's job is to create a visual background which the reader can people with the author's characters. . . . Any too detailed rendering of a specific character should be avoided, lest it go between the reader and the author, creating a sort of third-party intrusion. . . . In general I have endeavored to create a visual analogy of the chosen scene.

Such statements have been the excuse for a great deal of minimal illustration; but happily, the volume frontispiece and two illustrations for each of the fourteen comedies – pen-and-ink drawings with light color washes added – form one of Ardizzone's most conscientious and successful series.

Ardizzone's illustrations for *Exploits of Don Quixote* (1959) make it one of the most satisfying of the great number of English illustrated editions of this classic. Sketchy pen-and-ink vignettes, humorous but not comic, offer a running summary of the action. In reduction, they sometimes suffer from Ardizzone's "dirty" line. But the dozen superb full-page watercolors make this edition one that every lover of *Don Quixote* and of illustrated books would like to possess. In subdued plum and blue-gray and ocher, with forms indicated by brush lines and highlighted boldly in white, they do beautifully what Ardizzone failed to do with an intractable pen. From the first plate, Don Quixote cleaning his armor in a barn with chickens pecking about and his niece peering in at the door (fig. 140), to the last, Sancho Panza in a golden vest sitting under a canopy and holding court, one thinks how much the art of Ardizzone – with his ability to establish forms and character so thriftily and to blend humor, beauty, and event – resembles that of Thomas Rowlandson and Honoré Daumier when they put their hands to brush and color. The watercolor supplies a visual equivalent of the compassion overlaying Cervantes's humor like a transparent glaze.

In *The Oxford Illustrated Old Testament* (1968, 1969), Ardizzone's assignments were 1 Samuel, Jonah, and Ecclesiasticus 26–51 (in the Apocrypha). His effort to show the characters as ordinary human beings seems old-fashioned but welcome among the mixed styles of his juniors. But drawings such as the one of Jonah swimming into the mouth of the whale while his shipmates sail off (the Bible says they rowed) seem more appropriate for one of Ardizzone's books of Bible stories for children. And a small boy howling while his father holds him aloft by his shirt and whips his backside is far too jocose an interpretation of the brutal advice in Ecclesiasticus that advocates child beating.

The sixteen full-page line drawings with patches of pink

141. John Austen. Benjamin Disraeli, *Ixion in Heaven* (1925).

and gray-green in an edition of Dickens's *Short Stories* (1971) are as satisfactory as almost any series by Ardizzone, partly because of their size. Scenes such as those depicting members of a Pall Mall club sitting around a table and drinking, a railway snack bar, a Piccadilly pavement artist, and an evening of recreation in a middle-class boarding-house are in the right key, but they still seem too offhand. One finally comes to the melancholy conclusion that Edward Ardizzone could have done many more wonderful single illustrations and books of them, in black and white as well as in color, if only he had been less productive and more demanding of himself at all times.

John Austen

Having illustrated twenty-nine books in twenty-five years, John Austen (1886–1948) commands respect for his industry and professionalism. Beginning as an imitator of Beardsley, Austen improved his technique, but his engagement with literature was often superficial. He failed to convince that he was attuned to the serious aspects of such classics as *Hamlet* (1922) and *David Copperfield* (1935); in *Don Juan* (1926) and *Tristram Shandy* (1928), his drawings seem facetious rather than witty. His usual pen-and-ink figures with watercolor tints are impeccable, but they often have an arch banality akin to that of advertisements. Austen

never entirely shook himself loose from a preoccupation with manner or from mechanical exaggeration, as in the distance between large oval eyes. There is little individuality in or revealing interaction among his characters. Too many are depicted as carefully costumed figures, changing little with the widely different roles they play. To some extent, the responsibility for this stereotyping may lie with the American book-club publishers that engaged him to illustrate ten books between 1931 and 1943.

These generalizations have to be qualified by some specific comments. Austen's style was to some extent set by the suitability of the colored drawings in his own "miscellany" of eighteenth-century verse, *Rogues in Porcelain* (1924). A happy conjunction brought together Austen and Benjamin Disraeli. Austen's ladies and gentlemen in extreme Georgian dress point up the witty satire of Byron, George IV, Queen Caroline, and other London figures in the youthful Disraeli's *Ixion in Heaven* (1925) (fig. 141) and in his burlesque re-telling of the Persephone myth, *The Infernal Marriage* (1929). Elegant, affected, and satirical, the fifteen full-page designs, five in color, in Norman Douglas's then-celebrated *South Wind* (1929) make up one of Austen's most congenial series. His six delicate watercolors strike the right note of pastoral unreality in *As You Like It* (1930), but the actors stand around vacantly waiting for a director to tell them what to do. The shift to wood engravings (twenty-

142. Edward Bawden. William Beckford, *Vathek* (1958).

eight) in Aristophanes's *Frogs* (1937) produced attractive patterns on the pages. Published in the same year, the twenty color lithographs in Alain René Le Sage's *Gil Blas* are more masculine than most of Austen's illustrations tend to be, and the pen-and-ink headings in the two volumes are more expressive than usual.

Austen applied the bold wood-engraving technique of *The Frogs* to *The Comedy of Errors* (1939), with excellent results. The six tall blocks have strong black outlines and limited shading, supplemented by three or four engraved tint blocks that were printed in watercolors. They are playfully archaic, but never clumsily comic, and yet they offer serious realizations of the action. The twenty colored pen-and-ink drawings in a two-volume edition of Arnold Bennett's *Old Wives' Tale* (1941) reveal a somewhat increased sense of dramatic scene and concrete detail: gaslights, flowers under glass, and other Victoriana. But the twenty-seven black-and-white chapter-heading vignettes, mostly of town scenes viewed from above and at a distance, are closer to the gritty realism of the Staffordshire classic than are the color plates. For a modest edition of Jane Austen's *Persuasion* (1946), Austen made his last series of illustrations, eight color lithographs and sixteen chapter headpieces in pen and ink. With none of the earlier distracting overemphasis, Austen's interpretations of the eighteenth century seem highly appropriate, as in "Captain

Wentworth Taking Station" at the fireplace behind Anne in the midst of a drawing room full of bonneted women and waistcoated men. It is Jane Austen's milieu of decorum, criticism of women, and hunting of men.

Edward Bawden

Besides teaching art, Edward Bawden (b. 1903) specialized in decorative industrial design; literary illustration was intermittent. He was fortunate to be able to use color much of the time, and he got original effects with linocuts. *Peter Wilkins, a Cornish Man* (1928), the old favorite *voyage imaginaire* by Robert Paltock, contains seventeen tinted line cuts and twenty-three black-and-white drawings, all of which are wittily stylized. Bawden put himself to the test when he did one full-page and ten half-page watercolors (two to a page) for Shakespeare's *Henry the Fourth. Part 2* (1939). These realistic, sketchy illustrations do well enough for the comic passages, but Bawden's meanly drawn figures and faces could never be the embodiment of Shakespeare's Henry IV, nobles, and Prince Hal in time of crisis. The sixteen full-page color lithographs for M. G. L. Thomas's anthology *Travellers' Verse* (1946) depict imaginary scenes from the places mentioned; the one for Yeats's "Byzantium" is especially felicitous. The ten dream-sequence line drawings in Denis Saurat's *Death and the Dreamer* (1946)

143. Edmund Blampied. Robert Louis Stevenson, *Travels with a Donkey in the Cevennes* (1931).

are not appealing, mainly because of the mannequin-like dreamer; but when matched with the text, the Surrealistic designs command respect as an imaginative effort.

Bawden's chief popular success is his illustrations for Jonathan Swift's *Travels of Lemuel Gulliver to Lilliput & Brobdingnag* (1948). In a volume designed to be read, not hoarded, his twelve "bled" color lithographs make a cheerful splash. Throughout the Lilliput section, the difference in size is kept palpable because of the overprinting of little red figures hardly as big as Gulliver's thumb. His most innovative designs are in the Brobdingnag section, where the women, with their irisless eyes and pursed mouths, have the droll dignity of ships' figureheads. Bawden's 102 pen-drawn vignettes, mostly of groups of small figures, are helpful representations of the distant events related in *The Histories of Herodotus of Halicarnassus* (1958). The eight color lithographs in William Beckford's *Vathek* (1958) are appropriate for that outrageous oriental romance. The garish coloring and exaggeration of scenes, such as that of a genie in the shape of a shepherd appearing to Vathek and Nouronihar as they clutch each other in their magnificent litter (fig. 142), provide just the right touch. Gustave Flaubert's archeological revel among the picturesque and bestial antiquities of Carthage under Hamilcar in *Salammbô* (1960) is so lurid that Bawden's eight two-page six-color plates and thirty-nine black-and-white drawings in this transla-

tion might be a guide to a Hollywood production. Forty years after having illustrated *Peter Wilkins*, Bawden was one of the most effective contributors to *The Oxford Illustrated Old Testament* (1968, 1969). His sixty-six line drawings, he said, owe something to sketches of nomadic tribesmen that he made during his war service in the Near East. In more recent years, Bawden drew six color lithographs for Sir Thomas More's *Utopia* (1972) and seven for Samuel Johnson's *Rasselas* (1975).

Edmund Blampied

After having studied graphics in London, Edmund Blampied (1886–1966), a Channel Islands farm boy, returned to live in Jersey and draw his subjects, often anecdotal, from the country life of Jersey and France. He is best known for his prints – etchings, drypoints, lithographs – but he illustrated books, one with distinction. Jeffrey Farnol's *Money Moon* (1914) contains twenty-three pleasant color plates, the rural scenes much better than those showing city folk. Blampied's eight etched illustrations for *The Road Mender* (1924), three hypersensitive essays by Margaret Fairless Barber (Michael Fairless), are responsive to mood as well as deed.

Blampied's eight full-page etchings, some with the use of drypoint, for Robert Louis Stevenson's *Travels with a*

245

144. Douglas Percy Bliss. *The Devil in Scotland* (1934).

Donkey in the Cevennes (1931) contribute to one of the happiest fusions of image and text in an English illustrated book. They are admirable drawings – comparable with those of Forain, masterly in observation, and rich in subtle interplay of black, gray, and white. Blampied, the countryman and wanderer in France, chose eight subjects from this ever-fresh account of Stevenson's twelve-day ramble with Modestine, a she-ass carrier and companion: a portrait of the gentle and infuriating Modestine standing amiably after her overloaded pack has fallen to the ground; peasants eating in an *auberge* kitchen; Stevenson and Modestine in an upland gale; a Trappist monk offering a liqueur to the delicately drawn Stevenson, his face revealed for the only time in the series; man and beast on a mountain descent; Clarisse, a country-inn waitress; rustics in a café poring over a local map in order to advise the traveler; and man and beast on their last walk together in the late-afternoon sun and shadows beside a wood. These are true illustrations; they intensify the reading experience.

Blampied coalesced passages of Stevenson's plain prose into a single moment. The paragraph about the typical *auberge*, for instance, offered several options. Blampied put together "in the kitchen cooking and eating go forward side by side" and "the visit of a fat sow, grouting under the table . . . is no impossible accompaniment to dinner". At a rough table, a porcine fellow wearing a hat drains a white mug of wine while a rustic companion peers under the table at the sow, which is also closely watched by a cat (fig. 143). One of the persons whom Stevenson takes time to analyze as an individual is Clarisse, who in Pont de Montvert "waited the table with a heavy placable nonchalance, like a performing cow . . . her great grey eyes steeped in amorous languor". Blampied caught her perfectly, turning to look "without embarrassment or wonder" while one hand balances a tray and the other grasps a wine bottle that is on the table.

The watercolors over pen drawings in James M. Barrie's *Peter Pan and Wendy* (1939) must be mentioned because, although kept at the level of juvenile readers, they reveal Edmund Blampied as technically the equal of the colorplate masters Arthur Rackham, William Russell Flint, and Edmund Dulac. But he came too late to share their success.

Douglas Percy Bliss

The author of the valuable *History of Wood-Engraving* (1928) and for many years the director of the Glasgow School of Art, Douglas Percy Bliss (b. 1900) was an early participant in the revival of autographic wood engraving. He designed twenty-five "woodcuts" for *Border Ballads* (1925), which he also edited. Mainly headpieces, they run too much to black, and the engraving was unskilled; but

145. John Buckland-Wright. John Keats, *Endymion* (1947).

they are spirited interpretations. The nine full-page and assorted smaller illustrations for Samuel Johnson's *Rasselas* (1926) may bolster up the flagging spirits of modern readers who find *Rasselas* fatiguing. The pen drawings, even when colored, in Cervantes's *Spanish Ladies and Two Other Stories* (1928) and William Painter's *Palace of Pleasure* (1929) are ordinary, but the thirty-nine wood engravings in Bliss's collection of stories *The Devil in Scotland* (1934) return to the vitality of his designs for *Border Ballads*. They are still too black, but they evoke both the "strange world of the popular imagination" and the harsh windy world of rural Scotland. The humor is part of the grotesquery in the tales by Robert Burns (fig. 144), Sir Walter Scott, and Robert Louis Stevenson. The nine full-page pen drawings for *Farmer's Boy* (1935), a book of memories by John R. Allan, are unpretentious and evocative – the one of a boy standing on a hayrack and preaching to a congregation of fowls, for example. The wood engravings in *Some Tales of Mystery and Imagination* (1938) by Edgar Allan Poe lack the virtues of those in *Border Ballads* and *The Devil in Scotland*.

Douglas Percy Bliss did not make illustration his vocation, but his best work demonstrates the extent to which literary understanding can reinforce modest technical ability.

John Buckland-Wright

Born in New Zealand and educated at Rugby and Oxford, John Buckland-Wright (1897–1954) taught himself wood engraving after having read Gordon Craig's *Woodcuts and Some Words* (1924) and began illustrating books in 1930. Although he devoted too much of his time to engraving nudes for esoteric publications, Buckland-Wright was one of the most accomplished and productive interpretive illustrators of the twentieth century. His ten wood engravings for *The Collected Sonnets of John Keats* (1930) are heavy handed in conception and are in the style then popular. The ten full-page illustrations and six supplementary prints for E. Powys Mathers's anthropological play *Love Night: A Laotian Gallantry* (1936) have jungle settings of trees with writhing roots and vines, flowers, and lush plants. Most show handsome young Laotians in graceful stages of courtship. For Edward FitzGerald's translation of *The Rubáiyát of Omar Khayyám* (1938), Buckland-Wright turned to copper engraving; the eight pseudo-Persian plates lack individuality. The nine copper engravings in Apuleius's *Marriage of Cupid and Psyches* (1938), however, show a plausible approximation of classical elegance.

Among the seven wood engravings for Algernon Swinburne's *Hymn to Proserpine* (1944), all both ornamental and illustrative, the frontispiece of Proserpine bending to

247

Concealed Genius of the Home Secretary in his interrogation of that Consummate Actor Richard Mallard

Concealed Genius of that Consummate Actor Richard Mallard under the interrogation of the Home Secretary

146. G. K. Chesterton. Hilaire Belloc, *But Soft – We Are Observed!* (1928).

solace the dolorous singer, who lies on the shingle amid the ribs of foundered ships, is one of the really fine modern illustrations. But Keats's *Endymion* (1947) is Buckland-Wright's masterwork. It is an extremely difficult poem to interpret. Buckland-Wright called on all his mature resources to re-create in fifty-four main wood engravings the sensuous, luminous dream world of the shepherd Endymion, beloved of the moon-goddess Cynthia. He treated with great richness of texture foliage, rocks, water, shells, and human forms and irradiated every design with white. And these illustrations, apart from their beauty, are welcome because they are positioned in the book in just the right places to make concrete what the apostrophic couplets are saying. The Romanticism of Keats's verse captivated Buckland-Wright, and he found ways to captivate us. Among the fifty-four designs, the twelve large full-page blocks seem a shade less masterly than the smaller ones, but particularly fine are those that show the morning penetrating the "monstrous sea" – a young woman swimming down to the ocean floor, where a young man lies – and that interpret the words "until of the empyrean I have drunk my fill" – Endymion gazing at an extraordinary moon. The half-page design of Endymion lying with his arm thrust into a pool while a seated young woman watches him has harmonies that make it one of the loveliest of modern illustrations (fig. 145). The thirty-four headpieces and tailpieces in

Percy Bysshe Shelley's *Poems* (1949) are handsome but mainly decorative.

Buckland-Wright never again matched the creative force of his illustrations for *Endymion*. His twelve wood engravings, mostly love-making scenes, for Swinburne's tearfully erotic *Laus Veneris* (1948) are not so inventive or handsome as those in *Love Night*. The sixteen copper engravings that he made for *The Odyssey* (1948), eleven for Musaeus's *Hero and Leander* (1949), and nine for *The Iliad* (1950) seem thin and anonymous after the rich wood engravings, although the one in *The Odyssey* of a woman and a boy on a street of a seaport is an exception. The copper engravings in Swinburne's *Pasiphaë* (1950 [1951]) cannot be regarded as satisfactory interpretations because with one exception, they are based on the myth, not on Swinburne's mixture of eloquence and tastelessness. Simply as engravings, all have more color and charm of line than do any other illustrations that Buckland-Wright put on copper.

The series of ten colored wood engravings in Francis Beaumont's *Salmacis and Hermaphroditus* (1951) form a sequence of nude and seminude adolescent figures beside and in pools and streams encircled by plants and flowers. The large blocks, unified by the application of blue, green, and gold, are among the most attractive of the few significant colored wood-engraved illustrations done since the days of Edmund Evans. The eight large aquatints, another medium little used in modern illustration, for Phyllis Hartnoll's *Grecian Enchanted* (1952) are among Buckland-Wright's best interpretive efforts. The story follows the course of an ill-starred love affair in ancient Sicily and offers a variety of scenes, such as a cockfight, a rowing ship approaching land, and a flower market. Buckland-Wright also used aquatint for his eighteen perfunctory illustrations for Boccaccio's *Decameron* (1954), but he reverted to copperplates for Adrian Bury's *Syon House* (1955).

John Buckland-Wright had the intelligence, imagination, and art to illustrate the masterpieces of English literature with dignity and beauty. It is a pity that publishers did not ask him to illustrate more of them.

Edward Carrick. See Edward Anthony Craig.

Gilbert Keith Chesterton

Widely known as editor, critic, essayist, and writer of fiction, G. K. Chesterton (1874–1936) could have become a professional artist after having studied at the Slade School of Art, but he elected to become a writer. Yet he illustrated a goodly number of books, almost all by his friend Hilaire Belloc, an equally prolific author. For Belloc's books, Chesterton made almost 250 drawings. Superficially, they are much alike: humorous, satirical character studies that depict primarily single torsos or two figures interacting. All were drawn with a soft pencil and, in the English editions, printed in brown.

But these many drawings are not alike. They were drawn with great speed, but they are not sketchy; the drawing of faces, on which the attention is concentrated, is firm and final. The subjects are fictional, yet they seem taken from life. They are characters, not caricatures. Indeed, the subtlety of the nuances by which individuals are particularized and their social and occupational foibles are satirized, with as much geniality as wit, is astonishing. Random sampling will turn up many beautiful drawings done with great economy of line – the double spread in *But Soft – We Are Observed!* (1928) (fig. 146) will do – that are such extraordinarily expressive embodiments of the characters that they put to shame the shop-window figures in hundreds of illustrations. Amazingly, the illustrations were drawn before the text was written. Belloc, it is said, would develop a plan for a story; he and Chesterton would seclude themselves for a hilarious afternoon; and Chesterton would do all the drawings for the book, without which Belloc swore he could not write it. Thus Chesterton's illustrations are to an unusual degree integral parts of Belloc's good-natured satires.

Harry Clarke

An artist of conspicuous technique and mannerisms but no genuine originality of style or imagination, Harry Clarke (1890–1931) elaborated Aubrey Beardsley's discreet adaptations of Japanese undulating outlines, solid blacks, and finely patterned areas to such an extent that his drawings are often so crowded that they lose all movement. And, too often, the eroticism and diablerie that with Beardsley are decadence, with Clarke become decay.

The book with which Clarke is mainly associated is Edgar Allan Poe's *Tales of Mystery and Imagination* (1919). Although the tales are stretched to the borders of credibility and beyond, they vary in tone, and Clarke varied his illustrations accordingly. For example, for "Descent into the Maelstrom", a tale of the marvelous, he made a convincing vertiginous drawing of the narrator clinging to a water cask while his ship whirls above him upside down. But Poe and Clarke are chiefly remembered for the horror stories. The only defense against John Russell Taylor's dismissal, in *The Art Nouveau Book in Britain* (1966), of Clarke's illustrations as "uniquely nasty" is that the stories are, too. But visual explicitness is nastier than verbal. The black cat clinging to the corpse of the murdered wife that has been walled up in a cellar alcove is a prize example of a scene that should not have been illustrated.

The Years at the Spring (1920), an anthology of Edwardian and Georgian poetry, contains twenty-four illustrations, half of which are in color. Two or three of the color designs are good imitations of those by Edmund Dulac, but the impression that Clarke's strength was in the decorative quality of his black-and-white designs becomes a certainty in *Faust* (1925). His imagination, however, lacked the magnitude to do justice to Goethe. Clarke illustrated Algernon Swinburne's *Selected Poems* (1928) with ten designs, most of which are halftones reproduced by photogravure and reduced. Much of Swinburne's verse is far from the "boyish delight in something rich and strange" referred to by Humbert Wolfe in the introduction, and Clarke had a good excuse to make some erotic and unpleasantly macabre images. Other designs, especially those for "St. Dorothy" and "Hymn to Proserpine", deserve Wolfe's praise. But once more, as with the illustrations for Poe's tales, Harry Clarke seems to have been a skillful technician fabricating illustrations that are more ingenious than tasteful or imaginative.

Edward Anthony Craig [Edward Carrick]

Gordon Craig taught his son Teddy, Edward Craig (b. 1904), to draw and engrave on wood. Assistant to his father

147. Edward Anthony Craig. André Maurois, *A Voyage to the Island of the Articoles* (1928).

in his enterprises until 1927 or 1928, Craig had charge of the printing of his blocks. Under the pseudonym Edward Carrick, he was a proficient designer and engraver and would have been a significant book illustrator had he not found his métier in designing for the stage and cinema. Nevertheless, his four wood-engraved illustrations for André Maurois's *Voyage to the Island of the Articoles* (1928), three for Edith Sitwell's poem *In Spring* (1931), and five for *The Georgics of Vergil* (1931) are truly imaginative, and they were engraved with authority. Craig's witty presentation of Maurois's Routchko spending his last hours dictating is an example of an illustration that actually adds to the pleasure of the reading (fig. 147).

Eric Fitch Daglish

One of the earliest modern true white-line wood-engraver followers of Thomas Bewick, Eric Daglish (1894–1966) was, as the "F.Z.A." on his title pages indicates, a naturalist first and an artist second. His own books are primarily instructional, but in the books selected for the Catalog are many beautiful engravings – mainly of birds but with a scattering of toads, mice, and small deer – usually printed separately and pasted in. Almost none have any background or narrative function, and the use of black is sometimes overdone. Yet, typically, even among the sober represen-

tations of fish in *The Compleat Angler* (1927), there is a sparkling print of a nightingale. Half the designs in Henry Thoreau's *Walden* (1927) are of birds, and the inclusion of an alligator because Thoreau mentions one in passing suggests how little the sixteen attractive engravings have to do with the universal themes that the nonconformist Yankee fished from his little Concord pond. The nearest Daglish came to interpretive illustration was in Gilbert White's *Natural History of Selborne* (1929). Unless a reader has a strong interest in such matters as the migration of the ring-ouzel, the key in which owls hoot, or the late blooming season of hellebore, White's prose tends to be dry. Daglish's sixteen engravings add a welcome sense of strangeness to the familiar. He got unusual effects from white lines made with the finest of engraving tools, and often dared to place gray against gray, as in his block of field mice. Solid blacks and whites strengthen his designs, as in the prints of the green hellebore, a snowbound hare, and two cows standing in water. By means of the precision and beauty of his observations, Daglish helped to convey the wonder that White had felt throughout a lifetime of studying his Selborne environment and its inhabitants, and thus Eric Daglish was, in a true sense, an interpretive illustrator (fig. 148).

148. Eric Daglish. Eric Daglish, *The Life Story of Birds* (1930).

Thomas Derrick

Although he drew designs for about a dozen books, Thomas Derrick (1885–1954) was mainly a humorous decorator rather than a serious illustrator. He also was a rare modern practitioner of the woodcut. The woodcuts of Union soldiers on the frontispiece and title page of Ambrose Bierce's *Battle Sketches* (1930) achieve strong rhythmic effects; the remaining semihumorous headpieces fall between decorations and illustrations. In *Everyman* (1930), a fifteenth-century morality play, Derrick found his ideal text and created one of the unique illustrated books of the twentieth century. He broke the text into irregular sections, so that it extends over 100 large pages enlivened by seventy-two woodcut illustrations and one signed print. Most are bold single figures drawn with rigorous economy in 1-mm outlines with no backgrounds. Derrick occasionally broke up the pattern with two figures on a page, Death in solid black with white interior lines, and some decorative detail allowed to Kindred, Christ, Mary and the Infant Jesus, and Angel. One of the most amusing and instantly intelligible cuts is that in which Everyman seeks solace from those nearest him: "Gramercy, my friends and kinsman kind. / Now shall I show you the grief of my mind" (fig. 149). In *Everyman*, the secret of Derrick's success lies not in means but in effect – the absolute rightness of his synthesis of the panto-mimic quality of the earliest woodcuts, the sardonic humor of fifteenth-century marketplace play productions, and the religious faith of the anonymous medieval playwright and his audiences. The next year, Derrick took on a not dissimilar subject, *The Prodigal Son and Other Parables* (1931), which he treated with much the same bold outline designs (and calligraphic text) and humor and sincerity. The book might have been as original and moving as *Everyman* had Derrick not clothed the Good Samaritan and other biblical characters in contemporary dress, including bowlers, plus fours, and similar comic anachronisms.

John Farleigh

In *Graven Image* (1940), John Farleigh (1900–65), one of the best twentieth-century wood engravers, traces his career in the graphic arts. He gives not only important technical information about processes and insight into the economics of his uncertain profession, but also invaluable case histories of his work on specific books together with his relations with publishers, printers, and authors. It is one of the most enlightening records of English book illustration, particularly the fascinating account of Farleigh's association with George Bernard Shaw while illustrating *The Adventures of the Black Girl in Her Search for God* (1932). From the outset, Shaw listed moments in the *Black Girl* to

149. Thomas Derrick. *Everyman* (1930).

be illustrated, described how he thought they should be treated, made sketches for some, and offered shrewd criticism of the almost final drawings, which Farleigh submitted to him before having them photographed on blocks for him to engrave. Shaw, of course, was used to thinking in terms of scenes and pantomime on the stage. The girl appears in all but one of the designs. She is solid black with a powdering of white stipple to mark contours and white outlines where necessary. She is naked, beautiful, and modest.

With great candor, Farleigh quotes Shaw's perceptive comments. About the first sketch, Ecclesiastes talking to the Black Girl – a design of much dignity in its final form – Shaw said, "Ecclesiastes looks dead, like a figure in a frieze, because he is not looking at the girl." Farleigh admits, "The figure of Ecclesiastes *had* been taken from a frieze!" and adds generously, "I was learning the business of illustration from the best master possible." For the illustration of the Black Girl and Voltaire cultivating his garden, Shaw advised putting clippers in Voltaire's hand: "It would give him a perfect air of being taken by surprise. . . . As it is, he looks as if they were old friends and had been talking there for years. Stage management again!" For improving the design of GBS hurdling a fence in his attempt to avoid marrying the Black Girl (he marries her), Shaw suggested, "I think he must have one leg over the gate: nothing else will give the necessary impression of headlong flight" (fig.

150). The *Black Girl* illustrations were reprinted in the standard edition of Shaw's *Short Stories, Scraps, and Shavings* (1934) with ten more of Farleigh's wood-engraved illustrations and a number of headpieces. About these designs, Shaw contented himself with pointing out, "In the picture of my knocking down the grandfather's clock the action is ambiguous and rather suggests my propping it up," and he sketched how it might be done. Then drawing on his years as a music critic, he explained how to represent players of the French horn ("one hand *in the bell*") and the trumpet ("the action . . . is not a puff but a dry spit: it draws in his cheeks instead of bulbing them out").

Among Farleigh's other series of illustrations, his eleven wood engravings for *The Story of David* (1934) stir up interest without coming to grips with the moving and shameful deeds associated with that extraordinary biblical figure. But his ten full-page engravings and four smaller blocks catch nicely the astringent humor of Samuel Butler's *Way of All Flesh* (1934). D. H. Lawrence's *Man Who Died* (1935), a fable of Christ after the Crucifixion, is a pretentious piece of writing, and Farleigh's illustrations are correspondingly flamboyant. To the great English tradition of nature watching, Farleigh contributed the twenty-four lovely wood engravings that illustrate Ethel Armitage's *Country Garden* (1936). His designs of hellebore, birch trees, magnolia, and apples make this unaffected book a joy.

252

150. John Farleigh. George Bernard Shaw, *The Adventures of the Black Girl in Her Search for God* (1932).

Farleigh writes in the conclusion to *Graven Image* that he could not lay himself bare by printing a diary of his work on Shaw's *Back to Methuselah* (1939). It is a sore loss not to have Shaw's suggestions and sketches, if any. It seems, however, that Shaw let Farleigh evolve his own interpretations and then offered reactions. There are twenty-four designs: one full-page frontispiece to each of the five parts and nineteen designs of varying sizes. Farleigh says that his strategy was to transmit the essence of the play by blending "realism, allegory, and abstraction" rather than by visualizing scenes as they might be performed on a stage. It did not work. His failure arose mainly from his own high seriousness; the result is a pervasive humorlessness that is out of key with the play. No matter how long-winded Shaw is, humor flickers through his dialogue like the northern lights.

In 1948, Farleigh made sixteen crayon drawings for a happy bringing together of *Prometheus Bound* by Aeschylus and *Prometheus Unbound* by Shelley; the edition, though, was not published until 1965. Despite the risk of combining natural and abstract forms in the six illustrations for the first and ten for the second, Farleigh succeeded in making palpable the relation between Prometheus and the intimidating forces of the universe. The congruity of his designs with the lofty language of Aeschylus and Shelley is a tribute to their excellence. However, the ten wood engravings for

The Histories (1958) in the Heritage Shakespeare, which Farleigh shared with Edward Ardizzone and Agnes Miller Parker, lack the refinement of his earlier work.

Claud Lovat Fraser

Inspired by William Nicholson, Gordon Craig, and the chapbook woodcuts of the past, Claud Lovat Fraser (1890–1921) embellished many pages with simple drawings of much boldness and charm. He often drew with a reed, which produced thick, ropy, casual effects that closely resemble those of Nicholson and Craig. With two or three flat colors added, his designs have a bright posterlike appearance. Like Charles Ricketts and Craig, Fraser was a successful stage and costume designer. The effects of a gassing suffered at Ypres during the First World War cut short Fraser's career with only four fully illustrated books to his credit, and they are not interpretive in the usual sense.

The "embellishments" for Walter de la Mare's *Peacock Pie*, first published posthumously with the poems in 1924, were drawn in 1912. The sixteen color plates include a delightful frontispiece of a black servant wearing a green turban and a red coat with ocher cuffs and carrying a peacock on a tray. John Gay's *Beggar's Opera* (1921) is the book by which Fraser will be remembered. The eight color plates – the Beggar, Mrs. Peachum, Polly Peachum, Captain

253

151. Claud Lovat Fraser. John Gay, *The Beggar's Opera* (1921).

Macheath (fig. 151), Lucy Lockit, Peachum, Lockit, and one tavern set – are working designs for the production of the opera, which opened in June 1920 and ran until long after Fraser's death. For these designs, Fraser discarded his reed for a pen. The figures are not the usual costumed mannequins; they are Gay's inimitable personalities, not brought to life so much as made more intensely real as creatures of the stage. The designs for Carlo Goldoni's *Liar* (1922) are also a set of Fraser's theater drawings. The pink-and-blue frontispiece is quite as attractive as the illustrations in *The Beggar's Opera*, and the four pen drawings, which depict characters, perhaps would be, too, if only they had been blessed by Fraser's bright coloring.

Not a genuine book illustrator, Claud Lovat Fraser nevertheless contributed a great deal more than decorations to the books that he illustrated.

Barnett Freedman

All but three of the ten works that Barnett Freedman (1901–58) illustrated were commissioned by the Limited Editions Club of New York, a circumstance that may have influenced his work. After years of illness, he studied art and acquitted himself well on Siegfried Sassoon's *Memoirs of an Infantry Officer* (1931), a classic of trench warfare in the First World War. Among the twenty full-page drawings in pen and ink

with patches of color and the nineteen smaller black-and-white drawings, there are some as grim as the one of a pile of British dead, as realistic as the one of an underground dugout with coats hanging in the candlelight, and as unaffected as the one of a British soldier getting a haircut in a French barbershop.

For the remainder of his career as a book illustrator, Freedman shifted to lithography. Perhaps because he complicated the process by also using chalk, he did not get from it the full value of its resources. Also, presumably with the approval of his publisher, Freedman simplified backgrounds and in many illustrations abandoned them. Many of his designs are of single figures. The result is a substantial falling off of interest. Several of the sixteen full-page color lithographs and fifteen black-and-white lithographs for George Borrow's *Lavengro* (1936) have no human beings in them; the figures in the rest lack the vividness and dignity of Borrow's characters. For the six volumes of Leo Tolstoy's *War and Peace* (1938), Freedman supplied mainly color lithographs of individual characters. Some of the six color lithographs in *Henry the Fourth. Part 1* (1939) are among his best drawings, but none manages to seem necessary. *Oliver Twist* (1939) was his chance to surpass the efforts of his predecessors and prove himself a major illustrator. Instead, he was content to do eight color lithographs of Charles Dickens's leading characters without setting or

152. Barnett Freedman. Charlotte Brontë, *Jane Eyre* (1942).

action and for each chapter heading, a small black-and-white lithograph of a subordinate character or a simple scene.

Emily Brontë's *Wuthering Heights* (1940) and Charlotte Brontë's *Jane Eyre* (1942) are uniform in design, and each has sixteen color lithographs. The first follows the static single-figure scheme; the second finally brings Freedman closer to interpretation of text, but without getting him there. For instance, Freedman showed Jane standing in the hall outside her room, an illustration that conveys no meaning. Yet a moment later in the novel, she rescues Rochester from being burned to death. Among the illustrations, only that of Rochester's mad wife holding up a candle to look at herself wearing Jane's wedding veil conveys the intensity of this melodrama (fig. 152). The lithographs in Walter de la Mare's anthology *Love* (1943) are decorations, and those in a two-volume edition of *Anna Karenina* (1951) are, like those in the companion volume *War and Peace*, mainly of individual figures. The seven brown-and-green lithographs in de la Mare's *Ghost Stories* (1956) are relevant, but that is all.

Robert Gibbings

During the nine years that Robert Gibbings (1889–1958) was owner-manager of the Golden Cockerel Press, he pub-lished thirty-nine volumes illustrated by Eric Gill, John Nash, David Jones, Eric Ravilious, Blair Hughes-Stanton, Agnes Miller Parker, and other artists – as well as nineteen volumes that he had illustrated. He had, moreover, been one of the organizers of the Society of Wood Engravers in 1920. As publisher, he selected books and illustrators; as printer, he designed the books and supervised their printing. At a time of uninspired trade-book printing and illustration, his enthusiasm for fine illustrations harmoniously associated with fine typography had far-reaching influence. In 1933, because of the Great Depression, he had to sell the Golden Cockerel Press, and he turned to writing, illustrating, and teaching graphics at Reading University. Gibbings deserved the tribute that he received in *The Times Literary Supplement*: "More than any other one person he was responsible for the revival of wood-engraving that took place in this country between the wars."

After this tribute, it is distressing to have to admit that Gibbings was not a first-rate draftsman, wood engraver, or illustrator. He never mastered anatomy; his faces are little short of comic; and ugly, mechanically shaded natives disfigure the books about the Pacific islands that he wrote and illustrated. He engraved with a heavy hand and revealed little critical judgment about his illustrations. He cut blocks for books of poetry and fiction, books about the sea and nature in facile profusion but with little sense of commit-

153. Robert Gibbings. Llewellyn Powys, *The Glory of Life* (1934).

ment to the texts. The books that Gibbins illustrated are filled with miscellaneous cuts of scenes and objects, often small, black, and disconcertingly prosaic. The illustrations in more than forty books – including classics as rich in possibilities as Samuel Butler's *Erewhon* (1923), John Keats's *Lamia* (1928), Gustave Flaubert's *Salammbô* (1931), Sir Thomas Malory's *Morte d'Arthur* (1936), Herman Melville's *Typee* (1938), and William Shakespeare's *Othello* (1939) – do not have distinction enough to list the books in the Catalog. Several of Gibbing's most attractive wood engravings appear in books that he illustrated early in his career: Samson pulling open the jaws of the lion in the biblical *Samson and Delilah* (1925); the Boy in the Rose Chemise (who is really a girl) lying with his head in the poet's lap in *Red Wise* (1926) by E. Powys Mathers; a grove of pandamus trees with their roots above ground in *Iorana! a Tahitian Journal* (1932), which, by chance, he wrote after having done the illustrations; and a snake dangling from a tree (fig. 153), two kingfishers, and a large frontispiece of a sea gull in the folio edition of Llewellyn Powys's *Glory of Life* (1934).

Thereafter, in eight volumes that Gibbings wrote and illustrated, including the several about rivers beginning with *Sweet Thames, Run Softly* (1940), he failed to do justice to the rich opportunities for illustrations that he created for himself. Amid the profusion of insignificant visual memoranda of things and places in each volume are a few designs of some charm, but none that add meaning to the anecdotal accounts of people who held to ancient ways of life, which he admired.

Had Robert Gibbings limited himself to one-tenth of his output, he might have been a much better wood engraver, but there is little reason to believe that he might have been a sensitive interpretive illustrator.

Arthur Eric Rowton Gill

Calligrapher, sculptor, tombstone cutter, printer, type designer, and prolific writer of opinions, Eric Gill (1882–1940) engraved for ten years before he illustrated his first important work, *The Song of Songs* (1925), the first of several books of selections from the Bible. Gill's eighteen wood engravings reveal his lifelong bent for using nudes to adorn religious texts. His five copper engravings for *Procreant Hymn* (1926), an erotic poem by E. Powys Mathers in imitation of the Song of Solomon, are as chaste in line as they are voluptuous in spirit. The six wood engravings in *Passio Domini Nostri Jesu Christi* (1926), the Passion as related in the Gospel according to Matthew, are as fine a set of illustrations as Gill ever made. The one that depicts Christ carrying the Cross stands comparison with sixteenth-century woodcuts of the Passion.

154. Eric Gill. Geoffrey Chaucer, *Troilus and Criseyde* (1927).

For a folio edition of *Troilus and Criseyde* (1927), Gill engraved five large illustrations, four tailpieces, and a large number of side decorations of small figures, mostly amorous, in stylized leafy branches. These branches, a blending of the styles of William Morris and Art Nouveau, which Paul Woodroffe had prefigured in Tennyson's *Princess and Other Poems* (1904), grow monotonous in Gill's later books. The most satisfactory of the five designs is the second: Pandarus (oddly, a tall young man) bringing his niece Criseyde to the bed on which his friend Troilus has been lying sleeplessly and complaining since having gazed on her. Criseyde, in black, standing and Troilus reclining, holding her hand, and looking up at her from a bed with a striped coverlet are skillfully balanced (fig. 154). The block, however, was placed well before the scene in the text – a book too soon. Gill's illustrations for *Troilus and Criseyde* prove how attractive modern wood engravings can look in well-printed books and how insensitive Gill was to the delicacy, humor, and irony of Geoffrey Chaucer's great verse novel.

Between 1929 and 1931, a four-volume *Canterbury Tales* was published in a format uniform with that of *Troilus and Criseyde*. Gill engraved twenty-three headpieces that serve as illustrations, several tailpieces, and a large number of leaf-spray borders, most of which include figures. The designs are impeccable and witty. Gill should have been the perfect illustrator of *The Canterbury Tales* because he shared Chaucer's piety and carnal laughter. At the same time, his mannered style is medieval enough in spirit to be congruous with the language and content of the tales. Yet because Gill's headpieces are incidental decorations rather than illustrations, *The Canterbury Tales* was a wonderful opportunity that Gill never fully grasped.

The eleven wood engravings in the Latin *Canticum canticorum Salomonis* (1931) are different from the series in the English edition (1925). They are unusual for Gill in being tonal, worked from black by means of *criblé*. They make up one of his most attractive series, but their success as illustrations, as those of 1925, depends on whether the Song of Solomon celebrates mystical religious love or physical love. Gill's many illustrations for *The Four Gospels of the Lord Jesus Christ* (1931) are limited to figures subordinated to the lettering on the blocks of which they are a part. They were done in much the same spirit as the cuts in *The Canterbury Tales*. The small octavo *Hamlet* (1933), printed by Gill and his son-in-law René Hague, seems meant to rival Gordon Craig's edition for the Cranach Press, for which Gill engraved one block. In addition to the title page, with its sequence of small vignettes highlighting the action, a small square block appears above the first scene of each of the five acts. These genuine visualizations of the key scene of each act make their own imaginative

commentary. Hamlet naked amid high waves ("a sea of troubles", III.i), guided toward his father's ghost while a snake, a dragon, and predatory birds oppose him (IV), is the boldest invention of the series.

Gill arrived at his most rational equilibrium in a four-volume duodecimo edition of the New Testament (1934), with two full-page illustrations in each volume. Gill maintained his unique decorative values, the harmony between illustrations and typeface – Perpetua, which he had designed– and his disciplined engraving on wood in his eight vignettes, which reinforce significant passages of Montague James's translation. For the Gospels, Gill drew variations on an apt motif of an angel unrolling a scroll on which are revealed significant incidents in the Evangelists' accounts, such as Christ turning water to wine (John 2:7–11) and Christ's encounter with the woman of Samaria at Jacob's well (John 4:7–26). But Gill's waywardness spoils the effects of the four wood engravings for the four fifteenth-century English texts of two parts of the passionate medieval religious poem *Quia amore langueo* (1937). The first design is a depiction of the narrator, represented as a young woman, who is mentioned in only the first two lines, and not of Mary, who speaks the rest of the twelve fervent stanzas. In the fourth design, Christ pursues his true love, man's soul, with his wounded hands extended. Gill frivolously visualized the beloved as a young woman in a light frock looking into a mirror and holding a string attached to a balloon or to the moon as she flees. The composition and engraving of the four blocks are faultless, but Gill seems to have been only partly aware of the religious intensity of the poem.

English literature has no nobler testament than John Donne's *Holy Sonnets*, unforgettable cries of a deeply religious soul confronting death. Gill's four engravings, made for an edition that he printed in 1938, are so lacking in imagination and dignity that they are an affront to the text. Gill seems not to have taken seriously his preaching about the sanctity of art as work when he illustrated Shakespeare's *Henry VIII* (1939). His six wood engravings add nothing fresh even as decoration and have an unseemly facetiousness. Working in bed during the Battle of Britain and soon before his death, Gill made five small drawings of moments in *Glue and Lacquer: Four Cautionary Tales* (1941), translations from the Chinese of Têng Mêng-lung. The neat, witty designs, superbly engraved on copper by Gill's son-in-law Denis Tegetmeier, are a belated revelation of what Gill could do as a literary illustrator.

For an artist who was so passionately wrapped up in ideas, Eric Gill was disappointingly superficial in his interpretations of most of the texts he illustrated; yet the economy, clarity, and beauty of his work had a beneficial

155. Stephen Gooden. Aesop, *Fables* (1936).

influence on English book illustration because of its strong effect on twentieth-century wood engraving, typography, and book design and its emancipation from uninspired realism.

Stephen Gooden

The only English illustrator of modern times to use metal engraving extensively, Stephen Gooden (1892–1955) made an auspicious start with six delightful designs and a title page for an edition of Anacreon's *Poems* as early as 1923. He was, therefore, one of the senior members of the post-First World War generation. For each volume of a five-volume edition of the Apocrypha and Holy Bible (1924–27), he engraved a title page, a headpiece for the first page, and a tailpiece for the last page. For another edition of the Apocrypha (1929), Gooden's illustration of a brawny angel and a prophet proves him to have been at that early date one of the finest relief engravers in England. (He may have used a soft metal block instead of boxwood.) But he preferred intaglio engraving on copper, using drypoint etching for outlines. Besides being one of England's masters of the clean and economical engraved line, Gooden was one of the most intelligent and inventive interpretive illustrators.

At Gooden's suggestion, George Moore had the distinction of having him illustrate two of his books and decorate another with copper engravings. Not since the etchings of William Strang had English book illustration seen anything to match the naturalness and dignity of Gooden's plates. Among the nine full-page designs in *The Brook Kerith* (1929), those of Azariah and the boy Joseph walking, Joseph meeting his father on the road, Jesus feeding a lamb, Jesus admitting Paul beneath the arched stone and timber roof of the Essene hermitage, and others are among the most eloquent illustrations in a twentieth-century English book. Moore's suspenseless tale *Peronnik the Fool* (1933) hardly deserves the honor of Gooden's two full-page and six smaller engravings. Yet seldom has an illustrator treated a minor work of literature with so much respect as Gooden did in designs as fully imagined as the frontispiece of the peasant boy Peronnik leaning against a cow, Peronnik in half armor kneeling to be knighted by Sir Gilles, and the sorceress Redemonde, a woman of radiant beauty, descending steps within flying buttresses to the lawn where the boy-knight is announcing himself on a horn.

The twenty-six engravings for Edward Marsh's translation of Jean de La Fontaine's *Fables* (1931) are a technical advance over Gooden's earlier work. Among the finest plates are "Death and the Woodman", "The Fishes and the Flute-Player", and "The Dairymaid and the Jar of Milk". In the last, Perrette the maid trips along with a pot of milk balanced on her head, her petticoats aswirl. For

259

her, Gooden created a delightful quayside setting mottled in sun and shadow. After transporting La Fontaine to the twentieth century, Gooden spent two years on the illustrations for Sir Roger L'Estrange's seventeenth-century translation of Aesop's *Fables* (1936). He engraved ten designs that are both witty and brilliantly executed, together with a fine title-page portrait of Aesop, a full-page tailpiece, and a small pen-and-ink initial letter for each of the 201 fables. Whether the main illustrations took their cue from traditional designs or were Gooden's inventions, they elaborate L'Estrange's salty texts with rare pungency – such as Gooden's dressing the smith in the fable "The Smith and His Dog" in a British workingman's scarf and turning the ape in "An Ape and a Dolphin" into a gelada, so as to have its leonine mane and tail offset the baroque scales and floriated fins of the dolphin as the animals fly joyously over the waves. For "The Wolf and Kid" – in which "before he goes to pot", the kid persuades the wolf to play on his pipe (which brings the hounds) – Gooden sat the wolf on a sort of stile to play the bagpipes, while the kid dances on a stump (fig. 155). Gooden took playful liberties for surprise effects, but he always engaged in imaginative enhancement, not trivial elaboration. Nevertheless, the shift from small designs within formal borders to full-page designs for the last three illustrations is incomprehensible. The full-page engraving of a rampant lion as a final "tailpiece" seems equally ill-advised, especially since the same lion plus a gnat would have made sense as the illustration for the last fable.

The Gift of the Magi (1939), a short story by O. Henry, has ten illustrations that reveal Gooden as quite as skillful in pen and ink as the leading users of this medium. His four engraved illustrations and four decorative designs for *The Rubáiyát of Omar Khayyám* (1940) are far from what earlier artists imagined Edward FitzGerald had had in mind. In place of the usual young prince and girl are an elderly, almost bald Omar and a young male friend. Any notion of Victorian insipidity disappears with the presence of Death, at first wearing a mask, belted jerkin, and plumed turban. In the final quiet idyll – "And when the Angel with his darker Draught draws up to thee" – Death, now an unclothed skeleton, stands behind a willow with a single glass on a tray.

Few other English artists have published as many illustrations that offer as much insight, originality, wit, elegance, and beauty as those by Stephen Gooden in the service of his authors.

Joan Hassall

From 1937 to 1965, Joan Hassall (b. 1906) illustrated belles-lettres. She was primarily a wood engraver, although it is said that she also used pewter; for a while in the 1950s, she was forced to use scraperboard (board with a blackened surface that is removable by scraping for making white-line drawings). She apparently was influenced by the wood engravings of Thomas Bewick to work in the little and to fill each block with detail. After turning over the pages of the books she illustrated, one reluctantly concludes that her designs are too often crowded, dark, and insufficiently animated. She has said that her small blocks are superior to her large ones. This seems to be true not because of size, but because human beings appear in the larger designs, and she did not draw them well.

Elizabeth Gaskell's *Cranford* (1940) was the first major work of literature that Hassall illustrated. The twelve illustrations, hampered by the weight of their darkness, do not approach the smiling grace of the pen-and-ink work in the editions illustrated by Hugh Thomson, Charles Brock, and Henry Brock, nor do they offer any countervailing novel interpretations. After the Second World War, Hassall made a fresh start on more congenial subjects with Mary Webb's *Fifty-one Poems* (1946). The twenty-six headpiece scenes and tailpiece flowers, fruits, and birds are extraordinarily detailed to have been engraved on 1 or 2 inches of wood. The blocks did not print well, but the book is still one to cherish. Hassall returned to a fiction classic with Mary Russell Mitford's *Our Village* (1947), a companion volume to *Cranford*, and sketched the designs on the spot. Perhaps as a result, eight of the sixteen illustrations are scenes without action. After the gaiety of Thomson's 100 pen-and-ink vignettes and of Charles Brock's 25 pretty watercolors, Hassall's sober engravings seem dispirited. She was so unhappy with the poor printing of her blocks on the postwar "economy-standard" paper prescribed by the government (for which she should have made allowance) that she gave up her commission to illustrate *The Vicar of Wakefield*.

The Strange World of Nature (1950) by Bernard Gooch contains Hassall's finest engravings. A collection of nature essays, it permitted her to deal with lovely forms of wildlife, not awkward human beings. Among the twelve headpieces, the engravings of a toad and frogs, snails and glowworms, a snake and a frog (fig. 156), two water voles, a bird nursery, and two crossbills establish her as the equal of the brilliant twentieth-century wood engravers who have specialized in depicting natural-history subjects. Her scraperboard designs of houses preserved by the National Trust in *Sixteen Portraits* (1951) and some of the tailpieces for Margaret Lane's *Brontë Story: A Reconsideration of Mrs. Gaskell's "Life of Charlotte Brontë"* (1953) are among the rare artistic successes in this medium.

Again inviting comparison with Thomson and the Brocks, Hassall undertook as her major enterprise the illustration

156. Joan Hassall. Bernard Gooch, *The Strange World of Nature* (1950).

of seven uniform volumes of Jane Austen's works: *Pride and Prejudice* (1957), *Sense and Sensibility* (1958), *Mansfield Park* (1959), *Northanger Abbey* (1960), *Persuasion* (1961), *Emma* (1962), and *Shorter Works* (1963). The formula is the same for each of the six novels: a frontispiece and about a dozen small illustrations. *Shorter Works* contains a frontispiece and ten tailpieces, some of which approach illustrations. The total of eighty-four blocks is, by present-day standards, a considerable output of wood engravings to devote to one author. Alas, though, Joan Hassall seems to have been miscast as an interpreter of the feminine and domestic worlds of Gaskell, Mitford, and Austen. In any event, she never engraved a human being with anything like the authority of her enchanting engravings of snakes, snails, and voles – or the mouse in Robert Burns's *Poems* (1965).

Gertrude Hermes

Technically, Gertrude Hermes (b. 1901) is one of the most original wood engravers of the twentieth century. Her illustrations, however, are few. The influence that she has exerted, both by example and as a teacher of wood engraving at the Central School of Art, has been great. As an engraver, Hermes has been an innovator in two important respects. She has shown how realism in drawing may be transgressed in order to project an idea with a cutting edge

to it. Inseparable from this emancipation from the matter-of-fact concept of illustration, she has been a leader, with Blair Hughes-Stanton, in inventing exciting engraving techniques. Figures and forms in her designs fuse into one another in droll fantasy. White areas are cut out to leave completely arbitrary patterns of black and white, and tools of different shapes and sizes plow and jab the wood to create white-line textures and patterns unlike anything previously seen in wood engraving. The engravers and etchers of today are still exploring these linear and textural innovations.

The first book to which Hermes contributed illustrations, and indeed the only significant work of literature that she ever illustrated, was John Bunyan's *Pilgrim's Progress* (1928). She made four wood engravings, and Hughes-Stanton made six. The huge blocks are extravagant in concept and uncertain in execution. By 1931, Hermes's technique had improved, but she had not reached the top of her form. For *A Florilege*, edited by Irene Gosse, she did twenty large wood engravings of herbs with short quotations from the herbals of John Gerard and other early herbalists as "illustrations" or background music. This is a book of fascinating prints. Two slight short stories, *Strawberry Time* and *The Banquet* (1934), by Ralph Hale Mottram are the occasion for four engravings. Each has top and side curtains, as though for a stage. The best is one for *The Banquet*,

157. Gertrude Hermes. Ralph Hale Mottram, *The Banquet* (1934).

wittily showing a provincial wife at a company banquet seated at the head table next to a flirtatious lord, the chairman of the company for which her husband works (fig. 157). The intimacy of the couple and the gaiety of the flowers, fruit, and drink come through as a more spirited satire of the dull proceedings than is the story. The two cuts for a long poem by Naomi Mitchison, *The Alban Goes Out* (1939), are only decorative. In recent years, Hermes has turned to creating splendid large woodcut prints.

Blair Hughes-Stanton

One of the leaders in raising wood engraving in England to heights of technical mastery that approach wizardry, Blair Hughes-Stanton (b. 1902) began his career with six illustrations for John Bunyan's *Pilgrim's Progress* (1928) and ten for D. H. Lawrence's *Birds, Beasts, and Flowers* (1930). They mark a break with the past, but not a complete one; they still are experimental. In the words of the title page of John Milton's *Comus* (1931), Hughes-Stanton's seven wood engravings – his first distinguished work – are "a frontispiece and six characters in costume", not illustrations. But the masque is a "dainty piece of entertainment" in which even the "serious doctrine of virginity" is pranked out in language both quaint and sensuous. Comus in bejeweled rompers; the Lady in a long skirt, low-cut bodice, and

bustle; and Sabrina, goddess of the river, daintily appareled in a diaphanous apron festooned with daisies are witty translations into twentieth-century terms. The four full-page designs and one headpiece for Christopher Marlowe's *Doctor Faustus* (1932) are not so apt. Now that Hughes-Stanton had rid his designs of restrictive borders and was using more white behind his blacks and grays, his blocks make a lively show. But one look at Helen in a gauze shift makes clear that the artist was dealing with poetry that is too elevated for his artifices. And his faces are the least interesting, least skillfully engraved elements in his illustrations throughout his career. For Samuel Butler's *Erewhon* (1932), he engraved twenty-nine chapter headpieces. This satire of European society contains so much deadpan fantasy that the artist made a shrewd judgment when he elected to do representational designs without the mannerisms of those for *Comus* and *Doctor Faustus*, but with clear appreciation of the mischief that Butler was up to.

The Revelation of St. John the Divine (1932) and *The Lamentations of Jeremiah* (1933) are two of the most serious modern efforts at producing English illustrated books that in every respect reflect the splendor of their texts. For Revelation, Hughes-Stanton made forty-one wood engravings, twelve of which are full-page. Typical is that for Revelation 6: 2 : "And I saw, and behold, a white horse: and he that sat on him had a bow; and a crown was given

262

158. Blair Hughes-Stanton. D. H. Lawrence, *The Ship of Death and Other Poems* (1933).

unto him: and he went forth conquering, and to conquer." The dark archer in an oriental crown kneels with one knee on a charging white horse and pulls his bow. In the flux around him are the other three horsemen and the souls of the slain. With nothing but a few sharp tools, Hughes-Stanton turned a block of wood into a design that keeps faith with John's mystic words and creates new eloquence in patterns on the page. *The Lamentations of Jeremiah* is Hughes-Stanton's masterpiece. The twenty-one engravings in it are genuine illustrations that enhance the bitter monologue. By filling his designs with figures that gesture with arms, legs, and whole bodies, he expressed the vehemence of Jeremiah while he followed Lamentations through its five-chapter sequence. In no other book has Hughes-Stanton more completely come to grips with the text and tried both to account for the events narrated and to express the emotion in which they are steeped. In no other book has he drawn human figures with so much variety of posture and so much solidity and grace.

The eleven wood engravings in *Four Poems* (1933) by Milton include a full-page illustration each for "L'Allegro", "Il Penseroso", "Arcades", and "Lycidas". The Queen of Arcadia, a girdle of white flowers clinging to the diaphanous cloth that cascades between her quaintly crossed legs, is a delicious combination of fantasy and grace, but the gratuitous awkwardness of the gray naked male figures in the other three designs spoils the series. Hughes-Stanton engraved ten full-page and three smaller blocks for Lawrence's *Ship of Death and Other Poems* (1933). His naked men with short torsos and big feet still look odd, but they do suggest "slim naked men from Cnossos, smiling the archaic smile". The title-page design, a headpiece, and a full-page illustration (fig. 158) rise to the imaginative level of the moving cry of the dying Lawrence:

> to build the ship
> of death to carry the soul on the longest journey

> A little ship, with oars and food
> and little dishes, and all accoutrements
> fitting and ready for the departing soul.

The engravings for Lawrence's poems "Whales Weep Not!" and "Bavarian Gentians" are technically among the finest that Hughes-Stanton ever made. The twenty-one engravings of various sizes in *Ecclesiastes: or the Preacher* (1934) are primarily decorative. They also are primarily erotic. Love is, without doubt, one of the chief earthly vanities; yet it hardly seems to be the main theme of some of the weariest, most eloquent words ever written.

Among several minor works are scattered a few fine illustrations, but the nine nudes in Thomas De Quincey's *Confessions of an English Opium-Eater* (1948) are irrelevant, and the eight full-page color plates and twenty-one black crayon or pencil drawings in Jane Austen's *Sense and Sensibility* (1949) do not look like final designs. Since then, Hughes-Stanton has illustrated four books for an American publisher. The first was *The Wreck of the "Golden Mary"* (1956) by Charles Dickens and Wilkie Collins, with seven black-and-white wood engravings of large symbolic figures and too small human characters who are rescued after their ship sinks. Then followed three books with color designs: Joseph Conrad's *Youth* (1959), eight; Henry James's *Beast in the Jungle* (1963), sixteen; and *The Book of Genesis* (1970), twenty-four. These late illustrations – with color, linoleum blocks, and a good deal of abstraction combined with standard wood engraving – yield almost surrealistic effects, an example of artistic growth uncommon among book illustrators.

David Michael Jones

Born in Kent of a Welsh father and an English mother, David Jones (1895–1974) went to art school at fourteen, was wounded in the First World War, became a Roman Catholic, and added the middle name Michael. He joined the Ditchling Arts and Crafts Guild, where in 1924, he learned to engrave and carve boxwood, although not from Eric Gill, a member of the guild and Jones's close friend. By 1930, health troubles had ended his work as a book illustrator, and he turned to painting watercolors and writing poetry.

The numerous small square blocks that Jones engraved in a heavy woodcut manner for Jonathan Swift's *Gulliver's Travels* (1925) are timid beginner's work; the two white-line wood engravings of a pampered dog in Henry Fielding's *History of Pompey the Little* (1926) show improvement. The dozen wood engravings in *The Book of Jonah* (1926) follow the biblical account with a childlike boldness, but they are too imitative of Gill's style to be more than promising. In two designs for a Welsh version of *Ecclesiastes* (1927), Jones found his own wood-engraving style. He did not outline the figures in black, but modeled them by untidy white-line crosshatching against black. Although imperfectly printed because of Jones's shallow engraving, the ten wood engravings in *The Chester Play of the Deluge* (1927) are as original a series of illustrations as any in an English book. Jones's innovation was to integrate the elements of each design in a complex overall pattern by means of interlocking bands of solid black or white. The ten illustrations, which are arranged as five double spreads, depict the iniquities of the world that made God resolve to destroy humanity, Noah and his family during the building of the Ark (fig. 159), the animals going aboard, the stages of the Deluge, and Noah offering a sacrifice while his family and the animals kneel in thanksgiving.

Always exploring, Jones turned to copperplate engraving in his illustrations for *The Rime of the Ancient Mariner* (1929). These thin outlines with meager spots of shading are intrinsically little different from pen drawings, but their interpretive quality is extraordinary. The eight full-page plates convey the oppressive sense of the supernatural that permeates Samuel Taylor Coleridge's masterpiece. Two of Jones's designs – the ship becalmed on a sea that shimmers with heat while slimy things crawl about, and the Mariner with the dead Albatross hung around his neck – are unforgettable realizations of evil forces. In another key, the dead crew, having been "inspirited" to operate the ship, dancing with hands upraised as they sing, while in the moonlight the ship moves without wind and the horizon tilts, is a brilliant invention.

Jones's wood engraving "The Bride", which is used as the frontispiece to Walter H. Shewring's *Hermia and Some Other Poems* (1930), depicts a bride lighting a candle at the feet of the crucified Christ and combines piety and mystery. War prints were used as frontispieces to R. H. J. Steuart's *March, Kind Comrade* (1931) and to Jones's *In Parenthesis* (1937). The etching of a half-naked British soldier embraced by barbed wire in a battle-blasted wood is hauntingly evocative of Jones's reminiscences of the First World War. In the preface, he says, "I had intended to engrave some illustrations, but have been prevented [by his illnesses]." It was a great loss to English illustration.

David Jones's illustrations exemplify what it is so difficult to demonstrate; they penetrate deep into the spirit of their texts, and they are unique works of art. They are never ordinary because Jones, a poetic and artistic descendant of William Blake, was profoundly concerned about the destiny of humanity before he was the practitioner of an art form.

Edward McKnight Kauffer

The American artist and designer Edward McKnight Kauffer (1890–1954) is usually included among English illustrators because he worked in London from 1914 to 1941. He became a fellow of the British Institute of Industrial Artists and was best known for his posters. Kauffer's drawings for the first book that he illustrated, Robert Burton's *Anatomy of Melancholy* (1925), have been extravagantly praised. The formalized hellebore, familiar from reproductions, is the only design of even modest distinction; the rest of the several dozen abstract and semiabstract line drawings, mere decorative allusions to the text, are pointless and often embarrassingly facetious in conjunction with Burton's stately prose. Similarly, Kauffer's seven non-

159. David Jones. *The Chester Play of the Deluge* (1927).

160. Clare Leighton. Clare Leighton, *Four Hedges* (1935).

abstract pen drawings, reinforced by careless crosshatching and patches of color, are derisory as illustrations of Herman Melville's complex psychological tale *Benito Cereno* (1926). In Daniel Defoe's plain narrative *Robinson Crusoe* (1929), the eight arty hand-colored stenciled designs are hopelessly irrelevant. The ugly cold greens and blues and hot reds of the ten stencils in Arnold Bennett's *Elsie and the Child* (1929) might be considered to be in key with the shallow domestic drama, but ten line drawings with patches of wash convey almost nothing of what goes on in Bennett's sentimental *Venus Rising from the Sea* (1931). Two-color tints partly conceal the slipshod nature of Kauffer's twenty-one crayon drawings of the two main characters, and do nothing much else, in a two-volume edition of *Don Quixote* (1930). The nine full-page monotone drawings of automatons and machines in Lord Birkenhead's *World in 2030 A.D.* (1930) would seem more appropriate in an engineering magazine. Kauffer's later work in New York is beyond our concern.

Clare Veronica Hope Leighton

As early as 1923, Clare Leighton (b. 1899) was among the band of printmakers who were reviving autographic white-line wood engraving. Her early blocks are depressingly black, the drawing is weak, and the engraving is coarse. Yet her twelve full-page and numerous smaller blocks in the trade edition of Thomas Hardy's *Return of the Native* (1929) evoke belief, compassion, and foreboding. They depict the bleak beauty of the heath, the humors of the natives, and the strange events that befall these lonely Wessex folk. The sixteen wood engravings for Thornton Wilder's *Bridge of San Luis Rey* (1929) have none of the finality of the earlier illustrations, partly because Brother Juniper's search for the truth about the collapse of the bridge does not have the unity or tragic inevitability of *The Return of the Native* and partly because Leighton was not at home in Peru, as she was on Egdon Heath. Much the same explanation can be given in regard to her seven full-page illustrations and smaller headpieces and tailpieces of the exotic settings in Henry Major Tomlinson's *Sea and the Jungle* (1930). In a monumental edition of Emily Brontë's *Wuthering Heights* (1931), Leighton came close to identity of mood with that "horror of great darkness" that Charlotte said brooded over her sister's somber masterpiece. Mostly, however, she chose to develop rhythmic patterns that depict moments of tranquillity in the tale instead of moments of violence.

In 1933, Leighton's career entered a new phase with the publication of *The Farmer's Year*, which she had written as well as illustrated. In it, she emerged as an essayist with great respect for the men and women who work close to nature and as a prose writer of sensitivity. She also brought

161. Percy Wyndham Lewis. Naomi Mitchison, *Beyond This Limit* (1935).

her artistic powers to maturity and produced some of her best wood engravings, such as the one of three men pollarding willow trees beside a frozen stream. *Four Hedges* (1935) and *Country Matters* (1937) complete Leighton's trilogy of writings about rural England. They were published in the same format as that of H. E. Bates's *Through the Woods* (1936) and *Down the River* (1937), illustrated by Agnes Miller Parker. *Four Hedges* contains eighty-seven wood engravings, six of which are full-page; twenty, substantial; and sixty-one, single flowers and garden fauna. It is a serene book, in which women gathering apples (fig. 160) is an exciting event. In *Country Matters*, Leighton wrote with affection about hobos, gypsies, chair bodgers, and songsters in a pub, as well as about such polite activities as a flower show and a church Harvest Festival in her native Buckinghamshire. The fourteen chapters and seventy-two wood engravings demonstrate how the experiences that register vividly on a sensitive consciousness may require transmission by both word and image for adequate communication. For instance, on a May morning walk in the Chiltern Hills, Leighton follows the unseasonable noise of wood-chopping to "a small erection of discolored thatch, shaped like two playing-cards that had been placed against each other. There, before me, stood the most primitive of workshops." She has discovered chair bodgers at work, an old man working a foot-treadle lathe and a younger one

sitting on a shaving horse and shaping the chair legs in readiness for the lathes. She describes their craft in detail. Although this immemorial industry takes place within the hut, Leighton's engraving re-creates the scene outside and adds greatly to readers' feeling for it, as well as to their understanding.

Before leaving England in 1939 to live in the United States, Leighton illustrated Hardy's *Under the Greenwood Tree* (1940). The five large full-page engravings are a sort of prothalamion, five moments in the progression of the love between the tranter's son Dick and the schoolteacher Fancy, from a Christmas dinner to the dressing of the bride for the wedding. The fifty-seven headpieces and tailpieces for the short chapters follow the four-season organization of Hardy's re-creation of the rural past of Wessex.

The books that Clare Leighton wrote and illustrated after the Second World War deal mainly with her observations of places and people in the United States, of which she became a citizen in 1946.

Percy Wyndham Lewis

The role of illustrator was not a natural one for the polemical writer and artist Wyndham Lewis (1882–1957), but his twenty full-page and several smaller black-and-white vignettes for Naomi Mitchison's *Beyond This Limit* (1935)

162. Horace Bray. *Elia and the Last Essays of Elia* (1929).

should be mentioned. Phoebe, a Scottish wood engraver, starts across Paris to have tea when sudden anxiety about a broken heart and the ticket for the Metro turns her crocodile bag into a crocodile and the ticket collector into a sort of Charon on an underground trip filled with mythological characters. Lewis's Vorticist drawings of unreal human figures, birds, and animals have no warmth, but they respond to this brittle fantasy with wit and strangeness, as in a typically unreal scene in the British Museum (fig. 161). Lewis's break with traditional illustration did not win him contracts or a following; but like Mitchison's story, it was a refreshing gesture.

Thomas Esmond Lowinsky

"Decorated by Thomas Lowinsky" (1892–1947) often is the legend on those books that Lowinsky illustrated during his brief career as an illustrator. His drawing was unexceptional, but his careful open crosshatching and broken-line shading create a pleasant gray effect that is reminiscent of that of early German woodcuts. For John Milton's *Paradise Regained* (1924), he created three imaginative illustrations. The first, for Book I, shows a swathed, frowning tall figure wearing a crown of bones; he is surrounded by flying serpents, a bird with a skull for its head, and other strange, fantastic figures. The design represents Satan amazing his infernal crew with news of Christ's baptism by John the Baptist. Satan is the antagonist, a sinister force identified with death, yet not without dignity. For Book II, to illustrate a Hesperidian moment in the Temptation of Christ, Lowinsky invented a peaceful design of two Quattrocento women, one wearing acanthus-leaf-like sleeves, standing before a table and palm tree and holding flowers. The climax of *Paradise Regained* comes in Book IV. To test whether Christ is the Son of God, Satan carries him to the top of the Temple in Jerusalem and places him on the highest pinnacle in the expectation that he will fall. In Lowinsky's design, Christ stands serenely on an ornate ball – a daring image.

Lowinsky did not again equal the originality and independent interest of those three illustrations; he was more at ease with less exalted texts. Five formal full-page drawings of Victorian women and a smaller headpiece and tailpiece, with their sly sardonic touches, are exactly right for Edith Sitwell's *Elegy on Dead Fashion* (1926). Among the seventeen tailpieces for *Exalt the Eglantine and Other Poems* (1926) are a half-dozen modest designs that catch the accent of eccentricity and artifice in Sacheverell Sitwell's verse. The numerous neat and sometimes elaborately embellished woodcut-like designs for Wilhelm Meinhold's *Sidonia the Sorceress* (1926) give much needed help to the long narrative. For a translation of Voltaire's satirical

163. Robert Maynard. George Herbert, *Poems* (1923).

Princess of Babylon (1927), Lowinsky's eleven illustrations do not reach beyond being ornamental and amusing. The initial headpiece of an exotic bird, however, is almost a classic among pen-and-ink drawings.

Robert Ashwin Maynard and Horace Walter Bray

The partnership of Robert Maynard (1888–1966) and Horace Bray (1887–1963) at the Gregynog Press and later at the Raven Press included a remarkable sharing of the illustration of several books. They were among the earliest members of the new school of autographic white-line wood engravers that continued the tradition of Charles Ricketts, William Strang, Gordon Craig, and Eric Gill into the 1920s. Maynard (fig. 163) became a master of the burin and might have been one of the leading figures in book illustration had he not carried the responsibility of a head printer throughout his career. Bray (fig. 162), a good but somewhat less subtle engraver, was better at buildings and landscapes than at figures. Between 1923 and 1931, together and separately, Maynard and Bray embellished almost a dozen books with wood engravings in different styles and with moderate success. The headpieces among the thirty wood engravings for *Caneuon Ceiriog detholiad* (1925), a book of poems in Welsh by John Ceiriog Hughes, are as good as any English interpretive illustrations in the solid black-and-white woodcut mode of the period. In *The Private Presses* (1969), Colin Franklin wrote that Maynard and Bray's sixteen hand-colored figures in outline for Ernest Rhys's *Life of St. David* (1927) are "perhaps the bravest experiment in decoration from the private presses". In 1928, Maynard engraved for a Welsh translation of *The Rubáiyát – Penillion Omar Khayyám* – seven vignettes that combine textured effects with black and white, and Bray used the same technique with ocher and gray tints discreetly added in five full-page engravings for *The Book of Tobit from the Apocrypha* (1931). Bray seems to have been under the influence of Gill when illustrating this book and when doing a sort of chastely erotic pantomime of eight unshaded nudes for Shakespeare's *Venus and Adonis* (1931).

In 1931, too, Maynard engraved his most ambitious series, ten designs for John Milton's *Samson Agonistes*. The great poetic drama is ideal for illustration because it is relatively short, its scenes are defined but not detailed, its action is unified by the presence of Samson throughout, and its tension tightens from the start. Maynard's wood-engraved vignettes reflect the inexorable sequence from the opening scene of the blind Samson sitting outdoors; through a two-block double spread of Samson routing the Philistines in battle; his betrayal by Dalila in four fine related designs, including one of Samson being dragged off to prison by soldiers; another two-block spread of

164. Henry Moore. Edward Sackville-West, *The Rescue* (1945).

the blind Samson being summoned by his captors; and finally to Samson bringing down the temple. Maynard's designs are doubly distinctive because of, first, the tensions that he set up with his dynamic play of arbitrary blacks and whites, long clean lines, and variously textured grays and, second, the sense of Miltonic grandeur and biblical distance that is conveyed by these highly stylized effects. Robert Maynard's illustrations for *Samson Agonistes* are an example of the new wood-engraving technique used successfully for interpretive illustration of an important work of English literature, not primarily for decoration or display.

Henry Spencer Moore

The drawings of Henry Moore (1898–1986) are almost as well known as his sculpture, but few of them can be called book illustrations. *Shelter Sketch Book* (1940) reproduces his wartime studies of Londoners sleeping in the Underground, but with no text. *The Rescue* (1945) is a radio "melodrama" by Edward Sackville-West based on the end of *The Odyssey*, which was performed on the BBC in two parts on 25 and 26 November 1943, with music by Benjamin Britten. For the book, Moore made six illustrations, dated "1944", in mixed media of ink, crayon, and watercolor. Four were reproduced in color and two in halftone. The full-page "bled" plates, printed as inserts on coated war-

time stock, show Phemius, the poet-commentator, counseling Telemachus (fig. 164); Penelope at her loom talking to her attendant Eurynome; Odysseus sleeping in the Naiads' cave; Odysseus as a beggar sitting on the ground; a stone wall on which is Penelope's scratched outline of Odysseus's profile; and a lurid red, yellow, black, and white view of dead and dying suitors lying around like rag dolls. The inert drawings, very like those of the Underground sleepers, do little to realize a "melodrama" full of graphic possibilities. Sackville-West's text is an original imaginative effort of a high order and deserves to be reprinted in a fitting format.

Prométhée (1952), André Gide's translation from the German of Goethe, was published in Paris and is not part of English book illustration. For the color lithographs, Moore had the wise cooperation of Jonquières, a Paris book designer, and Mourlot, Picasso's lithographer, who transferred the drawings from plastic sheets to stones and printed them. The strangeness and monumental abstractness of Moore's designs make them harmonious accompaniments to the somewhat aloof allegory. The most impressive is the one of Prometheus and Minerva in front of the statue of Pandora.

Selections from Poems by Auden: Lithographs by Henry Moore (1974) is a pretentious piece of commercialism. The lithographs are often 1 foot tall. Seen close up, as in reading

165. Gwenda Morgan. Thomas Gray, *Elegy Written in a Country Church-Yard* (1946).

a book, a number suggest dark holes in the ground and rocky crevasses. A three-color mountain stretches across the bottom of the five-page "Dichtung und Wahrheit", although the poem is not about mountains. In a few designs, human figures can be made out: for "The Lesson", a naked couple looking like victims of a famine; and for "Lullaby", a horrible fat or pregnant woman in pajamas or underwear. Anyone who thinks that there is a connection between Moore's heavy and gloomy lithographs and Auden's bright and incisive verse should try mixing up the illustrations and then assigning them to the same poems as in the book.

Gwenda Morgan

For two short stories in book form, Theodore Francis Powys's *Goat Green* (1937) and Alfred Edgar Coppard's *Tapster's Tapestry* (1938), Gwenda Morgan (b. 1908) engraved on wood illustrations that are too matter-of-fact for books by these specialists in the bizarre. During the Second World War, she made eight wood engravings of country scenes for Marjorie H. Tiltman's "peace-in-war" essays, *A Little Place in the Country* (1944). They include intricate white-line tonal patterns of such subjects as farm buildings, a bowl of stylized flowers, and a walnut tree close to a cottage. In 1946, Morgan supplied an edition of Thomas Gray's *Elegy Written in a Country Church-Yard* with six

wood engravings whose charm and fitness lie in their unaffected development of the country theme in contemporary terms. They depict a country farmyard, a Stoke Poges churchyard by moonlight (fig. 165), a laborer returning to his family and cottage at evening, a farmer plowing with oxen at dawn, a family harvesting, and a contemplative soul stretched at the base of a great beech beside a brook. These wood engravings cast a fresh glow over the familiar classic.

John Northcote Nash

An influential painter, printmaker, teacher, and gardener, John Nash (1893–1977) never made the most of his opportunities as an illustrator. Although he was one of the pioneers of autographic wood engraving in the 1920s, off and on for thirty years he persisted in illustrating and decorating books by pen and ink, a medium that he never mastered. His designs deserved better treatment; they occasionally were aided by some cosmetic coloring by stencils. Nash failed to measure up to challenges such as Edmund Spenser's *Shepheardes Calendar* (1930), William Cobbett's *Rural Rides* (1930), and, except for a nice pen drawing of the stinking hellebore, Gilbert White's *Natural History of Selborne* (1951). Nash was by inclination an expositor and embellisher of pages, not an interpreter of texts. Thus his two most important series of illustrations

271

166. John Nash. John Nash, W. Dallimore, and A. W. Hill, *Poisonous Plants* (1927).

– both of which are composed of wood engravings – are in *Poisonous Plants* (1927) and in H. E. Bates's *Flowers and Faces* (1935). For the first, he engraved twenty blocks and a headpiece; for the second, five blocks, including a floral border for the title page. These are not literary works, but the bold distribution of light and shade in designs such as "Water Hemlock or Cowbane" (fig. 166) in *Poisonous Plants* and a marrow and sunflower in *Flowers and Faces* explains why, although a casual interpretive illustrator, John Nash had so stimulating an effect on illustrators who followed him away from the tight restraints of the post-Bewick tradition of wood engraving.

Paul Nash

Like his brother John an influential painter, printmaker, teacher, and designer between the First and Second World Wars, Paul Nash (1889–1946) has been highly praised for his book work. Most of his designs are abstractions, coarsely cut prints that perhaps are correctly described as woodcuts. They rarely include human figures as main elements. Not counting those that are stage designs, they use motifs related to their texts, but their function is largely decorative and symbolic. The series of eleven brush-and-ink, hand-colored drawings for a hand-press limited edition of Richard Aldington's poems of the First World War, *Images of War*

(1919), one of Nash's earliest efforts, is an exception. The drawing is crude; the color is violent; and yet the fusion of spirit between these poems of death, heroism, and horror by the poet-soldier and these raw records of trench warfare by the artist-soldier – Nash fought at Ypres – creates an enduring illustrated work. But Nash's woodcut engravings seem too limited in scope to be anything more than decorative in relation to a mighty subject such as *Genesis* (1924) and too ponderous to be an embodiment of the irony in *Abd-Er-Rhaman in Paradise* (1928), Jules Tellier's tale of disenchantment with the hereafter. They are, however, of historical interest as indicators of the direction in which illustration might have gone had the abstractionism of the period prevailed.

Nash's reputation as a book illustrator rests on his thirty pencil drawings tinted by stenciling in a 210-copy edition of Sir Thomas Browne's *Urne Buriall* and *The Garden of Cyrus* (1932). In 1944, Sir Herbert Read wrote in his book *Paul Nash* that *Urne Buriall* "will always be treasured for it is one of the loveliest achievements of contemporary art". In 1948, in his essay "Paul Nash as Book Illustrator and Designer", Philip James said, "This book, judged by all standards, is one of the greatest illustrated books of this or any age." We must look carefully at work that is admired so extravagantly. The artist who undertakes to match wit with the seventeenth-century Norwich master of curious

167. Paul Nash. Sir Thomas Browne, *Urne Buriall* (1932).

learning, quirky notions, rolling rhythms, and breath-taking images sets himself a formidable task. For instance, pyramids are a logical motif for a heading for Chapter V, but a gray pencil drawing with patches of pastel pink and yellow fails utterly to catch the accent of the famous "under the drums and tramplings of three conquests" passage. Nash and others have commented, especially, on one illustration in *Urne Buriall*. In "Aerial Flowers", an essay in his autobiography, *Outline* (1949), Nash states that his imagination was deeply stirred by Browne's sentence "Before Plato could speak, the soul had wings in Homer which fell not but flew out of the body into the mansions of the dead." Nash says:

I could see the emblem of the soul – a little winged creature, perhaps not unlike the ghost moth – perched upon the airy habitations of the skies which in their turn sailed and swung from cloud to cloud and then on into space once more. . . . Only recently I became aware that the reference might be to those underground burial sites whence came the urns which evoked that heavenly prose.

For the illustration, Nash made a drawing of what seem to be unfinished wooden shelves floating in the clouds and being visited by small flying saucers (fig. 167). (From this drawing, he also made a watercolor and an oil painting.) Read wrote, "In a drawing like 'The Soul Visiting the Man-sions of the Dead' Paul Nash evolved a completely original fantasy." The reader can decide whether Nash's drawing is a personal fantasy or an illustration of Browne's "heavenly prose". The illustrations for *The Garden of Cyrus* are chiefly expository. The four full-page designs of flowers – especially the thick-growth frontispiece and the fern, teasel, and sunflower diagram – are lovely botanical drawings, but clearly are not intended to be anything more.

Agnes Miller Parker

Few engravers on wood have been the equal of Agnes Miller Parker (b. 1895) when she was at the top of her form in the 1930s. Since she was at her best in books of essays dealing with nature, her engraving of flowers, birds, animals, and outdoor scenes may here be considered interpretive. Her brilliant engraving makes up for her often indifferent handling of human beings. Parker's first important work was a series of thirty-seven engravings for *The Fables of Esope* (1931), translated by William Caxton. Although her technique was still developing, her use of white lines, arbitrary whites, and patterned shading makes *The Fables of Esope* one of the cornerstones of the new school of autographic wood engraving. Her approach to her subjects was as fresh as her style. Among Parker's splendid additions to the Aesop gallery are a sinuous gray fox, seen from above in a

273

168. Agnes Miller Parker. H. E. Bates, *Through the Woods* (1936).

circular white cut-out with the counterswinging figure of the stork against a black ground; the grasshopper and the ant on a lateral pattern of reeds; and a grand rooster with a superbly engraved cat. Parker's engravings seem too sophisticated to be suitable for the flat English translation of *XXI Welsh Gypsy Folk Tales* (1933) collected by John Sampson, but at least one must be mentioned: a squirrel and a fox conversing on the bough of a tree while a blind man lies on the ground and listens.

The book that brought Parker critical acclaim on both sides of the Atlantic and did much to create a public awareness of the pleasures of wood-engraved illustrations was *Through the Woods* (1936) by H. E. Bates. It was a perfect vehicle for her microscopic observation of country things. Parker engraved seventy-three designs for *Through the Woods*, including one for the jacket and eight fine full-page blocks. "Chaffinches on Hawthorne", "Squirrel on Pine Tree" (fig. 168), and "Catkins of Hazel and Willow" are classics, and her smaller blocks are equally delightful. She loved woods and rivers and the creatures that live in them and drew them with passionate veracity. Her depictions of parasol clavaria, "spongecake" boletuses, and the deadly *Amanita muscaria* – "like a Russian cake with rich flecks of almond" – are botanically precise enough to guide mushroom pickers from Bromley to the Bronx. *Down the River* (1937), a companion volume by Bates, followed next.

Among the eighty-three wood engravings, Parker did many river subjects, such as fish, boats, and a weasel; but the finest engravings are those of birds and plants, especially the full-page "Herons", "Swans in Floodwater", glorious "Sea Gulls Flying", and full-page "Iris, Burweed, and Rushes" – one of the high points of artist-engraver achievement in any English book.

Among the successes of the 1930s must be included Parker's illustrations for Thomas Gray's *Elegy Written in a Country Churchyard* (1938). For it, she engraved thirty-two blocks, each of which faces one quatrain. Her blend of realistic and highly stylized engraving has an unexpected congruity with Gray's cheerless commentary on human destiny and polished verse in praise of humble rural virtues. Although Parker continued to illustrate books through the years, only the forty-eight small wood engravings in Herbert Furst's *Essays in Russet* (1944) are up to her highest standards. A dozen or more volumes by the Victorian naturalist Richard Jefferies, Thomas Hardy, William Shakespeare, and Edmund Spenser offered abundant opportunities for artistic fulfillment, but – because she found no way to avoid drawing human figures in naturalistic scenes, perhaps also for personal reasons – the many illustrations have little of the precision of observation and exquisiteness of execution for which Agnes Miller Parker will always be celebrated.

169. Mervyn Peake. Samuel Taylor Coleridge, *The Rime of the Ancient Mariner* (1943).

Mervyn Peake

Poet and novelist as well as artist, the talented Mervyn Peake (1911–68) also illustrated several books before a cruel illness cut short his career. Some of his pen-and-ink drawings – those for Lewis Carroll's *Hunting of the Snark* (1941), for instance – are comic without being funny. However, the twenty-one mostly outline drawings for Cyril Joad's *Adventures of the Young Soldier in Search of a Better World* (1943) and the eight for Quentin Crisp's *All This and Bevan Too* (1943) succeed in their satirical intent. Peake's only popular success as an illustrator was the series of seven reduced pen drawings for a humble little edition, printed on wartime paper, of Samuel Taylor Coleridge's *Rime of the Ancient Mariner* (1943). The edge-to-edge crosshatching is unfashionable, but the intensity of Peake's record of the Mariner's nightmare voyage transcends technique. He was psychologically and imaginatively able to identify with the obsessed, glittering-eyed survivor from the moment he intercepts the Wedding Guest, through his recounting of the disastrous, supernatural events on the ship, to the eerie and threatening climax, in which the Mariner awakens from his trance (fig. 169).

Among the hodgepodge of Peake's drawings in completely different styles in Christina Hole's scholarly *Witchcraft in England* (1945) are a few expressive illustrations,

especially a large Rembrandtesque wash drawing suggested by the passing remark "No one knew for certain who was, or was not, a witch," and a small line drawing of a woman being searched for Devil's marks. The thirty-two semierotic outline drawings in Maurice Collis's *Quest for Sita* (1946), a retelling of the Vedic epic *Rāmāyana*, verge on the ludicrous, and the broken-line figures in Robert Louis Stevenson's *Dr. Jekyll and Mr. Hyde* (1948) are pretentiously simple in execution and obvious in concept.

A Swedish publisher commissioned illustrations for *Alice's Adventures in Wonderland* and *Through the Looking-Glass* in 1946, but did not publish them until 1954, when they were also published in England. Peake had a highly developed sense of the grotesque, but how he could have conceived of Alice as a long-nosed, chinless, and short-haired boy in stocking feet stuns the mind. By any ordinary criteria, the two series are disasters. The twenty-two brush-and-ink drawings in Peake's *Rhyme of the Flying Bomb* (1962) are bold, unelaborated sketches, mostly white on black rectangles, that speak with the same apocalyptic voice as spoken by his ballad-stanza parallel of *The Rime of the Ancient Mariner*. In the poem, a sailor discovers, before he is killed by a cross-shaped flying bomb (and so achieves "the silence of the Cross"), that the baby he has found in a London street is the Christ Child. Not even half of these drawings are sufficiently developed to have warranted pub-

170. John Piper. *English, Scottish and Welsh Landscape, 1700–c. 1860* (**1944**).

lication, but one or two, such as that of the sailor leaping with the Child on his shoulder, were generated by the same intensity of emotion – and apparently at the same time – as the sometimes eloquent verse they accompany.

John Piper

As a matter of principle, John Piper (b. 1903) believes that illustrations should not be interpretive; and, anyway, he has preferred to draw topographical, architectural, and theatrical designs. His twelve full-page color lithographs and wrap-around cover design for *English, Scottish and Welsh Landscape, 1700–c. 1860* (1944), the first volume in Frederick Muller's New Excursions into Poetry series, mark a departure from the polished elegance of the wood engravings of the period. Few designs so rough, spontaneous, and moody have appeared in an English book. The black theatrical landscapes are scenes of desolation, inhospitableness, and ruin, completely out of sympathy with the poems, most of which celebrate the gentle aspects of the British countryside. "Park Place, Berkshire" typifies the neo-Romantic drawing of the times (fig. 170). The four colored drawings for Walter de la Mare's poem *The Traveller* (1946) are striking imaginary landscapes that follow the time sequence of the poem.

Omitting the fine architectural lithographs, stage sets,

and costume drawings that have appeared in books, next come Piper's line and tint-block drawings in Sir George Sitwell's *On the Making of Gardens* (1949); black-and-white reproductions and lovely color plates in Piper's *Romney Marsh* (1950); and eight full-page decorative color lithographs in *Elizabethan Love Songs* (1955). Some of the last are more than decorative; the head of the young Elizabeth I with Cupid seated in her brow is an apt borrowing of a seventeenth-century visual conceit to interpret Elizabeth's poem "When I was fayre and younge and favour gracëd me". Then followed eight full-page collage and watercolor semiabstract emblems of the Passion for *Judas* (1960), a religious poem by Ronald Duncan, and, for still another edition of Gilbert White's *Natural History of Selborne* (1962), twelve sketches, some unfinished and some of the same subject twice, in open disregard of the reader. Around 1948, Piper and Reynolds Stone shared their enthusiasm for nineteenth-century topographical guidebooks by collaborating on ten notable scenes of the Snowdon Mountains in Wales. Piper made the drawings, and Stone engraved them on wood. Twenty years later, they found a text – Robert Stuart Thomas's *Mountains* – to go with their blocks and a publisher for them. Most of them have too much black to be "factual engravings" with "clear observation of scenery". The largest, of Ffynnon Llugwy, is impressive.

171. Gwen Raverat. Laurence Sterne, *A Sentimental Journey* (1938).

Gwendolen Mary Raverat

As early as 1908, Gwen Raverat (1885–1957) joined Eric Gill in experimenting with white-line wood engraving, and she played a modest role in making this technique popular in England for both prints and book illustrations. *Modest* is the word that best describes her blocks, her talent, and her ambition. Sometimes using soft wood, she worked in the manner of Lucien Pissarro and got her characteristic gray effects by ragged uneven shading. In 1915, she made eight small blocks for her Cambridge friend Frances Cornford's *Spring Morning*. They are significant only for the date. In the subsequent books that Raverat illustrated, her blocks tend to vary unattractively in size and to make rectangular holes in the pages. Better planning for harmony, not uniformity, could have made the several volumes more appealing, for individually, her wood engravings are often charming – for example, that of a farmer asleep in a bare room with a candle on a chair, one of twenty-five blocks in Arthur Street's *Farmer's Glory* (1934). Among the thirty-three blocks in Cornford's *Mountains & Molehills* (1934), the full-page design of wild beasts circling a shepherd boy as he pipes is one of Raverat's finest wood engravings. It also is a perfect graphic restatement of the poem "Tapestry Song". The only book in which Raverat attempted to interpret a standard work of English literature

is *A Sentimental Journey* (1938). The ten wood engravings are spoiled by poor paper, the edition being a sixpenny Penguin. The engravings are uneven in interest, and some seem to be more in the spirit of Jane Austen than of Laurence Sterne; yet the frontispiece of Yorick sitting on a bed with the *fille de chambre* (fig. 171), a courtyard scene in Calais, the *fille de chambre* sewing Yorick's sock, and the servant La Fleur bringing Yorick's breakfast are among the successes of their day.

Eric William Ravilious

Because he was trained as and practiced as an industrial designer, Eric Ravilious (1903–42) was naturally more concerned with the decoration than with the interpretive illustration of books. His approach works well with period pieces such as Sir John Suckling's jolly *Ballad upon a Wedding* (1927). Ravilious's white-line engraving for the miracle of "The Song of Three Holy Children" in the Apocrypha (1929) is wittily literal. An angel appears to three naked males standing on the brick platform of a huge oven while flames spurt around the edges. The fourteen engravings for Shakespeare's *Twelfth Night* (1932) present the characters in Elizabethan dress, as though they were on stage. Heavily stylized and textured, the blocks make amusing decorations but limited illustrations. In his four

172. Eric Ravilious. Christopher Marlowe, *The Jew of Malta* (1933).

large engravings for Christopher Marlowe's *Jew of Malta* (1933), Ravilious created genuine illustrations. In the second design, Barabbas, holding a torch, receives bags of treasure and loose jewelry from his daughter, Abigail, who stands above him on the platform where he has hidden the wealth (fig. 172).

The four engravings in Thomas Hennell's *Poems* (1936) seem too formal to be appropriate for verse about "orts and ails and other country scroff". The final tailpiece, an airplane casting its shadow as a cross on the Atlantic Ocean, was sadly prophetic: Ravilious, a war artist, was lost on a flight off Iceland during the Second World War. The eleven oval designs in Ambrose Heath's *Country Life Cookery Book* (1937) are so rich and clever that they can be considered imaginative interpretations and probably Ravilious's finest wood-engraved illustrations. He made designs for several other similar books by Heath. Ravilious was in some ways an appropriate illustrator of the works of Gilbert White. In spirit, his wood engravings for the two-volume *Writings* (1938) have the decorum and formalism that are part of the style of the curate-squire of Selborne, but they lack his Anglo-Saxon earthiness. The final, memorial vignette – "GW 26th June 1793" – however, shows Ravilious at his best. Also in 1938, Ravilious illustrated *High Street* by James Maude Richards. It is a book of brief explanations of what goes on in small English shops. The twenty-four designs are lifted a little above the matter-of-fact by having been published as full-page color lithographs.

Albert Rutherston

The standard illustration by Albert Rutherston (1881–1953), professor of drawing at Oxford University for twenty years, is one or two broken-line figures framed by a wilting willow sapling with diamond-stitch patches of shading covered by splotches of two or three pastels. As light-hearted decorations for section breaks in *The Week-End Book* (1928) or for one of the single poems in the Ariel series, this formula does well enough. Rutherston rarely attempted to illustrate major works of literature. His designs for Shakespeare's *Cymbeline* (1923) present stage sets with names written above the characters in early-woodcut style. Rutherston's most ambitious effort was *The Winter's Tale* (1940). Superficially, the splashes of pink, yellow, and blue give the pastoral scenes an air of bright artificiality, but the drawing, especially of faces, is below professional standards. Fortunate in the number of books to which he was invited to contribute pen-and-ink drawings touched with color, Albert Rutherston was a book decorator of limited range, not a book illustrator.

173. Ernest H. Shepard. *Everybody's Pepys* (1926).

Ernest Howard Shepard

When We Were Very Young captivated the English-reading world in 1924. It was a rare double success, both literary and artistic, for both children and adults. It made the name of its illustrator, Ernest H. Shepard (1879–1976), almost as familiar as that of its author, A. A. Milne. With the publication of Milne's *Winnie-the-Pooh* (1926), *Now We Are Six* (1927), and *The House at Pooh Corner* (1928), Shepard's name became synonymous with enchanting pen-and-ink illustrations of children's books. After Milne, he turned to Kenneth Grahame. Shepard's illustrations for *The Golden Age* (1928) and *Dream Days* (1930) are disappointing, but his pen-and-ink vignettes for Grahame's classic, *The Wind in the Willows* (1931), created permanent images of Mr. Toad, Mole, Rat, and Badger, as John Tenniel's drawings had defined the creatures in *Alice's Adventures in Wonderland* and *Through the Looking-Glass*.

Shepard's 162 illustrations in *Everybody's Pepys* (1926), *Everybody's Boswell* (1930), and *Everybody's Lamb* (1933) are united by remarkable characters of the seventeenth, eighteenth, and nineteenth centuries who lived close to the heart of the London scene of their day. On each of the 547 pages of Samuel Pepys's *Diary*, vivid scene follows vivid scene, indicated by only a summary remark or a few tantalizing details and never by comprehensive description.

To deal with them, Shepard's fifty-eight full-page drawings strike a balance between Pepys's private life and the public affairs with which he was so surprisingly connected. The first eight designs indicate the riches that Shepard mined: Pepys at home dining in the garret with his pretty young wife; visiting his father in his tailor shop; sitting in the heaving wardroom of a naval vessel at sea; looking out from the high stern of a man-of-war off Holland; playing nine-pins on deck with his patron, Lord Sandwich; standing with his hat on at the foot of the high pulpit of St. Olave's to hear Dr. Mills preach; "King Charles I kissing country gentlewomen"; and Pepys reading by candlelight "while the wench sat mending my breeches by my bedside". All the illustrations are welcome in their completeness, but they are at the same time gracefully unlabored. The delight with which one recalls a drawing such as the one of Pepys and his wife "hearing of the mayds read in the Bible" (fig. 173) ultimately derives from the equivalence of mood, almost of flavor, between Pepys's text and Shepard's images.

Among the fifty illustrations in *Everybody's Boswell* and the fifty-four in *Everybody's Lamb* are some as memorable as any of those in *Pepys*: for instance, James Boswell sitting anxiously with Lady Diana Beauclerk while waiting for news of his election to Johnson's club, and Charles Lamb with that "excellent toss-pot" Ralph Bigod and other con-

174. Steven Spurrier. William Wycherley, *The Country Wife* (1934).

vivial friends. But neither series rises above the level of good twentieth-century illustration as consistently as does that in *Everybody's Pepys*. The same can be said of Shepard's illustrations for Laurence Housman's three volumes of plays about Queen Victoria – *Victoria Regina* (1934), *The Golden Sovereign* (1937), and *Gracious Majesty* (1941) – his own autobiographical accounts – *Drawn from Memory* (1957) and *Drawn from Life* (1961) – and other minor works.

Ernest Shepard is the only follower of Hugh Thomson who equaled him in lightness of spirit and mastery of that obdurate instrument, the pen. Apart from his ideal association with Milne and his classic drawings for *The Wind in the Willows*, he should be remembered for one of the few almost perfect English illustrated books – *Everybody's Pepys*.

Steven Spurrier

The 1934 edition of William Wycherley's play *The Country Wife* is lavish and colorful rather than distinguished. Yet the eight color plates and fourteen black-and-brown line drawings by Steven Spurrier (1878–1961) are imaginative efforts to capture the mood and atmosphere of this cynical Restoration comedy. The line drawings make little impression, but the watercolor plates are rich and sprightly. They were conceived as scenes on a stage, with the stage only suggested. Since there is no description of dress or setting

in the text, it helps immensely to have Spurrier's brightly colored scenes of the rakes and Pinchwife, whom they plan to cuckold – for example, Pinchwife and Sparkish, both gulled, meeting Alithea, Pinchwife's sister-in-law, and her maid at night by the light of a torch (fig. 174). Spurrier managed to make Sparkish a figure of ridicule; Alithea, lovely; and the torchbearer, a creature of the world of poverty that Wycherley ignored.

Spurrier illustrated *Nicholas Nickleby* (1940) with an attractive series of eight full-page color plates and sixty-five small black-and-white drawings notched into the chapter headings. He put some of Phiz into three designs by crowding his plates with figures: the theater scene "The Great Bespeak for Miss Snevellicci", the stage finale "The Indian Savage and the Maiden", and the riotous "Dotheboys Hall Breaks Up for Ever". The chapter-heading vignettes suggest that even Dickens can be visualized in fresh ways. The fifteen merry and unlabored designs, line drawings with splashes of color, do well enough for Robert Lynd's *Life's Little Oddities* (1941), but the eight in Shakespeare's *Sonnets* (1950) are not subtle or serious enough to be in accord with these flights of young genius.

Alan Reynolds Stone

After having attended Eton, Magdalene College, Cam-

175. Reynolds Stone. Leslie Paul, *The Living Hedge* (1946).

bridge, and a two-year apprentice program at the Cambridge University Press, Reynolds Stone (1909–79) found in wood engraving a means to express his love of natural forms and landscapes. His first book work, a graveyard scene for the title page of Walter de la Mare's *Ding Dong Bell* (1936), is impeccable. On the cream pages of Antonio de Guevara's *Praise and Happinesse of the Countrie-Life* (1938), freely rendered by Henry Vaughan, Stone's five white-line engravings of shrub, tree, grass, rock, flower, stone houses, and even gravestones gleam like jewels. The dozen headpieces for Jean-Jacques Rousseau's *Confessions* (1938) are elegant and idyllic. They translate Rousseau's Romantic notions about nature into English, especially the one of the author musing in a forest glade.

Stone breathed a modest fame into *The Open Air* (1946), an anthology of country life edited by Adrian Bell. His thirty or so little white-line wood-engraved vignettes of the English countryside so reincarnate the charm of Thomas Bewick's wood engravings that the book will be precious as long as it is preserved. A sturdy oak, a farmhouse snug in the lee of a hill, a deserted croft, a stone barn, an old churchyard, a wanderer resting among sweeping hills – these and other blocks, like some of Charles Tunnicliffe's and Joan Hassall's, evoke a beauty that the master ignored. But they are little tonal prints, with only general relation to the text and none of Bewick's salty anecdotal humor. For Leslie

Paul's reminiscences of a country boyhood, *The Living Hedge* (1946), Stone's small title-page engraving, four full-page blocks, and half-page design facing the last page might be considered his chief interpretive illustrations, for in all but one, a small boy is present in a scene mentioned in the text. The full-page engraving of a boy kneeling beside a shaded woodland rill establishes precisely the features and mood of the scene implicit in the words "and there still, welling clear and cold and mysteriously from a small bank which you could never find unless you knew where to look, was the beginning of a river" (fig. 175). The cut transmits the warmth of the sun on the bark of the old tree, the coolness of the dark spring, the spicy smell of the fern, and the peacefulness far away from town noises.

Among eight smaller blocks for another book of boyhood memories, Forrest Reid's *Apostate* (1947), that depicting the old graveyard with "Part Six" on a tilted gravestone is a modern classic of white-line engraving. In 1958, the Monotype Corporation of London printed 500 gift copies of *Boxwood* with sixteen of Stone's wood engravings, and in 1960, *Boxwood* was published commercially with five more of his engravings, four from *The Open Air*. Both editions have the subtitle *Illustrated in Verse by Sylvia Townsend Warner*. The small vignettes of rustic scenes are poems enough. Stone was an odd choice to illustrate Herman Melville's *Omoo* (1961). In the thirty-nine wood engrav-

176. Graham Sutherland. David Gascoyne, *Poems, 1937–1942* (1943).

ings, he made no attempt to follow the narrative; but he did far better than had Robert Gibbings in rendering the exotic Polynesian setting, as in a splendid view of Papeete Bay.

Graham Sutherland

The painter Graham Sutherland (1903–80), in his early years an etcher and engraver influenced by Samuel Palmer, turned to semiabstraction during the Second World War. At that time, he illustrated two books, each in a different, unconventional style. The five large lithographs in *Henry VI. Part 1* (1940) show stark, spotlighted figures against plain dark backgrounds with almost no indication of settings. The moments chosen are capriciously secondary ones. At the conclusion of the duel to test Joan (I.ii), the Dauphin cries, "Stay, stay thy hands! Thou art an Amazon." Sutherland pictured Joan in fencing posture with her back to the viewer. In the most interesting design of the five, two figures leap in the air, one above the other, to illustrate a stage direction: "The French leape ore the walles in their shirts" (II.i). Sutherland's lithographs are evocative, but not of Shakespeare.

David Gascoyne's *Poems, 1937–1942* (1943) contains five colored full-page drawings by Sutherland. In addition, the similar designs on the front and back covers might count as illustrations. These illustrations are perceptions of what

the poet is saying stated in terms of equal aesthetic validity. They seem to have been drawn in ink, chalk, crayon, and gray wash with touches of violet. In the drawing for the first group of poems, a cometlike form, suggesting the Christ of the verse, streams across a black void above a jagged wasteland touched with red-crayon flames. By the time Gascoyne came to write the fifth group of poems, "Time & Place", the Second World War had begun, and Gascoyne was writing about it. Taking his cue from these lines in "Zero – September 1939"

> Yet through
> The blackness of his dungeon there still peer
> Man's eyes, unmoving, lit by their desire
> To see the worst, and yet not die
> Of their lucid despair
> But in such vision persevere
> Through time into Eternity

Sutherland created a staring mask made up, as it were, of two rough pieces of iron (fig. 176). The effect is to roll the madness, primitivism, and terror of war into an image that is more powerful than are the poems that follow.

Denis Tegetmeier

Much of the illustrative work of Denis Tegetmeier (b.

177. Denis Tegetmeier. Henry Fielding, *Jonathan Wild* (1932).

1895), including some for the writings of his father-in-law, Eric Gill, is broadly comic. His six designs in Henry Fielding's *Journey from This World to the Next* (1930), seven in Fielding's *Jonathan Wild* (1932), and eleven (eight full-page) in Laurence Sterne's *Sentimental Journey* (1936) put him among the most workmanlike of modern English interpretive illustrators. For these books, he etched his drawings with a sharp clean line, virtually indistinguishable from that of an engraving. Without detailed descriptions to help him, Tegetmeier carefully visualized characters in action, and he reproduced perfectly the special accent of Fielding's and Sterne's unsentimental realism and raillery. In *Jonathan Wild*, the dupe Bagshot relieving Count La Ruse of his gambling winnings as Wild looks on is representative of Tegetmeier's etched work (fig. 177). His choice of passages to illustrate – and not to illustrate – is sometimes open to criticism. For instance, in the final scene of *Jonathan Wild*, the reader can do without a view of the body of the antihero dangling from the gallows, especially since his final gesture – picking the parson's pocket of a corkscrew – epitomizes the spirit of the novel.

Feliks Topolski

Although a native of Poland, Feliks Topolski (b. 1907) has lived in London since the beginning of the Second World War. He is well known as a portraitist, caricaturist, and theatrical designer as well as an illustrator. His book and magazine work has mainly been that of a traveler and a factual observer of the social scene. Twelve full-page portrait figures, some sepia wash and some red crayon, illustrate George Bernard Shaw's play *In Good King Charles's Golden Days* (1939). A few skillful twirls of the brush for masses, some seemingly careless swirling lines, a precise and expressive indication of eyes and features – and Charles II, Isaac Newton, Nell Gwynn, and Charles's other contemporaries stand before us as if drawn from life. In the same war year, for Shaw's play *Geneva*, Topolski drew savagely satirical portraits of fifteen real and imaginary figures, including Hitler, Mussolini, and Franco, and many line sketches. Among the latter are numerous good-humored designs, such as those that depict the sexy secretary Begonia Brown, GBS at ease at a rehearsal, and "Mr Shaw suggests a title-page".

Topolski was limited to pen-and-ink drawings for the paperback edition of Shaw's *Pygmalion* (1941). The drawings lost much of their *brio* through reduction and printing on wartime paper. Nevertheless, the approximately 100 dashing loose-line sketches are often electrifying in the way they seize on the essence of the text. The flower girl, a Covent Garden huckster and his donkey, Higgins and Pickering in conversation, the flower girl presented to

283

178. Feliks Topolski. George Bernard Shaw, *Pygmalion* (1941).

Higgins, Mrs. Pearce giving Eliza a bath, the magisterial Doolittle – Topolski snatched Shaw's characters out of the air, unerring as a salamander, as can be seen in the illustration of Eliza's entrance into society (fig. 178).

In 1950, Topolski made about forty line-drawing vignettes of great vivacity for *Prince Isidore*, a diverting novel of Naples in 1830 by Harold Mario Mitchell Acton. Whether it is a state procession, a naval battle, or an amorous dalliance, Topolski hit off his scenes with a play of lines that are less tangled than those in *In Good King Charles's Golden Days* but just as telling and dynamic. Unfortunately, Topolski's drawing became progressively more slapdash. It reached its nadir in an edition of Leo Tolstoy's *War and Peace* (1971), illustrated with what seem to be Topolski's first rough sketchbook notes and a few unrelated and much reduced pen drawings.

Charles Frederick Tunnicliffe

Because as often as not he dealt with the practical aspects of natural history and country life, Charles F. Tunnicliffe (b. 1901) drew primarily literal, almost photographic illustrations, some certainly from photographs. But like Thomas Bewick, the artist he most resembles, he introduced into his factual series occasional designs of considerable charm. In the collections of essays and similar works listed in the Catalog, however, many of the illustrations are sadly prosaic. Furthermore, Tunnicliffe used the facile but never wholly satisfactory medium of scraperboard to make the designs that appear in most of the books that he illustrated. In the two books for which he engraved his designs on wood, he proved himself one of the twentieth-century masters of the art.

Lone Swallows (1933) is the most appealing of the five books by the popular naturalist Henry Williamson illustrated by Tunnicliffe because of the variety of the twenty-four full-page scenes, such as gulls following a plow, birds among blossoms in a cottage yard, boys seeking out bird nests, and an owl among the ships on the Thames. Tunnicliffe turned to engraving on wood for his eighty-two designs in *A Book of Birds* (1937), edited by Mary Priestley. No doubt he was encouraged to do so by his publisher, who had just proved how acceptable Agnes Miller Parker's wood engravings could be in a trade edition. *A Book of Birds* is an anthology of brief passages from distinguished writers. Among Tunnicliffe's authoritative engravings of various sizes, those of the goldfinch, snipe, missel thrush, tawny owl, song thrush, woodcock, house sparrow and cat, and ivory-billed woodpecker are superb.

Perhaps because of wartime conditions, Tunnicliffe returned to using scraperboard. He was unquestionably a master of this dubious medium, as the fourteen full-page

284

179. Charles F. Tunnicliffe. H. E. Bates, *In the Heart of the Country* (1942).

180. Clifford Webb. H. G. Wells, *The Country of the Blind* (1939).

illustrations and fourteen chapter headpieces in H. E. Bates's wartime essays, *In the Heart of the Country* (1942), demonstrate. Few engravers could get more sensitive values from wood or more featly capture the peace and excitement of the author's chance meeting with a young fisherman than Tunnicliffe does in his scraperboard illustration of "The boy baited up with breadcrumb and began to pull little rudd out of the pond as easy as picking gooseberries" (fig. 179). *My Country Book* (1942), an autobiographic account, tells of Tunnicliffe's enthusiasm for drawing pigs and similar country subjects but says little about the practice of illustration. Among the many prosaic illustrations in Watson's *Walking with Fancy* (1943) and *The Leaves Return* (1947) are some of Tunnicliffe's most appealing drawings. Several, such as a black cat among blackberries and a fox in bracken, would have been beautiful had they been engraved on wood.

In his second major work as a wood engraver, *Wild Life in a Southern County* (1949), Tunnicliffe proved himself one of the best interpreters of Richard Jefferies. The eight full-page, nine half-page, and three smaller illustrations achieve a good deal of visual poetry through the subtleties of white-line engraving. Most of the designs are of birds, but the frontispiece of a hare and a half-page design of a village cobbler are part of the variety that Tunnicliffe extracted from the essays. In "The Hamlet", Jefferies wrote

about farm wagons and used ships at sea as his epic simile. Tunnicliffe created a heroic splay-wheeled farm wagon resting amid Canterbury bells, mint, and milkweed while pigs root in luxury and chickens and daws perch importantly on a cradle top beneath stately trees. For almost forty years, Tunnicliffe illustrated with unassuming and congenial line drawings more than a score of books of essays about life in the country by Alison Uttley. The books are too numerous and unpretentious to be listed in the Catalog. Among the illustrations are some delightful ones – a robin and a clump of snowdrops in *A Year in the Country* (1957), for instance. A collection of all the illustrations would compose an almost encyclopedic social record of rural England over nearly a century.

Several books contain color plates by Tunnicliffe. The fifty-two full-page watercolors in *Our Bird Book* (1947), on which he collaborated with Sydney Rogerson, especially proclaim Charles Tunnicliffe as a modern master of bird painting.

Clifford Webb

The heavy woodcut style that afflicted the revival of wood engraving during the 1920s influenced Clifford Webb (1895–1972) when he belatedly began illustrating adult books. (He had illustrated several children's books begin-

286

181. Ethelbert White. Richard Jefferies, *The Story of My Heart* (1923).

ning as early as 1931.) But he engraved with great clarity of line and strength of form the odd assortment of books with remote settings for which he had to invent scenes. Webb early demonstrated his ability to be an illustrator, not just a printmaker, in designs such as that of a tame boa protecting an Indian child by fighting a tiger in Ventura García Calderón's *White Llama* (1938). He then enriched his strongly patterned designs with a variety of graver texturing, as in the three full-page illustrations for H. G. Wells's paradoxical tale *The Country of the Blind* (1939). In the order that the events occur, the first shows the outsider Nunez looking down on the country of the blind – a stunning engraving of a difficult subject. Next, although printed as the frontispiece, Nunez defending himself without harming the blind men dramatizes his moral dilemma and proves that in the country of the blind, sight does not necessarily make one king (fig. 180). In this design, without abdicating his role of interpreter, Webb created one of the finest wood engravings made during this great period of autographic wood engraving. In the third creative illustration, Nunez sits on the floor and watches the blind Medina-saroté, whom he loves.

The illustrations in the books that followed at intervals of two or three years do not have the sensuous appeal of the three in *The Country of the Blind*. Their cool intellectual quality derives largely from the nature of their subjects and from the conscientious research needed to deal with such diverse works as *Gesta Francorum: The First Crusade* (1945), a novel translated by Somerset de Chair; Ivar Bannett's *Amazons* (1948); Julius Caesar's *Commentaries* (1951), an account of the Gallic Wars and the Civil War; and de Chair's *Story of a Lifetime* (1954), a life of Christ. For all except Caesar's *Commentaries*, Webb drew fewer than ten designs each, but they are often large, handsome, and genuinely satisfying to the reader.

Rex Whistler

Before his death as a tank captain during the Second World War, Rex Whistler (1905–44) was engaged in architecture and in the design of stage sets, murals, and book jackets, as well as in book illustration. Most of his book work is decorative and has been so described. His one remembered illustrated book is a luxurious two-volume 205-copy edition of Jonathan Swift's *Gulliver's Travels* (1930). The twelve full-page lightly hand-tinted illustrations take the form of scenes viewed through elaborate darker black-and-white frames. They have been described as engravings, but seem to be pen drawings. In their pseudobaroque elegance and playful spirit, they are closely related to Richard Bentley's series for *Designs by Mr. R. Bentley, for Six Poems by Mr. T. Gray* (1753). Each frame, acting as the wings of a theater but extending the action, adds a great deal of interest to the illustration proper; in the second design of Volume II, for example, Gulliver is shown Lagado, the capital of Balnibarbi, by Lord Munodi, while miserable citizens pursue their eccentric ways about the tenements in the ruins, as on a stage (pl. VI). The young Whistler's *Gulliver's Travels* series is one of the most charming in an English book, but for that reason, it cannot deal adequately with Swift's bitter indictment of humankind, especially in the second half.

Never again did Whistler have the chance to realize the great promise of this early book. While in training with the Welsh Guards, he made ten wash drawings in the eighteenth-century-French manner for Alfred Edward Woodley Mason's *Königsmark* (1952), which were published without text; twenty-two wash drawings for Simon Harcourt-Smith's tale *The Last of Uptake* (1942); and one color plate and ten humorous wash drawings for Edith Olivier's *Night Thoughts of a Country Landlady* (1943).

Ethelbert White

Although it is said that Ethelbert White (1891–1972) was one of the earliest twentieth-century advocates of white-line wood engraving, he was a practitioner in a nominal sense only. Like most other artists working on wood before 1930, he carried over to books the zest for broad, bold effects that they produced in their woodcut-like prints. These designs overpower the type, divorce the image from the text, and interfere with the reading of the book. This is true of White's seven illustrations for Carlo Goldoni's *Good-Humoured Ladies* as early as 1922 and half-dozen or so "wood engravings" for Henry Thoreau's *Walden* as late as 1938. Nevertheless, White's twelve designs for *The Story of My Heart* (1923) by Richard Jefferies are memorable in twentieth-century illustration. Jefferies was a man of vehement opinions. In Chapter X, he says, "If the whole of the dead in a hillside cemetery were called up alive from their tombs, and walked forth down into the valley, it would not rouse the mass of people from the dense pyramid of stolidity which presses on them." The heavy blacks of White's design do very well to illustrate this grim procession (fig. 181). And as Jefferies inveighs against the "must" of logic and says, "Nothing is straight, but all things curved, crooked, and unequal," White created a somber analogue from the twisted, lightning-shattered base of a great willow tree. In spite of the funereal borders and clutter of headpieces and tailpieces, Ethelbert White's illustrations for *The Story of My Heart* are a 1923 manifesto for autographic wood engraving.

CHAPTER ELEVEN

The Twentieth Century (III)
1946–1976

The last period of the twentieth century covered in this book extends from the end of the Second World War to the quincentenary of book publishing in England. There is no significance otherwise in the terminal date. The advance in population, affluence, education, technology, number of readers, and number of books was not reflected in the illustration of serious literature, although it was in that of children's books. The problem was economic, not artistic; readers, as well as talented illustrators, still delighted in pictures in the company of words. Combined with the high costs of book production was the competition for reading time from the automobile, motion pictures, radio, and television. Yet thanks to the Folio Society, the Limited Editions Club, Macdonald Illustrated Classics, and notable individual volumes, such as *The Oxford Illustrated Old Testament*, the cause of serious book illustration in England was not wholly lost. But the book clubs were probably to a considerable degree responsible for the unexciting and repetitive nature of the illustrations in many of their books, and artists sometimes seemed to be doing a minimal job. At a time when so little respect was shown to traditional values, it is strange that so little change occurred in book illustration. No Imre Reiner or Josef Hegenbarth turned up to introduce, say, an equivalent of the informality that distinguished the style of clothing of those years. That uncopyrighted literary classics, the staple of book clubs and illustrated trade editions, tend to be read by conservative readers explains only how such books were sold for thirty years after 1946.

Several artists who began their careers in the years between the wars were responsible for some of the best work in the postwar period and thus may have been a conservative influence. And some of the leaders of the period – Eric Fraser, Anthony Gross, Clarke Hutton, and Lynton Lamb – whose postwar publication dates place them in these thirty years, were much older than their apparent contemporaries, another explanation for the absence of innovation. Yet some artists of the new generation, instead of being pressed by diminished opportunities into

a defeatist casualness toward illustration, have manifested both a responsible understanding of the meaning and mood of imaginative literature and an earnest intention to make each design a serious visual statement of a significant moment in the text. Thus they share the state of mind that moved the great illustrators of the past, and they offer hope that book illustration in England may recapture some of its glory.

Wood engraving and lithography were the favored media of the postwar generation of illustrators, although good examples of pen-and-ink and watercolor designs are not wanting. John Buckland-Wright, Blair Hughes-Stanton, Agnes Miller Parker, Reynolds Stone, and other wood engravers whose careers spanned some of the second and third periods did much of their brilliant characteristic work during the third. The wood engravings of Frank Martin, Garrick Palmer, and Peter Reddick are not so decorative as those of their seniors, but at their best, they are excellent as straightforward, vivid realizations of narrative texts. These three artists did not, as did David Gentleman, seek to re-create the charm of the past but to use the traditional materials and tools to create fresh visions evoked by the texts of the books that they illustrated. One disappointment was the absence of women successors to Joan Hassall, Gertrude Hermes, Gwenda Morgan, and Parker.

More promising for the future, however, was the increased use of new direct processes to illustrate books, especially by autographic lithographs, sometimes in more than one color. Lithography can often produce a range of emotional effects, from dramatic power to subtle expressions, beyond the usual capacity of line drawings and wood engravings. It never has had a significant role in interpretive book illustration in England. The lithographs of Gross, Robin Jacques, Lamb, and Nigel Lambourne are sometimes admirable, although they never approach the high level of creative excitement that characterizes the lithographs of the great European illustrators who use that medium.

182. Eric Fraser. Ippolito Nievo, *The Castle of Fratta* (1954).

Writing about living illustrators is full of uncertainty – even as to whether they are still living. Some of the artists who are discussed in this chapter will illustrate more books and grow in stature. Others will do little or nothing to justify the promise discerned here. One certainty is that the judgments about contemporary illustrators will be subject to even more amendment than will be those about their predecessors in their 500-year-old craft.

Michael Ayrton

Although he illustrated books, Michael Ayrton (1921–75) gave his main efforts to painting, printmaking, sculpture, and art criticism. The ten lithographs in his earliest book, John Webster's *Duchess of Malfi* (1945), are extremely promising for a man in his early twenties. His sixteen color lithographs, plus another one for the wraparound cover design, in *Poems of Death* (1945) are somber and striking variations on the theme of enduring night. For *Clausentum* (1946), John Arlott's verse celebration of an ancient settlement near Southampton, Ayrton made seven drawings of buildings and places in a style much like that of his friends John Minton and John Piper. As late as Apuleius's *Transformations of Lucius* (1960), from *The Golden Ass*, Ayrton introduced a nervous jocularity that strains to catch the equivocal tone of the picaresque narratives. In 1951, he

illustrated *Macbeth* with eight full-page lithographs. In an introductory note, he wrote that they were conceived "in terms of a potential production of a play".

The nine comic figures for Wyndham Lewis's three novels published in two volumes under the title *The Human Age* (1956, 1955) are too simple to illustrate Lewis's eccentric trilogy. And Ayrton's designs for his *Testament of Daedalus* (1962), a prose and verse monologue by Daedalus after his flight from Crete to Cumae, were drawn at various times mostly as studies for sculptures and paintings or as separate prints dealing with the myth of Daedalus and Icarus. The text was written after the designs had been drawn. Only one or two of the sixteen large full-page monochromatic drawings for *Medea* (five), *Hippolytus* (four), and *The Bacchae* (seven) (1967) convey anything of the emotion of the noble poetry of Euripides. The rest celebrate violence through crude distortions of expression and anatomy and trivialize tragedy by making explicit some of the most brutal moments in the plays. A chorus of Corinthian women listening to Medea's plans to poison Jason's new favorite and kill her sons is more Euripidean than are most of the other designs.

Eric George Fraser

His career as a commercial artist required Eric Fraser (b.

183. David Gentleman. John Clare, *The Shepherd's Calendar* (1964).

1902) to draw with pen and ink most of the time, often on scraperboard with restrained suggestions of wood engraving. The results in his illustrations are not always attractive. The eight drawings for Ippolito Nievo's *Castle of Fratta* (1954) and six for Petronius's *Ephesian Matron* (1966), said to be pen and wash on linoleum, are much richer in effect. In the first, the whirling design of the smuggler Spaccafumo routing the three ruffians who have waylaid Leonardo (fig. 182) suggests that Fraser would now seem to be a superior illustrator had he been able to use this approximation of lithography – or, better, lithography – in all the books that he illustrated. Nevertheless, his black-and-white scraperboard designs are always clear and spirited, not perfunctory. Fraser's ten full-page line drawings with a pink partial tint added and twenty black-and-white headpieces and tailpieces in *The Art of Love* (1971) are among his most expressive designs, although their effort to match Ovid's wit is hindered by the heavy outlines and the burlesque of the classical style.

David Gentleman

Much fine work by David Gentleman (b. 1930) is in children's and informational books. For example, the many wood engravings, including thirty-one full-page designs in black and light brown and thirty-six smaller ones in black and white, in Johann David Wyss's *Swiss Family Robinson* (1963) add a good deal to this rewriting of *Robinson Crusoe* with a family substituted for a lone sailor. Their house in a hollow tree is a delight to adults as well as children. Gentleman used Thomas Bewick's technique, with modifications, to complement John Clare's verse in thirteen small wood-engraved vignettes for *The Shepherd's Calendar* (1964). They are done with modesty, charm, and humor – for example, the design for May, a boy racing gaily across a church burial ground, to illustrate the lines "The village children mad for sport . . . Oft leaping grave stones leaning hights" (fig. 183). The seventy pen drawings, twelve with tint added, for John Keats's *Poems* (1966) are disappointing, partly because the drawing of human figures and faces seems to be uncongenial for Gentleman. None of the few interpretive designs, including the central one in "The Eve of St. Agnes", a teen-age Madeline in a summery gown praying in what seems to be broad daylight, suggest the dreamlike mood of lines like those beginning "A casement high and triple-arched there was".

Philip Gough

Over thirteen years, Philip Gough (b. 1908) illustrated Jane Austen's novels with several color plates in each volume: *Emma* (1948), *Pride and Prejudice* (1951), *Mansfield Park*

184. Philip Gough. Jane Austen, *Northanger Abbey* (1961).

(1957), *Sense and Sensibility* (1958), *Persuasion* (1961), and *Northanger Abbey* (1961). His ten pen drawings for Anthony Trollope's *Last Chronicle of Barset* (1957) are merely amiable imitations of Victorian illustrations. The difference lies in the medium, not in the artist. For the series in Austen's novels, Gough made graceful outline drawings of properly costumed ladies and gentlemen sitting on authentic furniture, riding in vintage vehicles, and appearing near stately country houses, and then he washed his drawings with soft complementary roses and blues and ochers and greens. They are witty as well as good looking, as can be seen in an illustration in *Northanger Abbey* (fig. 184). With a quiet smile, Gough evoked the Regency atmosphere of the novels and the memory of Edwardian color plates. His immediate inspiration probably was the illustrations of John Austen and Rex Whistler. Gough eventually found more demand for his talents in juvenile books.

Rigby Graham

Critic and printer as well as graphic artist, Rigby Graham (b. 1931) has confined his illustrating mostly to pamphlet-length limited editions printed primarily in Leicester by private presses, including his own. He has followed his teacher John Piper in his techniques, subjects, and distaste for the painstaking illustration of his predecessors. Instead

of illustrating trade editions of the classics, he has contributed very free brush drawings, monotypes (single impressions on paper made from inked designs on other surfaces), line cuts, and silk-screen color plates of buildings, landscapes, and craft processes to books and booklets with short original texts, mainly of local history, poetry, and crafts. These modest items probably will become collectors' trove because of the delightful drawings, especially those in color; they are also fine examples of printing on hand presses, some on handmade paper.

What Graham says about his drawings in Frank Lissauer's *Lost Shepherd and Other Poems* (1974) applies to virtually all his literary illustrations: they "make no attempt to illustrate in the usual sense: they merely accompany the poems and offer a visual parallel to the mood and some of the ideas and feelings engendered" by the writings. They are appropriate – for instance, the village memorial to John Clare in Clare's *Lines Written in Northampton County Asylum* (1959), a bat flying and a hot sun seeming to spin between sharp hills in Algernon Swinburne's *Garden of Proserpine* (1961), and the local scenes called up by Shelley's *Lines Written among the Euganean Hills* (1961 [1962]).

By example as well as precept, Graham has been a constructive force in English book illustration. Thus most of the books he has illustrated are listed in the Catalog. The most substantial series are in Oscar Wilde's *Serenade* (1962),

185. Rigby Graham. Margaret McCord, *Abbeys and Churches* (1971).

the American folk ballad *A Song in Favour of Bundling* (1963), Oliver Bayldon's *Paper Makers Craft: Verse by Oliver Bayldon* (1965), David Tew's *Oakham Canal* (1968), Graham's *Slieve Bingian: A Cycle of Prints and Drawings* (1968), Penelope Holt and Edmond Thorpe's *Gold and Books* (1969), Margaret McCord's *Tower Houses and Ten Pound Castles* (1970) and *Abbeys and Churches* (1971), Mervyn James's *Mountains* (1972), David Rogers's *Peddars Way* (1974), and Marion Hunter's *Golden Orchid: Fantasy* (1975). Graham drew the designs for some of these books on the spot while the text was being written; yet they always are integral to the work, in which he was usually a publishing partner. The example shown from *Abbeys and Churches* is typical of his work (fig. 185).

Anthony Gross

Illustration has been only incidental to the career of Anthony Gross (b. 1905), who is primarily a painter, an etcher, and an art teacher. In his sixteen full-page line drawings for Emily Brontë's *Wuthering Heights* (1944), Gross evoked the feeling for the wild drama of the moorlands, but the roughness of the sketchy drawings seems ostentatious. His illustrations for a jumbo one-volume edition of John Galsworthy's *Forsyte Saga* (1950) are much more successful. The twelve full-page color plates and twenty-seven full-page black-and-white line drawings, produced by a special lithographic process, are both elegant and stylistically reflective of the text. They are pleasant interludes in the 800 pages of Galsworthy's unhurried narrative, and their general approach is right. *Forsyte Saga* makes at least three demands on an illustrator: it is steeped in the particularities of scene and time; it sometimes is transformed by the "impingement of Beauty"; and it is pervaded by an ironical view of the problems of people of property. Gross was assiduous in documenting the gradually changing scene with such details as chandeliers and cruets at formal dinners by gaslight, an oasis of quiet in Cheapside (fig. 186), bicycling costumes, the bulbous façades of Park Lane, and the arrival of the motorcar on carriage springs. At the same time, he effected an awareness of lovely ladies and muddled men in a society whose elegance, pretense, and transience are symbolized by the fragility of his drawings.

In direct contrast, the score or so line drawings in Henry James's essays *English Hours* (1960), mostly of buildings, have little in common with the formalities of James's prose. According to a note by Gross, his illustrations for Genesis 37–50 in *The Oxford Illustrated Old Testament* (1968, 1969) were based on sketches made in the Near East during the Second World War and in France on holidays. In addition, he used some etchings that he had on hand, including one

186. Anthony Gross. John Galsworthy, *Forsyte Saga* (1950).

abstract design and etchings that depict camel caravans on the march, sheep grazing, and harvesting scenes. But most of this second half of Genesis is taken up with the story of Joseph, one of the greatest dramatic narratives in all literature. To fail to deal with it seriously is to not illustrate Genesis.

Clarke Hutton

Color plates made Clarke Hutton (b. 1898) belatedly popular as an illustrator of books for adults as well as for children, with little differentiation in his technique. The modest line vignettes that often accompany the lithographic color plates help carry the stories forward without being illustrations. But the large color plates tend to appear ostentatious without engaging the text on more than a superficial level. In this respect, Hutton's seventeen full-page and about the same number of smaller color lithographs in John Bunyan's *Pilgrim's Progress* (1947) are superior to most of his later series. Many of Hutton's designs are portraits of characters; that of Elizabeth I in *Kenilworth* (1966) is one of the best of the twelve plates that Hutton did for Sir Walter Scott's historical novel. In general, Hutton's plates create a rich dim effect, but individually are too often ordinary drawings obscured by an overlay of dark colors. The twelve dark plates in *Villette* (1967) harmonize with the oppressive

atmosphere of Charlotte Brontë's fictionalized account of her experience in a Brussels girls' school. Another dozen plates in Jane Austen's *Northanger Abbey* (1971) exhibit more variety of tone, composition, and detail. Hutton imaginatively interpreted the words "Henry Tilney explains himself" by showing an aerial view of the small figures of Catherine and Henry walking down a country road with crows wheeling in the drab evening sky (fig. 187); this illustration reveals what Hutton might have done had he or his publishers not thought that the "market" required portraits of people. In 1974, Hutton livened up the eight plates in a volume of two plays by George Bernard Shaw, five for *Pygmalion* and three for *Candida*, several of which are surprisingly realistic. The striking design in *Pygmalion* of the metamorphosis of Eliza Doolittle proves that Hutton could have made his plates lighter and could have shown characters in moments of revealing animation.

Robin Jacques

In addition to being an illustrator, Chelsea-born Robin Jacques (b. 1920) has been a printer, a designer, an art director, and the author of a book about illustrating – all without formal art training. The characters in his careful pen drawings of heroes, heroines, eccentrics, and supporting cast are individualized without caricature. Jacques's

187. Clarke Hutton. Jane Austen, *Northanger Abbey* (1971).

technique reached maturity in Jonathan Swift's *Gulliver's Travels* (1955). The eight full-page illustrations and eight headpieces are simple, literal, and dignified tinted pen drawings; the one of Gulliver towering over the rooftops of the royal port of Blefescu with his two guides in his hands while, far below, natives on a ship, on the quay, and in windows stare up at him is an example.

An illustrated edition of a modern classic is so rare that it is a delight to see what Jacques did with James Joyce's *Portrait of the Artist as a Young Man* (1956). In his six illustrations, he depicted Mr. Dedalus sitting in pompous ease before the Christmas hearth, the bespectacled boy Stephen displaying his running form to the trainer Mike Flynn and to his Uncle Charles, Stephen being roughed up by his Belvedere schoolmates for having insisted that Byron was the greatest poet, Stephen being embraced by a prostitute in the presence of her doll, tight-faced Stephen passing the shrine of the Virgin among the poor cottages after he has been invited to become a priest, and Stephen unable to give a penny to a barefoot flower girl. The last illustration is a fine drawing (it slyly introduces the name Bloom on a shop window), but with almost 100 pages of rich episodes from which to choose, the incident is too insignificant to be the last choice. But all these too few illustrations are moments of insight into the tortured comedy of Stephen Dedalus's coming of age in middle-class Catholic Dublin.

Jacques's sixteen large full-page vignettes, including two double spreads, in Rudyard Kipling's *Kim* (1962) are meticulous line drawings shaded in his dotted manner and discreetly colored. Their rather tight photographic quality admirably serves Kipling's aim of presenting the real India, not *Lalla Rookh* exoticism, through the wanderings of the young secret agent. A little color would have helped Jacques's illustrations for *Vanity Fair* (1963), but his twenty-one line drawings do extremely well in realizing William Makepeace Thackeray's numerous leading male characters: Sir Pitt Crawley in his nightshirt; Captain George Osborne in his new uniform, despondent after Amelia breaks their engagement; faithful Dobbin surrounded by jeering boys after the wedding of Amelia and George; Jos Sedley, corpulent and complacent, being fitted for a waistcoat; and Rawdon Crawley seizing Lord Steyne by the neckcloth. Becky Sharp does not receive Jacques's usual gift of personality, and Amelia hardly appears.

In *Dubliners* (1967), Jacques again successfully met the challenge of illustrating Joyce. The fifteen full-page pen drawings, one for each story, were derived shrewdly from the text and are fastidiously drawn. The leading characters fill the foreground; and in harmony with the selective, symbolic nature of the short story, a few background bits – such as a broken fanlight, a corner of an obsolete tram, and

188. Robin Jacques. James Joyce, "Ivy Day in the Committee Room" in *Dubliners* (1967).

189. Charles Keeping. Erich Maria Remarque, *All Quiet on the Western Front* (1966).

the notice of a municipal election pasted on a wall – act as environmental signals. Jacques was extraordinarily faithful to Joyce's incisive descriptions, as in "Ivy Day in the Committee Room": Joyce says of two party canvassers that one was a fat man who had "a big face which resembled a young ox's face in expression, staring blue eyes and a grizzled moustache" and the other, "younger and frailer", had "a thin clean-shaven face"; Jacques made them absolutely right without falling into the error of caricature or of posed realism (fig. 188). Except in the last story, "The Dead", for which he drew a painstaking portrait of a bit-part servant instead of the principals, Jacques succeeded in *Dubliners* in doing what illustrators rarely manage to do: increasing the reader's knowledge of the characters and what happens to them.

The sixteen full-page vignettes in *The Poems of William Butler Yeats* (1970) are line drawings subtly colored by stencil. Together with nineteen smaller uncolored vignettes, they are the finest of Jacques's series of illustrations and among the finest of modern series. Beautifully finished, their exceptional quality derives from the sensitivity and aptness with which Jacques adjusted to Yeats's wide range of subject and mood during his long career. They include emblems and figures of misty Irish legends, the grim realism of a dead partisan in front of a brick wall for "Easter 1916", a bundled, worried man in the country

for "Ballad of Father Gilligan", and three fresh-faced girls for "Among School Children".

Jacques's thirty-five illustrations in *Folklore, Myths and Legends of Britain* (1973) are as well executed as his earlier work. Jacques clearly looked on ghosts and other manifestations of the supernatural with tolerance and amusement, for his designs are tinged with derision rather than with strangeness.

In recent years, Robin Jacques increasingly has confined himself to illustrating literature for young people, which is their good fortune but a loss to older lovers of illustrated books.

Charles Keeping

Like many of his contemporaries, Charles Keeping (b. 1924) has illustrated more books for young people than for adults. The color plates in them are lovely, amusing, and convincing, although some seem to be too sophisticated for any but precocious children. His best adult work has been lithographic. Keeping's twelve two-color lithographs for Emily Brontë's *Wuthering Heights* (1964) are effective because this novel lends itself to the expressionistic treatment of his rough, black, and enigmatic figures caught in broad sepia swirls and intersecting bands. He did not shy away from the violence and alienation that characterized the novel.

Keeping got his perfect assignment in Erich Maria Remarque's *All Quiet on the Western Front* (1966). His twelve full-page lithographs, too strong for ordinary fiction, are exactly right to transmit the agony and comedy of this classic of the First World War. Each design is wrought from a schema of slashing black figures, given body by a flat brown tint, and then charged with drama by patches of white. The series moves with great power from the depiction of the young soldiers playing cards, through terrible scenes of war – such as one of a scarecrow-like corpse hanging on barbed wire and another of the terrified narrator, Paul, stumbling on a dying Frenchman – to the profoundly moving illustration for the brief epilogue about Paul (fig. 189):

He fell in October 1918, on a day that was so quiet and still on the whole front that the army report confined itself to the single sentence: All quiet on the Western Front. . . . He had fallen forward and lay on the earth as though sleeping.

The twenty full-page pen-and-ink drawings for Feodor Dostoyevsky's *Idiot* (1971) depict figures and heads with exaggerated features against ugly black, hard-edged shapes, such as crosses and *L*s. They are regrettable. Even the five strong brush drawings done in red wash and line for the final section of *Folklore, Myths and Legends of Britain* (1973) show only isolated heroes. Victor Hugo's *Les Misérables* (1976) offered Keeping another grand challenge, and forty-eight full-page lithographs gave him exceptional scope to meet it. He devoted his energies to making tricky drawings of mainly single figures without accessories, settings, or backgrounds. These figures, some of which are inexplicably dark in parts, are often treated with a humorous exaggeration that is unsuitable to Hugo's monumental chronicle; indeed, exactly the same exaggeration appears in Keeping's illustrations for some children's stories.

Lynton Lamb

Few artists have been as well equipped to be book illustrators as Lynton Lamb (1907–77). He was not only a painter and art teacher, but also a book designer and author, and he wrote a thoughtful treatise on all aspects of illustration. As early as 1930, he began decorating books with simple wood engravings, but the books listed in the Catalog fall within the third period of the twentieth century. Like his contemporary Edward Ardizzone, Lamb adopted with almost doctrinaire rigidity a broken-line style that seems to have been achieved by means of a pen and dry brush. These drawings tend to be small, minimal, and matter-of-fact. They are effective in providing physical and social background to narratives and in documenting nonfiction works,

such as Lamb's *County Town* (1950), a collection of essays inspired by a town in Essex where he lived. His sixty-one vignettes of the prosy present – a brewery, bicycle riders, street loungers, a pub, a steam train on a viaduct, and so on – may become poetic in the future. Lamb's drawings also serve satisfactorily in children's books. But in works of imaginative adult literature, his gray drawings often seem to be dispirited.

When Lamb adopted lithography, sometimes combined with line drawings, as his medium, he was not always successful. The lithographs in Anthony Trollope's *Can You Forgive Her?* (1948), George Eliot's *Silas Marner* (1953), and Henry James's *Washington Square* (1963) do not add a great deal to the reader's understanding of the novels. Nevertheless, the eight full-page lithographs, with their strong contrasts, in Trollope's *Two Heroines of Plumplington* (1954) arouse interest better than do the many small line drawings. Furthermore, in this belated first edition of the 112-page novelette – its previous publication was in the 1882 Christmas number of *Good Words*, the month of Trollope's death – these lithographs are genuinely illustrative of, not merely supplementary to, the actual last chronicle of Barset. The one of the brewer Peppercorn calling on the banker Greenmantle in his inner office to tell him that their daughters are being gossiped about and that therefore they are "in the same boat" has little charm, but it embodies Trollope's ironic exposure of the social distinctions among the inhabitants of Plumplington and the delusions of importance of the two men. The melodramatic nature of Wilkie Collins's *Woman in White* (1956) enabled Lamb to fully exploit the resources of lithography for interpretive effects – stark whites clashing against the jet blacks and sinister grays to produce tensions that are necessary to the ten illustrations in this 500-page Victorian thriller. In the final plate, the exposed Count Fosco, sitting beside the open drawer of his desk, in which he has a gun ready to "scatter [Hartright's] brains about the fireplace", is a genuine villain, not the creature of a Hollywood make-up man's art, as he is in most editions.

With some reservations, *Tono-Bungay* (1960) by H. G. Wells contains Lamb's most satisfactory series of literary illustrations, sixteen full-page color plates and thirty-nine black-and-white drawings. They record the rise and fall of the entrepreneur Edward Ponderevo, as told by his nephew George, who disapproves of his uncle's unscrupulous promotion of patent medicines but nevertheless works for their success. Lamb's drawings mainly produce a sense of scene in which events take place and of the sort of people involved, but little of the specific episodes or of the effect of the action on the leading characters. Several of the color plates have no human beings in them. The black-and-white drawing

190. Lynton Lamb. H. G. Wells, *Tono-Bungay* (1960).

reproduced is one of the few that reflect character or action (fig. 190). Cigar in mouth, Edward Ponderevo, grown pompous with affluence, sits at his large clean desk. George Ponderevo stands, uneasy but alert. The adventurer Gordon-Nasmyth lounges in a chair, one of Edward Ponderevo's cigars in hand, while he offers a shady deal for making a nostrum out of "quap", an island mud – "the most radio-active stuff in the world" and theirs "for the taking". This design represents Lamb at his best as an interpretive illustrator of quiet character scenes.

For *The Oxford Illustrated Old Testament* (1968, 1969), Lamb illustrated Ruth, Psalms 73–106, Isaiah 57–66, and Tobit (in the Apocrypha). He returned to broken-line ink vignettes with skimpy or no backgrounds. Reduced in the printing, they seem weak in contrast with the more assertive drawings by other artists in these five volumes. But they also stand apart from most of the other illustrations because they convey the emotion, from lyricism to desolation, that characterizes these books of the Bible.

Nigel Lambourne

Few contemporary artists have had the opportunities enjoyed by Nigel Lambourne (b. 1919) to illustrate literary classics or the privilege to employ autographic lithography

so much of the time. Unfortunately, his drawings tend to look alike and not to be memorable, largely because his practice is to show one or two figures close up and, in the manner of Edgar Degas, at an odd angle, with some of the forms running off the page. The absence of localizing background or defining detail in illustration after illustration is devitalizing. Of the works of British literature that Lambourne has illustrated, Liam O'Flaherty's *Informer* (1961) comes off best, partly from the novelty of seeing a contemporary classic illustrated. There are eight lithographs of the characters in this grubby Irish masterpiece and one on the oyster linen binding, showing the informer looking at reward notices. Just as O'Flaherty's narrative transcends its thriller genre to become literature, so Lambourne's realistic drawings embody the tensions and violence of the story. For instance, Gypo, the dull-witted giant informer with the betrayal money on him, is upset by unexpectedly meeting Katie, his woman, in a pub. Without sentimentality or caricature, Lambourne showed the brute in the profile of Gypo and the faded prettiness in the sulky full-face of Katie (fig. 191). Then when the Revolutionary Organization avengers drag down Gypo by the force of sheer numbers, Lambourne showed his great bulk foreshortened and filling the page with one sinister figure throttling him. This may not be remarkable illustration,

191. Nigel Lambourne. Liam O'Flaherty, *The Informer* (1961).

but Lambourne's willingness to come to grips with the narrative on its own terms is refreshing.

John Lawrence

The twelve full-page vignettes in black and brown for Daniel Defoe's *History of Colonel Jack* (1967) by John Lawrence (b. 1933) are wood engravings done in a bold burin-and-scalper attack that extracts both textural variety and novelty from the block. At times, more cutting would have made forms and detail more intelligible, but the general effect of coarseness, excess, and violence of these engravings conveys an appropriate impression of Defoe's bruising picaresque "history" of illegitimate gentleman Jack. Lawrence's numerous small pen- or brush-and-ink vignettes for George Grossmith and Weedon Grossmith's humorous classic *The Diary of a Nobody* (1969) are vigorous and amusing, although they do not get inside the middle-class late-Victorian world of Mr. Pooter nearly as revealingly as do Weedon Grossmith's illustrations for the first edition (1892). But the forty illustrations for Laurence Sterne's *Tristram Shandy* (1970) reveal the characters to be as droll as Sterne would have us imagine them, in scenes made suitably bizarre by the artifices of wood engraving; a good example is the garden scene – Uncle Toby from his command post giving orders to Corporal Trim while the

Widow Wadman reconnoiters (fig. 192).

Marian Mahler [Mariana]

Textile designer, commercial artist, and illustrator of her own children's stories, Marian Mahler [Mariana] will be remembered for her illustration of one classic, Laurence Sterne's *Sentimental Journal* (1948). Her twenty-five full-page pen drawings and two double-spread end papers are entirely fresh visualizations of the droll scenes as they struck her delighted fancy. Underneath the jerky, wiry outlines, scratched-in foliage and shading, and improbable anatomy and architecture is sound draftsmanship; the overall effect is often that of a fine light etching that vibrates with tension. This broken-line style is exactly right as an accompaniment to Sterne's rapid, abruptly digressive prose. In what are often very funny drawings, Mahler got it all down: the servants dancing in the kitchen in Amiens, Yorick tenderly buying gloves from the *grisette*, the Abbé in the upper loge of the theater holding up his hands, the *fille de chambre* losing her balance, the notary knocking off the sentry's hat on the Pont Neuf, Yorick converting Madame de V*** from deism, Yorick consoling Maria by the roadside while his conveyance waits, and much more. Mahler conveyed Sterne's sense that something marvelous is always happening. She echoed the lyricism of Yorick's

192. John Lawrence. Laurence Sterne, *Tristram Shandy* (1970).

193. Frank Martin. Stendhal, *Scarlet and Black* (1965).

194. Charles Mozley. Maupassant, *The Tellier House* (1964).

The Lord Munodi takes him in his chariot to see the town of LAGADO.

Plate VI. Rex Whistler. Jonathan Swift, *Gulliver's Travels* (1930).

progress through the French towns and countryside, but included such dissonances as beggars and dogs biting fleas. The illustrations make tangible the gaiety of the rustics and the elegance of the beau monde; but the rustics are clownish, and the members of society, ugly.

Marian Mahler magically incorporated in her seemingly graceless drawings the passionate absorption in immediate surface experience, the special brand of sentimentalism, and the mocking sense of absurdity that keep Sterne's second masterpiece ever green.

Frank Vincent Martin

A pupil of Gertrude Hermes and Clifford Webb and himself a teacher of engraving, Frank Martin (b. 1921) naturally turned to the wood block when he began to illustrate books. His burin usually has served authors' interests rather than his own. Some of his neo-broadside cuts in Henry Fielding's *Jonathan Wild* (1956) are ineffective. As noted for Denis Tegetmeier, the illustration of Wild's body hanging after his execution is needless and tasteless. But the humor of Martin's depiction of Wild being captured in his own house is in the same key as Fielding's remark that in the Tower, the lieutenant-governor charged Wild "as exorbitant a price for lodging, as if he had a fine gentleman in custody for murder, or any other genteel crime".

Martin did an effective set of six black-and-brown full-page wood engravings and several headpieces for Thornton Wilder's *Bridge of San Luis Rey* (1956). They are a rare and welcome example of two-color wood blocks, and they achieve attractive atmospheric effects. A similar set in black and blue-gray for Oscar Wilde's *Salome* (1957) is heavily pseudoexotic, as are the twenty-six black-and-white designs that Martin did for Volumes II and IV of *The Book of the Thousand Nights and One Night* (1958). (Eric Fraser did twenty-six for Volumes I and III.) In these three series, Martin achieved lively decorative patterns, but he did not fully exploit the possibilities of wood engraving or enter seriously into imaginative interpretation. Far better in both respects are the thirteen full-page vignette wood engravings for Stendhal's *Scarlet and Black* (1965). They are honest evocations of events in this highly emotional novel, as is evident in the final illustration, which shows Mme. de Rênal visiting her lover Julien Sorel in the death cell after his attempt to kill her (fig. 193). Although made for a translation of a French work, Frank Martin's engravings form one of the best series of English illustrations of the postwar period.

John Minton

Had he lived longer and had the chance to illustrate more works of the imagination, John Minton (1917–57) probably would have shed the influence of John Piper and Graham Sutherland and become a book illustrator of considerable originality. As it is, his unlabored pen-and-brush drawings – with their dynamic line, knotted construction, and rough texture – decorate a number of books with honest informality. In 1948, Minton and Alan Ross brought out a two-man "note book" about Corsica, *Time Was Away*. The more than eighty drawings are related to the text, although often independent of it. The eight color plates make it a coveted travel book. "Clouded beauty of August thorn" in *The Country Heart* (1949), a revised edition of H. E. Bates's *O! More than Happy Countryman* and *The Heart of the Country*, evokes the tragic days of Dunkirk in 1940 as airplanes fought the Battle of Britain high above the peaceful countryside.

Charles Mozley

One of the most spirited lithographers of the 1960s, Charles Mozley (b. 1915) probably is not as well known for his designs in adult books as for his delightful color illustrations in numerous children's books. Some of the sixteen color lithographs and thirty-five pen-and-ink headpieces and incidental sketches in Anthony Trollope's *Duke's Children* (1954) are almost photographic scenes of suspended animation. The six lithographs done in the manner of the lithographs of Paul Gavarni, Henri Toulouse-Lautrec, and other French masters in *Concerning "Ulysses" and the Bodley Head* (1961), a publishing memento, echo the mocking tone of James Joyce and make us wish that Mozley had illustrated a complete edition of *Ulysses*. The eight pastel drawings for a book-club edition of George Bernard Shaw's *Man and Superman* (1962) seem meant to make a pleasant impression on a person "looking at the pictures" rather than on a reader. Dozens of the marginal sketches of people, which appear on almost every page of text, could have been sacrificed to make room for drawings of scenes with some Shavian humor and gusto. Encouragingly, for the trade edition of *Tellier House* (1964) by Guy de Maupassant, Mozley drew eleven large lithographs to illustrate the text, two for the covers, and one for the double-spread end papers. They transmit perfectly the incomparable Gallic flavor of this longish short story about a respectable Normandy madame and her five girls and clients and the celebration that follows a holiday they take to attend a child's Communion (fig. 194).

The thirty-six illustrations that Mozley drew for John

195. Garrick Palmer. Herman Melville, "Bartleby the Scrivener" in *Three Stories* (1967).

Galsworthy's *Man of Property* (1964) in the *Forsyte Saga* are his most impressive series. The twelve full-page "bled" lithographs, most in color, printed on the recto of leaves, twelve vignette sketches on the verso of the same leaves, and twelve smaller black-and-white line drawings show his exceptional ability to create personalities, moods, and milieux that are specific to a text. How perceptively he does this can be seen in the stiff demeanor of Soames, the man of property, and his wife, Irene, at the crisis of their marriage as they return to their house on Montpellier Square.

Mozley's twelve color plates and numerous full-page black-and-white drawings for H. G. Wells's *Invisible Man* (1967) revert to his earlier dependence on faces, single figures, and limited interaction. Faces are Mozley's strength and weakness. At their best, as they are only in the color plates, they combine realism with unostentation in an arresting way. But in the multiplicity of monochromatic drawings and a goodly share of the color plates, the ease suggests haste, the realism grows superficial, and the concentration on characters' appearance reduces setting and action to almost the vanishing point; the impression from book to book is one of repetition.

Garrick Salisbury Palmer

Three Stories (1967) by Herman Melville established

Garrick Palmer (b. 1933) as one of the best wood engravers of his generation to engage in book illustration. In the eight full-page blocks, he mixed starkly contrasting pure blacks and whites, white-line grays, and varied tonal effects by means of vermiculate texturing and extensive *criblé*. Off-literal drawing of faces and arbitrary patterning of shading give Palmer's designs a contemporary accent without eccentricity. Palmer's series for *Three Stories* is also witness to what interpretive illustration can be at its best. Every block is evocative of the sense of mysterious forces at work that runs through Melville's writing. In the first story, "Bartleby the Scrivener", the insubstantiality and incomprehensibility of the scrivener are made palpable by showing parts of the empty receding office through his head (fig. 195). And to illustrate the end of Bartleby in the Tombs, a notorious prison in New York, Palmer accepted the factual statement, "Strangely huddled at the base of the wall, his knees drawn up, and lying on his side his head touching the cold stones", but emphasized the horror by trussing the figure in writhing rhythms in a corner of the gray prison wall. The other two stories, "Benito Cereno" and "Billy Budd", are equally well served by wood engravings that are among the best examples of the reborn burin work of this time, tangible projections of physical aspects of the tales, and, most remarkable, images that are almost as emotive as Melville's prose, from which they rise.

The fifteen illustrations for a subsequent American folio

196. Peter Reddick. Thomas Love Peacock, *Crotchet Castle* (1964).

edition of *Benito Cereno* (1972), Melville's probing of the questions that arise as a result of a shipboard mutiny by African slaves, include one double spread of the slave ship and four full-page designs. The exceptional size of the blocks and the coarseness of the impressions suggest that they are woodcuts or linocuts. The illustration of the skull of the murdered Don Alexandro Aranda used as the ship's figurehead; the vertical view of Captain Delano stopping the admirable slave Babo from stabbing his escaping master, Captain Don Benito Cereno, as he lies in the *Bachelor's Delight* boat beneath the *San Dominick*; the depiction of Babo in chains; and the superb final, grim design of Babo's head on a post in the moonlit plaza in front of a Spanish church render events in Melville's convoluted tale with a power that is unusual in modern illustration.

Peter Reddick

Among illustrators of the second half of the twentieth century, Peter Reddick (b. 1924) is a major figure. His success stems from the unusually conscientious effort he makes to clothe imaginary characters and places in the semblance of reality. He takes pains to particularize faces and make them interesting. Then he transforms the traditionalism of his approach by means of bravura wood engravings that befit an artist of today using a technique of yesterday. His is true white-line engraving, in which forms and tones are fashioned out of black by tools of several sorts. Reddick uses multiple-tint-tool grays in the Russian wood-engraving manner, thick irregular blacks, and dotted white passages for rich textural effects; by canny shifts of direction of his shading, his dark designs take on a vivacity that would be lost at the hands of a Swain or a Dalziel. Some of his blocks would be helped by freer use of arbitrary whites to define main forms.

The first on the Catalog list of books illustrated by Reddick, Thomas Love Peacock's *Crotchet Castle* (1964) contains eight full-page vignettes. They depict thoughtfully selected scenes, and they were engraved with wit to match Peacock's satirical comedy of humors. Typical of Reddick's treatment is the illustration for the episode in which on one side of a chasm, the beautiful Miss Susannah sleeps in a tree that projects over a wild ravine, and the romantic Mr. Chainmail, a small figure in mid-leap high up against the sky – one hand clutching his stick, the other grasping his stovepipe hat, and his coattails flying – comes to her rescue (fig. 196).

The Mayor of Casterbridge (1968) is a prime example of how an artist can cooperate with a designer to produce a well-planned book without sacrificing his integrity. The thirty-six wood engravings for Thomas Hardy's classic are uniform in size, the same width as the text lines, which permits their often being inserted in precise conjunction with the words they illustrate – a rare phenomenon. These

197. Brian Robb. Aesop, *Fables of Aesop* (1954).

modest blocks are filled with characters who are sharply individualized by feature and dress and who are placed in rural surroundings of the most convincing authenticity. A sense of ceaseless variety arises both from the constant change of scene – kitchens, fairs, village streets, barns, graveyards, farmyards, lonely roads – and from shrewd shifts of point of view – close-ups of heads, half-figures, interiors seen from deep inside, village squares seen from above. For *The Return of the Native* (1971), the companion volume, Reddick engraved thirty-nine vignettes of various sizes, including three narrow double-spread landscapes. The vignettes, presumably drawn on the ground trod by Eustachia, Venn, Wildeve, and Clym, convey a sense of the inhospitableness of the heath and the insignificance of its inhabitants. However, the one or two scenes in which human beings are dominant, such as that of Venn sitting by the inn fireplace, show how much more interest the edition would have if many more scenes with people had been included.

The sustained originality of conception and masterfulness of execution of Reddick's forty wood-engraved illustrations for *Folklore, Myths and Legends of Britain* (1973) establish them as one of the finest series of the twentieth century. Unfortunately, they appear in a tall, 550-page book that is crammed with photographs, color plates of paintings, old prints, and illustrations by five other artists, whose work, like that of Reddick and of the many literary contributors, is not identified. Yet Reddick has the strength to stand apart. Indeed, the merely summary accounts of British folk tales, myths, and legends presented him with a congenial challenge. With only a few factual statements to go on, he steeped his scenes in supernatural strangeness. Among the most striking are those that show the Abbots Bromley horn dance, performed by men wearing ancient deer horns; the woman stricken because she had taken a shortcut past St. Cuthbert's remains in Durham Cathedral; the reveling of 200 witches and the Devil in North Berwick on All Hallows' Eve in 1590; and the meeting of St. Columba's monk with the Loch Ness monster.

After our limit of 1976, Reddick turned from wood engraving to sketchy etching-like line drawings to illustrate three of Anthony Trollope's Barsetshire novels: *Barchester Towers* (1977), *Framley Parsonage* (1978), and *Doctor Thorne* (1978). The forty or so unassertive half-page vignettes in each of the long quiet narratives depict the scenes with such refreshing variety and naturalness that they seem to have been sketched from life.

Brian Robb

Although he has been an art teacher, a lecturer on art history, and a critic as well as an illustrator, Brian Robb

198. Leonard Rosoman. Wilkie Collins, *The Woman in White* (1964).

(b. 1913) has consistently overloaded his drawings with scrawled shading. Still, his humorously literal delineations do justice to the extravagances of *12 Adventures of the Celebrated Baron Munchausen* (1947). These rather mechanical tall tales were written in England by Rudolf Erich Raspe, a German embezzler and refugee, and published there first in 1785. Robb was even more comfortable illustrating Laurence Sterne's *Sentimental Journey* (1948), mainly with headpiece and tailpiece vignettes, amusing sketches in the tradition of George Cruikshank. Robb's designs for *Tristram Shandy* (1949) are more ambitious than those for *A Sentimental Journey*. The approximately three dozen pen-and-ink vignettes include about ten full-page illustrations. Some of these drawings approach their Victorian precursors in suggestive expression, gesture, and mood. In the 600 pages, these successes are not frequent, chiefly because essential lines and accents are so often lost or obscured in thickets of shading.

The sketchy full-page frontispiece illustration and forty-three smaller vignettes in a paperback *Fables of Aesop* (1954) regrettably fall short in execution of what are refreshingly new images for the ancient fables. Take the fable of the frogs: after petitioning Jupiter for a leader and being dissatisfied with the log that he sends them, the frogs are then sent a crane (here a water snake). Over the centuries, this tale has had an illustration of the frogs either climbing on the log or being gobbled up by the crane. Instead, Robb visualized a frog agitator haranguing his *Führer*-hungry fellows. In just one vignette – for the fable of the ants and the grasshopper (fig. 197) – Robb drew the rapid, unpretentious, and essential statement of idea he earlier had been aiming at and could have achieved had he not used his pen to give prominence to strong dark and light tonal effects and done so with such gratuitous untidiness.

Robb's assignments in *The Oxford Illustrated Old Testament* (1968, 1969) were substantial: Numbers 20–36, Esther, Ecclesiastes, and The Rest of Esther (in the Apocrypha). In color, Robb's numerous brush drawings probably would register clearly and attractively. In halftone, they are gray and blurry; most of them look like working sketches rather than finished illustrations.

Leonard Rosoman

In Wilkie Collins's mystery *The Woman in White* (1964), Leonard Rosoman (b. 1913) engaged in a conscientious dialogue with the text that is unusual among late-twentieth-century artists. The thirty-two full-page watercolors are notable for the careful draftsmanship, the variety of composition, and the abundance and authenticity of detail. (There are also nine excellent but incidental line drawings of places and characters, but none in the last 100 pages.)

199. Cyril Satorsky. *Sir Gawain and the Green Knight* (1971).

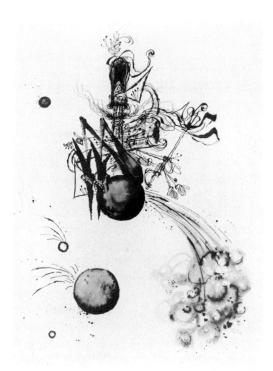

200. Ronald Searle. Rudolf Erich Raspe, *The Adventures of Baron Munchausen* (1969).

To illustrate a modest work of literature so generously with large color plates probably would have been impossible in 1964 without the support of a book club. But book clubs rarely receive such generous support in return from their artists. Some of the virtues of Rosoman's work can be seen in his illustration of the parting at the railway station between the housekeeper Mrs. Eliza Michelson and Lady Glyde, who is about to leave on her ill-omened trip to London (fig. 198):

The whistle of the train was sounding when I joined her ladyship on the platform. She looked very strangely and pressed her hand over her heart, as if some sudden fright had overcome her at that moment.

Besides his care to draw accurately the early steam locomotive, the costumes of principals and small background figures, and even the hatbox, Rosoman communicated the different social levels and emotional states of the two women. Altogether, Rosoman's performance is one of the finest of the period. His later contributions to *The Oxford Illustrated Old Testament* (1968, 1969) and to Aldous Huxley's *Brave New World* (1971) are disappointing. The nine lithographs in *Brave New World* are literal and oddly clumsy; Rosoman perhaps was betrayed by a sense of having to be clever.

Cyril Satorsky

The most impressive of the twenty-two illustrators of *The Oxford Illustrated Old Testament* (1968, 1969) is Cyril Satorsky. His designs for Leviticus, 1 Chronicles, and 2 Maccabees (in the Apocrypha) have an intensity, a directness, and a symbolic richness that set them apart from all the rest. They seem to be woodcuts or linocuts with white areas cut shallow to yield lithographic effects. In a note printed with the edition, Satorsky wrote, "I feel personally connected to every word in the Bible, as either factual or mythical history, in a way that reaches beyond language." This eloquent sincerity is manifest in every one of the designs. In 1 Chronicles 21:16, for instance, the simple statement that follows God's orders to the angel sent to destroy Jerusalem to stay his hand is "And David lifted up his eyes and saw the angel of the Lord stand between the earth and the heaven, having a drawn sword in his hand stretched out over Jerusalem." In Satorsky's illustration, David stands in the foreground, his clasped hands shown against the black silhouette of his body, and his large, narrow, and apparently neckless crowned head lying on his shoulders. Behind him stretch the square buildings of Jerusalem. His eyes turn up so that he can see a huge fist holding an amazing sword over the city. Above the angel's withheld sword, whose cruel cock-spur-like cutting edges

309

are parallel to David's head, the sky is aflame. For images at this level of imagination, one has to go to the art of the ancients and primitives.

Sir Gawain and the Green Knight (1971) confirms the rich promise of the Old Testament designs. Satorsky used the same bold technique in the design for the double spread of frontispiece and title page and for twelve tall illustrations. With heroic exaggeration, unconstrained distortion, and hearty humor, they form an almost perfect accompaniment to the unknown fourteenth-century poet's wonderful multi-layered seriocomic masterpiece of Gawain's coming of age in Camelot. Only Gawain's mature visage and the youthfulness of that of the wife of Sir Bercilak de Hautdesert (the Green Knight) seem to be errors of interpretation, and the very power of Satorsky's drawings made it impossible for him to match the beauty of the descriptions of nature. But the dynamic Z-shaped design in which Gawain, protected by the wife's magic girdle, is about to take the blow from the Green Knight and prove himself 98 percent pure (fig. 199) is evidence that this is one of the exciting series of literary illustrations by an artist of the postwar generation.

Ronald Searle

In many ways, Ronald Searle (b. 1920) would seem to be the ideal illustrator of the books by Charles Dickens. He draws with a free and vibrant line; he is strong on characterization; and his outlook is humorous. At first glance, his illustrations in three of Dickens's books – *A Christmas Carol* (1961), *Oliver Twist* (1962), and *Great Expectations* (1962) – seem to bear out this assumption. *A Christmas Carol* has eight color plates – seven of which are double spreads – fourteen pen-and-wash drawings, and various small headpieces and tailpieces. The most attractive of the color plates (used for the end papers) is a double spread of a boy and a girl standing in the open front of a poultry shop and gazing in awe at an enormous hanging turkey. The ranks of dressed birds, hares, eggs, and baskets convey the sense of plenty that Dickens loved to evoke. But in his interpretation of Dickens's characters, Searle was locked into caricature. Dickens's Scrooge is an extreme personality, but he experiences fear, shame, and good cheer. Searle's Scrooge is a comic grotesque like Mr. Punch, with an enormous beak of a nose that overhangs a chin that resembles a wooden shoe. In *Oliver Twist*, Searle followed George Cruikshank in representing Fagin with repulsive anti-Semitic exaggeration; Fagin in the death cell is a redrawing of Cruikshank's design. For *Great Expectations*, the companion volume, Searle, having no character to distort to such a degree, drew more-appealing illustrations.

Searle's approximately sixty brush-and-ink illustrations for Rudolf Erich Raspe's *Adventures of Baron Munchausen* (1969), however, are both funny drawings and brilliant interpretations. As the American humorist S. J. Perelman wrote, the drawings have an "explosive gaiety" and "coruscate like fireworks". How ably Searle matched or surpassed the flat prose fantasies of Raspe can be seen in his illustration of an incident recounted by Munchausen as having taken place during the siege of a town: "I stood close to one of our great guns. When it was fired, I jumped onto the ball with the plan of penetrating by this means into the town." Halfway there, Munchausen reflected that he would be hanged as a spy. Noticing a cannon ball shot by the enemy flying in the opposite direction, he jumped on it and returned safely to his side of the battle line (fig. 200).

II
A Selective Catalog of
Illustrators and Illustrated Books

CHAPTER ONE

The Fifteenth Century
1476-1500

Minor Printers

William de Machlinia (fl. ca. 1480–86)
[1484?] [*Horae ad usum Sarum.*]

Theodoric Rood (fl. 1478?–86) and *Thomas Hunte* (fl. 1473–86)
1486 J. Mirk. *Liber festialis.*

St. Albans Printer (fl. ca. 1484–86)
1486 *The Bokys of Haukyng and Huntyng and Blasyng of Armys.*

Major Printers

William Caxton (1422?–91)
[1481] B. Vincentius [Vincent de Beauvais]. *The Myrroure of the Worlde.*
[1483] J. de Cessolis. *Game and Playe of the Chesse.*
[1483, after 20 Nov.] J. de Voragine. *Legenda aurea.*
1484, 26 Mar. Aesop. *Fables of Esope.* Tr. W. Caxton.
[1484?] G. Chaucer. [*The Canterbury Tales.*]
[1486] St. Bonaventura. [*Speculum vitae Christi.*]
[1486?] *The Book Named Ryal.*
[1490] [*Horae ad Usum Sarum.*]
*

Blake, N. F. *Caxton and His World.* Deutsch, 1969.
Painter, G. *William Caxton: A Quincentenary Biography of England's First Printer.* Chatto & Windus, 1976.

Wynkyn de Worde (d. 1534)
1493 J. de Voragine. *Legenda aurea.*
1494 St. Bonaventura. *Speculum vitae Christi.*
[1494] [*Horae ad usum Sarum.*]
1495 St. Jerome. *Vitas patrum.*
[1495] Bartholomaeus Anglicus. *De proprietatibus rerum.*
1496 *Boke of Hawkynge & Huntynge.*
[1497] Aesop. [*Fables of Aesop.*] With Pynson. No copy with de Worde imprint extant.
1498 T. Malory. [*Morte d'Arthur.*]
1498 G. Chaucer. *Caunterbury Tales.*
1499 J. Mandeville. *The Wayes of the Holy Londe.*
1502 R. Le Fèvre. *Y^e Hystoryes of Troye.*
[1502?] *Robert the Deuyll.*
1504 [*The Four Sons of Aymon.*]
1505 *The Arte or Crafte to Lyue Well.*
[1505?] [*King Ponthus.*]
1506 P. Gringore. *The Castell of Laboure.*
1507, 4 Sept. J. de Voragine. *Legenda sc̄toꝶ.* Also with Pynson imprint.
[1507] *The Boke Named the Royall.* Also with Pynson imprint.

1508 J. Mirk. *The Festyuall.*
1508 *The Kalender of Shepeherdes.*
[1508] *The Dystruccyon of Jherusalem by Vaspazian and Tytus.*
1509 S. Hawes. *Pastyme of Pleasure.*
1509 S. Brant. *The Shyppe of Fooles.*
1509 *Kynge Rycharde Cuer du Lyon.*
1509 A. de La Salle. *The Fyftene Joyes of Maryage.*
[1509] S. Hawes. *Example of Vertu.*
1510 *Kynge Appolyn of Thyre.*
1512 Elias, Chevalier au Cygne. *The Knyght of the Swanne.*
1514 Simon the Anchorite. *The Fruyte of Redempcyon.*
1515 *The Cronycles of Englonde.*
1517 G. Chaucer. *Troylus and Cresyde.*
1518 *Olyuer of Castylle.*
1519 St. Catherine of Siena. *The Orcharde of Syon.*
1521 *The Passyon of Our Lorde.*
1521 St. Austin of Abingdon. *The Myrrour of the Chyrche.*
[ca. 1525 (ca. 1532?)] G. Boccaccio. *Tytus and Gesyppus.* Tr. W. Walter.
1532 G. Boccaccio. *Guystarde and Sygysmonde.* Tr. W. Walter.
*

Moran, J. *Wynkyn de Worde.* Wynkyn de Worde Society, 1960.

Richard Pynson (d. 1530)
[1492?] G. Chaucer. *Tales of Canterburie.*
1494, 27 Jan. G. Boccaccio. *The Falle of Princis Princessis & Other Nobles.* Tr. J. Lydgate.
[1495] St. Bonaventura. [*Speculum vitae Christi.*]
[1497] Aesop. [*Fables of Aesop.*] With de Worde.
[1497] *Hore intemerate beatissime virginis Marie.*
1500 *Missale ad usum Sarum.*
[1500?] Aesop. [*Fables of Aesop.*] A new set of cuts.
[1503?] *Beuys of Southamtowne.*
1504 *Missale ad usum Sarum.*
[1505?] P. Gringore. *The Castell of Laboure.* Tr. A. Barclay.
1506 *The Kalender of Shepherdes.*
1507, 4 Sept. J. de Voragine. *Legenda sc̄toꝶ.* Also with de Worde imprint.
[1507] *The Boke Named the Royall.* Also with de Worde imprint.
[ca. 1507?] J. Mirk. *The Festyuall.*
1509 S. Brant. *Shyp of Folys.* Tr. A. Barclay.
1512 *Missale ad usū Sarum.*
1513 Jordanus. *Meditationes.*
1513 G. delle Colonne. *The Hystorye Sege and Dystruccyon of Troye.*
[1513] *The Dystruccyon of Jherusalem by Vaspazyan and Tytus.*
[1515?] B. Spagnuoli. *Lyfe of Saynt George.*
1516 R. Fabyan. *The Newe Cronycles of Englande and of Fraunce.*
[1526] G. Chaucer. *The Boke of Fame.*
1526 W. Bonde. *The Pylgrimage of Perfection.*

CHAPTER TWO

The Sixteenth Century
1501–1600

Early Printers: 1501–1535

Laurence Andrewe (fl. ca. 1527–30)
[1529?] B. Vincentius [Vincent de Beauvais]. *The Myrrour of the Worlde.*

Richard Bankes (fl. 1523–45)
1523 *The IX Drunkardes.*

Robert Copland (fl. ca. 1508–48)
1528 R. Whitforde. *The Pomander of Prayer.*
[n.d.] [R. Copland?] [Rhymed life of Christ.]

Richard Fakes (fl. 1509–30)
[1521–23?] *A Glorious Medytacyon of Jhesus Crystes Passyon.*
1530 *The Myrroure of Oure Lady.*

Thomas Godfray (fl. ca. 1530–36)
1532 G. Chaucer. *Workes.*

John Herford (fl. 1534–48)
1534 *The Lyfe and Passion of Seint Albon.*

Charles Kyrfoth (fl. ca. 1519)
1519 *Compotus manualis ad vsū Oxoniēsiū.*

Julyan Notary (fl. ca. 1496–1520)
[1503?] *Hore beate Marie virginis secundum usum Sarum.*
1503 [1504], 16 Feb. J. de Voragine. *Legenda aurea.*
1504 *Cronycle of Englonde.*
1507 *Nycodemus Gospell.*
[ca. 1515] *Huon of Burdeux.* Tr. Berners.
[1518?] *The Kalender of Shepardes.*

Henry Pepwell (fl. 1518–41)
1521 *The Dyetary of Ghostly Helthe.*

John Rastell (fl. ca. 1515–36)
[1529] J. Rastell. *The Pastyme of People.*

Robert Redman (fl. 1523–40)
1531 Simon the Anchorite. *The Fruite of Redempcion.*

John Scolar (fl. ca. 1518–28)
1518 W. Burley. *De materia & forma.*
1518 R. Whittinton. *De heteroclitis nominibus.*

Peter Treveris (fl. ca. 1522–32)
1525 H. von Braunschweig. *Handywarke of Surgeri.*
1526 *The Grete Herball.*
1527 H. von Braunschweig. *Boke of Distyllacyon.*
1527 R. Higden. *Polycronycon.*
[1530?] A. Barclay. *Certayne Egloges.*
[n.d.] St. Austin of Abingdon. *The Myrrour of the Chyrche.*

Robert Wyer (fl. 1529–61)
[1533?] [*Horae ad usum Sarum.*]
[ca. 1540] G. delle Colonne. *The C. Hystoryes of Troye.*

The Middle Years: 1536–1562

1539 [Bible.] Great Bible. Ed. T. Cranmer. R. Grafton & E. Whitchurch.
1540 [E. Rösslin.] *The Byrth of Mankynde.* Tr. R. Jonas. T. Raynold.
[1545] [A. Vesalius.] *Compendiosa totius Anatomie delineatio aere exarata: per Thomam Geminum Londini.* J. Herford.
1548 T. Cranmer. *Catechismus.* W. Lynne.
1548 Urbanus Regius. *A Lytle Treatyse.* Lynne.
1548 E. Halle. *The Union of the Two Noble and Illustre Famelies of Lancastre and Yorke.* Grafton.
1548 P. Viret. *A Notable Collection of Diuers and Sondry Places of the Sacred Scripture.* Scoloker.
1548 M. Luther. *A Ryght Notable Sermon uppon the Twentieth Chapter of Johan.* Scoloker.
[1548] [C. van der Heyden.] *The Ordynarye for All Faythfull Chrystians. A Right Goodly Rule. 1548.* A. Scoloker for W. Seares.
[1548?] [C. van der Heyden.] *A Bryefe Summe of the Whole Byble.* Scoloker.
[1548?] J. Bale. *The Image of Bothe Churches.* R. Jugge.
[ca. 1548?] G. Lynne. *The Begynnynge and Endynge of All Poperie.* Herford for Lynne.
1556 J. Heywood. *The Spider and the Flie.* T. Powell.
1560–62 *Genealogie of the Kings of England.* G. Godet.
1562 G. Legh. *Accedens of Armory.* R. Tottel.

Later Printers: 1563–1600

John Day (1522–84)
1559 W. Cuningham. *The Cosmographical Glasse.*
1563 J. Foxe. *Actes and Monuments of the Church (The Book of Martyrs).*
1568 J. van der Noot. *Het Theatre.*
1568 J. van der Noot. *Le Theatre.*
1569 *A Book of Christian Prayers.*
1569 S. Bateman. *A Christall Glasse of Christian Reformation.*
1570 J. Foxe. *Actes and Monuments of the Church.* Second ed.
1575 R. Grosseteste. *The Testaments of the Twelve Patriarchs, the Sonnes of Jacob.* Tr. A. Gilby.
1577 J. Dee. *The Perfecte Arte of Navigation.*
1581 J. Derricke. *An Image of Irelande.*

*

Mozeley, J. F. *John Foxe and His Book.* Society for Promoting Christian Knowledge, 1940.
Oastler, C. L. *John Day, the Elizabethan Printer.* Oxford: Bibliographical Society, 1975.
Williamson, G. A. *Foxe's "Book of Martyrs".* Secker & Warburg, 1965.

Henry Bynneman (fl. 1556–83)

1569   J. van der Noot. *A Theatre for Voluptuous Worldlings.* Tr. E. Spenser et al.

1569   P. Boaistuau. *Wonders of Nature.*

1575   G. Turbervile. *The Booke of Faulconrie or Hauking. The Noble Arte of Venerie or Hunting.* For C. Barker.

1576   *The Mirror of Mans Lyfe, Englished by H. K.*

1577   R. Holinshed. *Chronicles of England, Scotlande, and Irelande.* For J. Harrison et al.

1581   J. Tixier de Ravisy. *Ioan. Ravisii Textoris Nivernen.*

1581   S. Bateman. *The Doome Warning All Men to the Iudgemente.* R. Newbery under assignment from Bynneman.

*

Eccles, M. "Bynneman's Books." *The Library,* 5th ser., no. 12 (1957).

Plomer, H. R. "Henry Bynneman, Printer, 1566–83." *The Library,* n.s. 9, no. 35 (July 1908).

Other Late-Sixteenth-Century Printers

1563   T. Gale. *Certaine Workes of Chirurgerie.* R. Hall.

1566   D. Lyndsay. *A Dialogue betweene Experience and a Courtier.* T. Purfoote & W. Pickering.

1568   [Holi-bible.] Bishops' Bible. R. Jugge.

1569   S. Bateman. *The Trauayled Pylgrime.* H. Denham.

1570   [Bidpai.] *The Morall Philosophie of Doni.* Tr. T. North. Denham.

1577   T. Beza. *A Tragedie of Abraham's Sacrifice.* T. Vautroullier.

1578   R. Dodoens. *Niewe Herball.* Tr. H. Lyte. G. Dewes.

1579   E. Spenser. *The Shepheardes Calendar.* H. Singleton.

[1581]   S. Bateman. *The New Arival of the Three Gracis, into Anglia about 1580.* T. East.

1582   T. Bentley. *The Monument of Matrones.* Denham.

1586   G. Whitney. *A Choice of Emblemes.* Leiden: F. van Ravelingen.

1588   H. Broughton. *A Concent of Scripture.* G. Simson & W. White.

1590   E. Spenser. *The Faerie Queene.* W. Ponsonby.

1590   T. Harriott. *A Briefe Report of the New Found Land.* Frankfurt: I. Wechel for S. Feierabend.

1590   *Three Lordes and Three Ladies of London.* R. Jhones.

1591   L. Ariosto. *Orlando Furioso.* Tr. J. Harington. R. Field.

1591   C. Paradin. *The Heroicall Devises.* W. Kearney.

1592   F. Colonna. *Hypnerotomachia Poliphili. The Strife of Love in a Dreame.* [J. Charlewood] for S. Waterson.

1597   J. Gerard. *The Herball: or General Historie of Plants.* E. Bollifant for J. Norton.

CHAPTER THREE

The Seventeenth Century
1601–1700

Anonymous and Minor Illustrators

1601   Pliny. *Pliny's "History of the World".* A. Islip.

1607   E. Topsell. *The Historie of Four-footed Beastes.* W. Jaggard.

1608   E. Topsell. *The Historie of Serpents.* W. Jaggard.

1615   G. Sandys. *A Relation of a Iourney [to] the Turkish Empire.* W. Barrett.

1615   T. Kyd. *The Spanish Tragedie.* J. White & T. Langley.

1618   W. Lawson. *A New Orchard and Garden.* R. Jackson.

1620   G. Boccaccio. *The Decameron.* I. Jaggard for M. Lowndes.

1620   T. Peyton. *The Glasse of Time.* L. Chapman.

[1620?]   *Syr Bevis of Hampton.* W. Lee.

1624   C. Marlowe. *The Tragicall History of Doctor Faustus.* J. Wright.

1629   J. Parkinson. *Paradisi In Sole Paradisus terrestris: or, a Garden of All Sorts of Pleasant Flowers.* H. Lownes & R. Young.

1631   G. Markham. *A Way to Get Wealth.* J. Harrison.

1633   P. Fletcher. *Piscatorie Eclogs.* Cambridge.

[1633?]   *Arden of Faversham.* C. W. [C. Wright.]

1634   E. Wotton, C. Gesner, T. Penny, and T. Muffet. *Insectorum sive Minimorum Animalium Theatrum.* T. Cotes.

1639   W. Barret. *Aesops Fables.* H. Gosson & F. Eglesfield.

1651   T. Hobbes. *Philosophical Rudiments of Government and Society.* R. Royston.

1653   I. Walton and C. Cotton. *The Compleat Angler.* R. Marriott.

1655   W. Shakespeare. *The Rape of Lucrece.* J. Stafford & W. Gilbertson.

1656   F. Quarles. *Argalus and Parthenia.* H. Mosely.

1658   T. Jenner. *A Work for None but Angels & Men, or A Book Shewing What the Soule Is.* T. Jenner.

[1658]   J. Payne. *Flora: Flowers Fruict Beastes Birds and Flies.* P. Stent.

1659   J. Playford. *Select Ayres and Dialogues.* W. Godbid for Playford.

1659   J. A. Komenski [Comenius]. *Orbis sensualium pictus. The Visible World.* J. Kirton.

1666   J. Davies. *The History of the Caribby-Islands.* T. Dring & J. Starkey.

1673   E. Settle. *The Empress of Morocco: A Tragedy with Sculptures. As It Is Acted at the Duke's Theatre.* W. Cademan.

1673   F. Kirkman. *The Famous History of Don Bellianis of Greece.* F. Kirkman.

1674   F. Quarles. *Divine Poems.* T. Strawbridge.

1674   F. Kirkman. *The History of Prince Erastus and the Seven Wise Masters of Rome.* Kirkman.

1676   J. Ray. *The Ornithology of Francis Willughby.* J. Martyn, Printer to the Royal Society.

1680   J. Bunyan. *The Pilgrim's Progress.* N. Ponder.

1684   J. Quarles. *Triumphant Chastity: or, Joseph's Self-Conflict.* B. Crayle.

1686 F. Willughby. *De historia piscium libri quatuor*. Oxford: Royal Society.

1687 *The Banquet of Musicke*. H. Playford.

1687 M. de Cervantes Saavedra. *Don Quixote*. Tr. J. Philips. T. Hodgkin. Sold by M. Whitwood & J. Newton.

1688 G. Wither. *Divine Poems . . . on the Ten Commandments*. R. Janeway.

1688 *Valentine and Orson*. T. Passinger.

1689 *Sir Bevis of Southampton*. W. Thackeray & J. Deacon.

1689 P. Ayres. *Mythologia Ethica: or Three Centuries of Aesopian Fables*. T. Howkins.

1691 L. Plukenet. *Phytographia sive stirpium illustriorum*. Privately printed.

1694 A. le Grand. *An Entire Body of Philosophy . . . of Renate Des Cartes*. S. Roycroft for R. Blome.

Emblem Books

[1612] H. Peacham. *Minerva Britanna: or a Garden of Heroical Devises*. H. Peacham.

1614 T. Combe. *The Theatre of Fine Devices*. R. Field.

1618 H. G. [H. Godyeare.] *The Mirrour of Maiestie*. W. Jones.

1626 T. Jenner. *The Soules Solace: or Thirtie and One Spirituall Emblems*. T. Jenner.

1633 H. A. [H. Hawkins.] *Parthenae sacra*. Paris: P. Cousturier.

1635, 1634 G. Wither. *A Collection of Emblemes*. R. Milbourne.

1635 F. Quarles. *Emblemes*. J. Marriott.

1635 F. Quarles. *Trinitas Emblemes*. Marriott.

1638 F. Quarles. *Hieroglyphikes of the Life of Man*. Marriott.

1638 R. Farley. *Lychnocausia sive Moralia Facum Emblemata*. M. Sparke, Jr.

1647 C. Harvey. *Schola cordis*. H. Blunden.

[1658] J. H. [J. Hall.] *Emblems with Elegant Figures*. Cambridge: R. Daniell.

1665 E. M. [E. Manning.] *Ashrea: or the Grove of Beatitudes, Represented in Emblemes*. For W. P.

1683 P. Ayres. *Cupid's Address to the Ladies. Emblemata Amatoria/Emblems of Love*. R. Bently & S. Tidmarsh.

1684 *Delights for the Ingenious in above Fifty Emblems Divine and Moral*. N. Crouch.

1686 H. Hugo. *Pia desideria: or Divine Addresses*. Tr. E. Aarwaker. H. Bonwicke.

Major Illustrators
Francis Barlow (1626?–1704)

1649 Sophocles. *Electra*. Tr. C. W. [C. Wase.] "At the Hague, for Sam. Brown." [London?] Attributed.

1652 E. Benlowes. *Theophila: or Love's-Sacrifice. A Divine Poem*. R. Norton for Benlowes. Sold by H. Seile & H. Moseley. With others.

1653 W. Denny. *Pelecanicidium: or the Christian Adviser against Self-Murder*. T. Hucklescott.

1660 J. Howell. *The Parley of Beasts, or Morphandra*. W. Palmer.

1660 Juvenal. *Mores Hominum, The Manners of Men Described in Sixteen Satyrs*. Tr. R. Stapylton. R. Hodgkinson. With others.

1666 Aesop. *Aesop's Fables With his Life In English French & Latine*. T. Philipott prepared the English text and R. Codrington, the French and Latin. W. Godbid for Barlow. Sold by A. Seile & E. Powell.

1668 J. Ogilby. *Aesopic's: or a Second Collection of Fables Paraphras'd in Verse*. With others. *Androcleus: or the Roman Slave*. With anr. or others. Published in one volume with *Aesop Paraphras'd*,

second ed., and *The Ephesian Matron, or Widow's Tears*. T. Roycroft for Ogilby.

1671 F. Barlow. *Seuerall Wayes of Hunting, Hawking, & Fishing according to the English Manner*. J. Overton.

1686 R. Blome. *The Gentlemans Recreation*. S. Roycroft for Blome. With others.

1687 Aesop. *Aesop's Fables*. Second ed., with illustrations for the "Life of Aesop". H. Hills for Barlow.

*

Croft-Murray, E., and P. Hulton. *Catalogue of British Drawings: XVI & XVII Centuries*. Trustees of the British Museum, 1960.

Evelyn, J. *Diary*. Ed. E. S. de Beer. Oxford, 1955.

Hodnett, E. *Francis Barlow: First Master of English Book Illustration*. Scolar; Berkeley: California, 1978.

Jenkins, H. *Edward Benlowes (1602–1676): Biography of a Minor Poet*. Athlone, 1952.

Sparrow, W. S. *British Sporting Artists: Barlow to Herring*. Lane, 1922.

———. "Francis Barlow: His Country Life and Field Sports." *Apollo*, January 1934.

———. "Our Earliest Sporting Artist: Francis Barlow, 1626–1704." *Connoisseur*, July 1936.

Francis Cleyn (1582–1657/58)

1632 P. Ovidius Naso. *Ovid's "Metamorphosis" English'd, Mythologiz'd, and Represented in Figures*. By G. S. [G. Sandys.] Oxford: J. Lichfield for A. Hebb.

1649 R. B. [R. Brome.] *Lachrymae Musarum; the Tears of the Muses*. T. Newcomb.

1650 T. Fuller. *A Pisgah-sight of Palestine*. J. Williams.

1651 J. Ogilby. *The Fables of Aesop, Paraphras'd in Verse and Adorn'd with Sculpture*. T. Warren for A. Crook.

1654 P. Virgilius Maro. *Works*. Tr. J. Ogilby. Warren for Ogilby. Ogilby, 1658. J. Tonson, 1697.

1660 Homer. *Homer His "Iliads."* Tr. J. Ogilby. T. Roycroft for Ogilby.

*

Beckett, F. *The Painter Francis Clein in Denmark*. Mémoires de l'Académie royale des sciences et des lettres de Denmark, 7th ser., vol. 5, no. 2. Copenhagen, 1936.

William Faithorne (1616?–91)

There seems no certainty that, excluding frontispieces, Faithorne designed the illustrations that he and his assistants engraved and etched. See the discussion in the text. The plates in the following books have been attributed to him.

1653 J. Taylor. *The Great Exemplar of Sanctity and Holy Life*. R. Royston.

1655 *Musaei, Moschi, & Bionis*. Ed. D. Whitford. T. Roycroft.

1675 J. Taylor and W. Cave. *Antiquitates Christianae: or, The History of the Life and Death of the Holy Jesus and Apostles*. Royston.

1693 S. Wesley. *The Life and Death of Our Blessed Lord and Saviour Jesus Christ: an Heroic Poem*. C. Harper & B. Motte.

*

Fagan, L. *A Descriptive Catalogue of the Engraved Work of William Faithorne*. Quaritch, 1888.

Jan Baptist Gaspars (1620–91)

1653 C. Sorel. *Lysis: or, the Extravagant Shepherd*. Tr. J. Davies of Kidwelly. T. Heath.

William Hole (fl. 1607–24)
1611   T. Coryate. *Coryat's Crudities*. W. S. [W. Stansby.]

Wenceslaus Hollar (1607–77)
1640   I. Ambrose. *Prima & Ultima: The First & Last Things*. J. Okes
for S. Broun.
1642   *All the memorable and wonder-strikinge Parlamentary Mercies
...Aᵒ 1641 & 1642*. T. Jenner.
1643   J. Drexel. *The Christians Zodiake*. Broun. Attributed.
[1646]   J. Vicars. *A Sight of ÿ Trans-actions of these latter yeares
Emblemized with engrauen plats*. Jenner.
1648   *True Information of the Beginning and Cause of all our Troubles*.
Jenner.
1665   J. Ogilby. *The Fables of Aesop, Paraphras'd in Verse*. T. Roycroft
for Ogilby. With anr.
1668   J. Ogilby. *Aesopic's: or a Second Collection of Fables Paraphras'd
in Verse*. With others. *The Ephesian Matron, or Widow's Tears*.
Published in one volume with *Aesop Paraphras'd*, second ed.,
and *Androcleus: or the Roman Slave*. Roycroft for Ogilby.

*

Borovský, F. A. *Wenzel Hollar: Erganzungen zu G. Partheys "besch-
reibendem Verzeichniss seiner Kupferstiche"*. Prague: Zemski Vybor,
1898.
A Description of the Works of Wenceslaus Hollar. Ed. G. Vertue. For
Vertue, 1745.
Eames, M. "John Ogilby and His Aesop." *Bulletin of the New York
Public Library* 65 (February 1961).
Hollar, W. *Ezop Vaclava Hollara*. Ed. M. Novotny. Prague: Sfinx,
1936.
Ogilby, J *The Fables of Aesop . . . (1668)*. Intro E. Miner. Los Angeles:
William Andrews Clark Memorial Library, 1965.
Parthey, G. *Wenzel Hollar: Beschreibendes Verzeichniss seiner Kupfer-
stiche*. Berlin: Nicolai, 1853, 1858.
Schuchard, M. *John Ogilby · 1600–1676*. Hamburg: Hartung, 1973.
In German.
Urzidil, J. *Hollar: A Czech Emigré*. [Czechoslovakia], 1942.
———. *Wenceslaus Hollar: Der Kupferstecher des Barock*. Vienna and
Leipzig: Passer, 1936.
Van Eerde, K. S. *John Ogilby and the Taste of His Times*. Folkstone:
Dawson, 1976.
———. *Wenceslaus Hollar: Delineator of His Time*. Charlottesville:
Virginia for the Folger Shakespeare Library, 1970.

Bernard Lens, Sr. (1631–1708)
1688   J. Milton. *Paradise Lost: A Poem in Twelve Books*. J. Tonson.
With others.

Sir John Baptist Medina (1659–1710)
1688   J. Milton. *Paradise Lost: A Poem in Twelve Books*. J. Tonson.
With others.

*

Boorsch, S. "The 1688 *Paradise Lost* and Dr. Aldrich." *Metropolitan
Museum Journal* 6 (1972).
Collins Baker, C. H. "Some Illustrators of Milton's *Paradise Lost*
(1688–1850)." *The Library*, 5th ser., vol. 3, no. 1 (June 1948).
Gardner, H. "Milton's First Illustrator." In *Essays and Studies*.
Murray, 1956. Reprinted in *A Reading of "Paradise Lost"*. Oxford,
1965.
Pointon, M. R. *Milton and English Art*. Manchester, 1970.

Henry Peacham (1576?–1643?)
[1612]   H. Peacham. *Minerva Britanna: or a Garden of Heroical
Devises*. H. Peacham.
[1639   Aesop. *Aesop's Fables*. Peacham.] Only title page extant.

*

Levy, F. J. "Henry Peacham and the Art of Drawing." *Journal of the
Warburg and Courtauld Institutes*, no. 37 (1974).

Dirk (Roderigo) Stoop (ca. 1610–86)
1665   J. Ogilby. *The Fables of Aesop, Paraphras'd in Verse*. T. Roycroft
for Ogilby. With anr.

CHAPTER FOUR

The Eighteenth Century (I)
1701–1775

Richard Bentley (1708–82)

1753   T. Gray. *Designs by Mr. R. Bentley, for Six Poems by Mr. T Gray*. R. Dodsley.

Nicholas Blakey (fl. 1749–53)

1751   A. Pope. *The Works of Alexander Pope*. Ed. W. Warburton. J. & P. Knapton, H. Lintot, J. Tonson, & S. Draper. With others.

François Boitard (ca. 1670–ca. 1717)

1709–10   W. Shakespeare. *The Works of Mr. William Shakespeare. In Six Volumes Adorn'd with Cuts*. Ed. N. Rowe. J. Tonson.

1711   F. Beaumont and J. Fletcher. *The Works of Mr. Francis Beaumont and Mr. John Fletcher*. Tonson.

1712   W. Rose. *The History of Joseph. A Poem in Six Books*. J. Knapton.

*

Hammelmann, H. A. "Shakespeare's First Illustrators." *Apollo Magazine Supplement*, August 1968.

Louis Philippe Boitard (d. ca. 1760)

1751   [R. Paltock.] *Peter Wilkins, a Cornish Man*. J. Robinson & R. Dodsley.

1751   [R. O. Cambridge.] *The Scribleriad*. Dodsley. With anr.

1751   R. Morris. *John Daniel, a Smith at Royston*. M. Cooper.

Hubert François Bourguignon. See Gravelot.

Louis Cheron (1655–1735)

[1717   P. Ovidius Naso. *Ovid's "Metamorphoses" in Fifteen Books. Translated by the Most Eminent Hands*. Tr. J. Dryden, W. Congreve, S. Croxall et al. J. Tonson. With anr. Attributed. See Cheron discussion.]

1718   R. Rapin. *Rapin of Gardens: A Latin Poem*. B. Lintot.

1720   J. Milton. *The Poetical Works of John Milton*. Tonson. With anr.

1724   P. Sidney. *The Countess of Pembroke's Arcadia*. E. Taylor. With anr.

1727   Plutarch. *Lives*. Tonson. With others.

1729   *A Select Collection of Novels and Histories*. Ed. S. Croxall. J. Watts. With others.

*

Croft-Murray, E. *Decorative Painting in England, 1537–1837*. Country Life, 1962, 1970.

Gravelot [Hubert François Bourguignon] (1699–1773)

1735   J. Dryden. *The Dramatick Works*. J. Tonson.

1737   *Songs in the Opera Flora*. J. Cooper & G. Bickham.

1738   J. Gay. *Fables. By the Late Mr. Gay. Volume the Second* [Second series]. J. & P. Knapton & T. Cox.

1739–45   C. Rollin. *The Roman History*. Knapton.

1740   W. Shakespeare. *Works*. H. Lintot, C. Hitch, J. & R. Tonson et al.

1742   S. Richardson. *Pamela: or, Virtue Rewarded*. S. Richardson. With anr.

1744   W. Shakespeare. *The Works of Shakespear*. Ed. T. Hanmer. Oxford: The University Press for Hanmer. With anr.

1750   H. Fielding. *Histoire de Tom Jones: ou L'Enfant Trouvé*. "Amsterdam: aux depens de la Compagnie." "A Dresde 1750. Chez George Conrad Walther." [Paris?]

1750   H. Fielding. *Histoire de Tom Jones: ou L'Enfant Trouvé*. "A Londre chez Jean Nourse." [Paris?]

*

Lanckoroński, M., and L. Lanckoroński. "Gravelot in London." *Philobiblon* 10 (1938). In German.

Salomons, V. F. *Gravelot*. Bumpus, 1911.

Louis du Guernier (1687–ca. 1735?)

1712   P. Ovidius Naso. *Ovid's "Art of Love"*. Tr. J. Dryden, W. Congreve et al. J. Tonson.

1714   A. Pope. *The Rape of the Lock*. B. Lintot.

1714   J. Gay. *The Shepherd's Week*. J. & R. Tonson.

1714   W. Shakespeare. *Works*. Tonson.

1716   B. Jonson. *The Works of Ben. Johnson*. Tonson et al.

[1717   P. Ovidius Naso. *Ovid's "Metamorphoses" in Fifteen Books. Translated by the Most Eminent Hands*. Tr. J. Dryden, W. Congreve, S. Croxall et al. Tonson. With anr. Attributed. See Cheron discussion.]

1727   Plutarch. *Lives*. Tonson. With others.

1735   G. Etherege. *Works*. Tonson.

Francis Hayman (1708?–76)

1742   S. Richardson. *Pamela: or, Virtue Rewarded*. S. Richardson. With anr.

1744   W. Shakespeare. *The Works of Shakespear*. Ed. T. Hanmer. Oxford: The University Press for Hanmer. With anr.

1744   [E. Moore and H. Brooke.] *Fables for the Female Sex*. R. Francklin.

1747   *The Spectator*. J. & R. Tonson & S. Draper.

1748   T. Smollett. *The Adventures of Roderick Random*. J. Osborn.

1749   J. Milton. *Paradise Lost*. Ed. T. Newton. Tonson & B. Draper.

1751   A. Pope. *The Works of Alexander Pope*. Ed. W. Warburton. J. & P. Knapton, H. Lintot, J. Tonson, & S. Draper. With others.

1752   J. Milton. *Paradise Regain'd. Samson Agonistes. Poems on Several Occasions*. Ed. T. Newton. Tonson & B. Draper.

1752   C. Smart. *Poems on Several Occasions*. W. Strahan for Smart. Sold by J. Newbery. With anr.

1753   J. Hanway. *British Trade over the Caspian Sea*. R. Dodsley et al. With anr.

1753   W. Congreve. *Works*. Tonson & S. Draper.

1755   M. de Cervantes Saavedra. *Don Quixote*. Tr. T. Smollett. A. Millar et al. With anr.

1758–60   T. Smollett. *A History of England*. T. Cadell.

1759   *The Tatler*. Tonson.

1770–74   W. Shakespeare. *Five Plays*. Vol. 1, *King Lear, Hamlet*; vol. 2, *Macbeth, Othello, Julius Caesar*. B. White et al.

*

Allentuck, M. "Sir Thomas Hanmer Instructs Francis Hayman: An Editor's Notes to His Illustrator (1744)." *The Shakespeare Quarterly* 27, no. 3 (Summer 1976).

Hammelmann, H. A. "Shakespeare's First Illustrators." *Apollo Magazine Supplement*, August 1968.

Merchant, W. M. "Francis Hayman's Illustrations of Shakespeare." *The Shakespeare Quarterly* 9 (Spring 1958).

Joseph Highmore (1692–1780)
1729   *A Select Collection of Novels and Histories.* Ed. S. Croxall. J. Watts. With others.

William Hogarth (1697–1764)
1724   L. Apuleius Madaurensis. *The New Metamorphosis.* Adapt. C. Gildon. S. Briscoe.
1725   G. de Coste La Calprenède. *Cassandra.* Tr. T. C. Cotterell. J. Darby & A. Bettesworth et al.
1725   J. Beaver. *Roman Military Punishments.* Privately printed.
1726   S. Butler. *Hudibras.* B. Motte; F. Fayram.
1730   L. Theobald. *Perseus and Andromeda.* T. Wood.
1755   M. de Cervantes Saavedra. *Don Quixote.* Tr. T. Smollett. A. Millar et al. With anr.
1760   L. Sterne. *Tristram Shandy.* R. & J. Dodsley.
*

Burke, J., and C. Caldwell. *Hogarth: The Complete Engravings.* Thames & Hudson, 1968.

Paulson, R. *Hogarth: His Art, Life, and Times.* New Haven, Conn.: Yale, 1971.

———. *Hogarth's Graphic Works.* New Haven, Conn.: Yale, 1965, 1970.

W. Hogarth. Engravings. Ed. S. Shesgreen. New York: Dover, 1973.

Webster, M. *Hogarth.* Studio Vista, 1979.

William Kent (1685–1748)
1720   J. Gay. *Poems on Several Occasions.* J. Tonson & B. Lintot.
1725   Homer. *The Odyssey.* Tr. A. Pope. Lintot.
1727   J. Gay. *Fables.* Tonson & J. Watts. With anr.
1730   J. Thomson. *The Seasons.* J. Millan & A. Millar.
1734   A. Pope. *An Essay on Man.* "For Lawton Gilliver."
1751   E. Spenser. *The Faerie Queene.* J. Brindley & S. Wright.
*

Eichholz, J. P. "William Kent's Career as Literary Illustrator." *Bulletin of the New York Public Library* 70, no. 10 (December 1966).

Jourdain, M. *The Work of William Kent.* Country Life, 1948.

Elisha Kirkall (ca. 1682–1742)
1712   W. Howell. *Medulla Historiae Anglicanae.* T. Childe, T. Varman, J. Osborn, & W. Taylor.
1719   W. Howell. *Medulla Historiae Anglicanae.* T. Childe, T. Varman, J. Osborn, & W. Taylor. A new set of blocks.
1722   S. Croxall. *Fables of Aesop and Others.* J. Tonson & J. Watts.
*

Hodnett, E. "Elisha Kirkall, *c.* 1682–1742." *The Book Collector* 25, no. 2 (Summer 1976).

John Miller [Johann Sebastian Müller] (ca. 1715–ca. 1789)
1755   J. Swift. *Works.* J. Bathurst et al.
1760   P. Miller. *Figures of the Most Beautiful, Useful and Uncommon Plants Described in the Gardners Dictionary.* P. Miller. With others.
1762   J. Thomson. *Works.* A. Millar. With others.

1773   [E. Young.] *The Passions Personify'd in Familiar Fables.* J. Whiston.
1773–77   C. Linnaeus [Carl von Linné]. *Illustratio Systematis Sexualis Linnaei.* J. Miller.

Nicolas Pigné (1690?–1718?)
1713   J. Milton. *Paradise Regain'd, Samson Agonistes, and Poems on Several Occasions.* J. Tonson. See Pigné discussion.

John Pine (1690–1756)
1719   D. Defoe. *Robinson Crusoe.* W. Taylor. Attributed.
1722   A. Behn. *All the Histories and Novels.* A. Bettesworth & F. Clay.
1723   *A Collection of Old Ballads.* J. Roberts.
1733–37   Horace. *Quinti Horatii Flacci Opera.* J. Pine.
1755, 1774   P. Virgilius Maro. *Bucolica et Georgica.* Ed. R. E. Pine. Pine.
*

Hutchins, H. C. *"Robinson Crusoe" and Its Printing, 1719–31.* New York: Columbia, 1925.

John Sturt (1658–1730)
1728   J. Bunyan. *The Pilgrim's Progress.* J. Clarke & J. Brotherton.

Isaac Taylor the Elder (1730–1807)
1765   S. Croxall. *The Fair Circassian.* T. Lowndes. With anr.
1766   J. Cunningham. *Poems, Chiefly Pastoral.* Newcastle: J. Cunningham.
1767   Metastio. *Works.* T. Davies.
1774   O. Goldsmith. *An History of the Earth and Animated Nature.* J. Nourse. With anr.
1775   *A Collection of Poems by Several Hands. Intended as a Supplement to Mr. [Robert] Dodsley's Collection.* J. Dodsley.
1781   S. Richardson. *Sir Charles Grandison.* W. Strahan et al.

John Vanderbank (1694–1739)
1729   *A Select Collection of Novels and Histories.* Ed. S. Croxall. J. Watts. With others.
1738   M. de Cervantes Saavedra. *Don Quixote.* J. & R. Tonson. In Spanish.
1742   M. de Cervantes Saavedra. *Don Quixote.* Tr. C. Jarvis. Tonson & R. Dodsley.

Gerard Vander Gucht (1697–1776)
1723   M. de Cervantes Saavedra. *Don Quixote.* J. Tonson.
1725   M. Prior. *A New Collection of Poems on Several Occasions.* T. Osborne.
1729   *A Select Collection of Novels and Histories.* Ed. S. Croxall. J. Watts. With others.
1735   J. Hughes. *Poems.* Tonson & Watts.
1735   W. Congreve. *Plays.* Tonson.

Samuel Wale (1721?–86)
[ca. 1750]   B. Cole. *Select Tales and Fables.* F. Wingrave.
1751   A. Pope. *The Works of Alexander Pope.* Ed. W. Warburton. J. & P. Knapton, H. Lintot, J. Tonson, & S. Draper. With others.
1760   I. Walton. *The Complete Angler.* C. Cotton. *Discourse on Rivers, Ponds, Fish, and Fishing.* T. Hope. T. Rivington, T. Caslon, & R. Withy, 1766.
1761   [R. Dodsley.] *Select Fables of Esop and other Fabulists.* R. Dodsley.
1762   J. Macpherson. *Fingal.* Becket & de Hondt.

1768 [F. de S. de La Mothe-Fénelon.] *Ethic Amusements*. Tr. D. Bellamy. "For the author."

1768 W. Wilkie. *Fables*. E. & C. Dilly.

1768 S. Richardson. *Clarissa Harlowe*. T. Lowndes.

1768 [F. de S. de La Mothe-Fénelon.] *The Adventures of Telemachus*. Tr. J. Hawkesworth. "For the Author."

[ca. 1768] *The Tyburn Chronicle*. J. Cooke.

1770 Plutarch. *Lives*. Dilly.

1774 M. de Cervantes Saavedra. *Don Quixote*. Cooke.

1778 F. Beaumont and J. Fletcher. *The Dramatick Works*. T. Evans & P. Elmsley et al. With others.

Anthony Walker (1726–65)

1751 A. Pope. *The Works of Alexander Pope*. Ed. W. Warburton. J. & P. Knapton, H. Lintot, J. Tonson, & S. Draper. With others.

1757 W. Somervile. *The Chace*. G. Hawkins.

1760 T. Smollett. *Sir Launcelot Greaves*. In *The British Magazine* 1 and 2. H. Payne.

1762 J. Ogilvie. *Poems on Several Subjects*. G. Keith.

1762 J. Philips. *Poems Attempted in the Style of Milton*. Tonson & T. Lowndes.

1764 J. Ogilvie. *Providence: an Allegorical Poem*. G. Burnet.

1764 C. Morell. *The Tales of the Genii: or the Delightful Lessons of Horam*. J. Wilkie.

John Wooton (ca. 1677–1765)

1727 J. Gay. *Fables*. J. Tonson & J. Watts. With anr.

CHAPTER FIVE

The Eighteenth Century (II)
1776–1800

John James Barralet (fl. 1770–1812)

1778 F. Beaumont and J. Fletcher. *The Dramatick Works*. T. Evans & P. Elmsley et al. With others.

1780 S. Gessner. *The Death of Abel*. J. Collyer.

Lady Diana Beauclerk (1734–1808)

1796 G. A. Bürger. *Leonora*. J. Edwards & E. Harding.

1797 J. Dryden. *The Fables*. Edwards & Harding.

John Bewick (1760–95)

1784 *Select Fables, in Three Parts*. Enlarged ed. Newcastle: T. Saint. With anr.

1789 H. Holbein. *Emblems of Mortality*. T. Hodgson.

1789 [J. H. Campe.] *The New Robinson Crusoe*. J. Stockdale.

1790 J. Trusler. *Proverbs Exemplified*. J. Trusler.

1791 J. Trusler. *The Progress of Man and Society*. Trusler.

1792 [A. Berquin.] *The Looking-Glass for the Mind*. E. Newbery.

1794 [J. H. Wynne.] *Tales for Youth: in Thirty Poems*. Newbery.

1795 J. Ritson. *Robin Hood: A Collection of All the Ancient Poems, Songs and Ballads*. T. & J. Egerton & J. Johnson.

1795 O. Goldsmith and T. Parnell. *Poems*. W. Bulmer. With others.

1796 W. Somervile. *The Chase*. Bulmer. With anr.

Thomas Bewick (1753–1828)

1776 *Select Fables, in Three Parts*. Newcastle: T. Saint.

1779 J. Gay. *Fables by the Late Mr. Gay*. Newcastle: Saint.

1784 *Select Fables, in Three Parts*. Enlarged ed., with additional engravings by J. Bewick. Newcastle: Saint.

1790 T. Bewick and R. Beilby. *A General History of Quadrupeds*. Newcastle: S. Hodgson, R. Beilby, & T. Bewick et al.

1795 O. Goldsmith and T. Parnell. *Poems*. W. Bulmer. With others.

1797 T. Bewick and R. Beilby. *History of British Birds. Vol. I, Land Birds*. Newcastle: Beilby & Bewick.

1804 T. Bewick. *History of British Birds. Vol. II, Water Birds*. Newcastle: Bewick.

1818 *The Fables of Aesop and Some Others. With designs on wood by Thomas Bewick*. Newcastle: Bewick. With others.

Thomas Bewick's role in the following books is uncertain.

1772 [P. S. Dufour.] *Moral Instructions of a Father and Son*. Newcastle: Saint.

1789 M. Consett. *A Tour through Sweden, Lapland, Finland, and Denmark*. Stockton: R. Christopher for Consett.

1795 J. Ritson. *Robin Hood: A Collection of All the Ancient Poems, Songs and Ballads*. T. & J. Egerton & J. Johnson.

1796 P. J. B. le Grand d'Aussy. *Fabliaux or Tales*. Bulmer for R. Faulder.

1798   J. Relph. *Poems. Embellished with Picturesque Engravings on Wood by Mr. T. Bewick.* Carlisle: J. Mitchell.

1798   O. Goldsmith. *The Vicar of Wakefield.* "For D. Walker, Hereford."

1806   Bible. Newcastle: Beilby & Bewick.

1818   W. H. Scott. *British Field Sports.* Sherwood, Neeley, & Jones.

*

Bewick, T. *A Memoir: Written by Himself.* Newcastle: Jane Bewick; Longman, 1862. Oxford, 1975.

———. *Vignettes.* Newcastle: Bewick, 1827. Ed. and intro. I. Bain. Scolar, 1978.

Bingley, B. "Bewickiana." *Signature,* n.s., no. 9 (1949).

Dobson, A. *Thomas Bewick and His Pupils.* Chatto & Windus, 1889.

Roscoe, S. *Thomas Bewick: A Bibliography Raisonné.* Oxford, 1953.

Weekley, M. *Thomas Bewick.* Oxford, 1953.

Wood Engravings of Thomas Bewick. Intro. R. Stone. Hart-Davis, 1933.

William Blake (1757–1827)

It is difficult to give exactly or simply the dates of composition and publication of some of Blake's own works. The books cited in the bibliography at the end of this list set forth fully the circumstances for each. Unless otherwise indicated, Blake was his own first publisher. Books for which he engraved plates after designs by others are not included.

[ca. 1785–88]   W. Blake. *Tiriel.* Quaritch, 1885. Oxford, 1967.

1786   T. Commins. *An Elegy, Set to Music.* J. Fentum.

[1788?]   W. Blake. *All Religions Are One.*

[1788?]   W. Blake. *There Is No Natural Religion.*

1789   W. Blake. *The Songs of Innocence.*

1789   W. Blake. *The Book of Thel.*

[ca. 1790–93]   W. Blake. *The Marriage of Heaven and Hell.*

1791   M. Wollstonecraft. *Original Stories from Real Life.* J. Johnson.

1793, 1818   W. Blake. *For Children. The Gates of Paradise.* "W. Blake and J. Johnson."

1793   W. Blake. *Visions of the Daughters of Albion.*

1793   W. Blake. *America: A Prophecy.*

1794   W. Blake. *Europe: A Prophecy.*

1794   W. Blake. *The Songs of Innocence and of Experience.*

1794   W. Blake. *The Book of Urizen.*

1795   W. Blake. *The Song of Los.*

1795   W. Blake. *The Book of Los.*

1795   W. Blake. *The Book of Ahania.*

1796   G. A. Bürger. *Leonora.* W. Miller.

1797   E. Young. *The Complaint, and the Consolation: or, Night Thoughts.* R. Edwards.

1797–98   T. Gray. *Poems.* Oxford, 1972.

1800   W. Hayley. *Little Tom the Sailor.* Folkstone: "The Widow Spicar."

1801   J. Milton. *Comus. A Mask.* Nonesuch, 1926.

1805   W. Hayley. *Ballads.* R. Phillips.

[ca. 1805–07]   W. Blake. *The Four Zoas.* Oxford, 1963.

1807–08   J. Milton. *Paradise Lost.* Liverpool Booksellers, 1906.

1808   R. Blair. *The Grave.* R. H. Cromek.

[ca. 1808–10]   W. Blake. *Milton: a Poem.*

1809   J. Milton. *On the Morning of Christ's Nativity.* Cambridge, 1923.

[ca. 1817]   J. Milton. *L'Allegro and Il Penseroso.* Nonesuch, 1926.

1818–26   W. Blake. *Jerusalem: The Emanation of the Great Albion.*

1821   A. Philips. "Imitation of Virgil's First Eclogue." In *The Pastorals of Virgil Illustrated by 230 Engravings.* Ed. R. J. Thornton. J. M'Gowan & F. G. & J. Rivington.

1824   J. Bunyan. *The Pilgrim's Progress.* Limited Editions, 1941.

1824 [1825]   *Remember Me! A New Year's Gift or Christmas Present.* Thornton.

1825, 8 Mar. [1826]   [Bible.] *Illustrations of the Book of Job.* J. Linnell.

[1825?]   J. Milton. *Paradise Regain'd.* Nonesuch, 1926.

1827   Dante. *Blake's Drawings for Dante's "Divine Comedy".* National Art-Collection Fund, 1922.

*

Bain, I., and D. Chambers. "Printing Blake's Engravings for Thornton's *Virgil*." *The Private Library,* 3rd ser., vol. 1, no. 4 (Winter 1978).

Bentley, G. E., Jr. *Blake Books.* Oxford, 1977.

Bindman, D. *Blake as an Artist.* Oxford: Phaidon, 1977.

———, and D. Toomey. *The Complete Graphic Works of William Blake.* Thames & Hudson, 1978.

Blake, W. *Engravings.* Intro. G. L. Keynes. Faber & Faber, 1950.

Blake in His Time. Ed. R. N. Essick and D. Pearce. Bloomington: Indiana, 1978.

Butlin, M. *William Blake.* Tate Gallery, 1978.

Erdman, D. V. *The Illuminated Blake.* Oxford, 1975.

Essick, R. N. *William Blake, Printmaker.* Princeton, 1980.

———, and R. R. Easson. *William Blake: Illustrator. A Bibliography and Catalogue of the Commercial Engravings.* Normal, Ill.; American Blake Foundation, Illinois State, 1972.

———, and M. D. Paley. *Robert Blair's "The Grave", Illustrated by William Blake.* Scolar, 1982.

Johnson, M. L., and J. E. Grant. *Blake's Poetry and Designs.* New York: Norton, 1979.

Lister, R. *Infernal Methods: William Blake's Art Techniques.* Bell, 1975.

Edward Francesco Burney (1760–1848)

1785   T. Smollett. *Humphrey Clinker.* T. Harrison.

1785   *Arabian Nights' Entertainments.* Harrison. With anr.

1786   S. Richardson. *Pamela.* Harrison.

1786   F. Sheridan. *Memoirs of Miss Sidney Bidulph.* Harrison. With anr.

1788   W. Shakespeare. *The Dramatick Writings of Will. Shakespeare.* J. Bell. With others.

1788 91   W. Shakespeare. *The Plays of William Shakespeare.* D. Bellamy & Robarts. With others.

1793   J. Gay. *Fables.* J. Stockdale. With anr.

1795   F. de S. de La Mothe-Fénelon. *The Adventures of Telemachus.* C. & G. Kearsley. With anr.

1796   J. Milton. *Paradise Regained and the Minor Poems.* Longman.

1797   C. Johnstone. *Chrysal: or, The Adventures of a Guinea.* J. Cooke.

1798   A. Pope. *The Rape of the Lock.* F. J. Du Roveray. With others.

1800   J. Milton. *Paradise Lost.* C. Whittingham.

1810   Homer. *The Iliad and Odyssey.* J. Johnson; T. Sharpe & Hailes. With others.

*

Peckham, M. "Blake, Milton, and Edward Burney." *The Princeton University Library Chronicle* 11, no. 3 (Spring 1950).

Richard Corbould (1757–1831)

Richard Corbould was one of the many contributors to the multitudinous volumes in the popular collections of literature published by Thomas Harrison, John Bell, and John and Charles Cooke. The list is too long, his contributions to individual volumes usually too few, and the quality of his work too ordinary to justify inclusion in the Catalog. Hanns A. Hammelmann and T. R. S. Boase list the eighteenth-century volumes in *Book Illustrators in Eighteenth-Century England* (1975).

1788–91 W. Shakespeare. *The Plays of William Shakespeare*. D. Bellamy & Robarts. With others.
1789 C. Smith. *Elegiac Sonnets*. T. Cadell. With anr.
1796 J. Milton. *Paradise Lost*. J. Parson. With anr.
1802 J. Thomson. *The Seasons*. R. Baldwin, F. & C. Rivington et al.

Daniel Dodd (fl. 1763–93)
1779–80 *Trials for Adultery*. S. Bladon.
1780 H. Fielding. *Amelia*. T. Harrison.
1780 H. Fielding. *Joseph Andrews*. Harrison.
1780 T. Smollett. *Roderick Random*. Harrison.
1781 J. Milton. *Paradise Lost*. The Poetical Magazine.
[ca. 1785] H. Southwell. *The New Book of Martyrs*. J. Cooke.
1788–91 W. Shakespeare. *The Plays of William Shakespeare*. D. Bellamy & Robarts. With others.
1793 S. Richardson. *Clarissa Harlowe*. A. Hogg. With others.

John Flaxman (1755–1826)
The italicized dates are the first London publication.
1793, *1805* Homer. *"The Odyssey" Engraved from the Compositions of John Flaxman R.A. Sculptor*. Longman.
1793, *1795* Homer. *"The Iliad" of Homer Engraved by Thomas Piroli from the Compositions of John Flaxman*. J. Matthews.
1793, *1807* Dante. *Compositions by John Flaxman Sculptor R.A. from the "Divine Poem" of Dante Alighieri, Containing Hell, Purgatory, and Paradise*. Longman.
1795 Aeschylus. *Compositions from the Tragedies of Aeschylus*. "Published for I. Flaxman by J. Matthews."
1805 Homer. *"The Iliad" of Homer Engraved by Thomas Piroli from the Compositions of John Flaxman*. Longman. Five new designs, three engraved by W. Blake.
1817 Hesiod. *Compositions from the "Works Days and Theogony" of Hesiod*. Longman. Engraved by Blake.

*

Bentley, G. E., Jr. *The Early Engravings of Flaxman's Classical Designs*. New York: New York Public Library, 1964.
Irwin, D. G. *John Flaxman, 1755–1826: Sculptor Illustrator Designer*. Studio Vista/Christie's, 1979.

Henry Fuseli (1741–1825)
1769 T. Smollett. *Peregrine Pickle*. R. Baldwin et al.
1789 [1791] E. Darwin. *The Loves of the Plants*. J. Johnson.
1791 E. Darwin. *The Botanic Garden*. Johnson.
1791–97 [Bell's] *British Theatre*. G. Cawthorn. With others.
1798 C. Allen. *A New and Improved Roman History*. Johnson.
1800 T. Gray. *Poems*. F. J. Du Roveray. With anr.
1802 J. Thomson. *The Seasons*. Du Roveray. With anr.
1802 J. Milton. *Paradise Lost*. Du Roveray. With anr.
1803 E. Darwin. *The Temple of Nature*. Johnson.
1805 W. Shakespeare. *The Plays of Shakespeare*. Ed. A. Chalmers. F. C. & J. Rivington et al.
1805 J. Milton. *Paradise Lost*. T. Sharpe.
1805 [1806?] C. M. Wieland. *Oberon: a Poem*. T. Cadell & W. Davies.
1806 [1807] W. Cowper. *Poems*. Johnson.
1810 Homer. *The Iliad and Odyssey*. Johnson; Sharpe & Hailes. With others.

*

Antal, F. *Fuseli Studies*. Routledge & Paul, 1956.
Ganz, P. *The Drawings of Henry Fuseli*. Parrish, 1949.
Henry Fuseli, 1741–1827. Exhibition catalog. Tate Gallery, 1975.
Powell, N. *Fuseli: The Nightmare*. New York: Viking, 1972.
Schiff, G. *Johann Heinrich Füsslis Milton-Galerie*. Zurich and Stuttgart: Fretz & Wasmuth, 1963.
Tomory, P. *The Life and Art of Henry Fuseli*. Thames & Hudson, 1972.

William Hamilton (1751–1801)
1777 J. Ogilvie. *Rona. A Poem*. J. Murray. With anr.
1786 T. Gray. *Poems*. Murray.
1788 W. Shakespeare. *The Dramatick Writings of Will. Shakespeare*. J. Bell. With others.
1797 J. Thomson. *The Seasons*. P. W. Tomkins. With anr.
1800 T. Gray. *Poems*. F. J. Du Roveray. With anr.
1802 J. Thomson. *The Seasons*. Du Roveray. With anr.
1802 J. Milton. *Paradise Lost*. Du Roveray. With anr.
1807 W. Shakespeare. *The Plays*. J. Stockdale. With anr.

Philippe Jacques de Loutherbourg (1740–1812)
1788 W. Shakespeare. *The Dramatick Writings of Will. Shakespeare*. J. Bell. With others.
1791–1800 Bible. T. Macklin. With others.
1805 *Scènes Romantiques et Pittoresques de L'Angleterre et du Pays de Galles*. R. Bowyer.
1812 D. Hume. *The History of England*. Bowyer. With others.
1816 [Bible.] Apocrypha. T. Cadell & W. Davies.

*

Joppien, R. *Philippe Jacques de Loutherbourg, R.A., 1740–1812*. Exhibition catalog, Kenwood House. Greater London Council, 1973.

Henry J. Richter (1772–1857)
1788–91 W. Shakespeare. *The Plays of William Shakespeare*. D. Bellamy & Robarts. With others.
1793 S. Richardson. *Sir Charles Grandison*. A. Hogg. With anr.
1793 S. Richardson. *Clarissa Harlowe*. Hogg. With others.
1794 J. Milton. *Paradise Lost*. J. & H. Richter.

Thomas Rowlandson (1756–1827)
1790 H. Wigstead. *An Excursion to Brighthelmstone*. G. G. J. & J. Robinson.
1791 T. Smollett. *Novels*. Edinburgh: J. Sibbald.
1791 H. Fielding. *The History of Tom Jones, a Foundling*. Edinburgh: Sibbald.
1792 H. Fielding. *The Adventures of Joseph Andrews*. Edinburgh: Sibbald.
1793 T. Smollett. *Humphrey Clinker*. Edinburgh: Sibbald.
1805 T. Smollett. *The Adventures of Peregrine Pickle*. Edinburgh: Sibbald.
1805 T. Smollett. *Roderick Random*. Edinburgh: Sibbald.
1808 [G. M. Woodward.] *Chesterfield Travestie*. T. Tegg.
1808–10 W. H. Pyne and W. Combe. *The Microcosm of London*. R. Ackermann. With anr.
1809 L. Sterne. *A Sentimental Journey*. Tegg.
1809 [R. E. Raspe.] *The Renowned Baron Munchausen*. Tegg.
1812 W. Combe. *The Tour of Doctor Syntax, in Search of the Picturesque*. Ackermann.
1815–16 W. Combe. *The English Dance of Death*. Ackermann.
1816 Quiz [pseud.]. *The Grand Master: or Adventures of Qui Hi? in Hindostan*. Tegg.

1816 [D. Roberts.] *The Military Adventures of Johnny Newcome*. P. Martin.

1817 W. Combe. *The Dance of Life*. Ackermann.

1817 O. Goldsmith. *The Vicar of Wakefield*. Ackermann.

1818 A. Burton [pseud.]. *The Adventures of Johnny Newcome in the Navy*. Simpkin & Marshall.

1820 W. Combe. *The Second Tour of Doctor Syntax, in Search of Consolation*. Ackermann.

1820–21 W. Combe. *The Third Tour of Doctor Syntax, in Search of a Wife*. Ackermann

1821 [M. A. von Thümmel.] *Journal of Sentimental Travels in the Southern Provinces of France*. Ackermann.

1822 W. Combe. *The History of Johnny Quae Genus*. Ackermann.

*

A Catalogue of Books Illustrated by Thomas Rowlandson. New York: Grolier Club, 1916.

Hayes, J. *Rowlandson: Watercolours and Drawings*. Phaidon, 1972.

Paulson, R. *Rowlandson: A New Interpretation*. Studio Vista, 1972.

Wark, R. R. *Drawings by Thomas Rowlandson in the Huntington Library*. San Marino, Cal.: Henry E. Huntington Library and Art Gallery, 1975.

Wolf, E. C. J. *Rowlandson and His Illustrations of Eighteenth Century English Literature*. Copenhagen: Munksgaard, 1945.

Charles Ryley (ca. 1752–98)

1782–86 W. Shakespeare. *Plays*. W. Lowndes. With others.

1783–87 C. Taylor. *The Picturesque Beauties of Shakespeare*. C. Taylor. With others.

1788–91 W. Shakespeare. *The Plays of William Shakespeare*. D. Bellamy & Robarts. With others.

Thomas Stothard (1755–1834)

1783 J. Ritson. *A Select Collection of English Songs*. J. Johnson. Engraved by W. Blake.

1783–87 C. Taylor. *The Picturesque Beauties of Shakespeare*. C. Taylor. With others.

1790 D. Defoe. *Robinson Crusoe*. J. Stockdale.

1792 L. Sterne. *A Sentimental Journey*. J. Good & E. & S. Harding.

1792 J. Bunyan. *The Pilgrim's Progress*. J. Mathews, Scatcherd, T. Whitaker, & G. Terry.

1792 O. Goldsmith. *The Vicar of Wakefield*. Harding & Good.

1792–93 J. Milton. *Paradise Lost*. T. Jeffryes.

1793 W. Haley. *The Triumphs of Temper*. T. Cadell.

1793–94 *The English Anthology*. Ed. J. Ritson. T. & J. Egerton.

1794 J. Thomson. *The Seasons*. Stockdale. With anr.

1794 S. Rogers. *The Pleasures of Memory*. Cadell, W. Davies, & C. Dilly. With others.

1794 [Church of England.] *The Book of Common Prayer*. Good & Harding.

1795 F. de S. de La Mothe-Fénelon. *The Adventures of Telemachus*. C. & G. Kearsley. With anr.

1796 A. Pope. *Essay on Man*. Cadell.

1797 S. Gessner. *The Death of Abel and New Idylls*. T. Heptinstall.

1797 W. Collins. *Poetical Works*. Cadell & Davies.

1798 W. Cowper. *Poems*. Johnson.

1798 A. Pope. *The Rape of the Lock*. F. J. Du Roveray. With others.

1800 W. Somervile. *The Chase*. T. Cadell, Jr., & Davies.

1801 H. Macneill. *Poetical Works*. Longman.

1802 E. Spenser. *The Faerie Queene*. Heath & Kearsley.

1804 R. Glover. *Leonidas*. Cadell & Davies; Longman. With others.

1807 W. Shakespeare. *The Plays*. Stockdale. With anr.

1810 Homer. *The Iliad and Odyssey*. Johnson; T. Sharpe & Hailes. With others.

1810 S. Rogers. *The Pleasures of Memory*. Cadell & Davies.

1813 W. Scott. *Rokeby*. Edinburgh: J. Ballantyne; Longman.

1814 R. Burns. *Poems*. Cadell.

1815 [1814–25] T. J. Dibdin. *The London Theatre*. C. Whittingham & Arliss. With anr.

1818–20 G. G. N., Lord Byron. *Works*. J. Murray.

1820 W. Scott. *Tales of My Landlord*. Rodwell.

1825 G. Boccaccio. *The Decameron*. W. Pickering.

1826 W. Shakespeare. *Dramatic Works*. Chiswick: Whittingham.

1830 S. Rogers. *Italy: A Poem*. Cadell & Moxon. With anr.

1834 S. Rogers. *Poems*. Cadell & Moxon. With anr.

1836 I. Walton and C. Cotton. *The Complete Angler, or Contemplative Man's Recreation*. Pickering.

*

Bray, A. E. S. *Life of Thomas Stothard, R.A.* Murray, 1851.

Coxhead, A. C. *Thomas Stothard, R.A.* Bullen, 1906.

Dobson, A. *Eighteenth Century Vignettes*. First series. Chatto & Windus, 1892.

CHAPTER SIX

The Nineteenth Century (I)
1801-1854

Henry Thomas Alken (1784–1851)

1821–22   *The Real Life of London: the Adventures of Bob Tallyho, Esq. and His Cousin the Hon. Tom Dashell by an Amateur.* Jones. With others.

1831   M. de Cervantes Saavedra. *Illustrations of "Don Quixote".* Tilt.

1835   C. J. Apperley [Nimrod, pseud.]. *Memoirs of the Life of John Mytton.* Ackermann. With anr.

1842   C. J. Apperley [Nimrod, pseud.]. *The Life of a Sportsman.* Ackermann.

1843   R. J. Surtees. *Jorrocks's Jaunts and Jollities.* Ackermann.

1843   C. J. Apperley [Nimrod, pseud.]. *The Chace, the Turf, and the Road.* Murray. With anr.

1846   R. S. Surtees. *The Analysis of the Hunting Field.* Ackermann.

*

Noakes, A. *The World of Henry Alken.* Witherby, 1952.

Sparrow, W. S. *Henry Alken.* Williams & Norgate, 1927.

Van Devanter, W. "A Checklist of Books Illustrated by Henry Alken." In *Homage to a Bookman.* Berlin: Kraus, 1967.

Hablot Knight Browne [Phiz] (1815–82)

1836   T. Sparks [C. Dickens]. *Sunday under Three Heads.* Chapman & Hall.

1837   C. Dickens. *The Posthumous Papers of the Pickwick Club.* Chapman & Hall. With others.

1838   [C. Dickens.] *Sketches of Young Gentlemen.* Chapman & Hall.

1838   R. S. Surtees. *Jorrocks's Jaunts and Jollities.* Spiers.

1838   D. Blake. *The Old English Squire.* Spiers.

1838   J. Grant. *Sketches in London.* Orr.

1839   C. Dickens. *The Life and Adventures of Nicholas Nickleby.* Chapman & Hall.

1839   C. Lever. *The Confessions of Harry Lorrequer.* Dublin: Curry.

1839   J. Fume [W. A. Chatto]. *A Paper. – of Tobacco.* Chatto & Windus.

1839   D. W. Jerrold. *The Handbook of Swindling.* Chapman & Hall.

1840   [C. Dickens.] *Sketches of Young Couples.* Chapman & Hall.

1840   T. Hook. *Precept and Practice.* Colburn.

1840   G. W. M. Reynolds. *Robert Macaire in England.* Tegg.

1841   C. Dickens. *Master Humphrey's Clock. The Old Curiosity Shop. Barnaby Rudge.* Chapman & Hall. With anr.

1841   C. Dickens et al. *The Pic Nic Papers.* Ed. C. Dickens. Colburn. With others.

1841   C. Lever. *Charles O'Malley.* Dublin: Curry.

1841   W. J. Neale. *Paul Periwinkle.* Tegg.

1841   [J. T. J. Hewlett.] *Peter Priggins.* Colburn.

1841   C. Pelham [pseud.]. *The Chronicles of Crime.* Tegg.

1841   F. M. Trollope. *Charles Chesterfield.* Colburn.

1842   W. H. Maxwell. *Rambling Recollections of a Soldier.* Dublin: Curry.

1842–47   W. Scott. *Waverley Novels.* Edinburgh: Cadell. With others.

1843   G. P. R. James. *The Commissioner.* Dublin: Duffy.

1843   C. Lever. *Jack Hinton the Guardsman.* Dublin: Curry.

1843   T. Miller. *Godfrey Malvern.* Miller.

1843   W. Carleton. *Traits and Stories of the Irish Peasantry.* Dublin: Duffy. With others.

1844   C. Dickens. *The Life and Adventures of Martin Chuzzlewit.* Chapman & Hall.

1844   C. Lever. *Tom Burke of "Ours".* Dublin: Curry.

1845   C. Lever. *Nuts and Nutcrackers.* Orr.

1845   C. Lever. *The O'Donoghue.* Dublin: Curry.

1845   C. Lever. *St. Patrick's Eve.* Chapman & Hall.

[1845]   G. H. B. Rodwell. *Memoirs of an Umbrella.* Mackenzie.

1847   C. Lever. *The Knight of Gwynne.* Chapman & Hall.

1847   R. S. Surtees. *Hawbuck Grange.* Longman.

1847   J. S. Le Fanu. *The Fortunes of Colonel Torlogh O'Brien.* Dublin: M'Glashan.

1847   W. H. Ainsworth. *Old St. Paul's.* Parry, Blenkarn. With anr.

1847   W. Carleton. *Valentine M'Clutchy, the Irish Agent.* Dublin: Duffy.

1848   C. Dickens. *Dealings with the Firm of Dombey and Son.* Bradbury & Evans.

1848   B. Jerrold. *The Disgrace of the Family.* Darton.

1848   H. Mayhew and A. S. Mayhew. *The Image of His Father.* Hurst.

1849   W. H. Ainsworth. *Crichton.* Chapman & Hall.

1849   G. P. R. James. *The Fight of the Fiddlers.* Orr.

1850   C. Dickens. *The Personal History of David Copperfield.* Bradbury & Evans.

1850   C. Lever. *Roland Cashel.* Chapman & Hall.

[1850]   C. Lever. *The Confessions of Con Cregan.* Orr.

1852   C. Lever. *The Daltons: or Three Roads in Life.* Chapman & Hall.

1852   F. E. Smedley. *Lewis Arundel.* Virtue, Hall, & Virtue.

1853   C. Dickens. *Bleak House.* Bradbury & Evans.

1853   F. E. Smedley. *The Fortunes of the Colville Family.* Hoby.

1854   C. Lever. *The Dodd Family Abroad.* Chapman & Hall.

1855   F. E. Smedley. *Harry Coverdale's Courtship.* Virtue, Hall, & Virtue.

1855   R. E. Egerton-Warburton. *Three Hunting Songs.* Chapman & Hall.

1856   C. Lever. *The Martins of Cro'Martin.* Chapman & Hall.

1857 [Dec. 1856]   W. H. Ainsworth. *The Spendthrift.* Routledge.

1857   C. Dickens. *Little Dorrit.* Bradbury & Evans.

1857   W. H. Ainsworth. *The Star-Chamber.* Routledge.

1857   H. Fielding. *Amelia.* Routledge.

1857   H. Fielding. *Joseph Andrews.* Routledge.

1857   H. Fielding. *Tom Jones.* Routledge.

1857   T. Smollett. *Roderick Random.* Routledge.

1857   T. Smollett. *Peregrine Pickle.* Routledge.

1858   M. S. Gatty. *Legendary Tales.* Bell & Daldy.

1858   W. H. Ainsworth. *Mervyn Clitheroe.* Routledge.

1858   A. S. Mayhew. *Paved with Gold: or the Romance and Reality of the London Streets, An Unfashionable Novel.* Chapman & Hall.

1858   G. W. Thornbury. *The Buccaneers.* Hurst & Blackett.

1859   C. Lever. *Davenport Dunn: A Man of Our Day.* Chapman & Hall.

1859   H. E. B. Stowe. *The Minister's Wooing.* Low.

[1859]   C. Dickens. *A Tale of Two Cities.* Chapman & Hall.

1860   W. H. Ainsworth. *Ovingdean Grange.* Routledge.

1861   G. Halse. *Agatha*. Harrison.

1861   C. Lever. *One of Them*. Chapman & Hall.

1863   C. Lever. *Barrington*. Chapman & Hall.

1864   [W. Eassie.] *Sir Guy de Guy*. Routledge.

1864–65   A. Trollope. *Can You Forgive Her?* Chapman & Hall.

1865   C. Lever. *Luttrell of Arran*. Chapman & Hall.

1865   W. H. Ainsworth. *Auriol: or, The Elixir of Life*. Routledge.

[1868]   H. K. Browne. *Racing and Chasing*. Ward, Lock, & Tyler.

1871   L. Benson. *The Book of Remarkable Trials and Notorious Characters*. Hotten.

1874   C. Dickens. *The Posthumous Papers of the Pickwick Club*. Chapman & Hall.

1876–78   C. Lever. *The Harry Lorrequer Edition*. Routledge.

[1876?]   Damocles [H. K. Browne]. *All about Kisses*. Clarke.

[1882–84]   W. Shakespeare. *Works*. Ward & Lock.

*

Bentley, N. *Hablôt K. Browne*. Art & Technics, 1949.

Browne, E. A. *Phiz and Dickens: As They Appeared to Edgar Browne*. Nisbet, 1913.

Buchanan-Brown, J. *Phiz: Illustrator of Dickens' World*. New York: Scribner, 1978.

Johannsen, A. *Phiz: Illustrations from the Novels of Charles Dickens*. Chicago, 1956.

Kitton, F. G. *"Phiz": Hablôt Knight Browne, a Memoir*. Redway, 1882.

Leavis, Q. D. "The Dickens Illustrations: Their Function." In F. R. Leavis and Q. D. Leavis. *Dickens the Novelist*. Chatto & Windus, 1970.

Matz, B. W. "'Phiz.' The Centenary of Hablot Knight Browne." *The Bookman* 48 (June 1915).

Steig, M. "Dickens, Hablôt Browne, and the Tradition of English Caricature." *Criticism* 11, no. 3 (Summer 1969).

Thompson, D. C. *The Life and Labours of Hablôt Knight Browne, "Phiz"*. Chapman & Hall, 1884.

Waugh, A. "Charles Dickens and His Illustrators." In *Retrospectus and Prospectus: The Nonesuch Dickens*. Nonesuch, 1937.

George Cattermole (1800–68)

1832–33   G. G. N., Lord Byron. *The Life and Works of Lord Byron*. Longman. With others.

1834   T. Gray. *Elegy Written in a Country Church-Yard*. Van Voorst. With others.

1841   C. Dickens. *Master Humphrey's Clock. The Old Curiosity Shop. Barnaby Rudge*. Chapman & Hall. With anr.

1841, 1844   R. Cattermole. *The Great Civil War*. Vol. 1, Cattermole; vol. 2, Heath.

[1845?]   *Scott and Scotland*. Ed. H. I. Stevens and A. Stevens. Stevens.

1846   E. C., baroness de Calabrella. *Evenings at Haddon Hall*. Colburn. With others.

John Heaviside Clark (ca. 1770–1863)

1814   *Foreign Field Sports, Fisheries, Sporting Anecdotes, &c. &c.* Orme. With others.

1819   M. de Cervantes Saavedra. *Don Quixote*. Tr. T. Smollett. M'Lean.

1819   A. R. Le Sage. *Gil Blas*. Tr. T. Smollett. M'Lean.

1819   S. Butler. *Hudibras*. M'Lean. With anr.

Edward Henry Corbould (1815–1905)

1838   T. Moore. *Lalla Rookh*. Longman. With others.

1842   *The Book of British Ballads*. [First series.] Ed. S. C. Hall. How. With others.

1842–47   W. Scott. *Waverley Novels*. Edinburgh: Cadell. With others.

1844   *The Book of British Ballads*. Second series. Ed. S. C. Hall. How. With others.

1844   *The Arabian Nights' Entertainments*. Harrison. With others.

[1845]   F. H. K., baron de la Motte-Fouqué. *Minstrel Love*. Lumley.

1853   E. Spenser. *The Faerie Queene*. Routledge.

1857   W. Scott. *The Poetical Works*. Routledge.

[1857]   *Reliques of Ancient English Poetry*. Ed. T. Percy. Routledge.

1858   J. Milton. *Comus: A Mask*. Routledge. With others.

1859   E. McDermott. *The Merrie Days of England*. Kent. With others.

[1859?]   R. Johnson. *Seven Champions of Christendom*. Blackwood.

1860   *A Book of Favourite Modern Ballads*. Kent. With others.

1864   J. Milton. *The Poetical Works*. Nelson. With anr.

1870   G. Chaucer. *The Canterbury Tales*. Routledge.

[1883]   G. W. M. Reynolds. *The Rye House Plot; or, Ruth, the Conspirator's Daughter*. Dicks.

Thomas Creswick (1811–69)

1842   *The Book of British Ballads*. [First series.] Ed. S. C. Hall. How. With others.

1842   O. Goldsmith. *The Deserted Village: Illustrated by the Etching Club*. Longman. With others.

1847   T. Gray. *Elegy Written in a Country Churchyard*. Etching Club. With others.

1857   A., Lord Tennyson. *Poems*. Moxon. With others.

1859   *Favourite English Poems*. Low. With others.

1863   *Early English Poems: Chaucer to Pope*. Low. With others.

George Cruikshank (1792–1878)

1815   W. Combe [Dr. Syntax, pseud.]. *Life of Napoleon: A Hudibrastic Poem*. Tegg & Allason.

1818   J. Kerr. *Ancient Legends*. Duncombe. With anr.

1821   P. Egan. *Life in London*. Sherwood, Neely, & Jones. With anr.

1822   D. Carey. *Life in Paris*. Fairburn.

1823   Brothers Grimm. *German Popular Stories*. Vol. 1. Baldwyn.

1823 [1824]   A. von Chamisso. *Peter Schlemihl*. Whittaker.

1823–24   *Points of Humour*. Baldwyn.

1824   J. Wight. *Mornings at Bow Street*. Baldwyn.

1824   *Italian Tales of Humour, Gallantry and Romance*. Baldwyn.

1824   [J. Whitty.] *Tales of Irish Life*. Robins.

1825   *Memoirs of the Life and Writings of Lord Byron*. Comp. G. Clinton. Robins. Attributed.

1826   M. H. Barker. *Greenwich Hospital*. Robins.

1826   Brothers Grimm. *German Popular Stories*. Vol. 2. Robins.

1827   J. Wight. *More Mornings at Bow Street*. Robins.

1828   J. P. Collier. *Punch and Judy*. Prowett. Limited Editions, 1937.

1828   W. Cowper. *The Diverting History of John Gilpin*. Tilt.

1830   T. Hood. *The Epping Hunt*. Tilt.

1830   [W. Clarke.] *Three Courses and a Dessert*. Vizetelly, Branston.

1830   R. Southey. *The Life of Nelson*. Murray.

1830   J. Y. Akerman. *Tales of Other Days*. Wilson.

1831 [1830]   J. Dalton. *The Gentleman in Black*. Kidd.

1831   D. Defoe. *Robinson Crusoe*. Major.

1831   T. Smollett. *Humphry Clinker*. Cochrane & Pickersgill.

1831   T. Smollett. *Roderick Random*. Cochrane.

1831   T. Smollett. *Peregrine Pickle*. Cochrane & Andrews.

1831   H. Fielding. *Tom Jones*. Cochrane.

1832   H. Fielding. *Joseph Andrews*. Cochrane.

1832   H. Fielding. *Amelia*. Cochrane.

1832 O. Goldsmith. *The Vicar of Wakefield*. T. Smollett. *Sir Launce-lot Greaves*. Cochrane.

1832 L. Sterne. *Tristram Shandy*. Cochrane.

1832 C. Anstey. *The New Bath Guide*. Washbourne. With anr.

1833 M. de Cervantes Saavedra. *Don Quixote*. Wilson.

1833 A. R. Le Sage. *Gil Blas*. Wilson.

1833 J. Wight. *Sunday in London*. Wilson.

1833 D. Defoe. *A Journal of the Plague in London, 1665*. Murray.

1834 W. Irving. *A History of New York*. Murray.

1835 W. Irving. *The Beauties of Washington Irving*. Tegg.

1835 M. H. Barker. *Tough Yarns*. Wilson.

1836 C. Dickens. *Sketches by Boz*. First Series. Macrone.

1836 W. H. Ainsworth. *Rookwood*. Macrone.

1836–39 W. Scott. *Waverley Novels*. Fisher. With others.

1837 C. Dickens. *Sketches by Boz*. Second Series. Macrone.

1838 C. Dickens. *Oliver Twist*. Bentley.

1838 J. Grimaldi. *Memoirs*. Ed. C. Dickens. Bentley.

1839 W. H. Ainsworth. *Jack Sheppard*. Bentley.

1839 [W. M. Thackeray; notes by C. Dickens.] *The Loving Ballad of Lord Bateman*. Tilt.

1840 W. H. Ainsworth. *The Tower of London*. Bentley.

1840, 1842, 1847 R. H. Barham. *The Ingoldsby Legends*. Bentley. With others.

1841 W. H. Ainsworth. *Guy Fawkes*. Bentley.

1841 C. Dibdin. *Songs: Naval and National*. Murray.

1842 W. H. Ainsworth. *The Miser's Daughter*. Cunningham & Mortimer.

1842 J. O'Neill. *The Drunkard*. Tilt & Bogue.

1843 W. H. Ainsworth. *Windsor Castle*. Colburn. With anr.

1844 M. H. Barker. *The Old Sailor's Jolly Boat*. Strange. With anr.

1844 W. H. Ainsworth. *St. James's*. Mortimer.

1844 G. Cruikshank. *The Bachelor's Own Book: Being the Progress of Mr. Lambkin, Gent*. Cruikshank. Sold by Bogue.

1844 G. Raymond. *Memoirs of Robert William Elliston*. Mortimer.

1844 C. Lever. *Arthur O'Leary*. Colburn.

1845 W. H. Maxwell. *History of the Irish Rebellion in 1798*. Baily Bros.

1848 E. G. Flight. *The True Legend of St. Dunstan*. Bogue.

1849 A. Reach. *Clement Lorimer*. Bogue.

1850 F. E. Smedley. *Frank Fairleigh*. Hall, Virtue.

1852 H. B. Stowe. *Uncle Tom's Cabin*. Cassell.

1852 C. W. Hoskyns. *Talpa: or the Chronicles of a Clay Farm*. Reeve.

1858 R. B. Brough. *The Life of Sir John Falstaff*. Longman.

[1859] A. S. Mayhew. *The Greatest Plague of Life*. Routledge.

1864 R. H. Barham. *The Ingoldsby Legends*. Bentley. With others.

1867 R. E. Raspe. *The Travels of Baron Munchausen*. Tegg.

1903 J. Bunyan. *The Pilgrim's Progress*. Oxford: Frowde.

*

Buchanan-Brown, J. *George Cruikshank*. Newton Abbot: David & Charles, 1980.

Cohn, A. M. *A Catalogue Raisonné of the Printed Works Illustrated by George Cruikshank*. Bookman's Journal, 1924.

George Cruikshank. Intro. W. Feaver. Exhibition catalog, Victoria and Albert Museum. Arts Council of Great Britain, 1974.

"George Cruikshank: A Revaluation." Ed. R. L. Patten. *The Princeton University Library Bulletin* (1973).

McLean, R. *George Cruikshank*. Art & Technics, 1948.

Isaac Robert Cruikshank (1789–1856)

1821 P. Egan. *Life in London*. Sherwood, Neely, & Jones. With anr.

1823 C. M. Westmacott. *Points of Misery*. Sherwood, Jones.

1824 M. de Cervantes Saavedra. *Don Quixote*. Knight & Lacey.

1825 *The Universal Songster*. Fairburn. With anr.

1825–26 C. M. Westmacott. *The English Spy*. Sherwood, Jones.

1829 P. Egan. *Finish to the Adventures of Tom, Jerry, and Logic*. Strange. With anr.

1830 W. W. Montagu. *Monsieur Mallét*. Griffith.

1830 S. T. Coleridge and R. Southey. *The Devil's Walk*. Marsh & Miller.

1833 [J. Birch.] *Fifty-One Original Fables*. Hamilton, Adams.

1837 C. Lamb and M. Lamb. *Tales from Shakespeare*. Pigot.

[1837] [J. Birch.] *Divine Emblems*. Ward.

1838 P. Pry [pseud.]. *Oddities of London Life*. Bentley.

1839 *The Lady and the Saints*. Bull.

[1840?] R. Cruikshank. *Cruikshank at Home*. Kidd.

1841 H. Playfair [pseud.]. *The Playfair Papers: or, Brother Jonathan, the Smartest Nation in All Creation*. Saunders & Otley.

[1841] M. H. Barker. *Jem Bunt*. How & Parsons. With others.

1842 G. Daniel. *Merrie England in the Olden Time*. Bentley. With anr.

1844 M. H. Barker. *The Old Sailor's Jolly Boat*. Strange. With anr.

Richard Doyle (1824–83)

1843 W. H. Maxwell. *The Fortunes of Hector O'Halloran and His Man Mark Antony O'Toole*. Bentley. With anr.

1845 C. Dickens. *The Chimes*. Chapman & Hall. With others.

1846 C. Dickens. *The Cricket on the Hearth*. Bradbury & Evans. With others.

1847 C. Dickens. *The Battle of Life*. Bradbury & Evans. With others.

1848 L. Hunt. *A Jar of Honey from Mount Hybla*. Smith, Elder.

[1849] P. Leigh. *Manners and Customs of Ye Englyshe, Drawn from Ye Qvick by Rychard Doyle*. Bradbury & Evans.

1850 W. M. Thackeray. *Rebecca and Rowena*. Chapman & Hall.

1851 J. Ruskin. *The King of the Golden River*. Smith, Elder.

1854 R. Doyle. *The Foreign Tour of Messrs. Brown, Jones, and Robinson*. Bradbury & Evans.

1854–55 W. M. Thackeray. *The Newcomes*. Bradbury & Evans.

1865 F. Locker [-Lampson]. *A Selection from the Works of Frederick Locker*. Moxon.

1870 W. Allingham. *In Fairyland*. Longman.

*

Hambourg, D. *Richard Doyle: His Life and Work*. Art & Technics, 1948.

Myles Birket Foster (1825–99)

[1847] T. Miller. *The Country Year Book*. Chapman & Hall. With others.

1850 W. Howitt. *The Year-Book of the Country*. Colburn.

1850 H. W. Longfellow. *Evangeline*. Bogue. With others.

1851 *Christmas with the Poets*. Bogue.

1851 O. Goldsmith. *The Poetical Works*. Cundall & Addey. With others.

[1851] H. W. Longfellow. *Voices of the Night*. Bogue. With others.

1852 H. W. Longfellow. *Hyperion*. Bogue.

[1852?] E. A. Poe. *Poetical Works*. Griffin. With others.

1853 W. Scott. *The Lady of the Lake*. Edinburgh: Black. With others.

1853 J. Thomson et al. *The Poetical Works*. Routledge. With others.

1854 W. Scott. *The Lay of the Last Minstrel*. Edinburgh: Black. With others.

1854 G. G. N., Lord Byron. *The Illustrated Byron*. Vizetelly. With others.

1854 M. Tupper. *Proverbial Philosophy*. Hatchard. With others.

1854 T. Gray. *An Elegy Written in a Country Churchyard*. Cundall. With others.

1855 J. Milton. *L'Allegro and Il Penseroso*. Bogue.

1855 W. Scott. *Marmion*. Edinburgh: Black. With others.

1855 M. Akenside and J. Dyer. *The Poetical Works*. Routledge.

1855 W. Cowper. *The Task*. Nisbet.

1855 O. Goldsmith. *The Traveller*. Bogue.

1856 *Sabbath Bells Chimed by the Poets*. Bell & Daldy.

1857 *The Poets of the Nineteenth Century*. Ed. R. A. Willmott. Routledge. With others.

1857 R. Bloomfield. *The Farmer's Boy*. Low. With others.

1857 R. Burns. *Poems & Songs*. Bell & Daldy. With others.

1857 T. Moore. *Poetry and Pictures*. Longman. With others.

1857 R. Pollok. *The Course of Time*. Blackwood. With others.

1857 G. Herbert. *The Poetical Works*. Nisbet. With anr.

1857 T. Campbell. *Gertrude of Wyoming*. Routledge. With others.

1857 W. Scott. *The Lord of the Isles*. Edinburgh: Black. With others.

1857 W. C. Bryant. *Poems*. New York: Appleton. Low, 1858. With others.

[1857] S. T. Coleridge. *The Rime of the Ancient Mariner*. Marston, Low, & Searle. With others.

1858 *Lays of the Holy Land*. Nisbet. With others.

1858 J. Beattie. *The Minstrel*. Routledge.

1858 W. Falconer. *The Shipwreck*. Edinburgh: Black.

1858 *The Home Affections, Pourtrayed by the Poets*. Ed. C. Mackay. Routledge. With others.

1858 J. Milton. *Comus: A Mask*. Routledge. With others.

1859 O. Goldsmith. *The Poems of Oliver Goldsmith*. Routledge.

1859 *Odes and Sonnets*. Routledge.

1859 E. McDermott. *The Merrie Days of England*. Kent. With others.

1859 T. Miller. *English Country Life*. Second ed. Routledge. With others.

1859 T. Warton. *The Hamlet*. Low.

1859 W. Wordsworth. *Poems of William Wordsworth*. Routledge. With others.

1859 W. Adams. *Sacred Allegories*. Rivington. With others.

1859 J. Thomson. *The Seasons*. Nisbet. With others.

1860 *A Book of Favourite Modern Ballads*. Kent. With others.

1860 J. Montgomery. *The Poems of James Montgomery*. Routledge. With others.

1861 *Household Song*. Kent. With others.

1863 T. Miller. *Common Wayside Flowers*. Routledge.

1863 *Early English Poems: Chaucer to Pope*. Low. With others.

1863 T. Taylor. *Birket Foster's Pictures of English Landscape. With Pictures in Words by Tom Taylor*. Routledge.

[1863?] *Old English Ballads*. Ward, Lock, & Tyler. With others.

*

Cundall, H. M. *Birket Foster, R.W.S.* Black, 1906.

Huish, M. B. *Birket Foster. Art Journal* Office, 1890.

Lewis, F. *Myles Birket Foster, 1825–1899*. Leigh-on-Sea: Lewis, 1973. Huish rewritten.

John Franklin (ca. 1800–68)

1836 *The Ancient Ballad of Chevy Chase*. Saunders & Otley.

[1841] W. H. Ainsworth. *Old St. Paul's*. Routledge.

1842 W. Scott. *The Talisman*. Edinburgh: Cadell. With others.

1842 *The Book of British Ballads*. [First series.] Ed. S. C. Hall. How. With others.

1844 *The Book of British Ballads. Second series*. Ed. S. C. Hall. How. With others.

[1844] F. H. K., baron de la Motte-Fouqué. *Wild Love and Other Tales*. Lumley.

1846 *Poems and Pictures*. Burns. With others.

1846 M. C. Gray. *Early Days of English Princes*. Grant & Griffith.

[1851] [Bible.] *The Parables of Our Lord*. Low. With others.

1853 J. Dryden. *Poetical Works*. Routledge.

1855 F. H. K., baron de la Motte-Fouqué. *The Four Seasons*. Lumley. With others.

1862 [Bible.] *The Psalms of David*. Low.

1862 W. H. Adams. *The Men at the Helm*. Hogg.

[1863?] *Old English Ballads*. Ward, Lock, & Tyler. With others.

1864 H. P. Dunster. *Historical Tales of Lancastrian Times*. Griffith & Farran.

Jean Ignace Isadore Gérard. See Grandville.

Sir John Gilbert (1817–97)

1840, 1842, 1847 R. H. Barham. *The Ingoldsby Legends*. Bentley. With others.

1841 W. Cowper. *Poems*. Routledge.

1842 *The Book of British Ballads*. [First series.] Ed. S. C. Hall. How. With others.

[ca. 1845?] *City Scenes*. Harvey & Darton.

1844 *The Arabian Nights' Entertainments*. New York: H. G. Langley.

1853 C. Mackay. *The Salamandrine*. Ingram, Cooke.

1853 H. W. Longfellow. *Prose Works*. Routledge.

1853 W. Scott. *The Lady of the Lake*. Edinburgh: Black. With others.

1854 W. Scott. *The Lay of the Last Minstrel*. Edinburgh: Black. With others.

1854 H. W. Ainsworth. *The Lancashire Witches*. Routledge.

1854 H. W. Ainsworth. *The Flitch of Bacon*. Routledge.

1854 M. Tupper. *Proverbial Philosophy*. Hatchard. With others.

1855 W. Scott. *Marmion*. Edinburgh: Black. With others.

1856 M. de Cervantes Saavedra. *Don Quixote*. Routledge.

1856 R. Burns. *Poems*. Routledge.

1856 H. W. Longfellow. *The Poetical Works of Henry Wadsworth Longfellow*. Routledge.

1856 J. Bunyan. *The Pilgrim's Progress*. Routledge.

1857 *The Poets of the Nineteenth Century*. Ed. R. A. Willmott. Routledge. With others.

1857 W. Scott. *The Lord of the Isles*. Edinburgh: Black. With others.

1857 W. H. Ainsworth. *Rookwood*. Routledge.

1857 [Bible.] *The Book of Job*. Nisbet.

1857 [Bible.] *The Proverbs of Solomon*. Nisbet.

1858 W. Shakespeare. *The Plays of William Shakespeare*. Ed. H. Staunton. Routledge.

1858 *The Home Affections, Pourtrayed by the Poets*. Ed. C. Mackay. Routledge. With others.

1859 W. Wordsworth. *Poems of William Wordsworth*. Routledge. With others.

1859 H. W. Longfellow. *The Courtship of Miles Standish*. Routledge.

1859 T. Miller. *English Country Life*. Second ed. Routledge. With others.

1859 C. Mackay. *Collected Songs*. Routledge.

1859 C. Mackay. *Ballads and Lyrics*. Routledge.

1860 J. Montgomery. *The Poems of James Montgomery*. Routledge. With others.

1861 E. Cook. *Poems*. Routledge.

1861 W. H. Ainsworth. *The Constable of the Tower*. Chapman & Hall.

1861 *English Sacred Poetry of the Sixteenth, Seventeenth, and Eighteenth Centuries*. Ed. R. A. Willmott. Routledge. With others.

1862 T. Campbell. *The Poetical Works*. Routledge.

1862 W. Shakespeare. *Songs and Sonnets*. Low.

1863 *Early English Poems: Chaucer to Pope*. Low. With others.

[1863?]   *Old English Ballads.* Ward, Lock, & Tyler. With others.

1864   J. Milton. *The Poetical Works.* Nelson. With anr.

1865   *Our Life Illustrated by Pen and Pencil.* Religious Tract Society. With others.

1865   T. C. H., viscount de La Villemarqué. *Ballads and Songs of Brittany.* Tr. T. Taylor. Macmillan. With others.

1866   A. Pope. *The Poetical Works.* Routledge.

1866   H. W. Longfellow. *Tales of a Wayside Inn.* Boston: Ticknor & Fields.

1866   C. Lamb and M. Lamb. *Tales from Shakespeare.* Routledge.

[1866]   J. Foxe. *The Book of Martyrs.* Cassell, Petter, & Galpin. With others.

1868 [1867]   J. Cundall [S. Percy, pseud.]. *Tales of the Kings of England.* Routledge.

1869   *A Thousand and One Gems of English Poetry.* Routledge. With others.

[1870?]   R. Southey. *Joan of Arc.* Routledge.

[1879?]   *The Book of Brave Old Ballads.* Ward, Lock, & Tyler.

Grandville [Jean Ignace Isadore Gérard] (1803–47)

1840   D. Defoe. *Robinson Crusoe.* Willoughby, Routledge.

[1840]   J. Swift. *Gulliver's Travels.* Hayward & Moore.

1842   *Fables: Original and Selected.* Willoughby.

*

Bizarreries and Fantasies of Grandville. Ed. S. Appelbaum. New York: Dover, [1974].

Grandville [J. I. I. Gérard]. *Das gesamte Werk.* Munich: Rogner & Bernhard, 1969.

Mespoulet, M. *Creators of Wonderland.* New York: Arrow, 1934.

William Harvey (1796–1866)

1824   A. Henderson. *The History of Ancient and Modern Wines.* Baldwin & Cradock.

1825   W. Shakespeare. *The Dramatick Works.* Bumpus; Sherwood, Jones.

1828   J. Northcote. *One Hundred Fables, Original and Selected.* [First series.] Lawford. With Northcote.

1829   [E. T. Bennett.] *The Tower Menagerie.* Jennings.

1830   J. Bunyan. *The Pilgrim's Progress.* Murray & Major. With anr.

1830–31   [E. T. Bennett.] *The Gardens and Menagerie of the Zoological Society Delineated.* Sharpe.

1831   *The Children in the Wood.* Jennings & Chaplin.

1831   C. Lamb and M. Lamb. *Tales from Shakespeare.* Baldwin & Cradock.

1831   D. Defoe. *Robinson Crusoe.* Baldwin & Cradock.

1831   T. Hood. *The Dream of Eugene Aram, the Murderer.* Tilt.

1833   J. Northcote. *Fables, Original and Selected.* Second series. Murray. With Northcote.

1836   W. Cowper. *Life and Works of William Cowper.* Ed. R. Southey. Baldwin & Cradock.

1836   G. White. *The Natural History of Selborne.* Whittaker.

1837   C. J. Latrobe. *Solace of Song.* Seely & Burnside.

1839–41   *The Thousand and One Nights.* Knight.

1840   T. Campbell. *Poetical Works.* Moxon.

1843   J. Milton. *The Poetical Works of John Milton.* Tilt & Bogue.

1845   J. Thorne. *Rambles by Rivers – The Avon.* Knight.

1847   W. Carleton. *The Black Prophet.* Simms & M'Intyre.

1850   J. Bunyan. *The Pilgrim's Progress.* Bogue. A new series of illustrations.

[ca. 1850?]   *The Beggar's Daughter of Bednall Green.* Willoughby.

1853   J. G. Wood. *The Illustrated Natural History.* First ed. Routledge.

1854   J. Gay. *Fables.* Routledge.

1857   *The Poets of the Nineteenth Century.* Ed. R. A. Willmott. Routledge. With others.

1857   T. Campbell. *Gertrude of Wyoming.* Routledge. With others.

1858   *The Home Affections, Pourtrayed by the Poets.* Ed. C. Mackay. Routledge. With others.

1858   *Lays of the Holy Land.* Nisbet. With others.

1859   A. Karr. *Tours Round My Garden.* Routledge.

1859   T. Miller. *English Country Life.* Second ed. Routledge. With others.

[1859], 1862, 1863   J. G. Wood. *The Illustrated Natural History.* Second ed. Routledge. With others.

1860   *A Book of Favourite Modern Ballads.* Kent. With others.

August Hervieu (fl. 1819–58)

1832   F. M. Trollope. *Domestic Manners of the Americans.* Whittaker, Treacher.

1836   F. M. Trollope. *Jonathan Jefferson Whitlaw: or, Scenes on the Mississippi.* Bentley.

1837   F. M. Trollope. *The Vicar of Wrexhill.* Bentley.

1840   F. M. Trollope. *Michael Armstrong, the Factory Boy.* Colburn. With anr.

Samuel Howitt (1765?–1822)

1800   S. Howitt. *The British Sportsman.* Orme.

1807   T. Williamson. *Oriental Field Sports.* Orme & Crosby.

1807–08   *Orme's Collection of British Field Sports.* Orme.

1811   *A New Work of Animals: Principally Designed from the Fables of Aesop, Gay, and Phaedrus.* Orme.

1814   *Foreign Field Sports, Fisheries, Sporting Anecdotes &c. &c.* Orme. With others.

1824   S. Howitt. *British Preserve. Drawn & Etched by S. Howitt.* Rodwell & Martin.

Thomas Landseer (1795–1880)

1830   R. Burns. *An Address to the Deil.* Kidd.

1830   R. Burns. *Tam O'Shanter and Souter Johnny.* Marsh & Miller.

Edward Lear (1812–88)

1832   E. Lear. *Illustrations of the Family of Psittacidae, or Parrots.* Lear.

1841   E. Lear. *Views in Rome and Its Environs.* M'Lean.

1846   J. E. Gray. *Gleanings from the Menagerie and Aviary at Knowsley Hall.* Privately printed.

1846   E. Lear [Derry Down Derry, pseud.]. *A Book of Nonsense.* M'Lean.

1846   E. Lear. *Illustrated Excursions in Italy.* M'Lean.

1851   E. Lear. *Journals of a Landscape Painter in Albania.* Bentley.

1852   E. Lear. *Journals of a Landscape Painter in Southern Calabria.* Bentley.

1863   E. Lear. *Views in the Seven Ionian Islands.* Lear.

1870   E. Lear. *Journal of a Landscape Painter in Corsica.* Bush.

1871   E. Lear. *Nonsense Songs, Stories, Botany, and Alphabets.* Bush.

1872   E. Lear. *More Nonsense, Pictures, Rhymes, Botany.* Bush.

1872   E. Lear and J. de C. Sowerby. *Tortoises, Terrapins, and Turtles Drawn from Life.* Sotheran, Baer.

1877   E. Lear. *Laughable Lyrics.* Bush.

1889   A., Lord Tennyson. *Poems.* Boussod, Valadon.

*

Field, W. B. O. *Edward Lear on My Shelves.* Munich: Privately printed, 1933.

Lehmann, J. *Edward Lear and His World.* Thames & Hudson, 1977.

Noakes, V. *Edward Lear: The Life of a Wanderer.* Collins, 1968.

John Leech (1817–64)

1840, 1842, 1847 R. H. Barham. *The Ingoldsby Legends*. Bentley. With others.

1841 P. Leigh. *Portraits of the Children of the Mobility*. Bentley.

1842 G. Daniel. *Merrie England in the Olden Time*. Bentley. With anr.

1843 A. Smith. *The Wassail Bowl*. Bentley.

1843 C. Dickens. *A Christmas Carol*. Chapman & Hall.

1843 W. H. Maxwell. *The Fortunes of Hector O'Halloran and His Man Mark Antony O'Toole*. Bentley. With anr.

1844 F. E. Trollope. *Jessie Phillips*. Colburn.

1845 C. Dickens. *The Chimes*. Chapman & Hall. With others.

1846 C. Dickens. *The Cricket on the Hearth*. Bradbury & Evans. With others.

1846 D. W. Jerrold. *Mrs. Caudle's Curtain Lectures*. Punch Office.

1847 C. Dickens. *The Battle of Life*. Bradbury & Evans. With others.

1847–48 G. A. à Beckett. *The Comic History of England*. Punch Office. Bradbury & Evans, 1864.

1848 C. Dickens. *The Haunted Man*. Bradbury & Evans. With others.

1849 D. W. Jerrold. *A Man Made of Money*. Punch Office.

1852 G. A. à Beckett. *The Comic History of Rome*. Punch Office.

1853 R. S. Surtees. *Mr. Sponge's Sporting Tour*. Bradbury & Evans.

1854 G. F. Berkeley. *Reminiscences of a Huntsman*. Longman.

1854 R. S. Surtees. *Handley Cross: or Mr. Jorrocks's Hunt*. Bradbury & Evans.

1858 R. S. Surtees. *Ask Mamma*. Bradbury & Evans.

1859 J. Mills. *The Flyers of the Hunt*. Field Office; Ward & Lock.

1859 S. R. Hole. *A Little Tour in Ireland*. Bradbury & Evans.

1860 R. S. Surtees. *Plain or Ringlets?* Bradbury & Evans.

1865 R. S. Surtees. *Mr. Facey Romford's Sporting Hounds*. Bradbury & Evans. With anr.

*

Field, W. B. O. *John Leech on My Shelves*. Privately printed, 1930.

Frith, W. P. *John Leech*. Bentley, 1891.

Rose, J. *The Drawings of John Leech*. Art & Technics, 1950.

Daniel Maclise (1806–70)

1836 F. S. Mahony [O. Yorke, pseud.]. *The Reliques of Father Prout*. Fraser.

1845 T. Moore. *Irish Melodies*. Longman.

1845 C. Dickens. *The Chimes*. Chapman & Hall. With others.

1846 C. Dickens. *The Cricket on the Hearth*. Bradbury & Evans. With others.

1847 C. Dickens. *The Battle of Life*. Bradbury & Evans. With others.

1847 G. A. Bürger. *Leonora*. Longman.

1857 A., Lord Tennyson. *Poems*. Moxon. With others.

1860 [1859] A., Lord Tennyson. *The Princess*. Moxon.

*

Daniel Maclise, 1806–70. Ed. R. Ormond and J. Turpin. National Portrait Gallery, 1972.

Turpin, J. "Daniel Maclise and His Place in Victorian Art." *Anglo-Irish Studies* (1975).

———. "German Influence on Daniel Maclise." *Apollo* 97 (February 1973).

John Martin (1789–1854)

1817 *The Characters of Trees*. Ackermann.

[1818?] *Sezincot House*. Privately printed for C. Cockerell.

1824 E. Atherstone. *A Midsummer Day's Dream*. Baldwin, Cradock, & Joy.

1826 *The Amulet: or, Christian and Literary Remembrancer*. Baynes. With others.

1826 B. Barton. *A New Year's Eve and Other Poems*. Hatchard.

1827 J. Milton. *Paradise Lost*. Prowett.

1828 E. Atherstone. *The Fall of Nineveh: a Poem*. Baldwin & Cradock.

1829 *Friendship's Offering*. Smith, Elder.

1830 J. Bunyan. *The Pilgrim's Progress*. Murray & Major. With anr.

1830 R. Martin. *The Last Days of the Antediluvian World*. Plummer & Brewis.

1830 H. Caunter. *The Island Bride*. Bull.

1833 J. Galt. *The Ouranoulogos*. Cadell.

1837 [Bible.] *Illustrations of the Old and New Testaments*. Churton. With anr.

1838 J. Martin. *Illustrations of the Bible*. Tilt.

1838 *The Book of Gems: The Poets and Artists of Great Britain*. Third series. Ed. S. C. Hall. Saunders & Otley. With others.

1838 G. A. Mantell. *The Wonders of Geology*. Relfe & Fletcher.

1840 T. Hawkins. *The Book of the Great Sea-Dragons: Ichthyosauri and Plesiosauri*. Pickering.

1844 T. Hawkins. *The Wars of Jehovah, in Heaven, Earth, and Hell*. Baisler.

*

Balston, T. *John Martin, 1789–1854: His Life and Works*. Duckworth, 1947.

Feaver, M. *The Art of John Martin*. Oxford, 1975.

Klingender, F. D. *Art and the Industrial Revolution*. Rev. ed. Carrington, 1968.

Pendered, M. L. *John Martin, Painter: His Life and Times*. Hurst & Blackett, 1923.

Joseph Kenny Meadows (1790–1874)

1834 J. T. de Trueba y Cosio. *The Romance of History – Spain*. Warne.

1838 [C. Whitehead.] *Autobiography of Jack Ketch*. Chidley.

1838 T. Moore. *Lalla Rookh*. Longman. With others.

1840 W. Shakespeare. *Works*. Tyas.

1847 [Bible.] New Testament. *Illustrated London News* Office.

1850 H. Mayhew. *Fear of the World*. New York: Harper.

1854 G. G. N., Lord Byron. *The Illustrated Byron*. Vizetelly. With others.

[1872] M. de Cervantes Saavedra. *Don Quixote*. Dean. With anr.

William Mulready (1786–1863)

1834 T. Gray. *Elegy Written in a Country Church-Yard*. Van Voorst. With others.

1843 O. Goldsmith. *The Vicar of Wakefield*. Van Voorst.

1857 A., Lord Tennyson. *Poems*. Moxon. With others.

*

Grigson, G. "The Drawings of William Mulready." *Image*, no. 1 (Summer 1949).

Heleniak, K. *William Mulready*. New Haven, Conn.: Yale, 1980.

James Northcote (1746–1831)

1828 J. Northcote. *One Hundred Fables, Original and Selected*. [First series.] Lawford. With W. Harvey.

1833 J. Northcote. *Fables, Original and Selected*. Second series. Murray. With W. Harvey.

Samuel Palmer (1805–81)

1846 C. Dickens. *Pictures from Italy*. Bradbury & Evans.

1853 W. Shakespeare. *Songs*. Royal Polytechnic Union. With others.

1859 W. Adams. *Sacred Allegories*. Rivington. With others.

1860 *A Book of Favourite Modern Ballads.* Kent. With others.

1861 *Household Song.* Kent. With others.

1883 P. Virgilius Maro. *An English Version of the Eclogues of Virgil.* Tr. S. Palmer. Seeley. Completed by A. H. Palmer.

1888 J. Milton. *The Minor Poems.* Seeley.

*

Binyon, L. *The Followers of William Blake: Edward Calvert, Samuel Palmer, George Richmond & Their Circle.* Halton & Smith, 1925.

Cecil, D. *Visionary and Dreamer – Two Poetic Painters: Samuel Palmer and Edward Burne-Jones.* Washington, D.C.: National Gallery of Art and Princeton, 1966.

Lister, R. *Samuel Palmer and His Etchings.* Faber & Faber, 1969.

Phiz. See Browne.

Frederick Richard Pickersgill (1820–1900)

1844 *The Book of British Ballads. Second series.* Ed. S. C. Hall. How. With others.

1844 P. Massinger. *The Virgin Martyr.* Burns.

[1852?] E. A. Poe. *Poetical Works.* Griffin. With others.

1857 *The Poets of the Nineteenth Century.* Ed. R. A. Willmott. Routledge. With others.

1858 *The Home Affections, Pourtrayed by the Poets.* Ed. C. Mackay. Routledge. With others.

1858 *Lays of the Holy Land.* Nisbet. With others.

1858 J. Milton. *Comus: A Mask.* Routledge. With others.

1860 J. Montgomery. *The Poems of James Montgomery.* Routledge. With others.

1861 *English Sacred Poetry of the Sixteenth, Seventeenth, and Eighteenth Centuries.* Ed. R. A. Willmott. Routledge. With others.

1870 H. Alford. *A Poem Illustrating the Lord's Prayer.* Longman.

1881 *Dalziel's Bible Gallery.* Routledge. With others.

Henry Courteney Selous (1811?–90)

1844 J. Bunyan. *The Pilgrim's Progress.* Holloway. With anr.

[1848?] F. H. K., baron de la Motte-Fouqué. *Sintram and His Companions.* Lumley.

1865 *Our Life Illustrated by Pen and Pencil.* Religious Tract Society. With others.

[1865] W. Shakespeare. *Cassell's Illustrated Shakespeare.* Cassell, Petter, & Galpin. With others.

1867 J. Hamilton. *The Parable of the Prodigal Son.* Nisbet.

Robert Seymour (1800?–36)

1837 C. Dickens. *The Posthumous Papers of the Pickwick Club.* Chapman & Hall. With others.

Robert Smirke (1752–1845)

1783–87 C. Taylor. *The Picturesque Beauties of Shakespeare.* Taylor. With others.

1802 *The Arabian Nights.* Miller.

1809 A. R. Le Sage. *Gil Blas of Santillane.* Bell.

1810 Homer. *The Iliad and Odyssey.* Johnson; Sharpe & Hailes. With others.

1818 M. de Cervantes Saavedra. *Don Quixote.* Cadell & Davies.

1819 S. Johnson. *The History of Rasselas, Prince of Abyssinia.* M'Lean.

William Clarkson Stanfield (1793–1867)

1832–33 G. G. N., Lord Byron. *The Life and Works of Lord Byron.* Longman. With others.

1833–34 W. Scott. *Poetical Works.* Edinburgh: Cadell. With others.

1836 W. C. Stanfield. *Stanfield's Coastal Survey.* Smith, Elder.

1836 F. Marryat. *The Pirate, and the Three Cutters.* Longman.

1840 F. Marryat. *Poor Jack.* Longman.

1845 C. Dickens. *The Chimes.* Chapman & Hall. With others.

1846 C. Dickens. *The Cricket on the Hearth.* Bradbury & Evans. With others.

1847 C. Dickens. *The Battle of Life.* Bradbury & Evans. With others.

1848 C. Dickens. *The Haunted Man.* Bradbury & Evans. With others.

1857 A., Lord Tennyson. *Poems.* Moxon. With others.

William Makepeace Thackeray (1811–63)

Thackeray is the author of all the books listed.

1840 [Mr. Titmarsh, pseud.] *The Paris Sketch Book.* Macrone.

1843 [Mr. M. A. Titmarsh, pseud.] *The Irish Sketch-Book.* Chapman & Hall.

1846 [Mr. M. A. Titmarsh, pseud.] *Notes on a Journey from Cornhill to Grand Cairo.* Chapman & Hall.

1847 [M. A. Titmarsh, pseud.] *Mrs. Perkins's Ball.* Chapman & Hall.

1848 *Vanity Fair.* Bradbury & Evans.

1848 *Our Street.* Chapman & Hall.

[1848] *The History of Samuel Titmarsh and the Great Hoggarty Diamond.* New York: Harper. Bradbury & Evans, 1849.

1849 *Doctor Birch and His Young Friends.* Chapman & Hall.

1849, 1850 *The History of Pendennis.* Bradbury & Evans.

1850 *The Knickleburys on the Rhine.* Smith, Elder.

1853 *The History of Henry Esmond.* Smith, Elder.

1855 *The Rose and the Ring.* Smith, Elder.

1856 *Sketches and Travels in London.* Bradbury & Evans.

1858, 1859 *The Virginians.* Bradbury & Evans.

1860 *The Four Georges.* New York: Harper. Smith, Elder, 1861.

1860 *Lovel the Widower.* New York: Harper. Smith, Elder, 1861.

1863 [1862] *The Roundabout Papers.* Smith, Elder.

*

Buchanan-Brown, J. *The Illustrations of W. M. Thackeray.* Newton Abbot: David & Charles, 1979.

Stevens, J. "Thackeray's *Vanity Fair*." *A Review of English Literature* 6 (1965).

Sturgis, R. "Thackeray as a Draughtsman." *Scribner's Monthly* 20, no. 2 (June 1880).

Van Duzer, H. S. *A Thackeray Library.* Privately printed, 1919.

John Thurston (1774–1822)

1798–1800 W. Shakespeare. *Plays.* Harding.

1800 R. Bloomfield. *The Farmer's Boy.* Vernor & Hood.

1802 R. Bloomfield. *Rural Tales.* Vernor & Hood.

1803, 1827 J. McCreery. *The Press: a Poem.* Liverpool: McCreery.

1805 J. Thomson. *The Seasons.* Wallis.

1806 J. Milton. *Paradise Lost.* Suttaby, Crosby, & Corrall.

1806 R. Bloomfield. *Wild Flowers: or, Pastoral and Local Poetry.* Vernor, Hood, & Sharpe.

1806 T. Percy. *The Hermit of Warkworth: A Northumbrian Ballad.* Scholey.

1808 J. Beattie. *The Minstrel.* Alnwick: Catnach & Davison.

1808 R. Burns. *Poetical Works.* Alnwick: Catnach & Davison.

1809 J. Thomas. *Religious Emblems.* Ackermann.

1812 G. Marshall. *Epistles in Verse, between Cynthio and Leonora.* Newcastle: Marshall.

1813 W. Somervile. *Hobbinol, Field Sports, and the Bowling Green.* Ackermann.

1815 [1814–25] T. J. Dibdin. *The London Theatre.* Whittingham & Arliss. With anr.

1817 J. Puckle. *The Club: in a Dialogue between Father and Son.* Johnson.

1817 T. Tasso. *Godfrey of Bulloigne: or, Jerusalem Delivered.* Triphook & Major.

1818 D. Hume. *The History of England.* Scholey; Baldwin.

1819 S. Butler. *Hudibras.* M'Lean. With anr.

Henry James Townsend (1810–90)

1842 O. Goldsmith. *The Deserted Village: Illustrated by the Etching Club.* Longman. With others.

1842 *The Book of British Ballads.* [First series.] Ed. S. C. Hall. How. With others.

1843 W. Shakespeare. *Songs.* Etching Club. With others.

1844 *The Book of British Ballads. Second series.* Ed. S. C. Hall. How. With others.

1847 T. Gray. *Elegy Written in a Country Churchyard.* Etching Club. With others.

1849 J. Milton. *L'Allegro.* Etching Club. With others.

1850 *The Germ: Thoughts Towards Nature in Poetry, Literature, and Art.* Aylott & Jones. With others.

Joseph Mallord William Turner (1775–1851)

1830 S. Rogers. *Italy: A Poem.* Cadell & Moxon. With anr.

1832–33 G. G. N., Lord Byron. *The Life and Works of Lord Byron.* Longman. With others.

1833–34 W. Scott. *Poetical Works.* Edinburgh: Cadell. With others.

1834 S. Rogers. *Poems.* Cadell & Moxon. With anr.

1834–36 W. Scott. *Miscellaneous Prose Works.* Edinburgh: Cadell. With others.

1835 J. Milton. *The Poetical Works of John Milton.* Macrone. With anr.

1837 T. Campbell. *Poetical Works.* Macrone.

1839 T. Moore. *The Epicurean.* Macrone.

*

Finley, G. *Landscapes of Memory: Turner as Illustrator of Scott.* Scolar, 1980.

Holcomb, A. M. "Turner and Scott." *Journal of the Warburg and Courtauld Institutes* 34 (1971).

Omer, M. *Turner and the Poets.* Greater London Council, 1975.

Wilton, A. *The Life and Work of J. M. W. Turner.* Academy, 1979.

Edward Henry Wehnert (1813–68)

1853 E. A. Poe. *Poetical Works.* Addey. With others.

[1853?] Brothers Grimm. *Household Stories.* Routledge.

[1855] J. Keats. *The Eve of St. Agnes.* Low for Cundall.

[1857] S. T. Coleridge. *The Rime of the Ancient Mariner.* Marston, Low, & Searle. With others.

1859 *Favourite English Poems of Modern Times.* Low. With others.

1862 D. Defoe. *Robinson Crusoe.* Bell & Daldy.

Richard Westall (1765–1836)

In several instances, plates are dated the year after the date on the title page.

1794 S. Rogers. *The Pleasures of Memory.* Cadell, Davies, & Dilly. With others.

1794, 1795, 1797 J. Milton. *The Poetical Works.* Boydells & Nicol.

1808 W. Scott. *The Lay of the Last Minstrel.* Longman.

1808 W. Scott. *Marmion.* Miller & Murray.

1810 W. Scott. *The Lady of the Lake.* Longman.

1810 Homer. *The Iliad and Odyssey.* Johnson; Sharpe & Hailes. With others.

1810 W. Cowper. *Poems.* Sharpe.

1812 W. Scott. *Glenfinlas and Other Ballads.* Longman; Miller, White, & Gale.

1815 Bible. Oxford.

1815 W. Scott. *The Lord of the Isles.* Longman.

1816 O. Goldsmith. *The Traveller, The Deserted Village, and Other Poems.* Sharpe.

1816 J. Beattie. *The Minstrel.* Sharpe.

1817 S. Johnson. *The History of Rasselas, Prince of Abyssinia.* Sharpe.

1817 J. Milton. *Paradise Lost.* Sharpe.

1817 T. Moore. *Lalla Rookh.* Second ed. Longman.

1818 O. Goldsmith. *The Vicar of Wakefield.* Sharpe.

1818 W. Falconer. *The Shipwreck.* Sharpe.

1819 B. de Saint-Pierre. *Paul and Virginia.* Sharpe; Longman.

1820 J. Bunyan. *The Pilgrim's Progress.* Hurst, Robinson.

1820 [Horam, the Son of Asman.] *The Tales of the Genii.* Bookes, Baldwin, Cradock, & Joy.

1820 M. de Cervantes Saavedra. *Don Quixote.* Hurst, Robinson.

1821 T. Gray. *The Poetical Works.* Sharpe.

1821 T. Campbell. *The Pleasures of Hope. Gertrude of Wyoming.* Longman.

1821 J. Thomson. *The Seasons.* Sharpe.

1822 F. Bacon. *Essays.* Sharpe.

1824 R. Burns. *Poems.* Sharpe.

1824 R. Southey. *Roderick. The Last of the Goths.* Longman.

1824–25 *The British Anthology: or Poetical Library.* Sharpe.

1827 R. Bloomfield. *The Farmer's Boy.* Longman.

CHAPTER SEVEN

The Nineteenth Century (II)
1855-1885

Frederick Barnard (1846–96)

1868   W. M. Thackeray. *The English Humourists of the Eighteenth Century*. Smith, Elder.

1871   T. Hood. *Petsetilla's Posy*. Routledge.

1872   C. Dickens. *David Copperfield*. Chapman & Hall.

1872   C. Dickens. *Martin Chuzzlewit*. Chapman & Hall.

1873   C. Dickens. *Bleak House*. Chapman & Hall.

1874   C. Dickens. *Master Humphrey's Clock and Other Stories*. Chapman & Hall.

1874   C. Dickens. *Barnaby Rudge*. Chapman & Hall.

1874   C. Dickens. *A Tale of Two Cities*. Chapman & Hall.

1875   C. Dickens. *Nicholas Nickleby*. Chapman & Hall.

1876   C. Dickens. *Sketches by Boz*. Chapman & Hall.

1877   C. Dickens. *Dombey and Son*. Chapman & Hall.

1878   C. Dickens. *Christmas Books*. Chapman & Hall.

1879   T. Hood. *Life in Lodgings*. Fun Office.

1879   J. Forster. *The Life of Charles Dickens*. Chapman & Hall.

1880   J. Bunyan. *The Pilgrim's Progress*. Strahan. With others.

1880   M. R. Mitford. *Children of the Village*. Routledge. With others.

1882   W. Besant and J. Rice. *All Sorts and Conditions of Men*. Chapman & Hall.

1883   F. Barnard and C. H. Ross. *Behind a Brass Knocker*. Chatto & Windus.

1883   E. C. Grenville-Murray. *People I Have Met*. Vizetelly.

1883   G. R. Sims. *How the Poor Live*. Chatto & Windus.

1885   R. B. Sheridan. *Comedies*. Boston: Osgood. With others.

1887   R. D. Blackmore. *Springhaven*. New York: Harper. Low, Marston, Searle, & Rivington, 1889. With anr.

1889 [1890]   D. C. Murray. *Joseph's Coat*. Chatto & Windus.

Charles Henry Bennett (1829–67)

1858 [1857]   *The Fables of Aesop and Others: Translated into Human Nature*. Kent.

1859 [1858]   *Proverbs with Pictures*. Chapman & Hall.

1859   J. Bunyan. *The Pilgrim's Progress*. Longman.

1860   H. Morley. *Fables and Fairy Tales*. Chapman & Hall.

1860   C. H. Bennett and R. B. Brough. *Shadow and Substance*. Kent.

1861   F. Quarles. *Emblems, Divine & Moral*. Nisbet.

1863   C. H. Bennett. *London People: Sketched from Life*. Smith, Elder.

[ca. 1872]   *Poets' Wit and Humour*. Ed. H. W. Wills. Ward, Lock, & Tyler. With anr.

*

Toilers in Art. Ed. H. C. Ewart. Isbister, 1891.

Ford Madox Brown (1821–93)

1857   *The Poets of the Nineteenth Century*. Ed. R. A. Willmott. Routledge. With others.

1868   *Lyra Germanica*. Second series. Longman. With others.

1881   *Dalziel's Bible Gallery*. Routledge. With others.

Randolph Caldecott (1846–86)

1873   F. Marryat. *Frank Mildmay*. Routledge.

1876 [1875]   W. Irving. *Old Christmas: Selections from the "Sketch Book"*. Macmillan.

1877 [1876]   W. Irving. *Bracebridge Hall: Selections from the "Sketch Book"*. Macmillan.

1878   C. Carr. *North Italian Folk*. Chatto & Windus.

1880   H. G. Blackburn. *Breton Folk*. Low, Marston, Searle, & Rivington.

1883   Aesop. *Some of Aesop's Fables with Modern Instances*. Macmillan.

*

Blackburn, H. G. *Randolph Caldecott: a Memoir*. Low, Marston, Searle, & Rivington, 1886.

John R. Clayton (fl. 1850s)

1853   J. Bunyan. *The Pilgrim's Progress*. Ingram, Cook.

1854   F. A. Krummacher. *Parables*. Cook.

1857   *The Poets of the Nineteenth Century*. Ed. R. A. Willmott. Routledge. With others.

1857   R. Pollok. *The Course of Time*. Blackwood. With others.

1857   G. Herbert. *The Poetical Works*. Nisbet. With anr.

William Stephen Coleman (1829–1904)

1858   J. G. Wood. *Common Objects of the Country*. Routledge.

1859   W. S. Coleman. *Our Woodlands, Heaths, and Hedges*. Routledge.

[1859], 1862, 1863   J. G. Wood. *The Illustrated Natural History*. Second ed. Routledge. With others.

[1860]   W. S. Coleman. *British Butterflies*. Routledge.

1864   J. G. Wood. *Our Garden Friends and Foes*. Routledge. With others.

Edward Dalziel (1817–1905)

1857   *The Poets of the Nineteenth Century*. Ed. R. A. Willmott. Routledge. With others. [D. Edwards, pseud.]

1857   B. W. Procter [Barry Cornwall, pseud.]. *Dramatic Scenes*. Chapman & Hall. With others.

1857   W. C. Bryant. *Poems*. New York: Appleton. Low, 1858. With others.

1865   *Dalziel's Illustrated Arabian Nights' Entertainments*. Ed. H. W. Dulcken. Ward & Lock. With others.

1866   *Ballad Stories of the Affections*. Routledge. With others.

1867   J. Ingelow. *Poems*. Longman. With others.

1868   R. Buchanan. *North Coast and Other Poems*. Routledge. With others.

1888   H. C. Andersen. *Stories for the Household*. Routledge.

1904   T. Parnell. *The Hermit*. Camden.

Edward Gurden Dalziel (1849–88)

1871–79   C. Dickens. *The Uncommercial Traveller*. Chapman & Hall.

1871–79   C. Dickens. *Christmas Stories*. Chapman & Hall.

1871–79   C. Dickens. *Reprinted Pieces*. Chapman & Hall.

1880   J. Bunyan. *The Pilgrim's Progress*. Strahan. With others.

1881   *Dalziel's Bible Gallery*. Routledge. With others.

Thomas Bolton Gilchrist Septimus Dalziel (1823–1906)

1857   *The Poets of the Nineteenth Century*. Ed. R. A. Willmott. Routledge. With others.

1857   B. W. Procter [Barry Cornwall, pseud.]. *Dramatic Scenes.* Chapman & Hall. With others.

1857   T. Campbell. *Gertrude of Wyoming.* Routledge. With others.

1857   W. C. Bryant. *Poems.* New York: Appleton. Low, 1858. With others.

1858   *The Home Affections, Pourtrayed by the Poets.* Ed. C. Mackay. Routledge. With others.

1858   *Lays of the Holy Land.* Nisbet. With others.

1863   J. Bunyan. *The Pilgrim's Progress.* Ward & Lock.

1864   H. W. Dulcken. *The Golden Harp.* Routledge. With others.

1865   *Dalziel's Illustrated Arabian Nights' Entertainments.* Ed. H. W. Dulcken. Ward & Lock. With others.

1866   *The Arabian Nights' Entertainments.* Warne. With anr.

1866   *A Round of Days.* Routledge. With others.

1866   *Ballad Stories of the Affections.* Routledge. With others.

1867 [1866]   *The Spirit of Praise.* Warne. With others.

1867   Aesop. *Aesop's Fables.* Ed. E. Garrett. Strahan. With others.

1867   J. Ingelow. *Poems.* Longman. With others.

1867   *Golden Thoughts from Golden Fountains.* Warne. With others.

1868   R. Buchanan. *North Coast and Other Poems.* Routledge. With others.

1881   *Dalziel's Bible Gallery.* Routledge. With others.

Paul Gustave Doré (1832–83)

1863   M. de Cervantes Saavedra. *Don Quixote.* Cassell, Petter, & Galpin.

1865   T. Hood. *Fairy Realm: Favourite Old Tales.* Ward, Lock, & Tyler.

1865   R. E. Raspe. *Baron Munchausen.* Cassell, Petter, & Galpin.

[1866]   J. Milton. *Paradise Lost.* Cassell, Petter, & Galpin.

1867   A., Lord Tennyson. *Elaine.* Moxon.

1867   A., Lord Tennyson. *Guinevere.* Moxon.

1867   A., Lord Tennyson. *Vivien.* Moxon.

1868   A., Lord Tennyson. *Enid.* Moxon.

1868   A., Lord Tennyson. *Idylls of the King.* Moxon.

1870   T. Hood. *Poetical Works.* Moxon.

1872   B. Jerrold. *London: A Pilgrimage.* Grant.

1876   S. T. Coleridge. *The Rime of the Ancient Mariner.* Doré Gallery; Adams.

1883   E. A. Poe. *The Raven.* Low.

*

Gosling, N. *Gustave Doré.* Newton Abbot: David & Charles, 1973.

Jerrold, B. *The Life of Gustave Doré.* Allen, 1891.

Roosevelt (Macchetta), B. *Life and Reminiscences of Gustave Doré.* Cassell, 1885.

Rose, M. *Gustave Doré.* Pleiades, 1946.

George Louis Palmella Busson Du Maurier (1834–96)

1863   E. C. Gaskell. *Sylvia's Lovers.* Smith, Elder.

1864   E. C. Gaskell. *Cranford.* Smith, Elder.

1864   E. C. Gaskell. *A Dark Night's Work.* Smith, Elder.

1864   *English Sacred Poetry of the Olden Time.* Religious Tract Society. With others.

1865   E. C. Gaskell. *The Grey Woman and Other Tales.* Smith, Elder.

1865   E. C. Gaskell. *Cousin Phyllis.* Smith, Elder.

1865   E. C. Gaskell. *Lizzie Leigh and Other Tales.* Smith, Elder.

1866   R. H. Barham. *The Ingoldsby Legends.* Bentley. With others.

1866   E. C. Gaskell. *Wives and Daughters.* Smith, Elder.

1866   A. Procter. *Legends and Lyrics.* Bell & Daldy.

1867   *Touches of Nature.* Strahan. With others.

1867   D. W. Jerrold. *The Story of a Feather.* Bradbury & Evans.

1867   E. C. Gaskell. *North and South.* Smith, Elder.

1868   W. M. Thackeray. *The History of Henry Esmond, Esq.* Smith, Elder.

1868   E. R. Bulwer-Lytton [O. Meredith, pseud.]. *Lucile.* Chapman & Hall.

1868   S. Brooks. *Sooner or Later.* Bradbury & Evans.

1873   G. E. Sargent. *Hurlock Chase.* Religious Tract Society.

1874   F. Montgomery. *Misunderstood.* Bentley.

1875   W. Collins. *The New Magdalen.* Chatto & Windus. With anr.

1875   W. Collins. *The Moonstone.* Chatto & Windus. With anr.

1875   W. Collins. *Poor Miss Finch.* Chatto & Windus. With anr.

1879   W. M. Thackeray. *Ballads.* Smith, Elder. With others.

1882   L. C. Lillie. *Prudence.* Low.

1882   C. Reade and D. Boucicault. *Foul Play.* Chatto & Windus.

1887   E. C. Gaskell. *Ruth.* Smith, Elder.

1888   E. C. Gaskell. *Mary Barton.* Smith, Elder.

1889   F. C. Phillips. *As in a Looking Glass.* Ward & Downey.

1892   G. Du Maurier. *Peter Ibbetson.* Osgood, McIlvaine.

1895   G. Du Maurier. *Trilby.* Osgood, McIlvaine.

1898   G. Du Maurier. *The Martian.* Osgood, McIlvaine.

*

Du Maurier, G. *Social Pictorial Satire.* Harper, 1898.

Ormond, L. *George Du Maurier.* Routledge & Paul; Pittsburgh, 1969.

Whiteley, D. P. *George Du Maurier.* Art & Technics, 1948.

Wood, T. M. *George Du Maurier: Satirist of the Victorians.* Chatto & Windus, 1913.

Sir Samuel Luke Fildes (1844–1927)

[1866]   J. Foxe. *The Book of Martyrs.* Cassell, Petter, & Galpin. With others.

1868   C. Reade. *Peg Woffington.* Bradbury & Evans.

1870   C. Dickens. *The Mystery of Edwin Drood.* Chapman & Hall.

1879   W. M. Thackeray. *Men's Wives.* Smith, Elder.

*

Fildes, L. V. *Luke Fildes.* Joseph, 1968.

Sir William Schwenck Gilbert (1836–1911)

1869   W. S. Gilbert. *The "Bab" Ballads.* Hotten.

[1873]   W. S. Gilbert. *More "Bab" Ballads.* Routledge.

1890   W. S. Gilbert. *Songs of a Savoyard.* Routledge.

Charles Green (1840–98)

1864   *English Sacred Poetry of the Olden Time.* Religious Tract Society. With others.

1869   *The Fine Old English Gentleman.* Castell.

1871–79   C. Dickens. *The Old Curiosity Shop.* Chapman & Hall.

1871–79   C. Dickens. *Great Expectations.* Chapman & Hall.

1897   W. Scott. *Waverley: or, 'Tis Sixty Years Since.* Black.

Ernest Henry Griset (1844–1907)

1866   J. Greenwood. *The Hatchet Throwers.* Hotten.

1867   J. Greenwood. *Legends of Savage Life.* Hotten.

1867   E. Griset and T. Hood. *Griset's Grotesques; or, Jokes Drawn on Wood, with Rhymes by Tom Hood.* Routledge.

1868   J. Greenwood. *The Purgatory of Peter the Cruel.* Routledge.

[1869]   Aesop. *Aesop's Fables.* Cassell, Petter, & Galpin.

[1869]   D. Defoe. *Robinson Crusoe.* Hotten.

1874   A. Bierce. *Cobwebs from an Empty Skull.* Routledge. With anr.

1884   E. Griset. *Our London.*

*

Lambourne, L. *Ernest Griset: Fantasies of a Victorian Illustrator.* Thames & Hudson, 1979.

Henry Holiday (1839–1927)

1876 L. Carroll [C. L. Dodgson]. *The Hunting of the Snark: an Agony in Eight Fits.* Macmillan.

*

Cohen, M. N. "Hark the Snark." In *Lewis Carroll Observed.* Ed. E. Giuliano. New York: Clarkson Potter, 1976.

Holiday, H. *Reminiscences of My Life.* Heinemann, 1913.

Arthur Boyd Houghton (1836–75)

1862 W. Collins. *After Dark.* Smith, Elder.
1865 *Dalziel's Illustrated Arabian Nights' Entertainments.* Ed. H. W. Dulcken. Ward & Lock. With others.
1865 *Home Thoughts and Home Scenes.* Routledge.
1866 *The Arabian Nights' Entertainments.* Warne. With anr.
1866 M. de Cervantes Saavedra. *Don Quixote.* Warne.
1866 *Ballad Stories of the Affections.* Routledge. With others.
1866 *A Round of Days.* Routledge. With others.
[1866] J. Foxe. *The Book of Martyrs.* Cassell, Petter, & Galpin. With others.
1867 [1866] *The Spirit of Praise.* Warne. With others.
1867 *Touches of Nature.* Strahan. With others.
1867 J. Ingelow. *Poems.* Longman. With others.
1867 *Golden Thoughts from Golden Fountains.* Warne. With others.
1867 H. W. Dulcken. *Old Friends and New Friends.* Warne. With anr.
1868 R. Buchanan. *North Coast and Other Poems.* Routledge. With others.
1869 R. Valentine. *The Nobility of Life.* Warne. With others.
1869 W. R. S. Ralston. *Krilof and His Fables.* Strahan. With anr.
1881 *Dalziel's Bible Gallery.* Routledge. With others.

*

Arthur Boyd Houghton. Intro. and check list by P. Hogarth. Victoria and Albert Museum, 1975.

Arthur Boyd Houghton: A Selection from His Work in Black and White. Intro. L. Housman. Paul, Trench, Trübner, 1896. Many reproductions of wood engravings after Houghton's drawings.

Reynolds, G. *A. Boyd Houghton.* Art & Technics, 1949.

Arthur Hughes (1832–1915)

1855 W. Allingham. *The Music Master: A Love Story and Two Series of Day and Night Songs.* Routledge. With others.
1857 *The Poets of the Nineteenth Century.* Ed. R. A. Willmott. Routledge. With others.
1866 A., Lord Tennyson. *Enoch Arden.* Moxon.
1867 G. MacDonald. *Dealings with the Fairies.* Strahan.
1868 G. MacDonald. *England's Antiphon.* Macmillan.
1868 F. T. Palgrave. *Five Days' Entertainment at Wentworth Grange.* Macmillan.
1869 [1868] T. Hughes. *Tom Brown's Schooldays.* Macmillan. With anr.
1871 G. MacDonald. *At the Back of the North Wind.* Strahan.
1871 C. Dickens. *The Christmas Carols.* Novello, Ewer. With others.
1871 H. Kingsley. *The Boy in Grey.* Strahan.
1871 G. MacDonald. *Ranald Bannerman's Boyhood.* Strahan.
1872 T. G. Hake. *Parables and Tales.* Chapman & Hall.
1872 G. MacDonald. *The Princess and the Goblin.* Strahan.
1872 C. G. Rossetti. *Sing-Song: a Nursery Rhyme Book.* Routledge.
1874 C. G. Rossetti. *Speaking Likenesses.* Macmillan.
1905 G. MacDonald. *Phantastes.* Fifield.

William Holman Hunt (1827–1910)

1850 *The Germ: Thoughts Towards Nature in Poetry, Literature, and Art.* Aylott & Jones. With others.

1857 A., Lord Tennyson. *Poems.* Moxon. With others.
1861 M. S. Gatty. *Parables from Nature.* [First series.] Bell & Daldy. With others.
1861 *English Sacred Poetry of the Sixteenth, Seventeenth, and Eighteenth Centuries.* Ed. R. A. Willmott. Routledge. With others.
[1862] D. M. Mulock (Craik). *Studies from Life.* Hurst & Blackett.
[1863] I. Watts. *Divine and Moral Songs for Children.* Nisbet. With others.
1867 *Touches of Nature.* Strahan. With others.
1867 M. S. Gatty. *Parables from Nature.* Second series. Bell & Daldy. With others.
1881 *Dalziel's Bible Gallery.* Routledge. With others.
1891 *Pearl: an English Poem of the 14th Century.* Nutt.

Charles Samuel Keene (1823–91)

1859 C. Reade. *A Good Fight.* In *Once a Week.* Frowde, 1910.
1861 *Lyra Germanica.* [First series.] Longman. With others.
1861 *English Sacred Poetry of the Sixteenth, Seventeenth, and Eighteenth Centuries.* Ed. R. A. Willmott. Routledge. With others.
1862 V. Morgan [H. Vaughan, pseud.]. *The Cambridge grisette.* Tinsley.
1864 F. C. Burnand. *Tracks for Tourists.* Bradbury & Evans.
1864 *Legends of Number Nip.* Tr. M. Lemon. Macmillan.
1865 T. C. H., viscount de La Villemarqué. *Ballads and Songs of Brittany.* Tr. T. Taylor. Macmillan. With others.
1866 D. W. Jerrold. *Mrs. Caudle's Curtain Lectures.* Bradbury & Evans.
1867 *Touches of Nature.* Strahan. With others.
1868 C. Reade. *Double Marriage.* Bradbury & Evans.
1879 W. M. Thackeray. *Roundabout Papers.* Smith, Elder. With anr.

*

Hudson, D. *Charles Keene.* Pleiades, 1947.
Layard, G. S. *The Life and Letters of Charles Samuel Keene.* Low, 1892.
Lindsay, L. *Charles Keene, the Artist's Artist.* Colnaghi, 1934.
Piper, M. "Charles Keene." *Signature,* no. 12 (1951).
The Work of Charles Keene. Intro. J. Pennell; biblio. W. H. Chesson. Unwin & Bradbury, Agnew, 1897.

Matthew James Lawless (1837–64)

1861 *Lyra Germanica.* [First series.] Longman. With others.
1862 *Passages from Modern English Poets.* Junior Etching Club. Day. With others.
[1862] H. Formby. *Pictorial Bible and Church History Stories.* Longman.
1867 *Touches of Nature.* Strahan. With others.

John Lawson (fl. 1865–89)

1866 *Ballad Stories of the Affections.* Routledge. With others.
1867 E. M. Norris. *The Early Start in Life.* Griffith & Farren.
1867 *Roses and Holly.* Edinburgh: Nimmo. With others.
1867 *Golden Thoughts from Golden Fountains.* Warne. With others.
[1867] *Ballads: Scottish and English.* Edinburgh: Nimmo.
1868 *Original Poems.* Routledge. With others.
[1868] *The Golden Gift.* Simpkin. With others.
1870 B. Hutton. *Tales of the White Cockade.* Griffith & Farren.
1872 B. Hutton. *The Runaway.* Macmillan.
1875 B. Hutton. *The Fiery Cross.* Griffith & Farren.

Frederick, Baron Leighton (1830–96)

1867 A. Sartoris. *A Week in a French Country-House.* Smith, Elder.
1880 G. Eliot [M. A. Evans]. *Romola.* Smith, Elder.

1881 *Dalziel's Bible Gallery*. Routledge. With others.
1889 D. Conyers [Mrs. J. White]. *"My Face Is My Fortune, Sir,"*
She Said. Simpkin.

*

Ormond, L., and R. Ormond. *Lord Leighton*. New Haven, Conn.:
Yale for the Paul Mellon Centre for Studies in British Art, 1975.

James Mahoney (fl. 1865–79)
1865 A. Trollope. *The Three Clerks*. Bentley.
1871–79 C. Dickens. *Oliver Twist*. Chapman & Hall.
1871–79 C. Dickens. *Our Mutual Friend*. Chapman & Hall.
1871–79 C. Dickens. *Little Dorrit*. Chapman & Hall.
1875 W. Collins. *The Frozen Deep*. Chatto & Windus. With anr.

Henry Stacy Marks (1829–98)
1857 G. W. Thornbury. *Songs of the Cavaliers & Roundheads,*
Jacobite Ballads, &c. Hurst & Blackett.
1861 *English Sacred Poetry of the Sixteenth, Seventeenth, and Eight-*
eenth Centuries. Ed. R. A. Willmott. Routledge. With others.
1861 *Lyra Germanica*. [First series.] Longman. With others.
1867 *Two Centuries of Song*. Low & Marston. With others.
1876 A. C. Leroy [Esme Stuart, pseud.]. *The Good Old Days*. Ward.

Sir John Everett Millais (1829–96)
1855 W. Allingham. *The Music Master: A Love Story and Two Series*
of Day and Night Songs. Routledge. With others.
1857 A., Lord Tennyson. *Poems*. Moxon. With others.
1857 *The Poets of the Nineteenth Century*. Ed. R. A. Willmott.
Routledge. With others.
1858 *The Home Affections, Pourtrayed by the Poets*. Ed. C. Mackay.
Routledge. With others.
1858 *Lays of the Holy Land*. Nisbet. With others.
1861 A. Trollope. *Framley Parsonage*. Smith, Elder.
1862 A. Trollope. *Orley Farm*. Chapman & Hall.
1864 [1863] [Bible.] *The Parables of Our Lord and Saviour Jesus*
Christ. Routledge.
1864 A. Trollope. *The Small House at Allington*. Smith, Elder.
1864 A. Trollope. *Rachel Ray*. Chapman & Hall.
1865 *Dalziel's Illustrated Arabian Nights' Entertainments*. Ed. H. W.
Dulcken. Ward & Lock. With others.
1865 T. C. H., viscount de La Villemarqué. *Ballads and Songs of*
Brittany. Tr. T. Taylor. Macmillan. With others.
1866 D. Defoe. *Robinson Crusoe*. Macmillan.
1867 [J. Ingelow.] *Studies for Stories*. Strahan. With others.
1868 J. W. von Goethe. *Egmont*. Chapman & Hall.
1869 A. Trollope. *Phineas Finn, the Irish Member*. Virtue.
1879 W. M. Thackeray. *The Memoirs of Barry Lyndon*. Smith, Elder.
1880 H. Martineau. *The Hampdens*. Routledge.

*

Fish, A. *John Everett Millais, 1829–1896*. New York: Funk & Wagnalls,
1923.
Gere, J. *J. E. Millais*. Art & Technics, 1948.
Hardie, M. *Catalogue of Prints: Wood Engravings after Sir John Everett*
Millais, Bart., P. R. A. in the Victoria and Albert Museum.
H.M.S.O., 1908.
Millais, J. E. *Millais's Illustrations*. Strahan, 1866.
Millais, J. G. *The Life and Letters of Sir John Everett Millais*. Methuen,
1899.

Thomas Morten (1836–66)
1861 G. Stewart. *The Laird's Return*. Hogg.

1865 *Dalziel's Illustrated Arabian Nights' Entertainments*. Ed. H. W
Dulcken. Ward & Lock. With others.
[1865] J. Swift. *Gulliver's Travels*. Cassell, Petter, & Galpin.
1866 *A Round of Days*. Routledge. With others.
[1866] J. Foxe. *The Book of Martyrs*. Cassell, Petter, & Galpin. With
others.
1867 *Two Centuries of Song*. Low & Marston. With others.

John William North (1841–1924)
1864 *English Sacred Poetry of the Olden Time*. Religious Tract
Society. With others.
1866 *A Round of Days*. Routledge. With others.
1867 *Touches of Nature*. Strahan. With others.
1867 J. Ingelow. *Poems*. Longman. With others.
1867 R. Buchanan. *Wayside Poesies*. Routledge. With others.

Sir Joseph Noel Paton (1821–1901)
1844 *The Book of British Ballads*. Second series. Ed. S. C. Hall. How.
With others.
1845 A. Park [J. Wilson of Paisley, pseud.]. *Silent Love*. Murray &
Stewart.
1863 W. E. Aytoun. *Lays of the Scottish Cavaliers and Other Poems*.
Blackwood. With anr.
1863 S. T. Coleridge. *The Ancient Mariner*. Art Union of London.
1866 P. B. Shelley. *Gems of Literature*. Nimmo.
1904 W. Shakespeare. *The National Shakespeare*. Mackenzie.

*

Strivelyne, E. *Noel Paton*. Macmillan, 1874.

George John Pinwell (1842–75)
1865 *Dalziel's Illustrated Arabian Nights' Entertainments*. Ed. H. W.
Dulcken. Ward & Lock. With others.
1865 O. Goldsmith. *Dalziel's Illustrated Goldsmith*. Ward & Lock.
1865 *Our Life Illustrated by Pen and Pencil*. Religious Tract Society.
With others.
1866 A. R. Le Sage. *The Adventures of Gil Blas*. Routledge.
1866 *A Round of Days*. Routledge. With others.
1866 *Ballad Stories of the Affections*. Routledge. With others.
1867 [1866] *The Spirit of Praise*. Warne. With others.
1867 *Touches of Nature*. Strahan. With others.
1867 R. Buchanan. *Wayside Poesies*. Routledge. With others.
1867 J. Ingelow. *Poems*. Longman. With others.
1867 *Golden Thoughts from Golden Fountains*. Warne. With others.
1868 R. Buchanan. *North Coast and Other Poems*. Routledge. With
others.
1868 C. Dickens. *The Uncommercial Traveller*. Chapman & Hall.
1868 C. Reade. *It Is Never Too Late to Mend*. Bradbury & Evans.

*

Hartley, H. "George J. Pinwell." *The Print Collector's Quarterly* 11
(April 1924).
Whiteley, D. P. *George J. Pinwell*. Art & Technics, 1949.

Dante Gabriel Rossetti (1828–82)
1855 W. Allingham. *The Music Master: A Love Story and Two Series*
of Day and Night Songs. Routledge. With others.
1857 A., Lord Tennyson. *Poems*. Moxon. With others.
1862 C. G. Rossetti. *Goblin Market and Other Poems*. Macmillan.
1866 C. G. Rossetti. *The Prince's Progress and Other Poems*. Macmillan.

*

Cary, E. L. "Dante Gabriel Rossetti, Illustrator." *The Print Collector's*
Quarterly 3 (October 1915).

Fredeman, W. E. *Pre-Raphaelitism: A Bibliocritical Study.* Cambridge, Mass.: Harvard, 1965.

Rossetti, W. M. *Dante Gabriel Rossetti as Designer and Writer.* Cassell, 1889.

Linley Sambourne (1845–1910)

1872   F. C. Burnand. *The New History of Sandford and Merton.* Bradbury & Evans.

1885   C. Kingsley. *Water Babies.* Macmillan.

Frederick Sandys (1829?–1904)

1861   *English Sacred Poetry of the Sixteenth, Seventeenth, and Eighteenth Centuries.* Ed. R. A. Willmott. Routledge. With others.

1865   G. Meredith. *The Shaving of Shagpat.* Chapman & Hall.

1866   *Pictures of Society.* Low. With others.

1866   D. M. Mulock (Craik). *Christian's Mistake.* Hurst & Blackett.

1867   *Touches of Nature.* Strahan. With others.

1876   G. W. Thornbury. *Historical & Legendary Ballads & Songs.* Chatto & Windus.

1881   *Dalziel's Bible Gallery.* Routledge. With others.

*

Frederick Sandys, 1829–1904. Brighton: Brighton Museum and Art Gallery, 1974.

Sandys, M. *Reproductions of Woodcuts by Frederick Sandys, 1860–66.* Hentschel, 1910. Reproductions of wood engravings after Sandys's drawings.

Frederick James Shields (1833–1911)

[1863?]   D. Defoe. *History of the Plague of London.* Marshall; Simpkin.

1864   F. J. Shields. *Illustrations for Bunyan's "Pilgrim's Progress".* Simpkin, Marshall.

1867   *Touches of Nature.* Strahan. With others.

*

Mills, E. *The Life and Letters of Frederick Shields.* Longman, 1912.

Shields, F. J. "An Autobiography." In *Toilers in Art.* Ed. H. C. Ewart. Isbister, 1891.

William Small (1843–1931)

1865   W. Wordsworth. *Poems.* Edinburgh: Nimmo. With others.

[1866]   J. Foxe. *The Book of Martyrs.* Cassell, Petter, & Galpin. With others.

1867   J. Milton. *Hymn on Christ's Nativity.* Warne. With anr.

1867   J. Ingelow. *Poems.* Longman. With others.

1867   *Touches of Nature.* Strahan. With others.

1867   *Golden Thoughts from Golden Fountains.* Warne. With others.

1867   *Two Centuries of Song.* Low & Marston. With others.

1867   *Cassell's History of England.* Cassell. With others.

[1867]   *The Illustrated Book of Sacred Songs.* Cassell, Petter, & Galpin. With others.

1868   C. Reade. *Christie Johnstone.* Bradbury & Evans.

1868   R. Buchanan. *North Coast and Other Poems.* Routledge. With others.

1880   J. Bunyan. *The Pilgrim's Progress.* Strahan. With others.

1881   *Illustrated British Ballads.* Cassell. With others.

1881   *Dalziel's Bible Gallery.* Routledge. With others.

1882   H. Fielding. *Works of Henry Fielding.* Smith, Elder.

1883   R. D. Blackmore. *Lorna Doone.* Low. With others.

1894   B. Harte. *A Protégée of Jack Hamlin's.* Chatto & Windus.

Marcus Stone (1840–1921)

1862   C. Dickens. *Pictures from Italy and American Notes.* Chapman & Hall.

1863   C. Dickens. *Great Expectations.* Chapman & Hall.

1865   C. Dickens. *Our Mutual Friend.* Chapman & Hall.

1866   A. Trollope. *Can You Forgive Her?* Chapman & Hall.

1869   A. Trollope. *He Knew He Was Right.* Strahan.

1869   F. E. [M.] Trollope. *The Sacristan's Household.* Virtue.

*

Baldry, A. L. *The Life and Work of Marcus Stone.* Art Annual, 1896.

Sir John Tenniel (1820–1914)

1844   *The Book of British Ballads. Second series.* Ed. S. C. Hall. How. With others.

[1845]   F. H. K., baron de la Motte-Fouqué. *Undine.* Burns.

1846   *Poems and Pictures.* Burns. With others.

1848   C. Dickens. *The Haunted Man.* Bradbury & Evans. With others.

1848   Aesop. *Aesop's Fables.* Murray.

1854   M. Tupper. *Proverbial Philosophy.* Hatchard. With others.

1857   B. W. Procter [Barry Cornwall, pseud.]. *Dramatic Scenes.* Chapman & Hall. With others.

1857   *The Poets of the Nineteenth Century.* Ed. R. A. Willmott. Routledge. With others.

1857   R. Pollok. *The Course of Time.* Blackwood. With others.

1858   E. A. Poe. *Poetical Works.* Low. With others.

1858   R. Blair. *The Grave.* Edinburgh: Black. With others.

1858   *The Home Affections, Pourtrayed by the Poets.* Ed. C. Mackay. Routledge. With others.

1860   S. Brooks. *The Gordian Knot.* Bentley.

1861   S. Brooks. *The Silver Cord.* Bentley.

1861   T. Moore. *Lalla Rookh.* Longman.

1861   *English Sacred Poetry of the Sixteenth, Seventeenth, and Eighteenth Centuries.* Ed. R. A. Willmott. Routledge. With others.

1864   R. H. Barham. *The Ingoldsby Legends.* Bentley. With others.

1864   *English Sacred Poetry of the Olden Time.* Religious Tract Society. With others.

1865   *Dalziel's Illustrated Arabian Nights' Entertainments.* Ed. H. W. Dulcken. Ward & Lock. With others.

1865   T. C. H., viscount de La Villemarqué. *Ballads and Songs of Britanny.* Tr. T. Taylor. Macmillan. With others.

1865, 1866   L. Carroll [C. L. Dodgson]. *Alice's Adventures in Wonderland.* Macmillan.

1867   *Touches of Nature.* Strahan. With others.

1867   W. H. Miller. *The Mirage of Life.* Religious Tract Society.

1869   C. Dickens. *Christmas Books.* Chapman & Hall.

[1869]   D. M. Mulock (Craik). *A Noble Life.* Hurst & Blackett.

1872   L. Carroll [C. L. Dodgson]. *Through the Looking-Glass, and What Alice Found There.* Macmillan.

1890   L. Carroll [C. L. Dodgson]. *The Nursery Alice.* Macmillan.

*

Ayres, H. M. "Carroll's Withdrawal of the 1865 *Alice*." *The Huntington Library Bulletin,* no. 6 (November 1934).

Bond, W. H. "The Publication of *Alice's Adventures in Wonderland*." *Harvard Library Bulletin* 10, no. 3 (Autumn 1956).

Carroll, L. [C. L. Dodgson]. *Alice's Adventures Under Ground.* Intro. M. Gardner. New York: Dover, 1965. Facsimile of the 1866 manuscript.

———. *The Diaries of Lewis Carroll.* Ed. R. L. Green. Oxford, 1954.

———. *The Letters of Lewis Carroll.* Ed. M. N. Cohen. Oxford, 1979.

———. *The Wasp in a Wig: A "Suppressed Episode of 'Through the Looking-Glass, and What Alice Found There'".* Ed. M. Gardner. New York: Clarkson Potter for the Lewis Carroll Society of North America, 1976.

Collingwood, S. D. *Life and Letters of Lewis Carroll.* Unwin, 1898.

Madan, F. *Lewis Carroll Centenary Exhibition*. Essay by H. Hartley on Dodgson's illustrators. Bumpus, 1932.

Mespoulet, M. *Creators of Wonderland*. New York: Arrow, 1934.

Monkhouse, C. *The Life and Works of Sir John Tenniel R.I.* Art Journal, 1901.

Robb, R. "Tenniel's Illustrations for the 'Alice' Books." *The Listener* 74, no. 1900 (1956).

Sarzano, F. *Sir John Tenniel*. Art & Technics, 1948.

George Housman Thomas (1824–68)

1855 O. Goldsmith. *The Vicar of Wakefield*. Low; Bangs.

1857 J. Bunyan. *The Pilgrim's Progress*. Nisbet.

1858 *The Home Affections, Pourtrayed by the Poets*. Ed. C. Mackay. Routledge. With others.

1859 E. McDermott. *The Merrie Days of England*. Kent. With others.

1860 [1859] T. Moore. *Lalla Rookh*. Routledge.

1860 *A Book of Favourite Modern Ballads*. Kent. With others.

1860 H. W. Longfellow. *The Song of Hiawatha*. Kent.

1861 *Household Song*. Kent. With others.

1863 *Early English Poems: Chaucer to Pope*. Low. With others.

[1863?] *Old English Ballads*. Ward, Lock, & Tyler. With others.

1864 D. Defoe. *Robinson Crusoe*. Cassell.

1866 W. Collins. *Armadale*. Smith, Elder.

[1866] J. Foxe. *The Book of Martyrs*. Cassell, Petter, & Galpin. With others.

1867 A. Trollope. *The Last Chronicle of Barset*. Smith, Elder.

[ca. 1870] *Poets' Wit and Humour*. Ed. H. W. Wills. Ward, Lock, & Tyler. With anr.

[1875] T. Gray. *An Elegy Written in a Country Churchyard*. Low, Marston, & Low. With others.

*

In Memoriam, George H. Thomas. Cassell, 1869. With about 100 reproductions of Thomas's wood engravings.

Frederick Walker (1840–75)

1861 C. Dickens. *Reprinted Pieces*. Chapman & Hall.

1861 *English Sacred Poetry of the Sixteenth, Seventeenth, and Eighteenth Centuries*. Ed. R. A. Willmott. Routledge. With others.

1862 C. Dickens. *Hard Times*. Chapman & Hall.

1864 *English Sacred Poetry of the Olden Time*. Religious Tract Society. With others.

1866 *A Round of Days*. Routledge. With others.

1867 R. Buchanan. *Wayside Poesies*. Routledge. With others.

1867 A. I. Thackeray (Ritchie). *The Story of Elizabeth*. Smith, Elder.

1867 A. I. Thackeray (Ritchie). *The Village on the Cliff*. Smith, Elder.

1867 *Touches of Nature*. Strahan. With others.

1868 W. M. Thackeray. *The Adventures of Philip*. Smith, Elder.

1882 W. M. Thackeray. *Denis Duval*. Smith, Elder.

*

Black, C. *Frederick Walker*. Duckworth, 1902.

Marks, J. G. *The Life and Letters of Frederick Walker*. Macmillan, 1896.

John Dawson Watson (1832–92)

1861 J. Bunyan. *The Pilgrim's Progress*. Routledge.

1861 N. Macleod. *The Gold Thread*. Strahan. With anr.

1861 *English Sacred Poetry of the Sixteenth, Seventeenth, and Eighteenth Centuries*. Ed. R. A. Willmott. Routledge. With others.

1861 E. Cook. *Poetical Works*. Routledge. With others.

1864 D. Defoe. *Robinson Crusoe*. Routledge.

1864 *English Sacred Poetry of the Olden Time*. Religious Tract Society. With others.

1864 H. W. Dulcken. *The Golden Harp*. Routledge. With others.

1865 *Dalziel's Illustrated Arabian Nights' Entertainments*. Ed. H. W. Dulcken. Ward & Lock. With others.

1865 *Our Life Illustrated by Pen and Pencil*. Religious Tract Society. With others.

1866 *A Round of Days*. Routledge. With others.

1866 *Ballad Stories of the Affections*. Routledge. With others.

1866 H. Southgate. *What Men Have Said About Women*. Routledge.

1866 *Pictures of Society*. Low. With others.

[1866] J. Foxe. *The Book of Martyrs*. Cassell, Petter, & Galpin. With others.

1867 *Touches of Nature*. Strahan. With others.

1867 H. W. Dulcken. *Old Friends and New Friends*. Warne. With anr.

Harrison William Weir (1824–1906)

1851 O. Goldsmith. *The Poetical Works*. Cundall & Addey. With others.

1854 F. W. C. Gerstäcker. *Wild Sports in the Far West*. Routledge.

1855 J. G. Wood. *Sketches and Anecdotes of Animal Life*. Routledge

1855 T. Campbell. *The Pleasures of Hope*. Low. With anr.

1857 T. Campbell. *Gertrude of Wyoming*. Routledge. With others.

1857 R. Bloomfield. *The Farmer's Boy*. Low. With others.

[1857] J. Bishop. *Animals, Beasts and Birds*. Dean.

1858 J. Milton. *Comus: A Mask*. Routledge. With others.

1858 *The Home Affections, Pourtrayed by the Poets*. Ed. C. Mackay. Routledge. With others.

[1859] T. Miller. *Sports and Pastimes of Merry England*. Darton.

[1859], 1862, 1863 J. G. Wood. *The Illustrated Natural History*. Second ed. Routledge. With others.

1860 J. Montgomery. *The Poems of James Montgomery*. Routledge. With others.

1860 *A Book of Favourite Modern Ballads*. Kent. With others.

1861 E. Cook. *Poetical Works*. Routledge. With others.

1861 *English Sacred Poetry of the Sixteenth, Seventeenth, and Eighteenth Centuries*. Ed. R. A. Willmott. Routledge. With others.

1867 Aesop. *Three Hundred Aesop's Fables: Literally Translated from the Greek*. Tr. G. F. Townsend. Routledge.

1868 *The Savage-Club Papers for 1868*. Tinsley. With others.

[1868] W. Cowper. *Table Talk and Other Poems*. Religious Tract Society.

1870 *Favourite Fables in Prose and Verse*. Griffith & Farran.

Joseph Wolf (1820–99)

1853 J. W. von Goethe. *Reynard the Fox*. Pickering. With anr.

1853 *The Poets of the Woods*. Bosworth.

1854 *Feathered Favourites*. Bosworth.

1856 C. J. Andersson. *Lake NGami*. Hurst & Blackett.

1858 *Lays of the Holy Land*. Nisbet. With others.

1859 W. Wordsworth. *Poems of William Wordsworth*. Routledge. With others.

[1859], 1862, 1863 J. G. Wood. *The Illustrated Natural History*. Second ed. Routledge. With others.

1860 R. H. W. Dunlop. *Hunting in the Himalaya*. Bentley.

1860 J. Montgomery. *The Poems of James Montgomery*. Routledge. With others.

1861 E. Cook. *Poetical Works*. Routledge. With others.

1861 *English Sacred Poetry of the Sixteenth, Seventeenth, and Eighteenth Centuries*. Ed. R. A. Willmott. Routledge. With others.

1862 C. A. Johns. *British Birds in Their Haunts*. S.P.C.K.

1866 J. Ingelow. *Poetical Works*. Longman. With others.

1867 Aesop. *Aesop's Fables*. Ed. E. Garrett. Strahan. With others.

1867 *Touches of Nature*. Strahan. With others.

1868 R. Buchanan. *North Coast and Other Poems*. Routledge. With others.

1872 A. E. Knox. *Autumns on the Spey*. Van Voorst.

1874 D. G. Elliott. *The Life and Habits of Wild Animals*. New York: Harper.

1894–1900 P. L. Sclater and M. R. O. Thomas. *The Book of Antelopes*. Porter.

*

Palmer, A. H. *The Life of Joseph Wolf, Animal Painter*. Longman, 1895.

Thomas W. Wood (fl. 1855–72)

[1859], 1862, 1863 J. G. Wood. *The Illustrated Natural History*. Second ed. Routledge. With others.

1864 J. G. Wood. *Our Garden Friends and Foes*. Routledge. With others.

Johann Baptist Zwecker (1814–76)

[1859], 1862, 1863 J. G. Wood. *The Illustrated Natural History*. Second ed. Routledge. With others.

1862 D. Defoe. *Robinson Crusoe*. Griffin, Bohn.

1867 Aesop. *Aesop's Fables*. Ed. E. Garrett. Strahan. With others.

1868 R. Buchanan. *North Coast and Other Poems*. Routledge. With others.

1869 W. R. S. Ralston. *Krilof and His Fables*. Strahan. With anr.

CHAPTER EIGHT

The Nineteenth Century (III)
1886-1900

Edwin Austin Abbey (1852–1911)

[1883] R. Herrick. *Selections from the Poetry of Robert Herrick*. Low, Marston, Searle, & Rivington.

1885 R. B. Sheridan. *The Rivals and the School for Scandal*. Chatto & Windus. With others.

1887 O. Goldsmith. *She Stoops to Conquer*. New York: Harper. Low, Marston, Searle, & Rivington, 1888.

1889 *Old Songs*. Macmillan. With anr.

1890 *The Quiet Life*. Low, Marston, Searle, & Rivington. With anr.

1895 *A London Garland*. Ed. W. E. Henley. Macmillan. With others.

1899 W. Shakespeare. *Comedies*. New York: Harper.

1902 O. Goldsmith. *The Deserted Village*. London: Harper.

*

Edwin Austin Abbey (1852–1911): An Exhibition. New Haven, Conn.: Yale University Art Gallery, 1973.

Lucas, E. V. *Edwin Austin Abbey – Royal Academician: The Record of His Life and Work*. Methuen, 1921.

Aubrey Vincent Beardsley (1872–98)

1893–94 T. Malory. *Morte Darthur*. Dent.

1893 B. Bøjrnson. *Pastor Sang*. Longman.

1893 C. Lamb and D. W. Jerrold. *Bon Mots*. Dent.

1893 *The Wonderful History of Vergilius the Sorcerer*. Nutt.

1894 O. Wilde. *Salome, A Tragedy in One Act Translated from the French of Oscar Wilde: Pictured by Aubrey Beardsley*. Mathews & Lane.

1894 J. Quilp. [J. Davidson?] *Baron Verdigris*. Henry.

1894 Lucian. *Lucian's "True History"*. Privately printed. With others.

1894 J. Davidson. *Plays*. Mathews & Lane.

1894–95 E. A. Poe. *Tales of Mystery and Imagination*. Chicago: Stone.

1895 J. Davidson. *The Wonderful Mission of Earl Lavender*. Ward & Downey.

1895 *A London Garland*. Ed. W. E. Henley. Macmillan. With others.

1896 A. Pope. *The Rape of the Lock*. Smithers.

1896 W. Ruding. *An Evil Motherhood*. Mathews.

1896 Aristophanes. *Lysistrata*. Privately circulated by Smithers.

1896 V. O'Sullivan. *A Book of Bargains*. Smithers.

1897 E. Dowson. *The Pierrot of the Minute*. Smithers.

1898 A. Beardsley. *Six Drawings Illustrating Théophile Gautier's "Mademoiselle de Maupin"*. Smithers.

1898 B. Jonson. *His Volpone: or The Fox*. Smithers.

1904 [1903] A. Beardsley. *Under the Hill: and Other Essays in Prose and Verse*. Lane.

*

Beardsley, A. *The Letters of Aubrey Beardsley.* Ed. H. Maas, J. L. Duncan, and W. G. Good. Cassell, 1970.

Clark, K. *The Best of Aubrey Beardsley.* New York: Doubleday, 1978.

Gallatin, A. E. *Aubrey Beardsley: Catalogue of Drawings and Bibliography.* New York: Grolier Club, 1945.

Pennell, J. "A New Illustrator: Aubrey Beardsley." *The Studio* 1, no. 1 (1893).

Reade, B. *Beardsley.* Studio Vista, 1967.

Walker, R. A. *A Beardsley Miscellany.* Bodley Head, 1949.

Weintraub, S. *Aubrey Beardsley: Imp of the Perverse.* State College: Pennsylvania State, 1976.

Robert Anning Bell (1863–1933)

1895 W. Shakespeare. *A Midsummer Night's Dream.* Dent.
1897 J. Keats. *Poems by John Keats.* Bell.
1898 J. Bunyan. *The Pilgrim's Progress.* Methuen.
1898 *English Lyrics from Spenser to Milton.* Bell.
1899 C. Lamb and M. Lamb. *Tales from Shakespeare.* Freemantle.
1901 W. Shakespeare. *The Tempest.* Freemantle.
1902 P. B. Shelley. *Poems.* Bell.
1902 O. Khayyám. *The Rubáiyát.* Bell.
1903 J. Milton. *Lycidas and Other Odes.* Bell.
1907 F. T. Palgrave. *Golden Treasury.* Dent.
1912 A. Meynell. *Mary, the Mother of Jesus.* Medici.

*

Taylor, J. R. *The Art Nouveau Book in Britain.* Methuen, 1966.

Sir Frank Brangwyn (1867–1956)

1895 M. de Cervantes Saavedra. *Don Quixote.* Gibbings.
1896 S. Crockett et al. *Tales of Our Coast.* Chatto & Windus.
1896 *The Thousand and One Nights.* Gibbings.
1898 M. Scott. *The Cruise of the "Midge".* Gibbings.
1898 M. Scott. *Tom Cringle's Log.* Gibbings.
1899 G. Cupples. *A Spliced Yarn.* Gibbings.
1900 M. de Cervantes Saavedra. *Exemplary Novels.* Gibbings.
1908 W. Raleigh. *The Last Fight of the "Revenge".* Gibbings.
1910 O. Khayyám. *The Rubáiyát.* Edinburgh: Foulis.
[1911] R. Southey. *The Life of Nelson.* Gibbings.
1913 A. W. Kinglake. *Eöthen.* Low, Marston.
1916 E. Phillpots. *The Girl and the Faun.* Palmer & Hayward.
1923 F. Brangwyn and H. Preston. *Windmills.* Lane.
1948 [Bible.] *Book of Job.* Leigh-on-Sea: Lewis.

*

Sparrow, W. S. *Frank Brangwyn and His Work.* Studio, 1915.

———. *Prints and Drawings by Frank Brangwyn: With Some Other Phases of His Art.* Lane, 1919.

Charles Edmund Brock (1870–1938)

1893 T. Hood. *Humorous Poems.* Macmillan.
1894 J. Swift. *Gulliver's Travels.* Macmillan.
1895 J. Galt. *Annals of the Parish.* Macmillan.
1895 H. Peek. *Nema and Other Stories.* Chapman & Hall.
1896 C. Kingsley. *Westward Ho!* Macmillan.
1897 W. Scott. *Ivanhoe.* Service & Paton.
1897 J. Austen. *Pride and Prejudice.* Macmillan.
1898 W. Cowper. *The Diverting History of John Gilpin.* Dent.
1898 W. Scott. *The Lady of the Lake.* Service & Paton.
1898 O. Goldsmith. *The Vicar of Wakefield.* Service & Paton.
1898 J. Austen. *Sense and Sensibility.* Dent.
1898 J. Austen. *Emma.* Dent.
1898 J. Austen. *Persuasion.* Dent.
1898 D. Defoe. *Robinson Crusoe.* Service & Paton.

1900 C. Lamb. *The Essays of Elia. Last Essays of Elia.* Dent.
1900 C. Dickens. *The Holly Tree. Seven Poor Travellers.* Dent.
1900 J. F. Cooper. *The Pathfinder.* Macmillan.
1900 J. F. Cooper. *The Prairie.* Macmillan.
1901–03 W. M. Thackeray. *The Prose Works of William Makepeace Thackeray.* Dent.
1904 E. C. Gaskell. *Cranford.* Dent.
1904 M. R. Mitford. *Our Village.* Dent.
[1904] C. Lamb and M. Lamb. *Mrs. Leicester's School.* Gardner, Darton.
1905 G. Eliot [M. A. Evans]. *Silas Marner.* Dent.
1905 C. Dickens. *A Christmas Carol. The Cricket on the Hearth.* Dent.
1906 W. Irving. *The Keeping of Christmas at Bracebridge Hall.* Dent.
1907 C. Dickens. *The Haunted Man. The Ghost's Bargain.* Dent.
1907 C. Dickens. *The Battle of Life.* Dent.
1907 J. Austen. *Northanger Abbey.* Dent.
1907 J. Austen. *Pride and Prejudice.* Dent.
1908 J. Austen. *Mansfield Park.* Dent.
1908 J. Austen. *Sense and Sensibility.* Dent.
1908 C. Dickens. *Doctor Marigold.* Foulis.
1909 J. Austen. *Emma.* Dent.
1909 J. Austen. *Persuasion.* Dent.
1910 R. D. Blackmore. *Lorna Doone.* Low, Marston. With anr.
[1910] W. Irving. *The Sketch Book.* Cassell.
[1910?] R. Herrick. *Love Poems.* Nister.
1911 D. M. Mulock (Craik). *John Halifax, Gentleman.* Cassell.
1930 C. Dickens. *Pickwick Papers.* Harrap.
1931 C. Dickens. *Nicholas Nickleby.* Harrap.

*

Kelly, C. M. *The Brocks.* Skilton, 1975.

Henry Matthew Brock (1875–1960)

1895 R. Pollok. *Tales of the Covenanters.* Anderson.
1895 F. Marryat. *Jacob Faithful.* Macmillan.
1895 F. Marryat. *Japhet in Search of a Father.* Macmillan.
1896 S. Lover. *Handy Andy.* Macmillan.
1896 W. M. Thackeray. *Ballads and Songs.* Cassell.
1898 J. Austen. *Pride and Prejudice.* Dent.
1898 J. Austen. *Northanger Abbey.* Dent.
1898 J. Austen. *Mansfield Park.* Dent.
[1898] E. C. Gaskell. *Cranford.* Service & Paton.
1898–1901 G. J. Whyte-Melville. [Seven works.] Thacker.
1899 W. Shakespeare. *King Richard II.* Longman.
[1899] W. Scott. *Waverley.* Service & Paton.
1900 J. G. Frazier. *Asinette.* Dent.
1900 J. F. Cooper. *The Pioneers.* Macmillan.
1900 J. F. Cooper. *The Last of the Mohicans.* Macmillan.
1900 J. F. Cooper. *The Deerslayer.* Macmillan.
1900 W. Scott. *Ivanhoe.* Dent. With anr.
[1900] J. Bunyan. *The Pilgrim's Progress.* Pearson.
1901 C. Dickens. *The Old Curiosity Shop.* Gresham.
1901 L. Wallace. *Ben Hur.* Pearson.
1902 O. W. Holmes. *The Autocrat of the Breakfast-Table.* Dent.
1902 O. W. Holmes. *The Poet at the Breakfast-Table.* Dent.
1902 O. W. Holmes. *The Professor at the Breakfast-Table.* Dent.
1903 D. W. Jerrold. *Essays.* Dent.
1903 L. Hunt. *Essays.* Dent.
[1903] C. Kingsley. *Westward Ho!* Pearson.
1904 D. Defoe. *Robinson Crusoe.* Pearson.
1905 J. Addison and R. Steele. *"Sir Roger de Coverley" and Other Essays from the "Spectator".* Dent.

1905 M. de Cervantes Saavedra. *Don Quixote*. Pearson; Seeley.

[1909] W. Irving. *Old English Christmas*. Foulis.

1912 O. Goldsmith. *The Vicar of Wakefield*. Seeley.

1924 J. G. Frazer. *Leaves from the Golden Bough*. Macmillan.

[1932] G. Borrow. *Lavengro*. Nelson.

1934 *A Book of Old Ballads*. Hutchinson.

Sir Edward Coley Burne-Jones (1833–98)

1857 A. Maclaren. *The Fairy Family: a Series of Ballads and Metrical Tales*. Longman.

1867 M. S. Gatty. *Parables from Nature*. Second series. Bell & Daldy. With others.

1881 *Dalziel's Bible Gallery*. Routledge. With others.

1892, 13 May W. Morris. *A Dream of John Ball*. Kelmscott.

1892, 12 Sept. J. de Voragine. *The Golden Legend*. Kelmscott.

1892 E. R. Bulwer-Lytton. *King Poppy*. Longman.

1892, 10 Nov. [1893] *The Order of Chivalry*. Kelmscott.

1894, 30 May W. Morris. *The Wood beyond the World*. Kelmscott.

1894 F. Huffer [Hueffer]. *The Queen Who Flew*. Bliss, Sands, & Foster.

1895, 16 Feb. *The Romaunce off [sic] Syr Perecyvelle*. Kelmscott.

1895, 25 May W. Morris. *The Life and Death of Jason*. Kelmscott.

1896, 2 Mar. W. Morris. *The Well at the World's End*. Kelmscott.

1896, 14 Mar. *Sire Degrevant*. Kelmscott.

1896, 8 May G. Chaucer. *The Works of Geoffrey Chaucer*. Tr. W. Caxton. Kelmscott.

1897, 14 July [11 Nov.] *Syr Ysambrace*. Kelmscott.

1897, 11 Dec. [1898, 24 Mar.] W. Morris. *Love Is Enough*. Kelmscott.

1898, 19 Jan. W. Morris. *The Story of Sigurd the Volsung and the Fall of the House of the Niblungs*. Kelmscott.

1898 Perlesvaus. *The High History of the Holy Graal*. Dent.

1935, 29 Oct. R. Bridges. *Eros and Psyche*. Gregynog.

1974–75 W. Morris. *Cupid and Psyche*. Cambridge: Carter. From forty-four of the original blocks.

*

Fitzgerald, P. *Edward Burne-Jones: A Biography*. Joseph, 1975.

Life, A. R. "Illustration and Morris' 'Ideal Book'." *Victorian Poetry* (West Virginia University) 13, nos. 3–4 (Fall–Winter 1975).

Morris, W. *Ornamentation and Illustrations from the Kelmscott Chaucer*. Intro. F. Johnson. New York: Dover, 1973.

Robinson, D. *A Companion Volume to the Kelmscott Chaucer*. Basilisk, 1975.

Sparling, H. *The Kelmscott Press and William Morris, Master Craftsman*. Macmillan, 1924.

Titlebaum, R. "The Creation of the Kelmscott *Chaucer*." *Harvard Library Bulletin* 27, no. 4 (October 1979).

William Morris and the Art of the Book. New York: Pierpont Morgan Library; Oxford, 1976.

Charles Conder (1868–1909)

1896 H. de Balzac. *La fille aux yeux d'or*. Tr. E. Dowson. Smithers.

1908 [1907] *The Story of Beauty and the Beast*. Tr. E. Dowson. Lane.

*

Gibson, F. *Charles Conder, His Life and Work*. Catalogue by C. Dodgson. Lane, 1914.

Ricketts, C. *Pages on Art*. Constable, 1913.

Rothenstein, J. *The Life and Death of Conder*. Catalogue by C. Dodgson. Dent, 1938.

Walter Crane (1845–1915)

1865 N. Hawthorne. *Transformation* [*The Marble Faun*]. Smith, Elder.

1868 *The Legendary Ballads of England and Scotland*. Warne. With others.

1893 W. Crane. *Eight Illustrations to Shakespeare's "Tempest"*. Dent. Without text.

1894 W. Morris. *The Story of the Glittering Plain*. Kelmscott.

1894 W. Crane. *Eight Illustrations to Shakespeare's "Two Gentlemen of Verona"*. Dent. Without text.

1895 H. C. Beeching. *A Book of Christmas Verse*. Methuen.

[1895] W. Crane. *Eight Illustrations to "The Merry Wives of Windsor"*. Allen. Without text.

1897 E. Spenser. *The Faerie Queene*. Allen.

1898 E. Spenser. *The Shepheard's Calender*. Harper.

1900 M. de Cervantes Saavedra. *Don Quixote*. Blackie.

1901 [C. Lamb.] *A Masque of Days: From the Last Essays of Elia*. Cassell.

*

Crane, W. *An Artist's Reminiscences*. Methuen, 1907.

———. *Of the Decorative Illustration of Books Old and New*. Bell, 1896.

Engen, R. C. *Walter Crane as a Book Illustrator*. Academy, 1975.

Massé, G. C. E. *Bibliography of First Editions of Books Illustrated by Walter Crane*. Chelsea, 1923.

Spencer, I. *Walter Crane*. Studio Vista, 1975.

Sir Harry Furniss (1854–1925)

1883 L. Sterne. *Tristram Shandy*. Nimmo.

1889 L. Carroll [C. L. Dodgson]. *Sylvie and Bruno*. Macmillan.

1893 L. Carroll [C. L. Dodgson]. *Sylvie and Bruno Concluded*. Macmillan.

1898 C. Dickens. *The Uncommercial Traveller*. Chapman & Hall.

1910 C. Dickens. *The Harry Furniss Dickens*. New York: Gleason.

*

Furniss, H. *Confessions of a Caricaturist*. Unwin, 1901.

Arthur Joseph Gaskin (1862–1928)

1895 J. M. Neale. *Good King Wenceslas*. Birmingham: Cornish Bros.

1896 E. Spenser. *The Shepheardes Calender*. Kelmscott.

Laurence Housman (1865–1959)

1892 G. Meredith. *Jump-to-Glory Jane*. Swann, Sonnenschein.

1893 J. L. I. Lie. *Weird Tales from Northern Seas*. Paul, Trench, Trübner.

1893 C. G. Rossetti. *Goblin Market*. Macmillan.

1894 J. Barlow. *The End of Elfintown*. Macmillan.

1894 L. Housman. *A Farm in Fairyland*. Paul, Trench, Trübner.

1895 L. Housman. *The House of Joy*. Paul, Trench, Trübner.

1895 C. N. Robinson. *The Viol of Love*. Lane.

1896 L. Housman. *Green Arras*. Lane.

1896 C. A. Housman. *The Were-Wolf*. Lane.

1896 L. Housman. *All-Fellows: Seven Legends of Lower Redemption*. Paul, Trench, Trübner.

1898 L. Housman. *The Field of Clover*. Paul, Trench, Trübner.

1898 T. à Kempis. *Of the Imitation of Christ*. Paul, Trench, Trübner.

1898 P. B. Shelley. *The Sensitive Plant*. Dent.

*

Guthrie. J. "The Wood Engravings of Clemence Housman." *The Print Collector's Quarterly* 11, no. 2 (April 1924).

Hodgkins, I. G. K. *Laurence Housman, 1865–1959; Clemence Housman, 1861–1955; Alfred Edward Housman, 1859–1936*. National Book League, 1975.

Housman, L. *The Unexpected Years*. Cape, 1937.

Thomas Sturge Moore (1870–1944)
1895 R. D. Blackmore. *Fringilla*. Mathews.
1899 M. de Guérin. *The Centaur. The Bacchante*. Tr. T. S. Moore. Hacon & Ricketts.
1902 W. Wordsworth. *Poems from Wordsworth*. Comp. T. S. Moore. Hacon & Ricketts.
1902 C. Perrault. *Histoire de Peau d'Ane*. Eragny.

*

Gwynn, F. L. *Sturge Moore and the Life of Art*. Richards, 1952.
T. Sturge Moore. Ed. C. French. Morland, 1921.

Sir William Nicholson (1872–1949)
1898 W. Nicholson. *London Types: Quatorzains by W. E. Henley*. Heinemann.
1898 W. Nicholson. *An Almanac of Twelve Sports: With Words by Rudyard Kipling*. Heinemann.
1900 W. Nicholson. *Characters of Romance*. Heinemann.
1923 J. Gay. *Polly*. Heinemann.
1929 S. Sassoon. *Memoirs of a Fox-Hunting Man*. Faber & Faber.

*

Browse, L. *William Nicholson*. Hart-Davis, 1956.
Steen, M. *William Nicholson*. Collins, 1943.

Sidney Edward Paget (1860–1908)
1892 A. C. Doyle. *The Adventures of Sherlock Holmes*. Newnes.

Frederick Pegram (1870–1937)
1895 B. Disraeli. *Sybil*. Macmillan.
1897 E. R. Bulwer-Lytton. *The Last of the Barons*. Service & Paton.
1898 W. Scott. *The Bride of Lammermoor*. Service & Paton.
[1898] *The Arabian Nights' Entertainments*. Service & Paton.
1899 W. Besant. *The Orange Girl*. Chatto & Windus.
[1900] M. Edgeworth. *Ormond*. Gresham.
1902 F. Marryat. *Mr. Midshipman Easy*. Macmillan.
[n.d.] C. Dickens. *Martin Chuzzlewit*. Blackie.

Lucien Pissarro (1863–1944)
1894 M. Rust. *The Queen of the Fishes*. Lane.
1896 [Bible.] *The Book of Ruth and the Book of Esther*. Hacon & Ricketts.
1904 S. T. Coleridge. *Christabel*. Eragny.

*

Fern, A. M. *The Wood-Engravings of Lucien Pissarro. A Catalogue Raisonné*. University of Chicago Library, 1960.

Charles de Sousy Ricketts (1866–1931)
1891 O. Wilde. *A House of Pomegranates*. Osgood, McIlvaine. In collaboration with C. H. Shannon.
1893 J. B. L. Warren, baron de Tabley. *Poems Dramatic and Lyrical*. Mathews & Lane.
1893 Longus. *Daphnis and Chloe*. Mathews & Lane. In collaboration with C. H. Shannon.
1894 Musaeus. *Hero and Leander*. Tr. C. Marlowe and G. Chapman. Vale. In collaboration with C. H. Shannon.
1894 O. Wilde. *The Sphinx*. Mathews & Lane.
1896 J. Milton. *Early Poems*. Vale.
1897 L. Apuleius Madaurensis. *The Excellent Marriage of Cupid and Psyches*. Tr. W. Adlington. Hacon & Ricketts.
1901 L. Apuleius Madaurensis. *De Cupidinis et Psyches amoribus fabula anilis*. Hacon & Ricketts.
1903 [Bible.] *The Parables from the Gospels, With Ten Original*

Woodcuts Designed and Engraved on Wood by Charles Ricketts. Hacon & Ricketts.
1903 T. S. Moore. *Danaë*. Hacon & Ricketts.

*

A Bibliography of the Books Issued by Hacon & Ricketts. Intro. C. S. Ricketts. Vale, 1904.
A Collection of Books Designed by Charles Ricketts. Zurich: L'Art Ancien, Bulletin 25, 1972.
An Exhibition of Books Designed by Charles Ricketts. Intro. A. E. Gallatin. Cambridge, Mass.: Houghton Library, Harvard University, 1946.
French, C. "The Wood-Engravings of Charles Ricketts." *The Print Collector's Quarterly* 14, no. 2 (1927).

Thomas Heath Robinson (1869–1950)
1896 E. C. Gaskell. *Cranford*. Bliss, Sands.
1896 W. M. Thackeray. *Henry Esmond*. Allen.
1897 L. Sterne. *A Sentimental Journey*. Bliss, Sands.
1897 N. Hawthorne. *The Scarlet Letter*. Bliss, Sands.
[1935] T. à Kempis. *Of the Imitation of Christ*. Hutchinson.

Charles Haslewood Shannon (1865–1937). See Ricketts.

Claude Allin Shepperson (1867–1921)
1899 W. Shakespeare. *The Merchant of Venice*. Longman.
1899 G. Borrow. *Lavengro*. Gresham.
1900 W. Shakespeare. *As You Like It*. Longman.
[1900] B. Disraeli. *Coningsby*. Gresham.
[1900] W. Scott. *The Heart of Mid-Lothian*. Gresham.
1902 L. Hunt. *The Old Court Suburb*. Freemantle. With others.
1905 E. Phillpotts. *Up-Along and Down-Along*. Methuen.
1909 R. Burns. *Poetical Works*. Gresham.
1913 E. V. Lucas. *The Open Road*. Methuen.
1916 J. Keats. *Poetical Works*. Gresham.

William Strang (1859–1921)
1884 W. Nicholson. *Seven Illustrations to the "Ballad of Aiken Drum"*. Castle Douglas: Gordon; Kirkcudbright: Nicholson. Without text.
1884 R. Burns. *Nine Illustrations to Burns' Poems*. Without text.
1885 J. Bunyan. *Fourteen Illustrations for Bunyan's "Pilgrim's Progress"*. Without text.
1892 W. Strang. *The Earth Fiend*. Mathews & Lane.
1894 W. Strang. *Death and the Ploughman's Wife*. Lawrence & Bullen.
1894 Lucian. *Lucian's "True History"*. Privately printed. With others.
1894 G. E. Lessing. *Nathan the Wise*. Glasgow: Maclehose.
1895 [1894] J. Bunyan. *The Pilgrim's Progress*. Nimmo. With text.
1895 R. E. Raspe. *The Adventures of Baron Munchausen*. Lawrence & Bullen. With anr.
1895 W. C. Monkhouse. *The Christ upon the Hill*. Smith, Elder.
1895 [1896] J. Milton. *Twelve Illustrations to Milton's "Paradise Lost"*. Nimmo. With "Arguments".
1896 S. T. Coleridge. *The Ancient Mariner*. Dunthorne. Without text.
1898 A. Sargant and W. Strang. *A Book of Ballads and Etchings*. Mathews.
1901 R. Kipling. *Thirty Illustrations to Rudyard Kipling's Short Stories*. Macmillan. Without text.
1901 W. Strang. *The Doings of Death*. Essex House.

1902   I. Walton. *The Compleat Angler*. Freemantle. With anr.
1902   M. de Cervantes Saavedra. *Thirty Etchings Illustrating Subjects from "Don Quixote"*. Macmillan. Without text.
1905   J. Milton. *Paradise Lost*. Routledge. With text.
1913   [Bible.] New Testament. Hodder & Stoughton.

*

Strang, D. *William Strang: Catalogue of His Etchings and Engravings*. Glasgow, 1962.
William Strang: Catalogue of His Etched Work, 1882–1912. Intro. L. Binyon. Glasgow: Maclehose, publisher to the University, 1906.
William Strang: Supplement to the "Catalogue of His Etched Work, 1882–1912". Intro. L. Binyon. Glasgow: Maclehose, Jackson, publishers to the University, 1923.

Edmund Joseph Sullivan (1869–1933)
1895   *A London Garland*. Ed. W. E. Henley. Macmillan. With others.
1896   G. Borrow. *Lavengro*. Macmillan.
1896   T. Hughes. *Tom Brown's School-Days*. Macmillan.
1896   R. B. Sheridan. *The School for Scandal. The Rivals*. Macmillan.
1896   I. Walton. *The Compleat Angler*. Dent.
1898 [1897]   W. Scott. *The Pirate*. Service & Paton.
1898   T. Carlyle. *Sartor Resartus*. Bell.
1900   A., Lord Tennyson. *A Dream of Fair Women and Other Poems*. Richards.
1900   G. White. *The Natural History & Antiquities of Selborne & A Garden Kalendar*. Freemantle. With anr.
1901   J. Bunyan. *The Pilgrim's Progress*. Newnes.
1902   L. Hunt. *The Old Court Suburb*. Freemantle. With others.
1902   R. Barr. *A Prince of Good Fellows*. Chatto & Windus.
1902   W. Irving. *The Sketch Book*. Newnes.
1902   T. Lodge. *Rosalynde*. Newnes.
[1904]   O. Goldsmith. *Letters from a Citizen of the World*. Gardner, Darton.
1905   H. G. Wells. *A Modern Utopia*. Chapman & Hall.
1908   F. H. K., baron de la Motte-Fouqué. *Sintram and His Companions*. Methuen.
1910   T. Carlyle. *The French Revolution*. Chapman & Hall.
1911   W. Shakespeare. *Works*. Dent.
1913   O. Khayyám. *The Rubáiyát*. Tr. E. FitzGerald. Methuen.
1914   O. Goldsmith. *The Vicar of Wakefield*. Constable.
1914   G. Borrow. *Lavengro*. Foulis.
1916   G. Outram. *Legal and Other Lyrics*. Foulis.
1922   A., Lord Tennyson. *Maud*. Macmillan.
1928   R. L. Stevenson. *Dr. Jekyll & Mr. Hyde. Prince Otto*. Macmillan.
1928   R. L. Stevenson. *Weir of Hermiston. The Misadventures of John Nicholson*. Macmillan.

*

Salaman, M. J. "Edmund J. Sullivan: A Master Book Illustrator." *The Studio* 88 (July–December 1924).
Sullivan, E. J. *The Art of Illustration*. Chapman & Hall, 1921.
———. *Line*. Chapman & Hall, 1922.
Thorpe, J. *E. J. Sullivan*. Art & Technics, 1948.

Hugh Thomson (1860–1920)
1884   A. St. Johnston. *Charlie Asgard*. Macmillan.
1886   J. Addison. *Days with Sir Roger de Coverley*. Macmillan.
1888   W. O. Tristram. *Coaching Days and Coaching Ways*. Macmillan. With anr.
1890   O. Goldsmith. *The Vicar of Wakefield*. Macmillan.
1891   E. C. Gaskell. *Cranford*. Macmillan.

1892   A. Dobson. *The Ballad of Beau Brocade and Other Poems of the XVIIIth Century*. Paul, Trench, Trübner.
1893   M. R. Mitford. *Our Village*. Macmillan.
1894   J. Austen. *Pride and Prejudice*. Allen.
1894   A. Dobson. *Coridon's Song: and Other Verses from Various Sources*. Macmillan.
1894   W. Scott. *St. Ronan's Well*. Black.
1895   A. Dobson. *The Story of Rosina*. Paul, Trench, Trübner.
1896   J. Austen. *Sense and Sensibility*. Macmillan.
1896   J. Austen. *Emma*. Macmillan.
1896   W. Somervile. *The Chase*. Redway.
[1896   Macmillan *Highways and Byways* series begins.]
1897   J. Austen. *Mansfield Park*. Macmillan.
1897   J. Austen. *Northanger Abbey. Persuasion*. Macmillan.
1898   E. C. Gaskell. *Cranford*. Macmillan.
1898   G. J. Whyte-Melville. *Riding Recollections*. Thacker.
1899   C. Reade. *Peg Woffington*. Allen.
1901   J. L. Allen. *A Kentucky Cardinal. Aftermath*. Macmillan. New York: Macmillan, 1894.
1901   J. Moffat and E. Druce. *Ray Farley*. Unwin.
1902   W. M. Thackeray. *The History of Samuel Titmarsh and the Great Hogarty Diamond*. Gardner.
1903   M. Edgeworth. *Tales*. Gardner, Darton.
[1903]   F. Burney. *Evelina*. Macmillan.
1904   F. J. H. Darton. *Tales of the Canterbury Pilgrims*. Gardner, Darton.
1905   W. M. Thackeray. *Henry Esmond*. Macmillan.
1906   G. Eliot [M. A. Evans]. *Scenes of Clerical Life*. Macmillan.
1907   G. Eliot [M. A. Evans]. *Silas Marner*. Macmillan.
1907   M. R. Mitford. *Our Village*. Macmillan.
[1909]   W. Shakespeare. *As You Like It*. Hodder & Stoughton.
1910   W. Shakespeare. *The Merry Wives of Windsor*. Heinemann.
[1911]   R. B. Sheridan. *The School for Scandal*. Hodder & Stoughton.
[1912]   O. Goldsmith. *She Stoops to Conquer*. Hodder & Stoughton.
1913   C. Dickens. *The Chimes*. Hodder & Stoughton.
[1913]   J. M. Barrie. *Quality Street*. Hodder & Stoughton.
[1914]   J. M. Barrie. *The Admirable Crichton*. Hodder & Stoughton.
[1918]   T. Hughes. *Tom Brown's School-Days*. New York: Ginn.
1920   N. Hawthorne. *The Scarlet Letter*. Methuen.
1933   C. Dickens. *The Cricket on the Hearth*. Limited Editions.

*

Balston, T. "English Book Illustration: 1880–1900." In *New Paths in Book-Collecting*. Ed. J. Carter. Constable, 1934.
———. "Illustrated Series of the 'Nineties – The Cranford Series." *The Book Collector's Quarterly* 11 (July–September 1933).
Spielmann, M. H., and W. C. Jerrold. *Hugh Thomson: His Art, His Letters, His Humour, and His Charm*. Black, 1931. With bibliography.

Frederick Henry Linton Townsend (1868–1920)
1890   S. J. (Duncan) Cotes. *A Social Departure*. Chatto & Windus.
1891   S. J. (Duncan) Cotes. *An American Girl in London*. Chatto & Windus.
1893   S. J. (Duncan) Cotes. *The Simple Adventures of a Memsahib*. Chatto & Windus.
1895   T. L. Peacock. *Maid Marian. Crotchet Castle*. Macmillan.
1896   T. L. Peacock. *Gryll Grange*. Macmillan.
1896   T. L. Peacock. *Melincourt, or Sir Oran Haut-Ton*. Macmillan.
1896   F. Marryat. *The King's Own*. Macmillan.
1897   T. L. Peacock. *The Misfortunes of Elphin. Rhododaphne*. Macmillan.

1897 C. Brontë. *Shirley*. Service & Paton.
1897 C. Brontë. *Jane Eyre*. Service & Paton.
1898 W. Scott. *Rob Roy*. Service & Paton.
1898 N. Hawthorne. *The House of the Seven Gables*. Service & Paton.
1899 N. Hawthorne. *The Blithedale Romance*. Service & Paton.
1899 S. J. (Duncan) Cotes. *The Path of a Star*. Methuen.
1902 C. Dickens. *A Tale of Two Cities*. Nisbet.
1905 R. Kipling. *"They."* Macmillan.
1907 R. Kipling. *The Brushwood Boy*. Macmillan.
1910 F. L. Barclay. *The Mistress of Shenstone*. Putnam.

Paul Vincent Woodroffe (1875–1954)
1898 W. Shakespeare. *Songs from the Plays of Shakespeare*. Dent.
1899 *The Little Flowers of St. Francis of Assisi*. Paul, Trench, Trübner.
1900 St. Augustine. *The "Confessions" of St. Augustine*. Paul, Trench, Trübner.
1901 St. Gregory. *The Little Flowers of St. Benet*. Paul, Trench, Trübner.
[1902] *Aucassin and Nicolette*. Tr. L. Housman. Murray.
1904 A., Lord Tennyson. *The Princess and Other Poems*. Dent.
1906 S. T. Coleridge. *The Rime of the Ancient Mariner*. Jack.
1908 W. Shakespeare. *The Tempest*. Chapman & Hall.

CHAPTER NINE

The Twentieth Century (I)
1901–1918

Lady Eleanor Fortescue Brickdale (1872–1945)
1905 A., Lord Tennyson. *Poems*. Bell.
1908 R. Browning. *Pippa Passes & Men & Women*. Chatto & Windus.
1909 R. Browning. *Dramatis Personae*. Chatto & Windus.
[1911] A., Lord Tennyson. *Idylls of the King*. Hodder & Stoughton.
[1912] *The Book of Old English Songs & Ballads*. Hodder & Stoughton.
[1912] W. Canton. *The Story of Saint Elizabeth of Hungary*. Herbert & Daniell.
1920 *The Golden Book of Famous Women*. Hodder & Stoughton.
1922 *Fleur and Blanchefleur*. O'Connor.
1924 *The Golden Treasury*. Ed. F. T. Palgrave. Hodder & Stoughton.
1925 *Christmas Carols*. De la More.
1927 D. C. Calthrop. *The Gentle Art*. Williams & Norgate.
                      *

Centenary Exhibition of Works by Eleanor Fortescue-Brickdale, 1872–1945. Oxford: Ashmolean Museum, 1972.

Herbert Cole (1867–1930)
1900 J. Swift. *Gulliver's Travels*. Dent.
1900 S. T. Coleridge. *The Rime of the Ancient Mariner*. Gay & Bird.
1901 O. Khayyám. *The Rubáiyát*. Lane.
1903 R. H. Barham. *The Ingoldsby Legends*. Lane.
[1908] J. Froissart. *Chronicles*. Dent.

Philip Connard (1875–1948)
1900 R. Browning. *The Statue and the Bust*. Lane.
1900 S. Phillips. *Marpessa*. Lane.

Edward Gordon Craig (1872–1966)
1906 H. Macfall. *Sir Henry Irving*. Edinburgh: Foulis.
[1928 W. Shakespeare. *Die tragische Geschichte von Hamlet*. Tr. G. Hauptmann. Weimar: Cranach.]
1930 W. Shakespeare. *Hamlet*. Weimar: Cranach.
1980 D. Defoe. *Robinson Crusoe*. Basilisk.
                      *

Craig, E. A. *Gordon Craig: The Story of His Life*. Gollancz, 1968.
Craig, E. G. *Woodcuts and Some Words*. Dent, 1924.
Fletcher, I. K., and A. Rood. *Edward Gordon Craig: A Bibliography*. Society for Theatre Research, 1967.
Nash, G. *Edward Gordon Craig*. Exhibition catalog, Victoria and Albert Museum. H.M.S.O., 1967.

Edmund Dulac (1882–1953)
1905 A. Brontë. *The Tenant of Wildfell Hall*. Dent.
1905 A. Brontë. *Agnes Grey*. Dent.
1905 C. Brontë. *Jane Eyre*. Dent.

1905   C. Brontë. *Villette*. Dent.

1905   C. Brontë. *The Professor*. Dent.

1905   C. Brontë. *Shirley*. Dent.

1905   E. Brontë. *Wuthering Heights*. Dent.

1907   L. Housman. *Stories from the Arabian Nights*. Hodder & Stoughton.

[1908]   W. Shakespeare. *The Tempest*. Hodder & Stoughton.

[1909]   O. Khayyám. *The Rubáiyát of Omar Khayyám*. Tr. E. Fitz-Gerald. Hodder & Stoughton.

1911   L. Housman. *Ali Baba and Other Stories*. Hodder & Stoughton.

[1912]   E. A. Poe. *The Bells and Other Poems*. Hodder & Stoughton.

[1920]   L. Rosenthal. *The Kingdom of the Pearl*. Nisbet.

1923   J. Milton. *Comus*. Hodder & Stoughton. Limited Editions, 1954.

[1936]   H. R. Williamson. *Gods and Mortals in Love*. Country Life.

1938   N. Hawthorne. *Tanglewood Tales*. Hodder & Stoughton.

1950   A. Pushkin. *The Golden Cockerel*. Limited Editions.

1951   L. Apuleius Madaurensis. *The Marriage of Cupid and Psyche*. Tr. W. Pater. Limited Editions.

*

Dulac. Ed. D. Larkin. Coronet, 1975. Useful for plates.

Sir William Russell Flint (1880–1969)

1908   T. à Kempis. *Of the Imitation of Christ*. Tr. R. Whytford. Chatto & Windus.

1909   [Bible.] *The Song of Songs Which Is Solomon's*. Medici.

1909   M. Aurelius Antoninus. *Thoughts*. Medici.

1909   W. S. Gilbert. *Savoy Operas*. Bell.

1910   M. Arnold. *The Scholar Gipsy. Thyrsis*. Medici.

1910   W. S. Gilbert. *Iolanthe and Other Operas*. Bell.

1910–11   T. Malory. *Morte Darthur*. Medici.

1911   R. Burns. *Songs and Lyrics*. Medici.

1912   C. Kingsley. *The Heroes*. Medici.

1913   G. Chaucer. *The Canterbury Tales*. Medici.

1922   *The Idyls of Theocritus, Bion & Moschus*. Medici.

1924   Homer. *The Odyssey*. Tr. S. H. Butcher & A. Lang. Medici.

1928   [Bible. Apocrypha.] *Judith*. Haymarket.

1929   [Bible. Apocrypha.] *The Book of Tobit and the History of Susanna*. Haymarket.

1955   R. Herrick. *One Hundred and Eleven Poems*. Golden Cockerel.

*

Flint, W. R. *Breakfast in Perigord*. Privately printed, 1968.

Palmer, A. *More Than Shadows: A Biography of W. Russell Flint, R.A., P.R.W.S.* Studio, 1943.

W. Russell Flint, A.R.A. Intro. G. S. Sandilands. Studio, 1928.

Lady Eleanor Fortescue Brickdale. See Brickdale.

Vernon Hill (1887–1953)

1911   S. Phillips. *The New Inferno*. Lane.

1911   S. Phillips. *Christ in Hades*.

1912   *Ballads Weird and Wonderful*. Lane.

Alfred Garth Jones (1872–1930)

1898   J. Milton. *Minor Poems*. Bell.

1901   A., Lord Tennyson. *In Memoriam*. Newnes.

1902 [1901]   C. Lamb. *Essays of Elia*. Methuen.

Jessie Marion King (1875–1949)

[1902]   G. Buchanan. *Jephtha: A Drama*. Paisley: Gardner.

1903   Perlesvaus. *The High History of the Holy Graal*. Dent.

1904   W. Morris. *The Defence of Guenevere and Other Poems*. Lane.

1906   J. Milton. *Comus: A Masque*. Routledge.

[1907]   J. Keats. *Isabella: or the Pot of Basil*. Foulis.

1911   J. Hogg. *Kilmeny*. Foulis.

1915   O. Wilde. *A House of Pomegranates*. Methuen.

1919   J. M. Neale. *A Carol. Good King Wenceslas*. Studio.

Henry Ospovat (1877–1909)

1899   W. Shakespeare. *Sonnets*. Lane.

1900   M. Arnold. *Poems*. Lane.

1901   W. Shakespeare. *Songs*. Lane.

1903 [1902]   C. E. Maud. *Heroines of Poetry*. Lane.

1903   R. Browning. *Men and Women*. Dent.

1906   [Bible.] *The Song of Songs*. Lane.

Evelyn Paul (1872–1945)

1910   S. Cunnington. *Stories from Dante*. Harrap.

[1910]   E. C. Gaskell. *Cranford*. Chapman & Hall.

[1913]   M. P. West. *Clair de Lune, and Other Troubadour Romances*. Harrap.

[1916]   Dante. *La Vita Nuova. The New Life*. Harrap.

1920   *The Romance of Tristram of Lyones & Beale Isoude*. Tr. E. Paul. Harrap.

1922   C. Reade. *The Cloister and the Hearth*. Harrap.

Arthur Rackham (1867–1939)

1905   W. Irving. *Rip Van Winkle*. Heinemann.

1906   J. M. Barrie. *Peter Pan in Kensington Gardens*. Hodder & Stoughton.

1907   R. H. Barham. *The Ingoldsby Legends*. Dent.

[1907]   L. Carroll [C. L. Dodgson]. *Alice's Adventures in Wonderland*. Heinemann.

1908   W. Shakespeare. *A Midsummer Night's Dream*. Heinemann.

1909   F. H. K., baron de la Motte-Fouqué. *Undine*. Heinemann.

1909   J. Swift. *Gulliver's Travels*. Dent.

1909   C. Lamb and M. Lamb. *Tales from Shakespeare*. Dent.

1910   R. Wagner. *The Rhinegold and the Valkyrie*. Heinemann.

1911   R. Wagner. *Siegfried and the Twilight of the Gods*. Heinemann.

1912   Aesop. *Aesop's Fables*. Heinemann.

1915   C. Dickens. *A Christmas Carol*. Heinemann.

1918   *Some British Ballads*. Constable.

1918   A. C. Swinburne. *The Springtide of Life*. Heinemann.

1921   E. Phillpotts. *A Dish of Apples*. Hodder & Stoughton.

[1921]   J. Milton. *Comus*. Heinemann.

1926   W. Shakespeare. *The Tempest*. Heinemann.

1928   W. Irving. *The Legend of Sleepy Hollow*. Harrap.

1929   O. Goldsmith. *The Vicar of Wakefield*. Harrap.

1931   I. Walton. *The Compleat Angler*. Harrap.

1931   C. Dickens. *The Chimes*. Limited Editions.

1932   J. Ruskin. *The King of the Golden River*. Harrap.

1933   C. G. Rossetti. *Goblin Market*. Harrap.

1934   R. Browning. *The Pied Piper of Hamelin*. Harrap.

1935   E. A. Poe. *Tales of Mystery*. Harrap.

1936   H. Ibsen. *Peer Gynt*. Harrap.

1939   W. Shakespeare. *A Midsummer Night's Dream*. Limited Editions.

1940   K. Grahame. *The Wind in the Willows*. Limited Editions.

1977   W. Shakespeare. *A Midsummer Night's Dream*. New York: Abaris.

*

Baughman, R. O. *The Centenary of Arthur Rackham's Birth, 1867*. New York: Columbia University Libraries, 1967.

Gettings, F. *Arthur Rackham*. Macmillan, 1975.
Hudson, D. *Arthur Rackham: His Life and Work*. Check list by B. Rota. Heinemann, 1960. With bibliography.
Latimore, S. B., and G. C. Haskell. *Arthur Rackham: A Bibliography*. Los Angeles: Suttonhouse, 1936.

William Heath Robinson (1872–1944)
1899   J. Bunyan. *The Pilgrim's Progress*. Sands.
1900   E. A. Poe. *Poems*. Bell.
1902   M. de Cervantes Saavedra. *Don Quixote*. Dent.
1904   F. Rabelais. *The Works of Mr. Francis Rabelais*. Richards.
[1908]   W. Shakespeare. *Twelfth Night*. Hodder & Stoughton.
[1909]   R. Kipling. *A Song of the English*. Hodder & Stoughton.
1914   W. Shakespeare. *A Midsummer Night's Dream*. Constable.
1935   T. à Kempis. *Of the Imitation of Christ*. Hutchinson.
*

Day, G. W. L. *The Life and Art of W. Heath Robinson*. Joseph, 1947.
Lewis, J. *Heath Robinson: Artist and Comic Genius*. Constable, 1973.
Robinson, W. H. *My Line of Life*. Blackie, 1938.

Noel Rooke (1881–1953)
1909   R. L. Stevenson. *Travels with a Donkey in the Cevennes*. Chatto & Windus.
1916   R. Brooke. *The Old Vicarage, Grantchester*. Sidgwick & Jackson.
1925   [Bible] *The Birth of Christ*, Golden Cockerel.
1946   I. A. Williams. *Flowers of Marsh and Stream*. Penguin.
*

Rooke, N. *Woodcuts and Wood Engraving*. Print Collectors' Club, no. 5 (1926).

Reginald Savage (d. 1937)
1898   R. F. Sharpe. *Wagner's Drama "der Ring des Nibelungen"*. Marshall, Russell.
1901   *A Book of Romantic Ballads*. Newnes.
[1903]   R. Herrick. *Hesperides and Noble Numbers*. Newnes.
1904   T. Hood. *Miss Kilmansegg and Her Precious Leg*. Newnes.
1905   C. R. Ashbee. *Echoes from the City of the Sun*. Essex.
1934   C. R. Ashbee. *Kingfisher out of Egypt*. Oxford.

Sidney H. Sime (1867–1941)
E. J. M. D. Plunkett, Lord Dunsany, is the author of all the books listed.
1905   *The Gods of Pegana*. Mathews.
1906   *Time and the Gods*. Heinemann.
1908   *The Sword of Welleran*. Allen.
1910   *A Dreamer's Tales*. Allen.
1912   *The Book of Wonder*. Heinemann.
*

Locke, G. *From an Ultimate Dim Thule: A Review of the Early Work of Sidney H. Sime (1895–1905)*. Ferret Fantasy, 1973.
———. *The Land of Dreams: A Review of the Work of Sidney H. Sime, 1905 to 1916*. Ferret Fantasy, 1975.

Sybil Tawse
[1910]   C. Lamb. *The Essays of Elia*. Chapman & Hall.
1914   E. C. Gaskell. *Cranford*. Black.
1915   *Tales from the Poets*. Ed. W. J. Glover. Black.
1920   A. Dumas. *The Count of Monte Cristo*. Black.
[1926]   L. A. Harker. *Miss Esperance and Mr. Wycherly*. Murray.

CHAPTER TEN

The Twentieth Century (II)
1919–1945

Edward Jeffrey Irving Ardizzone (1900–82)
1929   J. S. Le Fanu. *In a Glass Darkly*. Davies.
1939   H. E. Bates. *My Uncle Silas*. Cape.
1939   C. Dickens. *Great Expectations*. Heritage.
1941   E. Ardizzone. *Baggage to the Enemy*. Murray.
1946   F. Villon. *Poems*. Cresset.
1947   J. Bunyan. *The Pilgrim's Progress*. Faber & Faber.
1948   C. D. Lewis. *The Otterbury Incident*. New York: Putnam.
1952   A. Trollope. *The Warden*. Oxford.
1953   A. Trollope. *Barchester Towers*. Oxford.
1954   W. M. Thackeray. *The Newcomes*. Limited Editions.
1955   C. Dickens. *Bleak House*. Oxford.
1955   C. Dickens. *David Copperfield*. Oxford.
1956   W. M. Thackeray. *Henry Esmond*. Limited Editions.
1956   [Bible.] *St. Luke's Life of Christ*. Collins.
1956   R. S. Surtees. *Hunting with Mr. Jorrocks*. Oxford.
1958   W. Shakespeare. *The Comedies*. Heritage.
1959   G. K. Chesterton. *Father Brown Stories*. Folio.
[1959]   M. de Cervantes Saavedra. *Exploits of Don Quixote*. Blackie.
1960   C. Ray. *Merry England*. Vista.
1960   N. Mitchison. *The Rib of the Green Umbrella*. Collins.
1961   M. Twain [S. L. Clemens]. *Tom Sawyer*. Heinemann.
1961   M. Twain [S. L. Clemens]. *Huckleberry Finn*. Heinemann.
1962   J. Betjeman. *A Ring of Bells*. Murray.
1964   J. Buchan. *The Thirty-Nine Steps*. Dent.
1967   R. L. Stevenson. *Travels with a Donkey in the Cevennes*. Folio.
1968   D. Defoe. *Robinson Crusoe*. Nonesuch.
1968, 1969 [Bible.] *The Oxford Illustrated Old Testament*. Oxford. With others.
1970   E. Ardizzone. *The Young Ardizzone*. Studio Vista.
1971   C. Dickens. *The Short Stories*. Limited Editions.
1980   D. Thomas. *A Child's Christmas in Wales*. Boston: Godine.
*

Alderson, B. W. *Edward Ardizzone: A Preliminary Hand-list, 1929–70*. Pinner: Private Libraries Association, 1972.
Ardizzone, E. "The Born Illustrator." *Folio*, January–March 1962.
Hennessy, C. "Recent Graphic Work by Edward Ardizzone." *Image* 6 (1951).
Oakes, P. "The Lively Art of Ardizzone." *The Sunday Times*, 28 June 1970.

John Austen (1886–1948)
1921   R. H. Keen. *The Little Ape and Other Stories*. Hendersons.
1922   W. Shakespeare. *Hamlet*. Selwyn & Blount.
1924   *Rogues in Porcelain*. Comp. J. Austen. Chapman & Hall.
1925   P. Ovidius Naso. *Ovid's "Elegies"*. Tr. C. Marlowe. J. Davies. *Epigrams*. Etchells & Macdonald. With anr.

1925 B. Disraeli. *Ixion in Heaven.* Cape.
1925 *Everyman and Other Plays.* Chapman & Hall.
1925 Longus. *Daphnis and Chloe.* Bles.
1926 G. G. N., Lord Byron. *Don Juan.* Lane.
1927 A. France. *The Gods Are Athirst.* Lane.
1928 L. Sterne. *Tristram Shandy.* Lane.
1928 A. F., Abbé Prévost. *Manon Lescaut.* Bles.
1928 G. Flaubert. *Madame Bovary.* Lane.
1929 D. Defoe. *Moll Flanders.* Lane.
1929 B. Disraeli. *The Infernal Marriage.* Jackson.
1929 N. Douglas. *South Wind.* Chicago: Argus.
1930 P. Louys. *Collected Tales.* Chicago: Argus.
1930 W. Shakespeare. *As You Like It.* Jackson.
1930 V. David. *The Guardsman and Cupid's Daughter.* Toulmin.
1931 W. M. Thackeray. *Vanity Fair.* Limited Editions.
1933 C. Dickens. *Pickwick Papers.* Limited Editions.
1935 C. Dickens. *David Copperfield.* Limited Editions.
1936 T. Smollett. *Peregrine Pickle.* Limited Editions.
1937 A. R. Le Sage. *Gil Blas.* Limited Editions.
1937 Aristophanes. *The Frogs.* Limited Editions.
1939 W. Shakespeare. *The Comedy of Errors.* Limited Editions.
1939 O. Goldsmith. *The Vicar of Wakefield.* Heritage.
1941 A. Bennett. *The Old Wives' Tale.* Limited Editions.
1943 R. D. Blackmore. *Lorna Doone.* Heritage.
1946 J. Austen. *Persuasion.* Collins.
*

Grimsditch, H. B. "Mr John Austen and the Art of the Book." *The Studio* 88 (July–December 1924).
Richardson, D. M. *John Austen and the Inseparables.* Jackson, 1930.

Edward Bawden (b. 1903)
1928 R. Paltock. *Peter Wilkins, a Cornish Man.* Dent.
1930 R. Herring. *Adam & Evelyn at Kew.* Mathews & Marrot.
1931 C. B. [Cochran.] *Review of Revues & Other Matters.* Soncino.
1935 C. Bradby. *Well on the Road.* Bell.
1939 W. Shakespeare. *Henry the Fourth. Part 2.* Limited Editions.
1946 D. Saurat. *Death and the Dreamer.* Westhouse.
1946 [1947] *Travellers' Verse.* Ed. M. G. L. Thomas. Muller.
1948 J. Swift. *The Travels of Lemuel Gulliver to Lilliput & Brobdingnag.* Folio.
1949 E. Bawden and N. Carrington. *Life in an English Village.* Penguin.
1949 *London Is London.* Ed. D. M. Low. Chatto & Windus.
1953 J. Metcalf. *London A to Z.* Deutsch.
1958 W. Beckford. *Vathek.* Folio.
1958 Herodotus. *The Histories of Herodotus of Halicarnassus.* Limited Editions.
1960 G. Flaubert. *Salammbô.* Limited Editions.
1965 J. Swift. *Gulliver's Travels.* Folio. Complete text.
1968, 1969 [Bible.] *The Oxford Illustrated Old Testament.* Oxford. With others.
1972 T. More. *Utopia.* Folio.
1975 S. Johnson. *Rasselas.* Folio.
*

Bliss, D. P. *Edward Bawden.* Godalming: Pendomer, 1979.
Edward Bawden: A Book of Cuts. Comp. and intro. R. McLean. Scolar, 1979.
The World of Edward Bawden. The Minories, Colchester: Victor Batte-Bar Trust, 1973.

René Ben Sussan (b. 1895)
1926 J. Marston. *The Metamorphosis of Pigmalion's Image.* Golden Cockerel.
1929 J. Green. *Pilgrim on the Earth.* Blackamore.
1929 [Bible.] Apocrypha. Cresset. With others.
1934 R. B. Sheridan. *The School for Scandal.* Limited Editions.
1937 W. Shakespeare. *The Merchant of Venice.* Limited Editions.
1937 C. Dickens. *A Tale of Two Cities.* Limited Editions.
1948 H. de Balzac. *Old Goriot.* Limited Editions.
1952 B. Jonson. *Volpone: or, The Fox.* Limited Editions.
1953 R. B. Sheridan. *The Rivals.* Limited Editions.
1958 *The Chronicle of the Cid.* Tr. R. Southey. Limited Editions.
1972 G. Casanova. *Memoirs.* Limited Editions.
*

Pouterman, J. E. "René Ben Sussan." *Signature*, no. 6 (1937).

Edmund Blampied (1886–1966)
[1914] J. J. Farnol. *Money Moon.* Low & Marston.
1924 M. F. Barber [M. Fairless, pseud.]. *The Road Mender.* Duckworth.
1931 R. L. Stevenson. *Travels with a Donkey in the Cevennes.* Lane.
1939 J. M. Barrie. *The Blampied Edition of Peter Pan. Peter Pan and Wendy.* Hodder & Stoughton.
*

Allhusen, E. L. "Edmund Blampied." *The Print Collector's Quarterly* (February 1926).
Dodgson, C. *A Complete Catalogue of the Etchings and Drypoints of Edmund Blampied.* Halton & Smith, 1926.
Salaman, M. C. *Modern Masters of Etching: Edmund Blampied.* Studio, 1926.

Douglas Percy Bliss (b. 1900)
1925 *Border Ballads.* Ed. D. P. Bliss. Oxford.
1926 S. Johnson. *Rasselas.* Dent.
1928 M. de Cervantes Saavedra. *The Spanish Ladies and Two Other Stories.* Oxford.
1929 W. Painter. *The Palace of Pleasure.* Cresset.
1934 *The Devil in Scotland.* Ed. D. P. Bliss. Maclehose.
1935 J. R. Allan. *Farmer's Boy.* Methuen.
1938 E. A. Poe. *Some Tales of Mystery and Imagination.* Penguin.

Dorothea Braby (b. 1909)
1937 C. Whitfield. *Mr Chambers and Persephone.* Golden Cockerel.
1944 [Bible.] *The Ninety-First Psalm.* Golden Cockerel.
[1945] V. G. Calderon [V. García Calderón]. *The Lottery Ticket.* Golden Cockerel.
1946 [Bible.] *The Commandments.* Leigh-on-Sea: Lewis.
1948 *The Mabinogion.* Golden Cockerel.
1950 J. Keats. *Poems.* Folio.
1955 G. Jones. *The Saga of Llywarch the Old.* Golden Cockerel.

Horace Walter Bray (1887–1963)
1924 H. Vaughan. *Poems.* Gregynog. With anr.
1925 J. C. Hughes. *Caneuon Ceiriog detholiad.* Gregynog. In Welsh. With anr.
1926 E. Thomas. *Chosen Essays.* Gregynog. With anr.
1927 E. Rhys. *Life of St. David.* Gregynog. With anr.
1928 E., Lord Herbert of Cherbury. *Autobiography.* Gregynog.
1928 T. L. Peacock. *The Misfortunes of Elphin.* Gregynog.
1929 C. Lamb. *Essays of Elia.* Gregynog.
1931 [Bible.] *The Book of Tobit from the Apocrypha.* Raven.

1931 W. Shakespeare. *Venus and Adonis*. Raven.
1931 Euripides. *Plays*. Raven. With anr.
1932 G. G. N., Lord Byron. *The Vision of Judgement*. Published in one volume with R. Southey, *A Vision of Judgement*. Raven.

John Buckland-Wright (1897–1954)
1930 J. Keats. *The Collected Sonnets of John Keats*. Halcyon.
1933 A. C. Swinburne. *Dolores*. Privately printed.
1936 E. P. Mathers. *Love Night: A Laotian Gallantry*. Golden Cockerel.
1938 O. Khayyám. *The Rubáiyát of Omar Khayyám*. Tr. E. Fitz-Gerald. Golden Cockerel.
1938 L. Apuleius Madaurensis. *The Marriage of Cupid and Psyches*. Haarlem: Buckland-Wright.
1939 T. Gautier. *Mademoiselle de Maupin*. Golden Cockerel.
1939 F. L. Lucas. *The Vigil of Venus*. Golden Cockerel.
1944 A. C. Swinburne. *Hymn to Proserpine*. Golden Cockerel.
1946 M. Flinders. *Narrative of His Voyage*. Golden Cockerel.
1947 J. Keats. *Endymion*. Golden Cockerel.
1947 L. N. Andreyev. *The Seven Who Were Hanged*. Drummond.
1948 A. C. Swinburne. *Laus Veneris*. Golden Cockerel.
1948 Homer. *The Odyssey*. Folio.
1949 Musaeus. *Hero and Leander*. Sandford.
1949 P. B. Shelley. *Poems*. Folio.
[1949] J. B. Cabell. *Jurgen*. Golden Cockerel.
1950 Homer. *The Iliad*. Folio.
1950 [1951] A. C. Swinburne. *Pasiphaë*. Privately printed.
1951 F. Beaumont. *Salmacis and Hermaphroditus*. Golden Cockerel.
1952 P. Hartnall. *The Grecian Enchanted*. Golden Cockerel.
1954 G. Boccaccio. *The Decameron*. Folio.
1955 A. Bury. *Syon House*. Dropmore.

*

Gainsborough, R. "The Wood-Engravings of Buckland-Wright." *Image* 4 (Spring 1950).
Reid, A. *A Check-List of the Book Illustrations of John Buckland-Wright*. Pinner: Private Libraries Association, 1968.
Sandford, C. "John Buckland-Wright." *Folio* (Autumn 1954).

Edward Carrick. See Craig.

Gilbert Keith Chesterton (1874–1936)
Hilaire Belloc is the author of all the books listed.
1912 *The Green Overcoat*. Bristol: Arrowsmith.
1925 *Mr. Petre*. Arrowsmith.
1926 *The Emerald of Catherine the Great*. Bristol: Arrowsmith.
1927 *The Haunted House*. Arrowsmith.
1928 *But Soft – We Are Observed!* Arrowsmith.
1929 *The Missing Masterpiece*. Arrowsmith.
1930 *The Man Who Made Gold*. Arrowsmith.
1932 *The Post-Master General*. Arrowsmith.
1936 *The Hedge and the Horse*. Cassell.

*

Barker, D. *G. K. Chesterton: A Biography*. Constable, 1973.
Collins, D. "Memoir of G. K. Chesterton." *Illustrated London News*, June 1974.

Harry Clarke (1890–1931)
1919 E. A. Poe. *Tales of Mystery and Imagination*. Harrap.
1920 *The Year's at the Spring*. Ed. L. d'O. Walters. Harrap.
1925 J. W. von Goethe. *Faust*. Harrap.
1928 A. C. Swinburne. *Selected Poems*. Lane.

Edward Anthony Craig [Edward Carrick] (b. 1904)
1928 A. Maurois. *A Voyage to the Island of the Articoles*. Cape.
1931 E. Sitwell. *In Spring*. Privately printed.
1931 L. Virgilius Maro. *The Georgics of Vergil*. Jones.

Eric Fitch Daglish (1894–1966)
1925 E. F. Daglish. *Woodcuts of British Birds*. Benn.
1926 J. H. Fabre. *Animal Life in Field and Garden*. Butterworth.
1926 E. M. Nicholson. *Birds in England*. Chapman & Hall.
1927 I. Walton. *The Compleat Angler*. Butterworth.
1927 H. Thoreau. *Walden*. Chapman & Hall.
1928 D. Dewar. *Game Birds*. Chapman & Hall.
1929 G. White. *The Natural History of Selborne*. Butterworth.
1931 E. F. Daglish. *The Life Story of Beasts*. New York: Morrow.
1931 W. H. Hudson. *Far Away and Long Ago*. Dent.
1932 E. Thomas. *The South Country*. Dent.
1932 E. F. Daglish. *A Nature Calendar*. Dent.
1948 E. F. Daglish. *Birds of the British Isles*. Dent.

Thomas Derrick (1885–1954)
1930 A. Bierce. *Battle Sketches*. First Edition Club.
1930 *Everyman*. Dent.
1931 H. Belloc. *Nine Nines*. Oxford: Blackwell.
1931 [Bible.] *The Prodigal Son and Other Parables*. Longman; Oxford: Blackwell.
1932 F. Thacker. *Kennet Country*. Oxford: Blackwell.

John Farleigh (1900–65)
1925 J. Swift. *Essays*. Golden Cockerel.
1932 G. B. Shaw. *The Adventures of the Black Girl in Her Search for God*. Constable.
1933 W. de la Mare. *Stories from the Bible*. Faber & Faber.
1934 [Bible.] *The Story of David*. Black.
1934 G. B. Shaw. *Short Stories, Scraps, and Shavings*. Constable.
1934 S. Butler. *The Way of All Flesh*. Collins.
1935 D. H. Lawrence. *The Man Who Died*. Heinemann.
1935 M. L. Goldsmith. *John the Baptist*. Barker.
1936 W. J. Brown. *The Gods Had Wings*. Constable.
1936 E. Armitage. *A Country Garden*. Country Life.
1939 G. B. Shaw. *Back to Methuselah*. Limited Editions.
1941 C. Hole. *Haunted England*. Batsford.
1945 C. Hole. *Witchcraft in England*. Batsford. With anr.
1958 W. Shakespeare. *The Histories*. Heritage.
1965 Aeschylus. *Prometheus Bound*. P. B. Shelley. *Prometheus Unbound*. Limited Editions.

*

Farleigh, J. *Graven Image*. Macmillan, 1940.

Claud Lovat Fraser (1890–1921)
1921 J. Gay. *The Beggar's Opera*. Heinemann.
1922 C. Goldoni. *The Liar*. Selwyn & Blount.
1922 C. Cotton. *Poems*. Poetry Bookshop.
1924 W. de la Mare. *Peacock Pie*. Constable.

*

Drinkwater, J., and A. Rutherston. *Claud L. Fraser*. Heinemann, 1923.
Driver, C. E. *The Art of Lovat Fraser*. Philadelphia: Rosenbach Foundation, 1971.
Macfall, C. H. C. *The Book of Lovat*. Dent, 1923.
Millard, C. *The Printed Work of Lovat Fraser*. Danielson, 1923.
The Printed Work of Claud Lovat Fraser. Ed. G. L. Fraser and M. Easton. Exhibition catalog. Hull, 1968.

Barnett Freedman (1901–58)

1931 S. Sassoon. *Memoirs of an Infantry Officer*. Faber & Faber.
1936 G. Borrow. *Lavengro*. Limited Editions.
1938 L. Tolstoy. *War and Peace*. Limited Editions.
1939 W. Shakespeare. *Henry the Fourth. Part 1*. Limited Editions.
[1939] C. Dickens. *Oliver Twist*. Heritage.
[1940] E. Brontë. *Wuthering Heights*. Heritage.
[1942] C. Brontë. *Jane Eyre*. Heritage.
1943 W. de la Mare. *Love*. Faber & Faber.
1951 L. Tolstoy. *Anna Karenina*. Limited Editions.
1956 W. de la Mare. *Ghost Stories*. Folio.

*

Barnett Freedman, 1901–58 – A Catalogue of an Exhibition. Intro. S. Tallents. Arts Council of Great Britain, 1958.
Mayne, J. *Barnett Freedman*. Art & Technics, 1948.

Robert Gibbings (1889–1958)

1925 [Bible.] *Samson and Delilah*. Golden Cockerel.
1926 E. P. Mathers. *Red Wise*. Golden Cockerel.
1930 R. Gibbings. *The Seventh Man*. Golden Cockerel.
1932 R. Gibbings. *Iorana! a Tahitian Journal*. Boston: Houghton Mifflin; Duckworth.
1933 E. J. M. D. Plunkett, Lord Dunsany. *Lord Adrian*. Golden Cockerel.
1934 L. Powys. *The Glory of Life*. Golden Cockerel.
1934 W. Bligh and J. Fryer. *The Voyage of the "Bounty"'s Launch*. Golden Cockerel.
1936 R. Gibbings. *Coconut Island*. Faber & Faber.
1940 R. Gibbings. *Sweet Thames, Run Softly*. Dent.
1942 R. Gibbings. *Coming Down the Wye*. Dent.
1944 R. Gibbings. *Lovely Is the Lee*. Dent.
1948 R. Gibbings. *Over the Reefs*. Dent.
1951 R. Gibbings. *Sweet Cork of Thee*. Dent.
1953 R. Gibbings. *Coming Down the Seine*. Dent.
1956 C. Darwin. *Journal of Researches ... During the Voyage of H.M.S. "Beagle"*. Limited Editions.
1957 R. Gibbings. *Till I End My Song*. Dent.

*

Balston, T. *The Wood Engravings of Robert Gibbings*. Art & Technics, 1949.
Kirkus, A. M., P. Empson, and J. Harris. *Robert Gibbings: A Bibliography*. Dent, 1962.
The Wood Engravings of Robert Gibbings with Some Recollections. Ed. P. Empson. Dent, 1959.

Arthur Eric Rowton Gill (1882–1940)

1925 [Bible.] *The Song of Songs*. Golden Cockerel.
1926 E. Gill. *Id quod visum placat*. Golden Cockerel.
1926 E. P. Mathers. *Procreant Hymn*. Golden Cockerel.
1926 [Bible. Matthew.] *Passio Domini Nostri Jesu Christi*. Golden Cockerel.
1927 G. K. Chesterton. *Gloria in Profundis*. Faber & Gwyer.
1927 Juan de la Cruz [St. John of the Cross]. *The Song of the Soul*. Capel-y-ffin, Abergavenny: Walterson.
1927 G. Chaucer. *Troilus and Criseyde*. Golden Cockerel.
1929 A. Huxley. *Leda*. New York: Doubleday, Doran.
1929–31 G. Chaucer. *The Canterbury Tales*. Golden Cockerel.
1931 [Bible.] *Canticum canticorum Salomonis*. Weimar: Cranach.
1931 [Bible.] *The Four Gospels of the Lord Jesus Christ*. Golden Cockerel.
1933 W. Shakespeare. *Hamlet*. Limited Editions.

1934 E. Clay. *The Constant Mistress*. Golden Cockerel.
1934 [Bible.] New Testament. Tr. M. James. Dent.
1937 *Quia amore langueo*. Faber & Faber.
1938 J. Donne. *Holy Sonnets*. Hague & Gill.
1939 W. Shakespeare. *Henry VIII*. Limited Editions.
1939 E. Gill. *Sacred and Secular in Art and Industry*. Newport, R.I.: Stevens.
1941 Têng Mêng-lung. *Glue and Lacquer: Four Cautionary Tales*. Golden Cockerel.

*

The Engraved Work of Eric Gill. Ed. J. F. Physick. H.M.S.O., 1963.
Gill, E. R. *Bibliography of Eric Gill*. Cassell, 1953.
Speaight, R. *Eric Gill*. New York: Kenedy, 1966.

Stephen Gooden (1892–1955)

1923 Anacreon. *Poems*. Nonesuch.
1924–27 [Bible.] Apocrypha and Holy Bible. Nonesuch.
1929 [Bible.] Apocrypha. Cresset. With others.
1929 G. Moore. *The Brook Kerith*. Heinemann.
1931 J. de La Fontaine. *Fables*. Tr. E. Marsh. Heinemann.
1933 G. Moore. *Peronnik the Fool*. Harrap.
1936 Aesop. *Fables*. Tr. R. L'Estrange. Harrap.
1939 O. Henry. *The Gift of the Magi*. Harrap.
1940 O. Khayyám. *The Rubáiyát of Omar Khayyám*. Tr. E. Fitz-Gerald. Harrap.

*

Dodgson, C. *An Iconography of the Engravings of Stephen Gooden*. Mathews, 1944. Reproductions of all of Gooden's engravings.
Reid, F. "The Line Engravings of Stephen Gooden." *The Print Collector's Quarterly* 19 (January 1932).

Joan Hassall (b. 1906)

1937 F. E. B. Young. *Portrait of a Village*. Heinemann.
1939 R. Church. *Calling for a Spade*. Dent.
1940 E. C. Gaskell. *Cranford*. Harrap.
1946 M. Webb. *Fifty-one Poems*. Cape.
1947 E. Linklater. *Sealskin Trousers and Other Stories*. Hart-Davis.
1947 M. R. Mitford. *Our Village*. Harrap.
1947 R. L. Stevenson. *A Child's Garden of Verse*. Edinburgh: Hopetown.
[1947] A. Trollope. *Christmas Day at Kirkby Cottage*. Low, Marston.
1949 A. Trollope. *The Parson's Daughter and Other Stories*. Folio.
1950 B. Gooch. *The Strange World of Nature*. Lutterworth.
1950 A. Young. *Collected Poems*. Cape.
1951 *Sixteen Portraits*. Ed. L. A. G. Strong. Naldreth for the National Trust.
1951 A. Trollope. *Mary Gresley and Other Stories*. Folio.
1953 M. Lane. *The Brontë Story: A Reconsideration of Mrs. Gaskell's "Life of Charlotte Brontë"*. Heinemann.
1957 J. Austen. *Pride and Prejudice*. Folio.
1957 R. Church. *Small Moments*. Hutchinson.
1958 J. Austen. *Sense and Sensibility*. Folio.
1959 J. Austen. *Mansfield Park*. Folio.
1960 J. Austen. *Northanger Abbey*. Folio.
1961 J. Austen. *Persuasion*. Folio.
1962 J. Austen. *Emma*. Folio.
1963 J. Austen. *Shorter Works*. Folio.
1965 R. Burns. *Poems*. Limited Editions.

*

Hassall, J. *Wood-Engraving: A Reader's Guide*. Cambridge for the National Book League, 1949.
McLean, R. *The Wood Engraving of Joan Hassall*. Oxford, 1960.

Gertrude Hermes (b. 1901)

1928 J. Bunyan. *The Pilgrim's Progress*. Cresset. With anr.
1929 [Bible.] Apocrypha. Cresset. With others.
1931 *A. Florilege*. Ed. I. Gosse. Swan.
1934 R. H. Mottram. *Strawberry Time. The Banquet*. Golden Cockerel.
1936 N. Mitchison. *The Fourth Pig*. Constable.
1938 R. Jefferies. *The Story of My Heart*. Penguin.
1939 N. Mitchison. *The Alban Goes Out*. Raven.
1939 I. Walton. *The Compleat Angler*. Penguin.

Blair Hughes-Stanton (b. 1902)

1928 J. Bunyan. *The Pilgrim's Progress*. Cresset. With anr.
1929 V. Pilcher. *The Searcher*. Heinemann.
1929 [Bible.] Apocrypha. Cresset. With others.
1930 D. H. Lawrence. *Birds, Beasts, and Flowers*. Cresset.
1930 S. Gantillon. *Maya: a Play*. Golden Cockerel.
1931 J. Milton. *Comus*. Gregynog.
1932 [Bible.] *The Revelation of St. John the Divine*. Gregynog.
1932 C. Marlowe. *Doctor Faustus*. Golden Hours.
1932 S. Butler. *Erewhon*. Gregynog.
1932 W. J. Gwffyd. *Canidau*. Gregynog.
1933 J. Milton. *Four Poems*. Gregynog.
1933 D. H. Lawrence. *The Ship of Death and Other Poems*. Secker.
1933 [Bible] *The Lamentations of Jeremiah*. Gregynog.
1934 I. Graves. *Epithalamion*. Colchester: Gemini.
1934 A. Calder-Marshall. *A Crime against Cania*. Golden Cockerel.
1934 [Bible.] *Ecclesiastes: or the Preacher*. Golden Cockerel.
1934 T. Hubbard. *Tomorrow Is a New Day*. Williams.
[1934] C. Sandford. *Primeval Gods*. Boar's Head.
1935 H. M. Acton. *Pastoral: or Virtue Requited*. Colchester: Gemini.
1940 E. Wynne. *Visions of the Sleeping Bard*. Gregynog.
1948 T. De Quincey. *Confessions of an English Opium-Eater*. Folio.
1949 J. Austen. *Sense and Sensibility*. Avalon.
1956 C. Dickens and W. Collins. *The Wreck of the "Golden Mary"*. Kentfield, Cal.: Allen.
1959 J. Conrad. *Youth*. Kentfield, Cal.: Allen.
1963 H. James. *The Beast in the Jungle*. Kentfield, Cal.: Allen.
1970 [Bible.] *The Book of Genesis*. Kentfield, Cal.: Allen.

*

Fletcher, J. G. "Blair Hughes-Stanton." *The Print Collector's Quarterly* (October 1934).
Lewis, J. "The Wood-Engravings of Blair Hughes-Stanton." *Image* 6 (1951).

David Michael Jones (1895–1974)

1925 J. Swift. *Gulliver's Travels*. Golden Cockerel.
1926 [Bible.] *The Book of Jonah*. Golden Cockerel.
1927 [Bible.] *Ecclesiastes*. Gregynog. In Welsh.
1927 *The Chester Play of the Deluge*. Golden Cockerel.
1928 Aesop. *Seven Fables*. Lanston Monotype. Privately printed.
1929 [Bible.] Apocrypha. Cresset. With others.
1929 S. T. Coleridge. *The Rime of the Ancient Mariner*. Bristol: Cleverdon.
1930 P. Claudel. *The Satin Slipper*. Sheed & Ward.
1930 W. H. Shewring. *Hermia and Some Other Poems*. Ditchling: St. Dominic's.
1931 R. H. J. Steuart. *March, Kind Comrade*. Sheed & Ward.
1937 D. Jones. *In Parenthesis*. Faber & Faber.

*

Blamires, D. *David Jones, Artist and Writer*. Manchester; Toronto, 1972.
Gray, N. "David Jones." *Signature*, no. 8 (1949).
Hague, R. *David Jones*. Welsh Arts Council, 1975.
Ironside, R. *David Jones*. Penguin, 1949.

Edward McKnight Kauffer (1890–1954)

1925 R. Burton. *The Anatomy of Melancholy*. Nonesuch.
1926 H. Melville. *Benito Cereno*. Nonesuch.
1929 D. Defoe. *Robinson Crusoe*. Etchells & Macdonald.
1929 A. Bennett. *Elsie and the Child*. Cassell.
1930 T. S. Eliot. *Marina*. Faber & Faber.
1930 F. E. Smith, earl of Birkenhead. *The World in 2030 A.D.* Hodder & Stoughton.
1930 M. de Cervantes Saavedra. *Don Quixote*. Nonesuch.
1931 A. Bennett. *Venus Rising from the Sea*. Cassell.
1946 H. Melville. *Billy Budd*. Lehmann.

*

Haworth-Booth, M. *Edward McKnight Kauffer: a designer and his public*. Gordon Fraser Gallery, 1979.

Clare Veronica Hope Leighton (b. 1899)

1929 T. Hardy. *The Return of the Native*. Macmillan.
1929 T. Wilder. *The Bridge of San Luis Rey*. Longman.
1929 J. Auslander. *Letters to Women*. Harper.
1930 H. M. Tomlinson. *The Sea and the Jungle*. Duckworth.
1931 E. Brontë. *Wuthering Heights*. Duckworth.
1933 C. Leighton. *The Farmer's Year*. Collins.
1934 C. Holme (Punchard). *The Trumpet in the Dust*. Nicholson & Watson.
1935 C. Leighton. *Four Hedges*. Gollancz.
1937 C. Leighton. *Country Matters*. Gollancz.
1940 T. Hardy. *Under the Greenwood Tree*. Macmillan.
1941 G. White. *The Natural History of Selborne*. Lane.

*

Leighton, C. *Growing New Roots*. San Francisco. Book Club of California, 1976. With bibliography.

Percy Wyndham Lewis (1882–1957)

1935 N. Mitchison. *Beyond This Limit*. Cape.

Thomas Esmond Lowinsky (1892–1947)

1923 W. Shakespeare. *The Merchant of Venice*. Benn.
1924 J. Milton. *Paradise Regained*. Fleuron.
1926 E. Sitwell. *Elegy on Dead Fashion*. Duckworth.
1926 S. Sitwell. *Exalt the Eglantine and Other Poems*. Fleuron.
1926 W. Meinhold. *Sidonia the Sorceress*. Benn.
1927 F. M. A. de Voltaire. *The Princess of Babylon*. Nonesuch.

Averill Mackenzie-Grieve

1939 M. A. Fryer. *John Fryer of the "Bounty"*. Golden Cockerel.
1941 O. Rutter. *The Land of St. Joan*. Methuen.
1948 S. Johnson. *The New London Letter Writer*. Golden Cockerel.

Robert Ashwin Maynard (1888–1966)

1923 G. Herbert. *Poems*. Gregynog.
1924 H. Vaughan. *Poems*. Gregynog. With anr.
1925 J. C. Hughes. *Caneuon Ceiriog detholiad*. Gregynog. In Welsh. With anr.
1926 E. Thomas. *Chosen Essays*. Gregynog. With anr.
1927 E. Rhys. *Life of St. David*. Gregynog. With anr.

1928 O. Khayyám. *Penillion Omar Khayyám.* Gregynog. In Welsh.

1930 *The Stealing of the Mare.* Gregynog.

1931 Euripides. *Plays.* Raven. With anr.

1931 J. Milton. *Samson Agonistes.* Raven.

1932 R. Southey. *A Vision of Judgement.* Published in one volume with G. G. N., Lord Byron, *The Vision of Judgement.* Raven.

Henry Spencer Moore (1898–1986)

1940 H. Moore. *Shelter Sketch Book.* Editions Poetry.

1945 C. S. E. Sackville-West. *The Rescue.* Secker & Warburg.

1952 J. W. von Goethe. *Prométhée.* Tr. A. Gide. Paris: Jonquières.

1974 W. H. Auden. *Selections from Poems by Auden: Lithographs by Henry Moore.* Petersburg.

*

Clark, K. *Henry Moore's Drawings.* Thames & Hudson, 1974.

H. S. Moore, 1898– . Catalogue of Graphic Work, 1931–1972. Ed. C. Cramer, A. Grant, and D. Mitchinson. Geneva: Cramer, 1973.

Strachan, W. J. "Henry Moore's *Prométhée.* Experiments for a Book." *Image* 8 (1952).

Wilkinson, A. G. *The Drawings of Henry Moore.* Tate Gallery, 1977.

Gwenda Morgan (b. 1908)

1937 T. F. Powys. *Goat Green.* Golden Cockerel.

1938 A. E. Coppard. *Tapster's Tapestry.* Golden Cockerel.

1944 M. H. Tiltman. *A Little Place in the Country.* Hodder & Stoughton.

1946 T. Gray. *Elegy Written in a Country Church-Yard.* Golden Cockerel.

1956 Brothers Grimm. *Grimms' Other Tales.* Golden Cockerel.

John Northcote Nash (1893–1977)

1925 P. Ovidius Naso. *Ovid's "Elegies".* Tr. C. Marlowe. J. Davies. *Epigrams.* Etchells & Macdonald. With anr.

1927 J. N. Nash, W. Dallimore, and A. W. Hill. *Poisonous Plants.* Etchells & Macdonald.

1929 [Bible.] Apocrypha. Cresset. With others.

1930 E. Spenser. *The Shepheardes Calender.* Cresset.

1930 S. Schiff [S. Hudson, pseud.]. *Celeste and Other Sketches.* Blackamore.

1930 W. Cobbett. *Rural Rides.* Davies.

1931 W. de la Mare. *Seven Short Stories.* Faber & Faber.

1931 T. F. Powys. *When Thou Wast Naked.* Golden Cockerel.

1935 H. E. Bates. *Flowers and Faces.* Golden Cockerel.

1939 A. Bell. *Men and the Fields.* Batsford.

1951 G. White. *The Natural History of Selborne.* Lutterworth.

1953 R. Gathorne-Hardy, earl of Cranbrook. *Parnassian Molehill.* Cowell.

1972 G. White. *The Natural History of Selborne.* Limited Editions.

*

Lewis, J. *John Nash, the Painter as Illustrator.* Godalming: Pendomer, 1978.

Sarzano, F. "The Engravings and Book Decorations of John Nash." *Alphabet and Image,* no. 2 (December 1946).

Paul Nash (1889–1946)

1918 J. Drinkwater. *Loyalties.* Beaumont.

1919 R. Aldington. *Images of War.* Beaumont.

1921 J. Drinkwater. *Cotswold Characters.* Oxford; New Haven, Conn.: Yale.

1922 P. Nash. *Places.* Heinemann.

[1922] M. Armstrong. *Saint Hercules and Other Stories.* Fleuron.

1924 W. Shakespeare. *A Midsummer Night's Dream.* Benn.

1924 [Bible.] *Genesis.* Nonesuch.

1925 R. Graves. *Welchman's Hose.* Fleuron.

[1925] L. A. Leroy. *Wagner's Music Drama and the Muses.* Douglas.

1926 T. E. Lawrence [T. E. Shaw]. *Seven Pillars of Wisdom.* Privately printed. With others.

1927 W. Shakespeare. *King Lear.* Benn.

1928 J. Tellier. *Abd-Er-Rhaman in Paradise.* Tr. B. Rhys. Golden Cockerel.

1932 T. Browne. *Urne Buriall. The Garden of Cyrus.* Cassell.

*

Eates, M. *Paul Nash: The Master of the Image, 1889–1946.* Murray, 1973.

Graham, R. *A Note on the Book Illustrations of Paul Nash.* Wymondham: Brewhouse, 1968.

James, P. "Paul Nash as Book Illustrator and Designer." In *Paul Nash.* Ed. M. Eates. Lund Humphries, 1948.

Lewis, J. *John Nash, the Painter as Illustrator.* Godalming: Pendomer, 1978.

Nash, P. *Outline.* Faber & Faber, 1949. Autobiography.

Postan, A. *The Complete Graphic Works of Paul Nash.* Secker & Warburg, 1973.

Read, H. *Paul Nash.* Penguin, 1944.

Agnes Miller Parker (b. 1895)

1931 Aesop. *The Fables of Esope.* Tr. W. Caxton. Gregynog.

[1932] R. Davies. *Daisy Matthews and Three Other Tales.* Golden Cockerel.

1933 *XXI Welsh Gypsy Folk Tales.* Comp. J. Sampson; ed. D. E. Yates. Gregynog.

1936 H. E. Bates. *Through the Woods.* Gollancz.

1937 H. E. Bates. *Down the River.* Gollancz.

1938 T. Gray. *Elegy Written in a Country Churchyard.* Limited Editions.

1938 T. Hardy. *Far from the Madding Crowd.* Limited Editions.

1940 W. Shakespeare. *Richard the Second.* Limited Editions.

1940 A. E. Housman. *A Shropshire Lad.* Harrap.

1942 T. Hardy. *The Return of the Native.* Heritage.

1944 H. Furst. *Essays in Russet.* Muller.

1946 R. Jefferies. *The Spring of the Year.* Lutterworth.

1947 R. Jefferies. *The Life of the Fields.* Lutterworth.

1948 R. Jefferies. *The Old House at Coate.* Lutterworth.

1948 R. Jefferies. *The Open Air.* Lutterworth.

1948 R. Jefferies. *Field and Hedgerow.* Lutterworth.

1952 A. Roche. *Animals under the Rainbow.* Hollis & Carter.

1953 [1939] E. Spenser. *The Faerie Queene.* Limited Editions.

1956 T. Hardy. *Tess of the D'Urbervilles.* Limited Editions.

1956 J. C. Powys. *Lucifer.* Macdonald.

1958 W. Shakespeare. *The Tragedies.* Heritage.

1969 T. Hardy. *Jude the Obscure.* Limited Editions.

Mervyn Peake (1911–68)

1941 L. Carroll [C. L. Dodgson]. *The Hunting of the Snark.* Chatto & Windus.

1943 C. E. M. Joad. *The Adventures of the Young Soldier in Search of a Better World.* Faber & Faber.

1943 Q. Crisp. *All This and Bevan Too.* Nicholson & Watson.

1943 S. T. Coleridge. *The Rime of the Ancient Mariner.* Chatto & Windus.

1945 C. Hole. *Witchcraft in England.* Batsford. With anr.

1946 Brothers Grimm. *Household Tales.* Eyre & Spottiswood.

1946   M. Collis. *Quest for Sita*. Faber & Faber.
1948   R. L. Stevenson. *Dr. Jekyll and Mr. Hyde*. Folio.
1949   R. L. Stevenson. *Treasure Island*. Academy.
1954   L. Carroll [C. L. Dodgson]. *Alice's Adventures in Wonderland*. Wingate.
1954   L. Carroll [C. L. Dodgson]. *Through the Looking-Glass*. Wingate.
1961   H. de Balzac. *Droll Stories*. Folio & Cassell.
1962   M. Peake. *The Rhyme of the Flying Bomb*. Dent.

*

Peake's Progress: Select Writings and Drawings of Mervyn Peake. Ed. M. Gilmore; intro. J. Watney. Lane, 1978.
Sparling, H. *The Drawings of Mervyn Peake*. Davis-Poynter, 1974.
Watney, J. B. *Mervyn Peake*. Joseph, 1976.

John Piper (b. 1903)
1939   J. Piper. *Brighton Aquatints*. Duckworth.
1944   *English, Scottish and Welsh Landscape, 1700–c. 1860*. Ed. J. Betjeman and G. Taylor. Muller.
1946   J. M. Richards. *The Castles on the Ground*. Architectural Press.
1946   W. de la Mare. *The Traveller*. Faber & Faber.
1949   G. Sitwell. *On the Making of Gardens*. Dropmore.
1950   J. Piper. *Romney Marsh*. Penguin.
1951   W. M. Merchant. *Wordsworth's Guide to the Lakes*. Hart-Davis.
[1955] *Elizabethan Love Songs*. Ed. J. Hadfield. Barham Manor: Cupid.
1960   R. Duncan. *Judas*. Blond.
1962   G. White. *The Natural History of Selborne*. Folio.
[1968] R. S. Thomas. *The Mountains*. New York: Chilmark. Designs engraved on wood by Reynolds Stone, ca. 1948.

*

Betjeman, J. *John Piper*. Penguin, 1944.
Graham, R. "John Piper as a Book Illustrator." *American Book Collector* 22, no. 4 (January 1972).
John Piper: Paintings, Drawings, & Theatre Designs, 1932–1954. Intro. S. J. Woods. Faber & Faber, 1955.
West, A. *John Piper*. Secker & Warburg, 1979.
Woods, S. J. "John Piper as a Topographical Illustrator." *Image* 2 (1949).

Gwendolen Mary Raverat (1885–1957)
1915   F. Cornford. *Spring Morning*. Poetry Bookshop.
1933   Longus. *Les Amours Pastorales de Daphnis et Chloe*. Ashendene.
1934   A. G. Street. *Farmer's Glory*. Faber & Faber.
1934   F. Cornford. *Mountains & Molehills*. Cambridge.
1936   [E. A. Hart.] *Runaway*. Macmillan.
1938   L. Sterne. *A Sentimental Journey*. Penguin.
1939   H. A. Wedgewood. *Bird Talisman*. Faber & Faber.
1949   A. Trollope. *The Bedside Barsetshire*. Faber & Faber.

*

Furst, H. *Gwendolen Raverat*. Modern Woodcutters, no. 1. Furst, 1920.
Gwendolen Raverat. Intro. R. Stone. Faber & Faber, 1959.

Eric William Ravilious (1903–42)
1926   M. Armstrong. *Desert*. Cape.
1927   J. Suckling. *A Ballad upon a Wedding*. Golden Cockerel.
1927   N. Breton. *Twelve Moneths*. Golden Cockerel.
1929   *Almanach, 1929*. Lanston Monotype.
1929   A. Smith. *Atrocities of the Pirates*. Golden Cockerel.
1929   [Bible.] Apocrypha. Cresset. With others.

1930   H. Monro. *Elm Angel*. Faber & Faber.
1932   W. Shakespeare. *Twelfth Night*. Golden Cockerel.
1933   M. Armstrong. *54 Conceits*. Secker.
1933   C. Marlowe. *The Jew of Malta*. Golden Hours.
1935   L. A. G. Strong. *The Hansom Cab & the Pigeons*. Golden Cockerel.
1936   T. B. Hennell. *Poems*. Oxford.
1937   A. Heath. *Country Life Cookery Book*. Country Life.
1938   G. White. *Writings*. Nonesuch.
1938   J. M. Richards. *High Street*. Country Life.

*

Constable, F., and S. Simon. *The England of Eric Ravilious*. Scolar, 1982.
Harling, R. *Notes on the Wood-Engravings of Eric Ravilious*. Faber & Faber, 1946.
"The Printed and Published Wood-Engravings of Eric Ravilious." *Signature* 1 (November 1935). Bibliography and reproductions of Ravilious's wood engravings.
The Wood Engravings of Eric Ravilious. Intro. J. M. Richards. Lion & Unicorn, 1972.

Albert Rutherston (1881–1953)
1921   L. Housman. *Angels & Ministers*. Cape.
1923   W. Shakespeare. *Cymbeline*. Benn.
1923   G. Scott. *A Box of Paints*. Bookman's Journal.
1925   E. Sitwell, O. Sitwell, and S. Sitwell. *Poor Young People*. Fleuron.
1928   V. Mendel, F. Meynell, and J. Goss. *The Week-End Book*. Nonesuch.
1929   A. Huxley. *Holy Face and Other Essays*. Fleuron.
1930   Haggadah. Tr. C. Roth. Soncino.
1940   W. Shakespeare. *The Winter's Tale*. Limited Editions.
[n.d.] G. B. Shaw. *Androcles and the Lion*.

*

Gleadowe, R. M. Y. *Albert Rutherston*. Benn, 1925.

Lettice Sandford (b. 1902)
1932   E. Spenser. *Thalamos, or the Brydall Boure*. Manaton: Boar's Head.
1932   Sappho. *Poems*. Manaton: Boar's Head.
1933   B. Bingley. *Tales of the Turquoise*. Manaton: Boar's Head.
1933   Musaeus. *Hero and Leander*. Tr. C. Marlowe. Golden Hours.
1934   L. Apuleius Madaurensis. *Cupid & Psyches*. Golden Cockerel.
1935   E. Lascaris [pseud.]. *The Golden Bed of Kydno*. Golden Cockerel.
1935   B. Bingley. *The Painted Cup*. Golden Cockerel.
1936   [Bible.] *The Song of Songs*. Golden Cockerel.
1937   *The Golden Cockerel Greek Anthology*. Ed. F. L. Lucas. Golden Cockerel.
1939   C. Whitfield. *Lady from Yesterday*. Golden Cockerel.

Ernest Howard Shepard (1879–1976)
1924   A. A. Milne. *When We Were Very Young*. Methuen.
1926   A. A. Milne. *Winnie-the-Pooh*. Methuen.
1926   S. Pepys. *Everybody's Pepys*. Methuen.
1926   C. Dickens. *The Holly Tree*. Partridge.
1927   A. A. Milne. *Now We Are Six*. Methuen.
1928   A. A. Milne. *The House at Pooh Corner*. Methuen.
1928   K. Grahame. *The Golden Age*. Bodley Head.
1930   K. Grahame. *Dream Days*.
1930   J. Boswell. *Everybody's Boswell*. Methuen.
1931   K. Grahame. *The Wind in the Willows*. Methuen.

1931 J. Drinkwater. *Christmas Poems*. Sidgwick & Jackson.
1933 C. Lamb. *Everybody's Lamb*. Methuen.
1933 P. R. Chalmers. *The Cricket in the Cage*. Black.
1934 L. Housman. *Victoria Regina*. Cape.
1935 W. Fortescue. *Perfume from Provence*. Blackwood.
1937 E. V. Lucas. *As the Bee Sucks*. Methuen.
1937 L. Housman. *The Golden Sovereign*. Cape.
1941 L. Housman. *Gracious Majesty*. Cape.
1945 L. Housman. *Happy and Glorious*. Cape.
1956 G. MacDonald. *At the Back of the North Wind*. Dent.
1957 E. H. Shepard. *Drawn from Memory*. Methuen.
1959 K. Grahame. *The Wind in the Willows*. Methuen.
1961 E. H. Shepard. *Drawn from Life*. Methuen.

Steven Spurrier (1878–1961)
1934 W. Wycherley. *The Country Wife*. Hutchinson.
1940 C. Dickens. *Nicholas Nickleby*. Heritage.
1941 R. Lynd. *Life's Little Oddities*. Dent.
1950 W. Shakespeare. *The Sonnets*. Leigh-on-Sea: Lewis.

Alan Reynolds Stone (1909–79)
1936 W. de la Mare. *Ding Dong Bell*.
1938 A. de Guevara. *The Praise and Happinesse of the Countrie-Life*. Tr. H. Vaughan. Gregynog.
1938 J.-J. Rousseau. *Confessions*. Nonesuch.
1946 *The Open Air*. Ed. A. Bell. Faber & Faber.
1946 L. Paul. *The Living Hedge*. Faber & Faber.
1947 F. Reid. *The Apostate*. Faber & Faber.
1957 E. Linklater. *A Sociable Plover and Other Stories*. Hart-Davis.
1958 R. Hodgson. *The Skylark and Other Poems*. Hart-Davis.
1958 R. Stone and S. T. Warner. *Boxwood: Illustrated in Verse by Sylvia Townsend Warner*. Monotype.
1960 R. Stone and S. T. Warner. *Boxwood: Illustrated in Verse by Sylvia Townsend Warner*. Second ed. Chatto & Windus. Additional blocks.
1961 H. Melville. *Omoo*. Limited Editions.
1967 T. F. Powys. *Two Stories*. Hastings: Brimmell.
1969 B. Britten. *Tit for Tat*. Faber Music.
1978 I. Murdoch. *A Year of Birds: Poems*. Tisbury: Compton.

*

Goodison, J. W. *Reynolds Stone: His Early Development as an Engraver on Wood*. Cambridge, 1947.
Piper, M. E. *Reynolds Stone*. Art & Technics, 1951.
Reynolds Stone: Engravings. Intro. R. Stone. Appreciation by K. Clark. Murray, 1977.

Graham Sutherland (1903–80)
1940 W. Shakespeare. *Henry VI. Part 1*. Limited Editions.
1943 D. Gascoyne. *Poems, 1937–1942*. Nicholson & Watson.
1954 W. S. Maugham. *Cakes and Ale*. Heinemann.

Denis Tegetmeier (b. 1895)
1928 J. Taylor. *The Mysteriousness of Marriage*. Capel-y-ffin, Abergavenny: Walterson.
1930 W. Langland. *The Vision of William Concerning Piers the Plowman*. Cassell.
1930 H. Fielding. *A Journey from This World to the Next*. Golden Cockerel.
1932 H. Fielding. *Jonathan Wild*. Golden Cockerel.
1934 E. Gill. *Money and Morals*. Faber & Faber.
1936 L. Sterne. *A Sentimental Journey*. Limited Editions.
1938 E. Gill. *Unholy Trinity*. Dent.

*

"Teg": An Exhibition of the Work of Denis Tegetmeier. Oxford: Studio One Gallery, 1977.

Feliks Topolski (b. 1907)
1939 G. B. Shaw. *In Good King Charles's Golden Days*. Constable.
1939 G. B. Shaw. *Geneva*. Constable.
1941 G. B. Shaw. *Pygmalion*. Penguin.
1950 H. M. M. Acton. *Prince Isidore*. Methuen.
1971 L. Tolstoy. *War and Peace*. Folio.

Charles Frederick Tunnicliffe (b. 1901)
1932 H. Williamson. *Tarka the Otter*. Putnam.
1933 H. Williamson. *Lone Swallows*. Putnam.
1934 H. Williamson. *The Peregrine's Saga and Other Wild Tales*. Putnam.
1937 *A Book of Birds*. Ed. M. Priestley. Gollancz.
1942 H. E. Bates. *In the Heart of the Country*. Country Life.
1942 C. F. Tunnicliffe. *My Country Book*. Studio.
1943 E. L. G. Watson. *Walking with Fancy*. Country Life.
1946 C. H. Warren. *Happy Countryman*. Eyre & Spottiswoode.
1947 E. L. G. Watson. *The Leaves Return*. Country Life.
1947 S. Rogerson and C. F. Tunnicliffe. *Our Bird Book*. Collins.
1949 R. Jefferies. *Wild Life in a Southern County*. Lutterworth.
1949 R. Rogerson. *Both Sides of the Road: A Book about Farming*. Collins.
1952 C. F. Tunnicliffe. *Shorelands Summer Diary*. Collins.
1957 A. Uttley. *A Year in the Country*. Faber & Faber. See text about numerous others.
1965 J. McNeillie [I. Niall, pseud.]. *The Way of a Countryman*. Country Life.
1967 J. McNeillie [I. Niall, pseud.]. *A Galloway Childhood*. Heinemann.
1968 J. McNeillie [I. Niall, pseud.]. *A Fowler's World*. Heinemann.

George Claude Leon Underwood (1890–1975)
1926 J. B. Cabell. *The Music from Behind the Moon*. New York: Day.
1928 L. Underwood. *The Siamese Cat*. New York: Brentano.
1929 P. Russell. *Red Tiger: Adventures in Yucatan and Mexico*. Hodder & Stoughton.
1929 [Bible.] Apocrypha. Cresset. With others.

*

Neve, C. *Leon Underwood*. Intro. J. Rothenstein. Thames & Hudson, 1974.

Clifford Webb (1895–1972)
1936 M. Dixey. *Words Beasts & Fishes*. Faber & Faber.
1937 P. Miller [pseud.]. *Ana the Runner*. Golden Cockerel.
1938 V. G. Calderon [V. García Calderón]. *The White Llama*. Golden Cockerel.
1939 H. G. Wells. *The Country of the Blind*. Golden Cockerel.
1945 *Gesta Francorum: The First Crusade*. Tr. S. de Chair. Golden Cockerel.
1947 R. Wightman. *Moss Green Days*. Westhouse.
1948 I. Bannett. *The Amazons*. Golden Cockerel.
1951 Julius Caesar. *Commentaries*. Limited Editions.
1954 S. de Chair. *The Story of a Lifetime*. Golden Cockerel.

Rex Whistler (1905–44)
1930 J. Swift. *Gulliver's Travels*. Cresset.
1932 E. James. *The Next Volume*. Privately printed.
1932 L. Whistler. *Armed October*. Cobden-Sanderson.

[1933] W. de la Mare. *Lord Fish*. Faber & Faber.
1936 J. E. Agate. *Kingdoms for Horses*. Gollancz.
[1942] S. Harcourt-Smith. *The Last of Uptake*. Batsford.
1943 E. Olivier. *Night Thoughts of a Country Landlady*. Batsford.
1949 L. Whistler. *The World's Room*. Heinemann.

*

Rex Whistler: The "Königsmark" Drawings. Ed. L. Whistler. Richards, 1952.
Whistler, L. *Rex Whistler, 1905–1944: His Life and Drawings*. Art & Technics, 1948.
————, and R. Fuller. *The Work of Rex Whistler*. Batsford, 1960. With a *catalogue raisonnée*.

Ethelbert White (1891–1972)
1922 C. Goldoni. *The Good-Humoured Ladies*. Beaumont.
1923 R. Jefferies. *The Story of My Heart*. Duckworth.
1938 H. Thoreau. *Walden*. Penguin.

*

Balston, T. "The Wood-Engravings of Ethelbert White." *Image* 3 (1949–50).

CHAPTER ELEVEN

The Twentieth Century (III) 1946–1976

Michael Ayrton (1921–75)
1945 J. Webster. *The Duchess of Malfi*. Sylvan.
1945 *Poems of Death*. Ed. P. Pool. Muller.
1946 J. Arlott. *Clausentum*. Cape.
1946 T. Nashe. *Summer's Last Will and Testament*. Oxford.
1948 O. Wilde. *The Picture of Dorian Gray*. Castle.
1951 W. Shakespeare. *Macbeth*. Folio.
1953 M. Ayrton. *Tittivulus: or The Verbiage Collector*. Reinhardt.
1954 T. W. Day. *Here Are Ghosts and Witches*. Batsford.
1956, 1955 P. W. Lewis. *The Human Age*. Methuen.
1957 E. A. Poe. *Tales of Mystery and Imagination*. Folio.
1958 G. H. W. Rylands. *Distraction of Wits*. Cambridge.
1960 L. Apuleius Madaurensis. *Transformations of Lucius*. Tr. R. Graves. Folio.
1962 M. Ayrton. *Testament of Daedalus*. Methuen.
1967 Euripides. *Medea. Hippolytus. The Bacchae*. Limited Editions.

Eric George Fraser (b. 1902)
1948 T. Nashe. *The Unfortunate Traveller*. Lehmann.
1950 H. Bett. *English Legends*. Batsford.
1951 W. Shakespeare. *The Complete Works*. Collins.
1952 *Nero*. Tr. G. G. Ramsay. Folio.
1954 I. Nievo. *The Castle of Fratta*. Folio.
1957 Xenophon of Ephesus. *The Ephesian Story*. Golden Cockerel.
1958 *The Book of the Thousand Nights and One Night*. Folio. With anr.
1963 M. de Zayas y Sotomayor. *A Shameful Revenge, and Other Stories*. Folio.
1966 Petronius. *The Ephesian Matron*. Golden Cockerel.
1969 T. Bulfinch. *The Age of Fable*. Dent.
1971 P. Ovidius Naso. *The Art of Love*. Limited Editions.
1973 Homer. *The Voyage of Odysseus*. Blackie.
1973 *Folklore, Myths and Legends of Britain*. Reader's Digest Association. With others.
1974 P. Hill. *Joan of Arc*. Oxford.

*

Davis, A. *Eric Fraser*. Uffculme, 1974.

David Gentleman (b. 1930)
1963 J. D. Wyss. *The Swiss Family Robinson*. Limited Editions.
1964 J. Clare. *The Shepherd's Calendar*. Oxford.
1966 G. E. Evans. *The Pattern under the Plough*. Faber & Faber.
1966 J. Keats. *Poems*. Limited Editions.
1967 J. Clare. *Selected Poems and Prose*. Oxford.
1970 W. Wordsworth. *The Solitary Song*. Bodley Head.

Philip Gough (b. 1908)

1948　J. Austen. *Emma*. Macdonald.
1951　J. Austen. *Pride and Prejudice*. Macdonald.
1957　J. Austen. *Mansfield Park*. Macdonald.
1957　A. Trollope. *The Last Chronicle of Barset*. Oxford.
1958　J. Austen. *Sense and Sensibility*. Macdonald.
1961　J. Austen. *Persuasion*. Macdonald.
1961　J. Austen. *Northanger Abbey*. Macdonald.

Rigby Graham (b. 1931)

1959　J. Clare. *Lines Written in Northampton County Asylum*. Leicester: Orpheus.
1961　J. Clare. *The Natural World*. Leicester: Pandora.
1961　A. C. Swinburne. *The Garden of Proserpine*. Leicester: Pandora.
1961 [1962]　P. B. Shelley. *Lines Written among the Euganean Hills*. Leicester: Pandora.
1962　G. G. N., Lord Byron. *When We Two Parted*. Leicester: Pandora.
1962　A. Marvell. *Thoughts in a Garden*. Leicester: Pandora.
1962　O. Wilde. *Serenade*. Leicester: Pandora.
1963　*A Song in Favour of Bundling*. Leicester: Orpheus.
1964　*An Autumn Anthology*. Wymondham: Brewhouse.
1964　*Chidiock Tichbourne: His Last Letter to Agnes His Wife*. Wymondham: Brewhouse.
1965　O. Bayldon. *The Paper Makers Craft: Verse by Oliver Bayldon*. Cambridge: Twelve by Eight.
1967　H. Collinson. *Five Duets*. Aylestone: Cog.
1968　R. Graham. *Slieve Bingian: A Cycle of Prints and Drawings*. Aylestone: Cog.
1968　D. Tew. *The Oakham Canal*. Wymondham: Brewhouse.
1969　P. Holt and E. Thorpe. *Gold and Books*. Wymondham: Brewhouse.
1969　J. Cotton. *Ampurias: a Poem*. Berkhamstead: Priapus.
1969　A. Stramm. *Twenty-two Poems*. Wymondham: Brewhouse.
1970　M. McCord. *Tower Houses and Ten Pound Castles*. Belfast: Crannog.
1971　M. McCord. *Abbeys and Churches*. Belfast: Crannog.
1972　M. James. *Mountains*. Melton Mowbray: Brewhouse.
1973　C. Flores. *Correspondences*. Aylestone: Cog.
1974　C. Flores. *A Voice from Kalkara*. Leicester: New Broom.
1974　D. Rogers. *The Peddars Way*. Wymondham: Brewhouse.
1974　F. Lissauer. *The Lost Shepherd and Other Poems*. Leicester: New Broom.
1975　F. Lissauer. *A Visit to Ireland*. Aylestone: Cog.
1975　M. Hunter. *The Golden Orchid: Fantasy*. Wymondham: Brewhouse.
1975　R. Graham. *James Joyce's Tower, Sandycove*. Wymondham: Brewhouse & Hunter.
1975　R. Graham. *Edmund Spenser's Kilcolman*. Wymondham: Brewhouse.
1975　T. Hood. *Faithless Nellie Grey*. Wymondham: Brewhouse.

Anthony Gross (b. 1905)

1944　E. Brontë. *Wuthering Heights*. Elek.
1950　J. Galsworthy. *Forsyte Saga*. Heinemann.
1960　H. James. *English Hours*. Heinemann.
1968, 1969　[Bible.] *The Oxford Illustrated Old Testament*. Oxford. With others.
1971　Theocritus. *Sixe Idyllia*. New York: Chilmark.

*

Wayne, J. "The Graphic Work of Anthony Gross." *Image* 4 (Spring 1950).

Derrick Harris (1920–60)

1953　H. Fielding. *Joseph Andrews*. Folio.
1955　T. Smollett. *Humphrey Clinker*. Folio.
1959　H. Fielding. *Tom Jones*. Folio.

Clarke Hutton (b. 1898)

1947　J. Bunyan. *The Pilgrim's Progress*. SCM. Macmillan, 1948.
1965 [1964]　M. Twain [S. L. Clemens]. *The Prince and the Pauper*. Heritage.
1966　W. Scott. *Kenilworth*. Limited Editions.
1967　C. Brontë. *Villette*. Folio.
1971　J. Austen. *Northanger Abbey*. Limited Editions.
1974　G. B. Shaw. *Pygmalion. Candida*. Limited Editions.
1976　R. L. Stevenson. *New Arabian Nights*. Limited Editions.

Robin Jacques (b. 1920)

1945　C. Dickens. *Doctor Marigold*. Westhouse.
1946　W. Irving. *Alhambra Tales*. Lunn.
1946　*Selected Tales from the Arabian Nights*. Ed. H. Anderson. Lunn.
1946　P. de Heriz. *Fairy Tales with a Twist*. Lunn.
1947　J. K. Cross. *The Man in the Moonlight*. Westhouse.
1947　*Youth*. Ed. H. Bell. Westhouse.
1955　J. Swift. *Gulliver's Travels*. Oxford.
1956　J. Joyce. *A Portrait of the Artist as a Young Man*. Cape.
1962　R. Kipling. *Kim*. Limited Editions.
1963　W. M. Thackeray. *Vanity Fair*. Folio.
1964　O. Wilde. *Three Short Stories*. Macmillan.
1967　J. Joyce. *Dubliners*. Cape.
1968　A. S. Molloy. *Five Kidnapped Indians*. New York: Hastings House.
1970　W. B. Yeats. *The Poems of William Butler Yeats*. Limited Editions.
1972　G. Eliot [M. A. Evans]. *Middlemarch*. Folio.
1973　*Folklore, Myths and Legends of Britain*. Reader's Digest Association. With others.

*

Cross, J. K. "An Author Writes about His Illustrator." *Alphabet and Image*, no. 7 (May 1948).

Jacques, R. *Illustrators at Work*. Studio Books, 1963.

Charles Keeping (b. 1924)

1964　E. Brontë. *Wuthering Heights*. Folio.
1966　E. M. Remarque. *All Quiet on the Western Front*. Folio.
1969　W. Collins. *The Moonstone*. Heron.
1970　L. Cooper. *Five Fables from France*. Abelard-Schumann.
1971　F. Dostoyevsky. *The Idiot*. Folio.
1973　*Folklore, Myths and Legends of Britain*. Reader's Digest Association. With others.
1976　V. Hugo. *Les Misérables*. Folio.

Lynton Lamb (1907–77)

1948　A. Trollope. *Can You Forgive Her?* Oxford.
1950　L. Lamb. *County Town*. Eyre & Spottiswoode.
1953　G. Eliot [M. A. Evans]. *Silas Marner*. Limited Editions.
1954　A. Trollope. *The Two Heroines of Plumplington*. Deutsch.
1954　W. Sansom. *Lord Love Us*. Hogarth.
1955　C. Brontë. *Jane Eyre*. Macdonald.
1956　C. S. Emden. *Gilbert White in His Village*. Oxford.
1956　W. Collins. *The Woman in White*. Folio.
1958　W. Sansom. *The Icicle and the Sun*. Hogarth.

1959 C. S. Emden. *Poets in Their Letters*. Oxford.
1960 H. G. Wells. *Tono-Bungay*. Limited Editions.
1963 H. James. *Washington Square*. Folio.
1968, 1969 [Bible.] *The Oxford Illustrated Old Testament*. Oxford. With others.

*

Lynton Lamb: Illustrator. Comp. and intro. G. Mackie. Scolar, 1978.

Nigel Lambourne (b. 1919)
1949 L. Sterne. *A Sentimental Journey*. Folio.
1954 D. Defoe. *Moll Flanders*. Folio.
1959 G. de Maupassant. *Short Stories*. Folio.
1961 L. O'Flaherty. *The Informer*. Folio.
1964 F. Dostoyevsky. *The Brothers Karamasov*. Folio.
1969 P. Virgilius Maro. *Georgics*. Folio.

John Lawrence (b. 1933)
1967 D. Defoe. *The History of Colonel Jack*. Folio.
1969 G. Grossmith and W. Grossmith. *The Diary of a Nobody*. Folio.
1970 L. Sterne. *Tristram Shandy*. Folio.

Marian Mahler [Mariana]
1948 L. Sterne. *A Sentimental Journey*. Elek.

Frank Vincent Martin (b. 1921)
1956 H. Fielding. *Jonathan Wild*. Folio.
1956 T. Wilder. *The Bridge of San Luis Rey*. Folio.
1957 M. Sisson. *The Cave*. Hemingford Grey: Vine.
1957 O. Wilde. *Salome*. Folio.
1958 *The Book of the Thousand Nights and One Night*. Folio. With anr.
1965 Stendhal [M. H. Beyle]. *Scarlet and Black*. Folio.

John Minton (1917-57)
1947 H. Alain-Fournier. *The Wanderer*. Elek.
1947 R. L. Stevenson. *Treasure Island*. Elek.
1948 A. Ross. *Time Was Away*. Lehmann.
1949 H. E. Bates. *The Country Heart*. Joseph.
1950 R. Arkell. *Old Herbaceous*. Joseph.

*

Graham, R. "John Minton as a Book Illustrator." *The Private Library*, 2nd ser., vol. 1, no. 1 (1968).
John Minton. An Exhibition of Paintings, Drawings, and Illustrations. Arts Council of Great Britain, 1958.
Lewis, J. "Book Illustrations by John Minton." *Image* 1 (Autumn 1949).

Charles Mozley (b. 1915)
1954 A. Trollope. *The Duke's Children*. Oxford.
1961 *Concerning "Ulysses" and the Bodley Head*. Barnet: Stellar.
1962 D. Defoe. *Moll Flanders*. Zodiac.
1962 G. B. Shaw. *Man and Superman*. Limited Editions.
1964 G. de Maupassant. *Tellier House*. Cassell.
1964 J. Galsworthy. *The Man of Property*. Limited Editions.
1967 H. G. Wells. *The Invisible Man*. Limited Editions.
1971 S. Crane. *The Red Badge of Courage*. Dent.
1971 A. Pushkin. *The Captain's Daughter and Other Stories*. Limited Editions.

Garrick Salisbury Palmer (b. 1933)
1967 H. Melville. *Three Stories*. Folio.

1972 H. Melville. *Benito Cereno*. Barre, Mass.: Imprint Society.
1974 H. Melville. *Moby Dick*. Folio.
[n.d.] H. Melville. *Billy Budd*. Barre, Mass.: Imprint Society.

George W. Lennox Paterson (b. 1915)
1950 M. F. Barber [M. Fairless, pseud.]. *The Roadmender and Other Writings*. Collins.
1958 R. Burns. *Poetical Works*. Chambers.

John Petts (b. 1914)
1946 G. Jones. *The Green Island*. Golden Cockerel.
1953 G. Williams. *Against Women*. Golden Cockerel.

Peter Reddick (b. 1924)
1964 T. L. Peacock. *Crotchet Castle*. Folio.
1968 T. Hardy. *The Mayor of Casterbridge*. Folio.
1969 R. Browning. *Poems*. Limited Editions.
1971 T. Hardy. *The Return of the Native*. Folio.
1973 *Folklore, Myths and Legends of Britain*. Reader's Digest Association. With others.
1977 A. Trollope. *Barchester Towers*. Folio.
1978 A. Trollope. *Framley Parsonage*. Folio.
1978 A. Trollope. *Doctor Thorne*. Folio.

Brian Robb (b. 1913)
1947 L. Apuleius Madaurensis. *The Golden Asse*. Westhouse.
1947 L. N. Andreyev. *Judas Iscariot*. Westhouse.
1947 [R. E. Raspe.] *12 Adventures of the Celebrated Baron Munchausen*. Lunn.
1948 L. Sterne. *A Sentimental Journey*. Macdonald.
1949 L. Sterne. *Tristram Shandy*. Macdonald.
1953 H. Fielding. *Tom Jones*. Macdonald.
1954 Aesop. *Fables of Aesop*. Penguin.
1968, 1969 [Bible.] *The Oxford Illustrated Old Testament*. Oxford. With others.

*

Ardizzone, E. "Brian Robb." *Signature* 11 (1950).

Leonard Rosoman (b. 1913)
1952 C.-L. Philippe. *Bubu of Montparnasse*. Weidenfeld & Nicholson.
1958 A. Huxley. *Point Counter Point*. Folio.
1964 W. Collins. *The Woman in White*. Limited Editions.
1968, 1969 [Bible.] *The Oxford Illustrated Old Testament*. Oxford. With others.
1971 A. Huxley. *Brave New World*. Folio.

Cyril Satorsky
1968, 1969 [Bible.] *The Oxford Illustrated Old Testament*. Oxford. With others.
1970 C. Satorsky. *A Pride of Rabbis*. Baltimore, Md.: Aquarius.
1971 *Sir Gawain and the Green Knight*. Limited Editions.

Ronald Searle (b. 1920)
1951 R. Braddon. *The Naked Island*. Laurie.
1952 W. Cowper. *The History of John Gilpin*. Privately printed.
1959 Homer. *The Anger of Achilles: Homer's "Iliad"*. Cassell.
1961 C. Dickens. *A Christmas Carol*. Longman.
1962 C. Dickens. *Oliver Twist*. Longman.
1962 C. Dickens. *Great Expectations*. Longman.
1969 R. E. Raspe. *The Adventures of Baron Munchausen*. New York: Pantheon.

1970   K. Dobbs. *The Great Fur Opera: Annals of the Hudson's Bay Company, 1670–1970*. Toronto: McClelland & Stewart.

*

Ronald Searle. Intro. H. Brock; essay by P. Dehaye. Deutsch, 1978

Bibliography

Aldis, H. G. *The Printed Book*. Rev. J. Carter and B. Crutchley. Cambridge, 1951.

The Art of the Printed Book: 1455–1955. Intro. J. Blumenthal. New York: Pierpont Morgan Library, 1973.

Benesch, O. *Artistic and Intellectual Trends from Rubens to Daumier as Shown in Book Illustration*. Cambridge, Mass.: Harvard, 1943.

Berry, W. T., and H. E. Poole. *Annals of Printing*. Blandford, 1966.

Biggs, J. R. *Illustration and Reproduction*. Blandford, 1950.

Blagden, C. *The Stationers' Company, a History: 1403–1959*. Allen, 1960.

Bland, D. *A History of Book Illustration: The Illuminated Manuscript and the Printed Book*. Faber & Faber, 1969.

Bliss, D. P. *A History of Wood-Engraving*. Dent, 1928.

The Bookman's Glossary. Ed. J. Peters. Bowker, 1975.

Bryan, M. *A Dictionary of Painters and Engravers*. Bell, 1925–27.

Cave, R. *The Private Press*. New York: Watson-Guptill, 1971.

Chatto, W. A., and J. Jackson. *A Treatise on Wood-Engraving*. Knight, 1839.

Clair, C. *A Chronology of Printing*. Cassell, 1969.

———. *A History of Printing in Britain*. Cassell, 1965.

A Complete Catalogue of Limited Editions Club Books, 1929–1980. New York: Duschnes Rare Books, 1980.

Crane, W. *Of the Decorative Illustration of Books Old and New*. Bell, 1896.

Croft-Murray, E. *Decorative Painting in England, 1537–1837*. Country Life, 1962, 1970.

Eichenberg. *The Art of the Print*. Thames & Hudson, 1976.

Forty-Six Years of Limited Editions Club Books, 1929–1976. New York: Duschnes Rare Books, 1978. With four critical commentaries.

Franklin, C. *The Private Presses*. Chester Springs, Pa.: Dufour, 1969.

Garrett, A. *A History of British Wood Engraving*. Tunbridge Wells: Midas, 1978.

Glaister, G. A. *Glossary of the Book*. Allen & Unwin, 1960.

Godfrey, R. T. *Printmaking in Britain*. Oxford: Phaidon, 1978.

Gray, B. *The English Print*. Black, 1937.

Handover, P. M. *Printing in London from 1476 to Modern Times*. Allen & Unwin, 1960.

Hind, A. M. *A History of Engraving and Etching: From the Fifteenth Century to the Year 1914*. 3rd ed. Houghton Mifflin, 1923. New York: Dover, 1973.

———. *An Introduction to a History of Woodcut*. Constable, 1935. New York: Dover, 1963.

Hodnett, E. *Image & Text: Studies in the Illustration of English Literature*. Scolar, 1982.

Ivins, W. M., Jr. *How Prints Look*. New York: Metropolitan Museum of Art, 1943.

———. *Prints and Visual Communication*. Cambridge, Mass.: Harvard, 1953.

Jennet, S. *The Making of Books*. Faber & Faber, 1973.

Lamb, L. *Drawing for Illustration*. Oxford, 1962.

Levarie, N. *The Art and History of Books*. New York: Heinemann, 1968.

Lewis, J. *Anatomy of Printing: The Influences of Art and History on Its Design*. Faber & Faber, 1977.

Lindley, K. *The Woodblock Engravers*. Newton Abbot: David & Charles, 1970.

Linton, W. J. *The Masters of Wood-Engraving*. Stevens, 1889.

Mayor, A. H. *Prints and People: A Social History of Printed Pictures*. New York: Metropolitan Museum of Art, 1971.

Mumby, F. A. *Publishing and Books*. Cambridge, 1974.

Myers, R. *The British Book Trade: From Caxton to the Present Day. A Bibliographical Guide*. Deutsch and the National Book League, 1973.

Plant, M. *The English Book Trade: An Economic History*. Allen, 1965.

Praz, M. *Mnemosyne: The Parallel between Literature and the Visual Arts*. Princeton, 1970.

Steinberg, S. H. *Five Hundred Years of Printing*. Pelican, 1969.

Sullivan, E. J. *The Art of Illustration*. Chapman & Hall, 1921.

Thieme, U., and F. Becker. *Allgemeines Lexikon der bildenden Künstler*. Leipzig: Engelmann, 1907–50.

Vollmer, H. *Allgemeines Lexikon der bildenden Künstler des XX Jahrhunderts*. Leipzig: Seemann, 1955.

Weitenkampf, F. *The Illustrated Book*. Cambridge, Mass.: Harvard, 1938.

Williamson, H. S. "The Uneasy Marriage-Bed." *Signature*, n.s., no. 9 (1949).

CHAPTER ONE

The Fifteenth Century

Bennett, H. S. *English Books and Readers, 1475 to 1557*. 2nd ed. Cambridge, 1969.

Bühler, C. F. *The Fifteenth-Century Book: The Scribes, the Printers, the Decorators*. Philadelphia: Pennsylvania, 1960.

Duff, E. G. *The Printers, Stationers, and Bookbinders of Westminster and London from 1476 to 1535*. Cambridge, 1906.

Heilbronner, W. L. *Printing and the Book in Fifteenth-Century England*. Charlottesville: Virginia, 1967.

Hodnett, E. *English Woodcuts, 1480–1535. With Additions and Corrections*. Oxford for the Bibliographical Society, 1973.

CHAPTER TWO

The Sixteenth Century

Aldis, H. G. *Dictionary of Printers and Booksellers, 1557–1640*. Oxford for the Bibliographical Society, 1968.

Clair, C. "The Bishops' Bible, 1568." *Gutenberg-Jahrbuch* (1962).

———. *Christopher Plantin*. Cassell, 1960.

Croft-Murray, E., and P. Hulton. *Catalogue of British Drawings: XVI & XVII Centuries*. Trustees of the British Museum, 1960.

Cust, L. *Foreign Artists of the Reformed Religion Working in England from about 1560 to 1660*. Proceedings of the Huguenot Society, vol. 7. Aberdeen, 1903.

Dodgson, C. *Woodcuts Designed by Holbein for English Printers*. The Walpole Society vol. 27. Oxford: Walpole Society, 1939.

Duff, E. G. *A Century of the English Book Trade*. Oxford: Bibliographical Society, 1905.

Hind, A. M., M. Corbett, and M. Norton. *Engraving [and etching] in England in the Sixteenth and Seventeenth Centuries*. Cambridge, 1952–64.

Hodnett, E. *Marcus Gheeraerts the Elder of Bruges, London, and Antwerp*. Utrecht: Haentjens Dekker & Gumbert, 1971.

Strachan, J. *Early Bible Illustrations*. Cambridge, 1957.

Strong, R. *Holbein and Henry VIII*. Routledge & Paul for the Paul Mellon Foundation, 1967.

Williamson, G. A. *Foxe's "Book of Martyrs"*. Secker & Warburg, 1965.

Woodward, J. *Tudor and Stuart Drawings*. Faber & Faber, 1951.

Yates, F. A. "Queen Elizabeth as Astraea." *Journal of the Warburg and Courtauld Institutes* 10 (1947).

CHAPTER THREE

The Seventeenth Century

Allen, B. S. *Tides in English Taste, 1619–1800*. Cambridge, Mass.: Harvard, 1937.

Benesch, O. *Art of the Renaissance in Northern Europe*. Cambridge, Mass.: Harvard, 1945.

Croft-Murray, E., and P. Hulton. *Catalogue of British Drawings: XVI & XVII Centuries*. Trustees of the British Museum, 1960.

Dodgson, C. "Richard Gaywood." *The Print Collector's Quarterly* 15 (1928).

Foss, M. *The Age of Patronage in England, 1660–1750*. Ithaca, N.Y.: Cornell, 1971.

Freeman, R. *English Emblem Books*. Chatto & Windus, 1948.

Green, H. *Andrea Alciati*. Trübner, 1872.

Harrison, F. M. "Some Illustrators of *The Pilgrim's Progress*." *The Library* 17, no. 3 (1936).

Henkel, A., and A. Schöne. *Handbuch zur Sinnbildkunst des XVI. und XVII. Jahrhunderts*. Stuttgart: Metzlersche, 1967.

Hodnett, E. *Aesop in England*. Charlottesville: Virginia, 1979.

Jacobs, J. *The Fables of Aesop: Selected, Told Anew, and Their History Traced*. Macmillan, 1894.

Plomer, H. R. *A Dictionary of the Printers and Booksellers ... 1668 to 1725*. Oxford: Bibliographical Society, 1922.

Praz, M. *Studies in Seventeenth Century Imagery*. Warburg Institute, 1938.

Sparrow, W. S. *British Etching from Francis Barlow to Francis Seymour Haden*. Lane, 1926.

Vertue, G. *The Note-Books*. The Walpole Society vols. 18, 20, 22, 24, 26 and 30. Oxford: Walpole Society, 1930–55.

CHAPTERS FOUR AND FIVE

The Eighteenth Century (I) and (II)

Adhémar, J. *Graphic Art of the 18th Century*. Tr. M. I. Martin. Thames & Hudson, 1964.

Boase, T. S. R. "Illustrations of Shakespeare's Plays in the Seventeenth and Eighteenth Centuries." *Journal of the Warburg and Courtauld Institutes* 10 (1948).

Cohen, R. *The Art of Discrimination: Thomson's "The Seasons" and the Language of Criticism*. Routledge & Paul, 1964.

Eaves, T. C. D. "Graphic Illustration of the Novels of Samuel Richardson, 1740–1810." *Huntington Library Quarterly* 14, no. 4 (1951).

Geduld, H. M. *Prince of Publishers: A Study of the Work and Career of Jacob Tonson*. Bloomington: Indiana, 1969.

George, M. D. *Hogarth to Cruikshank: Social Change in Graphic Satire*. Penguin, 1967.

Halsband, R. *"The Rape of the Lock" and Its Illustrations, 1714–1896*. Oxford, 1980.

Hammelmann, H. A., and T. S. R. Boase. *Book Illustrators in Eighteenth-Century England*. New Haven, Conn.: Yale for the Paul Mellon Centre for Studies in British Art, 1975.

Lewine, J. *Bibliography of Eighteenth Century Art and Illustrated Books*. Low, Marston, 1898.

Lynch, K. M. *Jacob Tonson: Kit-Cat Publisher*. Knoxville: Tennessee, 1971.

Merchant, W. M. *Shakespeare and the Artist*. Oxford, 1959.

Papillon, J. M. *Traité historique et pratique de la gravure en bois*. Paris: Simon, 1766.

Pointon, M. R. *Milton and English Art*. Manchester, 1970.

Todd, R. *Tracks in the Snow*. Grey Walls, 1946.

Williams, I. A. "English Book-Illustration, 1700–1775." *The Library* 17, no. 1 (1936).

Wilton, A. *British Water Colours, 1750–1850*. Oxford: Phaidon, 1977.

CHAPTER SIX

The Nineteenth Century (I)

Bell, Q. *Victorian Artists, 1837–1910*. Routledge & Kegan Paul, 1967.

Bentley, N. "Dickens and His Illustrators." In *Charles Dickens, 1812–1870*. Weidenfeld, 1969.

Bliss, D. P. *Sir Walter Scott and the Visual Arts*. Glasgow: Glasgow School of Art, 1970.

Burke, W. J. *Rudolph Ackermann*. New York: New York Public Library, 1935.

Cohen, J. R. *Charles Dickens and His Original Illustrators.* Columbus: Ohio State, 1980.

Dickens, C. "Book Illustrations." *All the Year Round,* 10 April 1867.

Du Maurier, G. "The Illustrating of Books." *The Magazine of Art,* August 1890.

Gordon, C. "The Illustration of Sir Walter Scott: Nineteenth Century Enthusiasm and Adaptation." *Journal of the Warburg and Courtauld Institutes* 34 (1971).

Hardie, M. *English Coloured Books.* Methuen, 1906.

Howe, E. "From Bewick to the Half-Tone: A Survey of Illustration." *Typography,* no. 3 (Summer 1937).

Hunnisett, B. *Steel-Engraved Book Illustration in England.* Scolar, 1980.

James, P. *English Book Illustration, 1800–1900.* Penguin, 1947.

Kitton, F. G. *Dickens and His Illustrators.* Redway, 1899.

Klingender, F. D. *Art and the Industrial Revolution.* Rev. ed. Carrington, 1968.

Lewis, C. T C. *The Story of Picture Printing in England during the Nineteenth Century: or Forty Years of Wood and Stone.* Low, [1928].

McLean, R. *Victorian Book Design and Colour Printing.* Oxford, 1972.

The Mind and Art of Victorian England. Ed. J. L. Altholz. Minneapolis: Minnesota, 1976.

Muir, P. *Victorian Illustrated Books.* Batsford, 1971.

Prideaux, S. T. *Aquatint Engraving.* Duckworth, 1909.

Ray, G. N. *The Illustrator and the Book in England from 1790 to 1914.* New York: Pierpont Morgan Library; Oxford, 1976.

Tooley, R. V. *Some English Books with Coloured Plates. 1790 1860.* Batsford, 1954.

Wakeman, G. *The Production of Nineteenth Century Colour Illustration.* Plough, 1976.

———. *Victorian Book Illustration: The Technical Revolution.* Newton Abbot: David & Charles, 1973.

Wood, H. T. *Modern Methods of Illustrating Books.* Stock, 1887.

CHAPTER SEVEN

The Nineteenth Century (II)

Bibliography of British Book Illustrators, 1860–1900. Ed. C. Baker. Birmingham: Birmingham Bookshop, 1978.

The Cornhill Gallery. Smith, Elder, 1864.

Dalziel, G., and E. Dalziel. *The Brothers Dalziel: A Record of Fifty Years' Work, 1840–1890.* Methuen, 1901.

Du Maurier, G. *Social Pictorial Satire.* Harper, 1898.

Eckel, J. C. *The First Editions of the Writings of Charles Dickens.* Maggs, 1932.

Evans, E. *Reminiscences.* Ed. R. McLean. Oxford, 1967.

Fildes, P. "Phototransfer of Drawings in Wood-Block Engraving." *Journal of the Printing Historical Society,* no. 5 (1969).

Fredeman, W. E. *Pre-Raphaelitism: A Bibliocritical Study.* Cambridge, Mass.: Harvard, 1965.

Hall, N. J. *Trollope and His Illustrators.* New York: St. Martin's, 1980.

Harvey, J. *Victorian Novelists and Their Illustrators.* Sidgwick & Jackson, 1970.

Hunt, J. D. "Dickens and the Tradition of Graphic Satire." In *Encounters: Essays on Literature and the Visual Arts.* Ed. J. D. Hunt. Studio Vista, 1971.

Layard, G. S. *Tennyson and His Pre-Raphaelite Illustrators.* Stock, 1894.

Olmsted, J. C., and J. E. Welch. *Victorian Novel Illustrators: A Selected Checklist, 1900–1976.* Garland, 1979.

Reid, F. *The Illustrators of the Sixties.* Faber & Gwyer, 1928.

Toilers in Art. Ed. H. C. Ewart. Isbister, 1891.

White, G. *English Illustration: "The Sixties," 1855–70.* Constable, 1897.

CHAPTER EIGHT

The Nineteenth Century (III)

Aslin, E. *The Aesthetic Movement: Prelude to Art Nouveau.* Elek, 1969.

Balston, T. "English Book Illustration: 1880–1900." In *New Paths in Book-Collecting.* Ed. J. Carter. Constable, 1934.

———. "Illustrated Series of the 'Nineties – The Cranford Series." *The Book Collector's Quarterly* 11 (July–September 1933).

Burdett, O. *The Beardsley Period.* Lane, 1925.

Farr, D. *English Art: 1870–1940.* Oxford, 1979.

Howe, E. "From Bewick to the Half-Tone: A Survey of Illustration." *Typography,* no. 3 (Summer 1937).

Jackson, H. *The Eighteen Nineties.* Richards, 1913.

Johnson, J., and A. Greutzner. *The Dictionary of British Artists, 1880–1940.* Antique Collectors' Club, 1976.

Jullian, P. *Dreamers of Decadence: Symbolist Painters of the 1890s.* Tr. R. Baldick. Praeger, 1971.

Pennell, J. *Modern Illustration.* Bell, 1895.

Peppin, B. *Fantasy: Book Illustration, 1860–1920.* Studio Vista, 1975.

Rothenstein, J. *The Artists of the 1890s.* Routledge, 1928.

Schmutzler, R. *Art Nouveau.* New York: Abrams, 1978.

Sketchley, R. E. D. *English Book-Illustration of To-day.* Paul, Trench, Trübner, 1907.

Spencer, R. *The Aesthetic Movement.* Studio Vista, 1972.

Taylor, J. R. *The Art Nouveau Book in Britain.* Methuen, 1966.

Thorpe, J. *English Illustrations: The Nineties.* Faber & Faber, 1935.

The Turn of the Century, 1885–1910. Art Nouveau–Jugendstil Books. Exhibition catalog, Houghton Library. Cambridge, Mass.: Harvard, 1970.

CHAPTER NINE

The Twentieth Century (I)

Balston, T. *English Wood-Engraving, 1900–1950.* Art & Technics, 1951.

Garrett, A. *British Wood Engravings of the 20th Century: A Personal View.* Scolar, 1980.

Lewis, J. N. C. *The Twentieth-Century Book.* Studio Vista, [1967].

Salaman, M. C. *Modern Book Illustrators and Their Work.* Ed. C. G. Holme and E. C. Halton. Studio, 1914.

Waters, G. M. *Dictionary of British Artists Working 1900–1950.* Eastbourne: Eastbourne Fine Art, 1975.

CHAPTER TEN

The Twentieth Century (II)

The Art of the Book: 1939–1950. Ed. C. Ede. Studio, 1951.

Curwen, H. *Processes of Graphic Reproduction.* Faber & Faber, 1934.

Darton, F. J. H. *Modern Book Illustration in Great Britain and America.* Studio, 1931.

Feaver, W. "Wartime Romances." *The Sunday Times Magazine,* 20 May 1973. British art in the 1940s.

Garvey, E. M. *The Artist and the Book: 1890–1960.* Boston: Museum of Fine Arts and Harvard College Library, 1961.

Harrop, D. *A History of the Gregynog Press.* Pinner: Private Libraries Association, 1980.

Hassall, J. *Wood-Engraving: A Reader's Guide.* Cambridge for the National Book League, 1949.

Jones, T. *The Gregynog Press.* Oxford, 1954.

Klemin, D. *The Illustrated Book: Its Art and Craft.* New York: Clarkson Potter, 1970.

Leighton, C. *Wood-Engraving of the 1930's.* Studio, 1936.

Nash, P. *Room and Book.* New York: Scribner, 1932.

Quarto-Millenary: The First 250 Publications and the First 25 Years of the Limited Editions Club, 1929–1954. New York: Limited Editions Club, 1959.

Salaman, M. C. *British Book Illustration Yesterday and To-Day.* Studio, 1923.

Sandford, C., and O. Rutter. *Pertelote: A Bibliography of the Golden Cockerel Press.* Golden Cockerel, 1943.

Sleigh, B. *Wood Engraving Since Eighteen-Ninety.* Pitman, 1932.

CHAPTER ELEVEN

The Twentieth Century (III)

Boxwood & Graver. A Miscellany of Blocks. Penguin, 1958.

Folio: Quarterly Magazine of the Folio Society. Folio, 1954– .

Folio 21: A Bibliography of the Folio Society, 1947–67. Folio, 1968.

Graham, R. *Romantic Book Illustration in England, 1943–55.* Pinner: Private Libraries Association, 1966.

Guy, P. "Twenty-five Years of *Folio.*" *Penrose Graphic Arts Annual* (1973). Lund Humphries, 1973.

Jacques, R. *Illustrators at Work.* Studio Books, 1963.

McLean, R. *Modern Book Design from William Morris to the Present Day.* Faber & Faber, 1958.

Index

Figures in italic type refer to pages on which illustrations appear

Publishers' Acknowledgements

The Publishers express their thanks to the following for permission to reproduce illustrations from the books stated in the captions:

The Blake Trust (Plate I); Hodder and Stoughton Ltd (Plate III, Fig. 137); The Medici Society Ltd (Plate IV); Oxford University Press (Fig. 5, reproduced from *English Woodcuts, 1480–1535*); Ward Lock Ltd (Fig. 99); Macmillan Publishers Ltd (Figs. 105, 121, 123, 131, 132); Harper and Row, Publishers, Inc. (Fig. 113); George Allen and Unwin (Fig. 114); J. M. Dent and Sons Ltd (Figs. 116, 117, 148, 149); Methuen and Co. (Fig. 128); Routledge and Kegan Paul (Fig. 133); The Bodley Head (Figs. 135, 143); A. and C. Black (Publishers) Ltd (Fig. 139); Jonathan Cape Ltd (Figs. 141, 147, 188); The Folio Society (Figs. 142, 182, 189, 191, 192, 193, 195, 196); Mrs Phyllis Bliss (Fig. 144); The Golden Cockerell Press (Figs. 145, 153, 154, 157, 159, 165, 177, 180); The Society of Authors on behalf of the Estate of George Bernard Shaw (Fig. 150); The Heritage Club, a division of MBI (Figs. 152, 198); Harrap Ltd (Fig. 155); Lutterworth Press (Fig. 156); Penelope Hughes-Stanton (Fig. 158); The Trustees of the Wyndham Lewis Memorial Trust (Fig. 161); The National Library of Wales and the Gregynog Press (Figs. 162, 163); The Trustees of the Henry Moore Foundation (Fig. 164); The Trustees of the Paul Nash Trust (Fig. 167); Mrs A. D. Quickenden (Fig. 168); Chatto and Windus Ltd (Fig. 169); Aberdeen Art Gallery and Museums (Fig. 170); Century Hutchinson Ltd (Fig. 174); Feliks Topolski (Fig. 178); Macdonald and Co. (Publishers) Ltd (Fig. 184); Rigby Graham and M. A. McCord (Fig. 185); Mrs Marjorie Hutton (Fig. 187); Penguin Books Ltd (Fig. 197).

Plate V is reprinted by permission of William Heinemann Ltd; Fig. 136 is reprinted by permission of Miss Merle Taylor's executors; Fig. 140, © 1959 Edward Ardizzone; Fig. 171 is reprinted by permission of Faber and Faber Ltd from *The Wood Engravings of Gwen Raverat*; Fig. 172, © Estate of Eric Ravilious 1987, all rights reserved DACS; Fig. 175 is reprinted by permission of Faber and Faber Ltd from *The Living Hedge* by Leslie Paul; Fig. 176, © COSMOPRESS, Geneva and DACS, London 1987; Fig. 181 is included by permission of Gerald Duckworth and Co.; Fig. 183 is from John Clare, *The Shepherd's Calendar*, edited by Eric Robinson and Geoffrey Summerfield, published by Oxford University Press 1964; Fig. 186 is reprinted by permission of William Heinemann Ltd; Fig. 190 is the property of Mrs Lynton Lamb; Fig. 200, © 1969 by Ronald Searle (Methuen 1987); Fig. 115 is reproduced from *Lycidas and Other Odes*, Fig. 130 from *Sartor Resartus*, and Fig. 173 from *Everybody's Pepys*, all by kind permission of Bell and Hyman Ltd, London. The Publishers will be glad to hear from any copyright holders whom they have been unable to locate.

The Publishers also thank the following for editorial work and advice, and for help in providing prints, locating sources and identifying copyright holders:

Brian Alderson; the Bodleian Library; the British Library; John Commander; the Library of Congress; John Dreyfus; David McKitterick; the New York Public Library; Quevedo, booksellers, London; Bruce Ross-Larson; Stephen Ryan; Peter Stockham; Titles, booksellers, Oxford; Karin Turnbull.